RUSSIA IN MANCHURIA

(1892-1906)

By
B. A. Romanov
Translated from the Russian
by
Susan Wilbur Jones

OCTAGON BOOKS

A DIVISION OF FARRAR, STRAUS AND GIROUX

New York   1974

This work is a complete translation of *Rossiya y Manchzhurii* by
B. A. Romanov. It is publication 26 of the A. S. Enukidze Oriental
Institute, Leningrad, USSR, 1928.

Reprinted 1974
by special arrangement with the American Council of Learned Societies

OCTAGON BOOKS
A DIVISION OF FARRAR, STRAUS & GIROUX, INC.
19 Union Square West
New York, N. Y. 10003

Library of Congress Cataloging in Publication Data

Romanov, Boris Aleksandrovich, 1889-1957.
Russia in Manchuria, 1892-1906.

Translation of Rossiia v Man'chzhurii.
Reprint of the ed. published by J. W. Edwards for American
Council of Learned Societies, Ann Arbor, Michigan.

1. Russians in Manchuria.   2. Manchuria—History.   I. Title.
[DS783.7.R575   1974]   327.47'051'8   74-4181
ISBN 0-374-96903-5

Printed in USA by
Thomson-Shore, Inc.
Dexter, Michigan

Foreword

The Russian Translation Project of the American Council
of Learned Societies was organized in 1944 with the aid of a
subsidy from the Rockefeller Foundation. The aim of the
Project is the translation into English of significant works in
the field of the humanities and the social sciences which provide an insight into Russian life and thought.

Since Russian history is a continuum, the volumes translated are of various dates and have been drawn from both the
prerevolutionary and postrevolutionary periods, from writ-
ings published inside and outside of Russia, the choice depending solely on their value to the fundamental aim of the Project. Translations are presented in authentic and unabridged
English versions of the original text. Only in this way, it is
believed, can American readers be made aware of the traditions, concepts, and ideologies by which the thinking and
attitudes of the people of Russia are molded.

The first eleven volumes in the series were published
only after the original translators' texts were subjected to
a thorough editorial revision, annotation, correction, or re-
finement. With the termination of available funds on December 31, 1951 it is no longer possible to give the remaining
titles, of which this is one, the same degree of editorial
supervision accorded the first eleven volumes. This and the
other volumes in the series to be published are, however,
documentary materials which will be useful to scholars and
others more interested in their factual content than in the
niceties of their presentation. They are, therefore, deserving of publication.

With this reservation, it is believed that these works faithfully represent the Russian originals and serve to provide
that insight into Russian life and thought which is the aim of
the Russian Translation Project.

It should of course, be clearly understood that the views
expressed in the works translated are not to be identified in
any way with those of the translator or of the American
Council of Learned Societies.

Washington, D.C.
July 1, 1952

PUBLISHER'S NOTE

In publishing B.A. Romanov's "Russia in Manchuria," the press of the A.S. Enukidze Oriental Institute of Leningrad had as its primary aim the release of new, chiefly factual, material on no less pressing a question than that of Russia's imperialistic policy in the Far East.

And in the publisher's opinion, Romanov has been completely successful in adducing fresh material from our extremely rich archives--thus producing a factually rich and meticulously documented monograph on this major question of tsarist Russia's eastern policy.

Romanov focuses the analysis of his mass of documentary material upon the question of the export of Russian capital to the Manchurian area during the epoch preceding the Russo-Japanese war. He also exposes the imperialistic nature of the policy of the Russian autocracy in China as a whole and in Manchuria in particular, studying the evolution of local competition for the Manchurian market (not alone Russo-Japanese but Anglo- and American-Russian as well,) as an element in the broad scheme of the growth of world-wide imperialistic conflict.

This definition of his theme leads the author to the general problem of Russian imperialism as posed in our Marxist literature.

But in failing to explore the class struggle underlying tsarist Russia's whole imperialistic policy, Romanov plainly overrates the part played by individuals and brings nothing new to the solution of the general problem of Russian imperialism-- merely adhering to the concept of monopolistic capitalism in Russia as recently set forth in Comrade E. Granovsky's studies of other material.

Thus, both for what it does and for what it leaves undone, the publisher is confident that B.A. Romanov's book will be of interest not only to the relatively limited circle of specialists in oriental matters but to every Marxist historian as well.

iv

CONTENTS

AUTHOR'S FOREWORD

The present book is an outgrowth of what was originally planned as a collection of the articles published by me in 1923-1926 on the history of Russia's Far-Eastern policy during the late nineteenth and early twentieth centuries. The introduction and first two chapters were written before the idea of such a collection had been given up, and represent a revision of old texts for republication.[1] Numerous as were the alterations and additions that this entailed, such changes did not disturb the original plan beyond threatening to make the collection bulk larger. But as work on the third chapter progressed, the impossibility of holding to this plan became increasingly apparent. Upon closer study the material that I had collected by then (early 1927), refused to fit into the previous framework and I felt prompted to undertake a detailed rehandling. With the completion of the third chapter, however, the proposed compass of the publication had already been exceeded. It thus became necessary either to stop work and issue the book half done or to continue it on the scale of a full-length investigation. Unfortunately, in order to finish setting the third chapter, technical considerations made it necessary to print the first twelve folios and distribute the type, so that when the question of continuing the work was decided in the affirmative I could no longer go back over the pages (3-128) that had been written while only a "collection" was contemplated.[2] Chapters three to eight were, however, completely rewritten.

Such is the origin of the present "essays." They are linked by the single theme indicated in the title. The basic subject of investigation is only one of the questions of imperial Russia's foreign policy during that decade and a half. But the active policy of the autocracy in the 1890's and early 1900's was directly aimed at Manchuria and played its decisive part chiefly with reference to Manchuria in the development of Russo-Japanese conflict. It aided in shaping an international conjuncture conducive to war, ultimately deprived the Russian government of free manoeuverability in the world-wide imperialistic conflict then already defining itself, and

through war and the 1905 revolution projected Russia into the
lap of the Entente, where the autocracy duly met its fate in
1917. I believe, therefore, that my limitation of the topic
and of the chronological scope of my investigation neither de-
stroys the integral character of the present essays nor de-
tracts from the significance of their theme.

I have confidence also in their relevance to the general
problem of Russian imperialism central to our most recent
historiography. In selecting for monographic study the autocracy's foreign policy just at the epoch of imperialism, I
naturally had this problem in view, and in conducting my own
special studies could lean on the solutions already proposed
in the studies of M.N. Pokrovsky and his school. Following
step by step the work of Russian diplomacy, I made it my
task to study the methods and the resources at its disposal,
the program it attempted, the motive forces that in one way
or another affected the evolution of this program, and finally
the friction, or, rather, the deterioration increasingly ob-
servable at the top of the autocratic mechanism the closer
we came to war. And I conducted this study from the viewpoint of the anomalous situation inevitably created for the
autocracy by the sum of conditions typical of a developing
capitalism just entering the monopolistic stage:

In process of what I believe to have been a fairly intensive
study of materials remaining from the diplomatic intrigue of
the Russian government of that day, evidence accumulated
and became increasingly circumstantial as to the autocracy's
having (vainly) endeavored not only to adapt itself to these
conditions but even to inject itself into this development and
seize positions which would ensure sovereignty at home and
enable it to manoeuvre as freely as its fellows in the international arena of imperialism. Such evidence, relating chiefly to the Manchurian division of the Far-Eastern sector of
this arena, is accordingly set forth with the utmost possible
precision in my essays.

I have no illusions as to the exhaustiveness of my observations even within the limits of the material accessible to
me. But anyone who has occupied himself with questions of
modern history in terms of archival materials will appreciate
the difficulties that here confront the investigator, due to the
proportions and condition of the archival mass. The documents serving as basic source for this study were those of
the secretariat of the Third Department of the General Chan-

cellery of the Minister of Finance, set up in 1895, the moment the question arose of laying the trans-Baikal section of
the Siberian road through Manchuria, and promptly made to
function as a sort of diplomatic chancellery to the minister.
But I found a number of highly valuable documents in other
accumulations as well.[3] Owing to purely external circumstances I was prevented at the time from doing as much work
on the archival accumulation of the Ministry of Foreign Affairs in Moscow as I should have liked. But, granting my inability to make equal use of foreign office and finance ministry
files, it was perhaps fortunate for the present book that the
latter should have been the more accessible to me. It is far
from accidental that during the years studied, which fall almost entirely within Witte's ministry, the leading role in
directing Russian policy and in the work of Russian diplomacy
in the Far East should have been played by the Minister of
Finance. Material basic to the study of how and in what measure the economic policy of the autocracy attempted at that
time to state and solve Russia's problems in the sphere of
international relations is consequently not first to be sought
in the Ministry of Foreign Affairs. Moreoever, the latter
efficiently supplied the chancellery of the Minister of Finance
with abundant material in the form of copies of documents
(its own or borrowed) and from the summer of 1900, under
Lamsdorf, in some degree took on the character of a quasi-
subordinate organ, never making a move in the Far East
without the knowledge of the Minister of Finance, who, in turn,
had at his disposal there an executive and intelligence agency
of his own, and the whole machinery of the Chinese Eastern
Railway Company and the Russo-Chinese Bank.

The Manchurian epic is so closely linked with the name of
Witte that my ability to penetrate into the very laboratory of
his Far-Eastern policy greatly facilitated my defining and
proving the critical side of my investigation, to which I attributed essential significance on the following grounds: The
fact that Witte was a renegade from the camp of private capitalism, together with his experience and natural gifts, gave
him a place apart in Alexander III's government, since it
made him better fitted than the rest to undertake the adjustment of the autocracy's policy to new conditions. Director
of Russia's largest and best-paying railway joint stock company and therefore past master of the nationwide policy of
uniform railway-tariff economy, Witte assumed, along with

his minister's uniform, the responsibility for elaborating and
carrying out a grandiose plan for extending the territorial
base of Russian capitalism to include all Siberia.

The international-political significance of this plan at once,
and increasingly as time went on, drew Witte into active intervention in the foreign policy of the country. Witte's tendency to "get everything into his own hands" was no mere
character trait (as it must have seemed to his contemporaries)
but a response also to the objective need for reconciling a
domestic policy seeking to secure hegemony for the autocracy
in an environment of wild-cat capitalism with a foreign policy
undertaking in an imperialistic enviornment to acquire a market. The degree in which Witte's mediation proved successful would determine how far (under boom conditions of the 90's,
and with imperialism forging ahead on an international scale)
Russia's active policy in the Far East might also advance, in
close conjunction with finance capital, leaning on the St. Petersburg International Bank, and spearheaded by the Russo-
Chinese Bank--its associate the Chinese Eastern Railway
Company--and any private industrial enterprises agreeing to
remain under the aegis of the Russian Ministry of Finance
while operating in the Manchurian area. The larger the share
actually assumed in this banking-railroading-steamboating-
mining combine by the treasury, and the more hopeless, under
crisis conditions of 1900 and thereafter, any immediate prospects of strictly private-capitalistic exploitation of the riches
of Manchuria became, the more prominently did this policy
reveal its monopolistic nature. And such being its nature,
the longer it remained in force, the more warlike became the
character it assumed with respect to Manchuria, and maintained to the point of actual issue in war.

Meanwhile--being, in his official capacity as Minister of
Finance and particularly in his role of political director of the
"trust" founded and controlled by him, the inspirer of this
policy--Witte contributed by every means in his power during
his lifetime and posthumously by his "Memoirs" to the formulation and widest possible dissemination of the legend of the
exclusively peaceful character of his policy. This legend,
crude as it was, still shows such tenacity even now that to
uproot it will require a detailed application of the methods of
monographic study to every step and each devious turn the
policy took. In making just such a study my task, I could best
find the details I needed in the original correspondence of the

diplomatic chancellery of the Minister of Finance. Taking
every possible care not to overlook a single such detail, I
have aimed to expose with all candor the true nature and actual significance of the policy which the epoch of imperialism
dictated to the autocracy through the lips of its "faithful servant."

In releasing this book, I feel it my duty to thank the Board
of the Enukidze Oriental Institute of Leningrad for including
it among their publications. For the ability to undertake a
study of the archival material on which this book is based and
carry it to completion, I am indebted to the benevolent attitude
that I invariably met on the part alike of the administration
of the Tsentrarkhiv in Moscow and of the Central Historical
Archive in Leningrad. For finishing touches to the text I feel
particularly indebted to A.E. Presnyakov, who generously
undertook a preliminary criticism of the work in manuscript.

To the book is appended a map of Manchuria, on which
are plotted all actual or projected industrial, timber and railway concessions, Russian and foreign, mentioned in the text.
In drawing this map T.F. Kopylova did me an inestimable
service.

The Author.

September 30, 1928.

INTRODUCTION

BASIC FEATURES OF RUSSIAN POLICY IN
THE FAR EAST 1892-1917

The Manchurian question reached its full growth in the history of the international relations of the Russian Empire in
1895, assumed priority status and combat rank and became,
without interruption, the basic problem of Russian foreign
policy for the next ten years. As such, its rise was directly
and exclusively associated with the opening of construction
operations on the through route across Siberia, an enterprise
which threatened to change most substantially the tempo and
scale of Russia's active policy on the shores of the Japan Sea.
Whatever the occasion for building it may have been, whatever
the needs met and the interests served, it remains a basic
fact in the foreign policy of this country. Subsequent facts of
this policy fall into a compact and unbroken line, advancing
impetuous and unchecked from the moment when, after a
series of delays and piecemeal starts, the longstanding intention of linking the vast reaches of Siberia by rail with central Russia finally, in 1892, took form as a building plan.
The plan for a "great" Siberian railway, wide-gauge and continuous, to Vladivostok itself, long enough (over 7,000 versts)
to set a new world record, was not only officially confirmed
but scheduled for completion within a fixed time, worked out
in detail both on the technical and, of chief importance, on the
financial side. In such form, this plan was no longer regarded
as simply a broadening of the base of internal railway communication, let alone a mere commercially profitable shuttle between detached trading points in Siberia, but had acquired, it
would seem, world significance. At the point of a railway
line Russia was forcing an entry into the sphere of international
economic and political competition in the Pacific, in the hope
that its building would be followed by a "reversal" of direction

in communications between Europe and the Asiatic east to
her [Russia's] advantage." The Siberian railway was officially
proclaimed one of those "world events" that "usher in new
epochs in the history of nations, and not infrequently bring
about a radical change in established economic relations between states," and was regarded as a weapon that would so
strengthen the Russian navy in the Pacific so as to give Russia "control over the entire movement of international commerce in Pacific waters."[1]

That this plan, so pompously set forth in the report of
Witte, then Minister of Finance, was obviously drafted under
the immediate impress of the dire famine which gripped European Russia with unexampled fury in 1891, and that its fulfillment would in the first instance rest for the next few years
on the shoulders of that same Russian peasantry for whom a
short cut out of famine and landlessness to still largely un-
populated Siberia was now being provided, is another question.
Calculated to have a revolutionizing effect on the existing conjunction of world economic forces, this plan at the same time
inevitably proved to be of like significance in the development
of class relations within the country, now harnessed by the
railway as by a driving belt to the machinery of world imperialism in the Far East. The external fact in this sense
decisive--namely the Russo-Japanese war of 1904-5--would
have been unthinkable on just such a scale, or with so radical
a significance, for the Russia of Siberian water-routes and
post roads. The slogan "control over the entire movement
of international commerce in Pacific waters," enunciated by
Witte in 1892, embraced a program that would later push the
Russian government into laying more than 2,000 versts of the
Siberian railway entirely through Manchurian territory--an
act which accelerated, as nothing else would have, the fomen-
tation and issue in war of imperialistic conflict on the Russo-
Japanese sector.

The defeat of Russia in the Japanese war did not eliminate
her from Manchuria. It merely reduced, in Japan's favor,
the area of Russian influence there, while leaving in Russia's
hands the conducting medium for that influence, namely the
main line of the Chinese Eastern Railway through North Manchuria to Vladivostok. True, the monopolistic program, so
obstinately prosecuted with respect to Manchuria by Nicholas's
government right up to the war, and now a complete fiasco,
was dropped, and in the new international situation in which

Russia found herself after war and revolution the Manchurian
question lost acuteness and its immediately warlike character.
But the vast railway settlement in Northern Manchuria, in the
form of a zone of growing populated points with administrative
rights accruing to Russia from the concession of 1896, remained, as before--regardless of how much Russia may have been
weakened by the war--a threat to China that sooner or later
Northern Manchuria would be wrested from her; and the subsequent Russo-Japanese agreements of 1907-1916 ended in a
military alliance between these recent enemies that actually
looked to the partition of China. Only the October revolution
in Russia fully freed China from such predatory threats, open
or concealed, as had in the preceding period been linked with
Russia's program for "peaceful conquest" of east-Asiatic
markets, rendered peculiarly militaristic in respect to all
three Manchurian provinces by Witte's policy.

I

Despite the antiquity of Russian and European trade relations with China, (dating respectively from the seventeenth
and the sixteenth century,) the "opening" of China to foreign
capital, in the current sense of the term, strictly falls within the years 1842-44, when, as a result of the first Anglo-
Chinese "opium" war (1839-42), China was forced to "open"
five ports to European trade, clamp a flat duty of 5 per cent
on the price of goods and recognize the extraterritoriality of
English nationals (and, in 1844 of American and French nationals.) In round numbers, the turnover of European trade
with China at the moment (1844) came to about 28 million dollars in imports to China, and about 33 million in exports, in
the following percentage ratio: England's share of imports,
68 per cent, Russia's 19 per cent, America's 7 per cent,
the share of all other. powers (Holland, Portugal, France,
Belgium, Denmark, Sweden and Germany,) 6 per cent; and
England's share in exports 60 per cent, Russia's 16 per cent,
America's 20 per cent, that of the rest, 4 per cent.[2]
If we bear in mind that the Russian trade was at this time
concentrated in Kiakhta and went on chiefly across the overland Russo-Chinese frontier, and that in subsequent decades
it showed an obvious and consistent tendency to decline,[3] it
then appears that "China proper" (i.e., the eighteen provinces
within the Great Wall) was at that time almost wholly the

"sphere of influence" of the English (with as yet only a feeble accompaniment of American) capital.

Thus the whole future history both of the economic and of the territorial-political partition of the Chinese empire must be studied as a sign of the diminishing importance of the virtual monopoly which England had enjoyed since 1860, following the second war, 1858-60. That monopoly was strikingly expressed in the fact that at the head of the office of Chinese Maritime Customs, in the capacity of chief inspector, was the Englishman Robert Hart--a position in 1898 formally confirmed by treaty for such period as English trade in China should exceed that of any other single nation. The initial military onslaught upon China by England herself opened a series of attempts by other powers in the latter half of the 19th century on outlying provinces of the empire; by Russia on the Amur province (1858), on the Maritime (1860), on the western part of Ili province (1881), by France on Cochin China (1862), and Annam (1874), by Japan on the Ryukyu Islands (1879-1881), by England herself on Burma (1886), and Sikkim (1890)--attempts which, while leading to no direct clashes among their institutors, yet marked the starting points for future penetration by each deep into Chinese territory.[4]

By the 1890's the point in this area where imperialistic wires would cross was clearly Korea, a kingdom long since in vassalage to China, which, however, to avoid possible complications and clashes with Japan, had allowed Japan to conclude a treaty with Korea directly as with an independent power (1876). China had then just as pointedly not only kept out of all negotiations but had even prompted the Korean government to conclude like treaties with western powers, as a means of paralyzing the effectual inculcation of Japan's political influence at the court of Seoul (1879).

The Americans, from the early 1870's interested in penetrating into Korea, were the first to take advantage of China's stand: the American-Korean treaty of 1882 led off a whole series of like diplomatic acts by other European powers (England and Germany, November, 1883, Italy and Russia, June, 1884, France, June, 1886). This policy of a cross-system of international insurance for Korea received its crowning touch with China's invitation in 1883, to the post of head of the Korean customs office and adviser on economic questions, an official of the German consular service in China (Moellendorf) who immediately took over the foreign policy of his new-

found "country" as well--with a <u>volte face</u> to alliance with
Russia.

Moellendorf's plan, designed to preclude the possibility
of a repetition of Japan's military intervention at Seoul (the
1882 incident) by inviting Russian instructors for the Korean
army and giving Russia the ice-free port of Lazarev, evoked,
however, the menacing opposition of England. This opposition
was exemplified in her occupation of Port Hamilton on an islet
at the very entrance to the Korean gulf--and the plan fell through
in view of the specter of a naval clash then beyond Russia's
pwers and the creation of a sort of second Dardanelles (1885)
for her in Far-Eastern waters. But the renewed clash between Chinese and Japanese military detachments at Seoul
(1884) forced China to come to a temporary agreement with
Japan--pending better times--providing for bi-lateral abstention from introducing troops into Korea without reciprocal
notification (1885). In case China--relying on the support of
England, through Robert Hart who had obstinately pursued a
policy of paving the way for subordination of Korean custom-
houses to the Chinese office of customs--should during the
next few years show no intention of renouncing its rights over
Korea, Japan, on the basis of her priority in Korean trade,
was prepared to expel the Chinese and proclaim the formal
independence of Korea.

As for America and Russia--the former simply discounted
Chinese suzerainty, the latter, fully conscious of her "historic
mission" in the Far East, was bending all her energies toward
uniting her Maritime frontier with the center at the earliest
possible moment, if only by a combined rail and water communications system. In view of all of this it was impossible
to so much as dream that the Sino-Japanese agreement of
1885 would go even one step of the way toward solving the
complicated Korean question.[5]

Under such conditions, the decision to build an absolutely
continuous railway from Moscow to Vladivostok, a decision
made by the Russian government on February 23, 1891, and
announced in the special imperial rescript of March 17, 1891,
amounted to a direct threat of abrupt change in the correlation
of forces in the Far East, by enabling Russia to bring into
play there no longer only her local troops, perforce limited
to some tens of thousands and cut off from centers of supply,
but any section of her regular Imperial army, and to operate
there in unprecedented concentration. The Russian empire,

cumbrously climbing throughout the nineteenth century across
the continuous land mass of the Near, the Middle, and the
Far East, finally blocked in the Near East in 1878, halting at
Central Asia in 1885--had now found means in the Far East,
as was plain by the end of 1892, for advancing unchecked and
at record speed. The medial rate of construction on the
Siberian road topped all precedents, averaging 587 versts a
year and in 1895 reaching 1,254 versts.[6] Neither England,
much less America, had at its disposal at home, much less
in remote Asia, any serious land forces, and thus neither
could offer any direct resistance to this move of Russia's--
financed by the Paris bourse and absolutely independent of
the money markets of London or New York. Only Japan,
vitally interested in getting across to the continent, could
even attempt to challenge on land this nightmare prospect of
Russian "control over the entire movement of commerce in
Pacific waters,"--before it was too late.

The Sino-Japanese War of 1894-1895, rehearsed during
the 80's in sundry armed clashes at Seoul, was accordingly
Japan's attempt to get there first.[7] This war was what
formally tied the international knot cut ten years later by the
treaty of Portsmouth. It ranged the Far East once and for
all among problems of world policy faced by European powers.
While in progress it revealed, to everyone's astonishment:
first, China's utter incapacity for any sort of effectual military resistance even in the immediate vicinity of her own
capital, secondly, the indisputable height of military preparedness shown by Japan when she put an army of 70,000
into the field, and thirdly, the extreme chauvinism of the
Japanese government's plans. In substance the latter boiled
down to: 1) the establishment of a protectorate over Korea
(i.e., with a view to future seizure) on the hypothesis of its
independence of China, 2) the setting up of a great military
base on the coast of central China between Shanghai and Canton to safeguard economic penetration in that direction and
3) the seizure of Manchuria--through occupation of the whole
South Manchurian shore line, including the Liaotung peninsula.[8]

Such a combination of demands as appeared in the peace
terms proposed by Japan in the spring of 1895 sufficed to
bring the whole concert of Europe to the "bedside of the sick
man" China, and shattered any prospect of concerted intervention that the powers may have contemplated at the beginning of the war.

From England's point of view, the demand that appeared
least acceptable was the second, introducing Japan into the
preferentially English "sphere of influence" in central China.
For Russia, on the contrary, such a shift of Japan to the south
and to the sea had a positive connotation--the interlocking of
antagonistic Anglo-Japanese interests far from the contemplated Russian sphere in the north. England, again, in view
of the revealed impotence of China, was equally interested in
keeping Japan in Korea, shackling her there to Russia, and
thus paralyzing her in the south. Russia on the other hand,
however impeccable Japan's first demand respecting Korean
"independence" as minimum program for which the war had
been undertaken, must still see to it that Korea secured real
independence (from Japan) if only in the form of a dual Russo-
Japanese protectorate over this country, incapacitated, especially in her given international position, for independent
existence. This protectorate would be fortified, perhaps
by the occupation of some one of those convenient ports on
the Korean Gulf that Russia had long had her eye on.

Finally, Japan's third (Manchurian) demand, promising
to detain her in the north indefinitely, held very great attraction
for England. The prospect of giving Japan the actual means
to become an indestructible barrier in Manchuria against Russia and of letting her feed her fill there was destined to prove
the deciding factor in England's choice between the protection
of China from territorial seizures, proposed by Lord Kimberley at the beginning of the war (itself provoked by England's
covert backing of China on the question of Korean sovereignty)
and non-obstruction of Japan's solicitations--England's actual
choice.

For Russia, on the contrary, as Witte forced Nicholas II to
recognize at the last moment, Japan's occupation of Southern
Manchuria, with its threat of large sacrifices in future, was
not to be tolerated. Obviously Manchuria was at that time already regarded by Witte as the necessary next field for colonial
exploitation, designated: 1) indirectly to recoup the colossal
expenditures that Russia had been, and would still be, under
(partly at the cost of French credit) for effecting a transit
line and 2) to gratify the immediate export tendency of French
capital, which Witte probably even then had prospects of luring across the Urals for the promotion of the Siberian provinces
--to palliate the emergency existing at the Russian empire's
European base since its development of that new crack in
1891.

The grouping of powers in 1895 was thus defined. America from the outset evaded joint action with the rest, confining herself to counsels of moderation in Tokyo and Peking, at Korea's own request. England, originally--i.e., until Japan's terms were made known--prepared for an agreement with Russia, now plainly went over to the side of Japan, and only the suddenness of the event left her passive at the moment when the three remaining powers came out flatly for China. Russia--prepared, from the moment Japanese terms were announced, for immediate war with Japan, even if England should take her part--addressed the proposal for an ultimatum demanding Japan's renunciation of Manchuria: 1) to Germany, which, with an enthusiasm and alacrity that astonished the Russian government, declared her fleet at Russia's service, here glimpsing a loophole for future penetration to the Far East, where she had up to now only been watching for a chance to get in, and 2) to France, which, still wavering, one eye on England, very nearly enticed Russia at the last moment to content herself with compensations at China's expense, yet finally joined Russia, in order not to leave her paired off with Germany.

The bloodless victory thus scored by Russia in 1895--with the paradoxical essential circumstance that Russia guaranteed the French bourgeois his interest on the loan she had arranged for China in the French market to pay the Japanese indemnity, i.e., to arm Japan against Russia herself--caused such an unusual upsurge of imperialistic energy in Russian governmental circles as still further to widen the breach between Russia on the one hand and Japan and England on the other. In that same year, 1895, after passing Japan in the race of Manchuria and Korea, though at the same time recognizing her as a ranking European power,[9] Russia, as pointed out previously, also speeded work on the laying of the Siberian road-bed to a feverish tempo, founded the Russo-Chinese Bank (with 5/8 French capital) and produced the project for a trans-Manchurian line to connect Irkutsk with Vladivostok. In May, 1896--during the very days of the Khodynsky disaster --the results of the victory won were clothed in juridical treaty form. Alliance with China, personal bribery, on the installment plan, of the head of the Chinese ruling aristocracy, Li Hung-chang, a series of treaties guaranteeing the Russian government's ownership of the Chinese Eastern Railway authorized by China--quite obviously secured to Russia monopolistic

control in Manchuria and in perspective, "inevitable" future
penetration "deep into China."[10]

Furthermore, a Russo-Japanese protectorate over Korea
was indeed set up, on parity principles, for supervision of
her military and financial means. This protectorate, however,
took a predominantly Russian cast during the following years,
1897--in violation of the May agreements--through the medium of a Russian financial adviser having virtually the status
of minister of finance to the king of Korea and replacing a
comparable English official. In a form not so clearly political, the same tendency with respect to Mongolia found expression in the organization, in intimate conjunction with the
Russo-Chinese Bank, of a special syndicate for the exploitation
of Mongolia's mineral resources (June 1897).[11]

A tendency to broaden at once the interpretation of gains
achieved is shown both in the Manchurian question and in the
Korean. By the time governmental circles had blocked diplomatically the building of foreign narrow gauge railways in
Korea, and insisted on the Russian five-foot span, they were
already discussing the possibility of connecting--Russian
gauge without fail--the Chinese Eastern trunk-line not as yet
even under construction, with "one of the ports on the Yellow
Sea." The plan was then to open negotiations with China concerning a similar branch to the south, "for the time being"
only as far as Mukden, figuring that this would automatically
decide the whole question in advance. The fact that Russia
blanketed all these projects and acquisitions under the theory
of the necessity of protecting China from Japan, on the strength
of the treaty of alliance of May 22, 1896, did not alter the true
nature of what had happened. The partition of China into spheres
of influence and interest had begun and was progressing at a
very rapid rate, intermittently with imperialistic outbreaks in
other parts of the world. For these were the years (1897-1899)
when England, Germany, America, France, Russia, even Italy
were vying with one another to seize bases and suitable
markets for manpower, raw materials and manufactured goods,
one country as an investment, another for immediate exploitation.[12]

The relatively greatest successes in the Far East fell to the
lot of Russia and Germany, the latter acting virtually by preliminary agreement of the two emperors (the consent of Nicholas II to Germany's occupation of some port on the coast of
China had been given William II shortly before Germay's occu-

pation of Kiaochow). Germany, very late in developing col-
onially, first burst into China by force of arms, seizing (for
99 years)the exceedingly rich territory of Shantung.[13] Russia,
developing to the utmost her achievements of the past three
years, acquired a naval base at Port Arthur and a trade port
at Dalny, with outlying territory on the Liaotung peninsula.
It was obvious to all that this: 1) signified Russia's firm determination to establish full control over all Manchuria, and
2) gave teeth to her formally unbroken alliance with China by
the persuasive proximity of Russian naval forces to Peking,
which city, via the now authorized South-Manchurian railway
from Mukden to Port Arthur, the first Russian echelons from
Trans-Baikal and the Maritime Province could reach in some
five or six days.

Japan, powerless at the moment to obstruct the event, had
perforce to content herself with the recall of the Russian financial adviser from Korea and Russia's agreement "not to
hinder the development of industrial and trade relations" between Japan and Korea, with the preservation of the latter's
"independence" and the abstention of both sides from separate
intervention in her internal affairs (protocol of April 13/25,
1898). England, largely tied up by affairs in Africa, was
forced to a formal recognition of all North China (north, that
is, of the wall) as preferentially the sphere of Russian railway
building, contenting herself with the like recognition on Russia's
part as to England and the Yangtse basin (April 16, 1899).
Finally, France, safe with her own slice in the general sharing
(Kwangchowan), was only anxious lest England fail to increase
her influence by means of a loan to China, and--for the first
time in Chinese affairs--broached the question of an international loan.[14]

America took no part in the sharing out of China. As previously stated, these were the years when American capital
was seeking an outlet and bases beyond the continent--for the
time being, on neighboring oceanic islands.[15] And for precisely this reason America had at the time no choice but to
step forward and defend her (trade) interests in China against
threatened restriction of commercial freedom and of the equal
rights of nations in a country divided into closed spheres of influence. By proposing, in the autumn of 1899, that all the
powers that had just provided themselves with such "spheres
of influence" make declaration as to the preservation of full
equality of rights for all nationalities, including her own,

"within the bounds of the so-called spheres of influence or in
leased territories," America was in effect proclaiming for
the first time the principle of the "open door" with respect
to China. This principle, if constantly reiterated by her from
that time forth, would virtually, with the growth of Ameri-
ica's economic predominance on a world scale, lead to the
organization of China, "one and indivisible," into a continuous
"sphere of influence" for American capital.[16]

In a more candid note (of September 19 of the same year)
to the English government, which, as we saw, was in no
position to resist the onslaught of its young competitors, Hay,
the American Secretary of State, said point-blank that America "in no wise desired to bind herself by any acknowledgement
whatsoever of any power's exclusive rights within, or control
over, any province of the Chinese empire" founded on the
treaties of 1898--in the full conviction that for English as well
as for American capitalistic groups the policy of the open
door would alone permit "the preservation of their position in
the Chinese market and the broadening of their future operations."[17]

The anti-European Boxer movement, started in China back
in 1899, under direct influence of the partition which had been
carried out, and protected in some degree by the Chinese government, as personified in the nationalistic and reactionary
elements united about the empress dowager, assumed in the
spring of 1900 a character so threatening both to the lives of
Europeans directly and to the safety of European enterprises
in China, as to unite, for a time, all the powers, America
included, to combat the common danger. This ultimately led
to the savage retribution against China that found international-
legal expression in the famous "concluding protocol" of September 7, 1901, and, specifically, to the imposition upon
China of the so-called "Boxer indemnity" in the amount of
450 million lan (about 640 million rubles) with 39 years to
pay.

Having participated in the joint military expedition against
Peking and, furthermore, placed all Manchuria under occupation by her own troops in the name of protecting the railway under construction, Russia attempted to mask her further
imperialistic plans, as well as the military expedition of 1900
itself, under public assurances as to the protection of the
Chinese government from revolution while, simultaneously
with the general negotiations, she conducted separate parleys

with Li Hung-Chang about an agreement which should secure
to Russia a monopolistic right in the exploitation of the natural resources of Manchuria, authorize the laying of a Russian railway to Peking, and virtually clear Manchuria of
Chinese troops.

These parleys, needless to say demanding the observance
of complete secrecy, nonetheless became known to the third
parties interested and aroused protests, hence moved very
slowly and laboriously, and eventually led to the conclusion
of an Anglo-Japanese treaty of alliance in January, 1902--
by which date Russia had managed to repair all the damage
done the Manchurian lines in 1900 and opened temporary traffic along the full length of the Siberian road (with the ferry
across Baikal that had acquitted itself so well back in the
mobilization of 1900). The direct warning of this Anglo-Japanese treaty, in conjunction with America's simultaneously
taking a stand against Russia's economic pretensions in Manchuria (note of February 3, 1902) forced Russia to the hasty
conclusion of her treaty with China concerning complete evacuation of Manchuria (by September 1903) signed on March 26,
1902.

Though formally an exact symbol of the triumph of the conservative policy announced by Russia in 1900 which sought no
new acquisitions or privileges--even down to the proviso
(Article 2) as to its operativeness only in case "the conduct
of other powers shall not prevent"--the treaty of March 26,
1902 was in point of fact such a diplomatic defeat for Russia
as lent acuteness to more questions than the Manchurian--
under the conditions of profound social-economic crisis then
approaching the country. During these years (1901-1903)
the state of crisis revealed itself in outbursts of mass demonstration by the peasant and labor movement, signalizing peak
acuteness, and split the bourgeois-feudal governmental block;
the struggle at the top of the government in turn inevitably
affected the question of Russian eastern policy, previously to
a marked degree the object of this struggle and now its arena.
Fluctuations in the solution of the Manchurian question were
thus in the first instance reflections of this struggle (Nicholas II,
Pleve and the Bezobrazovists against Witte) in which from
the beginning of the 1903 victory plainly tended toward the
militaristic clique, a group whose foreign policy was inspired
by the thought of a Russo-German alliance against England
and apparently enjoyed the backing of Berlin on this point.

Meanwhile an exceptional inner equilibrium of the whole governmental organism was needed to preserve even outward balance in the international situation as it existed during the final months before the war in the Far East. America (Hay) well knew that her hand outstretched to China "would be less persuasive to the poor Chinese than the club that [Russia] held over them," but thought: "all the same we [Americans] must do all we can with the means at our disposal"--and went hand in hand with Japan in negotiations with China as to the opening of Manchurian "ports," fully intending to warn Germany and France, the moment war began, that if they interfered America would stop at nothing in order to aid Japan.[18] England, having back in 1897 loaned Japan 40 million rubles, and having in 1902 by the treaty of alliance guaranteed her a one-against-one war with Russia and the safeguarding of all her seacoasts and communications, now gave Japan all-out support in her preparation for war. And on the Manchurian question England took the position "of observer and critic,"[19] making no troublesome protests and verbally not even dismissing the idea of an agreement with Russia, confident, however, that the question would be advantageously settled by other means.[20]

Germany was still only waiting for a chance to divert Russia's war power to the Far East, away from the western border, relax the vice of the dual (Franco-Russian) alliance and renew the trade treaty with Russia that expired in 1904--on terms still more advantageous to herself.

Finally, Japan, uninterruptedly engaged in full scale preparations for war since 1895, when the Chinese indemnity had made a substantial addition to what still remained in her budget of the war fund amassed by 1894, back in 1898 rather expected to attempt armed protest against Russia's seizure of Liaotung. Japan--in 1900 able to put more troops in the field against China than any other power, since 1898 unsuccessful in obtaining Russia's diplomatic recognition of her position of dominance in Korea, now cut off from Manchuria by the broad zone of the Yalu River timber concession (which the Russians had unceremoniously converted into a "military screen against her" as Bezobrazov expressed it in his strategical projects)--Japan well knew that the "establishment of Russia's supreme authority in Manchuria would for Japan be tantamount to defeat in the struggle for existence." Japan also knew that in the future every added year and month of

Russia's consolidation in Manchuria would make the enemy's powers of resistance more difficult to overcome: for in the summer of 1903 regular traffic had finally opened along the Chinese Eastern Railway and apart from completing minor details the sole task remaining was to replace by a shore route the water break on the Siberian stretch at Baikal-- still an obstacle for Russia to cope with even after the opening of hostilities. And since Japan was, as before, left to face Russia entirely alone by land, it followed that if she did not propose to renounce once and for all the whole 1895 program but fight for it, she must do so at once.

Whereas Russia, in view of existing internal conditions, was discussing--on the one hand--whether the strain of a war economically beyond her and technically premature would not bring revolution "to the surface" (Witte-Lamsdorf) and whether it might not be better to abandon Port Arthur and all southern Manchuria, selling out, possibly to China (Kuropatkin) or to America (Subotich) or--on the other hand--whether a "little victorious war" wasn't just what Russia needed as a way out of the domestic political crisis (Pleve). And therefore, the discussion continued, wouldn't the thing be to draw out the negotiations started by Japan (July 30, 1903) on the Manchurian and Korean questions, while hastily completing our armaments and conserving positions occupied in Manchuria (Bezobrazov). The settlement of the Manchurian question in conformity with the treaty of March 26 regarding the withdrawal of Russian troops and in harmony with the program of the "open door" in Manchuria adopted by America, England, and Japan (wheth- er Russia consented to it before evacuation or was forced to do so afterwards) actually ruled out both variants of the Rus- sian plan put in operation in 1895-96: either direct annexation of Manchuria or organization as a market closed by monopolies and guarded by tariffs--and excluded all possibility of justify- ing the expenditure made.

Having persuaded Nicholas II not to reconcile himself to any such preliminary defeat, the Bezobrazov group, which had finally come into power in August 1903 (with the retire- ment of Witte) undertook 1) instead of withdrawing Russian troops from Manchuria, to prepare by a series of military measures for its possible annexation, and 2) to so organize its economic exploitation, with the aid of foreign capital, as to remove Manchuria from the national budget. After having with some ado redistributed during the summer of 1903 the

functions appertaining to the management of Far Eastern affairs, these persons, continuing to maintain the role of trusted personal agents of the tsar would not, or perhaps could
not, make up their minds to directly take over the apparatus
of national government. They did, however, disturb its normal functioning, thereby formally facilitating only the diplomatic unleashing of war.

In view of Japan's complete preparation for war, squeezed
out at the price of excessive strain on all her powers and resources and automatically demanding the realization of the
whole Shimonoseky program of 1895, and in view of her own
preparation lagging by some two years, as the experiment
of war afterwards demonstrated--for Russia it could only be
a question either of fully conceding all possible strategic
positions and renouncing her Manchurian program, or of going to war for it under conditions known to be unfavorable.
The conflicting parties in the Russian government in the
spring of 1903 were both agreed, however, that a miracle
might happen: one side felt that "by renouncing her seizures
in Korea" and freezing, albeit with some few additions, the
advantages gained in Manchuria, it might be possible to avoid
a war over Manchuria until better times (Witte), the other
that merely by manifesting a will to victory and in particular
to the defense of Manchuria along the Korean boundary line
they could keep the enemy at bay (Bezobrazov).

Both sides were also agreed that the treaty of March 26,
1902, was of itself, without supplementary concessions and
guarantees on the part of China, not capable of fulfillment--
and they differed only in defining the tenor of the desired
supplementary agreement (June conferences of 1903 in Port,
Arthur and August conference in Petersburg). But from the
viewpoint of the Anglo-American-Japanese coalition[21] which
kept China from making concessions of any sort, the question
was clear: until September 26 (October 8) 1903 (final evacuation by the treaty) Manchuria was juridically under actual
Russian occupation and had not reverted to China, but from
that date forward China entered fully into her rights--a viewpoint openly expressed in the joint signing, on one and the
same day (October 8, 1903) of American-and Sino-Japanese
trade treaties "opening" to foreigners the South Manchurian
ports of Antung and Tatungkow (both at the mouth of the Yalu)
and Mukden. The other side of the picture--the one which
apparently escaped the attention of Russian authorities--

here consisted in the fact that likewise in October Japan began spending her special war funds on getting her fleet into
fighting trim.

The circumstance that subsequently Japan still continued
to conduct negotiations with Russia, did not at once break
them off, in October, but waited until January, 1904, by no
means signified that even now Russia might still have prevented war by making concessions, and should any such question arise, the answer is to be found in the technical details
of Japan's mobilization. On the other hand in Russia thereafter, what with cleavage and even functional disorganization
in the foundering Bezobrazov ship of state, it is impossible
to insist on any practical distinction between the counsels
now offered by the respective supporters of "peaceful" and
"predatory" tactics.

The project fully worked out by Kuropatkin in November,
1903 for selling to China all of southern Manchuria at the
price of her conceding Russia the northern part (a project
to which even Witte committed himself) or Balashov's November proposals--to replace the whole Chinese administration in Manchuria by a Russian one, and Bezobrazov's--to
deprive the Peking government of the right to grant concessions there, or Bezobrazov's December reflections as to the
necessity of immediately entering into negotiations with Japan
on the subject of an alliance against England and America or,
when the war had already started, the discussion of the inertia
of future Russian economic policy in the Far East should Manchuria become Russia's (the Ignatiev conference, January-
May 1904) or, the excogitations suggested to Nicholas II by
Abaza in September 1904 regarding possible sources for obtaining an indemnity from Japan and methods for provoking
China (after Liaoyan) to a breach of neutrality in order to
facilitate "diplomatically" the annexation of Manchuria at the
end of the war (instruction to the vice regent, September 9)--
all this and more like it was argued back and forth on a plane
removed from actuality, and testified to a complete helplessness to comprehend the rigid international conjuncture in
which Russia's military weakness left her baffled by the immediate problem of the day, and to the hopelessness of the
domestic situation, battering at the supreme government like
some sort of fevered dream recurring intermittently with
paralytic symptoms.

Russia, having in spite of England come out against the

penetration of Japan to the continent in 1895; obtained the concession for a trans-Manchurian trunk-line, the strategic significance of which was sanctioned by the simultaneously signed
Chinese treaty of alliance against Japan, in 1896; seized, in
Liaotung, the key to all Manchuria in 1898; fenced herself
off from English railway competition in China in 1899; seeking, obtaining, and then conserving concessions in Korea,
next door to Japan, in 1898-1901; Russia, installing occupation troops at all key points in Manchuria, even those "open"
to foreigners (Yingkow) in 1900 and then aiming to get exclusive monopoly over the exploitation of whatever resources the
country might possess, and making the withdrawal of Chinese
troops an indispensable condition to the withdrawal of Russian
troops, in 1901; making a provisional agreement ("if the conduct of other powers shall not prevent" to evacuate Manchuria
within 18 months and meantime hastening to concentrate under
the treasury-created Manchurian Mining Association absolutely
everything that could possibly be taken on concession (directly
or through figureheads, with the consent of Peking or merely
of the local authorities) in 1902; delaying the evacuation and
suggesting to China negotiations as to supplementary terms
(1903), concluding an agreement with Austria on Balkan affairs (Mürzsteg, September, 1903) finally breaking off incipient
negotiations with China, halting the evacuation of Manchuria
(October, 1903) and transferring the administration of the Far
East to the Anglophobe and avowedly Germanophile Pleve-
Bezobrazov-Abaza-Alekseyev group, and retiring Witte--Rus-
sia was clearly headed straight for a clash not only with Japan
but with England and America as well, in a strictly European
conjuncture which had also changed.

    In 1895 as a third party with Germany and France, Russia
had in the physical sense, met Japan singly, and in the diplomatic sense England singly. Now on the eve of Russia's war
with a Japan prepared for it militarily, financially and diplomatically, France firmly kept to the path of agreement with
England, and any help from her was plainly out of the question.
Russia embarked upon the war in the Far East possessed of
an unprecedently powerful combination of enemies and a paralyzed alliance. France, having made Russia a loan of 350
million rubles in April, 1904 and in that month also signed
an agreement with England, took no subsequent part in financing the war, which Russia, after holding out for some time
on German loans, ended in its 19th month, August 1905, hav-

ing no resources at her disposal beyond the issue of her own
banks.

II.

The Russo-Japanese war of 1904-1905 was attended not
only by revolutionary upheaval at home, but also--in consequence of Russia's defeat--by a shift in the world grouping
of imperialistic powers. Internally it led to a more organic
adaptation of governmental machinery and policy to the needs
and interests of the bourgeois-land-owning classes (Duma of
June 3), with removal of or a certain limitation upon the
feudal group, which nonetheless retained influence through
the tsar and to some extent through the Council of State. It
also led to the solidarising of the peasant and workers movement and to its cleansing of any admixture of survivals--how-
ever narrowly limited--of the "tsarist legend."

The lines of international grouping--laid down while the
war was still in progress--bore a direct relation to the obvious weakness of Russia both in the Far East and in Europe.
After almost producing a Russo-German defensive alliance
(twice: in October, 1904, and in July, 1905), this weakness
in the first place secured for Germany an advantageous customs tariff, not subjected to revision until 1914, and measur-
ably freed her to expand both as to African colonies and in
the Near East; in the second place, it gave final impetus to
the Franco-English agreement (April, 1904), and assisted
in attracting the English money market to participation in the
loan made to Russia in 1906 for the liquidation of budgetary
deficiencies caused by war and revolution, and this--in the
third place--facilitated the agreement of Russia and England
upon Persian affairs in 1907 (as to zones of influence). The
liquidation loan of 1906 itself, at the same time in view of its
preferentially French composition, gave body to the Franco-
Russian alliance and now became the basis for a future Entente combination. Finally, the corresponding strengthening
of Japan in China virtually created there a second Russia,
with the sole difference that Japan constituted a much more
real threat and an energetic competitor--from the viewpoint
of the "open door" policy in behalf of which America had intervened in the settlement of the Manchurian question in
1903. The Ententization of Russia through her agreement
with Japan thus became a derivative of the situation that had
been building up for Russia in Europe.

The Russo-Japanese negotiations at Portsmouth, proposed
and conducted by America at just the moment and in just the
direction to counterbalance Russia against Japan in the Orient
and place the two in close proximity on land, led to their sharing Sakhalin Island and Manchuria, where Russia retained the
whole trunkline of the Chinese Eastern Railway together with
a narrow zone along it and just a spur of the South Manchurian
branch (from Harbin to Kuanchengtse station), the remainder
going to Japan.

Naturally this also defined the spheres of influence of the
two powers. Rich and promising Southern Manchuria, with
the mighty Fushun coal mines and the fine commercial port
at Dalny, placed in Japan's hands the key to all Manchuria
and enormously increased her chances in China as a whole.
Russia got Northern Manchuria with a railway line open to attack and breach at any point, requiring annual subsidies of
millions for operations, maintenance of a numerous guard,
and costs of civil government in a zone which included a
series of points (Harbin, etc.) "opened" by China to the free
trade and residence of foreigners--as late as 1914 considering themselves exterritorials and flatly refusing to participate
in the expenses of government. [22]

Relations with Japan, defined, to be sure, in the 1907
series of agreements as a sort of formal friendship, nonetheless did not at first lose sight of Russia's virtual powerlessness to put up even a show of resistance in the event of
a rupture. To all intents and purposes, nothing whatever remained of the Russian fleet in the Far East ("the Pacific
forces"). Any thought of loans for the maintenance of the
land units assembled during the war (around 130 thousand
men) had to be given up in view of an ascertained deficit for
1907 of 40 or 50 million (the cancellation of ransom payments
alone was 35 million rubles), the position of Vladivostok,
sole remaining outlet from Eastern Siberia to the ocean, appeared completely precarious[23]--the more so since, by the
peace treaty, the Chinese Eastern Railway could even formally
be utilized by Russia only for commercial purposes.

Thus--back in the epoch of the First Duma--the question
automatically came up of building through Russian territory
an Amur railway line, screened by the flow of the Amur from
immediate attack and providing strategic security for the
Maritime and Amur provinces--otherwise, in the event of interrupted communications along the Chinese Eastern Railway,

completely cut off from the rest of Russia and open to attack
both by the Chinese from Manchuria and the Japanese from
Korea. But the Amur road, as an element of the military
program in the Far East, would further necessitate the laying
of a second track on the Siberian trunk line, to judge from the
experience in the war just concluded, and this entire program,
according to rough estimates made at the time the bill for
starting construction was introduced in the Duma (June, 1908),
would require around 400 million rubles before 1912--the
date set for completion of the whole program.

Meanwhile, during the epoch when this program was being
elaborated, 1906-1908, Russia's economic and financial situation was extremely difficult. These were years when the
country never emerged from industrial depression, and when
poor harvests kept the whole domestic money market on the
strain and necessitated a search for new resources outside,
in particular a testing of the ground beyond the French market: in making their latest loan--the first on so large a
scale (800 million rubles face value)--the French had, actually,
bound Russia not to repeat the loan in less than two years; but
1909 was the redemption date for the short-term bonds of the
French war loan of 1904 in the amount of 350 million rubles,
and the new French loan inevitable by the end of 1908 must in
the first instance go to paying off these bonds. Thus, after a
ruinous war, the Far East again hung suspended over central
Russia primarily in railway form and threatened to halt for
some years all other domestic railway construction at the
expense of the treasury.[24]

Under such conditions, the Manchurian question proper,
though territorially reverting after Portsmouth to its initial
1896-1898 phase, had now entered an entirely different phase
politically and economically and must be settled under much
more complicated circumstances. Central to it, as before,
was the Chinese Eastern Railway. But in no other respect
was there even a formal resemblance. For the rest the whole
situation was radically altered. The road had lost all strategic
significance as a weapon of the alliance between Russia and
China against Japan, not only in view of the formal pledge in
Article VII of the Portsmouth treaty, but also because the
alliance itself had disintegrated.

Russia was now dealing with a China that was entering the
zone of national-revolutionary renaissance, was well aware
of Russia's weakness, and sought occasion to reduce her role

in Manchuria to the absolute minimum. Broad prospects of
branch railways inevitably gemmating from the main line
"deep into China," and of the development of the legal position
of the road, had fallen by the way and of necessity been super-
seded by a conservative and defensive policy, in strict conformity with the letter of the contract and of the charter. Instead of the anticipated flocking of Russians to the zone, the
thing actually to be reckoned with was a wave of Chinese colonization there, offering, in the event of complications, a
danger to the very possession of the road. To talk now of
reviving the former "pacific" and "apart from other countries"
policy was simply Utopian. [25]

In view of the instability of the general political situation
at home, (at least up to the 3rd of June, 1907) the above-mentioned gloomy financial prospects (up to the fiscal year of
1909) and the necessity of concentrating all of diplomacy's
flagging energy (in connection with the Franco-and Anglo-
Russian agreements of 1906 and 1907) on the western front--
the question to be answered was "whether to remain" in the
Far East, and if so, whom to lean on--or "whether to retire."
"To retire" simply meant to renounce future possession of the
Chinese Eastern Railway, as the only thing still left to us on
Chinese territory capable of breeding international conflict
momentarily: i.e., seek its pre-term purchase by the Chinese
government. Data exist to the effect that Russia did make
such a proposal, not, of course, to China, which lacked the
means, but to an American banking group (1908)--a proposal
which was presently referred back to the Russian government
in official form through the ambassador of the United States
of America (1909), as a project aiming not only to ease Russia's position, but also to limit "further seizures by Japan."
The proposal was to organize an international banking syndicate for the realization of a loan to buy up for China all the
Manchurian railways, their control and operation being reserved to the syndicate. Then followed a written memorandum
to the same effect, addressed by the government of the U.S.A.
to both of the interested parties (the so-called "Knox project.")

When Russia's answer to this was a polite refusal (January 8, 1910), it meant that she had made her choice between
America and Japan--in favor. of the latter. Back in the days
of the Russo-Japanese war, in expressing readiness to "support in everyway" any "lawful" solicitation of Japan's, America had recognized Japan's rights in Korea and in the Liaotung

peninsula, but had regarded as mandatory upon Japan the return of Manchuria to China and allegiance to her own "open
door" policy.[26] Yet even then (March, 1905) the view was
expressed that the "best barrier," one that neither Russia nor
Japan could surmount in future" would be the transfer to
China of the Manchurian railways under international guarantee.[27] Indications also exist that America was then already
aware of the danger of Japanese expansion developing at whirlwind speed after victory. Take for example the memorandum
of July 31, 1905, recently found in Roosevelt's papers relating
to the Philippines; a like implication must be read into Roosevelt's intervening at Portsmouth to block the Japanese indemnity
demand, which, if met, would have rudely altered the relative
balance of power established by the peace treaty. The proposals twice made by Americans to Japan after the peace, in
1905 and 1906, relative to the sale of the south-Manchurian
branch of the Chinese Eastern Railway tend in the same direction.[28]

Japan's refusal in both cases, and the feverish haste of
her strategic and economic operations both in Korea and in
southern Manchuria, so alarming to Russia, alarmed America
no less. Japan had responded to the demonstration staged by
the American fleet in the summer of 1908 by reassurances as
to the complete identity, in principle, of her policy and America's in the Pacific and in China (the Root-Takahira exchange
of notes, November 30, 1908),[29] but this had in no wise prevented her use of ultimative threats to China in pushing her
railway and industrial program in Manchuria (August, 1909,
agreements concerning the Antung-Mukden railway and the
Fushun and Yantai mines). How close the race was between
Japan and America on the Manchurian question may be gauged
by the fact that the above mentioned proposal of the American
ambassador in Saint Petersburg, barbed, formally, against
Japan, preceded literally by only a few minutes the Japanese
ambassador's more definite and to Russia more tempting
proposal. This proposal in essence precluded the American
project for the "commercial neutralization" of Manchuria:
the proposal of a "formal alliance" for the protection of mutual interests in Manchuria, where "only Russia and Japan
had spent money and shed blood."

Russia had by this time already ascertained that the amount
of the French loan arranged in 1908 would give her a free surplus of 100 million rubles beyond coverage of the old debt, had

decided to build the Amur road immediately, without putting
the Chinese Eastern Railway up for sale, and for the first
time since 1905 had reaped an abundant harvest. To have
refused the Japanese proposal, which promised to tranquil-
lize the whole Russo-Japanese border and free Russia's
hands with respect to China, would for Russia even have involved a certain risk--and on June 21/July 4, 1910, Russia
signed a secret agreement with Japan regarding demarcation
of spheres of influence in Manchuria, and mutual protection
of interests there.[30]   •
    This meant that Russia "was returning" to the Far East
in a far from passive role and in extremely aggressive combination with a power that had openly declared she was preparing for the dismemberment of China, since she "did not
believe in its rebirth." And the first trial of strength--having
as its purpose the restoration for the time being of her treaty
rights in Mongolia and Manchuria, easily transgressed by
China since Portsmouth, and as its occasion a renewal of the
basic trade treaty (Petersburg, 1881), at the expiration of its
normal ten-year term--turned out well for Russia: to ultimative demands in this sense made by Russia on January 30,
1911, China had no choice but to give a satisfactory answer.
In the agreement of 1910, Russia finally found a form of international settlement of the Manchurian question that stabilized
and clarified her position in the Far East as never before.
    Later on, the complicated and increasingly strained re-
lations existing between imperialistic powers on a world scale
further defined and simplified this position--by placing clearly
mapped zones between Russia and Japan in Manchuria and Mongolia. The Anglo-Japanese agreement, renewed for the third
time in 1911, now only reinforced Russia's position by confirming the entente orientation of Japan, and coincided with a
series of Russo-Japanese agreements on various questions,
including the full liquidation of claims connected with the war
of 1904-1905. America's attempts--both before and after the
Chinese revolution of 1911--to "internationalize" all China in
a financial sense (by the formation of a banking consortium for
a "reorganized" loan to China involving establishment of control over the administration of this "independent" country) and
under this banner to extend political control to Manchuria as
well--came to nothing, since France and England were, in the
nature of things, forced to take cognizance of the protests and
pretensions of their allies, Japan and Russia. America her-

self accordingly had no choice but to cease trying--until better times--under pretext of violation by the powers of China's
"administrative independence."[31] Despite the importance of
the Chinese national revolutionary movement inaugurated in
1911, the main axis of imperialistic rotation in those years
clearly passed through Central Europe and the Near East,
where the series of explosions occurred that touched off world
conflagration.

The secret agreement of June 21, 1910 was not yet the
"formal alliance" that Motono and Izvolsky had discussed in
November 1919. But this--and not the Portsmouth treaty--
was what settled the Manchurian question for Russia. In 1895,
as now, settlement required the alliance of two against the
third--a condition dictated by its politico-geographic nature.
For fifteen years Japan had been working to gain a firm foot-
hold on the north of the Chinese mainland and create for herself a base for the future development of her continental policy:
by 1910 she was not only formally in possession of Korea, but
had turned it into one solid ammunition dump and camp, planned
for the prompt reception and outfitting of an army of a million,
shuttled over light-armed from the Japanese islands.

In proposing an alliance with Russia under such conditions,
Japan was evidently hoarding her strength in expectation of
such a world conflict as would give her a free hand in all
China, and was not by any means contemplating only the easy
possibility of "annihilating" at any moment the pitiable Russian
forces extended all the way from Baikal to Vladivostok, as
might have been imagined before the conclusion of the June
convention.[32] Consequently even the alliance with Russia now
remained only a question of time, the more so since the failure
of the Knox project had in no wise halted America in her attempts
to penetrate the Russian and Japanese spheres of influence either
by means of financial control, as mentioned above, or by means
of branch railways (Chinchow-Aigun-Blagoveshchensk and Pe-
king-Kalgan-Urga-Kiakhta). Such moves by America gave the
June agreement a very real significance.

The Chinese revolution, the centrifugal tendencies of which
had been taken into account beforehand by the contracting parties, provided occasion for further development of the principles
underlying the June agreement. That is, with respect to Mongolia, which had painlessly seceded from China when she turned
republic in 1912, a secret agreement was at once concluded, giving Russia, as her sphere of influence, Western and Outer

Mongolia, and confirming Japan in Eastern and Inner Mongolia.[33]

The world war of 1914 crippled all European belligerents politically and in large measure economically in the Far East, leaving China to Japan and America. On the strength of her right as a general participant in the war, Japan expelled Germany from Shantung by force of arms, herself occupied it, and then presented a series of demands to China (the "21 demands") tending toward the future partition of the country, and violating its "independence" and "integrity."[34] America countered by memorializing China and Japan as to her non-recognition of any pledges China might make in breach of the principles of Chinese inviolability and the open door, but was in no position actually to obstruct further Japanese seizures.[35] It was partly in response to this nonetheless ominous move by America that Japan and Russia concluded a new secret agreement concerning mutual armed support against any power ("harboring hostile intentions against Russia and Japan") which might attempt to give political control" in China.[36]

The menacing two-power combination thus projected for the post-war period, militarily without peer in the Chinese area, hit a snag, however, after the February revolution, when the temporary government committed itself to borrowing from now allied America--and was jettisoned in October, 1917, along with all the other international-legal connections of pre-revolutionary Russia.

With the conclusion of the Soviet-Chinese political agreement of May 31, 1924 (whereby the USSR renounced consular jurisdiction in China, renounced the concessions obtained by Russia in the 1890's and 1900's, renounced the "Boxer Indemnity," and agreed to a joint management of the Chinese Eastern Railway and to the recall of Red troops from Mongolia), and with the conclusion of the Soviet-Japanese agreement of January 20, 1925 (based on full restoration of the territorial rights of the USSR after the long Japanese occupation of the Maritime and Sakhalin areas)--the Union of Soviet Socialist Republics was already formally entering the arena of international competition in the Far East as the proponent of a policy resolutely opposed both to America's policy of

the "internationalization" of China through banking consorti-
ums, and to the European-Japanese policy of "spheres of influence," and resting entirely on the vital interests of the
Chinese working masses, a radical departure from the policy
of pre-October Russia.   But that is another story.

Chapter I

ORIGIN OF THE MANCHURIAN QUESTION
1892-1895

I

In the autumn of 1903 when Russia's obstinate disinclination to evacuate Manchuria no longer appeared to leave room for the slightest doubt as to the inevitability of armed collision with Japan at any moment, War Minister Kuropatkin came forward with the project for a "compromise" settlement of the Manchuria question which would make "possible the restoration of friendly relations with both China and Japan" and would bring "tranquility to the affairs not of Russia alone but of the whole world." In a memorandum presented to Nicholas II on November 23, Kuropatkin proposed "giving back to China Kwangtun with Port Arthur and Dalny, relinquishing the southern branch of the Chinese Eastern Railway, and in exchange obtaining from China the right to North Manchuria plus 250 million rubles as reimbursement for Russia's expenditures on the railway and on Port Arthur."[1]

Copies of this memorandum were confided to only three persons outside the tsar: Alekseyev, then located at Port Arthur as viceregent, Lamsdorf, still holding on by main force to the post of minister of foreign affairs, and Witte, now languishing for the fourth month in disgrace and retirement. Nicholas made no response to this routine and verbose production: Kuropatkin made no mention of it in his journal, habitually exact as to such occurrences. To Alekseyev, the thought of selling the capital of our far-eastern viceregency to China, with which country all negotiations as to the evacuation of Manchuria had just been broken off (October 7, new style) can only have seemed heresy. And Kuropatkin's proposal went by the board. So far as we know, he did not even seek to renew it, either in subsequent reports or at the repeated conferences that still continued to take place during the two months before the opening of hostilities.

Nor was Kuropatkin, in point of fact, altogether the author

of his own proposal. The idea of the necessity of annexing North Manchuria had repeatedly been expressed by him before, but the idea of bartering for it all of South Manchuria here occurs in his papers for the first time and hence had very probably been borrowed from the circumstantial and consistently motivated letter-project sent him by General Subotich in October, 1903.[2] With Subotich this idea stemmed organically from his general conception of Russia's position in the Far East, Manchuria in particular.

Subotich honestly thought that: 1) the natural coloniational pressure upon Manchuria and Korea was from China and Japan, the chances for Russian colonization there consequently negligible, and opposition by Russia to yellow colonization "simply impossible;" 2) Russia, as a continental country "occupying in one unbroken strip the vast area of 1/6 of the terrestrial globe," was not even suited to the possession of colonies, and had, therefore, no need of specific "outlets" through "ice-free ports" to the Pacific Ocean when she held the port of Vladivostok, ice-locked no later than Petersburg and Kronstadt; 3) consequently, Russia could neither dream of any sort of supremacy there for her navy nor develop there the "peace policy" which during the last ten years had already cost "not less than a milliard rubles" and now (October, 1903) "in the momentary expectation of war" demanded a daily "contribution" of 200 thousand to keep the army in combat trim; 4) this situation had been created in 1895, when Russia passed abruptly from a state of fear lest she run the Ussury road too near the Manchurian border to considerations as to how she might "unimpeded" lay tracks "for a distance of 1,500 versts directly through Manchurian territory, 400-500 versts from the Russian bank of the Amur." From all of which, Subotich drew the "practical conclusion" that is behooved Russia to "liquidate her enterprise in Manchuria."

However, to effect this liquidation "as completely as might be desired [was] at the present time already impossible"-- "unfortunately," Subotich felt--due to the extent to which we had implicated ourselves in the past five or six years. But Subotich considered quite feasible the exchange of Southern for Northern Manchuria now appropriated by Kuropatkin. Only Subotich said nothing about any supplementary payment to Russia.

As we see, the two generals were approaching the same idea from different angles: one felt regret that so little could

be ceded, the other satisfaction that it would be possible to
keep just what was needed and still make a little something
on the side. But at the given moment, in face of the direct
threat of war, they may be thought of as standing together.

Quite unexpectedly, the Subotich-Kuropatkin project was
fully endorsed by the other two readers of the secret memorandum produced by the long-standing advocate of annexation
for Northern Manchuria, though up to that moment both had
stubbornly denied either the admissibility or the possibility
of any annexation of Chinese territory after the seizure of
Liaotung peninsula. Witte now told Kuropatkin "that a year
ago [i.e., in the autumn of 1902] he would have been against
the settlement proposed [in the memorandum] but that now,
after all that had happened, he saw no way out of the difficult
and uncertain position into which we had got ourselves other
than the one proposed, i.e., to secure Northern Manchuria
to Russia at the price of conceding South Manchuria and
Kwantung province. He, Witte, should the emperor so desire, would undertake to persuade Count Lamsdorf also of
the necessity for this decision."[3] But Lamsdorf needed no
persuasion: it turned out that he had "read...the memorandum...with pleasure...and would be very glad to see this
plan adopted."[4] Witte, for his part, "would undertake to
realize the 250 million rubles indicated [in the memorandum]
as payable for the southern branch and the constructions in
Kwantung and was completely agreeable to their being employed organizationally in the Far East. The returns would be
enormous.[5]

Witte and Lamsdorf, it must not be forgotten here, were
making a twofold concession in not only agreeing to the annexation of Northern Manchuria, but also, and no less, in acceding to the renunciation of all acquisitions in the south. Actually
they had, the year before, amicably discredited the latter
idea, then, it seems, seeking admission to the highest spheres.
Shortly after the publication of the Manchurian evacuation
treaty, in May, 1902, the Rosenthal press in Berlin had printed
--on fine paper and in an edition of only 25 copies--a brochure
entitled: "Manchzhurskii vopros. Posviashchaetsia S. I.
Vitte (The Manchurian Question: Dedicated to S.Yu. Witte).
A copy of this was received or obtained by Witte and passed
on to Lamsdorf; the latter was detailed to draft objections to
it and presented these to the tsar. Even without seeking to
unmask the pseudonymous author lurking behind the letter Z,

one may suspect that the aim of the brochure was to deal a
blow at the Witte-Lamsdorf policy not for the edification of
the general public but for a narrow and exalted circle, and
furthermore that the author did not lack support in this circle.

It would be difficult to explain in any other way the importance attached to the brochure by both of the ministers interested and under attack, the more so since the practical conclusions drawn by the brochure were known to be unacceptable to Nicholas. These practical conclusions boiled down to:
1) Russia's abandonment of Port Arthur; 2) "the conversion
of the Manchurian railways from strategic to purely commercial carriers" by laying a cut-off of the Siberian road between
Sretensk and Blagoveshchensk and annexing the extreme northern segment of Manchuria isolated by the new line; and 3)
the sale to China both of the Chinese Eastern trunk line and
of its southern branch. Russia would then "at a stroke return
to the traditional path of peaceful and friendly relations with
China...which was unthinkable while the Manchurian question
existed."

The whole sting and peril of the brochure, calm and correct
to a fault, lay however not in these conclusions but in the
fact that: 1) the author made a point of not considering them
"perfect" and not insisting upon them, and 2) attached chief
importance to his basic critical premises, from which he admitted the possibility of deriving other "practical" conclusions.
The author indicated as the basic defect of the Manchurian
evacuation treaty of March 26, 1902, that it did not in itself
settle the Manchurian question but left permanently open the
possibility of international complications, due to the co-exis-
tence in Manchuria of two administrations and two armed
forces, the Russian and the Chinese, between which "ceaseless conflicts" were inevitable, especially since both railway
lines were manifestly "not so much commercial as military-
strategic."

While mechanically returning the Manchurian question to
its original pre-1900 status, the treaty of March 26 in essence
absolutely failed to take into account the changed international
situation resulting from the Anglo-Japanese alliance, a situation giving China the "private support of our constant and irreconcilable enemies." In dedicating his brochure to Witte,
as "author of the Manchurian question" since he had "started
the ball rolling" ("the Manchurian railway contract of 1896 was

Your personal act,") the writer agreed to "take back everything he had said" "if the treaty of March 26 was the first
step in a sound and considered plan of action." In the contrary
event, do one of two things: either "get from China the greater
part of Manchuria or give up the risky practice of laying strategic lines through foreign territory where it takes a whole
army to guard them."

Lamsdorf's objections, which Nicholas considered a "splendid answer," were kept in the vein of a condescending expose
of the anonymous author's supposed ignorance and went no
farther than the pedantic, not always pertinent, recital of
official declarations and notes on the theme of the disinterestedness of Russia's policy, "her unalterable friendship" for
China and the latter's correspondingly special attitude toward
her. Typical of this manner was Lamsdorf's answer on the
Port Arthur point: "to this it may be objected that the return
of Port Arthur now, after all the sacrifices made, would surely be a step even more rash than the author deems its seizure.
'Rash step' is too mild a term--the return under present conditions of acquisitions already gained by Russia at a cost of
many million rubles--would be plain madness. Only persons
unacquainted with the state of affairs in the Far East could
advise such a solution."[6]

In paying tribute now, in November 1903, to this "madness," Witte encountered, ineluctable as his own shadow,
the stock rider to the idea of renouncing Liaotung--namely,
a reminder of the original decision to run the Siberian railway
straight across Manchuria. And, in their conversation of
December 2 "he, of course, took issue [with Kuropatkin] and
demonstrated the erroneousness of supposing that the occupation of Port Arthur was the consequence of building the trunk
line, at Witte's suggestion, through Northern Manchuria."[7]
And with characteristic trenchancy, as if he sensed a reluctance to understand, Witte explained: "Suppose I took some
guests of mine to the Aquarium, and they got drunk, found
their way to a brothel, and kicked up a row there. Would it
be my fault? I only intended going to the Aquarium. The
others led me on."

The cost of this "row"--on the assumption that the impending war would be victorious--one of the company, Kuropatkin,
estimated in 1903 at 700-800 million rubles of straight military expenditures.[8] Witte was able in 1909 to set this figure
at 2-1/2 billions.[9] In another, still later, calculation this

figure, including payments on loans concluded for the conduct
and liquidation of the war, grew to 7 billions.[10] But long before the war both speakers had distinctly realized that the
jaunt to the "Aquarium" was itself demanding enormous sacrifices quite apart from the "row." Back in 1901, Kuropatkin
had complained (to Polvtsov:) "our activities in the East have
now already cost us more than 800 million rubles and the end
of this interminable expenditure is not yet in sight."[11] At
that time Witte too had said: "Chinese complications have
cost us up to date a billion rubles," and "to continue this stu-
pid enterprise is impossible: it would set Russia on the road
to ruin--both financial and political."[12] In 1903 Witte spoke
of this same billion as having "weakened European Russia,"
but added that he "was not convinced that it would better have
remained unspent" and then jointly with Kuropatkin reported
to the tsar on the necessity of "moderating our expenditures
in the Far East."[13]

As to the Far East making a disproportionate drain upon
the rest of the Empire, there were essentially no two opinions,
and on the lips of such right-hand enemies of Witte as Bezobrazov and Company this idea even became polemic against
him: for example, their projects, the Far-Eastern viceregency and the Special Committee on Far Eastern Affairs,
were in part formally based on the necessity of isolating the
borderland in its budgetary aspect and transferring it to
"cost-accounting." It was in this connection that the ministry
of finance made a detailed balance-sheet in 1903, at the instance of Bezobrasov, "as to disbursements and receipts in the
provinces constituting the viceregency in the Far East for
1897-1902"--totals for items ordinary and extraordinary are
presented in the following form:

Years	Receipts	Disbursements	Difference	Average annual deficit
		In Rubles		
1897...	9,601,322	92,726,073	83,124,751	
1898...	12,573,550	123,952,316	111,378,766	
1899...	15,753,201	201,030,426	185,277,225	143.9 million
1900...	21,914,523	263,592,269	241,677,746	rubles
1901...	29,846,505	247,647,796	217,801,291	
1902...	196,885,609	220,816,797	23,931,188	
Total...	286,574,710	1,140,765,677	863,190,967	

Under the head of the Chinese Eastern Railway Company
the "balance sheet" for these same years gave the following
disbursements:

Years	Railway	Steamship Line	Port of Dalny	City of Dalny	Total
1897...	5,000,000	--	--	--	5,000,000
1898...	26,300,000	--	--	--	26,300,000
1899...	62,700,000	3,500,000	3,000,000	--	69,200,000
1900...	76,160,000	4,340,000	2,150,000	1,850,000	84,500,000
1901...	64,111,750	3,547,430	3,827,970	1,624,430	73,111,580
1902...	67,975,000	942,979	500,000	--	69,417,979
	302,246,750	12,330,409	9,477,970	3,474,430	327,529,559[14]

Not having these exact figures at his disposal, Kuropatkin
in January, 1903 set the building costs of the Chinese Eastern
Railway enterprises at 400 million rubles and estimated their
annual loss, over an indefinite period of non-earning, at 40
million rubles (20 million in interest lost on capital expended,
10 million rubles for maintenance of the guard and 10 million
rubles in operational loss.)[15] Thus around 40 per cent of
the notorious "billion" had been sunk in the so-called "Witte
enterprises." Inordinately costly, long unproductive, and
credited by rumor with "abuses" on an heroic scale, these
enterprises became the topic for more or less forceful and
malicious attacks on their omnipotent director.

In that same year of 1903, when construction on the Chinese Eastern Railway was nearing completion, the question
was seriously raised in government circles of withdrawing
the "enterprises" from the conduct of the minister of finance
and allocating their management in the normal way. While
defending, in a special report to his majesty (March 14),
the necessity of preserving the former arrangement, and
while giving a natural explanation of the protests that had
been made against it, even Witte himself did not deny that
the figure for treasury disbursements on the enterprises
really was "steep," that to complete all installations would
still require not less than 30 million rubles, that the cost of
the road per verst "figured high," and that the "first years"
of operation would undoubtedly close with "something of a"
deficit.[16]

In the presence of such a vexing of the question of the
"enterprises" into which he had admittedly put as much work

and as sincere effort" as "into any óne" of the problems of
state that had been "laid upon" him, [17] it is no wonder that
the nearer the danger of armed conflict approached a land
exhausted by domestic crisis, the more subjectively painful
for Witte became the idea expressed (and not for the first
time) in Kuropatkin's memorandum of November 23, namely
that the seizure of Liaotung, which Witte considered a gross
error and a violation of his own scheme of eastern policy,
had been the direct consequence of laying a Russian railroad
through Chinese territory. He therefore both combatted this
idea at the time, and later endeavored in every way possible
to obscure it from readers of his "Memoirs," written among
the ruins of his grandiose imperialistic dream--after the debacle. But a good half of the "enterprises" had been built up
around Port Arthur, for its sake, and in direct dependence
upon it. Does this mean that Witte in now consenting to relinquish this half was repudiating his own offspring? Meanwhile, as the war showed, Japan was fighting not only for
Korea but also for Port Arthur and for all Southern Manchuria:
consequently, after the war, did not Witte fall into one company with the so-called "true" culprits of the war--Bezobrazov,
Abaza, Alekseyev and the rest--as having been chief fashion-
er of the lever that this company grasped at the last moment?

The Chinese Eastern trunk line was Witte's own. Port
Arthur was a foundling, produced in defiance of all laws by
the "infantile" prehensile instinct and the crude "cunning" of
Nicholas II. The trunk line was an essential link in a systematic peace policy of primordial friendship based on mutual
reciprocity of interest between the two empires, a policy which
made Russia the center of that continental alliance system,
Franco-German-Russian and Russo-Chinese, in which Witte
saw the only possible means of saving an aging Europe, en-
vironed by powerful extra-European civilizations in their
prime, from attrition in armed peace or ruin in the event of
a European war. [18] The Port had been a seizure made in
broad daylight from an ally to whom inviolability had just before been guaranteed, a seizure which essentially upset the
whole structure.

This antithesis, promulgated by Witte with all the infectious-
ness of candor, served as basis for the concept of two intersectin
pre-war policies: his, Witte's, peaceful, and Nicholas's predatory. Nicholas--Port Arthur--the Yalu--the seizure of Man-
churia--war: was one. Witte--alliance with China--the trunk

line--evacuation of Manchuria--agreement with Japan: was
the other. But the theory that so annoyed Witte in Kuropatkin's November memorandum unbalanced these two parallel
series, gearing the trunk line to Port Arthur. Actually no
distinction can be drawn: the concession for the trunk line
was obtained by Russia on the pretext of alliance, friendship
and community of interests, but the whole Port Arthur scandal ran its course in the same terminology and without blood-
shed--Russian ships entered Port Arthur in order to keep the
English or the Japanese from seizing it (on the heels of Germany's seizure of Kiaochow,) and Russia then remained there
in order to pose as the efficient ally and protector of China
not only by land but by sea.

Formally not only was there no act hostile to China involved; Russia was on the contrary risking international complications in pedantically bracing the alliance. To reveal the
hostility of this act, to demonstrate that essentially there
could here be no question of China's good will, that actually
China, with no means of resisting possible coercion by Russia,
had been forced to cloak this seizure by her formal consent--
would have been easy, but such an answer did not satisfy even
Witte himself, since it did not parry the possible retort that
China had been just as powerless to withhold her consent to
the trunk line. And Witte, when it became possible to do so,
took refuge in an answer that aimed to bring out as simply and
graphically as possible a distinction that we have here ignored.

In "Prologue to the Russo-Japanese War," a book written
upon Witte's order and published in 1916, before the "Memoirs,"
this answer was confined to a single flat and laconic phrase to
the effect that Witte "by means accessible to him as minister
of finance had exerted pressure on the course of negotiations
concerning the lease of Port Arthur."[19] In the "Memoirs"
Witte no longer felt hampered in disclosing this absolutely
secret operation and told of his intervention in the course of
negotiations in great detail, describing how the Chinese plenipotentiaries Li Hung-chang and Chang Yin-huan procrastinated
about signing the agreement and only did so when Witte, to
avoid the bloodshed that would attend the forcible seizure of
Port Arthur by Russian troops, took it upon himself to promise
these plenipotentiaries "considerable gratuities."[20] It thus
turned out that the seizure of Port Arthur had been successfully put through under the fiction of "friendship for China,"
without bloodshed, only by means of a bribe, something which

could never be said of the concession for the Chinese Eastern
trunk line--and the requisite difference in the nature of these
two political acts now stood out in the proper relief. Witte
also concluded his story with a sentence highly significant in
the context: "this was the only time in my negotiations with
the Chinese when I resorted to interesting them through
bribes."[21] Thus did Witte differentiate the "Aquarium" from
the institution where his guests had behaved without regard
for propriety when already drunk.

However, upon an intensive reading of the second chapter
of Volume I of the "Memoirs," on the subject of "negotiations
with Li Hung-chang and conclusion of the treaty with China,"
there is one inconspicuous detail that attracts attention. The
negotiations with Li Hung-chang in Petersburg took place at
the apartment of the minister of finance and were opened and
conducted by Witte alone. Witte developed for the Chinese
representative the idea of the mutual utility of the agreement
proposed by Russia, while the Chinese "of course stated various obstacles." "But from the conversations with him" Witte
"understood that he would agree if he saw that our emperor
wished it."

Arrangements were made for the tsar to receive Li Hung-
chang in a private and unreported audience. Shortly after the
audience, Witte found himself in line at a palace "reception"
with others who had come to present birthday congratulations,
and when he approached Nicholas, the latter's "face lighted
up and almost in a whisper he said to me: 'Li Hung-chang
was in and I told him.'"[22] Why was a private audience necessary with an ambassador plenipotentiary attending the coronation as a matter of ceremony to present the official congratulations of the Chinese emperor, why was "absolutely no
mention made of it in official organs," and just what did
Nicholas "tell" him?

On March 7, 1908, when Li Hung-chang had been nearly
seven years in his grave, and Witte, in retirement, was
starting on his memoirs, Kokovtsov, minister of finance,
received an autograph note from Nicholas II to this effect:
"Send me for a purpose known to me 175,000 rubles (one
hundred seventy-five thousand)--from the so-called Li-Hung-
Chang fund. Nicholas. 7 March 1908." Nicholas had apparently lost no time: his requisition went in on the very day that he
received, in response to his verbal order, an autograph statement by Kokovtsov as to the ready money in the "so-called

Li Hung-change fund, carried as a special account of the minister of finance in the Russo-Chinese bank." From the statement it appears that on March 7, 1908, the balance in the
"fund" stood at 1,264,539 rubles.

"Li Hung-chang fund" is a later simplification. The original
designation had been: "special fund, designed to cover disbursements connected with the grant of the concession for the
Chinese Eastern Railway." A special dossier of disbursements from it was kept in the chancellery of the minister of
finance. Payments to the Chinese representative began a full
year before the "seizure" of Port Arthur. From 1897 to 1902
there were five such payments in all: the Port Arthur payment was second in point of time. A few payments proposed
beyond the five were for various reasons not made. In the
five installments the Chinese representative had received
1,700,947 rubles, 71 kopeks.[23]

As we see, the dossier on the "special fund" thoroughly
confutes Witte's testimony, above underlined, as to his
never having resorted to bribery in China except on that one
occasion. There can be no doubt that Witte's forgetfulness
on this point had a reason. Reticence on the part of author
of the memoirs might have explained plain silence--certainly
where any sort of political bribery was concerned, this being
the official secret of a former minister of finance. But in the
given instance, Witte's statement has a crudely tendentious
character: it represents bribery as the obligatory means for
liquidating the consequences of another person's "childishness"
and intentionally cloaks its having been, under the given conditions, the inevitable means for the tactical development of
Witte's own grandiose political plan--a means, furthermore,
not at all unusual but recurring in the most protean forms
throughout the whole diplomatic history of international relations between European and non-European countries alike.

It is easy to understand why Witte--who rate the Russo-
Japanese war of 1904-1905 as cardinal disturbing factor in
the fortunes of the Russian empire--should have had no desire, and seen no reason to be classed with the "authors of
the ill-starred war," as he expressed it, which he considered
Nicholas II, Bezobrazov, Abaza, Alekeseyev, and their ilk
to be, and in part even Kuropatkin along with them. But all
his efforts both then and post factum to keep clear of this
group and their "policy," even his version of Port Arthur,
were insufficient to obscure in essence the profoundly con-

flictive nature and the extreme riskiness--for the empire as
it was--of that policy of which Witte was himself both proponent
and artisan. In our review of the nodal aspects of this policy,
the dossier on the Li Hung-chang fund will frequently permit
a quite objective rending of the thick literary veil in which
Witte swathed his theory of a "peaceful" and a "predatory"
policy, mutually exclusive since ostensibly one pursued aims
and employed means that did not expose Russia to the danger
of war in the Far East while the other on both counts frantically
played with fire.

II

We have no facts to show that Witte had been interested in
the Far East, let alone occupied himself with it, previous to
his appointment as minister of means of communication in
February, 1892. But from that time forth, practically after
presenting his first report, he made the building of the great
Siberian road his specific concern.[24] Fully elaborated on
the technical side and settled in principle years before, this
question may be said to have descended to Witte as a going
concern and in almost final form. Piecemeal planning of
separate intra-Siberian lines had started immediately upon
the annexation of the Amur region (1858), had in 1875 been
promoted, in Posiet's project, to the concept of a continuous
railway from Volga to Amur, had then been interrupted by the
war of 1877-1878 and the financial crisis, and had in the early
80's been focussed exclusively upon the Volgo-Ural section
in view of the continued financial depression, but had in the
late 80's revived and assumed a quality of urgency, in direct
consequence of the turn that international relations in the Far
East had taken. The swing from the Near East to the Far
East after the Russo-Turkish war--as exemplified in the fact
that the Volunteer Fleet Society, with Alexander III (then
crown prince) as sponsor and Pobedonostsev as president,
put all its steamers on Black Sea--Pacific Ocean runs--coin-
cided with the above-mentioned (see pp. 7-9) aggravation of
the Korean question in its Sino-Japanese aspect and the concentration around it of the interests of the great powers.
Russia's attempt to seize a Korean port and introduce military instructors into Korea, a failure in view of England's
interference (1885) revealed Russia's weakness there and
made her next task the rapid improvement of her fighting

means, while the balance established between China and Japan with respect to Korea by the treaty of 1885 was still in force. Actually, in 1886, the governors-general of both western and eastern Siberia raised the question of the immediate strategic necessity of railway lines from Tomsk to Irkutsk and from Baikal to Sretensk, and in 1887 preliminary surveys were started not only for these but in the Ussuri sector as well. Yet despite repeated representations both by the governors-general and by the ministers of war and navy as to the urgency for constructing these lines, in view of the measures being taken by China to improve her military means, I.A. Vyshnegradsky, completely preoccupied with the accumulation of a metal reserve, obstinately refused an allocation for this purpose, until the news finally came that the Chinese government had engaged English engineers to make preliminary surveys for a railway through southern Manchuria along the Russian and Korean boundary to the Manchurian city of Hunchun (July, 1890)--and the question of building at least a single Ussury line again came up for discussion.

This time the question moved out of deadlock: Alexander III affirmed the necessity of "setting to work at once on the construction of this [the Ussury] road," whereupon Girs, minister of foreign affairs, declared that "Russia's position relative to China prompted the ministry of foreign affairs to consider the building of the Siberian road a question of paramount importance to Russia" (letter of August 31, 1890) and finally the Council of Ministers, voting on the allocation for the Ussury line, upon the motion of the minister of war, expressed itself as unanimously in favor of building a continuous Siberian railroad, in view of the fact that the termless, piecemeal building of separate lines was incompatible with the recognized urgency of the strategic aim (meeting of 12-21 February, 1891). Practically, however, they would have to keep strictly within the limits of the existing credit extraordinary for the building of new railways (about seven million rubles for 1891 and 1892) sufficient only to start work from the two extremities, (from Vladivostok in 1891, from Chelyabinsk in 1892). The rock against which the matter had beaten for five full years checked the impact of the rising whirlwind until itself thrown down: Vyshnegradsky resolutely sabotaged an enterprise that seemed to him risky--until himself dismissed. Meanwhile, the whirlwind, once raised, increased irresistibly in accordance with its own laws.

By-passing the question of financial possibilities, the Russian government proclaimed to all the world its determination
to build a "continuous railroad all the way across Siberia"
(rescript issued in the name of the heir-apparent, March 17,
1891). The Chinese government in turn responded (July, 1891)
by setting up an "Administration of imperial Chinese railways," and setting about the extension of its Peking-Tientsin
railway north to Shanhaikwan.[25] But in Russia that same
July, Gyubbenet (minister of roads) produced a complete plan
for building the Siberian road in six parts and over three periods, in an estimated twelve years, and at a cost of about 350
million rubles--with an economical disregard for a number
of indispensable technical provisions that manifestly fore-
boded the necessity before long of a complete relaying of the
roadbed practically all along the line. Such was the state of
affairs when Witte replace Gyubbenet and, as above stated,
was given authority to begin laying the road from Chelyabinsk,
together with an advance of 1,100,000 on the 7,000,000 ruble
credit. In view of the fact that Vyshengradsky not only refused
to support Gyubbenet's plan but also declared that it was figured
too high it would seem that politically the question had reached
maturity infinitely before the country was ready for it financially
or economically, having completed the accumulation of a gold
reserve precisely in a year of such bad harvests as threatened
not only to disturb the trade balance but to undermine for an
indefinite period the very solvency of the Russian countryside.
But even before the famine year of 1891, Vyshnegradsky had
not confined himself to a bare refusal of means from the treasur
but had expressed himself on the merits of the question. In
killing the requisition for the Ussury strip in 1890, he first of
all negated the seriousness of the danger that had been regarded
as attaching to China's intention of building a road into Man-
churia--on the strength of the Chinese government's apathy in
the matter of railway-building in general (wherein he proved to
be right)--and then denied the serious strategic significance
of one lone Ussury line. In general, Vyshnegradsky declined
to consider the question of railways in Siberia from any angle
except that of their commercial productivity and economic significance, and accordingly would only let building begin from
the west, things then being left to take their natural course.
And in 1891, when his argument as to the senselessness of
an isolated Ussury line was turned to the advantage of the
continuous Trans-Siberian road, he could still caution against

that "announcement" about starting work on a job inevitably requiring a large loan, the mere intimation of such an intention being bound to have repercussions on the Russian rate of exchange. Fear of the risk concomitant to the question was uppermost in Vyshnegradsky's mind and left him cold to the attractions of a course that meant risk and bold decisions. This man was clearly becoming less and less fitted to cope with the march of events and the demands of his immediate political environment.[26]

The transfer of Witte from the post of minister of roads to the post of minister of finance (in August, 1892) meant an abrupt volte face on the question of the Siberian road. It would obviously have been impossible for Witte even to consider continuing the policy pursued by his predecessor: this would have contradicted the very purpose of the new appointment. This appointment had expressly testified to an irrevocable decision to get out of deadlock at any cost and not be deterred by expense from an enterprise capable of effecting a re-annexation to the empire of that vast and promising area of 1,420,000 square versts, or throwing Siberian grain into the world market, systematically diverting the excess population of central Russia, and organizing about itself a diversified economic process. For the terrible economic picture revealed in European Russia must have had the effect of pushing the question of the great road forward, just as international complications over the Korean question and symptoms of English penetration into northern China had for some time exercised a pull on it.

One must also bear in mind that to produce a plan for building the "great Siberian road" and a project for its uninterrupted financing, thereby at a stroke removing the question from the state of deadlock in which Vyshnegradsky had kept it, was for Witte (in November, 1892) all the easier since he now had not only the actual Franco-Russian agreement of August 9-15, 1891, to go on, but also the recently accepted project (August 17, 1892) for a Franco-Russian military convention. These two acts virtually eliminated all financial risk earlier associated with the enterprise. It now had a sound financial base and the air of being the point of departure for a great political program with pretensions to world significance.[27]

It is imperative to note that the historian will seek in vain for any essential details of this aspect in the pages of Witte's "Memoirs." Here the foreground is occupied by the assign-

ment of the road's construction to the conduct of a special
committee having wide powers and the heir to the throne as
chairman. The latter circumstance Witte quite evidently
esteemed a happy move since it gave the committee virtually
the character of a sovereign organ and personally committed
the future tsar to a difficult and protracted affair otherwise
secure only for the length of Alexander III's lifetime and quite
likely to languish under his successor. And it is upon this
that Witte chiefly dwells in his "Memoirs," quoting as an
illustration of the expediency of the move the sympathetic
attitude of Nicholas II to the idea ("almost revolutionary")
of a systematic transplantation of peasants to Siberia.[28]
Again, in his voluminous report to his majesty (November 6,
1892) "On methods for constructing the great Siberian road
and on the calling of a conference to discuss this matter,"
Witte by no means confined himself to the financial and technical side of the matter, but endeavored to compass the question in its entirety, dwelling at some length on "principles
for guidance in the consideration" of construction methods.
And it can scarcely be accidental that the exposition of this
report in the "Prologue to the Russo-Japanese War," prepared under Witte's supervision, dwells almost exclusively
on such "principles" as had to do with the economic significance of the road in the restricted sense of the word, and
evades any broader aspects that had been mirrored with enthusiasm in the text of the report.[29]
    Now, in 1892, Witte is already enthralled by the world
scale of the task confronting him. He deliberately sidesteps
a narrowly financial treatment of his theme, leaving this
aspect until the very last. Small matter if "a continuous
railroad all the way across Siberia is a state enterprise in
the broad sense of the term," implying "the greatest possible
benefits in the field of economic, cultural and political interests" both for European Russia and for Siberia. The fact that
the great Siberian road would establish "uninterrupted European rail communication with the Great Ocean and the Asiatic
East," breaking a "new path and [opening] new horizons not
only for Russian but for world trade," "ranks it as one of
those world events that usher in new epochs in the history of
nations and not infrequently bring about the radical upheaval
of established economic relations between states."
    Witte was well aware of the fact--closely related to ideas
expressed in a memorandum by representatives of the Russian

merchant guild at Nizhegorod fair of 1889[29]--that a Siberian
trunk-line through to Vladivostok would project Russia into
the settlement of the problem of the Pacific, where all the
symptoms already existed of an economic struggle about to
get out of bounds. The Canadian railway, "now already" diverting a part of the silk and tea shipments that had formerly
reached Europe entirely through Suez, strikes Witte as an
"instructive example" for gauging the cost of the Siberian
railway, which in extent and in the character of the vast regions to be crossed, offers many analogies to the Canadian.[30]
But the latter only shortened transit between Europe and
Shanghai from 45 days through Suez to 35 across Canada,
whereas the Siberian will reduce it to 18 or 20 days.

On this basis, a "reversal in the direction of communication between Europe and the Asiatic East" is bound to occur, and to Russia's advantage "not only as intermediary in
the commercial exchange of the products of East Asia and
Western Europe" but also as "largescale producer and consumer, since she stands nearest to the nations of the Asiatic
east." Meanwhile "China, Japan and Korea, with a combined
population of not less that 260 millions, and a present international trade turnover of not less than 500 million rubles in
gold, are still far from having developed their trade relations
with Europe to the fullest possible extent, nay, rather, are not
yet out of the initial stage of their development." "It is therefore no wonder that nations European in civilization are exerting tremendous efforts to get possession of eastern Asiatic
markets, balking at nothing in the way of expenditures." And
Witte figured that "through the very fact of her immediate
proximity" to the eastern countries named, Russia would,
with the laying of the Siberian trunk-line, enjoy "important
advantages" in this respect "over all the other states of Europe."

To exemplify this general formula of the international importance of the Siberian project, Witte took Russo-Chinese
economic relations, where he was clearly feeling his way
through to an alliance not only defensive but offensive, though
still economic, against England. The latter country controlled
two-thirds of the exports going out of Chinese ports, and the
number of English ships in these ports was steadily increasing.
On the other hand, England was at the same time striving to
become a competitor of China in the production of tea, and
plantations in England's Asiatic colonies--India and Ceylon--
had already become the chief purveyors of tea to all Great

Britain. And again, as always, it was the railway network
in East India that gave England the overwhelming advantage
in hauling tea to ports themselves only half as far from Europe
as the Chinese ports. In consequence, the export of Chinese
teas to London and other consumer countries was "steadily
and rapidly declining," thereby presenting a "serious problem" both "to a considerable part of the Chinese population"
and "to the Chinese treasury" (in view of the high export
duty). Which meant that "in this connection the Siberian railway can be of great assistance to the Chinese tea industry, in
removing China's most dangerous competitor from the position
of middleman in the Chinese tea trade with European countries
and in securing for Chinese teas much faster delivery to Europe
not only as compared with their transport by sea from China
through London but also as compared with the speedier transport of East-Indian teas." "Wherefore," Witte concluded,
"not only Russia, but China as well has an interest in seeing
England's role in the transport of teas and in their merchan-
dising to European countries taken over by Russia, which at
the same time itself represents a wide, and, it may be said,
each day widening, consumer market for tea."

The specter of England was still before Witte's eyes when
he foresaw that "Russia might considerably expand her export
to China of cotton and woolen manufactured articles and likewise of metals"--wares which China was importing to the
amount of 80-90 million rubles in gold, "but not from Russia,
whose total export to China did not exceed 3 million rubles
in value, with the whole turnover along the Siberian border
of China not in excess of 17-18 million rubles."

The "political and strategic" importance of the great Siberian road Witte regarded as "obvious," and he dwelt on
this subject for only a few lines--which thus become all the
more precious. "Our power" in the east would increase in
proportion as the distance decreased, while the strengthening of economic ties would lead to the establishment of
"friendly" political relations with "eastern countries" on the
basis of "recognition of tangible mutual interests in the field
of the worldwide economic activity of mankind." He even
thought that the "opportunity" also opening up "for more direct relations with the North-American States" would disclose a "solidarity of political interests" between Russia and
that country. Finally, the Siberian railway "would provide
the Russian navy with everything needful and give it a firm

point of support in our eastern ports." "Wherefore, with the
opening of the road, this navy can be considerably strengthened
and, in the event of political complications, whether in Europe
or in the Asiatic east, will acquire a high degree of significance,
controlling the whole movement of international commerce in
Pacific waters."

Such was the first sketch of the "Aquarium," where Witte
intended taking his "guests." When they "got drunk," the
"row" started over their boasting about being "admirals of the
Pacific ocean" and refusing to listen to reason. By then (1898
and thereafter) others had already "led them on." In particular, a winged word of greeting from the admiral of the Atlantic to the admiral of the Pacific, tossed off by Wilhelm II during
one of his visits to Nicholas, became a fixed conventions with
these two "friends." And Witte could never recall without annoyance, after the debacle, this provocative sally of the "evil
genius" of a tsar susceptible to such flattery. Yet the magical
and alluring "control" "of the Russian navy" "over the whole
movement of international commerce" "in Pacific waters"had
also been on the "Aquarium" program when Witte invited his
guest there back in 1892.

Here among the flourishes of the original redaction of the
Russian political program for the Far East there was not, nor
could there be, any elaboration of concrete diplomatic questions,
any attempt to take account of the aggregate of international
political forces and how they would be massed in the Pacifíc
struggle. But the two major forces, England and China, were
boldly and distinctly figured in. Witte's picture of the Siberian
road as a weapon for a political alliance with China and as a
means of undermining England's colonial might was quite concrete. But as yet Japan and Korea stood out for him only in
very general outlines, lumped with China, as strips of one
field--largely still unplowed--the destined arena of Russia's
economic activity in the East. Relative to the U.S.A., Witte
was grossly in error.

As we see, this first redaction of the program offered alluring prospects but contained no concrete practical deductions as
to methods for realizing them. That it failed to satisfy Witte
from precisely this angle may be judged by the alacrity with
which he grasped at the first possibility that offered for filling
in this gap--oddly enough, a chimerical, quack project of the
notorious Badmayev's. Needless to say we shall find nothing
in the"Memoirs" this time either of a nature to clarify the sub-

ject. How Witte "met Badmayev through Ukhtomsky, whose
favor he had courted on one of his journeys to China": whether on the initiative of Ukhtomsky, or, as seems more likely,
that of Badmayev, or, not inconceivably, that of Witte himself, is destined to remain unknown.[31]

In any event, this Buryat-Slavophile and cattleman-poli-
tician--successively student at the Irkutsk gymnasia, orien-
tal-student at Petersburg University, then functionary in the
ministry of foreign affairs, and at one time reader in Mongolian at our capital's university, upon conversion to ortho-
doxy sponsored by no less a godfather than Alexander III, going straight from the philologist's bench (1875) into medical
practice, clinging tightly to Petersburg but still not severing
his connections with the east--Badmayev came forward in
February, 1893, with a project that was entirely agreeable
to the finance minister. One is tempted to think that in presenting to the finance minister (February 13, 1893) a voluminous memorandum on the urgent historic mission of Russia in the Far East, with the request that he report to Alexander III both this memorandum and concerning the results
obtained by Badmayev from his studies in Tibetan medicine,
which had apparently interested the tsar, Badmayev was
acting on an understanding with Witte.[32] The fact that Witte
at once transmitted the Badmayev memorandum to Alexander III,
in connection with an explanatory report of his own, and never
so much as mentioned the medicinal part of Badmayev's request, also suggests a preliminary understanding.[33]

Though it must be admitted that Badmayev, having built
up his argument historically, out of the very depths of the
Muscovite ages, failed to regulate the dose of his ideological
compound to the scale of his concrete proposals, and while
his memorandum undoubtedly pleased Alexander III, it evoked
in him a certain consternation: "this is all so new, unusual
and fantastic that it is hard to believe in the possibility of
success."

These proposals of Badmayev's boiled down to extension
of the Siberian road from Baikal not only to Vladivostok but
also southward, 1,800 versts into China, to the city of Lan-
chowfu, in Kansu province, and the preliminary creation
there of the secret political center for an uprising of the
Tibetan, Mongolian, and Chinese population against the Manchu dynasty, to be followed by a spontaneous appeal of the
merchant-feudal nobility of these peoples to the Russian (the

"white") tsar to accept them as his subjects. Badmayev proposed that he himself organize the preparations for this bloodless annexation of "the whole Mongol-Tibetan-Chinese east,"
acting through the agency of "a few thousand" Buryat-pioneer
frontiersmen dispatched by him, Badmayev, in all directions
as peddlers of articles in general demand and various sorts
of arms. "Upon acquainting himself with the contents of this
memorandum," Witte found that Badmayev "was expressing
very serious views," "that estabish a new point of view on
practical questions of policy that has particular significance
at the present time, since the building of the great Siberian
road...will exercise a potent influence...on the relations of
Russia...not only with the Asiatic East, but with the European
West as well."[34]

Unfolding to the tsar in Slavophile vein the idea of Russia's
peculiar political position between East and West, Witte expressed the fear that "European policy might attempt to arouse
against us the aggressive tendencies of China for seizure of
the poorly defended eastern section of the Siberian railway
and all adjoining territory, the maritime strip and Vladivostok not excepted." Meanwhile, should Badmayev's enterprise
produce the desired results, then "from the shores of the Pacific and the heights of the Himalayas Russia would dominate
not only the affairs of Asia but those of Europe as well." But
even in itself the "question of feeder branches into Chinese
territory" seemed to Witte "deserving of full consideration."
And Witte was prepared to place Badmayev's proposed undertaking on a practical footing at once, offering to "seek suitable means of support"--"quite unofficially"--for its carrying out.

However, the above-quoted sceptical resolution of the
tsar nipped in the bud any such "practical" settlement by
Witte of the political problem of the Siberian trunk-line. And
when, by the summer of that same year, the deal narrowed
down to what really interested Badmayev, namely the organization of his own "private enterprise," this took the form of
a "mercantile house, Badmayev and Company," quite impracticable without a treasury loan of 2,000,000 rubles for
10 years at 4 per cent--"for the proper organization and operation of a stock-breeding farm."[35] Badmayev gave assurances besides that the loan would "certainly be repaid as
soon as a multitude of enterprises well known to me, with a
turnover of tens of millions, shall have been firmly estab-

lished," and that the income alone from these enterprises
would enable him "gradually to approach the contemplated
aim."[36] And the tsar, having by this time apparently succeeded in accustoming himself to the "fantastic" project,
approved the loan.[37]

   Witte was here making his first experiment in working
toward "hidden political objectives" by peaceful means
through the medium of "private undertakings" on treasury
money. But justice must be done him: at the last minute
he tried "on various pretexts" to stop the loan, in full consciousness of his personal responsibility and of what he knew
to be the irrecoverable nature of the loan.[38] But it was already too late to reverse himself, the more so since for the
time being he had nothing with which to replace the pabulum
that he had himself offered and that the tsar's political imagination had assimilated. And the loan to Badmayev went
through. But immediately thereafter major events of an international character occurred in the Far Eàst, compelling
a close examination of the practical question of Russian
policy there in connection with the Siberian trunk-line, and
its irrevocable decision.

III

   Witte's November plan made it possible to initiate building operations at once along a stretch of more than 3,000
versts --quite literally without taking thought for the morrow.[39]
The operations of the so-called first stage were calculated
at seven to eight years (until 1900) but the question of the
second and third stages, a matter of nearly 4,000 versts,
was left open. It so happened that Witte's presentation to
the Siberian Committee of his project for further defining
this question and speeding up construction as a whole (traffic to be opened by 1899 along the whole line except for the
Amur section and Baikal, by 1901 everywhere except around
Baikal) took place in the spring of 1894, and the Committee's
decisive session occurred on May 3, old style. May 3 was
the very day when an uprising was launched in the south of
Korea under the slogan: "Down with the Japanese and all
foreigners," bringing in its wake the introduction first of
Chinese, then of Japanese troops, and creating the pretext
for Japan to start a war, ostensibly in defense of Korean independence.[40]

The joint demand of America, Russia, France, and England for simultaneous withdrawal of troops by both sides met with no success, the Japanese took possession of the palace at Seoul and established a regency over the reigning king (July 23, new style), sank an English transport carrying Chinese troops (July 25), and on August 1 reached the point of a formal declaration of war.[41] Russia's position in the matter was affected by the fact that ever since the suppressed Anglo-Russian clash on the Korean question in 1885 the primary thing for her to reckon with, in view of the exclusively economic successes of the Japanese in Korea, had been the indisputable dominant influence of English diplomacy in China on other than Korean matters, an influence to be feared all along the eastern border of China. Japan's intrusion now into Korea forced Russia to seek means for staving off a premature settlement of the Korean question, since "Korea's destiny as a component part of the Russian empire, on geographical and political grounds, had been foreordained for us to fulfill."[42] But Japan in turn "was fighting in Korea for her own future" and "for her own independence," which would be lost "the moment Korea came under the control of any European power."[43] Thus England again appeared in the position of <u>tertius gaudens</u> and the whole difficulty for Russia lay in disposing this adversary of hers to joint action.

Naturally, as soon as the war began, the Russian government was faced with the question of what attitude Russia was to assume in this war and what measures she should take if the winning side "conceived the design of encroaching on the territorial inviolability of Korea." This question was four times discussed during 1894-95 at special conferences of the ministers interested, and, consistently with the progress of hostilities, evoked radical differences of opinion which are of some interest from the viewpoint of subsequent Russian policy.[44]

The formal declaration of war had forestalled England's practically pre-arranged project for international intervention in the conflict, proposing the temporary partition of Korea into two spheres of occupation: the south, Japanese, and the north, Chinese. At the conference of August 9, Girs therefore saw fit to move that <u>conjointly with England</u> they strive to obtain cessation of hostilities, and a peace agreement, on the basis of "preservation of the <u>status quo</u> in Korea," "without in any way showing preference to either of the warring powers." This motion met with no objections and the decisions

of the conference were based upon it. But Witte then brought
up the point that at the close of the war "Great Britain, which
never missed a chance to reinforce her position in the Far
East, might intervene" and that "such intervention must not"
be permitted, wherefore it behooved us to be prepared to administer a rebuff to England in the event of her manifesting
ambitious intentions." And after him Vannovsky spoke on the
possibility of an Anglo-Chinese alliance after the defeat of
China, and the necessity of starting "in plenty of time" to
prepare the troops along the South-Ussurian frontier "for
action," whereupon Witte promised to open credit for the mobilization of the Ussuri armies. The decree of the conference
was accordingly supplemented to this effect.

The conference of January 20, 1895, met when the fortunes
of war had already been decided and the first Chinese plenipotentiaries had arrived in Kobe for the peace negotiations.[45]
And the question before it was: whether Russia should continue to act "jointly with the other powers" "in the matter of
Korea" or "whether we ought now to take an independent stand."
The situation was rather vague: on the one hand, Japan already held Port Arthur and Weihaiwei, was stubbornly con-
cealing her peace terms, and it was regarded as "highly possible" that "certain powers would present their demands to
the combatants," but on the other hand, Japan had testified
that she did not intend to encroach on the independence of
Korea, and England was behaving with perfect "correctness"
(reported Shishkin, assistant minister of foreign affairs).
Therefore the discussion of the question of possible guarantees for Russia against the strengthening of Japan, or the
chance of seizures by other powers, took on a somewhat
theoretical character. The occupation of the island of Kargo-
do at the entrance to Broughton strait, proposed by the ministry of foreign affairs, met sharp opposition from the chief
of staff, in view of the distance of this island from the continental base, and was feebly supported by the minister of
the navy, who in turn pointed out the possibility of Russia's
occupying "part of Manchuria" to counterbalance Japan's occupation of Ports Arthur and Weihaiwei.

The first practical proposal, a sort of development of his
August proposal, was introduced by Witte: namely, that,
while maintaining a policy of non-intervention, we increase
our naval forces in the Pacific--on the expectation that the
strengthening of our squadron "in view of possible compli-

cations" would rouse England to act toward a speedy ending
of the war; and again Witte promised to arrange the necessary credit. In his opinion, "nothing remained to us for the
time being but to act in conjunction with England," since, as
Count Kapnist, Director of the Asiatic Department, agreed,
only this course "offered any possibility of averting the disastrous consequences of the Sino-Japanese clash and gaining
the time necessary for the completion of the Siberian railway,
when we shall be in a position to step forward in the full pano-
ply of our material means and take our proper place in Pacific affairs."

Upon this occasion, the question of an agreement with England did not pass off as smoothly as it had done in August.
Objections were raised by the military: Chikhachev (minister
of the navy) doubted whether England would be interested in
defending the independence of Korea, and as an argument
against a general protectorate of the powers over Korea (the
variant allowed by Kapnist) pointed out the indispensability
of Korean ports for the berthing of Russian warships. Vannovsky agreed only "if we may be confident that this will not
react unfavorably upon our future relations with Japan"; and
Obruchev (chief of staff) frankly expressed himself as "particularly opposed to any joint action with England aimed at
arresting the progress of the Japanese, since, in his opinion,
the more China was weakened the better it would be for Russia," inasmuch as Russia's interest was the modification of
the Russian boundary of the Amur province. Grand Duke
Aleksey, who presided over the conference, proposed that
they nonetheless "endeavor" to arrive at an agreement, and
the conference resolved: 1) to increase the squadron, 2) to
endeavor to enter into an agreement, not only with England
but also with France and the rest, relative to exerting their
collective influence on Japan, with a view to preserving the
independence of Korea, and 3) should such an agreement
prove possible only regarding a joint guarantee of Korean independence by the powers, to reconsider the question.[46]

Meanwhile peace negotiations between Japan and China continued to drag and the conversations with powers recommended
by the conference could yield nothing until the Japanese terms
had been announced.[47] Not until March 13/25 did the delivery
of the text of these terms to Li Hung-chang take place at
Shimonoseki.[48] What we had up to that time considered the
main point--namely, the independence of Korea--was among

them. In relation to the rest, the ministry of foreign affairs
had no definite instructions. Except for England, which now
declined to support any interference whatsoever in the progress
of peace negotiations, the position of other powers remained
uncertain, but, meanwhile, to wait longer without arriving at
any decision meant to let the time for it slip by: the armistice
between China and Japan expired on April 8/20--and Prince
Lobanov, the newly appointed (March 6) Minister of Foreign
affairs, reported to the tsar on March 25 on the situation thus
created. He did not doubt that Japanese occupation of the
"peninsula on which Port Arthur was situated" would "from
the viewpoint of our interests" be "an extremely undesirable
fact," but if we should demand that the Japanese relinquish
Liaotung, and if they refused, ought Russia to "resort to coercive measures"--with the position of France and Germany
uncertain and England's attitude toward Russia's taking this
step known to be negative?

The utmost that Lobanov would himself undertake would be
to "indicate to the Japanese government in the most friendly
terms that the seizure of Port Arthur would be a lasting impediment to the restoration of cordial relations with China
and grounds for a breach of peace in the orient," as a preliminary, however, convincing himself that the powers would
subscribe to this step. Nicholas II "fully shared" Lobanov's
opinion, agreed not to demand the return of Port Arthur. "But
from a purely Russian point of view would it not be well to consider the occupation by us of port Lazarev or some other port
in eastern Korea," Nicholas added, i.e., posed the question
of compensations for the independence of Korea.49 In the
terminology of the conference of January 20, Nicholas had in
view Russia's now taking an "independent stand." But under
the given conditions, with Korean independence written into
the Shimonoseki treaty at the instance of Japan, Nicholas's
idea looked like the practicable means for reaching an agreement not with China but with Japan. To this choice between
China and Japan (in favor of Japan) the tsar had been pushed
by Lobanov himself.

With his report of March 25, Lobanov had also presented
to the tsar a special memorandum in which he posed point-
blank precisely that question: the choice as between China
and Japan of "Russia's future ally." "If our present position
in the Far East satisfies us" and "we aspire only to consolidate it," then a weak China will be Russia's best ally. But

"should we be compelled to seek the satisfaction of our urgent needs in the Far East through aggressive actions, the case would be altered." Lobanov considered these "needs" to be: 1) the acquisition by us of an ice-free port on the Pacific ocean and 2) the annexation of a certain part of Manchuria, indispensable for the more convenient laying of the Siberian railway ("imenno [precisely]," Nicholas underscored these lines.) But China: 1) possesses "no" port which could be ceded to Russia and 2) "surely will not voluntarily relinquish part of the Manchurian area." Since Japan "will in all probability at some time need our support" against England's dominant influence by sea, England being the "chief and most dangerous adversary in Asia" of Russia as well, as agreement with Japan seemed to Lobanov "not entirely impossible." Lobanov did not himself come out in favor of either one of the two combinations, merely proposing that they take "great care to avoid exerting any influence hostile to Japan without cognizance of the other powers, in order not to do future injury to our excellent relations with the Japanese government." But Nicholas came out categorically in favor of the satisfaction of "urgent needs": "For Russia a year-round free and open port is absolutely indispensable. This port must be on the mainland (in the south-east of Korea) and must without fail be linked with our previous possessions by a strip of land." And both these documents--as we have seen, with the tsar's exhaustive resolutions--Nicholar proceeded to transmit to Grand Duke Aleksey, presiding officer for the forthcoming conference of ministers.[50]

Five days later, however, on March 30, the conference opened under rudely altered conditions. Lobanov brought to the meeting some news that had just come in: 1) that Germany had professed her readiness "to join in any step that we might deem necessary to take in Tokyo to the end of impelling Japan to renounce not only her seizure of southern Manchuria and Port Arthur, but the Pescadores islands as well" and 2) that France had also agreed to "adapt her actions to ours." This, as Lobanov expressed it, "unexpected veer" in the German government's position returned to its initial state the question that had been virtually decided by Nicholas.

Grand Duke Aleksey, on the strength of the directive received, nonetheless dutifully defended and even developed the positions of the Lobanov memorandum and proposed entering into a "private" understanding with Japan relative to Russia's

seizure of a Korean port and of the strip of Manchuria along
the Amur--even "in advance of the completion of the Siberian
railway." But Vannovsky, retreating from the stand he had
taken at the preceding conference, instantly put in his word
against Japan and proposed, in the event of her refusing to
relinquish Manchuria (if only on the terms: southern Korea
for Japan, a Korean port for Russia,) "a resort to force."
Next Lobanov himself, to be sure without drawing any deduction, declared that the war undertaken by Japan had been
aimed not so much against China as against Russia and that
"to count on Japan's friendship was in any event impossible."

The whole burden of deciding the question was assumed in
the most energetic manner, and one which ruled out all objections, by Witte, who asserted his right, as minister of
finance, to have first say, since "in the event of an unhappy
decision of this question we risk losing all that has so laboriously been accomplished toward setting our finances in order."
He held "that the war had been undertaken by Japan in consequence of our having commenced construction on the Siberian
railway. All the European powers, and Japan too, apparently,
realize that the partition of China is not far off, and in the
event of such a partition, Japan's hostile activities are aimed
chiefly against us. The seizure of the southern part of Manchuria proposed by the Japanese will be a threat to us and
will probably lead to Japan's annexation later on of Korea as
well. When they get their indemnity of 600 million rubles
from China, the Japanese will fortify themselves in the localities they have seized, win over the highly warlike Mongols
and Manchus, and then start a new war. In such a state of
affairs, the mikado might, not inconceivably, in the course
of a few years, become emperor of China. If we now admit
the Japanese into Manchuria, then the guarding of our possessions and of the Siberian road will require hundreds of thousands of troops and a considerable increase in our navy, since
sooner or later we shall inevitably come into conflict with the
Japanese.

This raises the question: which would be better--to reconcile ourselves to Japan's seizure of the southern part of Manchuria and recoup ourselves after the completion of the Siberian road, or to make up our minds here and now actively
to prevent such a seizure. It would appear to be to our advantage to pass to the active form of procedure at once, and,
without aspiring for the time being to the rectification of our

Amur boundary or, in general, to seizures of any sort, in order not to have China and Japan both against us at once and be correct where Europe is concerned, definitely declare that we cannot permit Japan's seizure of southern Manchuria, and that, in the event of our demand not being met, we shall be forced to take suitable measures. There is a large probability that things will not even reach the point of war, when Japan and the European powers alike convince themselves that, if forced to it, we are actually prepared to act energetically. But if, contrary to all expectations, Japan fails to heed our diplomatic entreaties, then it will devolve on us to order our squadron to seize no points but open hostilities against the Japanese fleet and bombard Japanese ports. We should also be acting as the saviour of China, which country would value our service and afterwards agree to the rectification by peaceful means of our border. The victories of the Japanese over the Chinese do not necessarily demonstrate the strength of the former. In point of fact, so far as is known, the active Japanese army does not exceed 70 thousand men, and is, furthermore, dispersed over Korea, Manchuria, and the south. If, unexpectedly, matters should reach the point of war, such troops as we might have at our disposal at the given moment would probably suffice us. We might also count on some cooperation from the Chinese, and likewise from the Koreans, who are as hostile to the Japanese as ever."

Witte spoke a second time, and again stressed the point that he was prepared to concede Japan anything she pleased: Formosa, the Pescadores, "even Port Arthur, and, at a pinch, the southern part of Korea, only not Manchuria." In behalf of this point, "it would be to our advantage to resolve on war now, for if we do not, Russia will have much larger sacrifices to make in the future."

Grand Duke Aleksey and Obruchev attempted counsels of caution against "getting involved" in a war; Lobanov forewarned that in this connection war could scarcely be avoided; but the Ministers of the Navy and of War testified to the military preparedness and the relative adequacy of the Russian forces, and the question was decided as Witte desired.[51] Evidently the plan to lay the Siberian trunk-line through Manchuria, cost what it might, was so firmly lodged in Witte's head that for the sake of it he was taking a chance on immediate war and was prepared to renounce temporarily any annexations in Manchuria, thus "making" of Japan--as Grand Duke Aleksey

predicted--"a lasting and also a powerful enemy" and "compelling the Japanese, by force of circumstances, to make
common cause with the English."[52]

Formally the resolution was adopted by the conference,
but Lobanov did not present the book of minutes to the tsar
until four days later. Lobanov was clearly in doubt: he did
not wish to see Japan in Port Arthur, but he did not wish to
make an enemy of her either; he considered alliance with her
indispensable, but did not believe in the possibility of her
friendship. Two paths lay before him: one, staked out by
Nicholas, led to the annexation of a Korean port, the other,
urged by Witte, to the expulsion of Japan from the mainland,
i.e., as he saw it, to immediate war with her. But with Japan alone?--this question had, strangely enough, now slipped
from the field of vision, was not even touched on by anyone
at the conference. Directly after the conference, it was aired by the French ambassador in his conversation of April 2
with Lobanov. The ambassador had just returned from Paris,
and his words were to be interpreted not as his own personal
opinion but as the latest revised proposal of the French government. This proposal admitted two variants: compensations,
with France marking off for herself "a Chinese islet near the
island of Hainan," or "coercive measures relative to Japan."
"But," observed Count Montebello, "it must also not be lost
sight of, that such measures might prompt England to go over
finally to the side of Japan and give her the necessary aid
against us." The ambassador urged an immediate decision,
indicating the "extreme impatience" of his government. It is
very typical of Lobanov's position that he presented an account
of this talk with the French ambassador to Nicholas (on the
2nd), previously to submitting the minutes of the conference
for approval. And Lobanov had calculated correctly. Nicholas for yet a third time superscribed: "am agreeable to proposal 2, i.e., by agreement with France, not to oppose execution of a Sino-Japanese peace treaty, but at any cost obtain
our desired reward in the form of a free port."[53] This obviously created a psychological impediment to approval of the
decisions in the contrary sense made by the conference, whose
minute book Lobanov did not present to the tsar until the 3rd.[54]

It is known that Nicholas himself "expressed the intention
of giving a hearing to the members who had taken part in this
conference."[55] The summons to the palace of four of them
(Witte, Vannovsky, Lobanov and Grand Duke Aleksey) took

place on April 4. Witte "reiterated his opinion," "the others
either raised extremely feeble objections, or none at all" and
"in the last analysis" Nicholas accepted Witte's proposal and
then and there approved the minutes.56 Not one of the participants in this scene, decisive for the whole future development of events, left even the slightest record of it: no minutes
were drawn up whatsoever, and we have only these few lines
in Witte's "Memoirs." It is impossible, however, to examine
these lines except in their general context in Witte's story of
the whole episode of the intervention of the three powers as
it is set forth on pages 35-37 of Volume I. These pages, as
we shall presently see, suffer from inaccuracies which add
up to a certain tendency, distort the perspective, put the
reader on a false scent.

In Witte's version, it was this way. At the time of the
Sino-Japanese war, "the only person who had made a study"
of Far-Eastern questions was Witte himself. Not "our society" alone, but "even the highest state functionaries" Lobanov and Nicholas included were "complete ignoramuses"
as to these questions. "For this reason" it was his job "to
consider cautiously" what was to be done, when the Japanese
demands were made known. He raised the question of the necessity of obstructing the execution of these demands and,
"thanks to this," the tsar called a conference (presumably
that of March 30). At this conference, he, Witte, "developed the principle that Russia's whole interest for many, many
years had consisted in keeping China as she is;" and "developed" this principle "with extreme resolution and firmness."
He "was supported only by Vannovsky." "Obruchev took a
rather indifferent attitude toward the question." "The remaining members" "expressed no definite opinion." Then
Grand Duke Aleksey simply asked: "how I proposed to implement my desire." And Witte suggested issuing an ultimatum
to Japan. "But the conference arrived at no definite conclusion, since no one definitely opposed me, but at the same
time many members of this conference refrained from expressing agreement with my opinion." Lobanov "was silent throughout." Then come the above-quoted lines about the palace
meeting of April 4.

Some part of this version may simply be charged up to the
narrator's high opinion of himself. But by collating the
Memoirs version with the testimony of the documents we can
see how, with Witte, one aspect quite drops out, namely

Nicholas's clear and reasoned decision of the question, thrice recorded within a single week--in favor of an attempted annexation in Korea in exchange for the concession to Japan of Liaotung, and by agreement with her. This is why, with Witte, both Lobanov and Grand Duke Aleksey "remain silent," making it look as though only one proposal had been laid before the conference, namely Witte's. This is why even the conference of March 30 itself appears not as one of the regular series, planned back on January 20, and arranged for by Lobanov on March 25, but as suddenly arising out of his, Witte's, proposal. This is also why Obruchev, who had on January 20 come out alone as definitely against the straining of relations with Japan, and on March 30 as in favor of an agreement with her for the purpose of obtaining the Amur strip of Manchuria, was simply lumped with the "indifferent." This is the first thing that must be noted. The second is the formulation of Russia's "whole interest" and of that basic "principle" which Witte "developed" at the conference of March 30.

It was with intention that we quoted the record of Witte's speech from the conference minutes entire. Plainly, its principal thesis turned on the points: 1) that previous to the completion of the Siberian railway the Japanese must not have access to Manchuria, 2) that the completion of the Siberian railway will increase our chances "in the near future" on the occasion of China's partition, 3) that in the meantime (until the scandal of the ultimatum has died down) it will be well to refrain from correcting the Amur boundary and in general from any seizures, and 4) that our posing as the saviour of China may even lead to the correction of this boundary by peaceful means. In these four points there is not even a trace of those "many, many" years for which Witte claimed to have said he had been demanding the "integrity and inviolability" of China: they first appeared in the Memoirs after 1907, when this idea retrospectively converted itself in Witte's mind into a basic polemical dogma. And, finally, the third thing to note is his complete silence as to the "sudden" change created in the international situation by Germany's definite offer of her services in carrying out the program of action for which Witte had been fighting.

By combining these observations, it will, I think, also be possible to unriddle Witte's laconic record relative to the session that took place at the palace on April 4. It is not in

any sense true that what took place in Nicholas's presence
was a contest between two rivals points of view rather than
between two rival practical proposals: Witte makes it appear
that his proposal was the only one made, and that the "feeble"
objections of others were unaccompanied by any counter-proposals. In the second place, Nicholas was not merely acting
as umpire but was simultaneously the author of a definite
counter-proposal, so that it was with him that Witte had to
contend and against Nicholas himself that he must seek arguments. In point of fact, Witte's problem was not only to cap-
tivate the tsar by the attractions of his project, but also to
make it easier for him to give up the Korean port by working
on his "elemental desire to move upon the Far East and seize
lands in that region." (Vospominaniia, I, p. 35.) And if he
must also figure on a certain fear of the risk connected with
the martial project of defending Manchuria, then, supposing
the French should waver, they could still rely on the Germans,
who were prepared for any risk.

This is why one is constrained to suppose that Nicholas
"in the last analysis" agreed on April 4 to risk war not only
and not so much--or rather not in the least--because he was
carried away by the "principle" so pertinaciously developed
by Witte in the Memoirs, but because reconciled to the risk:
1) on the strength of all Witte's arguments, which can now be
restored on the basis of documents contemporary with the
event, and 2) by the rare perspectives that opened out in the
event of, and after, success, with the universally "recognized" "enlargement of our chances" "in the near future" on
the occasion of China's partition--provided Japan stayed out
of Manchuria and Korea, and provided we laid the Siberian
road across Manchuria and corrected the Amur boundary.
Did Witte also propose that Nicholas renounce once and for
all the idea of the "absolute" necessity of Russia's having an
ice-free prt--regardless of whether it was located in Korea
or Manchuria?

And so, on April 4, Witte had his way: Russia assumed
the "role of saviour of China," and faced war with Japan over
Manchuria. By the 5th, Wilhelm II already had telegraphic
transcripts of the instructions that Petersburg had sent to
Tokyo, and immediately ordered the German squadron in
Chinese waters to make contact with the Russian squadron.[57]
But intervention ended peacefully and produced the desired
result. The joint note of the three powers arrived, to be

sure, extremely late, when the Shimonoseki treaty in its original redaction had not only been signed by the plenipotentiaries (April 5/17,) but even ratified (April 26/ May 8.) The announcement of Japan's decision to restore Liaotung to China followed on April 28/ May 10, and necessitated her conclusion of a separate agreement with China regarding this modification of the treaty. In the elaboration of terms for the restoration of Liaotung the intervention of the three powers was again indispensable, and the agreement was not signed until October 27/ November 8, 1895.[58] Thus not only was Japan deprived of her only contemplated territorial acquisition on the mainland, but the diplomatic procedure involved was itself not without a certain formal humiliation for her.

On this occasion, Witte's gamble succeeded. Manchuria was won without bloodshed. Japan had been requested to withdraw from the scene and await the completion of the Siberian railway--across Manchuria. A grateful China came on the stage, prepared to correct "by peaceful means" the Amur boundary. But the Manchurian question ceased to be a mere boundary question. By Witte's admission, it was in no sense reduced, then and there, even to the question of a railway corridor to Vladivostok: Russia not only did not renounce her quest of an ice-free port; but even made Manchuria the point of departure for her policy of imperialistic penetration deep into China and Korea, with no bounds set in advance. As Witte was to express it in 1900, "it was not worth while to fence off our garden for Manchuria": "we shall follow the historic route to the south," "all China--all its riches are chiefly in the south."[59]

Thus was a third redaction of the "Aquarium" program evolved, and the way thither fought out, in 1895. Witte nowhere recalls, probably because at the time he did not even notice, that after having by his "sudden change" of front between March 25 and March 30 immensely facilitated Witte's steering of Nicholas into this path, Wilhelm II at once proceeded to cash in on his "right" to "gratitude" for this service. In his letter of April 14/26 to the tsar, Wilhelm was already lauding the "splendid precedent" set by Nicholas for "joint action by all Europe" against Japan, awaiting "with interest" the "future development of our deal," and offering to help "settle the question of possible territorial annexations for Russia," so that even Nicholas became "favorably" inclined to Germany's acquisition of a "port some place where

it will not inconvenience you." Nay more, Wilhelm promised
to "keep peace in Europe and defend Russia's rear, so that
no one can interfere with your activities in the Far East,"
and never wearied of repeating this on every suitable occasion
thereafter.[60] Which means that the "friendly agreement" between Russia and China relative to the laying of the Russian
railway through Chinese territory became possible at exactly
the moment when Germany's turn came for a "seizure" of
Chinese territory--and that this was no casual coincidence:
the "coaling station," as Nicholas understood Wilhelm's request, was by no means exorbitant compensation for such
perspectives as now opened out before Russia in Manchuria,
Korea and even in "all" China.[61]

Chapter II

"PEACEFUL" PENETRATION OF RUSSIA INTO MANCHURIA 1895-1896

I

The idea that the laying of the Siberian railway through Chinese territory beyond Baikal was one of Russia's "urgent" needs, arose in 1895 out of the Sino-Japanese war situation, quite empirically. Admiral Kopytov had, of course, been its persistent advocate during the years 1887-1890: first in a report "on the most advantageous direction for the main and continuous all-Russian, great eastern rr.," read before the Imperial Russian Technical Society and there accorded only two affirmative votes, then in a memorandum presented to Gyubbenet in April, 1890.[1] At the time, Kopytov's idea failed to gain currency: both Gyubennet's 1891 project and the project put into operation by Witte in 1892 envisaged the joining of Sretensk and Khabarovsk by a railway passing entirely through Russian territory. True, even in 1892 Witte did not mind discussing a "branch into China's domains" and even thought that the "building of such a branch would scarecely encounter serious obstacles in the immediate future." However, the railway here understood was not the main line but just a feeder branch for the purpose of "direct trade with the extremely populous inner provinces of China,"--one of those "feeder branches" of which Witte was already speaking in the plural number by the following year, 1893, in connection with Badmayev's Irkutsk-Lanchow project.[2]

Surveys of the Amur sector between Khabarovsk and Sretensk, not begun until the summer of 1894, demonstrated by the end of the season the full difficulties of proceeding in this direction, and moved Witte to think of obviating the revealed obstacles by striking across Manchuria.[3] No doubt, in advancing this idea in 1895 Witte took into account the helpless position in which China found herself during those first months of the Japanese war. That it had a concretely technical origin is, however, attested by its scale: both the director-manager of the Amur Company's steamship-transport and trade, Makeyev, in his report of February 10, 1895, to the Minister of Finance, and Witte himself in a memorandum to the Ministry of Foreign Affairs early in that same February (respecting the arrival of the Chinese embassy extraordinary to felicitate Nicholas II on his accession to the throne) proposed obtaining China's permission to lay a railway from the Novo-Tsurukhaitui guard station through Mergen to Blagoveshchensk, i.e., were quite obviously keeping to that minimal deviation from the Russian frontier then already designated in Russian military circles as the "rectification of our Amur boundary," and regarded in the Ministry of foreign affairs as obtainable at a price "by mere diplomatic correspondence."[4] It was duly included by Prince Lobanov in a list of "urgent needs" presented to Nicholas on March 25, 1895. But what both Makeyev and Witte understood by it at this point was not annexation but merely purchase of the right to build a railway.

Yet upon this relatively modest plan for partially straightening out the difficult Amur bend, no diplomatic action was taken previous to the peace of Shimonoseki. After the three-power ultimatum, on the other hand, it seemed altogether too little to seek, and suddenly, as if of its own accord, became metamorphosed into one long straight line from Chita to Vladivostok. By May 12, 1895, the minister of roads--apparently quite unbeknown to the other ministers[5]--was already petitioning the tsar for authority to "reconnoitre for a Manchurian line," foreseeing a saving of about 700 versts in length, as compared with the Amur line, and 35 million rubles in expenditures.[6] That some sort of Russian claims not to be brushed aside now hung over Manchuria was sensed, for example, even by the Americans. First of all, a Mr. Bush who had come to Peking "immediately after the peace of Shimonoseki," as representative of an American group, paid a call on the Russian minister, Count Cassini, for the purpose of openly warning him of the intention of his principals to undertake the building of a railway through Manchuria and to ascertain what the attitude of the Russian government would be to this in view of Russia's obvious preferential interests there.[7]

Russian nationals were also pressing the matter--primarily local ship-owners interested in having the railway somewhat farther from the Amur, which it was to parallel. In May, for example, Witte received through them a message concern-

ing a disposition on the part of the "mandarins" to feel that
it would be "better to move the Russian boundary a thousand
versts and have their old neighbor than to admit the Japanese
to the continent" and that "Russia's cooperation in connection
with the peace negotiations gave her full right to lay a road
in Manchuria through Nikolsk-Ninguta-Tsitsihar-Tsurukhai-
tui." Having communicated which items, this same Makeyev
expressed the opinion that a very favorable moment had arrived for negotiations as to the purchase of this right, since
China was "in terrific need of money."[8] But, glad as he was
to receive such communications from local volunteers, having at the time no official agency of his own, Witte did not
force the railway question proper in Manchuria and did not
cease to advance the means for survey operations in the Amur
sector. What must come first was the fundamental preparation of the grandiose and for those times not at all simple
political plan that in Witte's mind embraced the railway question proper.

The international conjuncture in the East was indeed at
this moment exceptionally favorable for that basic political
formula which, in Witte's eyes, made it the implement for
Russia's peace policy. But he had advanced this formula in
1892, when actually the conditions necessary to it were not
present: the idea of a mutually advantageous Russo-Chinese
economic alliance directed against England had been launched
in an atmosphere poisoned for Russo-Chinese relations by
the break-down of the Livadia treaty of 1879, chronic border
misunderstandings, and the Russian intrigues of the 1880's
in Korea, intrigues which left China in no doubt as to their
ultimate significance--and characterized in the matter of
Anglo-Chinese relations by England's support of China on
the Korean question and her political influence at Peking.

This support reached its culminating point, during the
most critical moments of the war of 1894-1895, in two huge
loans made one after the other by England to China that permitted the latter to keep on fighting after a fashion instead of
capitulating at once.[9] On the other hand, the sudden volte-
face of English policy to the side of Japan during peace-nego-
tiations, and Russia's correspondingly abrupt reversal to the
defense of Peking, now opened China's doors wide to Russia.
The basic and decisive fact with which it was first necessary
to reckon after the peace of Shimonoseki was that China, having just undertaken for the first time a loan of such vast pro-

portions (around 45 million rubles,) in gold bonds, must now within the next six months pay Japan around 70 million rubles, in another six months another 70 million rubles, and around 140 million rubles in the course of seven years, with an accrual of 5 per cent annum.[10] These sums, monstrous for China, could be obtained only by means of a foreign loan, and the question of such a loan was immediately raised by the Chinese government, simultaneously causing a flurry, during the first half of April old style, in the banking circles of Berlin, London and Paris.

It is also very curious that the Chinese apparently left Petersburg out: information here concerning the matter did not come from them, or at once. The first news about bankers' parleys, already begun, was from Berlin. On April 14/26, Charykov informed the minister of foreign affairs that the Chinese government had started negotiations--"chiefly in Berlin, but also in London"--for a loan to pay the indemnity, that in Berlin two bankers' conferences had already been held, and that the German government was greatly interested and was "exerting pressure" on the German bankers in favor of the loan. Charykov had already gone into the matter at the German ministry of foreign affairs, where they had not only confirmed the above but had also let him in on some of the details: namely, that the affair had run into competition from the Americans, who hoped to unload on China their accumulated reserves of silver, and that the Germans, not content to accept the office of Chinese maritime customs as guarantee, were proposing to set up a special administration in China "on the model of Turkey and Egypt."[11]

Witte at once went straight to Mendelssohn for details: it turned out that negotiations were in progress "regarding the formation of a group of German, French and English houses," but were not as yet concluded and that, in general, "nothing was settled."[12] Afterwards the negotiations among bankers on an international scale petered out, and the business shortly passed into Russia's hands. An attempt to draw her into the projected international combination was first made at the beginning of May, and came from Paris: the Paris-Netherlands Bank, which headed the French group for the Chinese loan, thinking that it might interest Russia from the political angle, proposed that Witte "organize a group of Russian banks to act collaterally with the French group": formally this "might warrant the presence of a Russian delegate in the administration

of the Chinese debt," but actually the bank was prepared to
assume the Russian share.[13] As we see, the French had adopted the idea launched by the Germans regarding a special "administration of the Chinese debt." The necessity for this apparently arose from the fact that what China might propose,
namely a simple guarantee of punctual payments on the loan,
with the revenue of the Chinese maritime customs as security,
seemed insufficient so long as the administration of these customs remained entriely in English hands. But Russia's participation in the loan, as the French suggested, would, under
such circumstances, boil down primarily to her sanctioning
the contemplated set-up, which, by its international character, would yield Russia no specific political advantages, but
would make her a common party to the attempt on the sovereignty of China. And Witte was left to decide whether to
decline participation in the loan, leaving it to the others, or
whether to propose his own guarantee, thereby relieving the
Chinese government of the necessity of authorizing an international financial control. However, Witte had not as yet made
up his mind; hence his answer to Paris was non-committal:
he was "insufficiently conversant with the matter to give any
answer to this proposal."[14] But a month later, word went
round that the Franco-Russian loan was a settled matter.[15]

Such fragmentary and colorless data as we have at our disposal regarding the course of negotiations on the subject of the
Chinese loan, do not as yet permit us to determine when and
under what circumstances Witte accepted the proposal of the
French or made choice of the exact form that his participation
in the operation was to take. What apparently proved decisive
was the fact that both the French and the Germans, without
breaking with each other, had nonetheless entered into separate negotiations with China, which, in turn, had from the
very beginning shown an inclination to do business in a "scattered" and "unsystematic" manner, calculating to gain by the
competition of separate financial groups.[16] It is, for example,
known that while negotiating the large loan, China was simultaneously bargaining in Berlin and London over two small loans
for local needs amounting respectively to 1 million and 400
thousand pounds sterling.[17] The Germans at the time thought
that Witte had "played chess" with them: he had explained
"at length," in repeated conversations with the German ambassador at Petersburg, that "he had no thought of taking part in
the loan," then had "quite unexpectedly" concluded it behind

their backs.[18] In reply to such an accusation, Lobanov indicated that Russia had entered into the unilateral combination
because the Germans themselves were then conducting separate negotiations with China; and when Radolin flatly denied
this, Lobanov averred that the French had not desired the
participation of the Germans.[19]

On the other hand, we know that on May 18, old style,
Hoskier was still telling Witte from Paris that "as yet there
had been no serious negotiations with the Chinese government
about the loan," and had suggested that Witte set about arranging a loan for the needs of Russia herself.[20] But Rothstein
spent May 29-30 in Paris and during those two days terminated with the French group negotiations that envisaged both
variants, i.e., a loan "with aid" of the latter and an "international" loan.[21] That the Germans were not sitting with
folded hands all this time is apparent from a document (unfortunately known to us undated) stating that the Chinese minister in Paris had notified the representatives of the French
group of the breaking off of negotiations with this group in
view of a preferable German proposal, and that the French
government had received notification from Berlin of the conclusion of a German operation on a basis of parity with English operators.[22] Insofar as data of this sort actually reflect
competition between the German group and the French, partly
as arising from the current abundance of free capital and
cheap money, the actual selection of the French demands no
particular explanation: it was absolutely out of the question
for Russia to do anything that would impair in the slightest
degree her relations with the French financial market as a
whole, particularly in a matter having political significance
as well, since she would thereby risk cutting off at the start
the actualization of her larger policy in the Far East from its
financial feeder base. And it must be assumed that in summoning Hottinguer, Netslin and Rêné Bris to Petersburg (on
June 9) for their presentation to the tsar on June 14, Witte
had something more in mind than the mere signing of a series
of documents about the loan.

On these documents agreement had been reached by June 23,
and the matter of a loan to China in the sum of 100 million
rubles in gold, under Russia's guarantee, might be regarded
as closed.[23] Then, on June 24, immediately after the loan
contract had been signed and the seals affixed, in the office
of the minister of foreign affairs and in the prese ce of Prince

Lobanov, Witte made "definite proposals" to the three above-
named bankers regarding the establishment, with their participation, of a Russian bank--under the auspices of the Russian government--"to operate, on the broadest principles, in
the lands of eastern Asia."[24] These definite proposals, made
in an atmosphere of international officialdom, were further
accompanied by the confirmatory promise not only of the minister of finance but also of the minister of foreign affairs there
present that they would give the bank full protection in its
practically unrestricted activity over that vast area, bound to
become an arena of international strife--strife of which the
bank was destined to be made the weapon. On a par with purely commercial operations, its appointed task was the "strengthening of Russian economic influence in China to counterbalance
the enormous importance that the English had managed to
achieve there, thanks chiefly to their having virtually taken
over the administration of the maritime customs."[25]

To this end, the bank was accorded suitably broad rights:
of trade, transport of commodities, conduct of any operational
services for the Chinese treasury, n.b. the receipt of taxes
and the issue of currency, acquisition of concessions to build
railways anywhere within the confines of China and to lay telegraph lines. In making a proposal on such a scale to foreign
bankers and giving his own "word" of promise as pledge of
government support for the bank in the event of international
clashes, Witte, by his own later admission, made the stabili-
ty of his country's credit and of her whole financial system
contingent on the keeping of this "word."[26] On the other hand
by securing to himself, through a Russian majority on the
bank's board of directors, adequate control over the general
trend of the bank's operations, Witte acquired in it a flexible
and manageable implement of his policy, with twofold protection: 1) as a private and 2) as a predominantly foreign,
institution of credit, an implement which made the future
development of this policy the last word in political method-
ology as practised by the major European powers in China.[27]

Negotiations with the French were concluded by the 30th
of September, 1895. The charter of the bank, which received
the name Russo-Chinese, was drawn up in Russia, signed by
the French founders on November 23 of the same year at the
Russian embassy in Paris, and ratified on the 10th of December.

In defining the bank's tasks "relative to the strengthening

of Russian economic influence in China" (in his report of
July 14) Witte pointed "in particular" to the fact that the bank
"might prove an extremely useful instrument in the hands of
the Russian government for the latter's effectuation of measures bearing an intimate relationship to the completion of
construction on the Siberian railway." He did not even enter
into the railway question until all details relative to the bank
had been settled (September 30,) and until the extremely protracted negotiations with Japan over the terms of the return
of the Liaotung peninsula to China had been brought to a conclusion (October 7/19 exchange of notes.) But now Witte--
not Lobanov--at once reopened the subject of a Manchurian
line, no longer to Blagoveshchensk, but straight across the
whole breadth of Manchuria to Vladivostok (October 30 report
to his majesty,) and undertook to draw up the project for a
concession to build the railway and for a directive political
memorandum to serve as instructions for the Russian minister at Peking during the conduct of negotiations.

Four days after the French had signed the project for the
bank's charter, on November 27, both of the above documents,
in absolutely finished form, were presented by Witte for the
tsar's approval, together with a report in Witte's own handwriting. "In view of the importance of the aim which is, in
the given case, being pursued" and in view of the "no slight
significance" attaching "in connection with the obtaining of
concessions in China" to "those gifts (often extremely substantial) which are in these cases made to the immediate ser-
vitors of the Chinese emperor," Witte suggested that he be
permitted to place a "suitable sum" at the disposal of the
Russian minister in Peking as the medium of these gifts, Witte
might recommend a "representative of the Russo-Chinese
bank (an official of the ministry of finance) who might accom-
pany the representative of the Russian railway company."28
Despite the tsar's subsequent approval, the matter of opening
negotiations in Peking was for some reason delayed. In any
event, it encountered opposition in Russian governmental circles, nor did it prove by any means simple diplomatically.

What must not be forgotten is the fact that the demand
which Russia was now about to present to China was, for all
its grandioseness, along the same lines as the like demands
casually pressed upon China by the Japanese after its disastrous defeat. The very decision to interrupt the course of
peace negotiations had been a last minute substitute for the

Franco-Russian project of seeking compensations at China's
expense, even without checking the Japanese, and did not dis-
place the compensation policy but only put a new foundation
under it in the form of China's "gratitude" for the service
done her by the powers in intervening. After manifesting a
less active interest at the decisive moment than the rest,
France was the first to return to the compensation psychology
--right at the start of negotiations over the return of Liaotung:
at least that was how Berlin understood the French ambassador on May 4 (new style), when he spoke of the Pescadores
islands as of course not having entered into the ultimatum by
the powers. [29] And next the French insisted on a supplementary pledge by Japan "to recognize the strait of Formosa as
a great international sea-way," lying "outside the sphere" of
"exclusive control or use" by Japan. [30]

Then Gerard, the French minister, got Peking to conclude
two conventions in addition (to the convention of 1887,) giving
France substantial rewards in the south of China. Besides
modifying the boundaries of French Tonkin at the expense of
Chinese Yunnan, China opened to French trade several cities
in Kwangsi and Yunnan, pledged herself to turn primarily to
French enterprisers and engineers for the exploitation of mines
in the provinces of Yunnan, Kwangsi and Kwangtung, and gave
France the right to extend both her existing railways in Annam
and her projected railways--through Chinese territory. [31]
The simultaneous completion of arrangements for the loan to
China, followed by the investment of French capital in a bank
dedicated to the support of Russia's descent from the north
with a railroad project of a magnitude hitherto unknown in
China, promoted France at this time to the role of leading
European marksman in the onslaught now opened upon China.
The "chess move" made by Witte on the question of the loan,
to meet this trend of France, was an adroit one, relating not
so much to the Germans, as they supposed, as to the otherwise inevitable competition of the French, who now became
the allies of Russia in the Chinese area also, their prime obligation being to provide French capital, as occasion arose--
but under the cloak of a Russian bank. [32] It would, however,
be a great mistake to suppose that Germany too did not at once
think of compensations. Somewhat later than France, in
October 1895, Germany secured two concessions: in Hankow
and Tientsin, and, likewise in October, passed from hesitancy
in the choice of a bay or two (on the north and the south simul-

taneously) to negotiations concerning such a cession, simultaneously with the Chinese minister in Petersburg (October 29, new style) and with the Tsungli Yamen in Peking.[33]

No wonder the Russian demand respecting the concession for a Manchurian line was regarded by Peking at the very least with a tendency toward caution. This disposition was the specific result of Russia's having procrastinated about presenting her demands and thereby created in Peking an atmosphere of alarm and uncertainty. According to observations made by the Russian minister to Peking (despatch of December 16, 1895,) "the feeling of gratitude cherished toward us by China is beginning to weaken and give place to a certain vague feeling of apprehension and distrust, evoked by a premonition that before long we are going to make extraordinary demands, the significance and proportions of which are still being kept from her," while "sundry foreign counsellors" only "aggravate" these apprehensions. The minister had "of late" even noted that the "Chinese ministers are far from showing the same readiness to fulfill certain relatively trifling demands of ours as was the case a few months ago."

The minister was evidently himself extremely uneasy and felt the necessity of warning Petersburg in the matter of the "extraordinary" demands that were at the time being projected along with the railway, for example by the governors-general of the Amur and the Steppe provinces (quite after the manner of the French): 1) for annexation of the section of Chinese territory to the north of the Sretensk-Blagoveshchensk line, 2) for the modification of the Ussurian boundary in our favor, to include the mouth of the Sungari, 3) for the revision of all articles in the Petersburg treaty of 1881, 4) for the cession to Russia of the Barlyk mountains, and 5) for a general revision of the whole boundary of the Semirechensk and Semipalatinsk provinces. To Cassini the impracticability of such demands was obvious and he categorically recommended concentrating on the one "chief" end in view--namely, the laying of the Manchurian railway.[35]

But the difficulty lay not only in Peking's growing "apprehensions" and "distrust" but also in the fact that the moment was approaching when competition among the powers would again run high there--on the question of a new loan. The term during which Article 16 of the contract of June 24 prohibited the Chinese government's seeking a new loan outside the French group expired on January 15, 1896, and meanwhile

the 100 million rubles then received fell far short of covering
even one figure of the war indemnity. The position of the Chinese government in expectation of this moment was scarcely
determined by fear of being left without the offer of any loan
at all. Furthermore, all other things being equal, it was
politically more advantageous for the Chinese government to
keep to the Anglo-German group, in order to restore the
balance whereof the disturbance in favor of the Franco-Russian side had already yielded large fruits, but as yet by no
means all fruits. The loan did, of course, actually fall this
time to the Hongkong-Shanghai and German-Asiatic banks.[36]
There was no lack of desire on the part of the French to assume the loan, but the deal fell through because of Witte's
refusal to provide the guarantee: he considered the revenue
of the maritime customs insufficient security for the loan,
did not wish to "dupe the public" and undermine his own credit,
"block his own way to a loan," reluctantly, under pressure
from the French ambassador, agreed to give "moral support"
to the loan, but on condition that this loan "be kept separate
from the previous one," that its sum be limited to the "actual
need" and that the rate of interest be not less than 6 per cent.[3]
It also embarassed him to bid a second time against "friendly"
Germany.[38] Naturally Russia's refusal to repeat the June
loan did not facilitate the impending negotiations with China
about the railway concession, either from the Chinese, or,
presumably, from the French angle.

But, as above stated, the decision to lay the Manchurian
line straight to Vladivostok met with opposition in Russian
governmental circles as well. Objections were raised by the
director of the Asiatic Department of the Ministry of Foreign
Affairs, Count Kapnist, and by Dukhovsky, Governor General
of the Amur Province, both in very close touch with the question on account of their official positions. Neither denied the
necessity of the short-cut through Manchuria, but both expressed themselves as definitely in favor of aiming not at
Vladivostok but at Blagoveshchensk. Kapnist censured Witte
on the ground that the new project had been inspired only by
a desire to lower the cost of construction, was wrongly linked
with considerations regarding the commercial interests of
Russia in Manchuria and in Northeastern China generally,
since these interests "are at the present time merely a question of the future," and was in no way borne out by "military-
political considerations," which, however, "are of the first

and utmost importance for Russia in the question of the Siberian railway in general."

From a military point of view, he believed the projected
line of 1,500-2,000 versts to be the only example in history
of a "military post road of such length through foreign territory," and furthermore it was at "an enormous distance from
our frontiers." But even from a purely "exploitational" point
of view, it would "in all probability" necessitate "the transfer to us of the whole internal administration of the country,"
"which would appear impossible without military occupation."
Even "the very building of the railway," would, in his opinion,
"call for the same coercive measure of armed occupation."
Meanwhile, "the seizure by us of all Manchuria or the greater
part thereof" would lead to the partition of China and in particular to the seizure by England of "such naval bases as
might secure to her in perpetuity predominance on the Yellow
Sea." Thus even "regardless of all strategic and military
considerations," Witte's proposal seemed to him to be "attended by enormous political risk" and to "offer no corresponding advantages," whereas the annexation, in case of need,
of the extreme northern corner of Manchuria along the Novo-
Tsurukhaitui-Blagoveshchensk cut-off would be a mere matter
of diplomatic correspondence.[39]

In all probability, Kapnist's memorandum was hastily
drawn up immediately after Witte's personal presentation of
the concession projects and, for Lobanov, of the memorandum of the minister of foreign affairs, but it did not deter
the latter from accepting both projects, which, as we have
seen, were afterwards duly approved by the tsar. Thus Witte
never actually had to answer Kapnist's objections. Dukhovsky's
note, composed after the memorandum had already gone to
Peking, but before the beginning of negotiations, reopened
the question when, though settled, it was still accessible to
reconsideration.[40]

Dukhovsky, too, regarded as unavoidable the "settlement
of a substantial Russian force in Manchuria," since China
would otherwise "have countless opportunities to interrupt
the operation of the railway" if the slightest political complication should arise, and "the laying of a 2,000-verst section
of the great Siberian railway through a region which will for
a long while be foreign to us" Dukhovsky deemed a "great
historical blunder." Dukhovsky accordingly proposed: 1) to
cut off the Manchurian corner along the Sretensk-Mergen-

Blagoveshchensk line, 2) continue the road through Russian territory along the Amur, turning the Amur province into a military base, and 3) obtain the concession for a road from Nikolsk-on-Ussuri to Ninguta and Bodune to meet the projected Chinese Shanhaikwan-Mukden-Kirin line, with a view to including this line as well in our concession later on. This third proposal of Dukhovsky's, plainly in contradiction of the spirit of caution and moderation expressed in the first two, facilitated debate exceedingly, and Witte's counter-memorandum was accordingly built chiefly on an examination of this contradiction, though also turning partly on the theory that Nicholas's above-quoted resolution upon Cassini's despatch of December 16, 1895 ruled out at the given moment any territorial acquisitions from China whatsoever.

But to point out the weaknesses of his opponents was not enough. Both Kapnist and Dukhovsky had reproached Witte with the same thing, namely that though well grounded from the viewpoint of China's interests and intelligible from the purely technical railroading angle, his project lost sight of Russia's own economic, political, and strategic interests as such. Needless to say, in a memorandum destined for the guidance of the Russian minister during negotiations with the Chinese, nothing else had been possible. But now Witte must argue his daring project on the basis of the sum total of Russia's own specific interests.

First and foremost, the laying of the road directly to Vladivostok would make that city port of entry for the greater part of Manchuria, "with the exception of the southernmost section immediately adjacent to the Yellow Sea," and this, with the closing of the free port, would give Russian trade the opportunity to consolidate itself not only in Manchuria but in the "adjoining provinces of China" as well, since "in the very nature of things, branches of this line would speedily be laid deep into China." But why could these branches not be laid from the Siberian trunk-line if it passed through Russian territory? Because then "their actualization would be postponed for a very long and besides absolutely indefinite time." Meanwhile, right now all the powers (England, France, Germany, Japan) were vying with one another to get hold of railway concessions and of contracts to supply railway materials to China,[41] and Russia, Witte felt, "must of necessity govern herself by the actions of her economic competitors." Otherwise "the principal railway lines of the northern provinces of

China, not excluding Manchuria, would fall into their hands,"
something which Russia "naturally could not permit, wherefore she must make every effort to divert into her own hands
the network of roads in Northern China."

Witte was completely convinced that once the trunk-line to
Vladivostok was in Russian hands, "no other line or branch
would be built in Northern China without Russia's consent,"
and this would enable Russia "from then on, until the consolidation of her economic influence in Manchuria," to prevent
the construction of a branch to the port of Newchang and thus
to protect Manchuria from the growing import of foreign goods
up-country by way of this port. Thus, as Witte saw it, Russia was, with the Manchurian road--under pressure of outward necessity--moving toward an economic share in China,
staking out for herself, as a market closed to outsiders,
Manchuria and more, but in danger of "letting" even Manchuria "slip" "forever from under Russian economic influence"
if she did not hurry. At the same time, Witte pointed out the
"political" and "strategic" significance of the direct trans-
Manchurian line--and its advantage over Dukhovsky's bend
through the Amur province--in that it permitted the construction of a military base in corn-producing Transbaikal and the
shuttling of troops thence "at any time by the shortest route"
not only to Vladivostok but also to any point in Manchuria "on
the shores of the Yellow Sea" and "in close proximity to the
capital of China." Who could fail to see that, in this respect
as well, wide prospects opened out before Russia, once the
"very nature of things" should have "speedily" laid Russian
branch-lines "deep into China"?

II

The opening in Peking of negotiations about the Manchurian
railway concession was delayed for four full months, occurred
(in April, 1896) at a moment, and under circumstances, altogether unfavorable, and ended in complete failure. The "vague
feeling of apprehension," noted by Cassini in the Chinese government back in December, proved to have been not at all
"vague": at the end of January, the viceroy of Chihli had presented to the Chinese emperor a report on the necessity of an
"immediate" extension to Chinchow of the Manchurian railway
started several years before and finished as far as Shanhaikwan,
and in reporting this fact Cassini explained it as a desire on the

part of the Chinese to "anticipate the impending negotiations with us."[42] The scale of the Chinese project was pitiable (the proposal was to build, in three years, only 190 versts in all:) essentially such a line did not rule out the Russian transit line or threaten it with competition, but formally the Chinese had acquired a serious argument against Russia's aspirations, and in any event had shown reluctance to meet them half way. It is definitely known that at this time Cassini already had the November instructions to hand, but did not "intend" starting negotiations until "the end of February."[43] But at the end of February even Petersburg was still awaiting in galling uncertainty "the moment when the further routing of the Siberian railway should be decided," while doubts on the subject of participation in a French loan to China led to victory for the Anglo-German group.[44] Negotiations were again deferred and were only opened after the signing of the contract with this group for the loan.

On the other hand, negotiations were now going on in two directions at once. Conducting them in Peking was extremely awkward--in full view of all competitors. Reports of Russian agents there give a telling picture of the stock-jobbing then rife in the capital of China, re-"opened" to Europeans, this time not for trade but for industrial exploitation. Needless to say, it was the English who had pushed the project for the Shanhaikwan line, later, of course, to fall under English control. But even the French, on whose "active cooperation" Cassini had still rested his hopes in the autumn of 1895, was now ranged among Russia's direct competitors: Gerard (French Minister to Peking showed by his whole behavior that he was guided solely by the desire to assure his own compatriots a "prominent part" "in the expected opening of China to foreign industry," and excited distrust by even including a Manchurian road among the "enticing proposals" with which he "bewildered the ministers of the Chinese emperor."[45]

What the Americans meant to do was no secret and at first glance seemed a very serious matter. The same American, Bush, who had tried to sound out the Russian minister in Peking during the spring of 1895, now appeared with a finished project of uncommonly broad scope, sponsored by an "extremely powerful syndicate representative of the foremost railroad, steamship and banking firms of America," capitalized at 250 million dollars. According to Bush's statement, this syndicate had founded a Company under the name American

China Development Company, capitalized, to begin with, at
one million dollars, which had set itself the task of "assuming the construction of all railways now awaiting construction
in China." The Company's attention had chiefly been arrested
by the Peking-Hankow and the Hankow-Canton lines, but in
addition it was deemed necessary to link the Chinese railway
system proper with the Siberian railway by means of a Manchurian line. Bush placed the matter in such a light as to
make it appear that, in order to carry out the plan as a whole,
it would be necessary for the Americans to enter into an agreement with Russia to assume the construction of roads in Manchuria and thus free China from the danger connected with
the "political substratum" of the Russian plans, thereby facilitating China's consent to the American,plan in its entirety.
Bush frankly expounded his project to Pokotilov and Cassini,
and offered to conclude a "secret understanding" with the Russian government whereby preference would be given to Russians in the acquisition of the American company's shares and
bonds, assuring them that the Americans would be "the most
trustworthy associates for Russia in this matter."

Collaterally, Bush was, of course, also carrying out negotiations with the secretary of Li Hung-chang, to whom he
entrusted the finished project of the concession treaty. But
here it was no longer a question of simply joining the Siberian
railway with the Peking-Canton trunk-line, but of the peaceful conquest of all Manchuria: the road was to run from "some"
port on the gulf of Liaotung through Newchang-Mukden-Kirin-
Tsitsihar to "some" point on the Siberian line, and from
Mukden to the Korean boundary; the company was to be given
the right to acquire "lands, timber and mines" at any point
in Manchuria and at points in Mongolia adjacent to the road,
and assigned a 30-year monopoly over all railway construction
in Manchuria.[47]

As we see, not only the political but the economic purport
of the American proposals was diametrically opposed to that
of the Manchurian railroad plan projected in Witte's memorandum against Dukhovsky: Russia not only did not get the
direct line to Vladivostok--a detail which might still be introduced into the proposed agreement--but would by this agreement knowingly exclude Manchuria once and for all from her
own sphere of economic domination, in that she would be
sanctioning a railway network immediately adapted to the import of foreign goods into Manchuria through south-Manchurian

and Korean ports. Meanwhile the instructions given Cassini
proposed endeavoring to obtain "the granting of a concession
both for a trunk line and for subsidiary Manchurian lines unconditionally to a Russian company," without any foreign participation.[48] And Cassini gave Bush no "encouragement."
But Cassini's own position when he presented himself at the
Tsungli Yamen on April 6 and again on April 18 and "in strong
language" attempted to dispose the ministers to agree to the
granting of the concession to a Russo-Chinese company, on
the plea that it would facilitate Russia's protection of China
"from the danger of new clashes with Japan or in general with
any power whatsoever," seemed equally hopeless.

The Chinese took twelve days to deliberate, and then definitely declared that they had "once and for all made a firm
and unalterable decision not to grant such concessions to any
foreign power or any foreign company," and only agreed "to
build the Manchurian road, possibly before long, with the aid
of Russian engineers and from Russian materials." Cassini's
retort that China lacked adequate means for this was, under
the circumstances described, simply ridiculous: in this respect, the Chinese "were being approached from all sides with
lavish offers." And after a three hour exchange of these
same identical ideas, it only remained for the minister to
threaten that such an answer would produce "the most painful
impression" on the Russian government, and to notify Petersburg that "if the Russian government recognized as not only
desirable but absolutely necessary our building of a railway
of our own, then the only thing left for us to do was give the
Chinese government definitely to understand that its refusal
would immediately entail the gravest consequences for China."[49]
Unprepared in any way and unconfirmed from the "suitable
sum," diplomatic negotiations in Peking, as we see, promptly
came to a standstill.[50]

But during those days when, in Peking the only thing left
was to pass over into the language of direct threats, Petersburg had the stage all set for bringing matters to the desired
conclusion by peaceful means: it was on April 18 that Cassini
had the above-mentioned unsuccessful three-hour conversation
with the Chinese ministers, and it was likewise on April 18
that Prince Ukhtomsky delivered in Petersburg, by special
train from Odessa, the first-chancellor of the Chinese empire, Li Hung-chang, formally the representative extraordinary of the Chinese emperor at the coronation of the tsar, but

actually, as it turned out, empowered to sign the most capital international acts.

Li Hung-chang's journey to Russia had been decided upn by the Peking government at the very beginning of February, and the choice of a person to be its represenative at the coronation ceremonies had been openly and quasi-officially motivated at that time by the necessity of settling the questions that were continuing to gather head between China and Russia. As Peking saw it, these were two in number: 1) the laying of a railway through Manchuria, and 2) the according Russia of an ice-free port for the berthing of her warships.[51] To flatly reject either Russia's "intention" relative to the railway or her "solicitation" relative to the port, the Chinese government seemingly regarded as impossible: precisely this interpretation might have been given to the half measures it took in the autumn of 1895 when it gave Russian engineers a permit to conduct surveys in Manchuria and authorized the building of winter berths for the Russian squadron in Kiaochow.[52] Concessions to Russia were unavoidable: the question was only one of dimensions and terms.

The choice of Li Hung-chang, most authoritative specialist on foreign affairs in the entire Peking government, could only be understood as China's decision to conduct negotiations in Russia, with the tsar's ministers directly. Accordingly, insofar as is known, the Russian minister in Peking did not even make an attempt to talk with Li Hung-chang about the railway.[53] Similarly, upon the departure of the mission extraordinary from Shanghai, the representative of the Russo-Chinese bank also confined himself strictly to the question of such services as the bank might offer the travellers in the matter of transfer operations.[54] The very itinerary of the mission was so calculated as to leave some time for negotiations before the beginning of the coronation ceremonies.[55] Thus it can scarcely be doubted that Petersburg thought of the direct negotiations with Li Hung-chang as something quite independent of the future progress and issue of the Peking negotiations, so long in deadlock. But with the shift of negotiations to Petersburg, the whole affair naturally fell into the eager hands of Witte, at once got under way, and became, if not a complete, still a decided, success. Li Hung-chang's visit had in large measure simplified the essentially extremely complicated and, owing to its scale, extremely difficult task confronting Russian diplomacy.

Petersburg knew perfectly well that it was impossible even
to dream of approaching a settlement without recourse to bribery.[56] But the technique of bribing Peking would have been no
simple matter, if only because it was not a question of secondary details and third-rate personages but of an unprecedently
grandiose economic, (nay more) political experiment, for which
the Chinese government literally had no precedents, and of
government dignitaries of such caliber that the smooth progress of the operation would have been rendered extremely difficult both by the very dimensions of the sum and by the necessity for observing absolute secrecy. In Petersburg, on the contrary , the impending operation was strictly localized in the
person of the ambassador extraordinary, whose personal qual-
ities--"energy and decision"--opened up possibilities of "arriving at final agreement on all questions pending"; it could be
surrounded by conditions of maximal secrecy; and while in
progress would take on all the flexibility and authority of direct oral negotiations, with no need to resort to code or diplomatic post.[57]

The personnel of the Chinese mission left nothing to be desired. Neither Peking's momentary idea of sending two plenipotentiaries to Russia (the celebrated Chang Yin-huan being
nominated as the second,) nor the attempt to replace the three
persons in Li Hung-chang's suite by Li Ching-fang (a son of
Li noted for his cupidity) and Lo Feng-loh (a no less grasping
confidential interpreter) had been crowned with success. Acting as "agent for financial affairs" with Li Hung-chang was a
Russian subject, an employee in the Chinese maritime customs
Victor Grot, who was especially commended to Witte's attention by the Russian minister in Peking.[58] At first glance, this
picture was spoiled by the presence of one Englishman, Li Hung-
chang's favorite doctor, Irving, and even he turned out upon
closer inspection to be an inveterate drinker and unfitted for
any sort of intrigue.[59]

Meanwhile, in Petersburg, not a stone was left unturned by
Russia to bring about the desired outcome of negotiations.
Witte, entrusted with them by the tsar, had had leisure to prepare both this entrusting of the matter to him, rather than to
Lobanov, and a plan of action. This time the man he put on the
job was not Badmayev (now, in 1896, a "sharp speculator,")[60]
but Prince Ukhtomsky, publisher of the "Saint Petersburg Journal," chamberlain, naively ecstatic newspaper panegyrist of
Russia's future in China, a great admirer of Witte, "very

close at that time to the sovereign,"[61] recently made director of the Russo-Chinese bank--and, as follow-up to Ukhtomsky, the central active figure of this bank, its real director-
manager, A. Yu. Rothstein. Ukhtomsky "during March repeatedly conferred and conversed with Witte" on the theme of
the continuation of the Siberian railway, and "at the end of
March had audience with the tsar and touched on the most important points of the question of his reception" (Li Hung-
chang's) and "on the necessity of a confidential rapprochement
with Li Hung-chang while he was still on his way to Russia."[62]
   It was not only, and not so much, to intercept the Chinese
mission on its exit from Suez and prevent its slipping off to
Marseilles that Ukhtomsky was commanded to meet him: the
Odessa-Petersburg itinerary had been settled on when the Chinese left Shanghai and there can scarcely have been any serious apprehension of a sudden and deliberate diplomatically
awkward refusal by Li Hung-chang to board in Alexandria the
Russian steamer specially provided for him.[63] The evidence
indicated that Ukhtomsky's job was rather to initiate negotiations with the ambassador extraordinary, and to establish
working relations with any persons in the suite who by their
proximity to the ambassador would be in a position to compose certain ticklish points that would inevitably arise: "after reporting to his majesty on this matter," Witte "sketched"
for Ukhtomsky "in its general outlines the program to be followed in conversations with the Chinese ambassador extraordinary, and authorized him, during the course of negotiations, to be lavish with certain promises to the influential
personages of the ambassadorial suite or through them to
their friends and associates in Peking itself."[64]
   There is no reason to doubt that, while accompanying the
mission all the way from Port Said to Russia, Ukhtomsky
achieved the "necessary confidential rapprochement" with
Li Hung-chang, nor, later on, up to the day of the old man's
death, did Ukhtomsky ever in case of need vainly see him, or
communicate by personal coded despatches, when pecuniary
influence on his "personal friend" was in order. As soon as
the mission had arrived in Petersburg and when the ceremonious meetings of Witte with Li Hung-chang, so saliently described in the Reminiscences, had just begun, Rothstein entered upon a discussion with Grot of the project for a "private
company," to build and operate the road--Grot, as it turned
out, having been "recommended" to Rothstein also by "Shang-

hai friends" of his Rothstein lured his collocutor with a million francs which he, Rothstein, "could have offered even in
1895 to Chinese partners" in the company under discussion--
and Rothstein's proposals "were well received"[65] by Grot.

True, Grot tried to insist on a Chinese company, while
Rothstein "argued that a Russian one would be preferable,"
but the text of the Rothstein letter quoted here leaves no doubt
of the fact that what they discussed founding was a mixed Russo-Chinese joint stock company, in which Chinese participation
could be represented (to a given quota, of course) by a total
number of actual shareholders not fixed in advance.[66] This
was not altogether what Witte obtained in further negotiations
with Li Hung-chang, which soon lost their ceremonial character and assumed a thoroughly business-like aspect.[67] The
agreement at which the parties arrived as the result of a full
month's negotiations--the Moscow treaty of May 22, 1896--
was the fruit, apparently, of obstinate struggle on both sides:
it represented concessions bought from the Chinese for less
than had been planned and yet exceeding the Russian demands
on which Rothstein's proposal had been built.

Formally, both sides defended their respective positions
in the main: China refused to authorize the Russian government's building a road through Manchuria--the Russian government, in turn, declined China's offer to effect a junction
with the Siberian trunk-line at the Chinese government's expense, but both governments would more or less participate
in the building and administration of the future line. Witte
attempted to obtain the concession for the line directly in the
name of the Russian government--and met with a flat refusal.[68]
On the other hand, the Chinese did not insist even on the organization of a Russo-Chinese railway joint stock company:
the concession was granted in the name of the Russo-Chinese
bank, without provisos, and the contract for the building and
exploitation of the road was to be concluded with the bank. A
special treaty on it was concluded between the two governments, in which the road became the basis of a defensive alliance between Russia and China against Japan, as being the
necessary weapon of the alliance.[69] Any attack by Japan on
Russian possessions in eastern Asia, or on the territory of
China, would put this treaty of alliance into effect, and during hostilities in such an event, all Chinese ports would be
open to Russian warships. A road through Manchuria to
Vladivostok would be built (by the Russo-Chinese bank) for

the express purpose of facilitating in time of war the access
of Russian troops to points threatened, Russia also having the
right to transport troops and supplies in time of peace. The
treaty was concluded for a term of 15 years from the moment
of the Chinese government's confirmation of a concession contract with the Russo-Chinese bank. On May 18, Li Hung-
chang received Peking's authorization to sign this treaty and
on the 22nd the text of it, drawn up by Lobanov, was signed
in Moscow. [70]

Li Hung-chang is known to have "stated various obstacles"[71]
during the negotiations with Witte. These obstacles of course
bore no relation to the alliance proper as proposed by Russia,
which, in the given political situation, was for the Chinese
government both an advantageous and a spectacular exit from
the state of profound humiliation to which the Manchu dynasty
had been brought by the Japanese war. They were "stated"
by Li Hung-chang in relation to satisfying the Russian demands
which were the price set for the alliance proposed by Russia.
As mentioned above, the Chinese mission expected to have two
basic demands made: 1) as to the construction of the road and
2) as to letting Russia have a port for the berthing of her war-
ships. Meanwhile, the treaty of May 22 was silent as to this
second demand, strictly limiting the right of user in Chinese
ports to periods when hostilities had been undertaken by Russia in defense of China against Japan on the basis of Article
5. Does this mean that Witte failed to extort Li Hung-chang's
consent on this point, or that no such demand was made?

If Witte's testimony is to be trusted, the only hitch in his
negotiations with Li Hung-chang--though he did not regard it
as such, and took every precaution to render it fictitious in
actuality--was his inability to obtain the railway concession
in the name of the Russian government directly. There exists,
however, indisputable documentary evidence that Witte then
demanded the Chinese representative's consent not only to a
north-Manchurian trunk-line but to a south-Manchurian branch
to "some port on the Yellow Sea"[72] as well. This demand
was apparently advanced by Witte in such insistent form as
to preclude a flat refusal: "Li Hung-chang agreed to its construction, but stipulated narrow gauge." Witte in turn "categorically rejected this proviso, recognizing that it was absolutely necessary for this branch to have one and the same
gauge as the main line"--and "these negotiations were without
result."[73]

This testimony, taken literally, still does not amount to proof that cession to Russia of a Chinese port was then discussed. But we do have here very valuable evidence that Witte in May, 1896, not only had in view the routing of the Siberian road by the shortest course but was also attempting a first step toward railway penetration into South Manchuria. At the very least it may be said that during the Petersburg negotiations Witte turned the question of a "port for the berthing of Russian vessels" into two questions at once: 1) inclusion in the sphere of Russian railway influence of the part of Manchuria that directly bordered on Korea and barred progress from the latter farther inland and 2) such connection of some ice-free port on the Yellow Sea with the Russian system of railways as would inevitably--with Russian guage, that is--make Russia virtually master of such a port and solve the question of a berthing for ships in the most prudent form politically and strategically.

Thus, Li Hung-chang raised objections on two points: on the formal appurtenance of the Manchurian trunk-line to the Russian government and on the question of the gauge of its South-Manchurian branch. And on neither point would he yield even for money. He yielded, however, on the main point: gave up the idea of a Chinese railway company and agreed to the Russian project. And this he did, actually, for money. The "obstacles" that he undoubtedly reared on this point as well were removed by Witte's "promise" that to him, Li Hung-chang, for successful accomplishment in the matter of building the road, 3 million rubles would be paid.[74] The matter was a delicate one, the transaction presented complications and did not yield itself to any true officialization as touching Li Hung-chang. For his signature to the treaty of May 22 as such, the old man received no cash in hand. Payment was promised at different and rather remote dates: the first million upon receipt of the imperial order for granting the concession to the Russo-Chinese bank and the document ratifying the main principles of the concession; the second upon the final signing of the concession and the confirmation of the exact direction of the line; and the third when the construction of the line was entirely completed. Guarantee of payment, apart from a verbal promise, Li Hung-chang had none, regardless of whether the business had been confined to Witte alone, or the promise further confirmed at the audience with the tsar. "This promise was officialized" only indirectly--as Witte re-

minded the tsar in 1900--"in the form of a protocol signed by
Undersecretary Romanov, Prince Ukhtomsky, and Rothstein,
on which protocol I, with your majesty's knowledge, wrote:
"agreed."[75] Thus, formally, the promise was confirmed by
the signatures of members of the board of directors of the
Russo-Chinese bank, which allocated three million rubles
"for the facilitation of negotiations as to the founding of the
Eastern Chinese Railway as well as for the effectuation of
this project." Apparently the protocol was hastily drawn up,
the day after the signing of the political treaty with the Russian government, to reassure Li Hung-chang at least as to the
official allocation of the promised sum, even if the protocol
did not specify payment to him, Li Hung-chang: from the
sense of paragraph 4 of the protocol Li could feel confident
that the "sums enumerated" would be debited to the new Chinese-Eastern Railway Company "under costs of construction."
But the protocol drawn up for the edification of Li Hung-chang
promptly passed into the maw of the ministry of finance, as
being a document from the bank's point of view fictitious, of
exclusively historic interest, and incapable of execution. The
purchase of the concession from Li Hung-chang in the name
of the Russo-Chinese bank enabled Witte virtually to get matters altogether into the government's hands, after establishing,
and by observing, the outward forms necessary to the maintenance of the fiction.

III

The imperial order for the concession was issued on August
16/28, and the contract for the road's construction signed on
August 27 (September 8) 1896.[76] The time for the first payment had arrived. Rothstein and Uhktomsky considered it
"imperative" to set about this "at once": "otherwise, the
Chinese may start serious sabotage, thinking that they have
been monstrously taken in." But to remit the money "to any
address" in Shanghai would, they feared, be to "publish the
secret, endanger Li's family and produce apathy in associates."
Consequently Ukhtomsky decided to go to Shanghai himself
and "hand over the full sum" in person. Telegraphing all this
to Witte in Yalta, Ukhtomsky requested him to "advance the
million from the State bank."[77] Witte replied that there was
no hurry until building actually started. As to the source of
the payment, Witte corrected Ukhtomsky: "the payment must

be drawn on the Russo-Chinese bank, " which "may obtain a
loan for this purpose from the State bank, this loan later being repaid, with interest, out of the bonded capital" (of the
Chinese Eastern Railway Company). [78]

As we see, in the very first case where a practical question of money arose in connection with the Chinese Eastern
Railway, two views clashed, its double nature was exposed.
Ukhtomsky saw the matter in essence, Witte's concept was
strictly formal. Ukhtomsky draws the whole payment straight
from the treasury's coffers; Witte rehearses the red-tape
required by the legal fiction. To Ukhtomsky it was plain that
the "bonded capital" of the road was a treasury subsidy of the
road's budget; Witte corrected this terminology. From the
bank's angle, there could be no doubt that the payment date
ought to be observed, but politically it was more prudent to
wait a bit, while the contractor was powerless to do harm
and it might still be possible to get something further out of
him. In point of fact, the protocol of May 23 proved completely fictitious in respect to paragraph four, and for the
rest was fulfilled as political necessity dictated: Li Hung-
chang was to get his first million from treasury funds, by
decree of the minister of finance, after considerable delay,
and accompanied by a new Russian claim; the other two he
was not to get at all.

In order to arrive at a full understanding of the above-
noted artificial and devious financial relations linking the
bank, the Chinese Eastern Railway Company and the treasury,
it will be necessary to revert to the epoch of the Moscow negotiations. On the very day of the Khodynsky catastrophe,
May 18, Witte presented for Nicholas II's approval the project
for an agreement between the Russian government and the Russo-Chinese bank as to the organization of the Chinese Eastern
Railway Company "to ensure the fullest government influence
on the construction and exploitation of the road, " and "virtually" put the concession "at the Russian government's disposal. " [79] In article four of this agreement, afterwards omitted
from the charter of the Chinese Eastern Railway Company and
thus kept secret, the relations of government and bank in the
capital stock of the future Company were defined as follows:

> The Russo-Chinese bank shall subscribe the whole
> capital stock of the Company (1,000 shares, at 5,000
> rubles each). Of this number not less than 700 shares,

designated for the Russian government, must thereafter
be kept as the Russo-Chinese bank shall decree until their
transfer to the possession of the government. The shares
designated shall, immediately after the closing of the subscription to shares be transferred by the Russo-Chinese
bank to the State bank. The remainder, not exceeding
300 shares, may be placed in private hands either during
the subscription or within six months thereafter. By the
State bank a loan without interest shall be made to the
Russo-Chinese bank on the security of the said 700 shares
deposited in the State bank, and likewise of such remaining shares as shall not by that time have been placed in
private hands. This loan shall be made in the amount of
the nominal capital value of the shares actually deposited.
Thereafter any dividend that may accrue on those shares
upon which the loan has been made shall be entered as
revenue of the Russian government. The government has
the right to acquire at any time at their nominal value the
shares in the Company upon which the loan was made,
crediting the loan made on them to the full amount of the
price paid for the shares. When the government shall
make an accounting with the Russo-Chinese bank upon the
acquisition of the said 700 shares for the treasury, in the
event of the Russo-Chinese bank so desiring, the government shall be obligated simultaneously to make an accounting with it upon the acquisition for the treasury of such of
the remaining 300 shares as shall by that time not have
been placed in private hands.

By the terms of this article, the <u>right</u> was reserved to the
bank to assume not in excess of 300 shares and even to issue
them to private holders. It may be conjectured that this, for
the Russian government, safe concession had in view possible
participation in the enterprise by French financial circles
connected with the bank and may almost have been introduced
by Rothstein, through whom the French were at just this time
receiving "detailed information about the negotiations with
Li Hung-chang," even knowing, for example, "what the purpose of Rothstein's trip to Moscow [had been]."80 The question whether the French would wish to avail themselves of the
right that was, in any event, reserved for them still remained
unanswered at that time, and the <u>obligation</u> of the

Russian government to relieve the bank's portfolio of the 300
shares reserved for them was inserted in the agreement in
case of their refusal. As soon as the bank's negotiations with
the Chinese government were over, the concession contract
signed, and the matter of organizing the Chinese Eastern
Railway Company itself reached, the question of French participation was decided in the negative. On November 4, 1896,
in presenting the project of the Company's charter to the
minister of finance for confirmation, the directorate of the
Russo-Chinese bank stated that "there appeared to be no necessity of giving any third parties shares in the Chinese Eastern Railway Company now seeking his confirmation, in consequence of which the bank found itself fully competent to
place the entire capital stock at the disposal, and into the
possession, of the Russian government, in conformity with
the agreement concluded on May 18 of the current year,
1896."[81]

On December 4, the charter of the company was confirmed
and December 17 set as the date for subscription to shares.
Notice of the subscription was printed in the Pravitel'stvennyi
Vestnik (Government Herald) of December 17 and, as the
opening of the subscription was set for 9 A.M., the outside
public was quite unable to participate.[82] At the appointed
hour a "considerable number of employees" gathered at the
banking rooms and the subscription was closed a few minutes
after opening."[83] Thus the capital stock of the Company in
the amount of 5,000,000 rubles duly became an item in the
"disbursements of the Russian treasury in the Far East."[84]

On the strength of article 9 of the Company's charter,
Witte simultaneously entered into an agreement with the Directorate of the Company as to the sum that the Company was
to pay the Russian government for the surveys it had conducted in Manchuria, and this sum was set at four million rubles.
Having, as we saw, run up against certain difficulties in the
matter of the Li Hung-chang account, and wishing to avoid
multiple bookkeeping operations in this connection, Witte resorted to the establishment of a "special" fund under his own
direct control, later known as the "Li Hung-chang" fund, and
solicited to this end an order not for publication.[85] In substance the operation authorized by this order consisted in the
transfer of three million rubles from the stock capital of five
million rubles, deposited by the State bank in the Russo-Chinese bank in the form of a loan on the shares of the Chinese

Eastern Railway Company, while one million reverted to
revenue of the treasury. After this operation only one million rubles of the capital stock would remain at the disposition of the directorate of the Chinese Eastern Railway Company.[82]

Such a withdrawal, at the outset, of four-fifths of the capital stock of the Company to the order of the treasury, which
had itself realized this capital, is to be explained by the conditions under which the concession contract was concluded
with the Chinese government. The basic, but inevitable, defect of the concession consisted in the provision that at the
end of eighty years the road was to pass, gratis, into the
possession of the Chinese government. But the Chinese insisted upon the inclusion in the contract of the right of pre-
term redemption of the road and article 12 of the contract
stipulated the right of the Chinese government to institute
redemption at the expiration of 36 years from the day of
the opening of traffic. Witte, in turn, demanded the extension of the time limit to 50 years, but under pressure from
Rothstein, who saw no possibility of getting the consent of
the Chinese to such an extension, was disposed to agree to
the 36-year time limit "in an extremity," "but only on condition that the redemption should be consummated on such
principles as to provide for the repayment to us of all sums
without exception that we shall have expended, together with a
fair increment."[87] Witte's idea in this last condition was to
make the redemption terms "in general" "as irksome as
possible."[88]

In accordance with Witte's conception, the redemption
terms for the Manchurian railway were made "much more
onerous than the redemption terms for Russian railways,
and therefore rendered the possibility of this redemption
very slight."[89] That is, the Chinese government was obligated, in connection with the purchase, to repay "all capital
invested in the concern and all debts contracted for the road,
together with the accumulated interest on them" (art. 12 of
the contract). According to a rough (and very low) estimate
made in the ministry of finance in November, 1896, the Chinese government would, after 36 years, have to pay in connection with the purchase around 700 million rubles.[90] But
if, notwithstanding, the pre-term purchase of the road did
take place, then this conversion of the greater part of the
stock capital into a "special fund" for repaying treasury

money spent for survey operations would permit restoration
to the Russian treasury of the sums assigned for the deferred
payment of Li Hung-chang intended to insure in some measure
the satisfactory conduct and completion of construction.

Foreknowledge of the possibility of all manner of untoward
happenings during the construction period itself is known to
have prompted Witte also to include in the concession contract the pledge of the Chinese Eastern Railway Company to
pay the Chinese government five million lan (about seven million rubles) on the day of the opening of traffic on the road.
Naturally this sum too, in the event of pre-term purchase,
would be subject to inclusion in the sum total of the redemption payment.[91] Thus a situation was created which put pre-
term purchase of the road beyond the Chinese government's
reach and, besides, linked it with the return to the Russian
treasury even of the ten million rubles paid from it for the
very right to build and operate the road.

The Russo-Chinese bank, though not assuming the slightest risk concomitant to financial participation in the Chinese
Eastern Railway enterprise, was nonetheless most vitally
involved in the interests of the road by the mere fact of having become its banker and having formally remained sole contractor with the Chinese government for the concession. In
view of the latter circumstance, it is impossible not to appreciate the shrewdness shown in fortifying the bank's position
in this respect by permitting the Chinese government to deposit five million lan in the bank and share accordingly in its
profits.[92] But while creating for the Chinese government a
substantial reason to be interested in the extensive development of the bank's activity, Witte definitely excluded both the
Chinese government and the Russo-Chinese bank itself from
any influence on the business management of the road.[93]

Needless to say, in becoming sole stockholder in the Chinese Eastern Railway Company and maintaining the right to
reserve for itself all bonded loans of the Company, as well
as assuming all supplementary operational costs and the
coverage of payments on loans, the Russian government became virtually full owner of the road.[94] But since the contract of August 27 allowed the adjustment of the Company's
charter to Russian railroad regulations, even formally the
competence of the government in the Company's affairs might
be defined very broadly. Article 27 of the Company's charter
called for presentation "for" the Russian finance minister's

"approval" of such questions as the election of the vice-president, the appointment of the chief engineer, heads of separate departments and engineers in general, the election of
members of the auditing committee, the establishment of
modes of investing the capital funds of the road, the definition
of the rights and duties of all senior employees of the road,
and of the form of administration of the road, as well as of
the direction and technical circumstances of the line's construction. Witte may be said to have obtained the right to
construct in Manchuria, and to operate for 80 years, a Russian government railway, shielded, on the plane of international relations, by the unexceptionable form of a private
joint-stock enterprise, whereof the actual residence and
ownership of the shares remained shrouded in impenetrable
mystery. 95

It is plain why Witte recognized the terms of the August
27 contract as also "extremely favorable from the viewpoint
of Russia's interests."96 For example: 1) the Russian 5-
foot gauge, 2) the one-third lower rate of Chinese assess-
ments on imports and exports by rail as compared with the
Chinese maritime customs, 3) full freedom of the Company
in the matter of railway tariffs, 4) full freedom of the road
from all Chinese taxes and levies. True, the contract did not
give the road the right of duty-free exploitation of coal mines
in Manchuria, but 1) Shui Ching-chen's written promise to
petition Peking for this was incorporated in the contract and
2) it would always remain possible for the road to employ
tariff measures to force the Chinese coal mines to sell coal
to the road at a reasonable price. All of which virtually guaranteed economic conquest of the whole region drawn into the
road's sphere of action.

But there were two points in the contract whereby the matter was not limited to mere economic conquest of this indefinitely vast Chinese area. Article 6 promised the transfer to
the Company of "lands actually necessary for the construction,
exploitation and protection of the line, as well as lands in the
environs of the road needed for providing the road with sand,
stone, lime, etc.,"--gratis, if the land was state property,
and for a fee if privately owned. Article 6 also gave the Company "an absolute and exclusive administrative right in its
lands" and "the right of erecting on these lands structures of
any sort." Article 5 established, quite generally, that "crim-
inal offences, lawsuits, and so forth in the territory of the

road were to be adjudicated by the local authorities on the
basis of the treaties." Both of these articles advanced the
concept of a "territory of the road," and raised the question
of how to organize its separate administration. The question here was in no sense a matter of applying the right of
exterritoriality granted Russian subjects by the treaties, but
one of juridically qualifying the nature of the new territorial
organization, in relation to which the treaty of May 22, 1896
had guaranteed the preservation of the sovereign rights of
China (article 4).

Article 5 of the contract was carried over into the Charter
of the Company, not subject to the Chinese government's confirmation, with only the slight further definition of the term
"local authorities" as: "Russian and Chinese" (article 7 of
the Charter).[97] Article 6 of the contract was embodied in
article 8 of the Charter, which made the Company responsible
for establishing its own constabulary in the territory of the
road. As justification for this clause, an explanatory note
to the project of the Charter indicated the complete analogy
between the territory of the road and "the districts set apart
in Chinese ports for the residence of Europeans (the settlements) which had their own police."[98]

This unprecedently extensive settlement, by its very nature as a railway holding, must, with the progress of construction, and still more with the exploitation of the road,
show a mighty tendency both toward the direct enlargement of
its territory and toward the broadening of its sphere of economic domination. And perspectives of an 80-year period of
the growth from within this social organism, as projected by
the acts of 1896, apparently precluded any possibility then
concretely conceivable to its initiators of an actual transfer
of the Chinese Eastern Railway gratis into China's full possession at the end of the 80 years. This is why all Witte's
efforts were primarily concentrated on preventing the curtailment of this period by pre-term redemption of the road, or,
in the event of redemption, to guard the interests of the Russian government not only on the financial side but also with
respect to the use of the road as a connecting link of the Siberian trunk-line, to be exploited first and foremost in the
interests of Russia. Article 3 of the Company's Charter,
enumerating the obligations assumed by the Chinese Eastern
Railway Company to the Russian government, was entirely
built up on the idea that the Russian government would, in the

given event, come forward as a "third person" and that the obligations with respect to this "third person" assumed by the Company for the 80-year period would automatically pass at term to the Chinese government.[99] That such a construction did not at all follow from the tenor of the contract of August 27 itself and would inevitably lead to conflict upon the first attempt to put it into effect was allowed to pass without comment in the documents preserved from this "happy" time.

Chapter III

"SEIZURE" OF CHINESE TERRITORY IN
SOUTHERN MANCHURIA 1896-1898

The May 22 treaty of alliance and the railway contract of August 27, 1896 settled irrevocably the problem of the great Siberian road: its last thousand and a half versts were to pass through foreign territory, and the uniting of Vladivostok and Moscow--according to the contract in six years' time, i.e., by 1903--became ostensibly a mere question of surmounting technical difficulties. Reconnaissance operations in Manchuria started by Russian engineers back in the autumn of 1895 had, up to the moment of negotiations, yielded no exact positive data, and it had thus proved impossible for Russia to designate in the contract, even approximately, the direction of the Manchurian line, the more so since it was then already apparent that the technical difficulties of construction would be exceedingly great. Surveys proper were only undertaken in the summer of 1897, and despite the speed with which they were conducted, the direction of the line and a plan for construction were not established until the spring of 1898. Almost two years had gone by since the day when the Chinese government gave its consent to the laying of the Russian road through Manchuria--to seal an alliance with Russia designed to brace the position of the Manchu dynasty and not only guarantee the inviolability of Chinese territory where Japan was concerned but also preserve peace along the whole 8,000-verst overland Russo-Chinese border.

For these two years Russia had little to show beyond the bare beginning of some of the simplest ground levelling operations on the North-Manchurian line--the line destined, in finished form, to serve as principal--and invincible, weapon of the alliance. But in the spring of 1898, just when construction operations might have got in full swing, a new and urgent task presented itself and was given precedence, namely the building of a South-Manchurian branch to Port Arthur. Something "unheard of" had happened: Russia had herself "craftily" transgressed the territorial inviolability of her ally, the "seizure" of Liaotung had taken place, "that fatal step which brought in its train all those future consequences that ended in our ill-starred war with Japan," "a seizure that destroyed all our traditional relations with China, and destroyed them forever."[1]

It would be futile to minimize the significance of the step taken by the Russian government in February 1898 in demanding that China lease Russia Port Arthur and Talienwan, with the territory adjoining them: Russia acquired for the berthing of her war ships two ice-free ports near Peking and outside the Japan sea--blocked by the Tsushima military base included in her budget for the next few years a supplementary ship-building program coming to 90 million rubles, charges for the equipment and fortification of the new ports in the sum of not less than 30 million rubles, and for the building of the new 900-verst railway not less than 100 million rubles; founded at treasury expense a commercial steamship line (the "Maritime Steamship Line of the Chinese Eastern Railway Company"); and in the end had to reckon with the political consequences of her step. The defeats of the Russo-Japanese war duly forced her to retrace this step and return territorially to the boundaries of the 1896 contract. But surely it still does not follow from this that the Port Arthur episode broke a political tradition or was in principal a contradiction of the Russian political program then just beginning to be put into effect and as yet far from having got into full swing.

As to Japan, the fact must not be lost sight of that by annulling the Russian "seizure" of 1898 and driving Russia back to the 1896 boundaries, she had, as a result of the war of 1904-5 got herself into the position projected in the first redaction of the Shimonoseki treaty of 1895, and not by any means back into that in which, through Witte's kind offices, she had found herself in 1896. As to China, and in particular as to the Russo-Chinese acts of 1896, it is not to be denied that basically both had stood the test to which the "seizure" of 1898 had subjected them: 1) the contract for the building of the railway had been carried through by the Chinese government, and the road had been built, even if China had not been able fully to guarantee its security from Khunkhuz attacks or from demolition by the Boxers, and 2) the treaty of alliance, personally revised by Witte to be operative against Japan alone, had indeed preserved China from renewed at-

tacks by Japan and was consistently prosecuted by the Russian government in respect to Korea up to the time when Japan finally settled the Korean question by military means
and Russia, following the war of 1904-1905, was compelled
to renounce her guardianship of even the specious independence of Korea. In the history of China's international relations as such, the Port Arthur episode is inseparable from
the whole factual complex of the policy of "spheres of influence" (Sphärenpolitik) and from the struggle for concessions
which had, since 1895, settled upon China, replacing the
policy of direct wresting of her border territories, and in
which Russia, at Witte's dictation, hastened to join, lest she
lose her share in what he believed to be the impending partition of China. [2]

It must, however, be taken into account that the appraisal
of the seizure of Liaotung so trenchantly formulated in Witte's
Memoirs gained the widest currency in Russia and--by some
miracle--the indirect acknowledgement of the very "author"
of this seizure himself, Nicholas II. [3]   Nor is it any less necessary to take into account that we are here dealing not with
Witte's retrospective appraisal alone: he had raised objections
to the occupation of a port on the Liaotung peninsula the very
first day the tsar assigned this question for discussion, and
had not withdrawn them.   On this one count, it will be imperative in our further investigation to give the utmost attention
to precisely those facts where Witte's personal participation
makes possible a study of the nature and an evaluation of the
role of that policy which designated itself "peaceful," which
had from the first ostensibly not aspired to seizures, and
which claimed to guarantee peace without renouncing, and
without sacrificing the attainment of, its ends.

I

If we turn to Witte's own Memoirs, we shall be convinced
that, up to November 14, 1897, when the conference with
Nicholas II on the question of Russia's future course of action
in view of Germany's occupation of Kiaochow took place, and
Count Muravev, minister of foreign affairs, read his project
for the occupation of Talienwan by Russia, the policy of the
ministry of foreign affairs in the Far East had evoked no
objections from Witte.   Nay more, he had himself taken so
active a part in it as to warrant his being credited with the

whole. It was no wonder that Witte ascribed prime importance to the seizure of Kiaochow in connection with Russia's
"sudden" change of course. But this fact will also necessitate our now reverting to the initial aspect of the political
situation that concerns us, and in which Witte played the decisive part--namely to the spring of 1895.

As was previously indicated, the idea of the necessity of
keeping Japan from entrenching herself in the north of China
was developed by Witte with all the fervor implied by his
general conception of the political role of the Siberian road,
in defiance not only of the objections of ministers but even
of the view of the tsar himself. In the spring of 1895, Nicholas II thrice in the course of one week expressed himself in
favor of acquiring an ice-free port on the Korean littoral and
was prepared to reconcile himself to the settlement of Japan
in southern Manchuria provided this port were united with
Russian territory by a "strip of land." There exists no
grounds for suspecting that, in turning Nicholas from Korean
compensations to the ultimative prohibition of Japan's occupation of the whole south-Manchurian coast of the Yellow Sea
and the Gulf of Pechili, Witte was negating the idea of an ice-
free outlet for the Russian railway to the ocean.

On the contrary, no doubt existed even for the Chinese
government that, in addition to asking to route the Siberian
line straight through Manchuria, Russia would also demand
suitable berthing for her warships, if only in the winter time,
since the use of Japanese harbors for this purpose had become
difficult and dangerous in consequence of Russia's openly
hostile move against Japan in April of 1895. In the autumn of
that year, such winter rights in the closed port of Kiaochow
had, as we know, been duly granted Russia for the approaching winter of 1895-1896. And during negotiations with Li
Hung-chang in the spring of 1896 Witte also tried opening the
subject of a railway branch to "some port on the Yellow Sea":
but the deal fell through over the question of gauge. The additional half foot, for which Witte stood firm as a rock, revealed to the Chinese in its full original scale the Russian
territorial program, and in view of the atmosphere of cor-
ruption in which the Peterburg and Moscow negotiations of
1896 proceeded, the significance of the obstinacy shown by
Li Hung-chang regarding this metrical detail must not be
under-estimated: Russia was shown the limit beyond which
she would not be allowed in Manchuria, that northern Man-

churia and nothing further must serve as the equivalent of
the defensive alliance proposed by Russia.

The tenor of Witte's negotiations with Li Hung-chang was
at the time veiled in profound secrecy except from a maximum of some ten persons involved in the technical side of
the deal, who preserved complete reticence to the end in the
matter of this professional secret of theirs. Nor do there
exist any traces of indiscretion on the part of those French-
men to whom certain details became known through Roth-
stein--probably not the actual course of negotiations, however, but only their practical results. Li Hung-chang as
well proved reticent in his Memoirs, if any scientific value
at all may be attached to the English edition. On the question immediately before us, that of the South-Manchurian
branch, Li Hung-chang proved as reticent as in his Berlin
conversations in the summer of 1896. In them he moreoever
asserted that Nicholas had rejected his offer of a Korean
port, and that in general there could never have been any
question of Russia's expecting any concession from China
as token of gratitude for intervention in the Liaotung question in 1895.[4] It may be conjectured that at the moment and
in London Li Hung-chang preferred to calm the English regarding the character and proportions of the concessions
made to Russia.[5] In any event, the texts of all three acts of
1896--the political convention of May 22, the financial protocol of May 23, and the railway contract of August 27--remain-
ed a genuine secret. And--for the international spheres in-
terested--this fact opened up a wide range of conjecture both
as to the claims made by Russia and the extent of her success.
Even after the publication on December 4, 1896 of the charter of the Chinese Eastern Railway Company how can these
conjectures have been confined to Northern Manchuria alone,
how can they have failed to relate to some version of the ice-
free port?

Under such conditions, a month and a half before the publication of the Company's charter, on October 18/30, 1896,
there appeared in the North China Herald the text of a "special convention between China and Russia," obtained in copy
by the Peking correspondent of this paper from the Russian
embassy, and thereafter known to literature as "Cassini's
convention." However one may regard the provenance of this
text, the fact must be borne in mind that until 1910, when the
French text of the treaty of May 22, 1896 finally found its way

into print in an accurate (albeit still uncertified) transcrip-
tion, "Cassini's convention" remained the sole semblance
of a documentary version of the Russo-Chinese agreement
as to Manchuria, and was, moreover, irrefutable except by
official publication of the treaty actually signed by Witte,
Lobanov and Li Hung-chang.[6] Meanwhile, this version was
not only not refuted, but, as the further progress of events
testified, came sufficiently close, in the main, to actuality,
being distinguished by persuasive concreteness as to detail.
That no such convention was signed by China and Japan in the
autumn of 1896 can scarcely be doubted in view of the treaty
of May 22--even if the published text of it reproduced point
by point some unsigned original existing in the Russian embassy at Peking in the autumn of 1896 (signatures were not
reproduced in the North China Herald). But to relegate
"Cassini's convention" to the category of purely journalistic
fabrications without more ado, as a bald fiction derived from
the real situation, would likewise appear to lack any direct
justification.

The tenor of this enigmatic document is as follows. Russia was given the right to build two railway lines finally uniting at Kirin: 1) a Vladivostok-Hunchun-Kirin line and 2) a
line "from some station on the Siberian railway" to Aigun-
Tsitsihar-Bodune-Kirin, and to operate them for 30 years,
at the end of which time the Chinese government would be
permitted to redeem them on conditions to be determined
later. If China should herself find it inconvenient to extend
the completed Peking-Shanhaikwan railway to Mukden and
thence to Kirin, Russia would be given the right to lay this
line from the north, starting at Kirin, China reserving the
right of redemption at the end of 10 years. Every possible
Chinese branch railway from Shanhaikwan--to Tsitsihar,
Yinkou, Kaipin, Port Arthur and Talienwan, was to be built
with Russian gauge to the end of facilitating trade between the
two countries. In principle the Chinese government would
assume the protection of all Russian railways in Chinese
territory, but in view of the difficulty of actually providing
such protection would permit the Russian government to
maintain at important stations its own cavalry and infantry
divisions.

The question of ports was settled by the "convention" in
the following manner: 1) foreseeing the possibility of an
outbreak of hostilities on the Asiatic mainland, China would

lease Russia the port of Kiaochow for 15 years, but Russia
would enter into direct possession of this port and would likewise occupy points commanding it only in the event of an immediate threat of hostilities--lest she arouse the envy or suspicion of other powers, and 2) China would be obliged to speedily fortify Ports Arthur and Talienwan, while Russia would
afford the aid necessary for the defense of these ports and
would prevent any power from seizing them; nor would China,
on her part, cede them to any power; should Russia be drawn
into war and circumstances require it, China would temporarily permit Russia to concentrate her land and naval forces
in these ports, but until such danger should arise, China
would reserve to herself complete control over the administration of these ports.

Finally, the "convention" accorded the right of prospecting and of exploiting mineral resources in Kirin and Heilungkiang provinces exclusively to Russian and Chinese subjects,
in every instance with the permission not of Pekinese but of
local authorities. Add to this that military instruction throughout Manchuria was guaranteed to Russia in the event of the
reconstitution of local native armies on the western model,
and, truly, as the North China Herald's correspondent concluded, "this document spoke for itself and gave Russia everything that she could possibly desire."[7]

It is plain to be seen that "Cassini's convention" envisaged
a Russian "sphere of influence" on an all-Manchurian scale--
southern as well as northern--and made the five-foot Russian
gauge the basic implement for such seizure, regardless of
which country, China or Russia, built a given branch or which
exploited it. The broken railway line in northern Manchuria
was assigned immediately and permanently to Russia, while
the southern lines were formally released to her only on condition of China's deciding not to build them. The scheme of
railway lines given in "Cassini's convention" is a sort of
combination of schemes also given in a known memorandum
of Dukhovsky's and partially in a project by the American,
Bush, that had found its way into the Russian embassy in
Peking back in the spring of 1896. In particular, the 30-year
time limit of the concession for the main line in northern
Manchuria is the same as in Bush's project. As in the treaty
of May 22, Russia's admission to ice-free Chinese ports was,
in a way, made contingent on the necessity for armed intervention by Russia in China's defense in the event of threatened
danger of war.

On the other hand, any intrusion by a third foreign power into Manchuria was absolutely precluded by the "convention," and all Manchuria put on ice for Russia--in full accord with the demand and the certitude expressed by Witte at the conference of March 30, 1895 that in the event of a Russian road being laid in northern Manchuria no other branch would be built in northern China without Russia's consent. Thus, the content of this "document" represents in its main outlines a concrete--if as yet far from complete--development of the aggressive Russian program linked with the building of the great Siberian road.

At the same time, the formal traits of the text of "Cassini's convention" are such as to prohibit its being regarded as the final copy of a diplomatic document: 1) while possessing a developed introductory section, "Cassini's convention" has no concluding section at all--signatures, dates, and so forth, 2) in the introductory section, China's representatives are unnamed, while Cassini is named as Russia's, 3) the "convention" text itself, in the exemplar from which the copy was taken, had not been broken down into articles and the numbering of articles is the work of the English publisher, not to mention the fact that 4) in the matter of style slight faults and incompletenesses are noticeable here and there in the text. These indications make it impossible to see more in "Cassini's convention" than the detailed rough-draft of a treaty not quite ready for signing in the form in which it was stolen from the papers of the Russian embassy in the autumn of 1896.

But in any case, it can hardly be doubted that when entering upon negotiations with the ministers of the Tsungli Yamen in April, 1896 Cassini had in readiness at least one finished project giving an exact enumeration of the concessions to be included in the forthcoming treaty, and the strictest contemporary critic would most probably have stopped at the hypothesis that "Cassini's convention" gave an essentially accurate account of the content of the Russian program. The question would then have boiled down to: just what part of what she had asked did Russia actually obtain from China. As will next be shown, this is precisely how German diplomacy stated the question when occasion offered for making a try for Kiaochow, a port apparently safeguarded by some ostensible Russian claim, or even right. "Cassini's convention" objectively erected in the international arena a presumption rela-

tive to Russia's staking of a claim to all Manchuria and the
approaches to Chihli province, and left no margin for hope
that the concession for a North-Manchurian trunk-line, as
formulated in the charter of December 4, 1896, would satiate
even briefly Russia's expansionist tendency in the Far East.

The position that Russian diplomacy took at this time on
the Korean question could only fortify such a view, and gave
rein to the daily anticipation of further steps by Russia in the
region of the prospected Manchurian zone as well.

II

The Sino-Japanese war, ending with the formal declaration
of Korea's independence of China (article I of the treaty of
April 5/17, 1895,) would appear to have created for Japan a
virtually dominant position in that country, the more precious
to Japan the more hopeless matters became for her in Manchuria. With the forcible exclusion of Japan from southern
Manchuria had come the collapse of that unified and integral
plan for Japan's railway defense against the spread of Russian holdings on the Asiatic littoral so widely publicized the
day after the signing of the Shimonoseki treaty. [8] This plan
had proposed: 1) to provide the Korean government with the
financial means to enable its building without delay a railway
line from the port of Fusan (in the south of Korea) to Gishu
(at the mouth of the Yalu, on the Manchurian border); 2) to
lay a railway from Chinchow to Newchwang and thence north-
ward to Mukden to connect with the great Siberian road; 3) to
persuade the Chinese government to build by some fixed date
a railway connecting the Korean and the Japanese line with
Peking; 4) to use the whole amount of the indemnity that she
was to receive from China for building the railways proposed
in these projects. As we see, Japan in 1895 meant to create
for herself in one bout that position on the continent which
she obtained ten years later at the cost of a second war and
by the most strenuous naval preparation.

The three-power ultimatum relative to Liaotung in April,
1895, had intensified the acuteness of the Korean question
for Japan extremely: to let slip through her fingers first
Manchuria, then the protectorate over Korea would for Japan have been tantamount to defeat in a war where she had
come off victor. But meanwhile Japanese diplomacy cannot
have failed to realize that the international situation in 1895

was more favorable to Russia than it had been ten years previously, in 1885, when Russia made her first attempt to lay hold of Korea. Though Russia had at the conclusion of the peace treaty agitated only the question of Liaotung, there could be no doubt that sooner or later, in one form or another, she would endeavor to frustrate Japan's plans in Korea as well, and this naturally tended to give Japan's activities in Korea an excessively nervous and stern character.

At the very beginning of the war the Korean government had been compelled to make a treaty of alliance with Japan, guaranteeing the Japanese army all manner of aid and provisioning within the country, and had accepted a loan of three million yen from Japan. Korea permitted the laying of Japanese telegraphic lines and underwent an occupation by Japanese troops that continued even after the end of the war. The Chinese resident at the royal court of Korea was now replaced by a Japanese minister who terrorized the palace at Seoul, abruptly set about the wholesale elimination of Russian sympathizers from the palace and from the administration, and ended by organizing a palace revolution (September 26, 1895) in the course of which the Korean queen was brutally murdered. By the end of the year the anti-Japanese movement in Korea, fanned to flame by the shameless depredations of the rabble of all sorts of war jobbers and contractors that had over-run the country, took on a sufficiently pronounced character so that the Russian representative in Seoul was able to extract from the situation thus created a success that seems to have taken Japan by surprise: on January 30, 1896, the Korean king fled from the palace to the compound of the Russian mission, where he settled down to await the building of a new palace under guard of a Russian military detail.[9]

The absolute value of the success that came Russia's way with the shifting of the royal residence and the opportunity thus opened for choosing ministers who were Russian sympathizers should not be exaggerated: the mainstay of the country's administration remained as inaccessible to foreign influence afterwards as before, i.e., the director of the Korean customs, with the lion's share of the treasury's cash revenues at his disposal, was the Englishman Brown. But having made this deduction, which applies equally to Japan, one may indeed speak of the "complete breakdown" of Japanese policy in Korea, where, as in Manchuria, the fruits of victory were threatening to slip from Japan's hands into

Russia's.[10] The memorandum signed on May 2/14, 1896, by Russian and Japanese representatives in Seoul was an agreement that gave precise official form to the victory won by Russia and in it not a vestige of Japanese privilege remained. In fact, the first two of the memorandum's four articles constituted mutual recognition of the situation created for the Korean government by the king's transit to the safety of the Russian mission as normal: the king's actual return to his own palace was left to the king's "own discretion," but the parties were pledged to give him friendly advice to this effect "as soon as all doubt as to his security shall have been dispelled" (i.e., when Russia so desired,) and relative to the current (Russophile) make-up of the ministry, article 2 simply asserted that the ministers "had been appointed by free choice" of the king. Articles 3 and 4 of the memorandum had the air of being concessions to Japan, permitting her to maintain not to exceed 200 gendarmes as guard of the telegraph line, distributed in small detachments along its whole extent, and not to exceed 800 soldiers as guard of the Japanese settlements in Fusan, Gensan and Seoul.

But: 1) Russia was permitted to maintain an equal number of troops at these points, 2) for Japan this meant the evacuation of all the rest of the troops then occupying the country, while for Russia it created a new right, 3) it was stipulated that all the foreign detachments enumerated should be withdrawn as soon as the perils requiring them "shall have passed" and "peace shall have been restored within the country,"-- which, in view of the Korean government's given situation, meant the reservation of political influence to Russia.[11] The question of the Russian government's endeavoring to consolidate and systematize this influence was left completely open by the Seoul memorandum, so that the primary task now facing Japan was to get from Russia certain guarantees in this respect. Such, apparently, was the origin of the so-called Moscow protocol signed by Lobanov and Yamagata on May 28/ June 9 of this same year as a result of negotiations proposed by the latter at the time of the coronation ceremonies. In substance, Yamagata's original idea had been a division of Korea along the 38th parallel, with the southern half, including Seoul, the capital, as Japan's share, and the northern as Russia's. But "Korea's destiny as a component part of the Russian empire, on geographical and political grounds, had been foreordained for us to fulfill," whereas "in conceding Japan

by treaty the southern extremity of the Korean peninsula Russia would be formally relinquishing, once and for all, the
most important part of Korea strategically and navally and
would thus voluntarily cramp her own freedom of action in
future,"[12]--and Lobanov rejected any such statement of the
question in view of the recognized "independence" of Korea.

The text of the open articles of the protocol was accordingly revised in the latter mode, laying on both governments
the following mutual obligations: 1) to counsel the Korean
government to balance its budget, 2) in the event of a resort
to foreign loans being necessary, to exert their influence on
Korea jointly, 3) to leave entirely to Korea the setting up and
maintenance of native militia and police in sufficient numbers
to maintain civil order without foreign aid, and 4) to permit
Korea to redeem both the existing Japanese telegraph lines
and those now authorized to Russia. For Japan the real significance of these obligations consisted in the fact of Russia's
renouncing separate counsels and aid to Korea in the financial
sphere and in the matter of setting up native armies. For
Russia it lay in the fact that the "principal integrity and independence" of Korea and the equal interest of both parties in
supporting it were confirmed--if the Moscow protocol worked
--"until Russia's firm consolidation in all respects on the
shores of the Pacific ocean."[13] And since there could be no
serious question of the actual independence of the Korean
government in the absence of troops and material means, it
was established by the secret articles of the protocol that the
contracting parties were not to introduce armies into Korean
territory without mutual consent and that in the event of such
necessity they were to agree in advance on the region of action
of their respective troops and on a neutral zone in between.[14]
Had the Moscow protocol been scrupulously observed subsequently, it might have been said to have kept Korea (until its
breach) in the position of a country evenly balanced between
being subject to the united influence of its neighbors and independent of separate pressure from either one--in a position
of equilibrium on the point of a needle.

However, Lobanov undoubtedly signed the protocol of
May 28 with every intention of disregarding the obligations
he had assumed. During those very days when the Moscow
negotiations with Yamagata were in progress, Moscow also
received an embassy from the Korean king asking for help.
And, strangely enough, the help Korea asked was on precisely

those points, all of them, that were included in the Russo-
Japanese protocol as objects of mutual action by Russia and
Japan. So far as we known, no bilateral act has remained
as monument of these Russo-Korean negotiations, only the
"points in reply to the Korean ambassador" as formulated
by Lobanov and approved by Nicholas.[15] Literally, these
ran as follows:

"I. The king during his sojourn in the Russian Mission
will be protected by a Russian guard. He may remain in
the Mission as long as he himself shall deem needful and
convenient; should a return of the king to his own palace
ensue, the Russian government may assume moral guarantee of his safety. The Russian detachment now located at
the Mission shall remain there at the orders of the Russian
minister, and in event of need may even be reinforced.

"II. For the settlement of the question of instructors,
there shall be dispatched to Seoul very shortly an experi-
enced Russian officer of high rank whom the Russian government will charge with entering into negotiations with
the Koreans on this subject; the said officer shall, first
of all, be charged to occupy himself with the question of
setting up a king's bodyguard. An equally competent person shall be dispatched from Russia for the study of Korea's economic situation and to ascertain the financial
measures necessary.

"III. The question regarding the sending of Russian
advisers to cooperate with the Korean government is answered by the preceding point. The above-mentioned
trustworthy persons will, obviously, under the direction
of the Russian minister, serve as such advisers in the
military and financial department.

"IV. The conclusion of a loan to the Korean government will be considered as soon as the economic situation
of the country and the needs of the government shall have
been ascertained.

"V. The Russian government agrees to the amalgamation " of its overland telegraph lines with the Korean
and will supply the assistance requisite to this undertaking. "

In making such promises to the Korean government, Lobanov, as it were, legalized, in the form of "points in reply,"

the separate program of action in Korea that was being undertaken behind Japan's back. As we see, this program did not
yet state the problem as literal "seizure" of the country whose
"independence" and "inviolability" had been proclaimed in the
statement by the Russian government that accompanied the
publication of the Moscow protocol.[16] But the contemplated
means to a "peaceful conquest" of Korea were bound to bring
Russian into conflict not only with Japan but with England as
well, inasmuch as the English customs director stood as a
stumbling-block in the path of the Russian financial adviser:
in gaining ascendancy over the person of the king and seizing
the archaic machinery of authority that was ready to hand,
Russia had laid hold on the basic resources of the country
and was actually threatening to establish her political authority there.

Thus, in May of 1896, Russian diplomacy was simultaneously working in three directions: 1) in North Manchuria it was
seeking a transit line to Vladivostok, 2) in Korea it was seeking some roundabout route to the protectorate, pending the
full development of its powers for her complete annexation,
and 3) in South Manchuria it was seeking an outlet to an ice-
free port. For the time being it had quite set aside its efforts in the fourth, and internationally most explosive, direc-
tion--a railway to Peking. On her way to the Yellow Sea
through Manchuria, Russia had, at the given moment, met
with failure. But on the first two points enormous diplomatic
success had been attained. On the Korean question in particular, this had been bought--in the provisional form of a favorable starting-point--at the price of the same "unheard-of
craft" with respect to Japan that Russia had somewhat tardily
countenanced in connection with the Liaotung question: having
taken an uncompromising tone with Japan back in April, 1895,
Russia decided to maintain it consistently until the end, not
admitting her to the mainland at all. Japan, hastening to
meet Russia both on Chinese and on Korean soil before the
completion of the Siberian road, had found herself ejected
from the Liaotung peninsula and outstripped politically on
the Korean.

By Witte's own admission, his part in negotiations on the
Korean question in May, 1896 had been quite secondary, the
principal role being Lobanov's.[17] However, the lion's share
of the work of developing the diplomatic success attained by
Lobanov from that day forth fell on Witte, since the basic

implement for the conquest of Korea became, by the whole
conception of the plan, the Russian financial adviser, whom
Witte from the first never conceived of otherwise than as
"minister of finance to the Korean king."18 Without the
slightest hesitation Witte took Korea into his fold, apparently
never doubting the correctness of the procedure--and this
whole Korean episode, ending in a puff of smoke, was con-
signed to the literary guardianship of the author of the Memoirs. The "treaty with Japan" (i.e., the protocol of May 28)
Witte considered "extremely successful" of itself, the more
so since "Japan's representatives gladly agreed to it," i.e.,
in the given case, as always, the policy that he, Witte, sponsored is presented to the reader as a policy of peaceful compromise. As Witte pictures it, the Moscow protocol said
that "we might have military instructors in Korea" and "were
to appoint an adviser on finance," thus firmly establishing
"the division of influence in Korea as between Russia and
Japan." One might almost fancy Witte did not know that Japan had replied to the above-described flagrant breach of
the promises made her in the Moscow protocol not by diplomatic representations alone but by a broadening of her armament program.19 The curiously mendacious elucidation of
the Korean episode ten years afterwards in the Memoirs was
for Witte a necessity in view of the idea there developed that
the sad end of the attempted peaceful conquest of Korea was
a direct consequence of Russia's seizure of Port Arthur,
since this seizure evoked such indignation in Japan that to
avoid war Russia had to sacrifice her position in Korea in
order to make matters right with her.20 At the time, Witte
appears to have been least concerned with the question of the
true value of the stake in Korea, to which there was no apparent risk attaching at the moment and which offered Russia most substantial advantages in her future clash with
Japan.

However, to maintain the advantageous position that she
had come by proved not so simple--for one thing because
she had no economic roots in Korea: Russian mercantile
interests there were absolutely negligible, Russian industrial
enterprise entirely lacking. The predominant economic influence in Korea was indisputably that of the Japanese, and
only very recently had representatives of European and American capital appeared on the scene in search of concessions.
In such a situation, it behooved the Russian government to

eschew the policy of isolationism and seek the support of allies on the spot.[21] At the same time, any delay in developing the political success achieved carried the threat of es-
tranging the Korean government from Russia and would open
the way to the exertion of other influences on the helpless
king. Finally, it had been absurd from the first even to think
of building her policy in Korea otherwise than with the aid of
some capital investment made without reference to immediate
commercial calculations. Had Russian diplomacy been confronted at the given moment with the Korean question in isolated form, probably such considerations would actually have
determined Russia's next few steps in Korea. But Korean
events had, so to speak, forestalled Russia to some extent,
giving her a more complicated situation to reckon with.

In point of fact, the question of making a loan to Korea
for a payment on the Japanese loan of three million--which
Russia, as we know, made contingent on "ascertaining the
economic situation of the country"--did not admit of a single
day's delay, its full political importance becoming apparent
in Seoul even before the return of the Korean embassy from
Moscow: in June, 1896 a loan was offered Korea by the French,
unbeknown to the Russian minister.[22] Lobanov sounded the
alarm immediately upon receipt of this information, requesting Witte to "accelerate" the dispatch of a finance official to
Korea, and advising the Korean government provisionally
"not to enter into any major financial transactions, especially
with English capitalists, until the arrival of the Russian finance
official."[23] Thus the Russian government would have had to
take decisive action in Korea at a moment when the matter of
permission to build the North-Manchurian railway was as yet
far from having reached a satisfactory conclusion. And meanwhile the mere ordering to Seoul of Pokotilov, then known to
each and all as factotum of Witte and of the Russo-Chinese
bank, made an open book of Russia's immediate policy in
Korea.[24]

The communications that came thick and fast from Pokotilov in Seoul during August, 1896 confirmed the necessity of
acting "without delay": 1) the king himself on the occasion
of his first meeting with Pokotilov asked for a loan of three
million to pay Japan off and obviate the necessity of burying
the Korean queen, "murdered by the Japanese," with Japanese
money, 2) rumors were already current in Seoul of the opening of a Korean national bank, and a visit from an agent of the

Hongkong-Shanghai (English) bank "to give advice" was expected. No wonder Pokotilov feared that the English might
participate in this bank, contributing "considerable amounts
of capital," and recommended that they immediately open in
Seoul a division of the Russo-Chinese bank and make the loan,
which, in his opinion, could find "adequate security" in the
customs revenues of Korea.[25]

However, notwithstanding many subsequent urgent dispatches from Pokotilov both in September and in October,
as well as a request from the ministry of foreign affairs
that he be empowered to "give Korea some sort of positive
assurances as to probable speedy material assistance on our
part," Witte categorically forbade any committments "until
November," and in November merely gave "in principle"
consent to the Russo-Chinese bank's making the loan, "when
this shall be recognized as opportune." In addition, Witte
made it the indispensable condition of such a loan that the
customs revenues of Korea be "under the immediate surveillance of Russia's financial representative," and requested
the ministry of foreign affairs to "direct every effort toward
effecting the transfer of the administration of the Korean customs to the superintendence of the Russian financial representative who shall be sent there."[26] Thus the step that it was
absolutely necessary for Russian diplomacy to take in Korea
without delay, for political reasons--the release of the Korean
government from Japan's financial control--Witte not only
postponed indefinitely but made conditional upon the removal
of English influence, in force, as we know, only in the administration of the customs office.

While freezing the questions of the loan and of the establishment of a Russian bank in Korea, Witte showed a disposition to place the question of railways there in a like position.
The question of building railroads in Korea had been raised
by the English and Japanese back in the 80's in connection
with the opening of Korean ports to foreign trade, but had been
shelved at that time, Russia apparently having some hand in
it.[27] Following the declaration of Korean independence, the
question again arose, and this time promised to get out of
deadlock. As above mentioned, the first railway concession,
for a Seoul-Chemulpo line, was awarded the Americans in the
spring of 1896, and, not without their influence, the king
issued an order for the adoption of the narrow, 4-1/2 foot,
European gauge on Korean railways (July 3, 1896,) and by

the time of Pokotilov's arrival in Seoul the French company
Fives-Lille of Chinese fame, which had just offered the Korean government a loan behind Russia's back, already had its
representatives there with concession proposals for railways
"out of Seoul in all directions," including our border, apparently counting on the resale of the Seoul-Yingkou line to Russia.[28] The French solicitations were, however, not supported
by the Russian chargé d'affaires in Seoul in view of "the exclusively political significance" of the contemplated lines,
and this circumstances was even made the topic of fruitless
explanations between the French ambassador and the minister
of foreign affairs in Peterburg.[29] Nonetheless, the French
got the concession for a Seoul-Yingkou line.

At this point Witte raised the question of the necessity of
asking the Korean government for a revocation of the order
of July 3 as to narrow gauge, and obtained an order making
the Russian gauge obligatory.[30] But Witte apparently still
refused even to think about starting to build Russian railways
in Korea, remaining absolutely unresponsible, for example
to a proposal of Mollendorf's that was communicated to him,
regarding the construction of a whole network of railways on
the peninsula through the facilities of an American syndicate
which had agreed to this on condition of a government guarantee of a 5 per cent return on capital expended.[31] And early
in 1897 a royal order was issued--as may readily be surmised,
at the wish of the Russian government--announcing the Korean government's decision to build no railways by concessionary methods beyond those already authorized.[32] Even
when Witte had renounced his passive tactic in Korean affairs
and it was disclosed that the American concessionary was
looking for a chance to sell his right, and moreover that work
on the Seoul-Chemulpo line had been started on the basis of
narrow gauge, and that the Japanese had come forward as
purchasers, Witte still confined himself to urging upon the
ministry of foreign affairs "energetic opposition" to the
transfer of the concession to the Japanese and to the infringement of the November order regarding Russian gauge, but
said that he himself "was apprehensive of stepping in, for
fear of losses."[33]

Witte was apparently also guided in part by financial considerations in his handling of the matter of the Korean loan.
The painstaking examination of the state of Korea's finances
conducted by Pokotilov in the autumn of 1896 led to the con-

clusion that 1) the organization of Korea's financial administration was itself absolutely primitive and bad from the
ground up, 2) at the given moment the Korean government by
some happy chance had at its disposal around a million and
a half yen of available cash and was consequently capable of
making a first payment on the Japanese loan and 3) the question still remained open as to whether Japan would agree to
accept this payment on the spot or whether she would stick to
the letter of the contract and insist upon payment at the two
dates set, in 1898 and 1899.

Hence, from a narrowly financial viewpoint, the correct
deduction was: 1) to let the question ride until the legal date
for the first payment, 2) in an extremity to direct matters,
without haste, toward a guarantee by the Russo-Chinese bank
of the 1898 installment, 3) let the Korean government itself
clear with Japan as to the possibility of pre-term payment,
and 4) in the meantime prepare the ground for bringing Korea's
whole financial administration under the control of the Russian financial adviser. In acquiescence with this point of
view: 1) Pokotilov's mission was recognized as accomplished,
and at the beginning of November, 1896 he left Seoul, 2) before leaving, he presented to the king and the minister of
finance a memorandum in the sense just indicated, proposing
a postponement of the question for six months and agreeing,
should this prove necessary, to make a loan on the security
of revenues from the land tax and from the customs (i.e.,
practically the country's whole revenue,) 3) "on a plausible
pretext," he neglected to leave this memorandum with his
collocutors, though exacting a written pledge from the minister of finance to accept a loan from Russia on the terms indicated.[34] The result was that five months after the Moscow
negotiations the Korean government had received nothing from
Russia except an oral, and at that a provisional, promise, and
had been left to itself for another six months. Absolutely unaware, apparently, of the political consequences of such a
dilatory tactic, Witte let himself be wholly swayed by "fear of
losses."

In January, 1897 when the post finally brought the ministry
of foreign affairs a detailed account of the Seoul negotiations
along with the text of the Korean pledge mentioned, and the
ministry, as usual, informed Witte of the fact and reminded
him, among other things, about sending a financial official,
Witte snapped: "Who will pay our agent is nowhere stated,

though I said at Korea's expense."[35] In his reply to Muravev, Witte chiefly expatiated on the unsatisfactory state of Korea's financial administration and economy and declared that "<u>preliminary</u> to the choice of a person [for the post of financial adviser] and to further agitation of the question of the loan" he begged to have the Russian diplomatic representative in Seoul ordered to prevail upon the king to give the Russian financial agent full support.[36] Muravev accordingly understood that Witte was dallying with the Korean question, and was doubtful as to just how he should go about putting the projected program into execution.[37]

Meanwhile, on February 8/20, 1897, the Korean king left the Russian mission and settled down in his own palace, and it soon became plain that Russian influence at the Korean court was unequal to this test. The decisive role in this connection must have been played by Japan's communication to the Korean government of the text of the Moscow protocol of May 28, secret articles and all: Russia's reluctance to fulfill the promises contained in "points in reply to the Korean ambassador" was explained, in a discouraging way, in the eyes of the Korean government, by this secret Russian agreement with Japan as to a joint Russo-Japanese protectorate over Korea.[38] Next, the English also took measures. Brown, director of customs, having from the outset made it his business to block the Russian loan, now prevailed upon the Korean government to start paying the Japanese loan from the Korean treasury's own means: by the expiration of the six-month term set by Russia, Korea had paid the Bank of Japan one million yen, and shortly afterwards it was announced that by the autumn of 1897 a second million would be payable in the same manner.[39] Disillusionment as to the trustworthiness of the Russian promises had so far possessed the king that in May of this same year he applied simultaneously to France and to Germany for aid and it was proposed to ask France in particular to send a shore detail and a permanent guardship to Chemulpo.[40]

When Witte at last emerged from a state of inaction and on May 9, 1897 presented to the tsar a report concerning the appointment of a financial agent to Korea, how to manage things so that this agent should occupy the position of adviser to the Korean government on financial matters was already far from simple. Not only did Witte himself decline to demand this formal status for him, to avoid protests and intrigues by rep-

presentatives of the powers, soliciting only the preparation
of a favorable footing for him personally with the Korean king,
but Muravev considered the situation in Korea so "greatly
altered" the he "felt reluctant to express any conclusion as to
what attitude the Korean government would take toward our
desire to appropriate to a commercial agent the role of adviser and as to what would be his official position in consequence."[41] The situation had altered not only "as compared
with last year when this question first arose" but as compared
with a month or two before, when Pokotilov, stationed in Peking
had, back in February, felt the necessity of bolstering up Korea's confidence in the financial support of Russia, and Muravev
had, early in March, endeavored to make Witte see the full
political significance of getting the control over Korea's finances into his own hands in time, give up his narrowly commercial approach to the matter, and dispatch a financial adviser without further delay.[42]

But on this last question--as to the adviser--Witte did continue to delay his decision for two full months longer, and only
took action on it when he himself thought necessary, without
responding in any way to his colleague's admonition.[43] But
to the advice of his Peking agent Witte paid full heed, and the
question of making a loan to Korea was scheduled "for decision
immediately upon the arrival [from abroad] of Rothstein."[44]
But if Witte was proceeding on the assumption that it would be
impossible to settle the question of the loan without Rothstein,
since a transaction with the Russo-Chinese bank was to be
concluded, then he proved to be mistaken: Rothstein apparently
preferred to leave his bank out of it and contrive another combination whereby the loan would virtually be made by the
treasury. This combination consisted in the establishment of
a special Russo-Korean bank, the fixed capital of which, in
the amount of 100,000 rubles, the Russo-Chinese bank would
reserve to itself, with the provision that the Russian government would have the right to redeem 51 per cent of the shares
within five years, while the three million rubles needed for
the Korean 6 per cent loan would be placed in the bank as a
permanent deposit from the fluid funds of the Chinese Eastern
Railway Company, with interest at 2 per cent per annum.
Such a combination naturally cannot have satisfied Witte, but
Rothstein again "for all his readiness to meet [him] half way"
could not "ignore the interests of stock-holders in the Russo-
Chinese bank, since [he was] convinced that for the first few

years the activity of the Russo-Chinese bank would be most
inconsiderable in view of an almost complete absence of Russo-Korean trade," and it might even be feared that the whole
thing would miscarry.[45]

And at this point P.M. Romanov, then director of the chancellery of the minister of finance, a man who, as Witte's
closest collaborator, knew all of the ministry's intrigue in
the Far East from the ground up, a member of the boards of
the Chinese Eastern Railway Company and of the Russo-Chinese bank, obviously well aware of the full significance of
further delays, made an attempt to dispose Witte to consent
to Rothstein's proposal, by stating the question on the political level:

> "It is my conviction," wrote Romanov on March 8, that
> Korea is for us of paramount importance; Northern Man-
> churia is important to us only insofar as it can provide
> access either to Liaotung or to Korea. But the Chinese
> are not soon likely to let us cut a railway through to a
> port on the Liaotung peninsula, for they know that this
> would place Peking absolutely at our mercy. On the con-
> trary, they will probably not seriously object to the laying
> of a railway from Bodune through Kirin to a Korean port,
> since this will guarantee them against seizure of Korea by
> the Japanese. But for us to obtain such permission from
> Korea it will first be necessary to gain an influence in her
> financial affairs, and in this connection we ought not to
> balk even at financial sacrifices, since it will repay us a
> hundred-fold in the relatively near future."--and Romanov
> added that "in any event the matter of the Russo-Korean
> bank requires an immediate decision (in the affirmative
> or in the negative)."

As we see, it was proposed that Witte: 1) renounce his
over-powering "fear of losses" and 2) choose between the
two variants that had, with the settlement of the North-Manchurian question, opened up for obtaining an ice-free port--on
Liaotung, or in Korea--in favor of the latter. Without a bank,
as a necessary political appurtenance, the possibility of any
aggressive policy in the Far East was by then no longer conceivable to the Russian ministry of finance, and to refuse the
Korean bank would mean to refuse the Korean policy--in favor
of the Liaotung policy. But what real data could Witte then

have had in favor of the latter to induce him to refuse Rothstein's terms? He accepted them that same day.[46] However,
to conclude from this that at the moment Witte completely
grasped the statement of the question of the future development of an aggressive policy in the Far East in the form given
it in Romanov's report--i.e., either Korea or Liaotung--and
was giving up simultaneous action in the two directions, that
consequently it now only remained to expedite the charter of
the Russo-Korean bank and hasten to dispatch an adviser to
Korea, and then start petitioning Peking for a railway through
Bodune and Kirin "to one [just which one?] of the Korean
ports," would be quite unjustified.

There are no perceptible signs that the sending of an adviser to Korea had, up to that time, been postponed because
of the bank and loan question remaining unsettled, nor that
the settlement in principle of this question resulted in any
practical steps in the matter of the adviser: as was said, two
months went by and only on May 9 of that year did Witte propose sending K.A. Alekseyev, a prominent official in the
Russian customs office, to Seoul, with a view to "the consolidation of Russia's influence on the Korean customs."[47]

Arrangements and preparations for the "Russian commercial agent's" departure dragged on for more than a month
longer, and Alekseyev left at the end of June, expecting to
make stops in London and Shanghai and reach his post at the
end of August, and having instructions: to act prudently and
without haste, to arrive at a full understanding of the financial
administration and economic life of the country, to ascertain
on what terms a Russo-Korean credit establishment might be
organized there, endeavor to get the Korean government to
establish a link with the Russian telegraphic network, and in
the last analysis "aim to have the customs administration
transferred in course of time completely into Russian hands."[4]
By the time of Alekseyev's departure it was, however, already
known that Russia's prospects in Korea were not so hopeless
and that in any event the king "was well disposed toward the
min. fin.'s agent."[49] But no one expected that with the arrival of the Russian agent in Seoul in September, 1897, events
would take so swift and abrupt a turn in Russia's favor as
actually happened: Korean events at that time again forestalled Russian diplomacy to some extent and necessitated its
reckoning with a yet more complicated situation. But this
time the brake was in Muravev's hands instead of Witte's,

and this time it was in the face of Witte's dogged insistence
that the attempt on Korea was halted. Both times the Korean
question proved to be closely linked with the Manchurian and
for that reason it has been necessary to linger over certain
details of Russo-Korean relations before passing to further
observations on Russia's progress in Manchuria.

III

A contemporary of the events described who had attentively
followed shreds of evidence as to the growth of Russian influence in Korea and was by the beginning of 1897 provided with
two such documents as "Cassini's convention" and the charter
of the Chinese Eastern Railway Company could scarcely have
predicted that the Chinese Eastern Railway would follow the
straight line Tsitsihar-Harbin-Nikolsk-on-Ussuri, and would
still less have believed that Russia's Manchurian program
was confined to this at the given moment. For lack of any
indications in the charter of December 4 as to the direction
of the authorized road, the route described in "Cassini's convention" acquired full authority: it made a bend at Kirin, as
later points of the "convention" showed, to allow for a continuation southward to Shanhaikwan, and in approaching the Russian
border at Hunchun came so close to the Korean as to make the
"convention" a commentary not only on the charter of December 4, but also on the Korean king's November order with respect to Russian gauge. If the contemporary observer felt obliged, on this account, to watch from day to day for further
moves by Russia in both directions, it would in nowise have
meant that he possessed a disordered imagination.

Negotiations concerning the Chinese Eastern Railway concession ended in the signing of a contract that failed to cover
all questions connected with its construction, one specific
omission being the question of the direction of the line. On
this count alone an immediate opening of operations was not
to be thought of. In the preliminary surveys two routes had
been under consideration: a northerly, to Tsitsihar-Hulanchen,
and a southerly, to Bodune-Kirin-Ninguta. The first was
shorter, and, as later became apparent, the physical difficulties involved were less serious, but the second struck nearer
the major centers of Mukden province and marked off as zone
of the road a preferable area economically.[50] This cardinal
question of the direction of the line necessitated special ne-

gotiations in Peking as a preliminary to serious surveys. But
there were other questions connected with the construction of
the road in Northern Manchuria that were in a similar position.
Their settlement Witte did not propose to allow out of his
hands and took measures to have it proceed in the most favorable atmosphere possible by linking the forthcoming negotiations with the delivery of the first of the three millions promised to Li Hung-chang. Witte had not hesitated to postpone
this payment at the time due, namely after the signing of the
contract of August 27, because "we shan't be doing anything
out there for several months, which means that [the Chinese]
can't hinder us," the more so that "by ill-advised haste we
might even lose money." In postponing the journey to China
that Ukhtomsky then proposed making for the express purpose
of settling with Li Hung-chang, Witte was already figuring
that if made later on it "might acquire another significance."[51]
Ukhtomsky's journey to China actually did take place in the
spring of 1897 and did acquire "another significance." But
until recently it attracted no attention, and Witte not only
passed it over in complete silence in his own Memoirs but
took care not to let any mention of it get into the Glinsky
Prologue to the Russo-Japanese War.[52]

The board of the Chinese Eastern Railway was formed on
December 27, 1896, and its first meeting devoted to questions
that appeared to be in prime need of clarification at Peking.
This first meeting took place on January 22, 1897, the very
same day when the question of Ukhtomsky's journey may be
regarded as having been finally settled, and was of a secret
character.[53] Here is what was entered as Point II of the
minutes of the meeting:

"II. Next S.I. Kerbedz proposed that the meeting express itself as to whether the Chinese Eastern Railway
Company ought not to enter at once into negotiations with
the Chinese government concerning authorization to build
a wide-gauge branch to one of the ports on the Yellow Sea.
Furthermore, recognizing for his part, that the immediate
effectuation of said branch was, in the interests of the
Company, extremely desirable, S.I. Kerbedz would suggest that in an extremity it might be possible to agree to
the construction of this branch with narrow gauge, should
serious objections on the part of the Chinese government
be encountered to its construction with wide gauge. In

S.I.'s opinion, to which other engineers present at the conference session also fully subscribed, the building of said
branch with narrow gauge could present no substantial drawbacks, since, in the event of its authorization, the Company
could arrange both a roadbed and complete false constructions for this line of wide-gauge type, and under such conditions the conversion of this branch from narrow gauge to
wide could, in event of necessity, be effected in the course
of a few days. In any event, in S.I.'s opinion, it would be
well to enter at once into negotiations on this question with
the Chinese government, utilizing for this purpose Prince
Ukhtomsky's journey to Peking, since so long as Li Hung-
chang and the empress dowager remained alive their support could be counted on; for this reason, and likewise in
view of the advanced age of the two latter, to postpone this
question for some years would be imprudent, as circumstances might change to the disadvantage of the Company.

   "Sharing the above-stated cogitations of S.I. Kerbedz,
S.V. Ignatsius, for his part, added that, thanks to the
powerful influence that the name of Russia enjoys in the
East and particularly in China at the present time, this
time would appear to be the most favorable for achieving
success in the matter under consideration. Meanwhile
there is reason to fear that in consequence of the endeavor
of our political antagonists this influence may in course of
time decrease and that then to obtain the said success
would be attended by considerably greater difficulties.

   "Apropos of the above, P.M. Romanov declared that
the question of laying a branch line from the Chinese Eastern Railway to one of the ports on the Yellow Sea already
had its history. During the negotiations that occurred in
Moscow in May of the past year between the minister of
finance and Li Hung-chang the question had duly been raised
of laying the said branch, on which occasion Li Hung-chang
had agreed to its construction, but with narrow gauge as a
proviso. Since the minister of finance had categorically
declared against this, recognizing that it was absolutely
necessary for this branch to have one and the same gauge
as the main line, these negotiations had been without result. In view of this, it was the opinion of P.M. Romanov,
who was upheld therein by E.K. Tsigler, that at the present
time the question of building said branch with narrow gauge
could scarcely be raised, since the Chinese government

had itself previously urged this and the minister of finance categorically rejected it. Such action would be undesirable if only because a firm policy should always be maintained in negotiations with the Chinese, since by this method we were likelier to be able to attain the desired result. Moreover, it should also be borne in mind that the concessions recently granted by the Korean government to French and American companies to build narrow-gauge lines: 1) from Seoul to the mouth of the Yalu, and 2) from Seoul to Chemulpo had, at the instance of the Russian government, been altered to the effect that said lines must be built with Russian gauge. It would therefore be inconsistent for the Russian government to agree to a Russian company's building a narrow-gauge line in the East, when foreign companies were at its instance being forced to build in that same East lines of the wide-gauge type.

"With the matter in this position, it was the opinion of P.M. Romanov that should it be deemed necessary to raise the question of building a branch line to connect the Chinese Eastern Railway with the Yellow Sea, then negotiations should be conducted on the basis of a wide, not a narrow, gauge line. But, for his part, P.M. Romanov saw no particular necessity for an immediate settling of this question. On the contrary, in his opinion, there would seem to be cause to fear that the raising of this question at the present time--before the agitation produced in our Far Eastern rivals by news of the organization of the Chinese Eastern Railway Company had fully subsided--might only injure the success of the Company's enterprise, complicating its already too difficult task. As to the apprehensions voiced in the Conference that later on it would be much more difficult to get the Chinese government's consent to the laying of the desired branch, P.M. Romanov not only did not share the said apprehensions in this respect but was, on the contrary, convinced that at some future time, when we shall have started building the Manchurian line, it will be incomparably easier for us to obtain the said consent than under present conditions.

"Though itself recognizing immediate effectuation of a branch line from the Chinese Eastern Railway to one of the ports on the Yellow Sea as extremely desirable, the Conference, nonetheless, in view of the arguments advanced by P.M. Romanov, deemed that the raising of this question

at the present time might cause considerable difficulties
both with the Chinese government and, above all, with
representatives of foreign powers, which might in turn
greatly complicate the Company's already difficult task.
In view of this, the Conference arrived at the conclusion
that the Company should move actively in this direction
only if there was full assurance that negotiations with the
Chinese government on this question would lead to the
desired result, or if the Chinese government itself raised
the question after entering into negotiations with the Company. In addition, E.K. Tsigler, supported by other members of the Conference, deemed that even should the Company immediately be given a concession to build said branch,
construction should still not be started on it simultaneously
with the main line, since this would put too great a burden
on the Company at the outset, and that in this respect, i.e.,
in respect to the date of starting, it would be more prudent
not to make any pledges to the Chinese government. During
further discussion as to what measures the Company could
immediately take to prepare the ground for the desired success in future without giving rise to any political misunderstandings, the Conference was arrested by the suggestion
of S.I. Kerbedz as to the possibility of soliciting from the
Chinese government a concession to build a branch from the
main line to the coal beds near Mukden. Taking into account,
on the one hand, that the necessity for building said branch
was fully explained by the need for coal to supply the demands
of the Chinese Eastern Railway, while in the event of this
branch being put through, the necessity of prolonging it to
one of the ports on the Yellow Sea would be self evident,
and that in any event its authorization would give rise to
fewer difficulties, the Conference arrived at the conclusion
that under existing conditions the most correct and most
prudent course would be to raise the question of authorizing
the Company to build a wide gauge branch from the Chinese
Eastern Railway to the coal-beds located in Mukden province,
with the terminus of said branch to be determined later in
accord with a more exact definition of the location of said
coal on the basis of surveys to be conducted.

"At the same time, the Conference supported the opinion
of A.I. Yugovich in recognizing as extremely desirable the
securing from the Chinese government of some guarantee
that, should it at any time be agreeable to the putting through

of a line from the Chinese Eastern Railway to one of the
ports on the Yellow Sea, the Company should then enjoy a
preferential right to the building of this line. "

As we see, before any other action had been taken, up
cropped the pretension to a "branch to the Yellow Sea, " quite
independently of any suggestion of Witte's (it would have been
still more curious had it not), by force of the logic of railroading in the superlatively undifferentiated aspect in which
it had figured in Witte's spring negotiations with Li Hung-
chang: the terminus was subjected to no further definition
and for the time being it remained immaterial whether the
road went to a Korean or to a South-Manchurian port. In this
ambiguous form, the plan not only met with no objections from
the august conclave but was accorded full approval by all members without exception. Differences of opinion came out only
on the question of the easier and surer route to its accomplishment, the practicing engineers apparently realizing the political significance of the plan and its hopelessness from the international viewpoint should the exceptionally fortunate moment
that hung by a slender hair be let slip (that is, if direct seizure
by force was to be avoided,) while the bureaucrat-politicians
on the one hand underestimated the impending increase in com-
plexity and intensity of international relations centering in
China, and on the other hand evaded the difficulties of the given
moment--just as though they could count on lack of foresight
in all the rest and keep the whole international situation on ice
while building up their own power.
    The Conference paid tribute to the second of the two views
as being that professed by the minister of finance himself, but
nonetheless weighed the chances of full success in the matter.
In any event, all present deemed it necessary to obtain real
guarantees of success if only in future and saw such a guarantee in the Chinese government's authorization of a branch into
Southern Manchuria as far as Mukden. In this form, the idea
of a branch to "some port on the Yellow Sea" left open as before the question of the site of its terminal point, since from
Mukden it could equally well be continued to a Korean or to a
Manchurian port. In March, 1897, when, apropos of the
Russo-Korean Bank question, discussion turned on a more
exact definition of the term "port on the Yellow Sea," it was
not without reason that the road to a Korean port was described

as going not round via Mukden, but straight through Kirin.[54]
The minimum program of the Russian government as shareholder in the Chinese Eastern Railway, it thus appeared,
called for immediate penetration to the very heart of southern
Manchuria.

This by no means signifies that such was at the given moment the program also of the ministry of foreign affairs as
the Russian government's official sworn representative. One
may well suspect the direct opposite, to judge from the fact
that Witte thought best to conceal from the ministry of foreign
affairs the true aims of Ukhtomsky's mission: for example,
when informing Muravev of the tsar's subsequent instructions
regarding Ukhtomsky's journey to Peking, he indicated only
the secondary, namely to transmit the tsar's gifts to the Chinese emperor and to clarify questions concerning legal tender
in Manchuria and the securing of fuel for the road.[55] Such
being the case, Palace Square never even suspected the attempt on Manchuria that was being devised under the same
roof, but over on the Moika, and naively taking silence for
heedless inaction, wasted their energy sermonizing in that
direction on the Korean question.[56]

With absolute disregard of Muravev's entreaties, however,
the Korean question went unexamined in the ministry of finance
until after Rothstein's return from abroad at the beginning of
March. But even the redaction of the questions destined to be
the subject of Ukhtomsky's negotiations in Peking was only
presented to Nicholas II for confirmation on March 14, 1897:
this too had apparently been kept waiting until Rothstein should
return. On the Korean question, as above noted, Rothstein
took a rather reserved attitude, regarding as unprofitable any
serious participation by the Russo-Chinese bank in the Russian
government's political arrangements in Korea: the Russo-
Korean bank, rather than a division of the Russo-Chinese, was
to serve chiefly as an instrument for mediating for the Korean
government loans from the resources of the Chinese Eastern
Railway, i.e., actually from the funds of the state treasury.
By this time, the route to a Korean port on the Yellow Sea had
apparently already been determined, which would to some
degree even justify the investment of Chinese Eastern Railway
capital in a Korean bank.[57] We possess no direct indications
of Rothstein's having also participated in the discussion of the
question of Ukhtomsky's instructions, but such participation
is suggested not only by the date of their confirmation but also

by the fact that at the proper time in January the discussion of certain questions subject to examination on the spot had been similarly postponed until his arrival.[58]

The instructions to Ukhtomsky included the following eight points: 1) to obtain authorization from the Chinese for the so-called southerly route of the Manchurian trunk-line, 2) to ascertain the attitude of the Chinese government toward the question of laying a Russian line which should connect the Chinese Eastern Railway with the proposed Chinese line from Tientsin through Shanhaikwan to Chinchow, and whether China would consent to the laying of a railway from the trunk-line to some Korean port, 3) to secure conscientious fulfillment by the Chinese of point 4 of the August 27 contract, 4) to request for the chief engineer of the road equality of rank with the three chiang chüns* of Manchuria and the right to deal with them directly, 5) to obtain authorization for the export of copper coins from inner China to Manchuria, 6) to secure for the Russo-Chinese bank the right to mint silver coins of compulsory acceptance for all payments in the Manchurian area, 7) to reserve the same status for bank-notes issued by the bank, 8) to obtain permission to establish agencies of the bank at points through which the road was to pass.[59]

In this its final form, the Russian government's minimum program as stock-holder of the Chinese Eastern Railway, as projected at the Conference of January 22, not only bristled with demands confirming the Russo-Chinese bank's dominance in Manchuria, but also gained in clearness, thanks to the differentiation of the two tendencies concealed in it: the Korean and the south-Manchurian--without any indications of their alternative nature. But here it was already not only a question of a railway outlet to the ocean through an ice-free port, but of an advance toward the capital of China without stopping at Mukden. It is not impossible that in making this change Witte had again been abetted by Rothstein: later on, the Russo-Chinese bank was at least not averse to taking over this South-Manchurian branch.[60] In making the decision to get to the ocean through Korea, the author of the instruction naturally renounced the outlet through Liaotung, but, as we see, this renunciation had nothing to do with giving up southern Manchuria and bartering it for Korea: it was just that at the last minute the opinion regained its hold on the Ministry of Finance

*Appears to refer to chiang chün--a four-star Governor-General of Chinese provinces. --Ed.

that it was worth taking a chance on Li Hung-chang and the
Empress Dowager while they were still alive, and fears of
the possible international consequences of such a monstrous
bid for territory by Russia were set aside.

The million, however, proved unequal to the load of such
an expanding program, and Ukhtomsky's mission ended in almost total failure. In the beginning everything went splendid-
ly. For Ukhtomsky an "unparalleled" welcome, "ceremonious,
cordial," had everywhere been prepared, and the handing over
of the million through agents "was effected at Shanghai with
every precaution" quite satisfactorily. "The old man [i.e.,
Li Hung-chang] was very tired of waiting" and "to have delayed longer in fulfilling [the promise] would certainly never
have done;" while "the soil for the conduct of negotiations"
seemed to Ukhtomsky for the first few days to have been "prepared by the exchange of preliminary despatches between our
old man and Shanghai as to the extent of the payment," and
from Peking, where the old man was installed, came "even
better news."[61] But in Peking, once the financial operation
proper had been concluded, it was another story. At Ukhtomsky's very first audience with the Tsungli Yamen the question
of the southerly route of the trunk-line ran into opposition,
the reason for which was thus figuratively expressed by Li
Hung-chang: "We have admitted you to the courtyard, now
you wish to get to the rooms where we house our wives and
small children;" and it was some time before he got a final
answer.[62]

Leaving this matter unsettled, Ukhtomsky next opened the
subject of connecting the trunk-line with the Shanhaikwan road,
thereby rousing such a storm of protests against Li Hung-chang
"for his devotion to Russian interests" that despite his customary rosy optimism in Chinese matters Ukhtomsky at once saw
the prudence "of confining himself to guarantees that this connection would not be granted to any other party.[63] Peterburg
raised no objections but still hoped to win the line to a Korean
port--but the Tsungli Yamen "would not even hear to"[64] the
Korean line either. Peterburg considered the question as to
this line more important than the connection to Shanhaikwan,
and easily reconcilable with Chinese interests, but it turned
out that "any such project was, to all appearances, regarded
by the Chinese as utterly impracticable, and it was noticeable
that the merest hint of any possibility of carrying out this plan
with our cooperation had a depressing effect on princes and

ministers."[65] In the concluding and decisive session of June 7 both of these questions were finally buried. But on other matters as well, in particular on the question of the southerly route, Ukhtomsky received only oral assurances, without later confirmation of any sort, partly of an affirmative, partly of a provisional character.[66]

As might have been expected, this unsuccessful excursion beyond the boundary of Northern Manchuria did not pass unmarked but introduced into Russia's future relations with China irremediable complications. The likelihood of such complications had been foreseen even as early as January 22 when the question of the two southern branches was discussed at the conference of the board of the Chinese Eastern Railway, and afterwards the Russian chargé d'affaires had also suggested to Ukhtomsky in Peking that "at the present time, when the feeling of distrust and suspicion among the Chinese toward our plans in Manchuria is still far from dissipated and when these feelings are being specifically encouraged in them by foreigners, the raising of the question of "extending our railway network to the shores of the gulf of Pechili might easily prove hazardous to the successful settlement of this question in future."[67] Evidence exists that as the last moment, under the influence of these suggestions, Ukhtomsky wavered, telegraphing Witte as to the chargé's opinion, but received the order from Witte to follow the exact sense of the instruction "in any event."[68] Since in the last analysis the Chinese declared that they had no intention of building their southern line any further north than Chinchow anyway, and that in any event they would not give such a concession to any foreigner, Russia contrived to take comfort from that--until better times.[69] Meanwhile, no sooner had Ukhtomsky left for Russia than Li Hung-chang entered a report as to the opening of construction on the Shanhaikwan-Kirin railway with means from the treasury, his report of July 19 was confirmed by secret order of the Emperor, and the director appointed for the future road was Hu Yui-feng, known "henchman of the Hongkong-Shanghai bank,"[70] and "undoubtedly under the influence of the English engineer Kinder," who had been in the railway construction business in China for over fifteen years.[71]

As to the meaning of what had happened there could be no two opinions: the Chinese had hurriedly drawn the English into Southern Manchuria to counterbalance Russia's attempt on it. Such was Peterburg's impression as to what had happened, so

was it likewise understood by Russian representatives in Peking : at both ends, the turn taken by affairs had been completely unexpected. Muravev indicated plainly to Witte that
the whole fault lay in "Ukhtomsky's imprudent and unseason-
able raising of the question of granting us the right to build
the two abovementioned connecting branches" and, finding
"the participation of English capital in the building of a railway in Manchuria extremely dangerous," telegraphed to Peking to "prevent Hu Yui-feng being given charge of this matter."72 And an exchange of letters took place between the
two ministers that is of some interest. Witte countered
Muravev's reproach with reproach: it was not a question of
protesting against a given Chinaman but of "roads in Southern
Manchuria either not being built at all or...their construction
being entrusted to no agency other than the Chinese Eastern
Railway Company."

In essence, Witte was attempting to disprove the charge
brought against him of having provoked China to a rapprochement with England against Russia by an untimely and unwar-
ranted move made a couple of years too soon--and employed
the crudest of evasions, arguing that: 1) "if the rousing of
feelings of distrust and suspicion in the Chinese regarding
our plans in Manchuria is to be linked with the raising of the
question of granting us the right to lay a road to the gulf of
Pechili, then it follows that the confidence of the Chinese in
us must have been shaken back in May of last year" (i.e.,
1896,) 2) since Ukhtomsky "had in all his negotiations with
the Chinese government acted merely as representative of the
private commercial interests of the Russo-Chinese bank and
the Chinese Eastern Railway," it followed that "Prince Ukhtomsky's mission has absolutely no political character and
therefore could not awaken the apprehensions of the Chinese
government," and 3) Ukhtomsky "had, furthermore, been
guided in his negotiations by the program given him, which
had before his departure for China been presented" by Witte
"to the consideration" of the tsar and been approved by the
latter.

Furthermore, Witte did not deny that "a change had lately
taken place in our relations with China, of which there could
be no better demonstration than the fact that the very raising
of the question of extending the Chinese Eastern Railway Company's network to the gulf of Pechili now seemed imprudent
and ill-timed," whereas in May, 1896 China had herself

agreed to a narrow-gauge South Manchurian line; but Witte
laid the blame for the "deterioration of our political influence
in China" on the fact that "our diplomatic mission in Peking
had remained for about a year without a minister."73 Since
the ultima ratio of this whole apologia of Witte's consisted in
his reference to the "sovereign's will," further criticism by
Muravev of the said unsuccessful diplomatic move was absolutely precluded. But the more awkward his position became
as official director of foreign policy without whose cognizance
not only were responsible decisions being made, but hazardous
steps taken, the more grounds had he for protesting in no uncertain terms against Witte's backstage meddling in foreign
affairs and his cultivation of double diplomacy.

In his reply, Muravev accordingly pointed out to Witte that:
1) if Ukhtomsky was guided by instructions confirmed by the
tsar, then by that very token he was no longer acting "merely
as the representative of private commercial interests," 2) the
two railway questions posed in the instructions made them in
essence a "political program," and 3) it was "hardly justifiable" to take as a criterion of our influence in China the "behavior of Li Hung-chang," who "could, especially under the
influence of any material considerations, make us the most
solemn and sweeping promises," and "upon returning to Peking
and being placed by his official position in entirely different
circumstances that same dignitary might easily repudiate the
promises made."74 Here Witte was clearly not only being
accused of political levity and diplomatic credulity but confronted with what he had perpetrated: an attempt to play his
own diplomatic game under the cloak of the tsar's personal
authority while formally acting in the interests of a private
enterpriser's monopoly.

Meanwhile Russian representatives in Peking took emergency measures toward liquidation of the immediate danger
of English entrenchment on Russia's road to the gulf of Pechili:
a resolute protest was made by the chargé d'affaires against
the permission of English participation in the building of a
railway north of Shanhaikwan, and as a result of persistent
explanations with Li Hung-chang and Hu Yui-feng the question
was reduced to the making of a small loan by the Russo-Chinese
bank for the building (though not on the security, of the road)
and the agreement of the Chinese not to turn to English banks.75
Though consenting to the loan, Witte nonetheless considered
any such settlement of the question "temporary" and resolutely

insisted on getting from China "positive assurances" of the
strict fulfillment of the statement made to Ukhtomsky.[76]
And when the ministry of foreign affairs gave instructions in
this sense to Peking, Witte requested that "a like categorical
protest" be made to the Chinese minister in Peterburg as
well.[77]

Witte not only did not intend to retreat before the threat of
English railway penetration into Southern Manchuria, but in
the given case his obstinate desire to consolidate the results
achieved by Ukhtomsky's mission had received added stimulus
from the fact that English capital ("by direct invitation of the
Chinese authorities") was now also reaching out toward the
mineral resources of Manchuria. In September, 1897 a representative of the English firm of Pritchard Morgan, the
American engineer Shackley, had gone out there from Peking
to prospect, whereas back in March of that year Witte had
received reassuring intelligences to the effect that this same
Pritchard Morgan's negotiations "as to a grant of the most
sweeping concessions for the working of ores throughout China"
had ended in the Tsungli Yamen's categorical refusal to grant
him concessions of any kind.[78] For the time being Witte had
no formal grounds for demanding China's recognition of Russia's industrial monopoly in Manchuria as well and had to fight
the Morgan "enterprise" by private means.[79] But to exact
such recognition from the Chinese had become, under the open-
door policy, a pressing problem, being alone capable of securing to Russia in future the undivided domination of the whole
Manchurian market, a domination threatened by the Peking
government's described change of policy. The only thing lacking was some suitable occasion for making such a demand.
And for this he did not have long to wait: before Shackley's
surveys, which managed to cover the whole Liaoyang-Mukden-
Fenghuangcheng-Tunghwashan area were even completed, the
episode of the murder of Catholic missionaries in Shantung
and the subsequent punitive descent of a German landing party
at Kiaochow had placed the Chinese government under necessity of seeking Russia's help--at the price of new concessions
in Manchuria.

IV

During those same days when Russia came directly up
against English interests on the soil of Southern Manchuria,

a sharper clash with them had occurred in Korea. Alekseyev's appearance there (at the beginning of September, 1897) was attended by the king's sudden return to Russia's side and the restoration of her partisans to power.[80] Alekseyev lost no time about acquainting himself with the economic situation of the country, and, having obtained in roundabout ways exact information as to the state of the customs administration, was soon able to present the king with evidence of Brown's self-interested handling of revenues received from customs.[81] The result of this was Alekseyev's appointment as financial adviser to the royal government and Brown's consequent dismissal, the two actions being officially embodied in a special contract.[82] What had in the spring seemed attainable at the price of pro-longed and careful efforts, fired by no particular hope of suc-cess, had come about in a very brief space of time and as if spontaneously: Russia had formally become master of Korea's finances and now had only to be industrious in developing her success.

Immediately this meant that she must actually take control of the customs administration, i.e., 1) obtain its transfer from Brown to Alekseyev and 2) get a Russian bank started to take over the deposit of customs collections from Japanese banks maintaining branches in the three chief (free) ports--Fusan, Gensan and Chemulpo--principally for this purpose.[83] Up-held by the English chargé d'affaires and Robert Hart's sug-gestions relative to protests by other powers, Brown showed no signs of being prepared to give up his post, and Witte kept requesting Muravev's "energetic cooperation" in Brown's re-moval.[84] For his own part, immediately upon receiving news of Alekseyev's appointment, Witte hastily revived the matter of establishing a Russo-Korean bank, shelved since spring: this time the bank started out with a capital of 500 thousand rubles instead of 100, and not only was there no further talk of the insignificance of Russian trade in Korea, but attention was called to the fact that "Russia's name and Russian money were already beginning to have a share in the exploitation of Korea's ore, timber, and other natural resources," and as an example Briner's concession was quoted, that timber conces-sion covering the whole course of the border rivers Tumen and Yalu so famed later on under Bezobrazov.[85] Finally, on the spot, Alekseyev undertook in conjunction with Russian soldiers and sailors "the elaboration of a definite plan of action" for studying the port of Gishu and surrounding territory as "best

point of egress to the sea."[86] Apparently, having run into
difficulties and even become convinced of the danger of forcing the Manchurian question now, Witte was all the more determined to get into Korea and stay there by every means at
his disposal, undaunted by the prospect of conflicts either
with England or with Japan.

But upon this occasion official Russian diplomacy definitely
declined to force the Korean question in any way, since it was
preparing for a hazardous step in the Manchurian. Even before the introduction of the Russian squadron into Port Arthur,
at the very end of November, Muravev declared that "it would
embarass him to instruct the chargé to insist on the transfer
of the Korean customs administration to Alekseyev" "in view
of the political events transpiring in the Far East," but it was
justifiable for the Russian ships to enter this port, as Japan
had raised the question of a revision of the "Brown-Alekseyev
agreement," on the strength of the Moscow protocol. Since
Muravev was convinced that "in the present political circumstances we are under absolute necessity of preserving amicable relations with Japan," it was inevitable that we should
meet her half way in Korea, above all on the question of the
financial adviser that she had herself indicated.[87] In any
event, Russian diplomacy had not found it possible to exert
pressure in both directions simultaneously, and had chosen
one--Manchuria. It would be a mistake to suppose that this
choice had been easy for it or that the matter had passed off
without hesitation or any attempt to contest it.

For a correct evaluation of the line of action undertaken
by Germany in October, 1897, it must be remembered that
she had made an active appearance in the Far East in 1895
for the purpose of getting a base in China and a chance at an
equal footing there with the other powers: the question of acquiring a port on the Chinese littoral had at once been put to
Nicholas II by Wilhelm following the three-power ultimatum
to Japan in April, 1895. The amazing thing is that Germany
should then have delayed her move so long, with the other pow-
ers--France, Russia and England--constantly getting ahead
of her.[88] Documents now published by the German ministry
of foreign affairs testify to the fact that Germany had entered
upon the diplomatic preparation of the question of China's
voluntary transfer to her of some port for the berthing of her
ships back in October, 1895, in December had brought the
matter before the Tsungli Yamen and met with a rebuff, had

renewed her entreaties in the summer of 1896 with Li Hung-
chang, likewise to no effect, and had then after some hesitation fixed her choice on Kiaochow, but had been convinced
by Count Cassini's representations that until Russia found herself a suitable bay in Korea, Kiaochow would remain the only
nearby harbor for winter berthing of her squadron (August,
1896) and in November was quite prepared to seize Amoy, incited thereto by none other than the Chinese minister in Berlin and Count Cassini, but had afterwards reverted to the
Kiaochow idea.[89]

The result of Radolin's attempt to open the subject of the
destiny of this harbor with Muravev in July, 1897 on the eve
of Wilhelm's trip to Peterhof, was, however, negative: Radolin was discreetly advised 1) to await a favorable juncture
and 2) to seek a port "more to the south," since Russia did
not plan to give up the Kiaochow berth that next winter.[90]
Nonetheless, at his meeting with Nicholas in Peterhof, Wilhelm renewed the attempt, asking Nicholas "whether Russia
had her eye on Kiaochow," to which the latter replied that
"Russia was interested in retaining access to this port until
she should have taken over the more northerly port that she
had already found for herself."[91] To Wilhelm's question as
to whether the tsar would object if "German ships, in case of
need, and with the preliminary consent of Russian naval authorities, should cast anchor in Kiaochow," Nicholas replied
in the negative. In addition, Muravev, to whom a record of
the conversation of the two emperors was shown, would appear
to have remarked that Russia had no intention of taking final
possession of Kiaochow, though he could not say when Russia
would be in a position to release the harbor--and that upon its
release, Russia would willingly turn Kiaochow over to Germany, so that England should not get hold of it.[92] Thus, by
the official German version, Wilhelm got nothing even at
Peterhof besides conditional consent to the temporary call of
German ships at the bay, which would continue to be in use
by Russia for an indefinite period. But this was, nonetheless,
a loop-hole, and Germany had made up her mind to take advantage of it: introduce the German squadron at once into
Kiaochow for wintering: not await a "favorable juncture," but
simply arrange matters with Russia and notify China.

On September 9/21 of the same year, when Radolin told
Muravev that "in accord with the Peterhof negotiations" it was
Germany's intention to inform China of the imminent intro-

duction of her squadron into Kiaochow "in case of need," but
that this should only take place after arranging with the "local
Russian authorities," Muravev accepted this communication
amicably and, without personal comment, promised to transmit it to the tsar.[93] But when, previous to any answer having
been received from Nicholas, this communication was made
to the Tsungli Yamen (September 19/October 1,) it produced
a "profound impression," the more so since the German minister 1) refused to indicate the duration of occupation of the harbor and 2) alluded to an agreement with Russia on the point in
question.[94] Even though Li Hung-chang did object that Russia
was not a party to the matter, and Germany herself well known
that actually there was no Russian "authority" in Kiaochow
and no one there to arrange with, it nonetheless remained to
obtain some sort of answer from Peterburg in order to start
operations on the spot with full diplomatic propriety. On
October 2/14 von Tschirsky told Lamsdorf that the necessity
for utilizing the berth at Kiaochow had arisen and, still without an answer, stressed the point that in entering upon negotiations with Peterburg, Germany considered that she was
thereby simultaneously also satisfying the point about arranging with the local authority.

There were three forms that the Russian answer might
take: Russia might refuse Germany the use of the berth, but
this would be an unmotivated--and, in view of the absence of
Russian ships there, even uncivil--repudiation of the Peterhof statement; or authorize it--but this would mean assuming
responsibility in some degree for a step which it would be impossible to make Germany retract later on; and so Lamsdorf
preferred to give the answer which, though evasive, was in
effect most likely to satisfy his collocutor, namely that Russia
had obtained permission to use Kiaochow only for the one winter of 1895-6, and could therefore not "dispose of" this harbor, about which, moreover, the Chinese held "special views,"
and that to him, Lamsdorf, the question would appear to be
how the Chinese would greet the sudden appearance there of
German ships. Only Lamsdorf couched this answer in the
form of a personal opinion, and promised to refer the whole
matter to Muravev.[95]

The murder of missionaries in Shantung had, as we see,
occurred opportunely, when, even without it, Germany's appearance in Kiaochow was in large measure diplomatically
prepared. It now merely provided a pretext to use the puni-

tive motif to occupy the port and seize adjoining territory, to
hurry matters up, and apply final pressure on Petersburg to
get a formal answer that would end any doubt relative to Russia's real position. The famous telegram of October 26/No-
vember 6 sent by Nicholas in reply to Wilhelm's inquiry of
November 6 added nothing new to what Lamsdorf had told
Tschirsky not long before: "I can neither approve nor disap-
prove your order to direct the German squadron to Kio-chau,
since I have just learned that this harbor was in our hands
only temporarily in 1895-1896." This was the official answer
sought, completely untying German's hands, since it constituted a formal renunciation of any Russian rights or claims
to Germany's chosen object of seizure in China. The order
to the German squadron in Chinese waters was given that
same day (November 7, new style,) and on November 2/14
Admiral Diedrichs was in Kiaochow.[96]

However, as the next few days were to demonstrate, Nicholas's answer not only did not exhaust the question of Russia's
attitude toward the step taken by Germany, but did not tally
in the least with the position of the Russian ministry of foreign
affairs immediately after the sending of the tsar's telegram:
the Russian representative in Peking had been ordered to up-
hold the German demands for punishment of the authors of the
murder, in order to render "needless" both the "sending of
the German squadron to Kiaochow" and "intervention by other
powers," and should the departure of the German squadron
nonetheless take place, the commanding officer of the Russian
squadron had been ordered to trail it into port "with the sole
purpose of confirming [Russia's] prior right to the anchorage."[97]

Muravev told Tschirsky straight out that "in his time" Russia had obtained China's pledge that in the event of the transfer
of Kiaochow to any foreign power, preference would be reserved for Russia, and that he, Muravev, "deplored" Germany's having taken a step that would eventuate in the "opening" of Kiaochow to all nations.[98] This "incredibly brazen"
declaration of Muravev's, as Wilhelm expressed it, first of
all aroused the suspicion that he might have conspired with
Hanotaux, in which case, unless the Germans wished to get
caught in a trap, they would have to beat a retreat.[99] Berlin
seriously raised the question of revoking the order already
given the German squadron and directing it to some other Chinese port (for example, Tsingtao,) but Wilhelm stood firm,
convinced that when confronted by "cold facts" Russia would

not go to war over Kiaochow but come to terms. However,
Hohenlohe's attempt to convince the Russian ambassador that
"there was no case in world history where a political question
had been discussed (between two monarchs) more openly and
faithfully than the question of Kiaochow," and that Muravev
had probably not been informed of the tsar's telegram in time,
was wasted: Muravev continued to hold his ground, quoting
the exact sense of the Peterhof negotiations.[100] Even "cold
facts" did not at once break Muravev's determination, facts
such as the landing of a German shore-party at Kiaochow on
November 2/14 and Hohenlohe's note of the same date to the
effect that Germany was only reckoning on the tsar's last
telegram, which annulled all preceding declarations "of any
sort."[101]

On November 4/16 Muravev, speaking for Nicholas, charged
the ambassador at Berlin to inform Wilhelm that the tsar was
"very much surprised" by the interpretation given his telegram,
and that Russia could not give up Kiaochow the moment foreign
ships entered this closed port, while the Russian chargé d'affaires in Peking received "notice" from Peterburg "that our
naval detachment had been ordered to winter at Kiaochow."[102]
It was obvious that further altercation along this line threatened
to grow over not only into a "straining" of relations but even
into conflict. In view of this, Berlin decided to seek support
in London, and ascertained that in that quarter there was no
objection to Germany's settling down on the Chinese coast--
the farther north the better.[103] London could wish nothing better than a clash between Russia and Germany in China, but that
made it all the more absurd for Russian diplomacy to get into
one, after doing its utmost to remedy the "imprudence" permitted of in the tsar's telegram and avert an abrupt breach of
the status quo close to the as yet undefended Russian zone.
And, seeing that further persistence would be vain, Muravev
undertook a retreat: the order of November 8/20 given the
Russian squadron was revoked and after that any claims to
Kiaochow were gradually forgotten.[104]

Germany smoothed over the whole episode by letting Russia
put her fleet in at Kiaochow for the winter, i.e., by granting
her the same privilege that Germany had previously been given,
while the harbor was still accounted Russia's.[105] If a transaction with friendly Germany relative to a port (of which the
Chinese government had, nevertheless, given Russia the use)
could take such a diplomatically outrageous turn, the fear

that now gripped Muravev and Nicholas lest England do the
same with Port Arthur becomes the more comprehensible.
Port Arthur was the port mentioned not only in "Cassini's
convention" as eventual base for Russia's war power, but
in the scheme of the Russian ministry of finance as a possible ice-free terminus for the Russian railway network.

On the same day that Witte submitted the charter of the
Russo-Korean bank to the examination of the Finance Committee as urgent, namely on November 11, Muravev presented a memorandum to Nicholas suggesting that it would
be well not to miss the opportunity for settling at once the
question of acquiring an ice-free port on the Yellow Sea.
The Kiaochow affair appeared to him altogether ended, not
only because counteraction of the German seizure had become
hopeless but also because by the testimony of naval authorities this port "would be useless to us in peace time" "both
on account of the distance from Vladivostok and on account
of its being completely cut off from Russia." Meanwhile the
"general state of affairs in the Far East created by the after-
effects of the Sino-Japanese clash and our intervention in
China's favor was not only unaltered but steadily continuing
to assume a more definite character that indicated the absolute necessity of Russia's being prepared for all manner of
untoward eventualities, to which end it would be necessary
for us to maintain a considerable fleet in the Pacific Ocean
and have a port completely at our disposal convenient for
winter berthing, fully equipped and amply provisioned." To
the question: "where shall this port be sought...in Korea,
and, if so, on the east coast or on the west, or on the Chinese coastal strip, and if so, exactly where," Muravev could
at first get no "entirely definite answer" from the department
of the navy, and the latter's proposal to buy a section of the
coastal strip in Fusan he did not consider a solution of the
question, since Fusan "had long been the object of Japan's
suppressed desires" and "any future attempt of ours at firmer
consolidation in Fusan would not only meet with a hostile reception from Japan but might easily lead to a serious clash
with her."

In general the Korean ports struck Muravev as inconvenient
because they were too remote from the Siberian trunk-line,
and the eastern ones in particular, being open to blockade by
the Japanese fleet, might well prove a trap for the Russian
squadron. While not declining to consider any "other port"

the navy department might indicate, Muravev for his part
would suggest that "the ships of our squadron set about occupying" Talienwan on the Liaotung peninsula. Besides the favorable natural features of the bay of Talienwan, Muravev noted
its being less distant from the Siberian trunk-line than the
Korean ports "if we bear in mind the proposal to connect this
main artery [and we have seen that this proposal actually had
previously been advanced by Witte] by special branch line with
Kirin and Mukden, " and at the same time he considered the
given moment specifically favorable to the acquisition of a
port on the Chinese coast.

On the formal side, China is herself "asking our defense
and protection" and "our seizure of Talienwan would therefore
be easily explainable in Peking as prompted by our desire to
have our squadron firmly based should further events trans-
pire in the Pacific to China's disadvantage." And in essence
such "decisive action" is dictated by the whole "behavior of
the Chinese government throughout the most recent period, "
when "no representation or counsel" of Russia's in Peking
"had achieved its objective" "with respect to any one of the
demands made by us": in particular Muravev pointed out
that 1) the question of the southerly route of the Manchurian
railway through Ninguta and Bodune "had remained open up to
the present time, " and 2) "in relation to our building branch
lines to connect with Kirin and Mukden, the Chinese government has already manifested the intention of retreating from
the assurances given us."106 As we see, Muravev tied his
proposal in with the "recent change in our relations with the
Chinese government, " the actuality of which even Witte did
not deny: Muravev's proposal also envisaged the abrupt removal once and for all of the obstacles the Chinese government had placed in the way of the effectuation of the Russian
program for Manchuria in the redaction given official form
by Witte in March, 1897 and presented to the Chinese government by Ukhtomsky in June.

Nicholas recognized the Muravev proposal as "fully justified" and on November 14 had it discussed at a conference of
the 4 ministers, where it met with a storm of protest from
Witte and practical objections from the minister of the navy
which disposed Nicholas to decide against occupying Talienwan
"in view of the Moscow treaty of May 22, 1896 with China, as
well as our prestige in the East."107 On the very eve of the
conference (November 13,) Witte had told the German ambas-

sador that Germany's seizure of Kiaochow would force Russia
to occupy some other more northerly Chinese port, and that
this would give Japan occasion to consolidate either on the
Chinese mainland or in Korea, which would inevitably lead
to a Russo-Japanese war, and had advised Radolin to give up
Kiachow and get something in the south of China.[108] And at
the conference of November 14 Witte's whole argument hinged
on the inevitability of a Russian seizure if the German seizure
was not averted. He even proposed not to "seek compensation
in hostile actions against China" but to "act against Germany:"
"to order our squadron to Kiaochow and direct it to stand by
until Germany left this port." And when Muravev alluded to
the "special circumstances" that would not permit Russia to
obstruct Germany, Witte shifted to such arguments as : 1) the
riskiness of the proposed step, which would set other powers
the "example," Japan in particular (in respect not only to
China but to Korea as well,) and 2) its prematureness and
the possibility of getting what we wanted later on by way of
an agreement "on grounds of economic interests."[109] Consequently from Witte's viewpoint there was nothing for it but
to make the purely negative deduction to refrain from all aggressive acts at the given moment, and for the given moment
he succeeded in disposing Nicholas to this conclusion also.

That the question of seizing a port on Liaotung was not in
consequence entirely eliminated but only postponed for a few
days, Witte blamed wholly on Muravev, who, it seems, had
inspired in Nicholas the obviously false fear of the English
making this seizure. Witte attributed this move of Muravev's
to personal motives alone, affirming that "he was given no
rest by the fact that, before his assumption of the post of
minister, Lobanov-Rostovsky and I had achieved such important results in Far Eastern policy" and that he "desired to
make sure of distinguishing himself in some way."[110] Witte
was so far unreconciled to this intrusion of the Russian empire's minister of foreign affairs into the sphere of its foreign
policy in the Far East that he could see nothing besides un-
scrupulous self-seeking on Muravev's part in the discord that
had arisen. In this sphere of purely personal attitudes Witte
now got back from Muravev as good as he had given in the
spring of that year: the next move in Manchuria, then unsuc-
cessfully made by Witte behind Muravev's back, had now been
made by Muravev behind Witte's back. The ensuing argument
as to the prematurity of the step then taken by Witte was now

turned by him against Muravev in such form as unmistakeably
to betray the instinct that was here guiding Witte: the ice-free
port on the Pacific would be acquired by Russia "on grounds
of economic interest" in the same way in which the "apparently
impossible" acquisition of the concession for the road through
Manchuria had come about, in other words this would be done
by him, Witte, "by means accessible to him as minister of
finance," and the date for the transaction would be determined
by him.[111] To regain at any cost his lost initiative thus became Witte's task in relation to the chain of events that followed his apparent parrying of Muravev's attack of November 14.

But even if he had for the time being prevented the "occupation" of a Chinese port by "ships of our squadron" as a handy
method of facilitating the settlement of other questions that
had by then accumulated between the Chinese government and
the Russian, this still did not mean that we should in general
refrain from utilizing for their settlement the panic that had
seized upon the Tsungli Yamen after the German raid. Immediately upon Peking's receipt of news of the German landing (November 3,) Li Hung-chang had dashed to the Russian
mission to ask for help, and had not left it until he was given
the telegram of the chargé d'affaires, coded for sending to
Peterburg. But as to the disinterestedness of the promised
aid the Chinese could entertain no illusions, if only from what
Pokotilov had on the very first day given them to understand.[112]
He had also first spoken to the chargé of the necessity of
profiting by the favorable moment.[113] Russia's immediately
subsequent decision not to send the squadron to Kiaochow, under the pretext of Peterburg's having already started negotiations with Berlin in China's behalf, necessarily put the Chinese still further on their guard and moved them to turn to
the Japanese minister for mediation.[114]

When, finally--after the occupation of Talienwan had become a closed question--Peking did receive Muravev's promise of "help in case of a major clash with Germany," "provided all questions that have latterly arisen as to railway and
other matters shall have been satisfactorily settled," Li Hung-
chang openly declared that "he was afraid to make us any
promises when we might not fulfill ours relative to aid against
Germany."[115] And in a report to the throne made at the same
time the Chinese ministers pointed out the danger of "flinging
themselves into Russia's arms" and proposed dispensing with
her intervention.[116] And when, after some indecision, the

Chinese nonetheless agreed to meet our demands on condition
of "the removal of the German detachment," it was already
too late: Nicholas had decided to occupy Port Arthur, and
the necessity of China's voluntarily "flinging herself into Russia's arms" to obtain riddance from the German occupation
had passed.[117]

But at this same moment the same necessity quite unexpectedly cropped up "on grounds of economic interests." On December 2, Li Hung-chang approached Witte with a request as
to Russia's guaranteeing a new loan of 100 million lan that
China without result had been seeking to conclude in foreign
markets ever since the spring of 1897.[118] The necessity for
China's concluding this loan lay in the fact that May 8, 1898
was the expiration date set by the treaty of Shimonseki for
preferential payment of the Japanese indemnity with allowance
for percentages previously paid off on the capital sum of the
debt which would reduce the actual disbursement to 21 million
lan, as well as in the fact that the time limits were also approaching for other payments (war orders, etc.)[119] Meanwhile, in preceding negotiations, the Chinese government had
invariably been met by the demand not only for a guarantee of
the loan by definite revenues but for authorization of foreign
control over their collection, and upon this specific point the
contemplated combinations had gone to pieces. In June, 1897,
when Li Hung-chang had approached Witte through Ukhtomsky
with such a request, Witte had not been seduced by the possible
political effect of a Russian loan and had demanded either real
guarantees in the form of control or "most substantial and
entirely material benefits for Russia," and the Chinese had
turned to other combinations.[120]

And now, in December, Witte encompassed his agreement
to undertake the loan with conditions altogether exceptional
and in no wise consistent with the professions he has so categorically made at the conference of November 14. Unembaras-
sed on this occasion by the example being set the other powers,
Witte demanded: 1) railway and industrial monopoly for Russia in all three provinces of Manchuria and in Mongolia,
2) grant of a concession to the Chinese Eastern Railway Company for a branch railway from the trunk-line to "that harbor
which shall be selected for this purpose by the Management
of the road, on the coast of the Yellow Sea, east of the port
of Yingkow," and 3) authorization for Russia to construct at
this harbor a port with right of entry for all ships under the

Russian flag.[121] Without binding himself by precise indication
of the harbor demanded, Witte was undertaking to finish in one
blow not only with Manchuria but with Mongolia, for the industrial exploitation of which Rothstein had by this time already
organized a special "syndicate"[122] with the cooperation of
the Russo-Chinese and International banks. Furthermore it
seemed to him such a sure thing that he ordered Pokotilov not
only to avoid pressing the loan but to leave the Chinese government to propose of itself the terms that had been dictated to it
by Russia.[123]

But in announcing his demands Witte also already knew for
a certainty that the occupation of Port Arthur was a settled
question and that this Mongolo-Manchurian diplomatic freight-
load would thus have two engines to pull it: not only financial
need but the threat of war as well.[124] The entry of Russian
war-ships into Port Arthur and Talienwan, even though represented to the Chinese government as a temporary measure
("up to the conclusion of the Kiaochow affair,") not only did
not contradict the sense of the terms set by Witte, but looked
like coordinated action, an accomplished fact that admitted
of no denial. From this moment Witte and Muravev, who had
until then been at loggerheads, worked as one over China,
and the difference that somewhat later flared up between them
was limited to the Korean question.

Witte's proposal and the simultaneous appearance of Russian ships in Port Arthur surprised the Chinese government
at a very delicate moment in its international relations: when
it had not yet given up hope of a German withdrawal from
Shantung, and when hope of financial support from England
had just been cut off (1/XII) by the Hongkong-Shanghai bank's
categorical refusal to make a loan. Under such conditions,
nothing remained for the Chinese but to receive the Russians
at Arthur with open arms, as friends coming to their aid at
a difficult moment and promising to withdraw after the accomplishment of their friendly mission, and then give reassurances
all round that Russia would leave when the need had passed.[125]
But, when it came to the terms of the loan, Li Hung-chang
upon first reading the Russian memorandum drawn up for him
by Pokotilov in accordance with Witte's telegram of December 4, "lingered particularly" over the point about the branch
to the Yellow Sea and evaded an immediate answer, thereby
provoking Pokotilov to threaten "that fulfillment of the demands
...Russia would in any event obtain in one way or another,

and that China would therefore do better to agree to the [Rus-
sian] proposals without delay."126 The more trusting the
continued attitude of the Chinese toward the occupation of
Port Arthur, the more "convenient" Pokotilov thought the
present moment "for categorical advice through the chargé"
that they accept the December 4 proposals, which he regarded as "perfectly natural" after China's acceptance of the German demands relative to monopoly in Shantung.127

For a week or two the Chinese did not budge from the position they had taken on the Port Arthur question; for example,
the first appearance of the English minister, on December 7,
to give notice that if China was going to grant "various concessions to other powers," then England would likewise present her demands, had no effect, the Chinese continuing to
withold permission for the call of English ships at Port Ar-
thur.128 But as soon as the English minister appeared at
the Tsungli Yamen to protest against the Russian loan and to
promise "his full cooperation in arranging a loan in England,"
with the further "condition that foreign control of the revenues
which were to serve as guarantee should become operative
only in case of irregularity in payments," the English simultaneously concentrating their squadron at Hamilton, and the
Japanese theirs at Tsushima, the Chinese changed their tune
and demanded Russia's written pledge to evacuate Port Arthur,
where, on the contrary, the English were now assured of a
"friendly reception."129 And in future Anglo-Russian conflict
was localized not on the question of the port, but on the question of the loan: what set the English on their feet was not
Nicholas's predatory attempt but Witte's proposed terms for
a "peaceful" economic agreement. Russian diplomacy, in
deference to Witte, had spaced the two questions somewhat--
that of the loan and that of the Liaotung ports--broaching the
former first and following it up with the latter.

The English proposal, even though encompassed by demands
for serious concessions in England's favor, gave the Chinese
government an opportunity for bargaining with the two competitors, and the demand for a written pledge from Russia
apparently started off this bargaining. In communicating this
demand by the Chinese, Pokotilov advised its fulfillment in
exchange for a written pledge on their part to meet the December 4 demands in full, thus converting the proposed loan into
a plain act of "charity."130 In full compliance with this counsel, Muravev telegraphed Pavlov on December 23 to notify

the Tsungli Yamen that 1) "we had never had an eye to territorial acquisitions and would quit Port Arthur and Talienwan
when political circumstances and the interests of Russia and
China should permit," concerning which, "notice" would also
be given the Chinese minister in St. Petersburg, 2) "in view
of our friendship with China, we count on the Peking government's granting to our use a completely secure anchorage on
the Pechili or Korean gulf to relieve us of the necessity of
berthing in Nagasaki,"--and to demand a "written pledge of
fulfillment of the verbal promises made regarding the instructor and railway questions, together with a guarantee of a concession for the connecting branch."[131] Presumably Muravev
had been left uninformed neither as to the actual fact of the
loan negotiations started by Witte, nor as to the terms set,
so that Muravev's demands in the given case appeared much
more moderate: they contained neither industrial monopoly
nor mention of Mongolia, and made no use at all of the loan
motif.

Notwithstanding all this, the Chinese ministers, in explanations with Pavlov on December 26, pointed out that the "only serious difficulty was the question of the branch to the Yellow Sea, which the Chinese government would prefer to build
itself," and Li Hung-chang, well knowing whence actually to
expect the blow, at once proposed to Witte to lay this branch
at China's expense to the mouth of the Yalu.[132] But Witte on
this occasion was no longer willing to confine himself to his
own recent project of a branch to Korea and flatly refused to
do any bargaining whatsoever. The instruction transmitted
by Muravev on December 30 to Pavlov, a verbatim reproduc-
tion of Witte's own manuscript rough draft, even comprised
somewhat more than the terms of December 4: besides the
maritime customs guarantee, the loan was to be still further
secured by "revenues from overland customs in connection
with the Chinese Eastern Railway and in the provinces of Manchuria as a whole, as well as by the whole salt revenue,"
which, taken with the industrial and railway monopolies, created a sort of third line of defense for the new Russian colony.
Witte's offer of a loan on such terms was couched in ultimatum form, and the treaty must be signed within two-weeks
time.[133] But before even a week had passed, the whole absurdity of so pretentious and acrimonious a posing of the loan
question became apparent.

It was already definitely known that Salisbury had just pre-

viously agreed to the English government's guarantee and
that negotiations with the English minister at Peking were in
full swing.[134] As to the political terms set by the English
the Russians had not succeeded in getting reliable information,
nor had the French, who were extremely jealous of the prospect of an English loan, but there was a stubborn rumor to
the effect that the prime condition set by the English was
restoration of Talienwan as an open port, and it was impossible not to relate this to the fact that two or three English
war-ships were stopping every day at Port Arthur.[135] To
figure on the Chinese accepting the Russian terms in toto before fully ascertaining the English would in such a situation
have been plain folly, and in any case it was also necessary
to figure on the possibility of China's accepting the English
offer.[136]

Inasmuch as the "seizure" of the Liaotung ports, which
Russia was prepared to renounce for the sake of "cutting"
Manchuria and Mongolia off from foreigners, was in effect
only part of the whole Russian declaration of December 4-
30, which naturally did not exclude from among the Yellow
Sea ports either of the two actually occupied, Muravev on
January 8, in case the loan should end badly, gave new instructions to Peking: 1) regardless of the two-week limit,
to refrain from breaking off negotiations should the Chinese
desire to enter into a discussion of the Russian terms, and
2) "being very careful not to harm our negotiations about the
loan," propose that the Chinese enter into a written agreement on the lease of the Liaotung ports, in view of China's
powerlessness to prevent their actual "opening" by the English after the withdrawal of the Russian ships.[137] But Peking learned on that same day that the English "were promising the Chinese ministers a huge bribe" to arrange the loan,
and on January 9 an order was issued by Peterburg to the
same effect, namely: "to distribute privately" "to Chinese
notables" "for the purpose indicated" a million rubles, and
Witte, fearing that an English loan might "completely sever
our friendship" (with China,) sent a follow-up telegram to
Pokotilov on his own responsibility: "if this sum proves inadequate, possible to increase."[138]

There were two days (January 12 and 13) when it looked
as though the Peking scales were starting to tip toward Russia and it only remained to meet the Chinese half way as to
the financial terms of the loan.[139] But at this point the affair

miscarried--in view of the menacing attitude now assumed
by England: on January 12 Staal sent word from London that
"public opinion had been disquieted by news from Peking relative to the supposed pressure that we had brought to bear on the
Peking government with the purpose of disrupting England's proposed loan" and that Lord Wolsley (Commander-in-Chief) had
publicly announced the "complete preparedness" of the British
army "should war break out;"[140] on the 13th the English minister in Peking threatened in the event of non-conclusion of
the loan with England to revive "various old claims" and declared that England would profit by Germany's example--there-
by producing on the Chinese ministers "a most forcible impression;"[141] on the 14th, Li Hung-chang diffidently suggested
halving the loan between England and Russia, but France at
once intervened to protest against the English loan terms,[142]
and on the 21st the Chinese minister to Peterburg informed
the Russian government of China's decision not to seek any
foreign loan whatsoever.[143]

Upon receiving from Muravev a copy of Staal's telegram,
Witte was in nowise disposed to admit that Russia was here
faced by the specter of war: in his opinion "a tumult so easily
raised would as easily subside, " since it was "unthinkable that
a serious clash could arise over the question of concluding a
loan with the bankers of this country or that, " and a "real"
"clash could only be provoked by a policy of seizures."[144]
Accordingly Witte refused to believe that England might prefer to 1) see Russia settle down on the powder-magazines of
Port Arthur, under her own observation from Weihaiwei, and
in the neighborhood of the open port of Talienwan, and 2) herself gain a number of substantial privileges in central and
southern China--if only she might thereby avert the cutting off
of Manchuria and Mongolia from the circulation of international
capital.[145] And when the "unthinkable" became an actuality
and China shrank in terror from the question of a Russian or
an English loan, Witte definitely ceased to understand what it
was all about and sought wisdom among his subordinates. He
knew that China would need money in March, 1896,[146] that to
allow the time limit for the preferential payment to Japan to
lapse would be madness, and that a domestic loan in so large
an amount was for China utopian, and he asked Pokotilov what
he thought "would come of it?"[147] Pokotilov's answer was the
only possible one--that this was a trick of China's for the purpose of gaining time and returning to the English loan.[148]

In shrinking from the threat of a war over the loan question
and giving up the thought of immediately putting Witte's monopolistic program in practice as a whole, Russian diplomacy
shifted to an attempt to carry it out at least in part. Data exist to the effect that at the very beginning of February, 1898,
Muravev returned to the project of leasing the Liaotung ports
--after a preliminary attempt to make an arrangement with
England. At least, among the documents of the ministry of
foreign affairs we find preserved a prospectus, confirmed by
Nicholas on February 5, 1898, for "demands that we might
present," from the text of which it appears that demands on
the English government were in question.149 These demands
were formulated as four points: 1) that the Chinese Eastern
Railway be permitted "the construction of a branch to the port
of Talienwan, or to some other port on the coast of the Yellow
Sea between Yinkow and the Yalu River, "should the laying of
a road to Talienwan present difficulties,"2) that this port "be,
if not wholly, at least to a sufficient extent in our hands, though
possibly open to foreign ships," 3) that "England be pledged
not to oppose our conclusion of an agreement with China, similar to the German Kiaochow agreement, granting Russia the
leasehold of Port Arthur without our appropriation of sovereign rights and for a less considerable term," 4) the lease to
be extended to Talienwan as well, provided that should be
chosen as "terminal open-trade port for our railway." These
demands were confirmed by the tsar on February 5, the very
day on which the English ambassador was expected at the ministry of foreign affairs at 1 o'clock noon to "open negotiations
on the question of the Chinese loan, in compliance with the
command of the sovereign," and on the previous day, February 4, Lamsdorf had been able to furnish Witte both a copy of
the English loan terms, as communicated to him by the English ambassador, and a project for "our objections to the
English proposals formulated in full accord with the observations" that Witte had that same day managed to make on them.150
     Whether any written agreement was concluded with England
on the enumerated principles remains as yet unknown, but it
may be conjectured that, having exchanged the documents indicated, each side granted the other future freedom of action.
Whether or not it was also known to the Russian ministry that
in connection with the English guarantee of the loan an Anglo-
Chinese agreement as to the non-alienation of the Yangtse region had been signed back on January 31, old style, and that

China had back on February 1, old style, given a pledge to
keep an Englishman at the head of the maritime customs as
long as English trade remained predominant in China--Mu-
ravev, following his explanations with the English ambassador,
now renewed (February 8) his correspondence with Peking as
to the lease of ports, proceeding from the position that Russia was "prepared to help the Chinese out of their embarassing situation" and "would not only create no obstacles to
China's conclusion of a loan with the English, but on the contrary cooperate in every way, directing her influence toward
getting England to mitigate the terms set."[151] "In return for
this substantial service" it was then to be suggested that the
Chinese conclude with Russia a lease-hold treaty to Port Arthur and Talienwan, and stated that these were conditions for
which "we...could under no circumstances withdraw."[152]

Such a statement of the question, following upon the defeat
just sustained in the loan negotiations, would have been impossible without some certitude that England would not wreck
things this time as she had wrecked the Russian loan. And in
future the Russian ministry's only concern was to keep forthcoming diplomatic procedure to the terminology of "our secret
treaty with China, signed by the late Prince Lobanov and State-
Secretary Witte," who now, incidentally, "fully recognized the
expediency" of the "arguments" formulated for presentation to
China and "fully sympathized in them" --and it now only awaited
notice from Pavlov in Peking of the arrival there of a "favorable moment" for opening negotiations.[153]

Negotiations in Peking began, as we know, on February 19,
just after the Chinese had signed the agreement with Hongkong-
Shanghai and German-Asiatic banks, and dragged on until
March 15 of that year.[154] The debarkation of a Russian landing party, in readiness at Port Arthur in case the Chinese
failed to sign the lease convention at the appointed time, was
averted by those same money promises with which we had
previously thought to buy the loan treaty. This time the method
proved effectual, but only because the Chinese government, after exhausting every expedient for drawing the English and
Japanese into the matter and having no success, was left face
to face with its obtrusive ally.[155] Thus was that odious symbol finally removed that had from the start been the only visible
object of strife within the Russian government, and "seizure"
of the Liaotung ports was cloaked under an "amicable agreement" as to the whole peninsula and a connecting line of very

nearly a thousand versts.[156] Upon receiving notice from
Muravev of the agreement of the Chinese to sign the lease
treaty, Witte "could but rejoice," "like any Russian," and
Muravev hastened to respond with "heartfelt gratitude" for
"the invaluable sympathy and cooperation without which it
would not have been possible to bring to a favorable issue so
difficult a matter."[157]

The acquisition of an ice-free outlet to the Pacific proved
possible for Russia not in the spring of 1895 and not on the
east coast of Korea, as tradition has it that Nicholas would
have wished, not in the spring of 1896, when Li Hung-chang
managed to frustrate Witte's attempt to secure Russia a
port on the Yellow Sea through laying a wide-gauge connecting branch to it, and not in the summer of 1897, when Witte
and Nicholas II, secretly from Muravev, finally fixed their
choice on a west-Korean port and brought panic to the Peking
government by disclosing their plan of cutting an offshoot
of the Russian trunk-line through South Manchuria to Peking
itself. It proved possible only in the winter of 1898 and at
the point in Southern Manchuria most remote from the Russian military base--with the "moral" support of France and
Germany and by agreement with England--at the price of
narrowing at the given moment the Russian territorial-political program that had just attained absolutely concrete formulation under Witte's pen.[158] To avoid a clash with England, Russia had to relinquish her monopolistic position in
Manchuria and Mongolia and write off the lost opportunity
of the summer of 1897 to restore her relations with China
politically by means of a loan. Nay more: a similar retreat
was undertaken by Russian diplomacy in Korea by way of an
agreement with Japan, which had, simultaneously with England, resorted to the threat of war, and had on the very
heels of England proposed her own terms of agreement.[159]
    Meanwhile, according to some indications, Witte up to the
last minute cherished the hope that he would succeed in combining the two component parts of his plan for a "peaceful"
advance upon Manchuria and Korea and in extending the Siberian railway line to the mouth of the Yalu at the Manchurian-
Korean boundary as projected by him back in the spring of
1897. This is by no means contradicted by the fact that Witte

for some reason refused to listen Li Hung-chang's request
(of December 27, 1897) that he route the connecting branch
to the Chinese port of Antung on the right bank of the Yalu
estuary, and arbitrarily confirmed, in the ultimatum of December 30, his demand that Russia be given a port on the
stretch "between the port of Yinkow and the mouth of the
Yalu."[160] This elastic formula, adopted by Witte back on
December 4, 1897, possibly as a concession to the tsar's
wish, just categorically expressed, regarding occupation
of the Liaotung ports, did not, however, prevent his interesting himself, as early as the middle of January, in the
"depth of water" and "ice-free-ness" of the Korean port of
Gishu.[161] And when, on February 4, 1898, Japan, in England's wake, made the transfer of the office of financial adviser in the Korean government to Japanese hands one of
her terms of agreement, Witte, already aware of the collapse
of the Mongolo-Manchurian part of his plan as associated
with the Chinese loan that had now passed into England's
hands, declared against making just this concession to Japan.[162] As he told both the German ambassador on November 13 and the tsar on November 14, 1897, to let Japan into
Korea now meant to make a Russo-Japanese war inevitable;
and to relinquish the financial management of Korea and lose
along with it the specially protected position of the Russian
bank there obviously meant the opening of Korea's doors
wide, primarily to Japanese influence.

The Russo-Japanese agreement, in which the question of
the financial adviser was formally left a tie, whereas Russia
bound herself "not to obstruct the development of trade and
industrial relations between Japan and Korea," was only signed
on April 13/25, 1898.[163] This is perhaps why the Liaotung
convention signed in March still carried a proviso, in the
Witte spirit, concerning the right to lay a connecting branch
not only to Talienwan but also to some other more convenient
point "between the city of Yinkow and the mouth of the Yalu,"[164]
whereas the so-called supplementary protocol of April 25/
May 7, 1898, i.e., concluded after the signing of the Korean
agreement, dropped this proviso and named as terminal points
of the new railway Port Arthur and Talienwan (with "and not
to any other port" underscored in article III").[165] The fact
that Korea had this time slipped from Russia's hands irrevocably was as irrevocably assimilated by Witte, and after

Alekseyev's recall (in March, 1898) Witte adopted an attitude
of quasi-boycott toward her, refusing to have any financial
dealings with the Korean government or in any way to support
Russian enterprise there.166 His whole attention was now
concentrated on China and on the grandiose construction work
that was now just starting on the whole 2,400 verst stretch in
Manchuria and that appeared all the more urgent on the southern sector "the more premature" Russia's having come into
possession of a remote military port was seen to be.

Chapter IV

"DISASTROUS" RETREAT BEFORE ENGLAND TO THE NORTH OF THE GREAT WALL 1898-1899

I

The Russo-Chinese acts of March 15 and April 25, 1898 (the convention and supplementary protocol) settled for Russia the question of the ice-free port and its connecting branch; they gave Russia "full and exclusive use" of the southern extremity of the Liaotung peninsula for 25 years, converted the remainder of the peninsula into a "neutral zone" where no concessions could be granted to foreigners without Russia's consent, and extended the terms of the contract of August 27, 1896 to the new branch line. But they left the Manchurian question wide open and the rear of the leased territory unsecured, while at the same time advancing Russia to sentry post at the very entrance to the gulf of Pechili. The Russo-German agreement which would have put at Russia's "complete disposal" the gulfs of Korea, Liaotung and Pechili in <u>immediate</u> vicinity to the German sphere of Shantung, thus <u>totally excluding</u> England from the Yellow Sea area, had not come off, and, close on Russia's heels, England took up a position at the entrance to the gulf of Pechili in Weihaiwei.[1] True, article III of the supplementary protocol of April 25 had established that "in the area served by the new railroad" no railway concessions would be granted to foreigners, which in a way guaranteed the commercial future and the military security of the road. But the weakness of this article lay in the fact that Russia agreed not to "obstruct" the Chinese government's building of an extension of the Shanhaikwan railway "to the nearest point of the new branch."[2]

It must not be forgotten that this approach to the province of Chihli was precisely the point at which China had in July, 1897 sought England's protection from Russian encroachment or that the participation of English capital in the building of this road had been only temporarily averted by the Russo-Chinese bank through the loan of 600 thousand lan (about one million rubles) made on the condition that in the event of the road's

being pledged in connection with subsequent foreign loans,
this loan must first be repaid.[3] Thus, what had happened in
the spring of 1898 to Weihaiwei by sea might at any moment
happen on land at the "nearest point of the new branch," to
the rear of Port Arthur.

As early as the middle of February, 1898, when the occupation of the Liaotung ports had just been composed on an international scale, Peterburg was informed that the Chinese
(and Li Hung-chang in particular) were again drawing the
English into the matter and had decided "to start work at once
on the extension of the road from Shanhaikwan to Chinchow
and simultaneously begin construction from the port of Yinkow to Mukden, borrowing for this purpose from the Hongkong-
Shanghai bank and entrusting the work on both lines to [the
Englishman] Kinder," and only to let the Russians build the
line north from Mukden.[4] It so happened that during these
same days the prospect again flickered before the Russian
government (for the third time already) of the collaboration
in Manchuria of American capital as well. This time word
came from Washington that our old friend the American Bush
had at the beginning of January, 1898 concluded a contract for
making a loan to the Chinese imperial railway administration
for building a line from Shanhaikwan to Mukden and Kirin and
from Port Arthur to Mukden on the condition that Americans
be called in to build and operate it, and furthermore that the
Americans were "not pursuing" any "political aims," "genuinely desired to work in conjunction with the Russian government" and would even "build the Russian type of railway [wide
gauge], fully recognizing Russia's sphere of influence in this
section."[5]

Needless to say, the English combination and the American
that at this moment threatened to reduce Russia's business in
Manchuria to the mere acquisition of an isolated anchorage
for her war-ships in the Liaotung ports were both greeted by
a categorical protest from Russia.[6] However Russia's subsequent attempt, as evidenced in the supplementary protocol
of April 25, article III, to find means for removing the danger
of a threat to her communication line between port and trunk
line by way of an agreement with the Chinese government
alone, still did not altogether settle the question. The Americans, coming forward as they had without any indications of
support from the United States government, could easily be
simply counted out as dangerous competitors. But the English

were an entirely different matter. England, after the seizure
of Port Arthur not only refused to believe "that the door to
Manchuria would be left open by a great power that had obtained
lock, bolt, and bar to it," not only comprehended that Russia
had now "attained a position that England would perhaps find
it difficult to dispute when the time came for Russia to shut
the door," but also expressed alarm lest "after assimilating"
Manchuria, Russia "would have the ability to start out for
Pechili, and between Pechili and the Yangtse there exists no
natural barriers."[7] From this standpoint, the fight for a railway "barrier" in southern Manchuria became for England a
fight for "the Yangtse valley." Under such conditions, and
with Anglo-Chinese negotiations proceeding successfully, to
continue her protests to the Chinese government and shun an
agreement with England, which country had evidently backed
China from the first on this question, would keep Russia under
threat of repeated conflicts such as the January one.

    And in point of fact, before six months had passed, England
did again start talking the language of war, as in January,
1898, on the question of which banker should get the next loan
for the Shanhaikwan railway and on what terms.[8] Having at
the proper time, early February, 1898, rejected England's
proposal for a "general agreement on all points where our interests touch hers" on terms of a "quite unusual character,"
Russian diplomacy felt obliged on this occasion, in July, 1898,
to itself propose to England their negotiation in general form
of the railway question in China--on the basis of spheres of
influence.[9] This proved not so simple a matter, and the Anglo-
Russian diplomatic tourney dragged on for nine full months.

II

    Preliminary negotiations, opened in London by Lessar in
July, 1898 and continued by Muravev in Peterburg, had by
September of that year clarified the basic points of a possible
agreement with only one exception, and this was to be made
the topic of future negotiations. The project proposed to
Peterburg by the English ambassador at the beginning of September presupposed two agreements. In one, which could be
signed immediately, the English appear to have presented the
terms which had been discussed, in their basic features, during the preceding negotiations, namely: 1) the controversial
Shanhaikwan line (to Newchwang) "was to be built, if necessary,

through a loan from the Hongkong-Shanghai bank," but "must remain a Chinese line, under Chinese control, and could not be mortgaged to any non-Chinese company whatsoever," 2) the Russian government and the English would mutually bind themselves not to seek for themselves or support their subjects in seeking railway concessions--England in Manchuria, or Russia in the "Yangtse area," 3) "no preferential railway rates or differential treatment would be established on railway lines in the aforementioned districts to which concession might be obtained by them [the governments,]" and 4) both governments "would urge" English and Russian banks "to compose their interests in exact conformity" with this agreement. The other "later agreement" was to "establish," "after further discussion of the matter," "a definition of the geographical boundaries between the two areas" referred to in the first agreement.[10]

As is apparent, the English cabinet hastened to avail itself of the readiness evidenced by the Russian ministry of foreign affairs during negotiations to yield on the two points most essential for England; 1) the legalizing of the English bank's financial participation in the Shanhaikwan railway, which would in any event mean Russia's renunciation of any influence whatever on this south-Manchurian line, even though not altogether restoring it to England's full possession, and 2) the establishment on all Manchurian railways, and consequently throughout Manchuria, of free competition between English and Russian trade on the basis of uniform tariffs and imposts for both, i.e., the actual extension to Manchuria of the "open door" principle.

In an effort to secure victory on these two points by the day of the opening of parliament (October 12) the London cabinet had originally been prepared to leave the question of exact demarcation in the background. But this question had, meanwhile, been raised by Russia, and it had become apparent that Russia inclined toward an expansive interpretation of her Manchurian zone. The latter circumstance, seemingly, even impelled the English a week later to present a second redaction of the agreement project, this time carrying a proviso as to the necessity for "exact definition" of the two areas--"previous to its signing."[11] And the business of concluding the agreement dragged on for more than six months.

The Russo-English agreement signed on April 16/28, 1899 fixed the boundary of the English and Russian railway spheres

at the "Great Wall," somewhat north of Peking. This was
more than England had originally proposed: the Russian sphere
beyond the Wall took in not only Manchuria but Mongolia as
well. Yet it was still not altogether what Muravev had proposed to obtain when he entered upon negotiations in the summer of 1898: he had then thought that "the line of demarcation
might be drawn through Peking."[12] Had Muravev been left
to himself, it is not difficult to conjecture that in further negotiations he would have made a point of fighting for the Peking
dividing line and would have prevented its being shifted north
from Peking to Shanhaikwan, located on the border between
Chihli province and Manchuria, just under the Wall itself: this
would have been the utmost that the Russian diplomatic department had felt competent to obtain. However, before matters
got as far as objections from England on this point, the idea
of the Peking line, advanced by Muravev even previous to receipt of the first English project, had at once evoked a protest
from the depths of the Russian ministry of finance, and negotiations took another turn, where complete failure awaited them.

As soon as the project for the Peking line of demarcation
became known in the ministry of finance, the first thing to attract attention there was this: that the diplomats had completely forgotten the existence of the Russo-Chinese bank,
which, not to mention a charter setting no territorial limits
to it in China, had actually by this time succeeded in interesting itself in several undertakings considerably to the south of
Peking. In December, 1897 the bank had concluded the contract for a loan to build a railway from Yulinpu to Taiyuanfu
(in Shansi province) and for the exploitation of iron and coal
beds in the vicinity of the road, had in May 1898 started negotiations with the Germans as to their participation in a loan
for building the Tientsin-Tsinanfu and Gishu-Chinhsien railways (i.e., for uniting Peking with the lower course of the
Yangtse) and finally, had within the past few days made arrangements for intermediary participation in the financial
operations of a Belgian-French syndicate in the matter of
building the Peking-Hankow railway; reckoning from this alone,
as an existing fact, the boundary of the Russian sphere ought
"by rights" to be drawn "approximately" at the Huang-ho.[13]
And when (on September 9, 1898) the actual text of the English
project arrived for the ministry's consideration, it became
clear that not only the bank but all the achievements and prospects of Russia's Manchurian policy for the past three years
were threatened.

Romanov (director of the ministry during Witte's absence abroad) at once thought necessary to open Lamsdorf's eyes to the fact in full detail that the English project "restricted to excess the rights already acquired by Russia in China and, without giving her any new advantages in exchange, consolidated the economic dominance of England in all of walled China [i.e., China proper,]" and hastened to send the text of the English terms to Witte in Berlin "by express courier."14 One can imagine what sort of impression they must have produced upon Witte, particularly the article about "railway tariffs and differential treatment," dooming Russian export trade in Manchuria, and the obligation to renounce support of the Russo-Chinese bank beyond the borders of Manchuria-- considering recent reproaches that the French had made even without this as to the disregard shown by Russian agents for French interests, which were, of course, by no means confined to Manchuria alone.15 In a brief telegram Witte accordingly gave orders for Lamsdorf to be "officially" informed that "in view of our obligations to the French banks and the Russo-Chinese bank" he found the English project "from an economic point of view" "impossible" and disastrous (désastreux)."16 This meant nothing if not a negation root and branch of the idea itself of a contractual demarcation of spheres of influence in China and a demand that negotiations be broken off.

Before the receipt of this September 16 telegram of Witte's, Peterburg had still thought of continuing negotiations: Romanov had undertaken the "task of drawing up a counter-project," and on September 14 Lamsdorf had given him the English ambassador's "supplementary explanation" relative to the boundaries of the "Yangtse area," to which Russia was to respond with her "definition of Manchuria."17 But instead of the project for a Russian answer, Romanov, now governing himself by the categorical reaction of his chief, confined himself on September 18 to explaining to Lamsdorf the impossibility of withdrawing from the Russo-Chinese bank the Russian governmental support promised the French for operations throughout China, as this "would be in the highest degree disadvantageous to Russian credit in the French market" and "absolutely incompatible with the primordial traditions of the financial policy of Russia, which even at the state's most difficult moments had always scrupulously fulfilled her financial obligations."18 And on the next day Peking was already apprised that the Eng-

lish project "would be rejected as excessively disadvantageous to Russia," that the English ambassador would in that
case "threaten" to make China accept a loan from the Hongkong-Shanghai bank secured by (and consequently controlling)
the Shanhaikwan-Yinkow railway, and that then Russia would
demand compensations from China, but that "the final answer
had not as yet been given."[19]

The final answer had indeed not then been given, and negotiations were resumed upon the return of the two ministers to
Peterburg, though not until mid-October.

III

As in the Liaotung episode of late 1897--early 1898, Muravev and Witte conducted negotiations four-handed and at that
with a tinge of disagreement perceptible to the English ambassador. At the beginning of February, 1898, as soon as the
possibility had been ascertained of avoiding a clash with England by conceding her the Chinese loan and giving ground to
Japan in Korea, and of obtaining the Liaotung lease, Muravev
had firmly maintained that "at the present time in the Far East
tasks are arising for Russia which will require of us full freedom of action and the preservation of friendly relations both
with Japan and with England."[20] And he now had no desire to
renounce the agreement with England and until the end of negotiations retained the air of a man slow to see political significance in bankers' interests, "being fully conscious that
our position on the shores of the Pacific is not yet secure"
and that the "fulfillment" "of highly complicated tasks" immediately connected with Russia's consolidation on Liaotung
was "possible only on condition of a peaceful flow of events
and complete abstention on our part from decisive actions capable of giving rise to any sort of political complications."[21]
Witte, guided by the "financial and economic interests of Russia," saw no absolute necessity for the agreement and in any
event considered the idea of a general and at the same time
exact demarcation of spheres of influence itself disastrous.[22]
As on the previous occasion Russian diplomacy by compromising with Witte had let slip the great Mongolo-Manchurian program with an ice-free port, and on the heels of that fiasco had
laid claim only to the port, so now it permitted Witte to attempt
to guard "all China, all its riches" from closure by the English
government to the Russian bank--and if that failed, to defend

himself at least from immediate railway penetration by the
English into Manchuria only, ostensibly because it seemed
to him hardly "worth while" "to fence" "the garden" just for
Manchuria. 23 But as Witte had previously lacked means to
overcome the stubborness (and Anglophobia) of the Chinese
government, so now he had no success in outflanking English
diplomacy per se.

Witte began by avowing, in an "absolutely confidential and
unofficial" talk with the ambassador on October 20, that "in
relation to such concrete questions [as railway affairs in
China] he did not see in a written treaty the best means of obtaining that frank and satisfactory agreement whereby both
governments obviously desired to consolidate their future relations," and that it was "almost impossible to draw up this
treaty [now proposed by England] in such a way as to forestall
all possibility of evading the fulfillment of its terms." And
he "then declared that in his opinion a much more reliable
foundation for our future relations might be laid in the form
of a general treaty," which "should state our steadfast intention of establishing our relations on the ground of a candid
and friendly agreement, and should likewise provide that in
the event of a question arising in any part of the world that
either government regarded as capable of occasioning a clash
between their interests, the two were to enter at once into
candid and friendly discussion of this question with the steadfast intention of obtaining its settlement without violation of
the legitimate interests of either party." 24

This idea of Witte's--as to a general political agreement
irrespective of China--was not taken up by the English and
further negotiations with the ambassador assumed the form
of detailed explanations by the two ministers of the unaccepta-
bility of separate points in the September agreement project,
and, meeting now with both ministers together, now with each
of them separately, the ambassador became increasingly
convinced that a difference of opinion existed between them
on the question of relations between the Russian government
and the Russo-Chinese bank. 25 But this was precisely where
the chief discernible impediment lay to getting the spheres of
influence exactly delimited in the agreement. And such a
situation facilitated the game for England exceedingly. She
must either bend her efforts toward getting the "open door"
policy demanded by Russia for the Russo-Chinese bank in
China proper adopted by her in relation to all Manchuria and

all Mongolia likewise (i.e., get Russia to accept the article
about uniform rates and imposts) or, if Russia wished to preserve an aloof position in Manchuria, see to it that she would
then not claim access to the rest of China. The resumé of
the Peterburg three-sided conferences presented by the English ambassador on November 18 was accordingly so drawn
up as to eliminate the proposal for a dividing line beyond which
the Russo-Chinese bank would not have franchise, and to give
principal prominence instead to the article ruling out tariff
and impost preferences for Russia in Manchuria.

"Though regretting that the idea of a delimitation of our
spheres of interest by means of a written agreement should
have encountered objections," the ambassador "had with satisfaction learned that Count Muravev and Count Witte were
both disposed to an agreement which should [1] recognize the
inviolability of China, and likewise our treaty rights, which
include among other things a prohibition against establishing
in concession treaties for railways any preferential tariff or
differential levy on goods or passengers contingent upon their
nationality; that they were prepared [2] to recognize and respect the open door policy, based on our treaty rights; and that
they [3] do not desire to demand for Russia an exclusive sphere
of influence or interests, or [4] demand more of a corridor
through Manchuria than is necessary for the defense of their
railway line." The ambassador accordingly proposed that
Russia give a written (unilateral) "engagement" in this sense.
In addition the ambassador agreed, in compliance with "the
desire of both ministers," to an exchange of notes which
"should confirm our mutual conviction that there exists no
actual antagonism between our mutual financial, commercial,
and other interests in China, and our steadfast purpose to
adjust them by free and friendly agreement," and to the signing of an agreement as to the Shanhaikwan railway in the spirit
of his September proposal. [26]

Thus, as the result of Witte's intervention in negotiations,
it was proposed that Russia formally renounce once and for
all any exclusive sphere of interests in China, nothing analog-
cal being proposed in return respecting England. Continuing
to nurse the assurance that "it would be more convenient
generally for Russia to preserve full freedom of action in relation to Far Eastern affairs" ("the more so that we have already restricted ourselves by the agreement with Japan"),
Witte found this November proposal of England's just as "un-

acceptable" as the September one. But in deference to Muravev's conviction "that in the present situation England would
never be content without a proper agreement," Witte decided
against "avoiding such an agreement," merely proposing "instead of the unilateral redaction" a project of his own in which
1) he combined all three of the English documents into one,
and 2) attempted to discard even the hint of any engagement
respecting "differential levy," preserving only the engagement to observe the "most favored nation" principle in relation to railway tariffs. Witte's project comprised the following mutual engagements:

"1) Both parties recognize as desirable the preservation
of the independence of the Chinese empire.

2) Both parties recognize the necessity of respecting
the existing treaties with China separately concluded by
them.

3) In accord with the spirit of the existing trade treaty
between England and Russia, both parties engage, in the
transfer of freight and passengers over railways operated
by them in China, to observe scrupulously the 'most favored nation' principle.

4) Each party, in districts which by virtue of economic
or geographic attraction come under its predominant influence, engages not to establish prohibitory measures
relative to the subjects of the other party.

5) Both parties engage to mutually examine all separate
questions touching railroading in China in which either
party professes its interest and to settle them in a conciliatory sense--in the interests of both.

6) In conformity with point 5, both parties will in relation to any specific road enter into some specific agreement."

It is easily observed that Witte's project was no mere
mechanical combination of the three installments of the English project or formal remodelling of the unilateral "engagement" into a bilateral "agreement," but was essentially designed to remove "the disadvantageous constraint of Russia
in future"[27] ensuing from the English project. Take, for
example, article 2 of the Russian project, binding the English
to respect the rights granted the Chinese Eastern Railway
Company, i.e., including articles 10 and 11 of the concession

which established a customs duty in two-thirds the usual
amount on goods imported or exported by the Chinese Eastern
Railway to and from Russia and tariff autonomy for the road.
Take also articles 3 and 4, formulated too generally to make
it impossible to give them the desired concrete interpretation
later on. And yet Witte's project left Manchuria completely
exposed to future English attempts after the manner of the
question of the Shanhaikwan railway now being composed, or
the Pritchard Morgan enterprise which had as yet come to
nothing. Muravev, in turn, accordingly drew up the following supplementary article ("for combination" with articles 3
and 4 of Witte's project which did not satisfy him:) though
not directly naming Manchuria, this would guard it from the
English:

> "Being convinced that there ought not to exist any anta-
> gonism between them in China, and guided by a desire to
> avoid any cause for conflict on questions where their in-
> terests meet, each of the two negotiating parties engages
> not to intervene in behalf of financial, commercial, eco-
> nomic and more particularly railroading enterprises in
> the region of predominant interests of the other negotiating
> party, and on the other hand not to create obstacles or in
> any way injure enterprises of this sort that the other party
> may possess or that it might wish to conduct in the region
> of its predominant interests. Both Russia and England
> affirm the rights acquired by each of them on the strength
> of private agreements with the Chinese government, and
> promise not to infringe on them."[28]

It is quite evident that Muravev's amendment did not simply return the question to England's September project, merely
avoiding geographical designations, while bringing out the
"region of predominant interests" concept, but also expanded
the purely railroad agreement to a scale approaching the program put forward by Witte in December, 1897. But naturally
it also gave England some protection from the Russians in the
Yangtse area, and Witte pedantically turned down this amendment on the ground that it "would impose a burdensome constraint on Russia in relation to all China."[29] As a result the
English ambassador was now given no answer and a hitch had
again occurred in negotiations.

IV

When, nearly a month later, Sir Charles Scott made inquiry of Muravev as to the fate of his second, November, proposal, he learned that the matter had been reported to the tsar
and that the "report on this question presented by Muravev
and Witte had been attentively read by his majesty, who had
said that since the views of the two ministers on some questions had not of themselves been fully reconciled, he must
invite joint discussion of the question in his presence." At
the same time, "the care which Muravev took to explain" to
the ambassador the "private character of the [Russo-Chinese]
bank caused" him "to suspect that this question had some connection with the difference of opinion between him and Count
Witte which the emperor wished to ascertain and remove."30
Whether such a conference with the tsar occurred, and, if
so, whether the matter was confined to Muravev and Witte
alone remains as yet unknown to us. But that the question of
an agreement at the moment described rested on the question
of support of the Russo-Chinese bank and that this had also
come to the fore in the disagreement within the Russian government there can be no doubt. It can likewise scarcely be
doubted that the tsar did not share Witte's position and was
only kept momentarily from definitely siding with Muravev
by embarassment at Witte's massive allusions to "obligations
to the French banks" and to the fate of Russian credit in France.
Kuropatkin, for example, whom Witte apparently tried to get
on his side, sending him at precisely this time the whole original correspondence on the matter of the agreement, was,
of course, up on the dispute and must have known which way
Nicholas was disposed--and Kuropatkin's reaction to the matter was brief, dry, and definite, being, literally: "have read
with attention. Conclusion: the Russo-Chinese bank has since
last year emphatically been scattering its efforts. Since the
Russian government is answerable for this bank, we may in-
voluntarily be drawn into most unpleasant scandals over concessions on the middle Yangtse (at Hankow,) on the lower
Yangtse (at Chinkiang) or over concessions between Chengting-
fu and Taiyuan-fu. To protect Russian interests in Manchuria,
which adjoins Russia for a thousand versts--this I can understand. But to be obliged to defend with Russian blood the interests of the Russo-Chinese bank on the Yangtse or to the
south of Peking in general is to me an incomprehensible and
disastrous thing for Russia."31

The Russian ambassador in London took approximately
the same attitude on the question, having from the start considered it "a calamity" that "agreements of the Russo-Chinese
bank should make it necessary for us to be firm on a point
where our interests had essentially nothing to gain."[32] Thus,
on the question at issue, Witte found himself practically a
minority of one in the government. Had this been a question
of a Russian private bank or a simple violation of the interests
of the French shareholders in the bank, that would have been
one thing. But Witte had referred to obligations to French
banks, and for the minister of foreign affairs to take upon himself the violation of any obligations to the subjects of an allied
state was not so easy: with such an argument, Witte even in
isolation remained altogether impregnable to Muravev.

And now, to find some exit from the impasse into which
the matter of an absolutely imperative agreement had been
driven, Muravev, "being completely uninformed as to the
tenor of our obligations to the French banks," requested Witte
to apprise him of the "nature" of these obligations.[33] Witte
was "quite prepared" to answer, and it turned out that obligations did exist and that to simply disregard them would be
extremely hazardous: 1) the whole procedure of negotiating
with French bankers about founding the Russo-Chinese bank
proposed by the Russian government had continued at all stages
in an atmosphere of high officialdom and with the participation
of the agencies of the ministry of foreign affairs, 2) by charter,
the bank had "large tasks" to perform, would function throughout China, would be under the patronage of the Russian government, and therefore from the start "gave no future promise of
the casual profits of a small banking office," 3) three members
of the board, without whose assent "no serious question was
settled in Board," "headed very large French houses having
common connections with a whole series of other French
houses and banks and together forming a powerful financial
group doing an extensive business in Russian stocks and devoted to Russian interests," 4) should they learn of a possible
"limiting of the bank's sphere of activity," instead of merging,
for example, with the Shanghai division of the National Discount
Office, "they would prefer to keep their own business" and 5)
in back of all this stood "those small rentiers who are the
chief owners abroad of Russian stocks," and a "damaging rumor about us" "would, besides harming us morally, cause
enormous material losses."[34] And it was impossible for
Muravev to refute this.

The proposal finally made to the English was the result of
a sort of tri-lateral rather than bi-lateral compromise. In
the Russian note of January 26, (old style) 1899 this compromise took the following form: 1) the idea of a line of demarcation, to which Muravev had inclined from the first, was accepted, but this line was drawn at the Great Wall, i.e., embraced not only Manchuria but Mongolia, the absence of which
from Muravev's summer proposals had astonished Witte; [35]
2) in conformity with Witte's idea, the parties made no engagement, with respect to the designated spheres, to refrain from
securing concessions (Russia, in particular, consequently remaining free to support the Russo-Chinese bank in the Yangtse
district) but only obligated themselves "not to obstruct" railway enterprises: England Russia's to the north of the Wall
and Russia England's in the Yangtse basin; 3) though in general meeting England half way by the designation of a dividing
line, and in particular by its designation at the Great Wall and
not at the latitude of Peking, the Russian project on the other
hand made no mention of any Russian obligations respecting
tariffs and imposts. [36]

This third--and last--phase of negotiations was opened by
Russia at a day and hour not of her own choosing but dictated
by the behavior of England. Back on January 12/25, 1899,
Witte had expressed to the English ambassador his "extreme
astonishment" upon learning that Muravev had still not delivered the "final agreement project;" but the project continued
to remain undelivered, until finally on January 25 Witte received
a telegram from London to the effect that on January 23 announcement had there been made of the opening on the 25th of the loan
subscription for building the Newchwang railway " upon security"
of the road. [37] The Hongkong-Shanghai bank was thus entering
upon an operation which back in September the English government had 1) not only dissociated from a mortgage on the road
but even 2) in a general way made contingent on Russia's con-
sent--and Russia now found herself faced by two accomplished
facts. And the inner weakness of her compromise project of
January 26 came out, as was to have been expected, when
England's reply to it arrived (February 22, old style).

The English noted, with some regret, the narrow, exclusively railroad, scale of the Russian project, and while expressing full acquiescence in its adoption as a point of departure,
hastened to explain that this circumstance [i.e., England's adoption of the Russian project] in nowise laid on either of the

negotiating parties any obligation to abstain from competing
for railway concessions in the other's sphere of interests,"
and that they did not suppose "that either Russia or England
would in its own sphere resolve to oppose the solicitations
mentioned" and consequently would only like to have included
in the agreement a "proviso adequately guaranteeing to the
Hongkong-Shanghai bank the construction of the Newchang
railway on the terms provided in the loan contract."[38] Having first let the tsar endorse the English note with his mark
of consent, Muravev, in full consciousness of defeat, then
did not deny himself the satisfaction of underscoring in a letter to Witte that "articles restricting England's pretensions
in the matter of obtaining concessions in the north of China"
(i.e., the amendment proposed to Witte's project by Muravev
on November 23) had been excluded from the Russian project
"in compliance with the desire of the ministry of finance,"--
and in such form the matter was passed on for Witte's conclusion.

It would appear that Witte got his own way within the limits
possible. In this new redaction not a vestige remained of the
provisions "disastrous" to Russian economic interests (the
renunciation of tariff and customs privileges in Manchuria)
or "impossible" in view of "obligations to French banks" (the
renunciation of universal support of the Russo-Chinese bank)
that he had stubbornly opposed admitting into the Russo-English agreement. Nor did it include any "disadvantageous constraints in future," as Witte had all along understood them.
But what had now happened demonstrated that the Russian redaction placed no constraints on England either, even in the
present, let alone in the future. Announced before the conclusion of negotiations, the Hongkong-Shanghai bank's loan
was destined not only for the Shanhaikwan-Newchang line that
had been the object for starting negotiations in July, 1898,
but also for a line to Hsinminting (50 versts from Mukden)
about which Peterburg had only learned from the London loan
prospectus. And the above-noted English interpretation of
the Russian project, as Muravev understood the matter, "left
no doubt of the fact that the government of Great Britain was
endeavoring to reserve in advance the right of railway enterprises in Manchuria."[39]

It thus came about that Russia was now bound to obstruct
no longer the building of English railways even in the "region
of the Chinese Eastern Railway," which had not long since

been specially protected from any such danger by article III
of the Russo-Chinese supplementary protocol of April 25, 1898,
the notorious agreement thus being converted as it were into
an instrument for "subsequent registration" of like English
acts in future as well. Meanwhile England's similar obligation
respecting Russian railways in the Yangtse basin would, at
the given moment, yield Russia precisely nothing of any real
value. And Witte could find no other exit but to draw a line
then and there through the verb "not to obstruct" in Muravev's
letter and write in "not to solicit" (thus falling into the very
trap that he had all along been trying to avoid and had avoided
for six whole months,) since, he admitted, such a redaction
of the project "would be more definite and at the same time
more advantageous from the viewpoint of Russia's interests."[40]
Such was the origin of the text of the so-called "basic note" of
April 16/28, 1899 concerning non-solicitation in its own favor
in the other's district and non-obstruction there by the other
party.[41]

True, Witte still tried to appear cheerful apropos of the
terrible deduction of the English note of February 22 concerning the right of Englishmen to build roads even to the north of
the Wall, "seeing no particularly serious obstacles to it,"
provided article III of the supplementary protocol of April 25,
1898 was not violated. He even proposed to continue to raise
objections to English participation in the building of the Newchwang railway, "not because this road lies to the north of the
Great Wall, but exclusively from the viewpoint of violation of
our agreements with China, since this road traverses the
region of the Chinese Eastern Railway."[42] But the matter of
the so-called "supplementary note" of April 16/28, 1899, where
by the sense both of the September and of the November English
proposals only a proviso concerning the Shanhaikwan-Newchwang
line was to find place, turned out quite badly. It now had also
to include the Hsinminting branch, the English loan on which,
as Muravev now reproached Witte, "had become an accomplished fact" "at the juncture when, in consequence of our declining the original English proposals for an agreement, our
negotiations with the Saint James cabinet threatened to end in
complete failure" and when, on the other hand, the English
were already acquainted with Witte's November counter-project,
"laying no obligation upon England to abstain from competing
for railway concessions not only to the north of Shanhaikwan
but anywhere in Manchuria."[43]

And from the Hsinminting branch had sprouted yet a third proviso "of the supplementary note" concerning Russia's right "to support Russian subjects and institutions in the solicitation of concessions for railways" "from the main Manchurian line" "to the southwest" through the region of English branches. This proviso was proposed and edited by Witte himself with a view to eliminating England's possible direct opposition to connection of the Chinese Eastern Railway with Peking, not "in future" (the words "dans l'avenir" were struck out of the text at Witte's request,) but here and now; and Witte simultaneously proposed that Muravev "obtain from the Chinese government an agreement to grant the Chinese Eastern Railway Company a concession for a railway to Peking."[44]

And so, after describing a sort of circle, Russian diplomacy arrived in the agreement of April 16/28 at practically the same point from which it had started in July-September, 1898. It won on the question of its treaty preferences in Manchuria and lost on the question of south-Manchurian branches. But the "disastrous" and "impossible" had returned to the final text of the agreement at the last moment--by a stroke of Witte's pencil. Russia was pledged "not to solicit on her own account or in favor of Russian subjects or others any railway concessions in the basin of the Yangtse:" this "or others," absent from all previous redactions of the agreement, exhaustively "forestalled" for Russia "any possibility of evading the fulfillment of its terms," inter alia, even in relation to French stockholders of the Russo-Chinese bank. Russia was neatly retired beyond the Great Wall, but on the other hand also obtained for the first time the international-legal recognition of her sphere of interests in all Manchuria (and Mongolia) from her greatest enemy. Russian policy in China was thus confronted not only by a barrier but also by a task strictly localized territorially.

Russia's lack of success in the clash with England over the loan to China in January, 1898, attended at the time by renunciation of monopolies in Manchuria and Mongolia, did not keep Witte, as we see, from a second attempt to compete with English imperialism on the territory of all China. In a brief space of time, Witte passed unhesitatingly from a monopolistic policy in Russia's sphere of influence to an open door policy outside this sphere, subjectively appearing, at first glance, as a sacrifice to the national duality of that banking neoplasm without which Russia could now not get along in China at all. Though

now for a second time forced to retreat before England to the
boundaries of just that sphere where he had suffered defeat
in January, 1898, Witte was evidently still disinclined to be
strictly limited by it, and, immediately after introducing into the supplementary note of April 16/28, 1899 the proviso
concerning Russian "south-western" Manchurian lines, on
April 17, ordered the representative of the Chinese Eastern
Railway in Peking to demand of the Chinese government in the
name of the Chinese Eastern Railway Company a concession
to build and exploit a railway to Peking from some point on
the trunk-line.[45]

Backed without particular enthusiasm by Muravev, who
naturally figured that "any complication in our relations with
China was extremely undesirable, and the more we restricted
our demands upon China the better it would be all round under
given political circumstances," this demand, in conjunction
with the agreement of April 16, 1899, set a new ordeal to
the policy of "friendship with China,"[46] for the third time (in
3 years). Even Li Hung-chang spoke openly of the partition
of China having come to pass.[47] But the new railway demand
now thrust upon the Chinese government partly as compensation
for its violation of pledges to Russia, partly for the good of
China's own interests, but supported by neither warlike nor
"peaceful" means, met with obstinate opposition from the Chinese and a request that China be left to look after her own
interests.[48] Nonetheless it was not withdrawn but held in
reserve by a pledge now obtained from China not to grant elsewhere the building of a railway "from Peking in a northerly
or northeasterly direction to the Russian border" and was included by Witte in Russia's future program as a direct continuation of the Manchurian railway construction plan, timed for
1902.[49]

From the viewpoint of Russo-English relations in the Far
East, the agreement of April 16 was known to be only a temporary measure postponing for no great length of time and, rebus
sic stantibus, even only up to a definitely determinable date,
the clash between the two in Chihli province. In respect to
China, it was one of the last of the impacts which, starting
in 1895, had with gathering speed produced their ruinous effect on the "integrity" and "inviolability" of the Chinese empire, and which along with the Boxer uprising brought her government to a state of "covert" war against foreign "features."

V

The agreement of April 16, it is true, "made a very bad impression on the French minister [in Peking]" but, despite Witte's threats of calamity, had no repercussion on the fortunes of Russian credit in the French market and apparently did not even "injure" Russia "morally" in the opinion of the "petty French rentiers."[50] And the stir raised by Witte over the Russo-Chinese bank, holding up Russo-English negotiations for nine full months, is perhaps not so much to be explained by Russia's compulsory solicitude about the interests of French share-holders in the bank as by the self-interestedness of the Russian share-holders. The truth is that only a few days before Muravev began his negotiations with the London cabinet concerning the demarcation of railway spheres in China, Witte had finished putting through a certain measure respecting the Russo-Chinese bank, undertaken in view of the fact that "the successful development" of its "activity" for the two and a half years and its "fully consolidated position in China" rendered it "capable of entering with success the field of railway building in China, side by side with foreign banks and syndicates." At the end of June, 1898 "in view of the bank's rapidly increasing needs for working capital," Witte confirmed the bank's decision as to a second issue of 12,000 shares and bought up the whole issue for the state treasury, which thus became owner of 16,2000 shares out of a total of 60,000 (i.e., more than 25 per cent). Besides this, Witte at the same time put through at a general meeting of the bank's stock-holders a supplement to the charter specifying confirmation of all members of the Board of the bank by the minister of finance.

It is perfectly obvious that with this provision the bank's transition to railway building and financing in the region between the Yangtse and Peking did not now get its support from the initiative of the French group of share-holders, but rested its full weight on the responsibility of the Russian government, which had "definitively consolidated the finance ministry's influence on the direction of the activity" of the bank.[51] Evidently Witte had here succumbed to the temptation to enter at his own risk the game of international interests in middle China, unrestrained by fear of the political risk connected with it, and had at this point, as in 1897, confronted Russian diplomacy with an unexpected fait accompli. In this connection the whole episode of the 1898-1899 negotiations takes on a somewhat different meaning from the one that Witte was always trying to give it; a different aspect is assumed both by the obstinacy that he showed in the course of negotiations and the ease with which at the last moment he himself relinquished his position, not only without asking the French members of the Board of the bank but even without so much as once mentioning them again.

With the English, Witte had been satisfied to argue from the "independence" of the bank and the impossibility of the government's violating its charter; but, as we have seen, the argument from French interests and the fortunes of Russian credit was the only one unassailable to Witte's antagonists in the Russian government at this moment. Thus the defeat that Witte met on the paths of his own diplomacy was essentially a defeat into which he led the Russian government, as a stockholder that had just invested in the Russo-Chinese bank very nearly three million rubles to make good its expansion to the south of Peking and sustain Russian railway building there.

In Chinese governmental circles it was understood that England had by the agreement of April 16 "got everything that she wanted even in Manchuria, while Russia could not even defend her Shansi railroad."[52] For Russian governmental leadership it would now have been absurd to continue a trans-mural enterprise begun through the bank, since it had now lost the ability to support it there diplomatically. Some evidence exists that the Russian directorate of the bank did endeavor to pull the bank out of the Shansi enterprise, and that Witte attempted to do this in such a way as to restore through banking agreements the south-Manchurian sector of the Russian front where the English had broken through in the agreement of April 16.

This attempt was associated with Pokotilov's coming to Peterburg for the examination of a number of questions that had arisen for the bank and the Chinese Eastern Railway out of conditions created by the new agreement, and got no farther than preliminary negotiations through Pokotilov and Tsigler (both members of the Board of the International bank), the Belgian Koch, who was afterwards to get into communication with his "friends in London." Russia proposed to buy up the loan given the Hongkong-Shanghai bank by the Chinese government in January, 1899, along with all rights accruing to the bank in the south-Manchurian line, on the understanding that the Russian government: 1) would give up building the direct Manchuria-Peking line, 2) would without fail build the line

from Shanhaikwan to Newchwang and would not employ differential rates on it, 3) would leave in the hands of the Chinese
administration the line from Shanhaikwan to Peking and not
lay it wide gauge, and 4) would concede the Shansi line to the
English.

Such an exchange of railway enterprises, in exact conformity with the basic note of April 16 and in complete abrogation
of the supplementary note of the same date, would cost the
Russian government, by Pokotilov's calculation, not more
than the nominal sum of the English loan (2,300,000 pounds
sterling,) since its bonds, under the influence of the Russian
demand for the Peking line, had managed to drop from 97 to
92, and an 8 per cent premium would fully satisfy holders of
the loan.[53] But the demand for the Peking line, held over only
temporarily and secured by the Russo-Chinese agreement of
May 20-June 5, 1899, also gave China the idea of buying up
the English loan secured by the south-Manchurian line as the
only effectual means of saving China from the virtual transfer
of Peking "to the hands of the Russian government" and the
"frightful compensations" that would "at once" be demanded
by all the rest of the powers.[54]

While profoundly confidential negotiations of the most preliminary sort were going on with Koch in Peterburg, Rothstein
in Ishl received a call from our acquaintance Grot, who had
come "at Li Hung-chang's behest to have a talk with him respecting the desire of the Chinese to buy out the English in
some way, the Chinese government [being] prepared, apparently, even to make financial sacrifices in the form of payment of the requisite premium to the English syndicate, provided they could get us to renounce the projected direct line
to Peking." This proposal of the Chinese would not only reduce
the cost of the Russian operation considerably but, in Rothstein's opinion, would also open up to Russia a new opportuni-
ty--"to demand more favorable terms in the sense of control
and participation in the administration of the railroad than
those that the Chinese had given the English."[55] But, though
projected to the mutual satisfaction of Russia and China, this
combination did not come off--apparently in view of non-agree-
ment on the part of the English. The English preferred to
retain the approach to the old Manchurian port on the gulf of
Pechili as an outpost on Russia's road to Peking. And a source
of possible Anglo-Russian conflict in future remained unremoved.

The Boxer uprising, striking in the summer of 1900 all the imperialistic powers in the deserted apartments of Peking palaces, brought out this and certain other fateful conflicts that greatly accelerated Russia's progress toward a military denouement of her Manchurian policy.

Chapter V

"TEMPORARY" OCCUPATION OF ALL MANCHURIA
1900-1902

I

Chinese events of the year 1900 overtook Russia in Manchuria when the colossal construction operations she had there
undertaken were in full swing. Railroad work, started simultaneously in five directions somewhat over two years before
(from Harbin to the south, east and west, and to Harbin from
Port Arthur and Nikolsk-on-Ussuri,) embraced about 1,300
versts of line, not counting station roads and temporary cir-
cuits; the river Sungari was in process of being made navi-
gable for the carrying of construction materials to the wharf
at Harbin, now transformed from a small hamlet to a huge
urban center; by sea, the construction administration of the
road had set up its own steamship line (13 ships), and capital
building operations had been inaugurated at the ports of Vladivostok, Newchwang, and Dalny, which were first treated as
warehousing points for construction materials and bulky railway inventory; work had been completed on the requisition of
lands (about 30 square versts) for the spaciously planned new
city of Dalny, having porto-franco rights; the colonization of
the zone of the road, not only by Russian laborers and employees and the frontier guard (totalling 6,000,) but in part
by natives, in part by immigrant Chinese (c. 60,000,) had so
far progressed as to call for the introduction of special organs of judicial administration (the chao-she-chui) to regulate
the mutual relations of newcomers and native population in the
territory of the road, these being maintained at the Chinese
Eastern Railway Company's expense; branches of the Russo-
Chinese bank spread to Harbin, Kirin, Mukden, Port Arthur,
Newchwang, drawing into their turnover the upper brackets
of local economic activity; exploitation of the Yantai and
Wafandan coal fields for the needs of the road, and the laying
of branches from them to the main south-Manchurian line, got
under way, etc., etc. The vast region stirred with a new life,
which with each succeeding day inevitably enhanced Russia's
chances in the future fortunes of Manchuria. [1]

173

Looking back over the road travelled during the past five-year period (1895-1899,) the Russian ministry of finance was moved to take stock of the correlative extent of Russia's participation in the world's colonial expenditures in general and in Far Eastern expenditures in particular. And it was revealed that "from the time of the Japano-Chinese war, Russia's extraordinary expenditures in the Far East" to 1899 inclusive aggregated 1,442 million rubles as against 379,760 million rubles spent by England (in part conjointly with Germany), and 225,562 million rubles of French investments in Chinese loans.[2] For certain Chinese Eastern Railway Company enterprises, this constituted only half the sum total of expenditures envisaged, the remote recovery of which depended entirely on conditions surrounding the exploitation of these enterprises within the confines of a complicated international situation that by no means promised smooth going in the Middle empire itself to begin with, and that had by the very end of the five year period produced a new and vigorous pretendant to Chinese markets in the person of America.

Having made a victorious end of the war with Spain, by the Paris treaty of December 10, 1898, the United States of America assumed her post at the sick man's bedside from the Philippines, and in September, 1899 demanded formal recognition by the powers of the "open door" principle, "guaranteed the United States by her treaties with China."[3] The government of the States on its part recognized the existing "spheres of interest" of individual powers, but relative to these spheres demanded of the respective governments a declaration: 1) that they would not "interfere with the rights of any treaty port or with vested interests" in their spheres, 2) that the existing Chinese customs tariff should be universally applied regardless of the nationality of the merchandise to be taxed, and 3) that railway tariffs and shipping duties in these spheres should be uniform for all nationalities and not higher than on that nationality's own goods. For Russia in particular such a demand meant an assault on the terms of the contract of August 27, 1896 and was bound to reduce her role to that of a carrier of foreign goods within the confines of Manchuria and nothing more.

At the same time, as above noted, for this assault the Russian government was by no means unprepared nor was such a possibility unforeseen: American capital had at short intervals thrice before tried courteously knocking at the doors of Man-

churia in search of railway concessions, setting itself no
less a goal than to monopolize the building of the whole Chinese railway network--a plan on which all that had been done
by 1900 was to clean out the reserve capital in the amount of
18 million rubles for financing one line, from Hankow to Canton.[4] Although the American demands related to the whole
area of China, still the third point of the American note of
September 6/18, 1899 actually contained the covert proposal
for a "neutralization" of the railroads of Manchuria, these
being at the given moment the only foreign railways in China,
and therefore acquired a sense specifically hostile to Russia.

The real point of this aspect of the American proposal escaped Muravev and likewise the Russian ambassador in Washington (Count Cassini,) both of whom reacted favorably to the
opportunity for here winning America's recognition of Manchuria as a Russian "sphere of interest" close on the heels
of England's. But to Witte the matter was at once suspect
and after waiting to ascertain the answers of the other powers
he proposed that Muravev reply: "1) that in respect to territory leased to the Russian government Russia's trade policy
was in point of fact an "open door" policy, as was evident
from the granting to Dalny of porto-franco rights, 2) that in
case the city of Dalny should in future be isolated from the
rest of the leased territory by a customs barrier, customs
duties were to be levied at the latter at a uniform rate for
all foreign goods, and 3) that in ports opened to foreign trade
by the Chinese government in parts of China not under Russian leasehold--questions of customs levies and port duties
were regulated by the Chinese government, and,that the Russian government did not purpose to seek any exceptional privileges for her subjects in this respect as compared with other
foreigners."[5]

From this projected answer of Witte's to the Americans,
the question of railway tariffs was, as we see, entirely omitted, since renunciation of the tariff autonomy given Russia in
Manchuria by the contract of August 27, 1896 and the convention of March 15, 1898, would, he thought--1) "deprive us of
a privilege having essential significance for our economic
interests in the Far East," 2) would not be compensated by a
like renunciation on the part of other powers respecting China
Proper, where the "main hauls will always be made for the
most part by water," and "Russian import trade will hardly
achieve large development in the immediate future." And

Russia's answering note of December 18/30, 1899 to the United States repeated almost verbatim Witte's project of the 14th.[6] The renunciation of Russia's railway and customs tariff privileges in Manchuria, Witte considered possible, "under pressure of extreme necessity," provided the powers "desiring to continue to profit by the special advantages that are reserved to...the Chinese Eastern Railway Company" "likewise participated in the enormous material expenditures" that Russia was under and would still continue to be under for the whole complex of railway enterprises in Manchuria.[7]

So it was Witte himself who first virtually formulated, when confronted by American pretensions, (and as yet quite theoretically) the problem of the commercial neutralization of Manchuria for which America was to come forward with a solution in 1909, at a moment when the Russian government was itself prepared to unload the Chinese Eastern Railway through pre-term redemption. In this question Russia was, thus, at the very end of the five-year period, meeting face to face the danger that she had thrice had occasion to avert by an agreement and which now, at Witte's instance, Russian diplomacy decided to outflank by a mere act of silence. This only postponed the conflict and did not decrease the risk of any future inclination on the part of Russian diplomacy to deviate from a strictly conservative policy in Manchuria.

Needless to say, such a policy was also dictated by those shocks on the economic home front with which the year 1899 had opened: by the beginning of 1900 the financial and industrial crisis, no matter how stoutly denied in the official press, was a fact, and indirect recognition of this fact was perhaps bespoken in the Russian government's flat refusal in January, 1900 to take advantage in any aggressive way of England's embarassment in the Boer War or "secure any appropriate compensations" linked with the allocation of special credits or an increase in the war and navy budgets.[8] But even back in the summer of 1899, immediately after the Russo-English agreement, there is noticeable in Witte's answers to Pokotilov, who was trying to get definite instructions respecting the future course of road and bank policy in China, a constraint about making decisions and a reluctance to anticipate the future course of events.[9]

It was, finally, impossible not to see that since the middle of 1898 everything even in China had been progressively shaping up to Russia's disadvantage. Discontent among the masses,

passing over into open rebellion against foreigners in the
spring of 1900, had paralleled the growing influence of England
and particularly of Japan on the Peking government, then in
the throes of convulsive searches for an exit from the pitiable
position to which the Manchu dynasty had sunk under the blows
of 1895-1898.[10] With Li Hung-chang's dismissal from the
central government and quasi-exile to the governor-general-
ship of Kwantung, Russia's real point of appui in Peking, even
for her Manchurian enterprise, had vanished and the strand
been broken that had in its time linked the fortunes of the road
with the apartments of the Empress Tzu Hsi.[11] Meanwhile,
precisely at the start of 1900, "certain hints" had begun to
reach Peterburg "concerning the approach of the date" for renewing this link and paying the second million rubles as stipulated in point two of the bank protocol of May 23, 1896.[12]
Peterburg was of course not going to break the old promise,
but neither did it hurry with the payment, resolving to postpone
it until Witte's own journey to the Far East, scheduled for
1901.

The Boxer uprising, attended by serious demolition practically all along the Manchurian road delayed this operation and
gave formal cause for annulling the obligation itself. And, as
with the first million in the summer of 1897, so now it was
proposed that the second million be given "another signification." The new international political situation tempted Witte
to pile on an additional load this time as well. But, this time
as well, complete and still more bitter failure awaited Witte's
try at diplomacy. Except that now, Lamsdorf having replaced
Muravev in June, 1900, Witte succeeded in actually taking control of the official diplomatic machinery and until his final diplomatic defeat in 1902 was virtually little less than tsar. For
the next two years Peterburg's "prehensile" instincts could
thus retreat before the triumphant "peace" policy, stripped
this time of so much as a sign of any double diplomacy.

II

When, at the middle of May, 1900, the whole diplomatic
corps and foreign colony in Peking, numbering not less than
1,000 persons, found themselves entirely without protection
under immediate threat of mobbing by the Boxers and perhaps
even by the regular Chinese troops, when (on May 15/28) railway communication between Peking and Tientsin was cut and

on May 22 (June 4) the ministers demanded that their governments "take measures for their relief," and the party in power
at the Chinese court was plainly a group of Boxer sympathisers
headed by Prince Tsun, Peterburg could no longer doubt that
"only the speedy advent of a strong detail could save the foreigners in Peking," that "the ministers could do no more"
and that the "admirals" of the handful of foreign ships berthed
at Taku "must take over."[13]

The shore detail hastily formed by the English Admiral
Seymour and dispatched to Peking on May 30/June 11, was so
negligible (about 2,000 men) and the panic in Peking so great,
that a "mandatory appeal" for the immediate dispatch of a
shore detail from Port Arthur, where Russia kept a garrison
of 12,000 men, was sent by no less than the English minister,
who would, presumably, be least inclined of all to admit Russian military power to Peking. And on May 25 Muravev suggested that Nicholas authorize the dispatch to Tientsin of a
Russian detail of 4,000, in part "to avert the danger of Japanese or other foreign troops being summoned to the defense."[14]
But it soon became plain that "events in China were assuming
an extremely dangerous character," that action could not be
restricted to a mere "safeguarding of the life and property of
the imperial mission's members and Christians residing in
Peking," and that foreign armed intervention would be confronted by the task of "suppressing a spreading revolt, of co-
ercing and wrestling with government armies, that was almost
tantamount to opening hostilities against China,"--and on
June 4 Muravev and Nicholas, taking as a point of departure
"the profound conviction that Russia's task in the East is absolutely at variance with the policy of the European states,"
made the following decision: 1) "on no account" to seek the
command of the combined detail for Russia and 2) "without
disruption of concerted action with the other European detachments," to limit the task of the Russian detachment of 4,000
to "safeguarding the security of the mission, defending the
life and property of Russian subjects" and "supporting legitimate authority in its struggle with revolution," on the supposition that the presence of the Russian detachment "would
prevent the powers' embarking on any political undertakings
without our consent."[15] This formula, preempting for Russia
in the Peking operation the role of secondary, rank-and-file
participant and watchful observer, was likewise adopted entire
by Muravev's successor Lamsdorf. Russian diplomacy had

no desire whatsoever of "hampering" its "freedom of action,"
and from the very start set itself, independently of the other
powers, the task of "renewing friendly relations" as soon as
possible with the Manchu dynasty's government.[16]

It might be all very well to seek solace at the time, as
Nicholas did, in the thought that the hatred of the Chinese
"masses" was directed against western-European missionaries
("these gentlemen are the root of all evil") and "shameless"
"commercial tyrannies" screened by the "holy name of Christ,"
or assert, as Witte did later on, in spite of the manifest fact,
that until "we mounted the expedition against Peking" (which
started on July 23, old style,) "all was quiet in Manchuria"
(where the determined general attack on the road began on
June 21)--but the basic fact had from the outset been obvious
to the Russian government in its full force: the unfinished
Manchurian railway, with 60,000 half alien Chinese laborers,
1,300 versts long, with a distributed guard of 4-1/2 thousand
men, virtually remained open to attack at times and places
quite impossible to determine in advance. And the thought
that support of the Chinese administrative machinery might
avert or localize the danger of demolition of the road by Boxers
played no small part in the Russian government's taking the
position above described. Of the fact that the seizure of the
Taku ports by foreigners on June 4/17 had brought on the overt
transition of the Peking government to official war propaganda
against all foreigners (the orders of June 8/21) Peterburg was
not apprised before June 20, and for a time the task of getting
at the local Manchurian administration, or even the government in Peking, may still have appeared capable of accomplishment.[17]

Hope that all was not yet lost reached Peterburg on June 14,
the very day when the first serious Boxer attack occurred in
Manchuria, on the road at Liaoyang:[18] by telegram of June 13/
26 from Canton, Li Hung-chang informed Witte that he had received imperial summons to an audience in Peking and asked
him to "give enlightened counsels" "which would aid [him] to
get out of this difficult position." Li Hung-chang in his capacity as "intimate adviser to the empress" Tzu Hsi--Russian
diplomacy could even have imagined nothing better, and from
this moment Russian diplomacy resolutely placed its stake on
Li Hung-chang. As before, on like occasions, Ukhtomsky was
set in motion and that same day two telegrams were sent to
the old man: one from Witte, promising not to declare war on

China and to give Li Hung-chang the full support of the Russian government and Russian armies if he would keep peace
in Manchuria through Chinese authorities and take measures
to safeguard mission and Russian subjects in Peking, the
second from Ukhtomsky, promising to come to China for an
interview in July.[19] And on June 15, "with a view to maintaining friendly relations with the local Chinese administration," Witte hastily opened for the chief engineer of the Chinese Eastern Railway "preliminary credit in the amount of
100,000 lan apiece for each of the three provinces of Manchuria" and authorized him to make the Chinese authorities
a sort of deposit, "promising to give them the rest if they
prevented rebellion against the road and its agents and put a
stop to disorders where they arose."[20] And finally, on
June 18, Witte had been able to communicate to the tsar,
along with Li Hung-chang's answering telegram, that for the
present at least [underscored in the original] it would be detrimental to introduce our troops into Manchuria," and had
asked "not to have the war department send troops to the pre-
cincts of the Chinese Eastern Railway Company" "without my
[Witte's] request."[21]

Needless to say, Peterburg entertained no illusions respecting an infallibly peaceful turn of events in Manchuria, and
even Witte himself had since the first of June been feverishly
reinforcing the guard of the road, augmenting it numerically
to 11,000 men by the moment of the opening of actual hostilities
forming artillery divisions besides, and trying to get the war
office to concede him petty officers on unlimited leave from the
mobilized Amur district.[22] But when the idea that it might in
some way be possible to avert an attack on the road proved un-
tenable, and Chinese troops in conjunction with Boxers demolished more than 200 versts of the south-Manchurian line
(June 22-24,) Witte himself requested the introduction of regular troops throughout the territory of the road, and, at times
susceptible to battle frenzy, counselled "greater troop con-
centrations in case of need." On this occasion he found "the
chief trouble" "in our unpreparedness," in the fact that "the
Siberian road is not as yet completed, nor the Manchurian
road as yet altogether completed while commercial fleet we
have none," whereas "100-150 thousand troops, if we had them
on the spot, would demolish it [China]."[23] And, slowly but
surely, Manchuria had by the end of September, 1900, as
even Nicholas now desired, "been permeated by our troops

from north to south," and by them occupied in its entirety.[24]

As can now be precisely established, at the very moment when the "peace" formula adopted by Russian diplomacy back in Muravev's time had palpably suffered shipwreck in Manchuria, it underwent a very fleeting test in the Peking theatre as well. On June 26, Witte's request had been followed by an order for the introduction of Russian troops into Manchuria; on the 29th, Lamsdorf was astounded by a bellicose thrust from Kuropatkin, who now talked "of the importance for Russia of an advance for the purpose of polishing off Peking" and proposed "that the general leadership of the detachments of all the powers be entrusted to Admiral Alekseyev."[25] Until then, Kuropatkin had functioned in complete solidarity with the other two ministers: his confidential communication of June 17/30 to the German military attache in Peterburg had, for example, even served to disillusion the German government as to the possibility of counting on the serious participation of Russian troops in the Peking campaign, a disillusionment all the more harrowing for Berlin in that only the day before, June 16/29, Wilhelm had declined to support Salisbury's proposal for summoning to the Peking theatre a Japanese army corps of 30,000, thinking to earn thereby the gratitude of the Peterburg cabinet.[26] Kuropatkin declared that Russia did not intend to "snatch" other people's "chestnuts from the fire" in Chihli province, and the Germans had at once sensed in this the familiar Lamsdorf-Witte "argument," the more so since the conversation with the attache occurred immediately after Witte had called on Kuropatkin.[273]

It is easy enough to conjecture that the purpose of this call made by Witte on June 17, the eve of his report to the tsar on the possibilities that had suddenly opened up for the Russian government in connection with Li Hung-chang's appearance on the scene and Ukhtomsky's forthcoming meeting with him, was to acquaint Kuropatkin with these news items and compromise with him the question of postponement of the military invasion of Manchuria, the postponement for which he asked Nicholas on the 18th. The Germans also took in essentially the same sense the declaration that Kuropatkin made to the military agent on June 22/July 4. Kuropatkin was on this occasion noticeably more amiable, no longer mentioned chestnuts, and did not in general negate the possibility of Russia's marching on Peking, but maintained that this undertaking was still premature in two respects: 1) the Russian (and

foreign) forces concentrated at Tientsin were insufficient for
an advance on Peking, therefore Alekseyev's immediate task
was to seize Tientsin and restore railway communication between Taku and Tientsin, and "in seven days time" when the
16 battalions from Vladivostok arrived to reinforce Port Arthur, then and "only then would the tsar decide according to
the circumstances the question of assignment of these forces
and of a possible attack on Peking," it being necessary to
bear in mind that "our interests are chiefly concentrated in
Manchuria, to keep which area under control will possibly require great sacrifices on our part," and 2) Russian participation in the Peking operations is impossible under English,
Japanese, or American command, while Prince Heinrich of
Prussia, "who would most naturally assume chief command"
is not at present in the locality. [28]

     This meant that Kuropatkin 1) was, under plausible pre-
texts, postponing the decision of the question of the Peking
expedition, 2) was making it wholly contingent on the Manchurian operation, and 3) was in full accord with Nicholas's
original decision of June 4, closing to himself the possibility
of demanding the appointment of a Russian chief in command
by himself offering this post to the Germans. The courtesy
implied in this demarche did not suffice to gloss over the
generally unfavorable impression made on the Germans by
Kuropatkin's words, and Berlin now began discussing whether
it might not be well to revert to the Japanese proposal just
refused. [29] It was in any event plain to the Germans that Russia was prepared to sacrifice the fate of ministers and foreigners in Peking to considerations of "higher policy," and
that the latter consisted in preserving her own "freedom of
action," which, side by side with refusal to participate in the
Peking expedition, might, in the event of a favorable turn of
affairs in Manchuria, even express itself in a volte face of
Russian war power to some separate action on the Peking
front: what Kuropatkin had said left room even for such dangers. [30]

     To correctly evaluate Kuropatkin's above act of courtesy,
it will be necessary to recall that June 22/July 4 was the very
day when Peterburg received official word of the murder of
Von Kettler, the German minister, in the streets of Peking
and of Wilhelm's "bellicose" demand for "exemplary chastisement and vengeance" on the Chinese and a triumphant advance
upon Peking for this purpose. [31] Kuropatkin's offer of the

chief command to Heinrich of Prussia was supposed to gild
the pill that was in different terms being simultaneously ad-
ministered to Germany both by Kuropatkin through the military agent and by Lamsdorf through Osten-Saken. Lamsdorf's telegram of condolence to Berlin of this same date,
June 22/July 4, did not contain a word of encouragement respecting the punitive expedition against Peking, did not mention Peking at all, but fully expressed the hope that, "notwithstanding the warlike tone of the emperor's words," Germany's
policy toward China would "in no wise" be altered, and gave
notice that before confirming its readiness to " proceed in full
accord with Germany," Russia would "first need to be convinced" that Wilhelm 1) would resist "any alteration of the
statu quo in China" or "any attempt at partition of the Celestial Empire," 2) would bend his efforts, "along with Russia,"
toward restoring a central government capable of maintaining
order in the country, and 3) despite all the manifestations of
anarchy, would not declare war on a "legitimate" Chinese government "powerless to wrestle with the revolt."[32]
    Small wonder that Wilhelm's rage knew no bounds and that,
taken together, the simultaneous declarations of Kuropatkin
and Lamsdorf sounded to him like "unprecedented double-
talk" (Zweizüngigkeit) and "cynicism": for what had they in
common? --Lamsdorf's invocations against the partition of
China, and Kuropatkin's anxiety about "controlling" Manchuria,
upon which control even the Peking expedition and the fate of
Peking residents were made contingent.[33] For Wilhelm no
doubt existed that he was here dealing, not with contradicitions
springing from a functional disorder in the Russian diplomatic
machinery, but with a unified policy resolutely pursuing its
own, and only its own, ends. After weighing the situation,
Wilhelm (June 26/July 8) went on to assert that Russia was
solely preoccupied with Manchuria and was evading the Peking
expedition not only for lack of troops but also in the hope of
entering Peking without violence in the capacity of savior of
China; and this was later corroborated from Peterburg (July 5/
18) by Radolin's assertion that Russia looked upon Chihli
province and Peking as part of her sphere of interests and
would therefore make every effort to avert even a temporary
occupation of this region by foreign troops and only move
when it became plain to her that the others had enough troops
to get along without her.[34]
    Kuropatkin's sudden declaration of June 29 as to "the im-

portance for Russia of an advance for the purpose of polishing
off Peking," and the necessity of her getting the chief command into her own hands, was not only "completely at variance" "with the elementary assumptions professed...in all
circular notices to foreign powers," but at the given moment
--should Nicholas accede to it--also threatened to ruin Witte's
attempt to come to an agreement with the Peking government,
separately from the others, through Ukhtomsky and Li Hung-
chang. After the taking of Tientsin (June 30) the question of
whether to go on to Peking or not automatically intruded itself,
and disagreement within the Russian government took on a
quite practical signification.

It can hardly be doubted that Kuropatkin had counted on
success with Nicholas or had even been gratifying the tsar's
wish; and there were a few days when matters almost got to
the point of Lamsdorf's retirement. But by persistence Witte
succeeded in obtaining (July 13 and 14) the postponement of the
Peking expedition until such time as it should have been definitely ascertained that "no other measures would bring about
peace."[35] And the next day, July 15, Witte was already making good use of the telegram (of the 13/26th) just received
from Li Hung-chang which had said that "if Ukhtomsky would
agree to come as soon as possible," he, Li Hung-chang,
"might be able to arrange with him as to some effectual means
for saving the situation,"--and suggested that the tsar let Li
Hung-chang have a Russian war-ship for the voyage to Taku-
Peking.[36] We are uninformed as to the "oral considerations"
respecting Ukhtomsky's journey that Witte communicated to
Nicholas in his off-the-record report of Sunday, July 16, but
they undoubtedly carried weight, and on the 18th all was ready
on the financial side for Ukhtomsky's journey.[37]

Of the success of Russian diplomacy's "separate" course
it is also possible to judge from the fact that Delcasse's proposal, received in Peterburg the next day, July 19/August 1,
to come to Peterburg in person to discuss the "Chinese problem" and the "conclusion of a highly stable alliance between
Paris and Peterburg" capable of "exerting an enormous influence on the majority decision of the powers" was politely
declined--"until such time as the many uncertainties of the
current moment shall have given place to a somewhat more
settled situation." As Lamsdorf explained to Nicholas, "it
would be awkward to bind Russia in advance by a promise of
full community of action with any power whatsoever," since,

on the other hand, by Admiral Alekseyev's avowal, "a rapid
movement on Peking was" in any case "quite impossible,"
and, on the other, "it was difficult to give even an approxi-
mate answer" to the questions: 1) "what proposals would Li
Hung-chang make to us through the medium of Prince Ukhtomsky, dispatched at his urgent request?" and 2) "might not
occasion offer for the imperial representative, Russian subjects and shore detail to get safely out of Peking before any
other foreigners?"[38] And finally the "separate" course apparently scored complete triumph when Nicholas gave his
consent to Wilhelm's proposal to appoint as commander-in-
chief of the united forces Field Marshal Waldersee (July 24/
August 6).[39] On this day Nicholas finally confirmed Lamsdorf in the office of director of the ministry of foreign affairs
and "dampened Kuropatkin's ardor by declaring that it would
not do to hurry the march on Peking," and in general Witte
felt that "a salutary change had occurred."[40]

What occurred a week later, on August 1/14--the entry
into Peking of a united detachment 20,000 strong--can in no
event have helped signifying a modification of the separate
course or, objectively, have failed to disconcert the Witte-
Lamsdorf plans. In the first place, they themselves, while
welcoming the assignment of the chief command to Germany,
were not at all desirous of having the Peking business drag
on until Waldersee's arrival and turn into a savage "pogrom."
In the second place, the French, too, after very nearly refusing to recognize Waldersee, had yielded only when "Lamsdorf whispered in their ear that nothing would come of this
command, since before his arrival with his troops either we
shall have reached Peking or the Chinese government will have
put in an appearance and negotiations have got started," i.e.,
Russian diplomacy even preferred in a way the hastening of
the Peking expedition, provided it forestalled the arrival of
Waldersee.[41]

Finally, there are no grounds for ascribing to Russian
initiative this "premature" movement of the united detail.[42]
Certain symptoms of aggressive and "prehensile" moods
manifest in Nicholas and Kuropatkin in connection with the
news of the taking of Peking were caught in time by Witte and
Lamsdorf and isolated behind decisions made in accordance
with their wishes at the palace conference of August 12, 1900:
1) respecting the evacuation of Manchuria, "immediately
settled order shall have been restored [there] and all neces-

sary measures taken for safeguarding" the Chinese Eastern
Railway, "unless, however, the conduct of other powers shall
constitute an obstacle of this," and 2) respecting the immediate removal of the Russian mission and Russian troops from
Peking to Tientsin and our readiness to enter into negotiations
with the lawful Chinese government "as soon as" it "shall have
resumed the reins of government."[43] Respecting China proper,
so far as is known, no further disagreements within the Russian government arose, the withdrawal of troops from Peking
started at the end of August, and by the time of Waldersee's
arrival (October 4/17, 1900) there were no Russian troops in
the Peking theatre to participate in those international punitive
expeditions which did not cease until April, 1901.[44]

As we see, to have counted on Ukhtomsky's reunion with
Li Hung-chang taking place in advance of the liquidation of
the siege of the foreign embassies in Peking proved as great
a mistake as to have counted on the possibility of avoiding
hostilities in Manchuria through Li Hung-chang's intervention.
Yet on this occasion the proposal for a withdrawal of troops
from Peking that Russia made to all the powers in a note of
August 12, 1900 was still calculated for the same diplomatic
effect: to set Russia apart, in the eyes of the Chinese government, from the rest of the foreign governments, all of which,
as was to have been expected (and as Peterburg probably
hoped) France not excepted, came out against subscribing to
the Russian proposal.[45] This proposal must have seemed all
the more suspect in that it had been preceded (August 3/16)
by a protest from Russia against the decision of the admirals
to forbid Li Hung-chang, in the event of his arrival at Taku,
any sort of communication with the shore: the Russian proposal of August was accordingly taken as a sign that Russia
already had some agreement with Li Hung-chang, on the
strength of which, in return for freedom of action in Manchuria,
she was pledged to support the diplomatic game of this as yet
unrecognized agent authorized by the Chinese government to
conduct negotiations with the powers.[46]

Germany assumed a particularly marked attitude of negation toward the Russian proposal to consider hostilities in
China ended, toward the question of the possibility of starting
negotiations with the Chinese government previous to the
punishment of the "authors" of the bloodshed that had taken
place, and toward the recognition of Li Hung-chang, and only
in the latter half of September, with French aid, was the for-

mula found that afterwards became the basis of the powers'
still long discussed "collective note," not presented to the
Chinese government until December 9/22, 1900.[47]
    The terms set in the collective note were immediately and
unconditionally accepted by China (December 13/26, 1900)
but the process of working out details and signing the so-called
"final protocol" dragged on for nine months longer, until August 25 (September 7,) 1901.[48] In this process, Russian diplomacy participated on an equal footing with the rest and "by
not detaching itself from the other powers" preserved to the
last "the ability to present its own demands at any time." The
main, and for the Chinese the most fearsome question--that
of compensating the powers for damage--was what most re-
tarded negotiations (of the ministers among themselves) and
was so settled as concerning Russia that Lamsdorf could later
refer to her military expeditions in 1900 as a rare example of
"a war completely paid for."[49] But even so this still did not
mean that Russian diplomacy, in subscribing to the collective
note of December 9 or to the final protocol of August 25, had
finally renounced all thought of a "separate" liquidation of the
"difficulties" in the relations between the Russian and Chinese
allies of 1896 created by the events of 1900. On the basic
question of monetary compensation, which, on the initiative of
England and America, at one time threatened to be solved by
the establishment of international control over the financial
administration of China, Witte from the start abandoned masked
freedom of action for Russia, proposing (on October 11, 1900)
to liquidate, in his projected "separate" agreement with the
Chinese government, the monetary compensation (which could
in such case be placidly included in the forthcoming general
agreement) through various "privileges of a value to correspond."[50] The only question was, just what "privileges" the
Chinese government would be able to offer. To arrange about
them was thus the only task remaining to Ukhtomsky's mission,
since the Peking question proper had been settled even before
his coming to China--by way of a "premature" general armed
action by the powers interested.

III

    When Ukhtomsky arrived at Shanghai (September 16, 1900,)
Li Hung-chang had already reached Tientsin and was only waiting for an opportunity to get to Peking and take over as viceroy

of Chihli until the powers should deign to recognize his diplomatic commission.[51] In Shanghai, Ukhtomsky was awaited
by Li Hung-chang's son Li Ching-fang, who had come to Russia in 1896 and had at that time taken an intimate part in negotiations over the deal concluded by his father. And on first
meeting Ukhtomsky, Li Ching-fang, after alluding to "his
father's command," at once "said that China would make us
full reparation at our desire and pay us a very substantial indemnity, but in such form as not to enhance the cupidity of
the rest of the powers." Russia need only "occupy the Chinese Eastern Railway manu militari" and declare "in principle" her "magnanimous refusal to appropriate the whole
region," (i.e., Manchuria,) since "this would buttress the
Chinese in the general negotiations." But in addition to the
promise "to reimburse us in installments for war losses and
demolition," Li Ching-fang professed China's readiness to
"accord us unconditional exploitation of the resources of
neighboring Mongolia and Kashgar, and collateral deflection
thither of the Russian tide of colonization, masking concessions to the Russian government itself under the patent of
sundry sham private companies."[52] Thus began, in an as yet
strictly private manner, those "absolutely independent negotiations" between Russia and China to which Russian diplomacy was "in no wise" prepared to "admit any interference by
the other powers."[53]

However, the political atmosphere was at this moment
still altogether unfavorable for the conduct of business negotiations with the central Chinese government. The court was
not only not contemplating a return to Peking, but was now
preparing to move out of Taiyuanfu, whither it had fled from
the foreign armies upon their first appearance at the capital,
and go to Hsianfu, still farther to the southwest, continuing
to "maintain an irreconcilable attitude toward foreigners,
preferring to negotiate with them at a distance, and figuring
that under such conditions the government would afterwards
have no trouble repudiating whatever obligations its representatives might assume." "Tsun's gang" was still all powerful
at court and the influence of the two plenipotentiaries, Prince
Ching and Li Hung-chang, "precisely nil,"--and to an experi-
enced eye the only apparent expedient was "to attend at once
to the security of our [Russian] interests in a strictly limited
region by dealing [through Admiral Alekseyev] with the provincial authorities direct," planning subsequently "to include"

these local agreements with separate chiang-chüns "in our
future treaty" with the central Chinese government. Pokotilov even advised "against pursuing the illusory central Chinese government, which was now less able than ever to exercise authority in the provinces," said "to leave it in peace"
and await the return of the court to Peking.[54]

In any event to talk further with the absolutely irrespon-
sible Li Ching-fang was, under such contions, utterly useless, the more so since the Chinese representative had for
a second time assailed Ukhtomsky with "bitter reproaches
for the non-delivery of the second payment" (as provided in
the Moscow protocol of May 23, 1896,) suggesting to him that
"if negotiations with Li Hung-chang could possibly have even
the slightest practical significance" then the "payment now of
something or other, even an insignificant amount, to raise
his hopes, was conditio sine qua, without which the old gentle-
man would lose all faith in our intentions ever to fulfill our
promise [to pay three million rubles in all,] even gradually,
in proportion to his services."[55] But Li's concession proposal itself was distinctly imperfect in that it referred only
to Mongolia and Kashgar and did not touch on Manchuria.

Even Peterburg was put on its guard: forbade the "outlay
of any large sums" until Ukhtomsky's personal meeting with
Li Hung-chang and "ascertainment of his [Li's] role in forthcoming negotiations, as well as the state of affairs in general,"
and--under the pretext that "events that had transpired had
broken all Li Hung-chang's own promises and inflicted stupendous losses upon us"--hastened to turn the old promise about:
"Li Hung-chang must now"--Witte now demanded--"so far as
he is able make amends for all that has occurred and earn
what was, with the tsar's consent, promised by me."[56] Preparedness on the part of the "grasping son of Li" to accept
these new conditions was at once manifest, provided he could
immediately get some money out of it, and if Ukhtomsky
"would procure" for him half a million in advance, Li Ching-
fang promised "on oath" to show the money to an intimate of
the empress and incite her to return to Peking "in expectation
of a large reward" and "insure the beginning of profitable negotiations there in the presence of the court."[57] Ukhtomsky
had even started bargaining about the amount, but Witte maintained that Li "could under present circumstances have no
influential relations with the court and was only "mystifying
us" and so cut the bargaining short, thereby projecting Li

Ching-fang into a state of "extreme disillusionment."58 Thus
a month went by, and matters remained at a standstill.

But on the 20th of October, when Pokotilov's first meeting
with Li Hung-chang in Peking took place, and Ukhtomsky proceeding via Port Arthur, had still got only as far as Tientsin,
Peterburg was already working full speed on the fashioning
of the "fundamentals of Russian governmental control in Manchuria," on which the separate agreements with local chiang-
chüns recommended by Pokotilov were to be based, and which
were then to pass over into the "future treaty" with the central
government and remain in effect for the whole period of Russian occupation.

It started with Mukden province. On September 24, Kuropatkin asked Alekseyev how he thought "order would be most
quickly and surely restored in the province of Mukden." He
began by pointing out that "it would be well to revert to administrative direction of this province by chiang-chüns with
the right to a police guard, mounted and otherwise, but not
to an army." Kuropatkin, however, no longer asked this
question on his own authority but referred to the fact that
"there exists a proposal as to the possibility and desirability
of opening the conduct of negotiations with separate chiang-
chüns, independently of negotiations to be conducted through
Peking."

A comparison of dates suggests that the initiative here
came through Witte: Kuropatkin telegraphed Alekseyev on
September 24, while Pokotilov's telegram of September 20,
on the urgency of addressing the provincial authorities as
such, was presented to Nicholas by Witte on the 23rd and
carries the tsar's notation: "many good ideas here." Alekseyev replied that the conduct of such negotiations was the
"perfect answer to the present situation and would facilitate
our task in Manchuria," and indicated as desirable: "to preserve in Mukden province as far as possible the existing administrative order, not interfering without special need in
matters of the chiang-chün's internal administration," 2) as-
sign to the chiang-chün a military commissioner and a representative of the ministry of foreign affairs and 3) effect the
appointment of the chiang-chün by mutual consent of Russia
and China. This opinion of Alekseyev's was both considered
by the spokesman for the Chinese Eastern Railway as "the
best solution" and "fully shared" by Witte.59 And when the
requisite preliminary agreement was signed by representa-

tives of the Mukden chiang-chün and an official from the diplomatic office, Korostovets, on October 27, 1900, and confirmed by the chiang-chün and Alekseyev on November 13, its
terms seemed "satisfactory" to Lamsdorf as well.[60]

Thus the suppression of the Chinese military authority in
southern Manchuria--and in Yinkow of the civil government
as well--confirmed in the "preliminary agreement" of October 27, 1900, and the treatment of the chiang-chün as an organ answerable to the Russian military command for the maintenance of order in the country, i.e., the clear violation of
the "independence" of the Chinese empire and the sovereignty
of the central Chinese government, evoked no disagreement
within the Russian government as a temporary, but also a
termless, measure.

Equally "unanimous" was the adoption of the "fundamentals
of Russian governmental control," touching all three provinces
of Manchuria, at a conference of the three ministers on October 31, 1900. To judge from the minutes of this conference,
the document there accepted had a twofold purpose: 1) to
serve as "regulations for this control," the government's instructions to itself, as it were, respecting modes and limits
for the exercise of the authority that had virtually fallen to it
in the occupied country, and 2) to formulate a program respecting which it was "imperative" "to endeavor to see that the
basic positions," "insofar as they touched China, should enter
into our forthcoming agreement with China."[61] The project
for this document was presented by Kuropatkin in fifteen articles so edited that they might be mechanically included in
the text of the bi-lateral Russo-Chinese agreement: (article 1)
respecting the preservation in Manchuria, as a "component
part of the Chinese empire," of the previous administrative
division and form of government, (article 2) the "temporary"
occupation of Manchuria by Russian troops "for the maintenance of settled tranquility" and "to guarantee the Chinese
government's fulfillment of obligations with respect to the
railway under construction and the branch to Port Arthur,"
(article 3) the Chinese government's renunciation ("the Chinese government renounces") "of its maintenance of troops
in Manchuria" "in view of the inefficacy of Chinese troops at
the present time to establish and maintain order in Manchuria,"
(article 4) reservation to the chiang-chüns and fu-tu-t'ungs of
such rights as they have had till now, except for the right of
commanding troops," and (article 5) the establishment "beyond

the railway line" of a police guard without guns and without
foreign members. Next came Kuropatkin's articles formulating the rights and obligations of Russian military and diplomatic organs in Manchuria: (article 6) the right of "supervision over the activity of the chiang-chüns and fu-tu-t'ungs"
and the obligation "to cooperate with them toward the restoration and maintenance of order," as appertaining to the commanding officer of the Amur military district for Tsitsihar
and Kirin provinces, to the central authority of the Kwantug
area for Mukden province, (article 7) subjects for supervision
"by army commanders," (article 8) cases in which army commanders are obligated to cooperate with the local authority,
(article 9) obligations of military commissars with respect
to the chiang-chüns (dealing with them in matters touching
Russian troops, surveillance in restraint of the reconstitution
of Chinese armies or the increase of the police guard,) and
(article 10) duties of the diplomatic agent (dealing with chiang-
chüns in all matters not under the jurisdiction of the military
commissars, protection of Russian subjects and Russian
enterprises).

Finally, the four remaining articles of the Kuropatkin project provided for: (article 11) a military court to try "local
residents" guilty of "attack on our troops or assault and battery of our military," (article 12) appointment to the offices
of chiang-chün and fu-tu-t'ungs "by agreement of the Chinese
government with our minister in Peking," (articles 13 and
14) exclusion of "questions of a political character" from the
transactions of army commanders and chiang-chüns, and
(article 15) efficacy of the "present principles" of control
"throughout the period of occupation,"[62]--Witte's additions
to this basic project with reference to the Chinese Eastern
Railway, the legal position of which was unspecified in Kuropatkin's project, distorted the diplomatic form and nature of
the project, since they obviously envisaged the definition of
relations not between the road and a restored Chinese civil
administration but between the road and the Russian occupation
authority.

Of these supplementary articles three were inserted between
Kuropatkin's articles 2 and 3 and (in the numbering of the final
text) mentioned: (article 3) that "the construction and exploitation of the Chinese Eastern Railway were under the ultimate
direction of the Siberian Railroad Committee and under the
supervision of the ministry of finance," (article 4) the right

of the local administration of the road to deal "directly" with
local Chinese authorities up to and including the chiang-chün
or to appeal to the aid of diplomatic agents or, through a
member of the Board in Peking, to the Russian minister,
(article 5) the relations of the guard of the road, as a "special army division," "subject to its own commander," to the
military authorities "to be defined on the same principles as
those of the Frontier Guard Detachment," it being "so far"
subject to army commanders only in the event of "use in
combat." As is evident, all three articles tended to mark
off a position of independence for the Chinese Eastern Railway as regarded the military authorities, in an environment
of military occupation, but the fourth, inserted by Witte between articles 6 and 7 of Kuropatkin's project, imposed upon
Russian military authorities the duty of "giving all possible
assistance to the railway administration."[63] The final redaction of the "principles" was a mechanical amalgamation
of all Kuropatkin's articles and all of Witte's, except for one
point: instead of the term of efficacy proposed by Kuropatkin
--"throughout the period of occupation"--Witte proposed "until conclusion of a final agreement with the Chinese government," and Witte's formula was the one adopted. Witte's purpose in making this change, as can now be precisely established, was to limit the efficacy of "exceptional measures"
associated with the military regime in Manchuria and the
hegemony of the war office and at the same time prolong the
possibility of "temporary" occupation of Manchuria, in case
of need, "for many years."[64] Thus, even of the "principles
of Russian governmental control," which in nowise deviated
from the Mukden agreement of October 27 that had pleased
Witte, it can hardly be asserted without reservation that they
"were drawn up under the dominating influence of the minister of war": absolutely everything in the form of additions
and corrections that Witte could possibly wish for had gone
into their composition.[65] But Lamsdorf signed the minute
book of October 31 with a proviso: "agreed, provided demands of a less categorical character touching Chinese armies
in Manchuria can be made, depending on circumstances [in
concluding the final agreement]." Witte, however, signing
after Lamsdorf, did not subscribe to this proviso.[66]

The more Peterburg focussed on the idea of establishing
some "temporary modus vivendi" through restoring the civil
powers of local Manchurian authorities by way of direct ne-

gotiations with the chiang-chüns, passing over the central government, the less urgent for Russia became the question of
a "separate" agreement, and on the other hand, the more urgent it became for China. To give Russia an opportunity to
develop and extend the practice of piecemeal filching of the
authority of the central government in each of the three Manchurian provinces would be tantamount to loss of the whole
region, and to get Russian diplomacy back on the path of an
agreement with Peking at all costs now apparently became the
object of Li Hung-chang's feverish efforts in his dealings with
Ukhtomsky. That it was a question, if not of direct annexation,
then of Russia's political and economic protectorate over Manchuria, had become manifest to the old man at his first meeting with Girs and Pokotilov in Peking (October 20 and 21):
Girs had declared point-blank "that he believed the removal
of all the old Manchurian governors to be imperative and
thought that it would be generally necessary to establish the
principle in future that no gubernatorial appointments be made
in Manchuria except by consent of the Russian government, "
while Pokotilov, apropos of Li Hung-chang's complaints as
to difficulties connected with guarantee of payments on the
claims of the powers, had hinted at the possibility of "resigning to Russia's management" the customs revenues at border
stations on the Chinese Eastern Railway, and to Li's remark
the "China would never consent" to resign "any revenues in
Manchuria, " had replied by threatening that, if so, "then we
should have to guarantee our interests as we deemed expedient,
without consulting the view of the Chinese government."[67]
  Nay more, it appeared that even Witte himself was not at
all prepared to simply "evacuate Manchuria in the near future,"
as the Chinese minister in Peterburg had given Li to understand, but would only agree to it "when everything had quieted
down and all our demands been met, " while the question of
customs on the Chinese Eastern Railway raised by Pokotilov
he did not even regard as a demand since Russia had "never"
"turned them over to the Chinese government."[68] Through
Ukhtomsky it was now announced to Li Hung-chang that what
Russia's demands in the separate negotiations "would boil
down to" was not only "security of the railway" but "the consolidation of our whole influence in Manchuria' (in Manchuria,
and not in Mongolia or Kashgar, whither, as we have seen,
Li Hung-chang had been trying to divert Peterburg's monopolistic appetites) and "in this Li Hung-chang must give us full

cooperation."[69] After that, it only remained for Li Hung-
chang to work fast, strive to get into his own hands the local
negotiations that had started in Manchuria, and rouse Russians diplomacy to a formal move in the Manchurian question
that would compromise her in the eyes of the others and complicate relations among the "allies" before they succeeded in
coming to an agreement about their "joint" demands on China.

The first step in the latter direction--the proposal that
Ukhtomsky act as agent of the Chinese government "in the
conduct of peace negotiations"--was neatly calibrated to Ukhtomsky's political denseness (he was prepared to consent), but
was so absurd otherwise that it got nowhere.[70] The second
project--transfer of the Manchu court, at the Russian government's invitation, to Mukden, "cradle of the Manchu dynasty"
--was apparently devised by Ukhtomsky himself and met with
Witte's approval, but was delicately declined by Li Hung-chang.[71]
The third, it would appear, was a direct response to Peterburg's demand for "consolidation of our whole influence" in
Manchuria: Li Hung-chang proposed that Ukhtomsky "give his
government for confirmation a treaty granting Russia, under
patent of companies ostensibly strictly private, rights of exploitation in all the colossal natural resources of Mongolia
and Manchuria." But 1) this "treaty" was not to be "given"
by Ukhtomsky alone (though chairman of the Board of the
Russ-Chinese Bank he was in China at the given moment an
absolutely "unofficial person") but conjointly with Pokotilov,
official representative of the Russian government in Peking,
and 2) at the same time "the old man confidentially requested"
him to inform Witte "alone" "that he felt inclined to set out
for Manchuria himself and, by all the means known to him of
directly influencing the chiang-chüns, bring peace to the people," calculating that "his appearance there, by inspiring
confidence at court respecting the territorial disinterestedness of a Russia desiring only to occupy railway and cities
with the necessary troops, would give impetus to peace negotiations by definitively allaying the apprehension of China's
dismemberment over Russia's supposed annexation of Manchuria."[72]

This last proposal of Li Hung-chang's was taken as primarily an attempt to "get money out of us and the officials in
Manchuria" and create a situation in which Russian diplomacy
would have a "much harder time coping with the relatively
energetic Li Hung-chang than with any other officials in Man-

churia,"[73]--and Witte found Li Hung-chang's proposed trip
"superfluous." But the treaty as to a monopoly over the exploitation of "all resources" would, he admitted at first glance,
be "very helpful" provided it was "confirmed by a decree of
the emperor," and he mentally related it not to "certain" private companies but to the Chinese Eastern Railway Company
alone.[74] But by the next day Witte had recollected that this
might be a pitfall, and was categorically telegraphing Ukhtomsky that Li Hung-chang's journey was "not to be thought of"
and that "a separate treaty we cannot conclude without knowing what the other powers will do, for we should be tying our
own hands."[75]

That Witte had correctly discerned Li Hung-chang's ulterior
motive was obvious from the sequel: Li Hung-chang continued
to "earnestly beseech" "a plain statement, for communication
to [his] government, that by decree of the sovereign Pokotilov
and Ukhtomsky had been authorized to examine and settle...
money and business questions connected with damage to the
Chinese Eastern Railway, exploitation of the resources of
Mongolia, Manchuria, and Kashgar, etc." ("then he, Li Hung-
chang, would at once arrange anything you please") and invariably did so through the Chinese minister in Peterburg.[76]
And when Witte confirmed his decision to Ukhtomsky, and, to
burn his bridges, gave orders (November 20) that the same be
communicated to the Chinese minister as well, Li Hung-chang
still did not subside, but expanded his proposal in the sense of
granting Russia the right to "have her own guard" over the
whole expanse of the new "concession," "if we reserve sovereign rights to the Chinese imperial government," and entered
into negotiations on this subject with the court at Hsianfu.[77]
But no answer had as yet come from there when the affair took
the turn Li Hung-chang desired--thanks to the intervention of
the Russian minister to Peking.

For a long time Ukhtomsky kept the tenor of his negotiations
with Li Hung-chang a secret both from Pokotilov and from
Girs, and only when finally convinced that Witte was prepared
to bring all the results of his mission to naught and that he was
"superfluous in Peking" did he turn outside for support. Girs
--"in view of the endeavor of Ching and Li to get us to actually
return Manchuria to China at the earliest possible moment"
and in view of the "decision" already made by Russia "to in
part fulfill their desire by the introduction of Chinese civil
government in the region" [the Tseng-Alekseyev agreement

of November 13]--declared definitely in favor of concluding
the agreement concerning "a concession for working mineral
resources and building railways in Manchuria" and "in the
whole region that falls within our sphere of influence" "right
now," "since, later on, China's consent might well be more
difficult to obtain."78

Girs's proposal was immediately scheduled by Lamsdorf
for discussion, and the "separate agreement" question thus
moved out of the stage of private negotiations. Witte abruptly
changed front and defended the "opportuneness" of an agreement made just in advance of the conclusion of peace by the
powers, while China was still in the submissive mood fostered
"by the policy of retribution and intimidation" practised by
Waldersee. Nor did Kuropatkin raise any objections. And
in a matter of ten days Peterburg had a separate agreement
program ready.99

Certain differences of opinion Lamsdorf had to allow for,
but it would nonetheless be erroneous to suppose that anyone
in the Russian government at that moment considered or even
mentioned the "actual return of Manchuria" to China, i.e.,
the restoration of "sovereign rights" to the imperial Chinese
government. All were agreed that it would not do to "annex"
Manchuria to Russia.80 But all three also insisted that the
separate agreement must "consolidate" the effects of the
"principles of Russian governmental control in Manchuria"
"unanimously" adopted back in October and now (December 4)
confirmed by the tsar.81 But this meant that not a single
official would be appointed in Manchuria by the Chinese government without Russia's consent, not a single policeman
over and above the number fixed by the Russian border command, not one soldier would be at the disposal of the Peking
staff to guard Manchuria's borders, and that in the country
"returned" to China would be stationed under the command of
Russian generals, a Russian armed force of a dual nature,
regular troops and troops of the frontier guard corps. One
difference of opinion, as we have see, was registered by
Lamsdorf back in October on the question of China's right to
maintain armies in Manchuria, a right which he was disinclined
to deny so "categorically": but Lamsdorf did not now renew
it. The only difference of opinion now evoked came from
Witte, but it was not developed by him in such a way that it
became a matter of principle and remained merely quantita-
tive. Kuropatkin, for the security of "Russia's link with

Vladivostok and Port Arthur," had ascribed "prime importance to the question of preserving our right to have troops
in Manchuria" and had proposed that, after reducing their
number from twenty-eight battalions to twenty by the spring
of 1901, they be kept, "after completion of construction" of
the railway, in Harbin, Kirin, Tsitsihar and Mukden to the
number of not less than eight battalions.

Witte, anxious to "avoid arousing suspicion of aggressive
aspirations on our part," "did not see the necessity of leaving within the confines of Manchuria as considerable a number of troops as had been proposed by the minister of war,"
but did not raise the question of withdrawing them from Manchuria entirely, even though he "foresaw" that "to leave our
troops" [regardless of their number] in Manchuria "for a
long, indefinite time" would arouse such suspicion; but how
short a time troops might remain there without arousing suspicion was a question to which even Witte himself had no answer.[82] And the difference of opinion did not at the given
moment flare up into a dispute. It was merely evident that
Witte's concern was not the reconstitution of Chinese armies
in Manchuria and not the elimination of Russian infantry,
cavalry and artillery units from the territory of an alien
state, but rather the relative number of troops in Manchuria
incapable under any circumstance of being subordinated to
him, Witte, (or any minister of finance), as head of the whole
agglomeration of banking, railway, steamship, and assorted
industrial enterprises, present and future, concentrated in
Manchuria.

And just as Kuropatkin, apprehensive, apparently, lest
the ministers of state attack the authority of the "principles
of Russian governmental control" rushed these to the tsar
for confirmation on December 4, even so Witte, seeking
means to replace one armed guard in Manchuria by another,
also rushed to the tsar that same day for authorization to increase the number of the "guard" of the Chinese Eastern Railway from 11,000 to 16,000 men and telegraphed Yugovich to
ask whether a still further increase would not be necessary
and whether he thought it "necessary for troops to be stationed
for a prolonged period" and if so, "where?" and "how many?"[83]
But Yugovich's answer was discouraging, and so Witte was
left in a quandry for the time being as to how to avoid "suspicion of aggressive aspirations on our part" without "actually
giving" Manchuria "back" to China.[84]

The question of Russia's compensation for "losses occasioned by disturbances and hostilities" provoked no disagreement at all. Witte proposed stipulating in the separate agreement: 1) Russia's right to recovery of military expenditures ("commensurately with the other powers"), 2) China's payment of damages to the Chinese Eastern Railway, private companies and enterprises, and private persons, and 3) those "privileges of like value" whereby the amount of the war compensation due the Russian government might be liquidated in whole or in part. And these "privileges" Witte for the time being defined more modestly than we should have expected. Witte demanded: 1) China's pledge "not to build without our consent any railway lines by her own means, and not to grant foreigners railway or any other concessions, in our whole sphere of influence" (i.e., "in Manchuria, the whole section of China to the north of the Wall, Mongolia, the Ili region and Kashgaria,") 2) "the ownership grant to us" of sections of the Shanhaikwan railway to the north of the Wall "in the direction of Peking," 3) the abrogation of self-government in the city of Chinchowting, not included at the time in the lease of Liaotung to the Russian administrative system, 4) the transfer of customs-houses at border points on the Chinese Eastern Railway to the management of the Chinese Eastern Railway Company, 5) interest payments and amortization on the 1895 loan by monthly instead of semi-annual installments. [85]

As we see, except in points three and five, Witte's concern was the complete exclusion of foreign concessions ("foreign influence") from China beyond the Wall, as sphere of Russian interest; to demand in the separate agreement any new concessions, such as Li Hung-chang proposed, Witte did not consider necessary. As he himself explained, "our interests respecting railway concessions" "will be fully guaranteed" if China makes a pledge neither to build railways herself nor to permit their construction by foreigners in our sphere of influence. But respecting the "right to exploit mineral resources" Witte confessed that "this could only acquire serious significance for us in the remote future, since at the present time Russia palpably lacked sufficient capital even for the exploitation of her own natural resources, and could therefore scarcely find means to work the ore-beds of China."[86]

Add to all this the demand, already featured in the 1897-98 negotiations, for non-admission of foreign instructors to

the army and navy of North China, the only demand now initiated by Lamsdorf, and the whole content of the negotiations
program as confirmed by Nicholas on December 13, 1900,
will have been accounted for.[87]

On December 9, the day the ministers in Peking presented
the "collective note" of the powers to the Chinese government,
Girs was ordered to obtain in Peking for the Chinese minister
in Peterburg "full powers" to conduct separate negotiations.[88]
The opening of separate negotiations came, as we see, somewhat late, and their conduct would have to proceed at a rapid
tempo to reach completion before China's general conclusion
of peace with the powers. The problem of "restoring" Manchuria to China without simultaneously evacuating Russian
troops naturally seemed to Russian diplomacy the most difficult point in the separate negotiations, and from the start
the only way out appeared to be the postponement of evacuation without postponement of the agreement. In this sense,
England's proposal to continue the occupation of Chihli province "until China should submit" to the demands of the powers
as presented to her in the "collective note" was a boon: "some
extension of occupation in Pechili"--Lamsdorf wrote Girs on
December 9--would give Russia "good legal ground for continuing" the occupation of Manchuria, whence Russia would
promise to withdraw her troops "only after the complete re-
establishment of order in China," and restoration "of the normal order of things could not be regarded as guaranteed until
the court should have returned to Peking, which would in turn
only become possible when foreign troops should have abandoned the empire's capital."[89]

The immediate future demonstrated that this had not been
the chief difficulty of the situation in which Russian diplomacy
had placed itself by choosing the path of separate agreement
with China, hoping thereby to obtain, even if not "annexation,"
still a new "consolidation of" Russia's "influence" in Manchuria.

IV

The separate negotiations program confirmed by the tsar
on December 13, 1900 decided against Kuropatkin the question
of "reserving Russia's right to have troops in Manchuria,"
and, retaining all the vagueness that still surrounded this
question in Witte's own mind, cautiously ("perhaps") recog-

nized the presence of "sufficient grounds" for leaving Russian troops in Manchuria merely "for a certain time." Nicholas did not of himself make any additions to the program.
But his one question: "would it be advisable to extend the
term of our lease to the Kwantung peninsula?"--which he did
not even wish "decided" "until the opinions of the departments
interested had been ascertained"--was in due time adduced
as an example of one of the "privileges" that might be demanded of China, again by Witte. Even Lamsdorf was not sure
that Witte would confine himself to the list of five "privileges"
he had presented, and the program of December 13 left the
possibility open that "our financial department" might still
"as a preliminary" "submit" the question of demanding "every
sort of concession" from China (in addition to the "already
projected" Peking line)--"for careful discussion."90 And it
did: on December 21 the program was communicated to the
ministers for resolution, on January 9 of the new year the
Chinese minister in Peterburg already had his powers to conduct negotiations, and the question of place was consequently settled as Witte had desired, but negotiations still could
not start because the "careful discussion" of Witte's anticipated survey took time and Lamsdorf had no project ready by
January 9 that could be presented to Yan Yu.91 But the fruit
of this careful discussion was no simple "list of privileges
which it would be advisable to bring up with the Chinese government during the forthcoming negotiations," but a"project"
ready for signing "consisting of two parts: a) the separate
agreement between the two governments and b) an agreement
between the Chinese government and the Chinese Eastern Railway Company," or, still more exactly, two separate agreement projects, each drawn up in full, and presented by Witte
to Lamsdorf one on the 9th, the other on the 11th of January.92

As Witte had from the start proposed, an opportunity was
afforded the Chinese government of avoiding direct payment
to the Russian government of "compensation" for "expenses
sustained in consequence of the disturbances," though not by
allowing any "exemptions" but by transfer of this debt to the
Chinese Eastern Railway Company, which would assume payment to the Russian government and incorporate the sum thus
paid in its figure for "damages" (article 9 of the separate
agreement). But in the project for the agreement with the
Chinese Eastern Railway Company the Chinese government
engaged93 to accept the opportunity afforded it by the Com-

pany for postponed payment of "damages," which it was proposed to compute not only on the basis of "demolition of a
considerable part of the railway" and "plunder of its property"
but also of "retardation" of construction (§§1 and 2)--with interest at 6 per cent per annum on the capital sum of the debt.
Toward the liquidation of this debt to the Company were applied
the five million lan that the Company was to have paid China
upon completion of construction (§12 of the contract of August
27, 1896) and all payments which the Company was to make
to the Chinese government in connection with the "privileges"[94]
now granted to the Company.

Even upon this occasion Witte did not abandon his pessimistic appraisal of the possibilities of Russian private capital being invested in the exploitation of China's mineral resources,
in railway building, or in "any" industrial enterprises "whatsoever": article 13 of the separate agreement merely bound
China not to "grant" such concessions to foreigners and not
to build railways herself either in Manchuria or in Mongolia
and the Kashgar, Yarkand, Khotan and Keriya districts. But
respecting the Chinese Eastern Railway Company, Witte did
not now draw back from the prospect of capital investments
(charged to the treasury) in a series of new enterprises of
this sort and in the expansion of previous ones, and demanded
for the Company the following "privileges": 1) the right to
work "all" gold deposits "located either on state or on private
lands" in Mukden and Kirin provinces and on the southern
slopes of the Little Khingan in Heilungkian province, and all
deposits of petroleum and nickel throughout Manchuria (§3),
2) the same right respecting "all deposits of coal" "in the
region served by" the Company's "roads," together with the
provisions that in the 10-verst zone along the railway line
and in the 5-verst district of the Company's mines no other
industrialists be permitted (§4), 3) the right to "select within 5 years" a parcel of 2,000 square versts of "fine timber"
in the basin of the Yalu River, with the right to lay roads
there and establish telegraph and telephone communication
(§5), 4) transfer to the Company of all lands in general (privately owned, with ransom at market prices) in the 10-verst
zone along the line of the Chinese Eastern Railway (§6),
5) reservation to the Company of parcels of land at Chinwang-
tao and Yinkow, at the mouth of the Yalu River and "on one of
the islands near this mouth"--for the construction of wharves,
warehouses, break-waters and dwellings (§7) and 6) conversion

of the temporary branch from the south-Manchurian line to
Yinkow into a permanent one (§8). All said lands were to be
transferred subject to "all rights" appertaining to the Company in lands set apart for construction of the Chinese Eastern Railway, i.e., they would become a component part of
the basic railway "settlement" provided for in articles 5 and
6 of the contract of August 27, 1896 and now increased to an
area of very nearly 30,000 square versts.[95]

Such was to be China's agreement with the Chinese Eastern Railway Company "concerning reimbursement for damages sustained in consequence of disturbances in Manchuria."
Actually, it laid a double load for the next few years on the
Russian national budget in consequence of 1) renunciation of
direct and guaranteed compensation to Russia in hard cash
for her war expenditures and 2) a not precisely definable,
yet considerable, increase primarily in the expenditure budget of the state "trust," now taking a sudden leap in stature,
that Witte desired to see in his Chinese Eastern Railway
Company.[96] It was adoption of Li Hung-chang's latest proposal (that of November 21, 1900) concerning "all natural
resources" and the right to guard them by force of arms, with
the addition, however, of the right of "administering" the new
concession areas. It is hardly an accident that the demand
for a line "to the Great Wall in the direction of Peking," firmly
rooted in Witte's mind since the moment of the April fiasco
of 1899, also stipulated in the form of a supplement to the
Chinese Eastern Railway Company concession, now found
place not in the project for the agreement with the Company,
but only in the separate agreement of the governments (article 14) not as an inoffensive economic "privilege," but as an
out and out "political" demand--so obviously was it aimed
against England. The remaining Chinese Eastern Railway
Company "privileges" were repeated in the separate agreement as well (article 10): but the very thing that made them
"political," namely the provisos concerning the withdrawal
of the new territories from general Chinese civil administration and their transfer to the railway "settlement" complex
was concealed in the corresponding paragraphs of the private
agreement with the Chinese Eastern Railway Company.

The question of the continuance in Manchuria of armed
forces not of the "trust" Witte now settled with complete fi-
nality. Namely, he excluded Chinese armies from Manchuria
once and for all, and the import of arms and munitions of war

was likewise permanently prohibited (article 4 of the separate
agreement) while the Russian regular armies would be withdrawn from Manchuria in three lots, as construction on the
basic trust enterprise, the railway, was completed and "regular traffic" upon it opened over the sections: 1) from Harbin
to Port Arthur and 3) from Harbin to the capital of Manchuria;
"after the absolute completion of all construction operations,"
Russia troops would also be withdrawn from Harbin (article
2). As Witte explained, this was of course only a withdrawal
of the regular troops to the wings of the possible Manchurian
theatre of war, since with the opening of traffic, they could
be brought on the scene, from Port Arthur or Chita or Vladivostok, to any point in Manchuria, in the "course of not over
24 to 48 hours."[97] And from an international viewpoint the
withdrawal of Russian troops from Manchuria by no means
disarmed the Russian government, which had simultaneously
been digging deeper into Manchuria and, under the mask of a
private-capitalistic trust, had now concentrated in its grasp
not only certain formal attributes of sovereign power but its
military and economic bases as well. That against which
even Li Hung-chang had cried out--the transfer "of all cus-
toms-offices that shall be established by the Chinese government" on the railroad and along the river Sungari "to the
management" of the Russian trust (whence the revenues would
come under its control as well) now found place in article 8 of
the separate agreement.

The foot and mounted police guard permitted the chiang-
chüns (article 4) was designated for the maintenance of "order and tranquility" not in the whole territory of Manchuria,
but only "outside the lands reserved" to our trust. Article 17
of the "principles of Russian governmental control" concerning the appointment of chiang-chüns and fu-tu-t'ungs "by consent" of the Chinese government and the Russian minister,
inserted by Kuropatkin, paled now before the formulation
given it by Witte in article 3 of the separate agreement: with
Witte, the "duty" "of instant removal" of any official "up to
and including the chiang-chüns" confronted the Chinese government upon the simple "declaration" of the Russian minister. "Responsibility" for the preservation of tranquility and
order now rested not on the chiang-chüns alone (see article 1
of the Tseng-Alekseyev agreement,) but also on the fu-tu-t'ungs
and "all local officials." What was absolutely new and, so
far as we know, hitherto unincorporated in Russia's Manchurian

program, but now contained in article 7 of the separate agreement, was the obligatory acceptance by Chinese authorities
"of all taxes and imposts" (not only from Russian subjects,
but without restriction) "in Russian currency."98 Needless
to say, the military commissar to the chiang-chün provided
for by Kuropatkin in the " principles" was tolerable to Witte
only "temporarily, until the withdrawal of Russian troops";
the only permanent organ now remaining to the chiang-chün
was the diplomatic agent, formally enabling the Russian government to communicate with the local authorities irrespective of the Peking government, while the administration of
the Chinese Eastern Railway was left entirely free to either
avail or not avail itself of the services of the agents (article 5).

A monument to Witte's absolutely individual desire to obtain for Russian subjects the right of free trade in Manchuria,
contested even in the ministry of finance itself (see above,
p. 284, note 1,) remained in the project for the separate agreement, article 6, concerning the right of Russian subjects "to
trade anywhere in Manchuria" and acquire necessary real estate. This meant turning all Manchuria into one continuous
"open port" not only for Russians, but for other foreigners
as well, on the strength of the "most favored nation" principle,
and meant altering the whole basic sense of the agreement,
which consisted precisely in the exclusion of "foreign influence"
from Manchuria: this product, apparently, of a certain diplomatic ignorance vanished soundlessly and without a trace in
subsequent redactions of the agreement.99 All this, Witte
duly proposed to give up for the "restoration of the authority
of the Chinese government in Manchuria, which would remain
a component part of the Chinese empire and preserve the same
administrative organization and the same form of government
that had existed before the occupation of this province by Russian troops" (article 1).100

In point of fact, the grandiose pretensions to "consolidation
of the whole influence" of the Russian government in Manchuria
contained in Witte's project presupposed not restoration of the
pre-war status quo but gradual contraction of the region of occupation and ultimate withdrawal from Manchuria not of the
Russian forces in general but only of the regular troop under
the control of the Russian minister of war. The content of
Witte's project, for the rest, boiled down, first, to consolidation of the economic and political power of the Chinese Eastern Railway Company on principles of monopoly and restriction

of the Peking government's "sovereign" rights in Manchuria,
and, secondly, to a formal broadening of Russia's "sphere of
interests" to take in all China beyond the Wall. This so cardinal departure from the program formulated by Muravev only
a year before, on the eve of the Boxer uprising, now struck
an international situation such as to make the new program
either a challenge or utterly impracticable.[10]

Witte's project underwent some revision and limitation
even before presentation to the Chinese minister. Negotiations
opened only on February 7, 1901, and on March 11 were broken
off by the Chinese government, which refused to sign the treaty
proposed by Russia--under friendly pressure from Germany,
England, Japan, the United States, and even Italy. They were
renewed in July, 1901, suspended in October and again renewed
in December, 1901. What was finally signed by Russia and
China on March 26/April 8, 1902 preserved nothing of the original scheme except: 1) the declarative first article concerning
the "restoration of the authority of the Chinese government,"
and 2) China's general pledge to observe the contract of August 27, 1896 and safeguard the security of the railway and of
Russian subjects in Manchuria, and Russia's concrete pledge
to "withdraw all her troops" from the three provinces of Manchuria at three six-month intervals (article 2). But even the
latter Russian engagement only roughly corresponded to Witte's
previous idea of terminanting the occupation "after the absolute
completion of all construction operations" on the railroad, and
if the Russian government managed not to let the power to set
the final moment of occupation slip from its grasp, this was
only at the price of the celebrated proviso stipulating fulfillment of this obligation "should no disturbance arise and should
the conduct of other powers not prevent."

As to the right of the Chinese government to maintain armies
in Manchuria, article 3 of the treaty of March 26, 1902 proceeded, counter to Witte's project, from the explicit assumption of such a right, and merely proposed: that, for the period
"before the withdrawal of Russian troops," the Russian military authorities and the chiang-chüns "arrange" as to their
number and disposition, and for the period "following the complete conclusion of evacuation" the Chinese government "discuss" the question of increasing or decreasing their number--
"upon seasonable notification of the Russian government"--to
avoid "an increase in expenditures for military needs extremely
undesirable to both governments." And, finally, article 4 of

the treaty killed Witte's idea of a Russian south-Manchurian
line "in the direction of Peking" or, "in its stead," her "right
to finish and exploit" the Shanhaikwan-Yinkow-Hsinminting
railway, for it stipulated the return of this railway, seized
by Russian troops during hostilities, to the Chinese govern-
ment.102 Everything else in Witte's project that was to have
"consolidated" Russia's "whole influence" in Manchuria had
bit by bit been lost during the sixteen months that had passed
since the day when Li Hung-chang succeeded in luring Russian diplomacy to separate negotiations by the bait of "the
natural resources of all China beyond the Wall."

Russia's military occupation of Manchuria, justified only
by right of conquest and unsanctioned by any treaty with the
Peking government, continued for exactly 21 months (from
June 26, 1900 to March 26, 1902). The longer such a termless, naturally suggesting an endless, occupation lasted, the
more easily might the Manchurian question turn into the subject of acute international conflict for Russia, and the likelier
was the formal preparation of a military clash between Russia
and Japan over Manchuria to succeed.

V

Back in the summer of 1900, when Witte was busy repre-
senting the battle instincts that had flared up in Kuropatkin and
Nicholas respecting not only China but Korea as well, he was
chiefly concerned to keep the conflict with Japan from following the formula: "if you take Manchuria, we shall take Korea."103
But even when, after the taking of Peking, he had succeeded
in stowing both militarists in the framework of the August 12
program, and Nicholas had promised "not to move" even if
Japan "got into Korea,"--Japan continued to disturb him as
the "danger point." "Complications with European powers"
he did not fear, but he did fear Japan's "getting into Korea,"
which would be "essentially troublesome [regardless of Nicholas's promise]," since it might "arouse us." And Witte then
hit upon the idea of "making a proposal as to the neutralization
of Korea."104 Diplomatically, the affair was so handled that
the question of neutralization was raised by Korea herself,
and with this accomplished fact to conjure with, Russian diplomacy asked the Japanese government whether it would not
prefer to settle the Korean question "through a direct understanding with Russia."105 If the essence of the proposed ar-

rangement was to have been Russia's making certain concessions in Korea in exchange for freeing her own hands to some
extent in Manchuria, it was a flat failure. Japan's answer,
given Lamsdorf on January 9, 1901, was to the effect that
until the "status quo ante" had been restored in Manchuria
she preferred to let the Korean question wait, and return to
its discussion when "no longer swayed by outside considerations."[106] This was one warning that reached Peterburg in
good time: to propose the neutralization of Korea to Japan
would be impossible without simultaneously proposing the
neutralization of Manchuria, or so long as Russia was en-
camped in the latter according to Witte's prescription.

Another warning was linked with the serious alteration in
Germany's attitude toward Russia. The separate policy of
Russian diplomacy in Chinese events of 1900 (particularly the
withdrawal of Russian troops from Peking) had evidently been
a blow to the "personal agreement" of the two monarchs, and
the so-called "Yangtse agreement" (Jangtse-Abkommen) signed
by Germany and England on October 3/16, 1900, might be regarded as a symptom of a new and hostile orientation of the
Berlin cabinet toward Russia.[107] But the widening of the gulf
between Russian and German policy in Chinese affairs Peterburg accounted a necessary hostage for Russia's success in
her separate negotiations with China, and Witte, as we know,
had abruptly chosen the path of an immediate opening of negotiations just for fear Germany might suddenly renounce her
policy of terror in China.[108] It was therefore impossible to
take Radolin's announcement to Lamsdorf on January 3/16,
1901 of Germany's complete disinterest in Manchuria as anything but an attempt at entrapment.[109]

Finally, a third warning was linked with the publication in
the Times (January 3, new style, 1901) of a notice concerning
the Tseng-Alekseyev agreement. Peterburg might not have
known that this item would lead to diplomatic intervention
generally, or by just what powers in particular--the Chinese
government received in rapid succession the protests of Germany, England, Japan and America against the conclusion of
any separate agreements of a "territorial or financial" character.[110] But it could not have helped noticing that the Times
version, by garbling the text of the October 27 agreements,
1) gave it a permanent character and 2) left unmentioned the
retention of Russian troops in Mukden province, and was therefore interpreted as signifying that a post of Russian resident,

similar to the resident in "native principalities of India," had
been established in Mukden (i.e., the "commissar to the chiang-
chün,) and that this agreement placed Manchuria "de facto" under a "Russian protectorate," "since on the strength of a previous agreement [i.e., the contract of August 27, 1896] Russia
already enjoyed the right of maintaining as numerous a force
as was necessary for the protection of the railway." In other
words, the whole tumult raised in the press, as well as the inquiries subsequently addressed to Lamsdorf through diplomatic
channels, derived not from the concept of a prolonged occupation of Manchuria by Russian regular troops but from the concept of a normal and permanent order that had ostensibly been
introduced in Manchuria and that rested on the elimination of
Chinese armies and the presence of the guard of the Chinese
Eastern Railway, stipulated in a "previous agreement." The
warning that might have been drawn from this would have consisted in the recognition that the precise date when Russian
occupation would be lifted was not the crux of the matter.

Nonetheless the project for the separate agreement that was
finally approved by the three ministers in private session on
January 26, 1901 was based on the text presented by Witte. In
view of the "alarm" occasioned in Japan by the "mere rumor
of negotiations presumably started by us" and "false reports
in the foreign press," Lamsdorf "deemed it necessary to restrict the project to mere basic principle," and thought they
might defer "various details" until the "private" negotiations
of the Chinese Eastern Railway Company and the Russo-Chinese bank in Peking, and of local Russian authorities with the
chiang-chüns, and in general "endeavored" to give the agreement "the most peaceable character possible" in the hope that
its "publication" might "even produce a politically very favorable impression abroad."[111] Thus, the first thing to be dropped
(temporarily) was the whole second part of Witte's project (the
agreement with the Chinese Eastern Railway Company). And
the project for the separate agreement of the governments,
after thrice undergoing editorial alterations (January 16, 22, 25),
assumed at the conference of the three ministers on January 26,
1901 the following final form:[112]

"Art. 1. His majesty the Emperor of all Russia, desiring to give new proof of his pacific and friendly feelings toward the emperor of China, notwithstanding the fact that the
first attacks on peaceful Russian settlements were made

from border points in Manchuria, agrees to the restoration
of the authority of the Chinese government in the said province, which shall remain a component part of the Chinese
empire and retain the same administrative organization and
the same form of government that existed before the occupation thereof by Russian troops.

"Art. 2. In conformity with art. 6 of the contract concluded on August 27, 1896 between the Chinese government
and the Russo-Chinese bank concerning the construction and
exploitation of the Chinese Eastern Railway, the Company
of said road has the right of independent administration of
lands reserved to said road, and consequently also to the
maintenance of a guard to this end. Considering, however,
that in the present still unsettled state of affairs in Manchuria
the said guard is insufficient to insure future construction
on the Chinese Eastern Railway,[113] the Russian government is temporarily retaining in Manchuria a detachment
of its troops pending the establishment of tranquility in the
said province and his majesty the Chinese emperor's execution of the enactments contained in articles 9, 10, 11,
12, 13 and 14 of the present agreement.[14]

"Art. 3. Russian troops during the whole period of their
sojourn within the borders of Manchuria shall, in event of
necessity, give full cooperation to the Chinese authorities
in the matter of maintaining order and tranquility in the
province.[115]

"Art. 4. In view of the fact that Chinese troops stationed
in Manchuria have taken the most active part in hostilities
directed toward Russia,[116] the government of the celestial
emperor, desiring to give a guarantee of future maintenance
of the peace in Manchuria pledges not to maintain armies
there until construction on the Chinese Eastern Railway shall
have been completed and regular traffic over it established.[1]
Thereafter, the number of Chinese troops maintained in Man
churia shall be fixed by agreement with the Russian government. The import of arms and ammunition into Manchuria
is prohibited.

"Art. 5. With a view to the maintenance of tranquility
and the normal order of things in Manchuria where it adjoins
Russia, the government of the celestial emperor pledges itself to remove upon the Russian government's representation
those chiang-chūns and other higher administrative officials
appointed by the central government whose functioning shall

not be in harmony with established friendly relations between the two Empires.[118]

"For policing and the maintenance of civil order in Manchuria outside the lands reserved to the Chinese Eastern
Railway Company, a foot and mounted police guard shall
be organized under the auspices of the local governors
(chiang-chüns,) its numbers to be fixed by agreement with
the Russian government. In the arming of the police guard
guns are not to be permitted nor may foreign subjects serve
in its ranks.

"Art. 6. In accord with the solemn assurances it has
repeatedly given, the Chinese government pledges not to
authorize foreign instructors either for the ranks of the
army or for the personnel of the North China fleet.

"Art. 7. With a view to securing more lasting order
and tranquility in the neutral zone established by article
5 of the convention of March 15, 1898 to the north of the
Russian-leased province of Kwantung, the two negotiating
parties shall permit the local authorities subject to them
to enter into an agreement on this topic between themselves.
With the same end in view, the right to autonomous government accorded the city of Chinchowting by article 4 of
the supplementary protocol of April 28, 1898 shall be ab-
rogated.[119]

"Art. 8. The Chinese government shall not grant anywhere throughout the area of the Chinese provinces contiguous to Russia, namely: Manchuria and Mongolia, or
in the area of the Tarbogatai, Kuldja (Ili), Kashgar, Yarkand, Khotan, and Keriya districts of the Kansu-Sinkiang
province that borders on Russia, any concessions for railway construction, the working of mineral deposits, or for
any industrial enterprises whatsoever, to foreign powers
or their subjects without the consent of the Russian government. The Chinese government shall not build railways by
its own means anywhere in the said provinces without consent of the Russian government nor shall it grant parcels
of land for the use of foreigners, with the exception of the
open port of Newchwang.

"Art. 9. The government of his majesty the Chinese
emperor shall compensate the Russian government for expenses incurred in consequence of disturbances in China
in a sum commensurate with the Russian government's
actual disbursement and with compensation of the other

powers. The amount of the Russian government's compensation, as well as the time-limit and guarantee of payment of this compensation are to be determined by joint discussion of the matter with interested powers.[120]

"Art. 10. The Chinese government shall enter into an agreement with the Board of the Chinese Eastern Railway Company concerning compensation of said Company for losses sustained by it in consequence of the demolition of a considerable part of the railway, the pillaging of property of the Company and of its employees, and the retardation of construction of the road.

"Art. 11. The compensation of the Chinese Eastern Railway Company mentioned in the preceding article may, by agreement between the Chinese government and the Company, in part or in full be effected by grant to the Company of certain privileges, modification of existing concessions, or the issue of new concessions.[121]

"Art. 12. The government of the celestial emperor obligates itself to grant the Chinese Eastern Railway Company a concession for the construction and exploitation of a railway line from some point on the Chinese Eastern Railway, or its South-Manchurian branch, to the Chinese wall, in the direction of Peking, on the same terms as the concession to the Chinese Eastern Railway, the principal consent of the Chinese government to this demand having already been expressed in 1899.[122]

"Art. 13. The Chinese government shall enter into an agreement with the Russo-Chinese bank concerning compensation for losses to the bank occasioned by demolition of the property of this institution and its employees as well as suspension of the bank's operations.

"Art. 14. Claims of Russian subjects and Russian private institutions and enterprises to compensation for losses occasioned by the disturbances in China the Chinese government pledges to pay as they shall be examined by the Russian Mission in Peking and transmitted to this government."

It is easy to see that the "basic principles" in the final redaction not from Witte's project, i.e., its 3rd and 6th articles, were not inconsistent with the general tendency of this project. Of these, art. 3 passed without a ripple, uncontested either by Witte or by the Chinese; article 6, concerning instructors,

could naturally not have been taken over by Witte from the
December 13 program, since his project did not allow for
Chinese troops in Manchuria at all. But now that Lamsdorf
had mitigated the "prehensile" tendencies of Witte's project
(respecting the "sovereign rights" of China) and introduced
into the final redaction permission for China to have armies
in Manchuria after completion of construction of the Chinese
Eastern Railway, the insertion of art. 6 became a necessity
even from Witte's point of view.[123] Some toning down of
these tendencies is also noticeable in Lamsdorf's art. 5,
which, at least verbally, did not obtrude the concept of the
"responsibility" of all Manchurian officialdom from top to
bottom for possible assault on any of the employees of the
Chinese Eastern Railway. Lamsdorf would also have liked
to expunge from the final redaction the whole article about
the line in the direction of Peking, no doubt recalling the
consternation that a like demand had induced in Peking during
the summer of 1899; but article 12, with this demand, he was
forced to reinstate in the final redaction--Witte insisted.[124]

After the temporary postponement of the agreement with
the Chinese Eastern Railway Company, Witte's project also
quite naturally lost in the final redaction of the separate agreement the enumeration of concessions to be granted the Chinese Eastern Railway and the mention of transfer of the Russian government's future "Boxer compensation" to the capital
of the Chinese Eastern Railway (in the form of additional concessions). But an accusatory trace of Witte's concession
plans remained in the form of art. 11 of the final redaction:
true, it was formulated facultatively, but the Chinese did not
even conceive of it otherwise than as actually compulsory,
and, of course, protested against it.[125] As summarized, the
dose of "conciliation" injected into Witte's project by Lamsdorf was nicely calculated to give it the proper aspect for
"publication."

But respecting the date of withdrawal of Russian troops
Lamsdorf, obviously under pressure from Kuropatkin, took
refuge in a less categorical formula than Witte's . The latter
had linked total evacuation with total completion of the construction of the road (true, "if order is undisturbed"), while the
final redaction simply made it contingent generally upon the
"establishment of tranquility" in Manchuria, and particularly
upon the fulfillment of articles 9-14, i.e., upon the Chinese
government's being so good as to meet all of Russia's eco-

nomic demands. However, from the formal standpoint, even Witte's project scarcely admitted of an interpretation whereby Russia would be obliged to evacuate Manchuria upon completion of the road regardless of China's fulfillment of all its other, and in Witte's project even more numerous, economic obligations with respect to Russia. In any case, the objections of the Chinese had nothing to do with the question of the evacuation date but were directed at certain other points that had managed to come safely through into the final redaction from Witte's project.

Peterburg never even thought of putting the separate agreement through, even in this "conciliatory" redaction, "without taking certain measures to influence" Li Hung-chang: he was now promised the whole of that same million rubles (again in installments, however) and during negotiations all of Russian diplomacy's efforts were concentrated on him personally.1. But through him also came objections. These were based on the theory that, the powers having come out against the agreement, this would first of all require alterations to obviate "international complication."127 Neither the "friendly counsels" nor the threats (of remaining in Manchuria permanently) that issued from Peterburg had the slightest effect on Hsianfu, and when representations by the powers gave place to Japan's announcement to Peking that she was "prepared to support China under any circumstances" the latter's objections at once increased in number and assurance.128 The Chinese objected: 1) to that part of art. 8 which gave Russia Mongolia and other provinces besides Manchuria, 2) against payment of damages to the Chinese Eastern Railway, as specified in art. 10 for "retardation" of construction, 3) to art. 11, in which they sensed not an option, but an obligation to settle with the Chinese Eastern Railway through the medium of concessions, 4) to art. 6, concerning instructors, 5) to art. 4, and pressed the right of maintaining Chinese armies in Manchuria before completion of construction, even if not in the zone of the road, 6) to the prohibition of import of arms into Manchuria, also in art. 4, and 7) to art. 12, in part, requesting that at least the one phrase: "in the direction of Peking" be struck from it.

Witte saw no hope in acceding on all points indiscriminately, since "after meeting all the objections now advanced, we should have no guarantee that other pleas would not immediately be brought forward."129 And he proved to be right: a cor-

rected text of the agreement, embodying practically all the
changes desired by the Chinese, was transmitted to Peking
on February 28 on the understanding that it was to be signed
within two weeks, and on March 11 Yan Yu got orders from
Hsianfu not to sign it.130 On the day this news was received,
March 12/25, the Japanese minister called on Lamsdorf and
made "friendly representation" "concerning the danger of concluding any special agreement with China now," particularly
in view of the fact that "some of the articles of the treaty appeared to Japan to transgress the sovereign rights and the inviolability of China as well as certain treaty rights of the
other powers,"--and after that there was nothing left for Russian diplomacy but to reserve "freedom of action" to itself
"in any event."131 On the 15th, Witte made a despairing
attempt to still get some "definite answer" as to whether "China
would or would not sign the agreement before Monday," but
Lamsdorf and Nicholas had already consoled themselves by
the thought that such a turn of affairs was even "in some measure to our advantage from a political point of view" and that
"Russia would lose nothing by it."132 The decision of the
Peking government was irrevocable: Li Hung-chang had the
air of a man who had really "done what he could in the way
of incessantly memorializing the throne as to the importance
of expediting the conclusion of the treaty with Russia," but he
had been "absolutely alone and unsupported in furtherance of
this principle," and now promised that "when peace with the
powers generally shall have been concluded, China, in the
interests of lasting friendship, will gladly sign separate demands at Russia's pleasure."133

What it was in these demands that could bring all the powers
to their feet even after the conclusion of the general treaty
with China, was expressed with superlative clearness by Hay,
the American Secretary of State, in his tardy statement to the
Russian government, on March 15, after everything was over,
when, in a chat with Cassini, he said--in referring to the
"harsh criticism" with which "public opinion in the United
States" had greeted the "insensibility he had shown for the
American commerical and industrial interests threatened by
those agreements that we were endeavoring to obtain in Manchuria"--"We fully recognize Russia's right to adopt any measures that she shall deem necessary and expedient to prevent
a repetition of the painful events of last year. We would even
understand if she should pursue this path as much farther as

she might deem necessary for her interests and projects, provided we had the assurance that our trade would not suffer and
that the 'door' would remain open." No wonder Hay's words
seemed to Cassini deserving of "our exceedingly serious attention." Hay of course said nothing new about the "open
door" or "industrial and commerical interests." What struck
Cassini was that part of Hay's statement (underscored by us)
which he could not take otherwise than as an open admission
that the "U.S.A. had strangely altered its <u>ideas respecting</u>
<u>the inviolability of the Celestial empire, and would lightly</u>
<u>sacrifice them</u> insofar as the powers would guarantee Ameri-
can trade all the benefits of the open door."[134] This still
did not mean that the rest of Russia's partners in Manchuria
would go as far. But that even such a view was possible might
well have served as still another, also not unsalutary, warning
to Russian diplomacy in the event of a renewal of this first,
now discredited, attempt to "return" Manchuria to China.

VI

Suspension of the negotiations begun in February was naturally not of itself enough to create a situation in which the Russian government could actually "await with tranquility the further progress of events," as it declared for general consumption in a message of March 24, 1901.[135] Such an agreement
as had been proposed by Russia in February could only be
signed under circumstances of complete secrecy. Russian
diplomacy had, however, miscalculated, since secrecy by no
means depended on Li Hung-chang alone; yet even when an
exact translation of the text of the Russian project found its
way into the hands of the English minister in Peking, he was
unconvinced of the authenticity of the document until after a
confidential talk with Li.[136] Unless the assurances that
Lamsdorf had given Charles Scott back on January 25/Febru-
ary 6, respecting the "temporary" character of the then sen-
sational Tseng-Alekseyev agreement, had perhaps also referred to the project now obtained, then Lamsdorf's statement
of March 12/25 to the Japanese minister that this project also
"has a temporary character" and "affects neither the sovereign
rights and the inviolability of China in Manchuria, nor the
treaty rights of any other power" plainly had the air of an
empty denial, and Lamsdorf here failed to deceive anyone.
<u>Diplomatically</u>, this whole embarassing episode might have

been liquidated by the official assurances orally given the
English, American, and German ambassadors in Peterburg
(March 30/April 12) that no "proper project of an agreement"
had ever even existed and that he, Lamsdorf, even lacked
the authority to sign anything.137 But politically Russian
diplomacy now found itself in a more difficult position than
had been the case in January.

A new circumstance had entered in, radically changing
the orientation of the Russian government: then, at the beginning of January, there had still been hope of removing Japan
from the ranks of Russia's Manchurian competitors through
a special understanding with her on the Korean and Manchurian
questions. In March, when negotiations were terminated, not
only had Japan registered definite refusal to make any concessions of any sort to Russia in Manchuria until full restoration of the pre-war status quo, but her minister to Peterburg had made what was for Japan at that time an unprece-
dentedly daring move, and her promise to China that she
would "under any circumstances" "assist in obtaining the
evacuation of Russian troops from Manchuria at the proper
time"138 was reliably known. No wonder the "tranquility"
promised in the message of March 24 proved to be merely a
temporary literary screen for the alarm that Lamsdorf soon
had to sound apropos of the apparently quite immediate danger
of armed conflict with Japan over Manchuria.

In May, 1901, on the basis of a dispatch from our naval
agent, Lamsdorf was already suggesting to his colleagues that
"Japanese government circles, influenced by rumors of Russia's plans in Manchuria, had from the very first of the year
been so belligerently inclined that, had not the imperial government's circular message supervened, announcing its renunciation of conclusion of a separate treaty with China, Japan would not have hesitated to open hostilities against Russia then and there." And now, in May, the "war party" in
Japan was "steadily" gaining "influence," and "conflict with
Japan might easily arise on the most insignificant pretext,
even could Japan not also rely on the effective cooperation of
England and the other powers." But the attitude of Japan
"may become more accentuated at the end of the Peking conferences, and also at the close of the current year [1901] when
the re-equipment of her army shall have been completed,"--
and from this, Lamsdorf made the simple practical deduction
that "in evaluating the measures we shall have to take in Man-

churia" it will be necessary to account all diplomatic negotiations with Japan as "undependable to avert probable complications the moment a <u>break with Russia</u> becomes in the eyes
of the Japanese government not a <u>means</u> but a <u>directly contem-</u>
<u>plated end.</u>"139
     Another circumstance that might have opened Russia's eyes
still wider to the complete hopelessness of any active plans
whatsoever that she might have in Manchuria, apparently escaped the attention of Russian diplomacy entirely. It was not
only a case of Japan's approaching the end of her strictly military preparations for war with Russia, but also of London,
Tokyo and Berlin having been at work ever since January, 1901
preparing the necessary international combination. On January 25/February 7, the eve of the Peterburg conference that
confirmed the final redaction of the Russian demands respecting Manchuria, Lansdowne posed point blank to the German
ambassador in London the question of whether Germany,
"conjointly with England and Japan," would agree to force Russia to call a halt to her "independent and aggressive" policy
with respect to China. But at their next meeting Lansdowne
did not renew his question and Hatzfeldt for the moment refrained from making the statement that had been dictated by
him from Berlin: "we desire the preservation of universal
peace that we may ourselves live in peace; in the event of
this desire not being realized and England finding herself in
a state of war with a third power, we engage to remain neutral
toward England."140 But an opportunity was soon (February 3/
16) offered Eckardstein, secretary-in-chief of the German
embassy in London, to make an analogous declaration, and in
a more effective context, in response to a feeler from Hayashi.
     Hayashi had said that in the event of an attempt by Russia
to establish herself in Korea, Japan "would go the limit,"
provided she was assured of the neutrality of England and Germany. As to Manchuria, Japan would go to war only if she
could count on the "active" support of England and had assurance of the "benevolent" neutrality of Germany. Hayashi had
also remarked that "on land we are easily a match for Russia,"
that naval preparations alone were incomplete. Thereupon,
without waiting for a direct question from the Japanese,
Eckardstein hastened to say that "the idea prevalent in Tokyo
as to the existence of a secret agreement between Germany
and Russia respecting Korea was absolutely unfounded, and
that in general there existed no treaty between them respecting

eastern Asia."[141] Nor was there any reason to suspect this
of being a matter of Eckardstein's own personal policy.

In reading the cited report of the secretary-in-chief, Bulow
noted opposite Hayashi's statement to the effect that, had this
idea (about a secret agreement) not existed in Tokyo from of
old, Japan "would long since have adopted an energetic mode
of action respecting Russia": --"Why not now?"[142] And on
February 20/March 5, after a private dinner, Hatzfeldt intimated to Hayashi that Germany had in eastern Asia "no engagements that would oblige her, in the event of a Russo-
Japanese or other clash, to side with the enemies of Japan"
and that Germany "would remain absolutely neutral" if Japan
alone or Japan and England together should be forced to "stop
Russia in China by resort to force." Inasmuch as Hatzfeldt
had, back on February 15/28, succeeded in making an analogous
declaration of neutrality to the English as well, he was not
in the least surprised that Hayashi was now already able to
inform him of his appeal to England for the aid of her fleet
and of Lansdowne's expressed readiness to discuss this question in cabinet council.[143] Germans in London willingly
credited the Foreign Office version that, had the English not
been compelled to maintain an army of 200,000 in South Africa, they would long since have taken an entirely different
tone respecting Russian "encroachments," but these same
Germans notified Berlin of their suspicions, amounting to
certainty, that Salisbury held a different view from that of
his colleagues and not only did not consider English interests
in northern China sufficiently vital to risk war, but even
looked upon the concession of northern China to Russia as a
starting point for a possible general agreement with Russia,
which he was even said to have discussed with Peterburg in
July, 1900.[144]

And, in reply, Berlin flashed back instructions to convince
the English that Russia was at present as much hampered by
a financial crisis as they were by Africa, and that, in the
event of war, Witte "foresaw" the collapse of the gold standard and his own downfall, (but, meanwhile, Witte was the
"most powerful main in Russia") and that Russia would not
carry things to the point of war: --an argument openly designed
to reassure the "irresolute" English premier.[145] But, once
started, matters in London took their course, and on February
22/March 7 Lansdowne was already asking Hatzfeldt whether,
in the event of a Russo-Japanese war, Germany would agree

to make declaration to Paris, conjointly with England, that
the two of them would remain neutral, in order to localize
the war, but that in the event of intervention by a third power
they would jointly "reconsider their position."[146] But when,
upon receiving a non-committal answer from Hatzfeldt, Lansdowne repeated his question on March 4/17 to Eckardstein and
the latter counter-questioned him as to what Germany might
expect from England in exchange, Lansdowne the very next
day opened the subject of a possible "defensive agreement
between Germany and England."[147] Berlin immediately responded with a counter-proposal that England join the Triple
Alliance, provided Japan also joined, and Eckardstein took it
upon himself to speak of a tripartite alliance to Hayashi.[148]
--Thus the Japanese move of March 12/25, 1901 in Peterburg
was backed not only by the recognized preparedness of the
three powers to give Peking advice unfavorable to the Russian government, and not only by Japan's conviction of the
superiority of her armed forces, but also by the reports of
Japanese diplomatic agents respecting "absolutely private"
negotiations, in which even the word "alliance" had at last
been uttered.

The breaking off of negotiations, and Russia and China's
quasi-mutual renunciation of the separate agreement, the
Manchurian "encroachments" of which had given rise to the
"defensive" triple alliance idea, could naturally not of itself
impede in the slightest degree the future ripening of the idea.
This was delayed during the critical days of March, and the
government message of March 24, depicting with provocative
malice and imbecile frankness the course of events and the
conduct of the powers during the whole Boxer period, and
highlighting the wolfish appetites of all except Russia, which
country had, so it said, been prevented from returning Manchuria to China, gave no evidence of any change in the political
position of Russia. And at the beginning of April Hayashi received instructions from Tokyo to renew the interrupted conversations, without as yet opening official negotiations, merely
by way of "sounding out" "how far" "future collaboration with
England in the settlement of the Chinese problem"[149] might
go. The question Tokyo posed, that is, was not of Japan's
joining the "triple alliance," where the Germans had ended
up in March. Yet Hayashi also approached the Germans:
would they enter into an agreement, "along with Japan and
England," concerning maintenance of the "open door" and

the inviolability of China, an agreement differing from the Anglo-German treaty of October 3/16, 1900 in that it would obligate all three to defend these principles from attacks either by a fourth or by the other powers.

Knowing that the Germans had been careful to exclude Manchuria from the sphere of efficacy of the treaty of October 3/16, Hayashi acceded to its exclusion from the new agreement now proposed ("no matter if it gives Manchuria to Russia") providing, however, "that the existing treaty rights [of the powers] be observed." As the future revealed, Hayashi acceded to such an "Americanization" of the treaty with respect to Manchuria on account of the Germans, for the English had, he said, repeatedly pointed out the impossibility of their associating themselves with any agreement respecting China "unless it was simultaneously subscribed to by Germany."150 But reflecting that such a "special" agreement regarding eastern Asia would make it unnecessary for England to join the European triple alliance, Berlin took the stand that, until such affiliation, "let England and Japan be content with our neutrality."151 And that is where Hayashi's "sounding out" of the Germans ended. And Germany's refusal to join England against France at Morocco (in May, 1901) apparently played no small part in England's shift to the idea of a dual alliance with Japan, unless importance here be attached to the efforts in favor of just such a combination that Eckardstein still continued for some time in London at his own risk and peril, for fear of a Russo-Japanese rapprochement.152

Thus, at the end of May 1901, Lamsdorf sounded the alarm and raised his question of whether Russia was ready for war with Japan militarily and financially without himself even suspecting that this was just the moment when the contemplated anti-Russian combination was starting to degenerate from a triple into a dual one, and that after the defection of the Germans, the other two would have no further need of any restrictions respecting Manchuria. And the question of the return of Manchuria to China again came up. Naturally Witte was the one most exercised about the matter. After all that had happened, there could be no question whatsoever of standing on ceremony with China in the spirit of friendship and the treaty of alliance of May 22, 1896. But the occupation of Manchuria, like "any definite measures likely to occasion or hasten a break with Japan" carried the threat of "colossal expenditures" which "would lay a heavy burden on

the Russian people, and chiefly on the great-Russian population of the central governments," and to meet which "we
should again have to suspend satisfaction of many daily
needs of the population, and such procedure in a country
with an incompletely integrated economy and passing through
a period of outfitting in many branches of industry might have
the most serious consequences." Therefore "the thing for us
to do" now, since the breaking off of negotiations and "in view
of the Chinese government's present attitude toward us," is
"energetically protect our material interests in the matter of
compensation for losses," and, in any case, "not make al-
lowances for China to the detriment of the Russian people"
("though personally pitying the Chinese, my sympathies go
out still mo̊re to the people of Russia"). Our only problem
now is "to avoid war with Japan."

Of course Witte could not bear the thought of withdrawing
from Manchuria entirely: "we cannot and must not leave ["to
the mercy of fate"] either the southern branch of the Chinese
Eastern Railway, or the Port Arthur, or the Dalny, but we
must not go farther." "The surest means" of avoiding war
would be: "to consider the Chinese Eastern Railway a private-
company business and confine our role in Manchuria exclusively to safeguarding this enterprise," "by abolishing our
military administration" and renouncing "political occupation
of Manchuria." But, as if this were not enough, Witte next,
in effect, proposed to have done with the Russo-Chinese
treaty of alliance of 1896 and revert to the Lobanov combination that he had so stubbornly discredited and then killed
in the spring of 1895, namely: if Japan should demand Korea
for herself, then attempt to "shift the question of Korea's independence to an international footing," but "should Japan
nonetheless seize Korea" not to regard even this as "casus
belli."[153] Such a statement of the question would in future
inevitably lead, as with Lobanov, to an amicable agreement
with Japan--at China's expense. But such an agreement was,
of course, impossible until restoration of the status quo in
Manchuria, and to set about its restoration now became the
pressing problem.

How convinced Witte was of the immediate practicability
of such an agreement with Japan became evident upon the
first attempt to put the new plan into effect. The first concrete proposal respecting the evacuation of Manchuria was
made by Witte on June 11, was completely developed by him,

was passed at a special conference on June 28, and, having
encountered no objections from the military, was accepted
(July 5) by Nicholas as well. Witte proposed immediate return to Chinese administration of the railway lines in South
Manchuria and Chih-li province seized by Russian troops,
provided China 1) reimburse Russia for expenditures on their
operation and repair (about one million rubles), 2) give "formal pledge" of their completion and operation "on the exact
basis" of the Russo-English agreement of April 16, 1899 and
the loan treaty of September 28, 1898 with the British and
Chinese Corporation, 3) likewise pledge that "no start would
be made on continuation of these railways without our consent, or on the laying of branches to them, or on construction
of the bridge over the Liao river to Yinkow and transfer there
of the terminus of the railway" and 4) would not permit a foreign guard on these lines. But quite suddenly, at the last
moment, Witte also incorporated in these conditions a "political" "demand as to granting the Chinese Eastern Railway
Company the concession for a railway from the trunk-line to
the Great Wall in the direction of Peking,"--the same demand
that Li Hung-chang had himself objected to in February, at
the outset.[154] Meanwhile, according to military advices, the
English and Japanese were, in this region, now entering upon
activities suggesting that they themselves were not preparing
to withdraw from it and that between them they even had "some
general plan in connection with the Manchuria question,"[155]--
a circumstance which made Witte's present attempt to restore
one of the points of the rejected separate agreement project
even bolder and more risky.

    However, when the question of such a partial evacuation
of Russian troops had got well under way in Peterburg, Lamsdorf introduced a new proposal, which apparently stated the
question in full. On July 19, 1901, Lamdsdorf declared the
"imprudence" of making its statement "dependent on the future
course of event," and proposed that, "on our own initiative,"
we set about the "gradual" evacuation of Manchuria and, without previous notice to anyone, annouce it "through publication
of a special government message."[156] Kuropatkin was quite
unable to see the real political significance of such a gesture,
insisted upon leaving North Manchuria (the Chinese Eastern
Railway trunk-line included) under Russian protectorate, attempted to demonstrate that such a gesture would be generally
discredited anyway: "we shall, in effect, be removing one

set of troops but replacing them by another...for Europe,
America and Japan it is not a question of glossing over or
of form, they are sure of just one thing: that we do not actually intend to make full transfer of Manchuria to China,
since we are keeping the railways in our own hands and shall
have plenty of Russian troops upon these railways."[157]
Evidence exists, however, to the effect that Witte also, while
enthusiastically welcoming Lamsdorf's proposal in terms of
inter-ministerial epistolary discussion, still refused to believe in the absolute necessity of withdrawing from Manchuria
unconditionally, and, passing the professional Russian diplomats by, made an attempt through the Japanese minister in
Peterburg to renew the negotiations that the Tokyo government had refused in January 1901. From a long conversation
with Witte, Sutemi "carried away the definite impression that
Witte wished at all costs an agreement between Russia and
Japan respecting Korea" on the following principles: "Korea
to remain neutral territory (Gebiet.) Japan, however, to be
given the right to keep administrative and financial advisers
to the Korean government, as well as higher police officials
and their agents. Japan to pledge, in return, her official
recognition of Russia's predominance (Vorherrschaft) in
Manchuria."[158]

If such a proposal was actually made by Witte at the beginning of July, o.s., then it can hardly be doubted that
"Russia's recent declaration to Tokyo" of her readiness "at
any minute" "to arrange a large loan for the Japanese government in Paris" was also very closely linked with Witte's
political move.[159] This proposal for a frankly fictitious
"neutralization" of Korea--though capable, even in Hayashi's
opinion, of satisfying Japanese public opinion--came somewhat late, since 1) it was no longer addressed to the government of "Russophile" Ito, but to the war cabinet of General
Katsura, who had replaced Ito at the beginning of June, and
2) it would be somewhat subject to repercussions from the
fact that in London, back on July 2/15, Hayashi had been approached with proposals not only to "conclude a fixed, long-
term agreement," but also, as formulated this time by
Salisbury himself, an "alliance whereby each of the allied
countries would be pledged to give military aid in the event
of attack on one of them by the united forces of two or more
states."[160] But this proposal of Witte's, in turn, may also
quite possibly have had something to do with the fact that

notwithstanding Lansdowne's second reminder to Hayashi, on July 18/31, of its being "an opportune moment to start negotiations on the subject of concluding a long-term alliance," the Japanese government delayed for another two months before finally giving Hayashi official authority to enter into such negotiations.[161] But events then took a turn for Russia such that even the sweeping gesture proposed by Lamsdorf on July 19 was never made: unless something happened at this point that we still did not know, then it was pure coincidence that on the next day, July 20, Li Hung-chang again appeared on the scene in Peking with a tempting proposal. On this day Li Hung-chang, without as yet getting in touch with Girs, summoned Pozdneyev and "declared that he would like to have Manchuria cleared of Russian troops as soon as possible, and therefore wished to raise the question of revision of the agreement about Manchuria," but, as a preliminary, wanted to know how Witte would react to this. And only upon receiving a favorable answer from Witte a week later did he also address Girs.[162]

And Russian diplomacy, forgetting all, fell for a second time into the temptation of trying its luck on the road of direct negotiations with the Chinese government.

VII

Li Hung-chang had summoned his Peterburg "friend" to a renewal of negotiations concerning withdrawal of Russian troops from Manchuria at a moment when it was still not too late to take advantage of a diplomatic situation considerably more favorable than that of November 1900 for obtaining Russia's pledge "not to deprive China in Manchuria: 1) of military authority, 2) of the right to all profits from the country, and 3) of independence."[163] Pozdneyev may have been right that personally Li Hung-chang wished to prevent further postponement of the question of the evacuation of Manchuria in order to "take advantage of the absence of the court" for the easier "conduct of an affair" which promised him an opportunity to make quite a lot of money.[164] Girs may also have been right at the moment in believing Li Hung-chang when he said that he "would not demand any alterations in the February project," and in relying on his first impression that Li "was prepared to sign the [old] agreement without any preliminary discussion," for fear "we might no

longer recognize the February text as adequate and might
want new terms harder on China."165 But the fact of the
matter was that Li Hung-chang's move had placed Russian
diplomacy in an ultimative position.

Lamsdorf could not know that Salisbury, as has been indicated, had only now cast doubts aside in choosing between an
agreement with Russia at the expense of China and an agreement with Japan against Russia, and Li Hung-chang could not
even suspect that Tokyo was at that very moment meditating
for the last time before taking the final step in choosing between the English proposal and the opportunity for reaching
a capital agreement with Russia but objectively a plain refusal of the negotiations proposed involved a great risk for Russian diplomacy. It was expected that "in the very near future"
the project for the "concluding protocol" between the powers
and China, finally worked out at the cost of prolonged efforts,
would be signed, and at the beginning of September, new style,
as China had already been officially informed, the first
echelons of allied troops were to be withdrawn from Peking;
and this meant that Russia must expect the statement on an
international scale "of the question of the future fate of Manchuria" to be "next in turn." And Lamsdorf felt sure that
"neither England nor Japan would let slip the extremely
tempting opportunity" to ply Peterburg either with "inquiries"
or with "reminders of Russia's repeated promises" to restore
Manchuria "to China." Lamsdorf now even recognized himself that Russia's mere declaration of her "intention" to set
about "the gradual recall of Russian troops" from Manchuria
"as soon as circumstances should permit" "would scarcely
serve to set public opinion definitely at rest," and saw an
exit from all these difficulties in the proposed "amicable
agreement [with China] on Manchurian affairs," "the more
so" since, in the event of refusal, Li Hung-chang "might
seek aid of the other powers to prod Russia into an immediate
return of Manchuria to China."166 Peterburg was more or
less convinced that, in one way or another, directly or through
intervention of the powers, Russian diplomacy was in the
position of being forced by China to enter into negotiations if
it wished to avert a blow "either to Russia's dignity or to her
immediate interests."

The treaty project proposed by Lamsdorf was not a repetition of the February one as Li Hung-chang had expected and
as the English minister in Peking had learned "from an abso-

lutely reliable [Chinese] source" back on August 1/14, immediately after Li Hung-chang's receipt of the favorable
answer from Witte.[167] Contrary to the opinion of Girs,
Lamsdorf regarded "the agreement in the previous redaction"
as "out of the question," and drafted his project entirely anew
so that its 4 articles (in place of the former 11) mechanically
combined the statements: concerning the transfer of Manchuria to the Chinese government (art. 3), with the terms
Witte had recently projected for the return of the Chinese
railways to their former owners (art. 4.).[168] The new project included Russia's agreement (with the stereotyped proviso: "shall no new complications arise and shall the conduct of the other powers not prevent") "to withdraw its troops
gradually from the confines of Manchuria, planning to have
not more than...[space for figure] thousand of these troops
left there in 1902 and to withdraw the remainder of said
troops in the summer of 1903." But the new project no longer
linked complete evacuation with the "absolute completion of
all construction operations on the Chinese Eastern Railway,"
as Witte had originally wished, nor did it take into account
the strategic considerations that Kuropatkin had just advanced
in favor of maintaining the Russian occupation in the northern
part of Manchuria and moving the line of defense to the Bodune-
Hunchun line, with its reduction in length by more than half.[169]

Kuropatkin's attempt to introduce into the treaty even now
the promise: 1) "to evacuate in the present year (1901)" the
"southwestern part of Mukden province to the Liao-Ho river,
with transfer to China of the railways," 2) "to evacuate next
year (1902) the remainder of Mukden province," and 3) only
"in 1903 set about the evacuation" of the "southern part of
Kirin province and the city of Kirin," was not crowned with
success, and on August 22 Girs was ordered to "enter into
explanations with Li Hung-chang as to the content" of the
project for an agreement concerning the complete evacuation
of Russian troops, in a redaction even somewhat more sub-
dued than that of August 4.[170] This project actually tallied
with the above-mentioned three points in Li Hung-chang's
instructions, and even surpassed Li Hung-chang's own expectations. At least, when he saw Girs on August 18, before
Lamsdorf's project had been delivered to Peking, Li Hung-
chang, though quoting his three points, had, nonetheless,
offered to give Russia a secret note pledging 1) that the "number of Chinese troops [in Manchuria] would not be increased

without preliminary agreement" with Russia, and 2) that
"foreigners would not be granted concessions in Manchuria."[171]
And when Girs, in fulfillment of Lamsdorf's instructions,
demanded Li Hung-chang's presentation of a "missive" certifying his authority and guaranteeing secrecy of negotiations
until the signing of the agreement, Li that same day (August
18) presented Girs with an imperial order in his name and
Ching's in this sense.[172] Thus the matter of the separate
agreement was apparently not to encounter impediments from
the Chinese government, and officially got under way in time
to forestall even those "reminders" by the powers that were
to be expected after the evacuation of Peking.

But then a month went by, and Li Hung-chang had by September 23, after minute study of the Russian project only
been able to think up four corrections to it, three of them
purely editorial, and one so insignificant as to be immediately
accepted by the Russians.[173] Meanwhile, the concluding
protocol of August 27/September 7 had already long since been
signed, the evacuation of Peking had commenced, and from
Manchuria came incessant reports picturing "in extremely
dark colors" a "state of affairs" that threatened "the country
with devastation and ruin, economic life there being at a
complete standstill" and suggesting to Peterburg the "necessity of settling the question of the future fortunes of Manchuria
as soon as possible either by restoring power and meaning
to the Chinese administration or by taking the country under
its own direction and governance."[174] Negotiations had actually gone at a snail's pace up to this time, but when Witte
(September 28) quoted advices to this effect, and expressed
to Lamsdorf his impatience in this connection, they were
already "approaching a favorable conclusion," and Lamsdorf,
to avoid reproaches, ordered Lessar to "enter upon final
explanations with Li Hung-chang on the Manchurian agreement."[175]

But on September 30, when Lamsdorf thus reassured
Witte, Izvolsky had just sent word from Tokyo that "Komura
was extremely troubled by news from Peking as to the renewal
of the Manchurian negotiations," and Lamsdorf, overtaking
his own reassuring letter of the same date, informed Witte
by telegram that "if Li thinks he can turn to the other powers
for advice in the present matter, Russia will be forced to
break off negotiations at once."[176] And when Li Hung-chang,
just as though he had been eavesdropping on the two Peter-

burg ministers, informed Lessar on October 2 that the project for the evacuation agreement had been "approved by the
court" and that he, Li, would immediately request an edict
for its signing," Lessar now "rejoined that this was out of
the question."177 So this project acceptable to both sides
was never again discussed during Li Hung-chang's lifetime,
and when, after his death (October 21, o.s.,) the question
of a new negotiating agent was looked into, Peterburg already
had "reason to believe that certain interested powers would
now not only not obstruct our conclusion with China of an
agreement on Manchurian matters, but were even, apparently,
prepared to advise the Chinese to clean up this question as
soon as possible," and Lamsdorf himself was already devising means to delay the renewing of negotiations.178
    The described vicissitudes of the Manchurian agreement,
unconnected with its tenor as such, find complete explanation
in the fact that simultaneously and collaterally with these
negotiations the Russian government had set to work in Peking,
through the representative of the Russo-Chinese bank, on the
bank's "private" agreement with the Chinese government, the
content of which thus became a stumbling block for Russian
diplomacy. To do Pozdneyev justice, when, on July 27, 1901,
with Nicholas's approval, Witte replied to an inquiry of Li
Hung-chang's that it "might greatly assist" the withdrawal of
troops from Manchuria "if the Chinese government would
give the Russo-Chinese bank a pledge not to grant anyone any
railway or industrial concessions in Manchuria before offering them to the bank," and Lamsdorf, through Girs, demanded
of Li Hung-chang "the preservation of absolute secrecy,"
Pozdneyev at once warned Witte that "preservation of secrecy
in Peking was, in the given case, impossible."179 But the
most attentive investigation will fail to disclose in the correspondence of those days even the slightest indication that
this warning had any effect on Peterburg. Apparently no
suspicions were aroused in Witte even by the fact that Li
Hung-chang, despite Witte's precise indication of the necessity for a preliminary agreement with the bank, innocently
suggested also including consent to the banking monopoly in
the government treaty concerning the transfer of Manchuria,
and, as we have already seen, tried afterwards to foist a
like proposal on Girs.180
    Peterburg merely insisted pedantically that the Russo-
Chinese bank's treaty with the Chinese government had "noth-

ing to do with the question of the evacuation of Manchuria,"
that the Russian minister "should not participate in this matter at all" (except for "the full support" in such cases given
to "Russian private enterprises") that the Chinese government's promise of complete secrecy would be sufficient, and
said not to promise Li Hung-chang even the whole million but
only three hundred thousand rubles--and everything else would
go differently than it had in February-March, 1901.[181]
Meanwhile, as before, Lamsdorf thought "our main job" was
to keep foreign concessionaries "from getting a chance at
important industrial enterprises" in Manchuria, and this was
why both Witte and Lamsdorf regarded the banking agreement
as "secret" and felt that it must be concluded "previous to
conclusion of the agreement concerning the return of Manchuria."[182] Witte and Lamsdorf were resurrecting in its
entirety the former diplomatic combination, and must have
had some sort of superhuman optimism to think that this time
they would with impunity manage to carry the "parallel" negotiations on both agreements to completion, cloaking their
game in a private and state secrecy known to be "impossible"
to maintain.

    From his first talk with Li Hung-chang about the details
of the banking agreement (August 21), Pozdneyev carried
away the "conviction" that Li Hung-chang would "exert every
effort to negotiate it simultaneously with the general agreement but that its [the banking agreement's] conclusion before
the latter would require pressure from Girs; in that talk Li
Hung-chang had in turn "demanded a precise statement as to
whether China would or would not have the right to give concessions to foreigners," regarding this as the question of
"first importance" to himself.[183] And future Russian tactics came down to "working on Li Hung-chang through a
certain promise [known to Pozdneyev] in such a way as to
give him no reason to believe that we specially valued the
agreement or were in any hurry to conclude it."[184] But the
Chinese had even less reason to hurry about giving all possible concessions to the Russo-Chinese bank, and only on
September 24/October 7 did Li Hung-chang suggest that
Pozdneyev show him the banking agreement project.[185] Upon presentation of the project to Li Hung-chang, on September 27, Pozdneyev "went through a very stormy scene with
him," at the conclusion of which Li Hung-chang declared that
he "would never dare to assume responsibility for an agree-

ment that would turn all Manchuria over to the bank" and
"unquestionably call forth the protests of foreigners," and
that he "could only conduct negotiations as to mining concessions."[186] There were no more stormy scenes but at the
next interview (October 2) Li Hung-chang was still so obstinate in his denial of the promises he had given Ukhtomsky
and so persistent in asserting that "the agreement, in this
form, would not be confirmed by the emperor" "and would
call forth the protests of the powers" that Pozdneyev could
only suppose "that China had on the Manchurian question
made some sort of secret pledges to foreign powers."[187]
Needless to say, the trouble here was not formal pledges
but Li's certainty that the foreigners would never consent
to his "turning all Manchuria over to the bank," and Lamsdorf had been right in his earlier suspicions that what lay
back of Komura's alarm at the end of September over news
of the renewal of Russian negotiations was Li Hung-chang's
own direct appeal to the Japanese "for advice." And a few
days later this suspicion, that Li Hung-chang had broken his
promise about keeping the negotiations secret, was twice
confirmed: on October 9 Peterburg received a passing report, of uncertain origin, that "Li had appealed to the governments of England and Japan to intervene in the Manchurian
matter, but had met with failure," and on October 12 even
Li Hung-chang himself admitted to Pozdneyev that the text
of the agreement "was, he had no idea how, already known
to the Japanese government."[188] But, for the time being,
the danger of foreigners taking "steps inconsistent with Russia's dignity" had passed, and to the very day of his death
Li Hung-chang had to continue the footless talks on the banking agreement, now inserting trivial corrections in the text,
now accepting it in its entirey, now pleading the necessity
for consulting Ching, until finally his "double-dealing" reduced Witte to threats that he would "pay him nothing" if he
did not "within the next few days" simply sign the agreement.[189]

Toward the very end, apparently, Li had exhausted all his
pretexts and tried "changing the system": on the last day, he
had assured Pozdneyev that "on the banking agreement he and
Ching were in agreement, but it must be signed simultaneously
with the general agreement, and though he and Ching found
the general agreement sound, the court feared the protests of
foreigners and therefore would not authorize its signature,"
and Li had asked Pozdneyev to wait two weeks, until Ching's

return from court, where he had gone to report in person
as to the necessity of signing both agreements. 190 But when,
after the old man's death, Witte asked Pozdneyev what he
"thought of doing" now, and whether there would be any
chance of his "interesting some influential person, as Li
Hung-chang had been interested," it became apparent that
they must start all over again from the beginning, since not
only had "the loss of Li Hung-chang and Sui Ching-chen [who
had perished in 1900] left our whole party absolutely without
support, but there apparently existed among the highest central officials not a single person capable of courageously and
responsibly dealing with foreigners," and it was as yet "too
soon" to "interest anyone materially."191

The death of Li Hung-chang had created for Russian diplomacy in Peking an entirely new subjective situation, and the
fate of the stalled negotiations must really have caused the
Peterburg optimists serious anxiety, unless they thought
they had not yet played all their trumps.

VIII

If, while Li Hung-chang was still alive, negotiations had
been confined to the evacuation treaty alone and the return
of the railways, the Chinese government would scarcely have
spun out its paltry emendations as it did until convinced of
the impossibility of doing anything about the general agreement without first taking up negotiations with the bank (September 24) and Lamsdorf was entirely justified in parrying
Witte's impatient complaints (September 28) about prolongation of the undefined situation in Manchuria by simple reference to how the whole thing had been held up by "some lag in
Pozdneyev's negotiations about securing concession rights
in Manchuria for the Russo-Chinese bank," since, "until
completion of these negotiations, our minister was powerless to sign the said [general] agreement."192 Unless some
other factor entered in, it was again a coincidence that Li
Hung-chang should, on September 24, have taken the decisive
step of asking Pozdneyev for the text of the bank treaty project and his credentials for signing it, while in London the
next day, September 25/October 8, Hayashi received orders
by wire from Tokyo to take an equally decisive step--namely,
to wind up the "private" conversations with Lansdowne, and,
in deference to his wish, "formally" enter upon "negotiations"

concerning the treaty of alliance, on the basis of such general positions as Hayashi had succeeded in compromising with Lansdowne in "conversations" even more "frank" than their first chat, which took place, as we have seen, on July 18/31, and at the initiative of England: and Hayashi had even then not concealed the fact from Lansdowne that, although "Japan's interests in Manchuria were a secondary matter, still, in view of the danger that after seizing Manchuria Russia might endeavor to annex Korea, Japan did not intend to let Russia into Manchuria, and in the event of war breaking out between herself and Russia [consequently not over Korea alone, but at the same time over Manchuria], desired that the latter be unsupported by other powers."[193]

This capital fact undoubtedly lay beyond Russian diplomacy's field of vision. But at the very beginning of September, old style, Peterburg had been precisely informed of the prospective journey of former Japanese premier Ito, who would "by-pass England" and go "directly to France, his secret plan being to find out how Russia would receive the proposal through Paris of a project of alliance with Japan."[194] Russian diplomacy's attention was so riveted on the figure of Ito that, even after the publication of the Anglo-Japanese treaty of alliance (January, 30-31, o.s., 1902), the firmly established version in Peterburg circles, later released by Witte to the public at large, was that "Ito had been very coldly received in Peterburg," was "treated en quantité négligeable," "got no definite answer from us," "immediately afterwards betook himself to England, was there received with open arms," and that "Japan's treaty of alliance with England was concluded shortly thereafter."[195] It is easy to see how the hints and direct indications that reached Peterburg, as above noted, in September-October 1901, to the effect that Peking was taking Tokyo and London into the secret of the Russo-Chinese negotiations about Manchuria, might have caused Peterburg no serious uneasiness: to the accompaniment of just such advices Ito was already on his way east from Tokyo (via America), lured by the loan that Witte had set as bait for him in Paris back at the beginning of July 1901--Peterburg having taken measures at the last moment so that Delcasse would not give Ito a direct answer but prepare him "in general outlines" for the political conditions to the loan that he might expect in Russia.[196] And the circumstance that Li Hung-chang's attempt (at the beginning of Oc-

tober) to enlist the intervention of Japan and England had
met with no success might well suggest that the textual content of the bank agreement had remained a secret, the more
so since Li Hung-chang's own confession to Pozdneyev on
October 12 had related only to the general agreement concerning the withdrawal of troops.[197]

In any event, on October 31, when Lamsdorf started discussion of the situation created by the death of Li Hung-
chang, he proceeded on the supposition that the main secret
(concerning the bank agreement) had not yet leaked out and
that they might now expect to have trouble over it with newcomers into the Peking government since the former chancellor's death.[198] But now, at the end of October and the beginning of November, Ito must already be in Paris, and the expected Franco-Russian negotiations with him had presumably
begun.[199] Under such conditions, the involuntary interruption of the Peking negotiations must even have been somewhat of a convenience for Russian diplomacy, offering a pretext to state all questions as it chose upon renewal: either
change nothing, or make a whole new start, as circumstances
might dictate after the meeting with Ito. And by another coincidence the Chinese themselves revived negotiations only
after a month's interval, when Ito had already visited Peterburg, and was on his way back to Paris, via Berlin.[200]

Ito stayed ten days in Peterburg (November 11 to 21, o.s.),
outwardly was received "brilliantly," "in an uncommonly
friendly way," and "with peculiar thoughtfulness," and by
the end of his stay had conversed several times not only with
Lamsdorf, who, "while remaining marvellously correct
throughout," "naturally" "could answer Ito only in generali-
ties," but also with Witte, who, "not" being "a diplomat,"
spoke "more frankly and definitely" to him.[201] Taken together, such few data as we have at our disposal concerning
this moment (scarcely to be termed decisive in the fortunes
of Russo-Japanese relations, considering the irretraceable
steps Japan had then already taken in London) do nonetheless
conduce tó the conclusion that Russian diplomacy (in whose
eyes the moment must indeed have seemed decisive, since
our diplomacy did not even suspect how far Anglo-Japanese
negotiations had already gone), failed to recognize the true
state of affairs, i.e., on what terms it would have been possible at this moment to make the Japanese government renounce its still to be completed preparation for war with
Russia over Manchuria.

It had been ascertained in an "oral exchange of opinion" between Lamsdorf and Ito on November 19, that Japan wished to "eliminate the influence of any other foreign power from Korean affairs" and alone have freedom "to advise the Korean government and aid it" "even by armed force in the event of disorders in the country or clashes with other powers," and in return was prepared to allow Russia freedom of action in China "henceforth," should "events of the past year [1900]," as was "very possible," "repeat themselves" there "in the near future." This did not mean, of course, that Ito had immediately offered Russia freedom of action respecting Manchuria, and in just this connection Ito had hinted that what Russia had in Manchuria--the Manchurian railway--was hers thanks exclusively to the Sino-Japanese war.

Taking this hint to mean that for the time being (i.e., "henceforth" until the proper circumstances arrived for Russian intervention in China) the Manchurian road might serve as sufficient compensation to Russia for yielding to Japan in Korea, Lamsdorf parried it by remarking that the road "answers Japan's interests even better than Russia's." And in reply Ito proceeded to advance the idea of granting Japan "tariff privileges." But his further observation--that Lamsdorf would still have to "convince" the finance minister of this--apparently testified to the fact that Ito had either already tried to talk Chinese Eastern Railway tariffs to Witte and had failed, or else himself realized perfectly that the last of all concessions, for Witte on a par with the question of internationalization of Russian railways in Manchuria, was the renunciation of tariff protection for Russian trade in Manchuria. As Witte subsequently formulated it in his Memoirs, Japan was prepared to "reconcile herself" "to the seizure of Kwantung province" and to the building of the road to Port Arthur, "provided we withdrew our troops from Manchuria" and "then introduced the open door policy in Manchuria."[202]

But when, at their second meeting (probably on the 20th or the 21st), Ito presented his "terms" in written form, they proved, upon scrutiny, to be "merely a list of extremely sweeping privileges that Japan desired to bespeak for herself," and Ito, quite naturally, proposed that Lamsdorf himself "formulate" such demands as he would deem "adequate compensation for the rights to be acquired by Japan in Korea."[203] But Ito for some reason did not stay and wait for Lamsdorf's

answer in Peterburg, and the Russian counter-project had
to be sent after him through the Japanese mission in Berlin.
The project drawn up by Lamsdorf was presented for Witte's
consideration on November 27, and after making two slight
corrections (at once accepted by Lamsdorf without demur),
Witte agreed to the rest of the changes that Lamsdorf had
introduced into Ito's text, and, as a result, the Russian
text, as collated with the Japanese, took the following form: 204

"1. Mutual guarantee of the independence of Korea.
"2. Mutual engagement (or Japan engages) not to use
any section of Korean territory for strategic purposes
[against each other.]
"3. Mutual engagement (or Japan engages)205 not to
make on the shores of Korea any military preparations
threatening free passage through the Korean gulf.
"4. Recognition by Russia of Japan's freedom of action
in Korea in [political] industrial and commercial respects,
and likewise of Japan's preferential [exclusive] right, by
agreement with Russia, but alone, to aid Korea with counsels [and by act] directed toward assisting her in fulfillment of the obligations falling on any well-organized government, even military assistance here included insofar
as it shall appear necessary for the suppression of uprisings or disorders of any sort capable of endangering
peaceful relations between Japan and Korea.
"5. In the event provided for in the preceding article,
Japan engages to send to Korea only the absolutely necessary number of troops and to withdraw troops as soon as
their mission shall have been accomplished. It is, at the
same time, understood that Japanese troops shall never
cross the boundary of a tract, exactly defined and located
in advance, along and in proximity to the Russian border.206
"6. On her part, Japan recognizes the preferential
rights of Russia in the provinces of the Chinese empire
contiguous to the Russian border and pledges in no way
to hamper Russia's freedom of action in these provinces.
7. The present agreement shall replace [all] previous
agreements."

A comparison of the Japanese text and the Russian leads
to the deduction that both ministers reprobated Japan's exclusive freedom of action in Korea and absolutely repudiated

it in the political respect, but, for Russia, demanded, respecting the provinces of China contiguous to the Russian border (not Manchuria alone, as could be seen, but the whole
gamut covered by the statement, known to the Japanese, that
had been made by Russia and rejected by China back in February 1901) a freedom of action unrestricted in the political
respect, not partial, but complete ("in no way") and not
upon the occurrence of any new incidents in China, as Ito
had orally agreed, but now. In their counter-proposals,
Witte-Lamsdorf were clearly deviating from the formula:
"you take Manchuria, we take Korea," which Witte had
feared Japan might suggest back in the summer of 1900, and
were approaching the formula: "we take Manchuria to do
anything we like with, and give you Korea, with some restrictions."

One indirect indication exists that Witte not only approved
the diplomatic formulations of Lamsdorf's project, but had
himself in his personal meetings with Ito in Peterburg ("especially the second") "not" being "a diplomat," "frankly"
and "more definitely" expressed himself in the same sense.
Four months later, Ito thus recounted that second chat with
Witte: when Witte "was precisely formulating all the Russian imperial government's tasks in Manchuria, and Marquis
Ito asked him what compensations Japan might hope for in
Korea, such being the case, Witte answered: "meet all our
demands in Manchuria, then--anything you like (tout ce que
vous voulez.)"[207] And in reading this passage of the report
of his agent in Japan Witte jotted opposite Ito's quoted words:
"rot." Which means that Witte had not promised "anything
you like" respecting Korea, and that the restrictions he had
in mind even in the chats with Ito were duly inserted by Lamsdorf in the Russian counter-project since they did not risk,
and did not in point of fact encounter objections from Witte.[208]

But even supposing Ito reported accurately a phrase that
Witte perhaps let slip in a "frank" chat, even so it would not
have typified his real attitude toward the fate of Korea at the
given moment. As touching Korea, Witte attached no serious
significance to the projected treaty. The penetration of Japan to Korea he regarded as an extremely transitory phase,
and one that would create an advantageous future point of
departure for Russia: "when the construction of the road is
fully completed and our influence in the north of China consolidated" Japan will be "in large measure weakened" "by

enormous expenditures" in Korea, which will facilitate Russia's "reconquest of Korea, should circumstances require
it." So the Germans took it that Peterburg had found it impossible to deceive Ito by a "brilliant reception" explicable
only by the necessity of Russia's "arresting premature aggravation of the opposition between Russia's interests and
Japan's"-"until the year 1904." 209 Meanwhile Russian
diplomacy in now demanding "freedom of action" in Manchuria,
seriously set out, as it were, from the assumption that Japan had calculated the date no less accurately than Peterburg
and Potsdam, but it did not grasp the full force of the ineradi-
cable controversy that would exist between Russia and Japan
so long as Manchuria was to some extent in Russia's hands
and Korea in Japan's, which fact, as we have seen, Hayashi
had duly exhibited to Lansdowne in the summer of that year. 210

Small wonder that Ito upon receiving in Berlin such an
awkwardly drawn up counter-project "frankly" replied to
Peterburg that the formulations of pp. 4 and 6 alone gave
him "serious reason to doubt the expediency of recommend-
ing" the Russian project to the Tokyo government "as a basis
for future negotiations."211 Unless it is to be supposed that
when Ito left Peterburg on November 21 he had sent Tokyo
no word as to the tenor of his Peterburg talks, the question
arises: on November 25/December 7, when the Genro council in Tokyo passed, in the emperor's presence, by an "enormous majority" the decision to sign the Anglo-Japanese
treaty, did it not make this decision in the knowledge of what
Russia wanted in Manchuria--not in the words of Lamsdorf,
who had talked chiefly about Korea, but in those of Witte,
who, if Ito's private statement is to be believed, "frankly"
and "precisely" expounded in their second chat what he wanted
there (evidently the question of "compensating" Japan in Korea,
over and above the simple status quo ante, came up immediately
afterwards). 212 In any event, the only thing that Ito even mentioned for Japan in Manchuria was the "open door," which
Witte's diplomacy was at this very time obstinately working
to shut tight and would, after Ito's departure213 so continue
to do without respite. Ito's answer, courteously declining
to consider an agreement, was misunderstood by Peterburg
at the time, and Russian diplomacy, never suspecting that
Ito had hurriedly left Peterburg on November 21 with the
final project of the treaty of alliance with England, received
the day before, already in hand, could for some time longer

not get away from the idea that the Japanese government was
taking an attitude of reserve toward the renewed Russo-Chinese negotiations pending a "detailed report" from Ito.[214]

When, on November 28, immediately on the heels of this,
and three days after Tokyo's decision, Ching in Peking summoned Pozdneyev for explanations on the bank agreement,
and Russian diplomacy had occasion to continue negotiations
with China while transported by the illusion of possibly buying
Japan's complete non-intervention in Manchuria for incomplete concessions to her in Korea, business went on as if
nothing had happened. The formula: "first the bank agreement, then the general" remained in force; "no foreigners
in Manchuria"--ditto. But negotiations continued to move at
a slow tempo, not only because the general agreement was
shackled to the banking, but also because Witte had decided
to really give battle to the Chinese by rejecting their proposed corrections to the general agreement project. Bol-
stered up by Ito's coming, Peterburg's optimism was so im-
perturbable that from the first manifest signs of diplomatic
agitation among Russia's enemies, in December 1901, to the
actual publication of the Anglo-Japanese treaty of alliance at
the end of January 1902, Ito's two collocutors stubbornly kept
to their chosen course.

Ching proposed "certain alterations, in part divesting the
financial [i.e., banking] agreement of its monopolistic character," these taking the form of the basic clause: "shall China
herself be incapable of exploiting concessions, then all such
concessions shall be given to the Russo-Chinese bank."[215]
Ching's correction derived immediately from the second
paragraph of the instructions given Li Hung-chang (China's
right "to all profits from Manchuria") but was now of course
rejected by Witte for fear "foreigners would come in under
cover of the Chinese government or Chinese concessionaries."
Instead, the idea was proposed to Ching of founding a "special
Chinese division" of the bank, which would manage concession
matters in Manchuria but which could "subsequently be made
fictitious with no great difficulty"--and then for one full month
(until January 5) a "waiting attitude" was adopted "in the expectation that the Chinese would take the initiative;" and the
Chinese of course also held their peace.[216]

Instead the Chinese resumed conversation with the minister
as to the general agreement, and by December 15 the following emendations of the Russian project had been proposed to

Peterburg: 1) evacuation of Russian troops not by the autumn of 1903 but by the end of 1902 in three four-month cycles, 2) the number and disposition of Chinese troops to be fixed by mutual consent of both parties only "for the period preceding the withdrawal of Russian troops," and the increase or decrease of Chinese troops in Manchuria after evacuation to be effected not by mutual consent but merely "with seasonable notification" of Russia, 3) prohibition of "guns" for the Chinese police guard to be dropped, 4) China's "engagement" that foreign armies shall not occupy territory of railways returned to China to be dropped and replaced by her engagement "not to permit" foreign (not armies, but) powers to occupy it, 5) all of Russia's expenditures on returned railways to be repaid by China (not simply upon Russia's indication of the amount, as was tacitly implied in the Russian project, but) "upon discussion with the Russian government."[217]

We do not know whether these emendations were presented to Kuropatkin, for example, for consideration, but sufficient to seal their fate was the fact that not one of them was accepted by Witte--on the pretext of their "inexplicit redaction, which would subsequently enable them [the Chinese] to evade observance" of the treaty.[218] But Lessar, encountering no objections from Peterburg, had decided to postpone any answer to the Chinese, even an unfavorable one, on these emendations, until Ching should renew discussion of the bank agreement. But when Pokotilov called on Ching on December 30, immediately upon returning to Peking after a long absence, to persuade him that "an immediate signing of the [bank] agreement was much more to China's interest than to ours," Tokyo had already given Peking to understand that an "exchange of ideas on the question of the Manchurian agreement"[219] was in progress between Japan, America and England. So Pokotilov's appeal sounded like a sort of double paradox, and remained without effect.

Tidings as to a triple agreement, Peterburg, through inquiries immediately lodged by Lamsdorf with Cassini in Washington and Izvolsky in Tokyo, found to be false: Izvolsky complacently asserted that "Japan" had "flatly refused" "some sort of agreement" as to intervention in the Russian negotiations, and agreed that "the behavior of our American friends had been somewhat disingenuous," but Cassini "sounded out" Hay, and Hay "assured Cassini that Russia might positively

count on the friendly attitude of the U.S.A. in the present
matter." Since the French minister in Tokyo had, furthermore, received advices from Peking that "Japan had refused
to subscribe to the English minister's proposed...plan for
joint intervention in the Manchurian question, a refusal no
doubt to be explained by the Tokyo cabinet's hope of an agreement with us about Korea," and since from what could be
gathered, Ito would not reach Tokyo to give the "details"
"until the end of February, new style," Peterburg again ascribed no significance to English diplomacy's supposed blank
shot and believed what it preferred to.[220] Upon now renewing, in January, after a month's interruption, the bank agreement negotiations, Witte, as before, actually refused on any
account to renounce either the bank's monopoly or the elimination of foreigners from all enterprises in Manchuria and
was only prepared to make such modifications of formula as
would meet half way Ching's desire to "save the Chinese
government's face before its subjects." By January 15, as a
result, the two sides were locked in a disagreement that took
the following form in the controversial section of the project:[221]

   "...henceforth either the Chinese government will itself
   function [in Manchuria] on its own resources, i.e., without
   any form of participation by foreign capital or foreign subjects, or the Chinese and Chinese companies functioning
   independently and on their own resources, i.e., without
   any sort of participation by foreign capital or foreign subjects, will with the Chinese government's authorization
   exploit all sorts of mining, railroading and other industrial
   enterprises in Manchuria, and in such cases the Russo-
   Chinese bank, as an institution for the financing of these
   projects. If no such Chinese companies and persons shall
   appear, then preferential right of exploitation shall be
   given the Russo-Chinese bank. If the bank refuses, then
   exploitation may be authorized to other persons or companies, which shall utilize exclusively the services of the
   Russo-Chinese bank, as banker, but infallibly on the same
   terms on which they were offered to the bank.... This
   treaty does not relate to other commercial matters, concerning trade in open ports (and does not in the least affect
   trading rights granted by treaties)."

Finally, when, on January 18, 1902, Peterburg was fur-
nished with intercepted telegrams of January 10/23 and 11/
24 from the Japanese minister in Peking to Tokyo, to the
effect that both Yuan Shih-kai and Wang Weng-shao had let
him know of the prospective signing in the immediate future
of both Russian agreements and that he and the English and
American ministers had agreed to make representation to
Ching "this very day,"--even then Peterburg still did not
lose "faith" that Pokotilov and Lessar "would succeed in
bringing about the desired results."221 Similarly, Witte,
upon receipt, on January 21, of Pokotilov's telegram that
Ching was prepared to renounce the clause about trading
rights and further define the idea "own resources" by the
term: "exclusively,"--he still did not give in, "fearing
that the indefinite redaction Ching was striving for might
enable foreigners to overrun Manchuria."223 Nay more,
neither Lamsdorf nor Witte considered the question of the
bank agreement ended even after Hay's "singular" act in
tendering the Russian government the note of protest of
January 21 (February 3) 1902, aimed exclusively and specifically at the Russo-Chinese bank's "monopoly" in Manchuria,
the "assumption" of which by the Russian government would
appear to be a "denial of the assurances repeatedly given
the U.S.A. by the Russian ministry of foreign affairs respecting the Russian government's intention of adhering to
the open door policy in China."224

Peterburg decided in short order to make believe it did
not know what Hay was talking about and, in replying, Russian diplomacy 1) declared that "of any transgression of the
open door principle" "there is not nor can there be any question," 2) merely spoke of the Russo-Chinese bank's demands
for "concessions" as "in nowise exceeding those made with
like frequency by other foreign companies," 3) deemed "extremely strange [the demand] that doors open to certain
powers be closed to Russia," 4) inquired "whether Russia
could have assurance that in the event of the Russo-Chinese
bank's refusal to secure any concessions in Manchuria, other
powers would not also start endeavoring to obtain like favors
from China...in that same Manchuria?" and 5) refused "to
recognize the right of the United States government to run
single-handed the lease of individual concessions all over the
sub-celestial empire,"--as though the American note had
been talking not about monopoly but about certain specific

concessions.[225] And meanwhile Lessar in Peking continued
to urge Ching not to listen to foreigners, and he of course "resolutely" and "self-confidently" replied that the "Americans
were not protesting against the political agreement, and that
he as minister had nothing to do with the bank agreement,"
and refused Lessar's now pointless request for a "written
statement" that "the intervention of other powers in our
agreements cannot be tolerated."[226] And only Ching's refusal of further negotiations on the banking agreement, transmitted to Pokotilov on January 29, put an end to Witte's pain-
fully protracted attempt to "consolidate Russia's whole influence in Manchuria"[227] his way. But the direct result of
this attempt confronted the Russian government on the very
day after its termination: on January 30/February 12 the
Japanese minister to Peterburg confided to Lamsdorf the
text of the Anglo-Japanese treaty of alliance that had been
signed in London on January 17/31.[228]

   The sudden blow dealt Russian diplomacy by the Japanese
minister's communication at once knocked it out of position
with respect to the evacuation treaty as well.[229] When, on
February 12, Liang Fang in Peking transmitted to Lessar
Ching's request "for acceptance without alterations" of the
December emendations to the general agreement and hinted,
as Lessar understood it, that "if the evacuation agreement
was not concluded soon the foreign powers would take advantage of this fact to intervene in the matter," Witte immediately withdrew all his objections to the compromises
asked by the Chinese and expressed himself as definitely in
favor of signing the agreement, "even if less perfect in form
and to some extent in substance," if only to obviate "a new
impediment in the form of an outrage to our national pride,"
in the event of interference by the powers, and the Russian
minister was immediately given instructions to "endeavor to
accelerate the progress of negotiations respecting evacuation
terms."[230] Only on one point, put forward by the Chinese
at the very last moment, did Russia attempt to exhibit some
firmness. After having obtained Russia's consent to all the
compromises demanded, the Chinese had spoken of expung-
ing from the text of the treaty the notorious proviso "making
evacuation conditional on general tranquillity and the conduct
of the other powers," "which [in their opinion] nullified our
promise of evacuation," and the affair dragged on day after
day and was threatening to go to pieces altogether when Witte

finally made up his mind to end it, "even if substantial expenditures were required to do so."[231] On March 18, Pokotilov
"promised to pay Wang Wen-shao 20,000 lan and promised
another 10,000 lan in driblets," and on March 26 the evacuation agreement was signed by the Chinese keeping in the
proviso that actually gave the Russian government a formal
pretext to retain its troops in Manchuria until the Russo-
Japanese war itself.[232]

The separate policy undertaken respecting China from
the first days of the Boxer uprising, back in Muravev's
time, after the purchase of Liaotung had forbidden even the
thought of any new acquisitions in the Far East until Russia
had grappled with the old, and in particular the monopolistic
policy that Witte then revived respecting Manchuria, and
even, in case of need, respecting all the border provinces
of China, produced and for more than a year maintained a
political temperature exceptionally favorable to the ripening of an international combination in the Far East disastrous
to Russia. Consistently refusing all agreements hampering
her freedom of action, whether with France, England, or
Germany, each of which had separately, for different reasons,
sought such an agreement with Russia, Russian diplomacy,
relying on "bribable" Li Hung-chang, had set itself the task
of getting out of difficulties that arose, not by resort to arms,
but the "peaceful" way, and, should this succeed, prove herself outside the concert of powers in relation to China. However, the necessity of introducing troops and opening direct
hostilities in Manchuria to safeguard the railway, rendering
diplomatically useless even abstention from participation
in the Peking expedition, had actually brought Russia to a
state of war with China and lined the Russian government up
with the rest of the claimants to compensation for war losses.
In spite of having resolved back at the beginning of 1900
to call a halt to any future expenditures beyond those provided
for in plans of developed works in the Far East (even these
being visibly disproportionate to Russia's economic position),
Witte met half way Li Hung-chang's proposals, actually his
own suggestion, concerning political and economic compensations, and these last were not only linked with partial or
full renunciation of pecuniary compensation, but would

necessitate the Russian treasury's preparing itself in addition for new capital investments in the exploitation of new enterprises in Manchuria. Furthermore, Witte also simultaneously set in motion negotiations with provincial authorities in Manchuria, occupied at his request, which negotiations were conducted according to a program approved by him that transgressed the "inviolability" and the sovereignty of China--and Russian diplomacy started basic negotiations with the Chinese central government, in January 1901, at the very moment when one such temporary provincial agreement was made public property and became the occasion for a diplomatic union of several powers directed against any "separate" agreement of Russia with China until conclusion of the general treaty with the latter of all "victor" powers.

Carried away by the idea of "consolidating" Russia's "whole influence in Manchuria," now that circumstances had again brought him face to face with Li Hung-chang, Witte set at naught everything that now made the situation of 1895 and 1896 unrestorable: America's demand for the "open door," confirmed when the United States became a party to the concerted actions of the powers at the outset of the uprising,[233] Japan's categorical refusal to make any Korean agreement with Russia until full restoration to make any Korean agreement with Russia until full restoration of the status quo in Manchuria, conveyed to Peterburg before the separate negotiations opened, the unsuccessful attempt to come to terms with England about a railway line from Peking to Manchuria. There was not much that the original project of the "separate" treaty did not encroach upon as it issued from the depths of the ministry of finance: the sovereignty of China in Manchuria, expropriation of territory to the Chinese Eastern Railway Company on the most generous scale (including lands at the Korean border along the notorious Yalu river, and a naval base at its mouth) diffusion over this whole territory of a Russian armed guard and Russian administration, railway lines to Yinkow and Peking, elimination of all foreigners from industrial enterprise both in Manchuria and in all provinces of China bordering on Russia, and a ban on railway building there such as Russia had just (i.e., in 1900) obtained in Persia and in the northern strip of Asia Minor, legalization of open military occupation of Manchuria until full completion of the railway, which would make a second occupation of the country, should need arise, a question of a few days. No wonder that, even though somewhat toned down by Lamsdorf and, as he thought, made more "pacific," such a plan did not really prove amenable to any "soft-pedalling" and was sent crashing by joint effort of the powers.

Accurately informed of Japan's mounting and all but completed war preparations, and apparently never suspecting the steps being taken in Berlin, London, and Tokyo toward a tripartite alliance, or even conversion of the European triple alliance into a quintuple one, Russia started to make trial of a new plan--to get along without any agreement with China and come to an understanding with Japan at China's expense on the basis of renunciation of "political seizure" of Manchuria in connection with compromises on Russia's part in Korea (July 1901.) But during those very days England too was definitely veering toward a dual alliance with Japan, leaving Germany out, since her presence inconvenienced Japan also, and immediately thereafter Peking made a move that fitted in: Peterburg could not resist China's request to renew separate negotiations, and objectively Li Hung-chang's July move was a weight on England's side of the scales. Provided Tokyo still actually had doubts as between England and Russia, advices concerning the tenor of the new Russian terms for the evacuation of Manchuria must have ended them. Russia's concern was to get "all Manchuria" into the "bank's clutches," and, again, to exclude foreigners, get the railway as nearly finished as possible, and bring the complex of railway troops up to the contemplated norm--maintaining her occupation of the country for the next year and a half, or still longer, should that term not suffice. Continuing to build its whole calculation on Li Hung-chang's personal involvement, and seeking in this a guarantee of secrecy for the two-fold government and bank negotiations, Russian diplomacy hurried to have in hand by the time of Ito's arrival a completed Chinese treaty, which would also serve as an object "of subsequent record" for Japan.

Li's death subjectively threw out this calculation: but Peterburg did not know that when Li gave up talking and got down to business and asked for the test of the bank agreement (September 24) and stormily protested against the Russian demand (September 27) the Tokyo government had already made its irrevocable choice in favor of England. Though building their own calculations respecting Japan on the hope of gaining time to complete all military and railroad preparations, and on the knowledge that Japan had "already more than once conquered Korea" and "more than once" "withdrawn," Ito's Peterburg collocutors (Witte and Lamsdorf) did not accede to all Japan's terms, even respecting Korea, without objections.[234] Meanwhile, several days before Russia's answer, the text of the Anglo-Japanese treaty had been approved by Tokyo and that same international combination been put in force as to the object of which Japanese diplomacy had at the outset declared: that in the event of Russia's attempt to consolidate herself in Korea, Japan "would go the limit," granted the neutrality of England and Germany, but that over Manchuria she would only go to war granted the "benevolent" neutrality of Germany and the "active" support of England.[235] But, as even Peterburg knew after Hay's move (March 15, 1901,) the Manchurian question, not as a question of who should bear the expense of military and civil administration in Manchuria, but as a question of the "open door" there, had now given Japan a new fellow-traveller in the person of the U.S.A., whose appearance relieved her of the necessity of seeking the "benevolent neutrality of Germany" at any price.

On the other hand, Berlin was now anxious to have Russia entertain "no doubt" as to the Germans not having been active or even silent partners in preparing the Anglo-Japanese alliance. Berlin was "very glad" that Lamsdorf had taken the news of what had happened "very seriously," and rejoiced "still more" that he had himself at once opened the subject of the necessity of "other powers consolidating" to avoid war, now possible "at any moment."[236] Actually a rapprochement with Germany was now in order for Russia, and Alwensleben had not long to wait before Lamsdorf himself brought up the question of a joint "declaration" which should state that "shall the signatory powers sustain damage to their rights or interests by China or any other power, they will discuss what measures it will be necessary to take."[237]

Chapter VI

ON THE LAST LAP BEFORE WAR
1902-1904

I

Had the question of executing the treaty of March 26/
April 8, 1902 (whereby Russia must withdraw her field troops
from Manchuria by September 26/October 9, 1903) not been
complicated from the outset by the clause Witte bought at the
last moment respecting the provisory character of this obligation, and had not this treaty itself been the fruit of the
obvious diplomatic defeat that had overtaken the vast imperialistic plan that the Russian government had for seven
years overtaxed its powers to prosecute in order to outstrip
and block the other imperialist powers in China, diplomatic
preparation for building up the military resources that Japan
had during these same years accumulated for the realization
of her Shimonoseki program of 1895 would have proved much
more difficult. But the question of a timed evacuation of
Chinese territory was bound up with the matter of the future
policy of Russia in Manchuria, and outgrowing its local international significance confined to the Far East, where no possible solution would of itself eliminate a military clash between
Russia and Japan, now, with the conclusion of the Anglo-
Japanese alliance, the question passed over into the sphere
of European international relations proper, for Russia so
complicated that there too it constituted a key card in the
larger game.

The 22 months (from March 26, 1902 through January 26,
1904) that elapsed between the signing of the ill-starred Manchurian evacuation treaty and the Japanese squadron's "sudden" attack on the Russian fleet at Port Arthur, and during
which Russia withdrew more than half her troops but kept the
rest in Manchuria some four months longer, were a crucial
and important time, having the power of "creating an epoch,"
of reorienting the international relationships of Europe. The
basic fact in this sense--England's reversal to definite rapprochement with France against Germany--was denoted at

248

the very beginning of 1902, and German diplomacy, having
let slip the last chance to attempt to prevent this in the summer of 1901, found itself obliged to direct all its efforts in
future toward circumventing threatened "isolation" in the
European theatre and to seek such a rapprochement with
Russia as would at the same time enable Germany, just deprived of her Italian ally, to escape the "griffin's claws"[1]
after breaking up the Franco-Russian alliance. With the
prospect thus opened before Russia of being drawn into an
Anglo-German conflict in the more or less immediate future,
Nicholas II's government was confronted by the necessity for
a drastic decision: had the time come either to reorient Russia's long-standing policy respecting England or to scrap the
alliance with France to return to the traditions of a three-
emperor alliance? For, if not, the Russian government
would be called upon to exert incredible dexterity in handling
both the foreign policy and the state economy of a country
incapable of extricating itself from dependence on the "aid"
of European financial markets.

But in that case, for England and Germany in equal measure, the problem of profiting by the colossal numerical
might of the tsar's empire would become a problem of getting
the Russian government into such a position that it would no
longer have the ability (objective or subjective) to maintain
a neutral position between the combatants to the end: which
meant that to weaken Russia was the natural and surest
method of play for both parties--and Russia's great war in
the Far East, already some years in preparation, alone
opened up any prospect in this sense. The conclusion of the
Anglo-Japanese alliance, diplomatically prepared with the
cognizance, and even with some participation, of German
diplomacy, opened this play from the English side, and even
Izvolsky, stationed in Tokyo, was for some time cured of his
naive optimism and now grasped that "henceforth the node of
Russo-Japanese relations would no longer be here but in London and any understanding between us and Japan was now
hardly possible without the full knowledge and approval, and
even perhaps the more or less direct participation, of the
Saint James cabinet."[2]

Lamsdorf's proposal of a joint move of the continental
powers headed by Russia and Germany to counterbalance
the Anglo-Japanese treaty of alliance, which was understood
by Russian diplomacy and Peterburg as an instrument of war,

and the renewal in this way of the former Russo-German
"Hand in Hand politik" in the Far East, tallied exactly with
those steps which, following the above-noted brief interval
in their "personal agreement," the two emperors had already
taken since their Danzig tryst (in August 1901)[3] to meet each
other half way. The Danzing invitation, adroitly extended
by Nicholas's diplomacy in the matter of a separate agreement with China was still fresh, had been accepted by Nicholas (at the end of May) when Berlin had just learned the sense
of General Pendezec's negotiations with the Peterburg staff,
i.e., that France "had been the first to succeed in utilizing
Russia's [grievous] economic situation to obtain future political concessions" (the Paris loan of 1901, stipulating immediate start on construction of the strategic Sedletz-Bologoe
line) and the Danzig meeting itself objectively acquired the
sense of providing some insurance of the balance of power
in Europe and preparing the diplomatic soil for renewed
separate agreement negotiations in Peking.[4]

In any event, it is beyond doubt that at Danzig there was
talk of Germany's supporting Russia in the Far East, and
Lamsdorf and Witte were even prepared for the possible
necessity of producing documents to let the German government in on the nature of the demands which they were then
counting on putting through in profound "secrecy" at Peking.[5]
Of course the Russians also spoke of the desirability of a
Russo-German alliance, said that the idea of a continental
group had a great future, that the time was not yet ripe for
it, but that the tsar would strive toward its realization, that
there was no point where the interests of Russia and Germany
would conflict, whereas England's policy was egoistic and it
was impossible to come to an agreement with the English
about anything; Lamsdorf even "twice" expressed himself
to the effect that "an alliance between Germany and Russia
would be the greatest good fortune and that it was an end
that must be achieved," and although such talks went no further, still even this was a good deal for the first time, and
Prince Heinrich, who visited Nicholas at Spala that same
October, warned Bülow that it would not do to "force" the
budding friendship and that after these two meetings it would
be better to leave Nicholas for a while"in peace."[6] At Spala,
Nicholas had made it plainly understood that his chief interest
at the moment was the Siberian railway, that he hoped to have
it entirely completed in five or six years and that for this he

needed French money--and the Germans must have grasped
that a break with France was absolutely impossible for Nicholas just now, however well developed his consciousness of the
necessity for a union of the monarchic states to confront the
revolutionary movement.[7]

No wonder Lamsdorf's proposal concerning a joint declaration apropos of the Anglo-Japanese alliance evoked some astonishment in Berlin: there the treaty of January 17/30, 1902
was regarded as "Russia's harsh but not entirely unmerited
chastisement for flirting with England, for her passivity during the Boer war, for her indifference toward Germany, her
insensibility to Wilhelm's tokens of benevolence," and finally,
Lamsdorf's perturbation was taken as a clear sign that Russia's "Achilles heel" had been uncovered--"particularly in
the Far East;" and in point of fact it turned out that Russia
did wish to derive immediate profit from the alarming situation created for her, in the form of restoration of neither
more nor less than the Asiatic triple alliance of 1895.[8] This
was a little too much, and Berlin answered Lamsdorf in the
negative, explaining, furthermore, that German diplomacy
would make no direct diplomatic moves in the Far East,
since such moves would only force America to join the anti-
Russian combination openly, and make Germany's negligible
fleet in the Pacific the first target for its blows; and then
(Bülow asked the Russian ambassador) where was the guarantee that under certain circumstances Russia would not be
compelled to attack Germany in Europe along with France?
and had not Russian diplomacy not so long ago (in the Boxer
uprising) taught Germany "moderation" respecting China?

That German diplomacy would by its refusal affront Nicholas as well did not act as a deterrent, since it was evident
that, with the "growing Russophobia" in world politics,
Nicholas's far-eastern program, as just announced by him
at Spala (neither to take, nor for anything on earth let others
have either Manchuria or Korea) would in any case get nowhere; that Nicholas would not feel inclined to remain wholly
at the mercy of France alone, nor would Witte, who had at
the beginning of 1902, for "political" reasons, according to
information from Peterburg sources, for the first time in a
long while sought the next loan not in the French but in the
German market; and, finally, that Lamsdorf was campaigning
for his "little declaration" primarily as a means to his own
rehabilitation. Furthermore Berlin also received in

January 1902 (and communicated to Peterburg) advices as
to Anglo-French negotiations having started between Chamberlain and Cambon on all colonial questions, and, however
much Osten-Saken might assert: "the Anglophilism of any
French minister will go no farther than Russia permits, "
the "personal confidence" of Nicholas in Wilhelm, which
Berlin considered the "top card" in its "political game, "
must have gained new values from the incipient "coquetting"
of the French with England. 9

Nicholas fully realized the seriousness of the refusal received by Lamsdorf, but, relying on the mutual "assurances"
voiced (at Danzig) "respecting the solidarity of their mutual
interests in the Far East, " expressed hope that "accord"
might still be reached, whereupon Wilhelm had Nicholas informed that he "must keep his hands free to cover the tsar's
rear flank in Europe and secure him from threat of attack in
Europe either by sea or by land. " As a result, the whole
episode far from spoiling the game, merely served to weaken
Lamsdorf's position and strengthen direct relations between
the emperors, and from conversations with the Russian naval
attache, Wilhelm was soon satisfied that the Reval meeting
set for that summer would be an important step forward
from Danzig and in general that Peterburg was "very much
afraid of something": in Pauli's frank speeches it had
"struck" Wilhelm that Russia was "very ardently" seeking
his favor. 10

Actually, the meeting at Reval in July (24-26) 1906 took
place under circumstances less favorable for Nicholas than
had been the case in Danzig days. Following Sipyagin's assassination, Nicholas came there in a "more reactionary"
mood, talked much of the necessity of "fighting anarchism, "
as of a topic of peculiarly close concern to him personally,
in a chat with Bülow openly branded Tolstoy "the evil genius
of Russia, " and, not altogether apropos, stated that a consti-
tution would be the "end of Russia." The only foreign policy
question he dwelt on with Bülow was the Far East: he was
markedly irritated with Japan and declared that the "consolidation and propagation of Russian influence" in the orient he
regarded as "the specific tasks of his reign."11 There can
be no doubt that the promise respecting "coverage of the
rear" would have been repeated by Wilhelm, that the theme
of the "yellow peril, " in combatting which Wilhelm had assigned preeminence to Russia back in 1895, was one topic of

the emperors' chats, and that in this connection they also
talked of amalgamating the Russian and German fleets to
counterbalance the Anglo-Japanese fleet.[12]

But in the Danzig days, despite the doubt and distrust of
Witte's course then already "fermenting" in Nicholas, a
treaty closing Manchuria to foreigners was still in prospect
and Russian diplomacy counted on getting its way by means
tested during the lucky years of 1896 and 1898 through Li
Hung-chang. Whereas now, in July, 1902, Nicholas went to
Reval with a Russo-Chinese treaty respecting which it was
anybody's question why he had not signed it in March of the
year before, thus obviating the formation of the tripartite
anti-Russian group in the Far East, and how, exactly, he,
Nicholas, now proposed to avert a sudden attack on defenseless Port Arthur by the Japanese, or on the South-Manchurian
branch by Japanese-organized Chinese troops, and in general
what his future plans were (the question that the above-
mentioned Berlin brochure asked Witte)   and in particular
what he thought of the Japanese seizure of Korea and its
conversion into a Japanese Hinterland to southern Manchuria:
would he, as before (Spala, October, 1901)   regard this as
casus belli, and how unfavorably would the Russian fleet
compare with the Japanese if the Germans made it possible
for him to reckon his whole Baltic fleet for use in the Pacific,
assuming responsibility for Kronstadt and refraining from
direct intervention in the struggle in the Far East so as not
to draw the British fleet in, the latter, by the strict letter
of the Anglo-Japanese treaty of January 17/30, being pledged
to appear only should Japan be attacked by two powers?[13]

The Reval meeting gave, as both sides had wished, an
actual demonstration of "unity," yet this demonstration took
the form not of an open "declaration" by the German government on Far-Eastern affairs, as Russia had probably hoped,
but of an exchange of personal telegrams between the emperors, in which the sense of what had taken place was put
on record--for transmission to the English when occasion
offered--in terms formulated by the German side and testi-
fying to unalterable determination and accord of the two continental powers against any attempt of theirs to reorganize
for purposes of war.[14]

In connection with the Franco-Russian declaration of
March 3/16, 1902, which might have been taken as an extension of the Franco-Russian alliance to the Far East, such a

demonstration testified to the fact that Russia had as yet no
intention of simply backing down before the Anglo-Japanese
threat, and the publication of the Russo-Chinese treaty of
March 26, 1902 concerning the evacuation of Manchuria
could, after all that had happened, scarcely be taken as a
reassuring symptom by any one of the three adversaries of
Witte's Manchurian plans united in the Far East.[15] Outwardly it had unquestionably been a diplomatic victory for
the group of three but any immediate belief that Russian
diplomacy would even on this occasion not attempt by hook
or by crook to actually close the door to Manchuria was unjustified unless the contrary should be demonstrated by a
clear-cut reversal of Russia's whole conduct in Manchurian
affairs. The atmosphere of alarm in the Far East was not
in the slightest degree dissipated by the signing of the treaty
of March 26. And the pointed conversation that took place on
April 10/23, 1902 between Lamsdorf and Scott apropos of the
treaty could only be taken as a sign of Russia's profound
exasperation and a warning that the Manchurian question was
not yet closed. In case the English were further prepared to
refrain from examining "with a magnifying glass" any "decrees" not wholly satisfactory to them, Japan, placed by her
alliance in the position of an English infantry, but also deriving from it, as was generally admitted, extraordinary reserve
power and assurance in view of the war in preparation, proceeded, immediately after the "reassuring" Russo-Chinese
treaty, to the realization of the third part of her naval program, amid a tumult of rumors about the imminent and now
inevitable war.[16]

Furthermore, even when it had already become known that
France did not consider herself bound by the declaration of
March, 1902, still, even to maintain the alliance with France,
and, as he explained to Wilhelm at Wiesbaden not long before
the war (in October, 1903) thus prevent the French making
trouble and "going over to the English," Nicholas was evidently unwilling to place Russia under the necessity of making
a definite choice, in the event of an Anglo-German war, between the two new groups projected. But such a position in
Europe required at all cost the avoidance of war with Japan
in the East at that time. Had this not already been wholly a
paradox since the Anglo-Japanese treaty, it would still have
been possible only through an open and comprehensive agreement on such a scale as to give Japan a real guarantee of

the tenability of her position on the mainland, where she
would first of all have to be admitted, and not permit of
being turned into a mere necessary implement of brief
respite for Russia--that she might drive Japan a second
time from the mainland as soon as she got her strength back.
But such an agreement would, in turn, have required of the
Russian government a most serious revision of the whole
Far Eastern plan, which had grown directly out of the railway plan of 1891-92, which had been put into effect in 1895
and prosecuted during subsequent years by means, and in
expectation, of the export both to China and to Korea of
Russian and foreign capital (under Russian control) for the
industrial exploitation of these countries started at that time,
and which had furthermore from first to last threatened to
increase out of all proportion the military-political pressure
of Russia on the Peking government.

These two plans, absolutely unparalleled in scale and in
the drain on European Russia involved, had been expected to
take not less than ten years, and were the product of circumstances essentially different from those prevailing in 1902.
Both of them were patently and consciously directed against
England (the second even more against Japan) and moreover
against an isolated England and an isolated Japan, and both
(already amalgamated in 1895) were indebted for their definite success in their Manchurian division to the support of
France and Germany, the first capital investments in them
having been made when there was not only no question of an
industrial and financial crisis, but when it might even have
appeared that the economic development of the mother country would itself take new impetus from their unfolding. Russia's main enterprise, the interests of which had since 1895
chiefly dictated Russian policy in the Far East--namely,
the Chinese Eastern Railway--had by 1902 roughly attained
its whole contemplated length and been opened to "temporary"
traffic along its full 2,400 versts. But the road could not
be released "for exploitation" (even at a pinch) before the
summer of 1903, and, despite ceaseless labor from then on,
57 million rubles' worth still remained "to be done" on the
in January 1904, not to mention the fact that the Circum-
Baikal road had in 1902 been put over to 1905, and that in
1902 the Baikal ferry caused complete interruption of railway
traffic for 12 days.[17]

Thus, both of the capital facts above noted: the incipient

rebuilding of European international relationships, and the domestic crisis of somewhat earlier origin that had now succeeded in revealing to the dynasty and the government its alarming social-political side, presented themselves to the Russian government full-grown, too late for all practical purposes: to yield territory and stop construction on the Chinese Eastern Railway seemed "madness,"[18] but to accelerate operations, even could a breakneck tempo have been developed, would be to no purpose, since the advantage was with Japan and would remain there--she had only to watch the progress of these break-neck construction operations, even could a breakneck tempo have been developed, would be to no purpose, since the advantage was with Japan and would remain there--she had only to watch the progress of these break-neck construction operations toward completion and choose the moment to stop Russia in her course.

Furthermore, the question of punctual observance of the dates set in the Russo-Chinese treaty of March 26, fruit of the reiterated assaults of international supervision of the fate of Manchuria, also, as was obvious, remained subject to the control of all three of the powers that had united on the "open door"-in-Manchuria platform, and became, with the Anglo-Japanese treaty of January 17/30 a formal auxiliary instrument of war.

On the other hand, the clause making the evacuation dates conditional was an added danger, since the dates of the March 26 treaty had themselves been set partly for considerations connected with the technique of evacuation, partly with a view to having them correspond with the dates for completion of railway construction and allow time to recruit a whole guard corps of 25,000 to 30,000, in full fighting trim, to replace the field troops withdrawn: meanwhile the 18-month time limit for evacuation at which the contracting parties had arrived instead of the 12-month term proposed by the Chinese--inadequate even in Witte's opinion--was, as the future demonstrated, insufficient for bringing the road to full mobilization efficiency.[19] But the notorious proviso immeasurably increased the chances of war still further because it opened to Russia the formally unimpeachable possibility of use for making essential corrections and additions to the treaty, which not only represented Russia's diplomatic defeat but at the given moment actually satisfied nobody in the Russian government. In all justice, "responsibility" for the defeat fell on

Witte as actual guiding spirit of Russian diplomacy in Far
Eastern affairs since 1900 and "author of the Manchuria
question" as a whole from the first moment of its statement
in 1895. The treaty of March 26, 1902 greatly facilitated
the opening up of a government crisis in this sector just
when Nicholas broke the ominous calm by undertaking to
salvage his autocracy through supplying his government's
powerlessness to do so by personal intervention in its current operation, and when the whole situation both international and domestic would have appeared to demand fault-
less precision and accord in the functioning of governmental
machinery all along the fighting front.

II

No sooner had Peterburg learned, on January 30, 1902,
that the business of the formal contractual "transfer" of "all
Manchuria" to the Russo-Chinese bank was off, and that the
Chinese regarded as final their refusal of further negotiations
in Peking along this line, than Witte took measures to secure
for the Russian government the right to every imaginable
industrial concession in Manchuria, by means of separate,
concrete agreements with provincial authorities. Witte's
concern was to institute this operation on a broad basis and
not let it slip from his hands, instead of heedlessly leaving
the business to the manipulation of the private-capitalistic
element, whereby concessions (i.e., "a considerable share
of participation in capital and in the management of affairs")
actually might well pass into the hands of "foreign subjects"
and "into undesirable hands" in general.[20]
    In September 1901, when Witte still had full confidence
that Manchuria could be barred to the import of foreign industrial capital by a general treaty with the central Chinese
government, he had manifested extreme punctiliousness even
respecting the Russo-Chinese bank and been minded to link
its Board with the Russian government by a special treaty,
from the text of which nothing should be omitted that could
under any circumstances permit the bank to depart from the
role of "figurehead" or from complete subordination to the
minister of finance.[21] Now, on January 30, 1902, in asking
Lamsdorf whether he was agreeable to the transfer of all
concession negotiations to the provinces, Witte particularly
stressed the point that this business must be entirely con-

centrated in the Russo-Chinese bank, and that in future the
support of Russian diplomatic agents in Manchuria must be
extended not to "Russian private (underscored by Witte) enterprisers" as heretofore, but strictly to agents of the
bank.[22] First, of course, concessions already "let to Russian subjects" were set aside, but on the other hand orders
were given that every "large scale" and "supremely important" thing as yet unclaimed be secured in the name either
of the bank or of "its reliable agents" ("with right of transfer"--to the bank, of course), and that "this business be
prosecuted" "as energetically as possible" from the very
first day. Enumerated "as examples" of what "to secure"
were: "gold, iron, petroleum, nickel, coal, exploitation of
timber along the Yalu," but it was also proposed that concessions be taken "for other large scale enterprises."[23]

Haste appeared necessary if only on account of reports
that "many foreigners in Shanghai have Manchurian concessions, purchased from the Chinese," and whereas "last year
they considered their chances lost, now they are convinced
that Russia is through in Manchuria, and will dash there in
the spring to get new concessions."[24] Meanwhile, the local
machinery of the bank was very limited, and, above all, not
in the least adapted to the new function on the technical side,
and Witte soon decided to draw the Chinese Eastern Railway
Company in as well, allowing Pokotilov and Yugovich to function in parallel, set their own bounds by mutual agreement
on the spot, and, if necessary, bring in not only "reliable
persons from among Russian subjects" but also Chinese "sub-
servient to the company or to the Russo-Chinese bank," exacting their "signed promise, under penalty of a huge forfeit,
not to transfer elsewhere, without the company's consent,
concessions obtained by them, and in general not to involve
in the exploitation of such concessions persons of other
nationality than Russian or Chinese."[25]

But it was furthermore ascertained that Yugovich was inclined not to scatter his efforts but continue the negotiations
that he had up to that time successfully conducted for the
road concerning products of immediate interest to it from
the operational point of view--coal and timber, preferring
for the rest to confine himself to mere cooperation with the
bank. And, seeing what Peterburg was here aiming at, Yugovich in turn came forward with the proposal that the road
start buying up "in generous quantities" (naturally unestimated)

"large sections of land in proximity to stations that would
subsequently have commercial importance," arguing not only
the attraction of "revenue from increment in property values"
but also the "political" significance of future "Chinese settlements on our lands with rights of extraterritoriality."[26]
Thus, even before the signing of the evacuation treaty of
March 26, a program of action had been assembled requiring
in the very near future new investments from treasury resources to set up a whole series of "mammoth" enterprises
in a foreign country by way of future "reinforcement of the
whole influence" of Russia in Manchuria.[27]

For the Russo-Chinese bank in Manchuria a new era appeared at this moment to be opening up. As may be inferred
from certain fragmentary data, the bank had, up to this time,
not been persona grata to the Russian occupation authorities
either military or diplomatic. Back in February 1901 in
connection with negotiations with the chiang-chün of Kirin
respecting a provincial loan (of 300 thousand lan for three
years) the bank had counted on reserving to itself the preferential right "over other enterprisers" to obtain concessions for the working of mines in Kirin province, and would
undoubtedly have got this, had it not been for the intervention
of the diplomatic agent Lyuba, who "thought this preference
would create for the bank special monopolistic rights in the
country to the detriment of our private enterprisers, and
therefore refused to agree to the insertion of this point [in
the loan agreement] though allowing the bank to enjoy said
right on general principles."[28] And the agreement Lyuba
concluded (on March 2, 1901) with the chiang-chün of Kirin
as to the operation of "mines and pits" accorded the right of
such operation "only to Russian and Chinese subjects" and
the bank "along with" them.[29]

But all certificates of permission (as yet only for reconnaissance) must be issued "through agreement with an official of the ministry of foreign affairs,"   and by September
1901 "all the gold-bearing districts in Kirin province" had
been "assigned" and the bank was left out.[30] The same
type of agreement was signed in September 1901 by an official
of the ministry of foreign affairs and the chiang-chün of
Tsitsihar respecting Heilungkiang Province (especially the
gold fields on the right bank of the Argun and Amur and in
the Huang-ho, Tulu-ho and Hulan-ho basins) the assignment
of regions for prospecting and working being included in the

agreement itself--with the bank again left out.[31] Evidence
exists that this was not due simply to indifference on the
bank's part. For example, one agent of the bank reacted
thus in February 1902 to the news of the bank's new mission:
"exploitation of the resources of Manchuria I regard as profitable for the bank and very important for the government
too bad that the latter--or rather--its representatives in the
East, should have only remembered about the Russo-Chinese
bank now that negotiations respecting the Manchurian convention have gone badly; during the past year enormous concessions in Kirin and Tsitsihar provinces have been let to a
variety of scoundrels, while the bank was unable to get anything, and in view of our relation to the Port Arthur authority
there would be no special point in asking there for anything."[32]
But even later, when the bank had already set to work, the
Russian consul in Kirin tried to withhold "support" from it
and "support the applications of outside persons," and Lyuba,
while not refusing to solicit concessions for the bank, made
efforts to conceal from the bank's agent the names of localities that might serve as the object of solicitations.[33]

However, the bank's immediate difficulties now lay, not
in the behavior of Russian authorities, but in an alteration
in the Chinese administration's attitude toward the concession
method of exploiting the entrails of the earth--just when Witte,
to save the situation, had placed his stake on the speed that
was to outstrip his nightmare fear of a wave of foreign enterprise engulfing Manchuria. Simultaneously with refusal to
conclude a general agreement with the bank, the Peking
government gave orders to the Manchurian chiang-chüns to
cease all issuance of prospector's permits to Russian subjects, and in the new mining regulations, published on
March 4/17, 1902, reserved to itself exclusive right to confirm permits issued by local authorities, and required exact
indication in concession applications of the locality of proposed
operations. Thus the agents of the bank were immediately
incapacitated for obtaining anything in their own names or
even in the name of Chinese figureheads except within roughly
defined regions, or without binding themselves by precise
indication of the sort of mineral.

The bank must both place itself in exclusive and more or
less blind dependence on the Chinese middle-man, and, should
it actually strive to corner all concession documents of Chinese holders indiscriminately, risk "being hooked by sharp

speculators."[34] Meanwhile, foreigners (Americans and
Englishmen) instead of relying on Chinese agents, had undertaken "detailed explorations" "with the assistance of ex-
perienced technicians" that stopped only at the Tunhwa-shan
district of Mukden province and the Yalu basin, and it was
becoming plain that "our only guarantee of success would be
adoption of a like system," and moreover that to work "through
the bank's actual powers in Manchuria" was, obviously, "absolutely impossible."[35] The first three months of work had,
thus, clearly demonstrated the whole futility of further effort
without special organization, and, in the middle of June,
Pokotilov categorically demanded "a practical solution as
soon as possible of the question of sending Manchuria trained
mining engineers and technicians," to place the matter of
"obtaining" concessions "on a rational footing."[36]

So far, the bank had by its own means succeeded in obtaining little, and by the end of June 1902 results of makeshift
attempts by two or three local agents of the bank had assumed
the following form. In Mukden province, a Chinese merchant
and broker known to the bank (Lian Cheng-chen or, in Russian, Livachana) had, on a salary, been instrumental in obtaining information about, and making applications for, 16
gold, silver, iron, coal and copper beds, but a working permit (in the name of a Chinese company) had been obtained
only for one gold field in the Shimyaotsukow district (area
75 sq. versts,) and the chiang-chün's report on working the
silver, iron, and coal there still remained unconfirmed in
Peking, while his promised reports respecting gold in
Mamakholo and coal in Iloo still remained in project. The
Russo-Chinese bank's financial participation in the matter
had amounted to 5,000 lan in disbursements for gifts to Chinese officials during negotiations, and 3,000 lan loaned to
the Chinese company that got Shimyaotsukow. Beyond this,
the bank had, in the spring of 1902, succeeded in reviving
the "Anglo-Russian Exploration Company" deal made back
in 1899, whereby the bank (1,000 shares) and the English
(Ross, 800 shares and "Gilbert and Co.," 200 shares)
would participate in working gold fields in the region between
Yinkow and Shanhai-kwan. At the beginning of 1902 Ross had
transferred his 800 shares to the bank, and the bank had become holder of 90 per cent of the total capital stock, and in
June 1902 a prominent Korean promoter, the American, Hunt,
had been admitted to the stock company, on condition that

his engineers conduct explorations in the districts reserved
to the company. 37

In Kirin province, the bank's agent had in the entire five
months only succeeded in: 1) reaching an oral agreement with
the local Tao-t'ai Wêng whereby he would "enter into association with the bank" for working the mineral resources of the
province, but "final agreement" respecting "allotment to him
of a share in the profits commensurate with the value of the
parcels acquired" had been postponed until his receipt of the
"expected permits," and 2) obtaining the written promise of
the Chinese official in charge of mining concerns in the Hunchun district and "personally possessed of considerable rights
there," not to transfer these rights to anyone without consent of the bank "for some months." In Tsitsihar province,
the bank had during these months simply failed to do anything
"for lack of a suitable agent."38

But, insignificant as the results of the bank's concession
operation may now have appeared, it was, on the other hand,
at that time ascertained that the bank must prepare to take
upon itself those prospecting assignments that had already
been distributed among Russian private enterprisers, what
with the time limit expiring in Kirin province within the next
few months, and the local authorities making no secret of
their intention to transfer the old permits to new persons
(Chinese at that,) on the basis of the new mining regulations.
Respecting Astashev's gold mines, the bank had, following
the owner's death, started negotiations with the heirs concerning transfer to the bank, but even as to other Kirin ap-
plicants the bank had suspicions that they either could not,
or did not desire to, invest capital in their concessions.39
But whether or not such suspicions may have been justified,
the bank was in any event confronted by the serious task of
keeping afloat, and perhaps even of financing, these enterprises on principles of some participation.40

Thus, by the summer of 1902, when the time for starting
to prepare for the evacuation of troops from the western part
of Mukden province was already at hand, the firm establishment of the bank in Manchuria that Witte had undertaken
raised the question of adapting the bank to the scale and tech-
nicalities of the urgent task laid upon it by government decree. With these circumstances one is practically obliged to
connect the new, third, issue of 20,000 Russo-Chinese bank
shares voted by a general meeting of the stock-holders on

June 22, 1902, in the amount of 3,750,000 rubles. That this was entirely assumed by the Russian ministry of finance only emphasizes the connection: the cornering of concessions and implementing of their exploitation, destined to assume dimensions dictated not by immediate commercial calculation but by a desire to guard Manchuria from the political consequences of the appearance there of foreign capital beyond the control of the Russian autocracy's government, was obviously chiefly a political undertaking, and its economic perspectives were, just as obviously, associated with a considerable risk.[41]

But there were also, perhaps, extrinsic reasons besides why Witte at least formally released the bank from direction of concession operations and delegated this to the "Manchurian Mining Association" ("Anchu" for short,) founded (July 5, 1902) for the particular purpose. This in no way alienated the bank from possible profits or from the practical direction of operations, yet relieved it of all risk.

Actually, the Association was founded by three share-holders: A.I. Putilov, director of the chancellery of the minister of finance, L.F. Davydov, official of the special chancellery for the credit division, and the "Prussian subject" A. Yu. Rothstein, "for prospecting, obtaining concessions and securing from private persons and companies those already assigned, and for exploiting mineral wealth of various kinds in Manchuria," with a fixed capital of one million rubles, and with limited liability of the stockholders.[42] In point of fact, Witte proposed to supply this capital in installments as needed, in the form of loans on the security of the shares of the associates, "from the means of the State bank," which "would at any time have the right to reserve these shares for itself or to sell them," and the whole financial risk was thus entirely assumed by the Russian government.[43] Profits, on the basis of the Association's treaty with the Russo-Chinese bank, which was pledged to "give the Manchurian Mining Association every support both in terms of influence and of experience and personnel, and likewise to effect all the Association's money payments for as moderate a compensation as possible," were to be halved between the Russo-Chinese and the State banks.[44]

Furthermore, Rothstein had obviously joined the Association not in the least as a "Prussian subject" but as director-manager of his bank and "as" its "spokesman."[45] And, as may be seen from the whole Manchurian Mining Association

correspondence, Rothstein also primarily embodied in his
own person that "experience" whereby the Russo-Chinese
bank was, by treaty, obliged to aid the Association.[46] It is
not impossible that in the given instance Rothstein was repeating what he had already done once before in connection
with founding the Russo-Korean bank , when he had declared
point blank that "for all his readiness to meet" Witte "half
way," he "could not ignore the interests of the Russo-Chinese bank's stock-holders."[47] Yet this would not prevent
Rothstein's investing the capital of the Russo-Chinese bank
in the enterprises of the Association, should this be to its
commercial interest, and wide opportunities along this line
had been opened up by the Russian government's latest investment in the capital stock of the bank and by the organization
of the Association itself.[48]

The Directorship of the Association began by organizing
three prospecting expeditions headed by mining engineers,
which during the autumn of 1902 conducted a preliminary
survey of all mineral beds up to that time in the Association's
possession and succeeded in providing the material for drawing up some plan of future operations, whereupon two chief
engineers were appointed to institute and direct the work of
exploitation. But the whole financial-organizational part was
entirely reserved to the Russo-Chinese bank, one of its Manchurian directors was appointed chief agent of the Association,
and the bank "continued in Manchuria to behave toward the
Chinese authorities as if carrying on the mining business independently, inasmuch as on the spot it was deemed preferable for the Manchurian Association to work under cover of
the bank temporarily."[49] But, by all the existing data, Witte
still did not seriously propose to make the mining industry of
Manchuria a permanent monopoly of the treasury. He only
figured that "in the present state of affairs in Manchuria, it
would be extremely difficult to attract private capital to
enterprises in this country," but "obviously, later on, under
more favorable conditions, it will be possible, should this
appear advantageous, to transfer all or part of said concessions to private persons or companies in return for suitable
remuneration," and in his own circle he directly counted on
"attracting foreign capital" "for the work of exploitation."[50]
There can be no doubt that in this case the Russo-Chinese
Bank, should it so desire, would be first in line, and the
only question was, on what terms the tsar's government

would admit private (Russian or foreign) capital to participation in the exploitation of enterprises already on their feet,
considering that Rothstein, as director of the financial policy
of the Association, had at once set out to obtain an absolute
majority in companies where participation of the Association
(under cover of the bank) was proposed.[51]

During the nineteen months that remained between the organization of the Association and the war, the business situation in Manchuria showed no signs of a rise, and the Association was doomed to work to the end of its days with nothing
to count on beyond the State bank's loan of a million on the
security of shares and the interest credited by the Russo-
Chinese bank to that same million. Closer contact with the
actuality and (in July 1903, when the Association had already
stopped buying up rights) an attempt to compute future expenditures for exploitation and draw up a plan of operations, revealed a minimum need of three times the sum allowed.[52]
After deducting what had by December 1902 been rejected,
or shelved as unpromising, by prospecting expeditions, the
corpus of the Association's concession rights having serious
business interest--whether inherited from the Russo-Chinese
bank or obtained through the medium of the bank since the
founding of the Association--included the six following "large-
scale" enterprises (one in Heilungkiang province, two in
Kirin, and three in Mukden.)[53]

Obtained directly in the name of the Association were: 1)
the concession right to prospect for, and mine, gold at
Chapigou (in the basin of the upper Sungari,) by treaty of
November 13, 1902 with Artashev's heirs, with engagement
to form a stock company, 20 per cent Chinese participation
in the capital stock indispensable,[54] 2) the concession right
to prospect for gold in the Kwangshan district along the right
bank of the Amur (from the Wi-ho to its confluence with the
Sungari) and along the left bank of the Sungari (from the Tulu-
ho to the confluence with the Amur) transferred by the
Russian Gold-Mining Company to the Association on April 1,
1903,[55] and 3) the concession to prospect for gold in the
Sansin district of Kirin province (along the lower Mudan-
kiang and along the river Taoken,) transferred to the Association by A.A. Troitsky and L.M. Kutuzov on May 23, 1903.[56]

Participation formally appertained to the Russo-Chinese
bank in the three enterprises in Mukden province: 1) in the
Chinese company "Hwasin," organized to work the western

section of the Fushun coal beds with a capital of 160,000 lan, 60,000 of which had been invested by the Russo-Chinese bank and 54,700 through the bank by the M.M. Association,[57] 2) in the Chinese company "Gishensin" ("Mukden Mining Company") organized to work twelve beds, with a capital of 400,000 lan, of which the bank had put in 150,000 (Chinese share-holders 200,000 and the Mukden provincial treasury 50,000),[58] and 3) participation in the above-mentioned "Anglo-Russian Company."[59]

Though it had by July 1, 1903 spent 427,000 rubles, the Association had not yet succeeded in embarking upon regular exploitation of even one of these concessions. And initial installations and working funds to get two of them in operation would require, by calculation of the Management of the Association: for Chapigou, 600,000 rubles, and for the Anglo-Russian Company's auriferous sands in the Telin district and mineral gold fields at Chashan in the Ninyuan district of Mukden province, one million rubles.[60] In the very near future the Association projected "transferring" the exploitation of these to stock companies it was organizing: to the "Chapigou gold-mine stock-company," capitalized at six million rubles. The charter of the first of these companies was even confirmed at the beginning of July, 1903, and the organization meeting of the stockholders duly took place on August 14.[61] But the company, by admission of the management of the Manchurian Mining Association itself, appears to have been "fictitious," inasmuch as shares in the amount of 1,300 thousand rubles were transferred to the Association as payment for the concession, and the rest, to judge from the list of shareholders, were just about as "fictitiously" distributed in driblets to certain persons close to the ministry of finance.[62] The meeting took place two days before Witte's dismissal (August 16) and its protocol thus remained unconfirmed and the company unconstituted. From this moment, the M.M. Associations at once drops into a decline and, had it not been for the Russo-Chinese bank credit, would have been obliged to suspend current payments.[63]

The Manchurian Mining Association, devised by Witte as a desperate attempt to compensate the failure that had overtaken the policy of "peaceful" conquest of Manchuria by diplomatic means, was cut short by events without even having time to cast aside the "mask" of the Russo-Chinese bank in Manchuria, much less actually to institute a wide system of

stock companies--companies in which in future it would apparently have had to remain to some extent an actual partner
in order to maintain the Russian national character of the
whole organization which was to have enabled autocratic Russia, through railroads, waterways, bank and "mammoth"
industrial enterprises working in harmony, to obtain a share
in the imperialistic partition of China without resorting to a
direct grab of territory.

III

On January 30, 1902, the same day when Witte suddenly
bethought himself to set the Russo-Chinese bank to work as
the government's implement for a sweeping expropriation of
all the most desirable morsels of Manchurian territory while
Russian occupation was still in full force there, and stop the
filching of Manchurian concessions by Russian "private enterprisers,"--who should appear on the scene, as just such an
enterpriser, with pretensions to the exploitation of the Manchurian forests along the Yalu, where Witte had plans of his
own, but the not unknown Matyunin. On January 30 Matyunin
presented himself to Lamsdorf as proprietor of "concessioned
Korean timber-lands" on the left bank of the Yalu, and complained that back in July he had asked Muravev "about stopping Chinese depredations" in these woods and "about reserving [for him] prior right to the Manchurian timber concession
in this same region, likewise subject to ruthless and uncon-
trolled depredations by the Chinese," and that "nonetheless"
the "filching of timber" had continued. "Recognizing the
present moment as incomparably favorable for inaugurating
a timber enterprise on the Yalu," Matyunin asked Lamsdorf
"about assisting him to obtain a timber concession to the
right tributaries of the Yalu" and "about communicating with
the navy department touching the despatch of a guard-ship to
the mouth of the Yalu during the rafting season of the current
year, as soon as [its] agent is sent there from Port Arthur
with the requisite personnel to construct the log barrier.[64]
Furthermore, Matyunin also produced the draft of a telegram to Lessar, which had, so he said,"in principle been
approved by His Highness Prince Alexander Mikhailovich."
But Lamsdorf knew even without this that this former official
of his ministry was only here as a figurehead, and lost no
time in reporting the matter to Nicholas, while the latter,

after confirming the projected telegram to Lessar, wrote:
"Matyunin's request should be complied with, and all possible
cooperation accorded his undertaking as a whole."[65] Thus
Witte in giving instructions to Pokotilov to try to get the timber concession on the Yalu for the Russo-Chinese bank and
in explaining to Lamsdorf the distinction between the bank
and "private enterprisers" (both on February 4) was acting
with his eyes open.[66] In the person of Matyunin, those "undesirable hands" that Witte had more than once diverted from
the Korean forests on that same Yalu were reaching out for
Manchurian concessions. A force politically hostile to him
was entering Manchuria, a force impossible to combat by
any commercial methods.

The beginning of this Korean timber concession scandal
that made such a stir at the time, dates, as we know, from
the epoch when Witte, in search of an ice-free port and opportunity for Russia's further railway expansion after the
successes of 1896, was frustrated in Manchuria by the Chinese and, in the autumn of 1897, started at top speed on the
"peaceful" conquest of Korea, where, it was stated, "Russia's
name and Russian money" had already begun to participate
"in the exploitation of mineral, forest, and other natural
resources."[67] The last was simply a high-sounding phrase:
the only Russian concession Witte here had in mind was the
one taken out in 1896 by Briner, a "Vladivostok merchant of
the first guild," for lumbering operations along the rivers
Tumen and Yalu. But even this lone concession, in the autumn
of 1897 when Russian diplomacy still stood at the Manchurio-
Korean cross-roads, and Witte had not yet ceased to be interested in the investigation of ice-free ports on the Korean
littoral at the mouth of the Yalu, was by Briner offered for
sale and (through Rothstein, whom it did not attract in the
least) might have slipped into foreign hands, had not Vonliarliarsky and Bezobrazov, with the aid of Count I.I. Vorontsov and Grand Duke Alexander Mikhailovich, arranged its
purchase by his majesty's Cabinet.[68]

When the purchase of the concession was formally consummated (May 11, 1898), Russian diplomacy had already abandoned the Korean plan: Nicholas now hesitated to directly
oppose his own ministers and renew the "peaceful" conquest
of Korea at his own risk--and the Briner concession was
salted down by means of its fictitious sale to Matyunin, on
condition of his "transferring" it at any moment to a third

person or company "at the instruction" of Mr. V.B. Fredericks (Minister of the Imperial court).[69] Nicholas was be-
guiled into investing the Cabinet's capital in the deal not only
by the commercial profits of lumbering but also by political
considerations. These were of two kinds. First, on the
concession area of 5,000 sq. versts, extending the whole
length of the Manchurio-Korean boundary, "our military van-
guard" could be deployed, "garbed as lumberjacks, mounted
police, and employees in general," to the number of "20 or
more thousand men," and "communications, provisioning
centers, and bases" set up (what Witte, as indicated above,
had calculated on reserving for the Chinese Eastern Railway
in 1901), since the south-Manchurian branch would otherwise be easily accessible to attack from Korea by the Japanese, and Port Arthur cut off.[70] Second, it was represented
to Nicholas that foreigners were already scrambling for concessions in Korea, and that if Russia did not join in, Korea
would be forever lost to her, or, after "conquest [of Korea]
by force of arms," Russia would only get "the job of policing
other people's property." Meanwhile this "new method of
conquering backward countries" would not work out if Russia
were to depend on "individual Russians" (even Witte considered
any such "new method" acceptable only for the Far East).
Nicholas was therefore called upon to take the "first step" by
participating in the "East-Asiatic Company" "for exploitation
of the natural riches of Korea and East Asia."

The company was given the character of a "political" institution, "directed by the sovereign will of the Russian emperor,"
for the development "of the Russian principle" in Korea "and
perhaps even for the implanting of Russian ideas." It could
only accomplish this "entirely confidential aim" with the participation, as founders, of persons "of unquestioned devotion
to the government" and prepared to "serve the tsar of Russia" without demanding an "immediate dividend" or balking
"at necessary disbursements for expenses of national rather
than commercial significance."[71] From the outset this project savored of the "svyashchennaia druzhina" (consecrated
personal military guard). (I.I. Vorontsov and A.M. Bezobrazov were former members),[72] conscripted to rally loyal
capital about the tsar to do battle for "purely Russian" interests in the distant colony where the tsar, they said, was
himself forced to export his own capital in order to keep up
with the times and achieve "on the basis of economic interests"

the same thing that had formerly been achieved by cavalry
attack and military occupation, and also to attract foreign
capital under his own direction.[73] How could any Russo-
Korean bank, even "of official character," but "pursuing
the aim of material gain exclusively" and headed by Rothstein, a Jew and not even a Russian subject, compare, as
the conducting medium for "purely Russian" "aims quite
specifically of a political character," with a perspective so
alluring to the imagination as this: such a bank "will never
be capable of becoming" "a serviceable implement" "in the
hands of the government."[74]

No sooner had Nicholas launched the "East-Asiatic company" project (March 1900) under renewed pressure from
the "staff"[75] of four, than it became evident 1) that this was
by no means a matter of Korea alone, and 2) that to fit the
new organization into the frame of the existing governmental
mechanism was not so simple, since it did not itself desire
to occupy a subordinate and modest place in the Witte-directed
"trust" in the Far East consisting of the Russo-Chinese bank,
the Chinese Eastern Railway Company, and subsidiary enterprises, while any status outside this "trust" would be denied
it by Witte. The substance of the "project for implementing
the East-Asiatic Industrial Co." presented by Bezobrazov,
as "temporarily in charge of the organization of the company,
by special decree," was as follows. The company was founded
on stock company principles, with a capital of two million
rubles at 5,000 rubles a share. The "dominance" of the
Cabinet was secured by the "concentration" of "more than
half" the capital "in reliable hands." What else was to have
been done is unknown: at the moment, Bezobrazov's concern
was that "no expenditures" be "at present" demanded of the
Cabinet. This was achieved by the provision that "until final
investigation and verification of the commercial expediency
of the enterprise," associates would pay in 1,000 rubles per
share, and 200 shares would go to the Cabinet: 100 without
payment, in return for the Briner concession transferable
to the Association, and the other 100 to be paid for from
the 150 thousand rubles expected from the sale of a part of
it (Dagelet island).

The other 200 shares were to be equally divided between
two "groups" of "reliable" persons: the first group consisted
of fifteen persons close to the court, "blue bloods"* (Count

*"White-boned ones" in Russian--Ed.

Vorontsov, Prince Yusupov, Colonel Vonliarliarsky, Count
Hendrikov, Assistant Counsellor I.P. Balashov, Count Or-
lov-Davydov, Prince Shcherbatov, Count Nostits, P. Ia.
Dashkov, Colonel Serebryakov, Kristi, Captain Abaza,
Count Sumarokov-Elston, Prince Kozlovsky, Mih. VI. Rod-
zianko) the second, of the less select, so to speak, who
were to act as "specialists," to use the project's terminology
(Yakov Pyotrovich Beliaev, director-manager of the mercantile house of "Beliaev and Co.," hereditary honorable
burgess Nicholas Nikoforovich Fedorov, owner of a saw-mill
in Vyshnaya Volochka, commerce counsellor Matvey Osipo-
vich Albert, director-manager of the Neva Shipbuilding Plant,
councillor diplomatic service Nicholas Gavrilovich Matyunin
and "certain other persons as required").[76]

Nicholas was visibly in doubt: on the one hand, he had been
assured that at this moment the fate of Korea was being irrevocably decided, yes, and more than that ("a decision must
be made as to whether or not the Russian cause in the Far
East is to be allowed to perish.... We can now by clever
management postpone the war with Japan for a long time and
get a firm footing on the Japan Sea");[77] on the other hand,
Fredericks raised doubts respecting the "productivity of the
investment."[78]

And then (at the beginning of June) "the psychological moment came").[79] Fredericks, it may be surmised, turned to
Witte for help, and exhaustive arguments were presented to
Nicholas (arguments that drove their opponents completely
into a corner) in favor of a compromise decision such as to
upset the "staff's" whole scheme: 1) if "direction" "by an
agency of government close to the supreme power" was in
question, the Cabinet "by its organization and appointment
indisputably did not have the means at its disposal to influence
the transaction," 2) "the founder themselves, no doubt recognizing the incompetence of the Cabinet in like matters, state
that dominant influence...must be yielded to a person elected
by the founders, possibly someone quite unknown to the Cabinet" (the downright juggling so characteristic of Witte: "election" was nowhere mentioned, and Nicholas could have been
perfectly sure that without his knowledge and desire no
"yielding" of "predominant influence" would occur), 3) "in
reality" the Cabinet "would be reduced to" playing the part
of an "executive' organ of the association to be founded when
in the course of things the pecuniary cooperation of the Cabi-

net was required" (another argument wide of the mark: the
holder of Cabinet shares, chosen by Nicholas himself, would
only be his reporter, and the Cabinet his, the tsar's, "executive organ" as it should be), 4) the "payment of a free bonus"
of 250 thousand rubles to the Cabinet (as above stated, 100
shares at 500 thousand rubles were to be transferred gratui-
tously, whereas only 250 thousand rubles had been spent by
the cabinet) was not only "unacceptable ethically" but also
(here we again recognize Witte) "cannot be regarded as permissible legally" and would "reduce the association's capital,"
which was, even without this, far from commensurate with
the breadth of the tasks being assumed by the association,"
5) it is untrue that any further expenditures will not be required: there will be 400 thousand rubles to make up on the
second hundred shares, 6) the conclusion to be drawn from
this was therefore that "if the founders wish to secure leadership in the enterprise to the government [which, as we shall
presently see, they did not wish] then the safest thing would
appear to be to draw in the ministry of finance [underscored
in the memorandum], which..., of course, could solicit and
obtain instructions respecting the national tasks of the enterprise," not to mention the fact that it "possesses numerous
means both for guaranteeing the material success of the
undertaking through finding absolutely dependable capitalists
[how else could this be understood than as Witte's continuing
to put forward that same Russo-Chinese bank?], and for the
necessary supervision and direction."[80]

But this was the very root of the matter: the druzhina did
not wish to recognize any other direction than that of Nicholas
himself, and wished neither to lose "its banner" in collaborat-
ing with no-one knows who, nor to let third persons profit.
Vorontsov himself now entered the lists against Fredericks,
being his predecessor in the ministry of the court, no less
wise in years and in experience, and enjoying no less authority
with Nicholas, and he did so as representative of the whole
druzhina. Vorontsov presented point-blank a sort of ultimatum:
"the formation of the company hangs on your majesty's decision. The persons on the list in your majesty's possession
are going into the affair with the idea of serving you and Russia; unless it is plain to us that we are working for you and
under your patronage, very likely the majority will give the
affair up, not desiring, after loss of their colors, to spend
time and labor on augmenting the means of x, z or y, with

the views of the gentlemen ministers subject to change. The participation of Your Majesty...is therefore extremely neces- sary." Vorontsov even set a time-limit: "tomorrow"--"the day after tomorrow" he, Vorontsov was leaving for Marien- bad. Thus a "psychological moment" was created, and the pressure produced its effect: Nicholas consented. [81] Inas- much as the charter of the company had been printed in ad- vance and inasmuch as Nicholas's resolution said that "the Cabinet shall be enjoined to buy 200 East-Asiatic Company shares in the name of Captain, 1st rank, Abaza," "exami- nation" of the charter in the ministers' committee was a mere formality. But during these first days of June, "events" in the Far East were developing into open war with China, and on this basis Witte won a postponement--"this matter not to be brought before the committee of ministers until events in the Far East shall have quieted down." [82] And the psychological moment was off.

What happened in "staff" may easily be imagined. Bezo- brazov flew into a perfect rage. Witte's removal was dis- cussed in "staff" and everything blamed on him. He and his dreams were responsible for the fact that all Manchuria was in revolt; but "praise God, revolt and various general mani- festations had now begun, since this meant one more chance to hope for desired changes: we suffer not from China's big fist but from St. Petersburg's." The whole [Far Eastern] question was wrongly stated: instead of acting at the periphery [running the road through Korea to Gishu][83] we set out for the center of the Chinese world," "the whole trouble came from the Manchurian railway and in particular from the branch to Mukden and from that Polish-Jew of a right-hand man who ran things there;" "instead of bringing our own best powers into play, we left the work to Jews and Poles whom S. Yu. [Witte] commissioned to be our color-bearers." "If we now had in northern Korea those telegraph and road communica- tions that were proposed in good season, not only would Port Arthur have secure communication lines, but, even more im- portant, we should not be compelled to exert such pressure on China or to concert with Europe." Of course Witte "blamed" everything on the "late Muravev's policy," but "Muravev's real crime was absence of policy, the active forces being the Russo-Chinese bank and the Manchurian contractors," who "did not keep us posted, did no business (except Jewish geschäfte) and among the yellow peoples only prepared us an unenviable position in company with the rest of the international speculators."

"And what will happen next?" "Military success generally is only half-success in a national undertaking," and, "does a plan exist and do the necessary powers exist for wise use of the successes of our bayonet work?" For the ground is now being prepared for future successes or failures in the Far East and prepared irrevocably: we shall either come out on top and consolidate the Russian cause politically and economically or we shall fall prey to the Jewish consistorium and the tricks of European diplomacy." This in the Far East: but what about the center, Peterburg? "Speculation" "will keep on" and "demoralization" "in business circles" based on justifiable "lack of confidence in the subordinate departments": "S. Yu. created a system which did not work even in peace time, lay heavy on the productive forces of the country, bred a mass of malcontents and dispossessed persons, while in war time this system spontaneously evokes fear of the possibility of state bankruptcy."[84]

But it was now evident even to the "staff" that the turn events had taken in the east gave such prominence to the Manchuria question that this was no time to speak only of Korea. Their passing thoughts at the moment by way of a "principal statement of the question" (of the Company) "under new conditions" consisted in 1) "occupying Manchuria, but under no circumstances parts densely populated by the Chinese," 2) abandoning the authorized line to Mukden and running a branch "from Kirin by way of Port Shestakova through Korea to Port Arthur," and 3) consigning Japan to Amoy and then proclaiming the inviolability of Korea," and for this purpose taking the initiative in a "continental European agreement" directed against England and headed by Germany.[85] Translated into the familiar idiom of ministerial discussion in those days, this meant limiting ourselves "to the non-return" to China of sparsely settled northern Manchuria (Kuropatkin) and obviating occupation of Korea by the Japanese (which "might" "actually" "arouse us," as Witte had thought in the autumn of 1900) by proposing the "neutralization" of Korea (Witte.)[86] That the extension of the Chinese Eastern Railway along Korea's northern boundary was to be effected not on the basis of conquest or annexation of this strip, but on the concession basis is obvious, if only from the fact that until the very end the "staff" continued to

discuss and petition the retention of the Korean timber concession, rather than the annexation of northern Korea.

Under these "new conditions" the "statement of principles
of the East-Asiatic Company question" was then further defined in three respects. First, it had already been "drafted"
to "function in the Far East within the confines of the Empire
and beyond--in Korea and Manchuria," 2) the Company's
function "must be economic-industrial and not financial-
speculative," wherefore, "cooperation with other institutions,
even operating under the Russian flag, was absolutely impossible"[87] and "preference between the two competitors will
naturally be given the one that can offer more political and
moral guarantees of dependability" (what were these two if
not the Russo-Chinese bank and the East-Asiatic Company),
and 3) inasmuch as "the Company could, even before its rise,
confidently expect in subordinate bureaucratic spheres non-
sympathy, dislike, and opposition at the first opportunity,"
it would, apart from "monopolistic rights being obligatory"
(though only "beyond the Russian border," "in order not to
let yellow-skins witness a struggle, even on the economic
level, of Russians among themselves) be necessary now,
i.e., before the organization of the company, "to organize
a preliminary conference of persons who would in time participate in responsible executive work," the "chairman" having
the right of immediate report to the tsar, and "to have created
by special decree of his majesty the office" of "state-secretary"--"for communication with subordinate departments.."[88]

As we see, immediately after the affront sustained, the
"staff" resolutely reorganized, primarily to combat the enemy
within, and projected the very organization, now defensive,
but afterwards offensive as well, which it stubbornly strove
to attain, and did attain as soon as "things had cleared a
little" and "[the tsar's] decision had finished brewing."[89]
And, as principal and specially created weapon for the battle
"with the departments," the "state-secretary" was projected,
"outside the departments"--the post in which Bezobrazov duly
ended up, "when decision had brewed."

We have seen how the "all-powerful Witte now too put on
the brakes," regardless of the fact that in personal relationships the tsar's decisions never "brewed" so very fast either:

the plan Witte proposed was: to get ahead of everybody by
"separately" coming to an agreement with Li Hung-chang
by "peaceful" means, not about Manchuria alone, but about
a series of gold-bearing Chinese provinces, and, by drawing
Japan into this separate plot, tear her away from any other
groups at the price of concessions in Korea (and, who knows,
perhaps not in Korea alone?). But now the first period of the
separate negotiations was over, and Witte's plan had failed:
Japan had not come to the hook, and at the last minute the
Chinese had obviously cheated, and not only was the question
of a continental agreement against England never raised, but
everyone not too lazy took a hand in the affront, even including
Germany.[90] And the clouds of suspicion that had gathered
over Witte's whole "system" the year before "started to brew"
in Nicholas's brain in the summer of 1901 when he urged
Bezobrazov to attempt to put through the Company charter by
"agreement" with Witte, and Witte (for the third time already)
again killed it by a trick.[91] Witte was here under no illusion
as to what he was risking and what price he might have to
pay. "Times" were thoroughly "bad," "many failures, and
a poor harvest to boot." "This is made the theme for suggesting to the sovereign that the financial policy needs changing from the ground up--look at the results of my policy, they
say. But how change it? Of course, they do not know."

And, needless to say, Witte was, as always, convinced
that for Bezobrazov the "only" question was "to clear the
road for himself [i.e., remove him, Witte] and fish in
troubled waters," and Nicholas would, so to speak, be not
so much a party to the sport as the victim and the implement.
But Nicholas, as we know, resolutely negated the "troubled
waters" suspicion (even Witte himself considered Bezobrazov
"honest") and agreed, for example, with Kuropatkin, that
Bezobrazov was himself his implement for "goading" his
ministers.[92] It is now known that Nicholas had not lost hope
of getting a little something, autocrat fashion, even out of
the "failures": for example, from his heart he desired the
personal overthrow of L.S. Poliakov, and interested himself in the possibility of liquidating a failure of the Poliakov
combine in such a way as both to preserve enterprises and
break up the "Hebrew nest in Moscow."[93] Witte had even
"prostrated" the zemstvos: "under my influence, they say,
Russia's autonomy has been destroyed, they say I wish the
sovereign to be remote from the people, and authority to pass

to the officials and, consequently, to the ministers." 94 Now,
since the "trick," Bezobrazov has been closeted with Nicholas "by the hour" "not less than twice a week," retailing to
him "all manner of nonsense and every sort of ephemeral
plan" and saying "it is necessary that I be removed from the
East altogether,"and the tsar has already "casually" launched
such ideas as "ought not the Chinese Eastern Railway to be
transferred to the ministry of roads." The slavish subser-
vience of Witte to foreign capital is illustrated by the statement that he would have "sold the English all the minerals
of Siberia in order to conclude a loan with Rothschild." In
the crisis situation, Witte himself "was not in the least
alarmed at the state of affairs in essence," was "profoundly
convinced that if we stuck to the existing economic policy, in
a year or two everything would again get back to normal,"
but Nicholas clearly "was in some perplexity." 95

For the ministers, back in the spring of 1901, to alarm
Nicholas by the thought that "a break with Russia" now appeared Japan's "immediate aim," and propose that he simply
withdraw unconditionally from the Manchurian theatre, was
one thing, and Nicholas did then give away to "perplexities." 96
But when it was ascertained that in the East all was still far
from lost, and that first China and then Japan were themselves
seeking an agreement with Russia, at this point the "perplexities" relaxed. The Witte-Lamsdorf diplomacy, as above related, again set to work, and was unprepared to relinquish
its positions: Witte again insisted on the Peking line, did
not even think of turning Manchuria over to foreigners, and
though saying for form's sake that the Japanese might some
time be admitted into Korea, did not actually admit them (and
let Ito leave empty-handed). 97 Witte's manoeuvre in connection with the East-Asiatic Company charter proved well calculated: by apparently denying the Company a monopoly, relieving the treasury of pecuniary investments and obtaining
shares on the basis of transfer of the Soochan forest to the
company, thus permitting development only on the initial deposits of the "reliable" private persons and giving them
ready occasion to assert themselves in connection with their
non-confirmation as founders, Witte actually wrecked the
undertaking. 98 In February 1902 the time limit expired for
the first deposit on shares, Bezobrazov collected nothing,
and was "ordered" by Nicholas to "liquidate the concern." 99

Liquidation proved a rather singular process, consisting in Bezobrazov's "endeavoring to get them [affairs] on their feet and on a business basis so that they can be taken off my hands," viz.: 1) "respecting the Korean peninsula, the plan ...is to create in Korea itself a coalition centering in a vast Cabinet concession [to all mines] and oppose this concession to Japanese solicitation," and "if Pavlov [chargé d'affaires in Seoul] does not get embroiled with Mr. Gavr. Gintsburg in process, the success of the combination is practically guaranteed;" 2) "respecting our Korean timber concession, its amalgamation with the Manchurian is requisite," and then "the construction of a barrier at the mouth of the Yalu river for collection of the assessment" that is to provide means for exploitation; 3) "next in turn" we shall enlarge on "Manchurian affairs and the charter of the East-Asiatic Industrial Company"--and for the last time Bezobrazov inquired whether he ought not again to attempt to find a "modus vivendi" through an understanding with Witte.[100] Ten days later, however, Bezobrazov was "fully convinced" of the impossibility of any understanding and "seriously lost heart:" "although I profoundly hate and despise Count Witte and his system, I must withdraw as soon as possible in order not to make it awkward for those associated with me"--inasmuch as he was "bete-noire" to the Witte-Sipiagin group."[101]

And, in withdrawing, this is how Bezobrazov resuméd the "principle" of the cause he must abandon. The aim of the Company was: to be "a reservoir for Far Eastern concessions." "Personal exploitation of concessions it did not envisage but only an intermediary role for the allocation of concessions to firm and fully reliable hands." But "the realization of this idea has up to the moment encountered the opposition of Count Witte," who "was unsympathetic to the principle of the organization of an independent company capable of obtaining independent information and creating competition for the Russo-Chinese bank." And what is the Russo-Chinese bank? It is "an uncertain quantity," "a mixture of exchange banking with the monopolistic right to obtain and hold various concessions," "with a show of dependence" on the government and "private and financial" dependence "on a group of foreign capitalists"--and "it would be hard to tell which spring is the more powerful." "The monopolistic right" carries with it "the indisputable ability to create a mass of abuses," and "things will be unalterable and irreparable" "by the time it

has been borne in upon us that through this bank we are working principally for foreign interests." And therefore it is
"highly desirable" "to confine the bank within its strictly
banking limits, leaving the manipulation of concessions to
another private-semi-official company with a wholly Russian
and trustworthy personnel."[102] As we see, the liquidation
was more like a mine-laying operation. But Bezobrazov,
who thought that now, "with Witte's appointment as chairman
of the conference on agriculture" (January 18) "no struggle
[with him] would be possible," never suspected that two
mines had exploded under his enemy the day before, on the
30th, in the form of advices: as to the downfall of the Russo-
Chinese bank's monopoly in Manchuria, and as to the signing
of the Anglo-Japanese treaty.

Under these conditions, Matyunin's appearance with a
claim to the Manchurian timber concession bore witness that
Witte had failed to uproot the idea of an organization prepared
to take upon itself the fight for the autocracy's interests and
to safeguard it from the disastrous consequences under threat
of which "Witte's" whole "system" had placed it. Behind
Matyunin, as before, might be seen the figure of the tsar's
enterprising brother-in-law, and Nicholas's resolution placed
at the service of the concessionary the whole machinery of the
diplomatic office in those parts. However, neither Gintsburg
in Korea (of whose mission Witte did not even know) nor
Matyunin in Manchuria can have immediately represented
serious competition for the bank, for one thing because the
bank lacked.the desire, and the Manchurian Association the
means, to "get" all Manchuria into their hands.[103] As to
the financial side of the Matyunin undertakings, about Gintsburg we have no data at our disposal beyond the fact that he
counted on the American, Hunt, and that by the "preliminary
pledges" he was only obliged to give Matyunin, in all, 1/10
of the shares of such companies as he "should organize."[104]
But Matyunin's Manchurian undertaking was during 1902 provided with a Cabinet sum of 130,000 rubles.[105] However,
it encountered insurmountable difficulties on the spot, and,
being, to say the least, boycotted by the Russo-Chinese bank,
obtained nothing from the chiang-chün of Mukden except a
year's "chopping ticket" for the right to cut wood on the Yalu
in locations not yet being worked by anyone, and up to the
moment of Bezobrazov's coming to Manchuria in 1903 dragged
out a miserable existence.[106]

Furthermore Witte had not only determined not to put
himself out for Matyunin by setting the bank or the Chinese
Eastern Railway to work, but even endeavored to conceal
from Nicholas the Russo-Chinese bank's actual participation
in the collection of Manchurian concessions by organizing on
State bank capital a state Association with constituent functions which should carefully avoid timber and concentrate on
mines. Now, however, after the Manchurian evacuation
treaty, to expect to extricate himself by such petty compromises and by future concession on the minor question of a
"reservoir for Far Eastern concessions" would have been
naive on Witte's part. His diplomacy had "lost" in the Far
East, and Japan, without delay, proposed that Russia confirm this fact in a special treaty which should recognize only
Russia's railway interests in Manchuria but give Japan full
freedom of action in Korea, with Russia's abnegation of any
intervention in Korean affairs and without Japan's analogous
abnegation respecting Manchuria.107

But when "cabinet" unity, perfunctorily imposed and with
difficulty maintained by Witte (the "Witte-Sipiagin group")
vanished with Balmashev's shot on April 2, 1902, the "Witte
system," which had earlier perplexed Nicholas and was now
being checked by the Zubatovshchina and x-rayed by Plehve
through the police department without any embroidery, was
called to account for what was happening within the country
as well: Nicholas now just "assumed control," without even
understanding how the "system" worked, and undertook to
throw out the technical director, a man who had for over ten
years faithfully and truly served the autocracy with the whole
force of his natural abilities and all the experience that he
had brought over from the private-capitalistic "camp."

In this "system" Witte had sought and found means of
neutralizing up to a given moment the dangers that lurked
for the autocracy in the rank growth of capitalistic relations
in the country-- particularly in the internationalization and
concentration that prevailed at the peaks of Russian capital-
ism--through the autocratic machinery's avid accumulation
of financial and economic might. While choosing this path in
pursuit of preservation of the autocracy of its domination
within the country, Witte sought to reinforce its positions in
the struggle with the outer imperialistic environment by
erecting plans for "peaceful" conquests in China on export of
capital: first, capital completely at the disposition of the

autocratic authority for meeting the state budget, and second, private capital, Russian (though he pinned no hopes to it) and foreign, insofar as it would consent to work in the Far East under the control, and in conformity with the political views, of the Russian government. But this "system" in point of fact only aggravated contradictions, irremovable owing to the class-serfage nature of the autocracy, on the home front, where the class struggle was just now assuming an ever more organized form, and where the imperialistic plans of foreign policy, demanding continuous financing for not less than ten years, under conditions of impending crisis, had laid the whole burden on the treasury, and instead of "peaceful" conquests had subjected the autocracy to diplomatic failures that obviously worsened its chances in the inevitable war. When, in this situation, Witte never ceased to pretend that he was not a party to it and that on the whole nothing irremediable had happened, and even undertook as before, a "peaceful" settlement of the foreign crisis, it would be astonishing if they had again believed him.

In the given connection there is no need to watch how decisions now "brewed" and "psychological moments" arrived (in any event, the Reval meeting here played no small part), but by October 1902, when Witte returned from his trip to the Far East, the Far East was just what people did not care even to converse with him about; and in sending Bezobrazov there on a "mission of a very confidential nature" in November 1902, Nicholas had prepared Witte even for dismissal on January 1, 1903.[108] And when this was successfully averted, nothing more was ever said about cabinet sums, share deposits, founders or charters: Nicholas simply ordered Witte (on January 19, 1903) as minister of finance, to open a credit of 2 million rubles to Bezobrazov in the Russo-Chinese bank at Port Arthur at the treasury's charge.[109] And the question now was actually not whether Witte would or would not attempt to hamper the founding of a new "reservoir for concessions," unconnected with the concern already existing in the Far East: Bezobrazov, commanding a sum twice as large as the Manchurian Mining Association could now without any stock company proceed to the collection of concessions under false names.[110] The question was whether Witte would submit to the will of the tsar and accept the program of action that Nicholas was putting forward by way of revision of the treaty of March 26, for that same old "strengthening of

Russia's whole influence in Manchuria." If he did accept it,
he must also accept the control and leadership of the "staff"
that had long ago sounded the alarm and prompted the program now put forward. And if he did not accept it, what way
out of the crisis could he for his part propose?

At the start, Witte was even prepared to cease "competing"
with the East-Asiatic Company through the Manchurian Mining
Association, if only to lure Bezobrazov out of the Far East
to this hook and cut short the examination he had there undertaken of the "state of affairs" in Manchuria, was even prepared
to cooperate in obtaining in Peking the concession to the
Yalu-kiang forests, if only to get credit for a success pleas-
ing to the tsar and, as he express it, get "in on the thing."[111]
But as soon as it became known to him that Alekseyev was
himself disconcerted by the pace Bezobrazov had developed
in Manchuria and the reckless projects he was divulging right
and left for "turning Manchuria into a sphere of Russia's
exclusive interest" by simply ignoring the Chinese administration and physically annihilating with the aid of Khunghus any
foreign enterpriser who appeared there; and when it then
occurred to him that with Admiral Alekseyev's aid he might
yet overthrow Bezobrazov, whom he justly regarded not only
as his chief personal enemy, strong primarily by Nicholas's
favor, but as a natural calamity generally for any enterprise,
Witte felt victory almost within his grasp, and attempted not
only to oppose, with the whole "mangy triumvirate," the
program proposed by Nicholas (at the conference of March 26,
1903) but at the same time to get out of the fusion of the M.M.
Assn. with the future lumbering (only) company.[112]

This long shelved (since 1898) program, under given conditions absolutely fantastic and "rather childish,"
while figuring on the actual fulfillment of the evacuation
treaty, still consisted in: "organizing a company for the
exploitation of timber resources in the valley of the Yalu
river (both banks) "seeking means of safeguarding" this
"Russian enterprise," "attracting " American and French
capital to its exploitation, and all this in pursuance of the
idea "that now, with the evacuation of Manchuria, the screen
in the Yalu basin gains special significance in the sense of
averting a clash with Japan, and, should a clash occur, in
the sense of an obstacle to concerted attack by the Japanese
and the Chinese on our railway" (in the hope, as Bezobrazov
once finished off, "of morally unstringing the Japanese"

while still in process of crossing the border through this region).[113] Furthermore, Nicholas proposed to "declare" at once that if China did not give the Russians a concession to the Yalu-kiang forests, and Japan did not take measures against the "appearance" of Japanese on the Korean bank of the Yalu, then Russia would halt the evacuation of Manchuria, whereby he greatly facilitated the "triumvirate's" task of demonstrating the whole danger (and at the same time the military absurdity) of the project as a whole.

All three, with the support of Grand Duke Aleksey, amicably attacked the tsar on the theme that this was just the sort of project to risk evoking the protests of the powers and lead to war with Japan, and, without dismissing the private company question, put through the resolution: 1) to "restrict" its function to "exploitation of forests along the Yalu river," 2) to permit the participation of foreign capital, and avoid involving the treasury in "considerable expenditures," and 3) to establish it "on purely commercial principles."[114] Furthermore Witte, without blinking an eye or reproaching anyone in particular, declared that "a limit" should "at last be set" "to the financial sacrifices of the empire for the needs of its remote borderlands" and that, in general, "Russian commercial enterprises in Manchuria" "should be conducted without any expenditures on the part of the treasury" (as if the M.M. Assn. did not even exist). But Witte, to use Kuropatkin's expression, "got his way" even in respect to the question raised by Nicholas of "uniting all the functions of state authority in the East in order to put an end to the existing painful dissension between department representatives," which was now also amicably killed by the assurances of the triumvirs that "differences of opinion" among them were "never" "expressed in the form of lack of coordination between departments," since they always acted "by the direct instructions" and "under the immediate guidance" of the tsar himself.[115]

Thus, on March 26, 1903, the day when the second cycle of evacuation was to be concluded, it looked as if the tsar had been kept from suspending the evacuation and from real conflict with the powers, and an agreement reached, after the five-year boycott, in the form of a compromise to his personal desire, to obtain for him only the legal ability, with small aid from the treasury, of engaging in the wood business on the international market in company with his intimates,

provided he renounce any other undertakings there--in other
words, as if the "emperor's" policy had in person triumphed
over the "Bezobrazov" policy.116 However, the next few
weeks were to demonstrate that Witte had not succeeded in
deceiving anybody about anything. Witte had expected that
Bezobrazov, suddenly recalled by the tsar from the East,
would return compromised by a report drawn up by one of
Witte's trusty agents and signed by Admiral Alekseyev (but,
it turned out, then not sent), and upon Bezobrazov's return
Witte had politely urged him to abandon commercial matters,
of which, he said, Bezobrazov had no understanding.117
Kuropatkin, upon his departure for the Far East at the beginning of April 1903, was charged by the tsar to "cover up the
tracks of" "this Bezobrazov's" "activity."118

And so April went by--and a "psychological moment" again
arrived. But this time the obstinate ministers were confronted
by two accomplished facts: 1) a change of course, and 2) an
administrative reform, incapable of being reduced to commercial pastimes. On May 2, 1903, Nicholas, without asking his ministers, ordered Alekseyev by telegram to "prepare" to put a new course into effect ("under my immediate
direction") whereby, "in connection with the final decision
to execute the treaty of March 26, 1902 to the letter," "the
penetration of foreign influence into Manchuria is not to be
permitted in any form whatsoever" (but to this Witte would
also have subscribed).119 And for this purpose: 1) "broad
development of the activity of Russian enterprisers is to be
allowed in Manchuria [not in Korea?],...particularly in
regions which are important politically or militarily" (as
we shall presently see, Witte was also trying for this) and
2) "in minimal time and without balking at the necessary
expenditures, our fighting power in the Far East is to be
placed in complete equipoise with out politico-economic
tasks, giving a demonstration palpable to all of our determination to defend our right to exclusive influence in Manchuria"
(this was news).120

Nicholas was clearly hurrying not only with the new course
(that same day a telegram also went to Kuropatkin, saying
that "in connection with measures" projected for his department, his "immediate" "attendance" upon the tsar was deemed
"necessary")121 but also with the overhauling of the machinery:
notified Alekseyev that he was to "concentrate" in his own
person the "supreme and responsible control in the Far East

over all departments" (a vicegerency), and, still on the
second of May, appointed Bezobrazov his "state-secretary,"
then on May 7 assembled his ministers, to talk with them
not simply through some "non-official adviser," but through
the functionary that Bezobrazov had now become, and inform
them as to what had happened, explaining why it was impossible that the future conduct of policy in the Far East remain
in their hands.[122] Furthermore, as to the essential thing,
i.e., the necessity of rushing the defense in the Far East
and concentrating it in the hands of a vicegerent, it was
proposed that the ministers merely listen; they were permitted to speak only on the "private company," which had
somehow become a topic of third-rate importance the instant
it had ceased to be sole instrument of the "personal" policy
of the tsar.[123] At the meeting of May 7, Bezobrazov proposed point-blank to give up bothering about the Manchurian
timber concession, and even "to postpone the fullscale organization" of the projected company; Witte again endeavored to
maintain, despite its obviousness to all, that "according to
the principles of our financial economy the treasury ought
not to participate in the stock capital of the company"; but
this time Plehve, not without malice, proposed, as if reassuring Witte, "that they wait about attracting foreign
capital to the concern" in order "to prevent the penetration
into Manchuria of largescale economic interests of foreign
states" "before the creation there of actual security for our
own interests;" and in this case what else was there for it
but to "define the extent of the treasury's participation in the
stock capital of the company [not as the "modest dimensions"
of March 26, but] as corresponding to the actual interests of
the state."[124] That the immediate settlement of the limits
of this participation was upon this occasion still entrusted
to Bezobrazov and Witte was an altogether paltry concession
as compared with the fact that it had been proposed (in the
telegram of May 2) that Alekseyev discuss the general principles of economic policy in the Far East not with Witte but
with Bezobrazov alone.

Thus, what happened on May 2-7, 1903, in no wise fits
the formula then released by illustrious Prince Meshchersky
and much relished in Peterburg ministerial circles, to the
effect that a "conspiracy had been organized against the
sovereign and his ministers, and that it was headed by Niko-
lay Aleksandrovich (as we should now say, Romanov) with

Bezobrazov, Abaza and so on as fellow conspirators."125
The fact was exactly the contrary: what had until then been
the "tsar's unofficial" policy and "at war" with the "tsar's
official," as Vorontsov had complained to Witte, had now
finally replaced the former "tsar's official" as present
"tsar's official" policy.126 In the shape in which it was formulated on these days in May, it set itself the same task
the the "imperial" policy promulgated by Witte had previously
pursued. The capital distinction between the new course and
its predecessor lay in the fact that the problem of the military
preparedness of Russia in the Far-Eastern theatre for actual
defense of the old program was brought to the fore: not defense of direct annexation, the seizure of Manchuria, but of
its economic conquest and protection from "inundation" by
foreigners.127 While the new course proceeded from the
idea that "enormous sums" had been spent on Manchuria
"and the whole thing was up in the air" (since "should Japan
today take a notion to seize Port Arthur and our road, we
could offer no resistance by land," and were "at the given
moment absolutely dependent on Japan"),128 advocates of
the former course were "convinced" "that the forces we have
are quite sufficient for the defense of what we already possess" and "that Japan will never touch us unless we wish to
make further seizures."129 The task of Russian diplomacy
even now, in May 1903, seemed to Witte quite "simple":
"we must abandon the thought of seizing Korea"--and "that's
all."130
　　Meanwhile, Nicholas had definitely veered to the new
course in May, immediately after his "imperial" diplomacy,
keeping to the old course, had, in April 1903, at full speed
and at the same point, run hopelessly aground for the third
time, in Manchuria--not in Korea.

IV

　　That the treaty of March 26, 1902 had exhausted the sum
total of questions at issue between Russia and China even
from the viewpoint of "defense of the interests" of the Chinese
Eastern Railway alone, even Witte did not affirm. Upon returning from the East in the autumn of 1902, he himself raised
the question, for example, of the necessity of extending the
railway concession to the line from Kwang-chung-tse to
Kirin, since for the full security of the Chinese Eastern Rail-

way "in the event of political complications with China" it
would be necessary, "preliminary to the withdrawal of our
field troops from Manchuria," for troops of the border
guard "to occupy" "all the principal cities." Meanwhile,
"after the evacuation of Manchuria, we shall only have the
right to maintain detachments in that country along the line
of the railway, on pretext of its protection," and Kirin is the
"most principal" center, with "important ordnance, commis-
sary, and ammunition depots" and a "military arsenal," and
if the Kirin station "could be located on a height commanding
the city" and provided with "even a small battery, it would
be in a position to threaten the whole city with destruction."[131]

In March 1903, when the time for the evacuation of Kirin
approached, and the question of a branch to it was still unsettled, the commander of the trans-Amur district border-
guard, the finance minister's subordinate, asked permission to occupy this position synchronously with the departure
of the Russian troops, before the Chinese should have time
to occupy it, and Witte of course raised no objection.[132]
When (in February 1902) Yugovich submitted the idea of a
generous purchase of lands in the region of large stations,
Witte readily grasped this "political" idea and developed it
into a complete plan for widening the zone and for its colonization not only by "persons of the tradesman-industrial class,"
Russian and Chinese (but not foreigners, who "must not be
permitted to acquire any foot-hold at all in the region of the
road,") but by the organization of "whole soldiers' settlements" of non-coms transferred to the reserve.[133] Finally,
a project for having the road operated "by troops," through
the medium of railway battalions, and for the subordination,
"as a whole, of all Russian employees" of the road "to the
regulations for railway employees in war time" was now
brought forward by Witte, in view of the imminent withdrawal
of field troops.[134] But that the "settlement of the Manchurian
question" for now was in "literal fulfillment" of the treaty of
March 26, Witte regarded as "beyond question."[135] This did
not mean, however, that Witte had once and for all renounced
the direct annexation of Manchuria: "if serious complications
shall subsequently arise in the Manchuria returned by us,"
then, in "re-introducing our armies there" "we shall have
good ground" for setting about "the establishment there of a
normal Russian administration."[136] It is easily seen that
by such a statement of the question, Witte was himself open-

ing the loop-hole for revision of the treaty of March 26 that
he had himself bought at the last moment when the act was
being signed.

As we know, respecting the northern section, Kuropatkin
had from the very beginning of the "temporary" occupation
of Manchuria regarded as imperative, if not annexation,
then the maintenance of occupation and of the Russian "governmental control" established back in the autumn of 1900.[137]
So now, Kuropatkin simply declined to be responsible, as
minister of war, for the "outward security" of Russia's Pacific possessions if the trunk-line of the Chinese Eastern Railway to Vladivostok remained in the position of a "thread
easily broken," and threatened in such case to "insist on the
immediate construction of a new railway through Russian
territory from Sretensk to Khabarovsk," though then "all
past expenditures will have been in vain."[138] When, back
in July 1902, during the first period of evacuation, Kuropatkin had criticized the signed treaty, and attempted to mention
the necessity "in view of evacuation" of getting the Chinese
government to agree "on no account to admit instructors
from Japan or other nations for the purpose of training Chinese troops in Manchuria," and to permit the maintenance
of military commissars "to keep an eye on the development
of the Chinese armed forces,"--Lamsdorf had categorically
refused to raise, for the Russian government, the question
of "unsatisfactoriness of the statement he had himself worked
out."[139]

But when the first cycle of evacuation was happily concluded,
and Mukden province west of the Liao, along with the railroads,
had been turned over to the Chinese administration, the question of the "unsatisfactoriness" of the March 26 treaty was
raised anew, and this time not by Kuropatkin alone. The projected semi-annexation of North Manchuria must now be
definitely and finally accepted or rejected: in the second cycle,
by March 26, 1903, the treaty obliged Russia to clear not only
the remainder of Mukden province, respecting which no disagreement existed among the triumvirate, but also all of Kirin
province, for which Witte was not quite prepared even in part,
while Kuropatkin's scheme established a line of demarcation
"from the confluence of the Nonni with the Sungari, near
Bodune, to the moth of the Tumen."[140] This disagreement
within the triumvirate got on practical ground at the most
unfortunate moment, when redoubled circumspection toward

the "admiral of the Pacific ocean" was requisite before the
emboldened Bezobrazovists, and demonstration of the solidarity of the suspected "department." A review of the Manchurian question as an aspect of Russo-Chinese relations
particularly suggested itself because this question had been
brought up as an aspect of Russo-Japanese relations by the
latest Japanese proposal (that of July 22/August 4, 1902)
the Korean points in which prompted a statement in its
entirety of the whole question of the "general trend of Russian policy in the Far East."[141]

A new fact that now had also to be taken into account was
the impending extension to Manchuria of the competence of
the office of Chinese maritime customs and the arrival in
each of its provinces of "one or more" officials of the "foreign staff" of this office, assigned there "for service connected with the affairs of the native customs house" by agreement with Sir Robert Hart.[142] Finally, as to the situation
on the spot, in Manchuria itself, a clear idea on the question
of Peterburg's future policy was there even less possible to
get; and this further increased the chaos in which the country had existed for over two years.[143]

In undertaking a review of the general question of Russia's
future policy in the East, Lamsdorf did all he could to make
this review as imposing as possible and to propose a program
to Nicholas that should rest on the authority of all four of the
ministers interested (i.e., Tyrtov, minister of the navy,
included) and all three of Russia's representatives in the
capitals of China, Japan and Korea. Rozen, who had been
in Japan in 1897-8 and now again held the appointment there,
Pavlov (Korea) and Lessar presented extensive memoranda.
In January 1903 all three assembled in Peterburg, had a
preliminary, but quite official conference with Lamsdorf
(January 11) and then participated in an equally official conference with the ministers (January 25).[144] Both questions:
the agreement with Japan and the evacuation of Manchuria
were discussed, and resolutions upon them passed unanimously. As a peacemaker, Lamsdorf was indisputably successful, and compromise was reached at the price of mutual
concessions. Rozen, who had originally, in his memorandum,
come out very definitely against the agreement with Japan
and in favor of the annexation of Manchuria, at the conference
spoke only of "temporarily prolonging the occupation or at
least maintaining a large number of troops on the railway
line."[145]

Witte, who had just come out for the necessity of "exact
fulfillment" of the evacuation treaty, showed up even before
the opening of the conference in the camp of those who, like
Lessar, rebelled against the annexation of Manchuria, but
would like to "surround" its evacuation "with the necessary
guarantees that, after the Russian detachments left, Russia's
lawful interests in Manchuria would be transgressed neither
by the Chinese emperor's government nor by the other powers:"
the conference of foreign ministers, for example, unanimously
rejected the "finance minister's proposal to link the evacuation of Manchuria with obtaining China's agreement to pay
the war [the Boxer] indemnity in gold;" [146] naturally even at
the minsters' conference of January 25 Witte did not say
another word about "exact fulfillment" of the Chinese treaty,
and in the guarantees discussed objected "in essence" only to
the point about forbidding Chinese to settle along the Chinese
Eastern Railway line. [147] Kuropatkin too had before the
opening of the conference expended a great deal of effort to
get Lessar to consent even to the maintenance of the Russian
occupation "along the line of the road, in the alienated zone,"
and Lessar honestly fulfilled his agreement by mentioning at
the conference of January 11 the possibility of "replacing"
the guard by "army divisions." [148]

The conference of ministers thus disagreed with Kuropatkin on the question of the annexation of North Manchuria and
did not adopt his proposal to include among guarantees the
prohibition of Chinese settlement along the Chinese Eastern
Railway line. But they were quite ready to meet Kuropatkin
half way when he himself then proposed a compromise formula, which boiled down to: 1) not promising the Chinese
to meet the March evacuation date, even in the event of their
consent to the guarantees demanded (in view of the fact that
it was desirable for technical reasons to confine themselves
to the clearing of Mukden province alone before March 26,
1903, then clear the southern part of Kirin province "in the
summer" of 1903, and "not fix a time" for further evacuation
"until the results of clearing the south had been ascertained")
and 2) when its turn came, "making not only the clearing of
Heilungkiang, but also that of the northern part of Kirin
province conditional on the demand concerning maintenance
of a certain number of troops along the railway line and along
the rivers Amur and Sungari." [149] The question of the agreement with Japan was even more simply and easily put through
at both conferences.

That the Japanese proposal was "unacceptable" (Pavlov) and "overly exacting" (Witte) all were definitely agreed; but, following some hesitation at the foreign ministers' conference of January 11, where Rozen came out against agreement with Japan on the Korean question, the conference of January reached "complete unanimity" respecting the "advisability" of such an agreement and even respecting the fact that the Japanese terms "offered a basis for future negotiations."

However, Lamsdorf took it upon himself to propose "refraining" from negotiations "at present," "in order not to give the Japanese reason to assume any urgent desire on our part to come to an agreement with them," and "waiting for the Tokyo government to make the first move in renewing negotiations," --and this again met with "general consent,"150 even though Witte had, back in December 1902, contended for immediate agreement with Japan, even at the price of temporary concession to her of Korea.151 Thus a refurbished program for the "imperial" policy was put together that buttressed the outward unity of the "cabinet" but did not settle a single one of the questions set for discussion. On the Manchurian question in particular, it proposed such a revision of the March 26 treaty as would inevitably conduce to the postponement of evacuation for a palpably indefinite time. The minimum for this postponement was fixed, by unanimous agreement with Kuropatkin, at partial clearing (the south only) of Kirin province "during the summer of 1903"157 (instead of by March 26). But it was not difficult to foresee (and was of course plainly realized), that China's non-acceptance of all or part of the supplementary engagements to the treaty was quite likely, and that the question would then return to its starting point--"temporary" but termless occupation. Naturally, with the Manchurian question stated on the basis of gaining time, Lamsdorf could propose nothing else as to the Korean question than to await a new proposal on Japan's part, in the hope of making "the new agreement complement and develop those now existing, which were to retain their validity," instead of letting Russian "compromises" pre-determine in essence the settlement of the Korean question."153 "Imperial" diplomacy, on January 25, 1903, made a decision that irrevocably committed it to a course of "delays, remaining for the most part inexplicable," as the Japanese note of January 23/ February 5, the last before the opening of hostilities, expressed it.

Any haste about presenting China with the note agreed on,
at the January 25 conference, respecting guarantees was un-
dreamed of (if only to permit completion of evacuation on
time in the event of a satisfactory answer from the Chinese):
it was not handed to Ching until April 5, 1903, when the final
evacuation date was already past.[154] The accepted list of
guarantees had apparently been communicated to the not very
subtle chargé d'affaires in Peking (Lessar had likewise not
hurried back) only as a basis; the project of the note was
drawn up by Planson and then approved as a whole from
Peterburg, the list of demands now being augmented.[155]
Attempts by Alekseyev and then even by Nicholas himself,
at the conference of March 26, to augment this list still further were unsuccessful, and the redaction of this diplomatic
act was left entirely to the responsibility of the triumvirate.[156]
Still having nothing to present, Planson had on March 19
pretentiously informed the Chinese of what was coming,[157]
and somewhat earlier Peterburg had been forewarned that
the Chinese "would show the note to foreign representatives,"
and that Japan's consul in Tientsin and her former minister
of foreign affairs (Aoki) would conduct "secret negotiations
with Yuan Shikai, preparing a joint-action project which
would be presented to the empress in the event of non-execu-
tion of the evacuation," that "all official Peking was now
discussing what our intentions were."[158]

For this reason alone, it can scarcely have been any great
surprise to Russian diplomacy that the Chinese government
found the demands presented to it on April 5 "entirely foreign
to the convention of March 26" and like a "new special agreement," and responded with the proposal that they discuss
"any questions relating to Manchuria"--"after the evacuation."[159] And when in the course of two or three days the
content of the Russian note of April 5 became known in the
diplomatic quarter of Peking, England and America immediately protested to Russia about her infringement of "treaty
rights." Particular alarm was caused, needless to say, by
the point about "open ports" and consuls in Manchuria, and
to Hay it seemed the more provocative in that, not long before, the project of an American-Chinese trade treaty had
been communicated to Russia which provided for the "opening" of Mukden and Takushan to foreign trade.[160] The energetic efforts of Japanese diplomacy in Washington just then
were based exclusively on this point, since "if there was

ever a favorable moment for Japan to obtain the withdrawal
of Russia from Manchuria it was now when Russia contemplated attacking the commercial and other interests of all
powers interested in the affairs of the Far East."[161] No
denials by Lamsdorf and no assurances of his that such a
demand by Russia "was absurd at first glance" and that "Russia was above all endeavoring to attract American capital
and trade" could have weight in view of the fact that the text
of the Russian terms had been obtained by the American ambassador to Peking from the Japanese, who, in turn, had
got it from Ching himself.[162]

Just as had happened two years before, Russian diplomacy
was caught red-handed in an attempt to transgress the "treaty
rights" of the powers and shut the door into Manchuria, so
that Hay, for example, had an opportunity to place Cassini
in an extremely ridiculous position by referring to the fact
that Planson in Peking "had himself admitted in a conversation with two colleagues" that the text of the note obtained
by Conger "had actually been transmitted by him to the
ministers of Wai-wu-bu."[163] And the future conduct of the
Chinese in negotiations with the U.S.A. as to the opening of
Manchurian "ports" only confirmed the supposition that Russia was continuing to exert pressure on Peking on this point
and the Chinese did not at last "formally promise" "to open
the ports" "as soon as the evacuation of Manchuria was over"
(i.e., to "sign on October 8 [new style] the trade treaty including this engagement) until Russian diplomacy had itself
renounced its claim on this point.[164] While protesting to
the Russian government in company with America only against
the infringement of "treaty rights" (i.e., against the points
about ports and the elimination of foreigners from the administration in Manchuria) the English government in company
with Japan simulateneously: 1) offered China "support such
as had been given her during negotiations over the Manchurian
convention" (in 1901 and 1902), respecting "[in general] any
conditions whatsoever not justified by the Manchurian convention," 2) accounted the demands made by Russia "absolutely unacceptable" and 3) warned the Chinese against
"compliance on the less important points" to avoid the "much
more important compromises" otherwise "inevitable."[165]
This means that the revision of the Manchurian agreement
was reprobated by England root and branch and, moreover,
in full agreement with Japan: the latter was assured that

England "fully understood the seriousness of the condition demanded by Russia," while Japan on her side promised "not to take any steps" [for the "settlement" of the Manchurian question] without notifying her ally.166 This created an impasse for Russia's "old course": "imperial" diplomacy's attempt to retreat at once, after China's first refusal, from some of its demands failed to advance matters, for the Chinese government did not assume as many as one even of the "less important" obligations, gladly following England's advice on this point.167

Back in November 1902, Witte had suggested to Nicholas that Japan must regard Manchuria as "unconditionally and forever lost" to her, but on the other hand that "Korea might temporarily even be conceded to her entire, provided Japan would give us suitable compensations in return" (presumably in Manchuria).168 And now, in May 1903, Witte continued obstinately to insist on having it his own way: don't make "seizures" in Korea, and Japan will stay quiet. But meanwhile, in Japan, not only were the newspapers now saying that "on the day Russia's supreme authority is established in Manchuria, the closed door policy will also be established," and that "for Japan this would be tantamount to defeat in the struggle for existence" (Asahi) but even the government, according to some advices, was prepared to create a "breach of peaceful relations" with Russia by making some demand respecting Manchuria that it would be absolutely impossible for her to entertain: and how else than as a direct provocation was the demand apparently contemplated at the beginning of May to be taken namely "numerical restriction of the railway guard inside Manchuria"?169

Now this unrestricted right of the Chinese Eastern Railway had from the outset been the only trump card at the disposal of the authors of the March 26 treaty on all occasions when they had to defend the possibility of evacuating the field troops and at the same time maintaining the security of the road. The purpose of the demand of Komura (or of whoever wished to produce an effect on Peterburg by such a communication) must have been to place in a hopeless position just those persons who constantly masqueraded as friends of Japan when they were in fact her chief enemies: might not Komura have known that Witte, at whom chiefly this thrust must objectively have been aimed, had, since the Chinese note of April 9, already "accepted" Kuropatkin's demand for "non-withdrawal

from North Manchuria of nine battalions of infantry together
with corresponding divisions of other types of armament."[170]
   If such a plan was actually discussed in Tokyo, it could
not have been put into execution without the consent of the
English cabinet. But as yet London was apparently still not
entirely alien to the thought of a possible understanding with
Russia, and even as late as July 1903 Lord Cranborne was
to declare in the House of Lords that "the Russian government well knows we should be exceedingly glad to arrive at
an understanding" but that "it is first necessary that readiness of the part of the Russian government exist" and next
"a clear picture of precisely what the Russian government
is endeavoring to obtain is requisite on our part": but this
was what England "has been absolutely incapable of grasping." Cranborne further observed, however, not without
malice, that "it would be well to disabuse themselves of
the idea that the Russian government was any such homo-
geneous quantity as might a priori be presumed in a despotic
state; that, on the contrary, in the Russian government there
appeared to be at least two parties with which one had to
deal."[171] But when, on July 15/28, 1903, Japan (making it
no secret from the London cabinet) decided to propose to
Russia "that they enter into an examination of the state of
affairs in the Far East where their interests met;" when
Russia on July 23/August 5 accepted this proposal; when,
finally, on July 30/August 12 Kurino handed Lamsdorf the
Japanese project of agreement and when, of course, it turned
out that Japan 1) in nowise regarded Manchuria as "indisputably and forever lost to her" and 2) desired to protect
her own and even foreign interests in Manchuria and not pre-
determine its future fortunes in Russia's favor alone, so
broad a statement of the question of an understanding (on
Korean and Manchurian affairs simultaneously) brought Japanese diplomacy up against both variants of the Russian
course. Now, as before, neither of them was restricted to
the defense of Russia's railway interests alone in Manchuria,
whereas Japan was only prepared to recognize Russia's
"special interests in railway enterprises."[172]
   The difference between these two variants, replete with
subjective significance for the warring personages in the
tsar's government, was not so great as it apparently seemed
to themselves or so hard and fast as outsiders took it to be.

VI

No possibility exists of even hypothetically answering the
question: what, strictly, did the triumvirate figure on in
proposing that the Peking government assume, for no particular reason, sundry obligations supplementary to the treaty
of March 26, 1902, among them some that were known to be
unacceptable to three powers and that must still further complicate an international situation in the Far East already
strained to the breaking-point. The historian is equally
powerless to answer a second question: how did the triumvirate figure on continuing their diplomatic game, supposed
to have as its aim the attainment of lasting peace with China
and Japan, when it made up its mind (at the conference of
April 13, 1903) to "seize" (i.e., openly maintain Russian
field troops at) such strategic points as Harbin, Tsitsihar,
Fuliardi, Ninguta, Hailar, Hunchun, the course of the Sungari and the Tsitsihar-Blagoveshchensk highway.173 After
May 2, 1903, what the historian has to deal with is already
the "new course," and what the spokesmen for the old course
might have devised had it been granted them to carry the
matter still farther is no longer a subject for conjecture in
the pages of an historical investigation. But the old personages did not leave the stage even now, nor were they even
"eliminated from Far Eastern affairs": they were merely
transformed into "knowledgeable secretaries," "under the
sovereign's direction," as Bezobrazov forced home to Lamsdorf the new position created for the ministers after the conference of May 7, so that long afterwards they still claimed
the right to preen themselves on having up to the last moment
fought for the "peaceful" way out and opposed the "adventure"
undertaken by new advisers, who had, it seems, "hypnotized"
the tsar.174

Nicholas, so Bezobrazov said, had "his own method of acting," a method of "logical gradualism" whereby "there remains much tar in the honey and the job is spoiled." Under
tar, Bezobrazov comprehended (this was in July 1904) that
same whole "mangy triumvirate" of "patented scoundrels"
whom he had "in due course zealously unmasked," who had
"made a great, great lot of trouble," and who did not cease
to exasperate the Bezobrazov imagination even after Witte
had been properly "removed" and the "understanding" (among
the triumvirs), should, by Bezobrazov's calculations, have

"ceased to exist."[175] Which means that the "scoundrels" were unreconciled to the last, did not accept the new course or make common cause with the Bezobrazov "gang."[176] They even attempted to hold some sort of line of their own, as will presently be seen.

That to overtake Japan now in respect to military preparedness--as Nicholas had apparently conceived the design of doing when he charged Alekseyev (on May 2) to give "in a minimal time" "a demonstration palpable to all of our determination to defend our right to exclusive influence in Manchuria"--was a hopeless task, all the members of the triumvirate plainly realized. At the conference of May 7, Witte declared that on the question of the timber concession, "after explanations with Bezobrazov, he was not in essential disagreement with him," but to the "increase of our war power" in the Far East he objected, since "new allocations for this object on the part of the state treasury would deal a crushing blow to the economic position of the Russian people."[177] Lamsdorf, echoing Witte, denied Russia's "material ability" "to refuse to withdraw another step from the provinces occupied by Russia," adding by way of consolation that "time was Russia's only ally and would be her true helper" "provided she showed no impatience."[178] Kuropatkin too discussed "our unpreparedness for war as compared with Japan" in June 1903 and again in January 1904, on the eve of the rupture, considered it imperative to "delay" the war for one year and four months," (to finish work on the railway), or "at least for four months," merely to "send all reinforcements."[179] Hence, all three deduced that war must be avoided but not one of them either at the conference of May 7 or afterwards up to the very late autumn of 1903 proposed to revert wholly and at once to the punctual execution of the March treaty, without surrounding evacuation with any guarantees, even though they were not averse to talking in a general way about the necessity of "keeping the treaty" out of pique against Bezobrazov.[180] It is safe to say that the very concept of "fulfilling" the treaty of March 26 had become somewhat confused in Peterburg now that the second evacuation date had, by the joint efforts of all concerned, been missed; for example, the above quoted instructions to Alekseyev, drawn up no doubt by Bezobrazov, and signed on May 2 by Nicholas, announcing the new course, even spoke of a "final decision to execute the treaty of March 26 to the letter."

No wonder it was a case not only of the English being unable to understand what Peterburg now wished respecting
Manchuria, but of incomprehension on the very part of the
new "deputy" responsible to the tsar for the progress of
affairs in the Far East, future Vicegerent Alekseyev. The
latter was at the start disturbed by the inner contradiction
of the task laid upon him: "to discharge to the letter the
obligations assumed by us in the convention of March 26, "
at the same time allowing for "full protection, however, of
our interests in Manchuria, " and began to "incline" toward
the idea "of the advisability of maintaining the occupation, "
since, "with the admission of foreigners into Manchuria the
latter will be definitively lost to us." Hence Alekseyev made
the further, the only possible, deduction--prompted by "our
diplomacy's" unsuccessful experiment ("blunders, " to use
Alekseyev's expression)--"that now is no time to conduct
any sort of negotiations with the Chinese; we must pay no
attention to them and reinforce our position in Manchuria."181
And in point of fact to start negotiations with the Chinese
about anything previous to the evacuation of Manchuria for
a fourth time after such attempts had thrice ended in failure
would have been ridiculous, to say the least. One of Witte's
correspondents in Dalny summed up the impression he had
gained from conversations with Alekseyev as being that he
"actually favors the annexation of Manchuria, but from
motives of discretion will perhaps not express this extreme
view unless he finds the war minister sumpathetic to it, but
will merely insist upon a prolonged military occupation."182
Thus was the annexationist position of the future vicegerent
in the Far East described pending the congress at Port Arthur of Kuropatkin, Bezobrazov, and the other persons with
whom, at Nicholas's desire, Alekseyev was to discuss the
future policy of Russia in Manchuria: in any event "his views"
were progressively "approaching" "somewhat to the ideas
developed by Bezobrazov."183 When, on June 3, Bezobrazov
"with God's help" prepared to leave Peterburg for Port Arthur,
the auspices there awaiting him were apparently not too bad.

But in Bezobrazov's rear as well, in Peterburg, things
"in general and in all departments" now seemed "all right
for the time being." Actually Bezobrazov had, during the
three weeks between the conference of May 7 and his departure, succeeded in accomplishing a good many things. First
there was Lamsdorf, who gave him the most trouble; he had

planned to resign, but after two long and harrowing visits
from Bezobrazov ended with excuses, saying "that, perhaps,
had he known many things earlier he might have done better,
but he had not known, and bore no ill will."[184] Lamsdorf
not only remained in his post but even showed some signs of
"reviving," and arranged to have Bezobrazov give him a
"list of the minimal demands" "that would be presented to
China and for which the ministry of foreign affairs would have
the necessary means to provide argumentational support."[185]
Second, Witte, with whom it turned out to be much easier
and simpler for Bezobrazov to "come to an understanding."
Witte had at the conference of May 7 already pretended that
he recognized as desirable an "increase in our fighting power
in the Far East" provided it kept within the "limits" (210
million rubles, distributed over five years) of the "budget"
just confirmed (April 2).[186]

And after the conference, when Bezobrazov came to him
for a "talk touching the pecuniary means" for this, Witte,
instead of the expected rebuff, at once met the new state-
secretary half way and put him on the road to curtailing expenditures for defense of the western border by showing
him 22 million rubles allocated to the Bobr-Narevsk strategic
railway and at the same time flattering him by the disclosure
of this military secret.[187] And before his actual departure,
Bezobrazov, in Vonliarliarsky's presence, also "reached an
understanding" with Witte respecting the new enterprises
started in Manchuria, in particular as to "agreeing on a joint
procedure for the Fushun mines" (part of which, as we know,
appertained to the M.M. Assn.)[188] Third, Bezobrazov "came
to an understanding" with Witte "touching the reorganized association," a treaty as to which was notarially concluded on
May 31, 1903, and Vonliarliarsky officially constituted its
representative for Peterburg and Balashov for the Far East.[189]
Fourth, Abaza and Bezobrazov, helpless in such matters, at
once turned over to Plehve the working out of the question of
a new administrative organization for the Far East: for the
time being, of course, Nicholas's resolution on the minutes
of the conference of May 7 had ordained that "Far Eastern
matters requiring joint discussion of the departments" be
"henceforth considered in special conference such as the
present one," and had laid the "management" of these conferences upon Abaza.[190] And finally, fifth, Bezobrazov
succeeded in obtaining, behind the war ministry's back,

Nicholas's consent to the sending of two brigades to the Far East.[191] After this, it only remained for Bezobrazov to "pray God" to "aid" him "on the spot as well, to execute to the extent of my ability the will of my sovereign," and for this it would apparently suffice if he got to Port Arthur before Kuropatkin to put Alekseyev into a proper frame of mind, since Alekseyev passed even with the Bezobrazovists for a man who "will always look to his own profit," and was capable, for all he knew, of joining Kuropatkin.[192]

Though "with Bezobrazov's departure for Port Arthur" "there was" indeed "a lull in the discussion of questions raised as to the Far East where decision on the spot in the conference of the war minister, Admiral Alekseyev and the state-secretary was expected."[193] Peterburg cannot be said to have withdrawn them from discussion entirely. True, conferences were no longer called, but by proxy for Nicholas, Abaza carried on conversations with Grand Duke Aleksey Aleksandrovich, Witte and Lamsdorf, while Lamsdorf in turn communicated with our Tokyo and Peking representatives by telegraph. So far as may be judged from the incomplete data at our disposal, casting its shadow over everything was the question of how to proceed so as to avoid complications with foreign powers, of whose vigilant check on every future move of Russia's in the East no one on Peterburg could possibly have any doubts. Lamsdorf proposed point-blank that Lessar "ascertain exactly what foreign claims in Manchuria to look out for in the forthcoming working out of final guarantees," and Lessar made a straightforward attempt to ascertain from his Peking "colleagues" what, properly, was comprehended under the "open door" principle the observance of which was now being demanded of Russia.[194] But it turned out that his "colleagues" "had no fully defined view as to what must be comprehended under this appellation," and so Lessar offered Peterburg his own reflections on the question of "foreign activity in Manchuria."

Lessar broke the question down thus: was this desirable for Russia 1) in the form of foreign trade and 2) in the form of the opening of foreign industrial enterprises there, and whether it would be possible, and how possible, to obstruct it in relation to trade and in relation to industry respectively. Foreign trade in Manchuria, Lessar recognized as "absolutely undesirable" but saw only one means of preventing it--the annexation of Manchuria and its inclusion in the Russian cus-

toms boundary, and this in turn he regarded as impossible.
On the contrary, the attraction of foreign capital to Manchurian industry in the absence of capital in Russia herself for the
purpose, Lessar considered desirable "for the economic ele-
vation of the region" "even in the event of the annexation of
Manchuria": but he also feared "considerable difficulties"
in this connection since "the only reason so much is said
about Manchuria is that Russia's reluctance to admit foreigners
is attributed to the exceptional wealth of the region" and
"should enterprises [there] become free, very few persons
desirous of engaging [in them] would appear" since "actually
it is no richer than other parts of the country."[195] But the
matter was complicated by the fact that "foreign industrial
activity" in Manchuria "would" inevitably "take on a political
coloration" and "be directed toward the weakening of the
position that we enjoy on the basis of treaties," and Lessar
as a result proposed "contenting ourselves with continuation
of occupation of the whole province or a part thereof, leaving
it to the Chinese emperor at least nominally" and concluding
a "special treaty" whereby China would engage "to refrain
from opening new points to foreign trade in said country and
from permitting the organization of settlements and regularize the question of industrial concessions in conformity with
our interests."[196]

A far "bolder" and "riskier" settlement of the question
was now proposed by Rozen, likewise interrogated by Lamsdorf, from Tokyo. Respecting Korea, he proposed a "supplementary agreement" with Japan as to the "demarcation of
respective spheres of interest in Korea, giving us northern
Korea, and Japan southern Korea with the capital, and allowing her...the right to supply the Korean government with advisers, but, of course, under the restrictions indicated in
your [Lamsdorf's] telegram touching the erection of fortifications." His expectation that Japan would accede to such
a "compromise" on Korean matters, Rozen (quite astonish-
ingly) based on the effect of a radical settlement of the Manchurian question in the form of "taking all Manchuria under
our protectorate" (modelled on Bosnia and Herzegovina) and
"declaring" to the powers "our initiation throughout Manchuria
of the same free access to foreign trade and capital that they
enjoy in the home provinces of the Russian empire," with the
engagement to introduce in Manchuria a tariff "lower than
China's," and excluding the port of Yinkow from the area of

the protectorate.197 How Lamsdorf reacted to these two
proposals is unknown, but Witte privately expressed himself
to the effect that Rozen's project was "bold," "extremely
unilateral" and rather risky," and as to Lessar's reflections
replied that "in general" he "shared" them, but would postpone a detailed exposition of his own point of view as yet--
until the projected guarantees had been worked out at the
conferences with Alekseyev at Port Arthur.198 Both ministers
were, however, in another connection compelled to express
themselves rather definitely and at once.

At the same time and in the same context these same questions were, as is now known, also in process of settlement
by Nicholas with the aid of Abaza, who had remained behind.
They gave precedence to the question of an agreement with
Japan, Nicholas expressing himself as in favor of "resigning
Korea to the Japanese." Since, as before, Nicholas abode
by his "intention of executing the treaty of March 26," Abaza
feared "we might find ourselves in difficulties and not have
Korea surrounded," and in drafting the "bases of our future
relations with Japan" included paragraphs "on the economic
establishment" of Russia in Manchuria, and on Russian concessions along the Tumen and Yalu rivers. The time was
even set when, without waiting for Japan to take the initiative,
we might "start discussing Korea with Japan": namely, "as
soon as the [two] brigades dispatched had reached the trans-
Baikal."199 As we see, Nicholas no longer even dreamed of
Korea: he was prepared to follow Witte's repeated counsels
in this respect, even while renouncing the waiting tactics
adopted by the triumvirate in January 1903.200

There is as yet no evidence that Nicholas informed the
ministers of his decision. But there is evidence that Lamsdorf was not averse to "bestowing Korea on the Japanese"
either, provided "it be announced that in future we shall remain in Manchuria."201 But both Witte and Lamsdorf were
invited by Abaza, as proxy for the tsar, to express themselves
as to whether the rights of porto-franco should be restored
to Vladivostok. With one voice the two replied that this question was directly linked with the Manchuria question, and as
to Manchuria stated: Lamsdorf ("on his own initiative") that
"for three years he had been of the opinion that it would be
well to take Manchuria and now felt that a clear and firm
decision must be arrived at," and that "should it be decided
to take Manchuria, then, when they announced the fact to

Japan would be a good time to bestow Korea upon them;"
Witte--that "it would be advisable to state clearly and firmly
what Russia wanted in Manchuria," and that "the tax-free
import of foreign goods into the Amur province and Manchuria
might kill the market for Russian goods," that "in general it
was better to admit foreign capital than foreign goods," and
that "in Manchuria it would be best to close the ports."202
If Witte actually "shared" "Lessar's reflections" "in general"
as to the impossibility of shutting off the access of foreign
goods to Manchuria otherwise than by annexing Manchuria
and including it in the Russian tariff boundary, then what did
this advice of his to Abaza mean?

If such a confusion of tongues took place behind Bezobrazov's
back in Peterburg, neither did things at the June conferences
in Port Arthur turn out so "satisfactorily" for Bezobrazov as
might have been expected. Bezobrazov got no support whatsoever there from Alekseyev, who not only no longer even
mentioned the annexation of Manchuria but showed himself
even more moderate than Kuropatkin. Namely: 1) even on
so sacred a question as "activity on the Yalu," Alekseyev,
in defiance of Bezobrazov, expressed himself as in favor of
giving it an "exclusively commercial character," 2) in defiance of Kuropatkin, expressed himself as against the annexation even of northern Manchuria only, 3) originated the
motion that the treaty of March 26 be "executed" (with guarantees, of course, stipulated), 4) did not support Kuropatkin's seventeen points for such guarantees, deeming it necessary to "reduce" their number "to a minimum," since otherwise it might appear that "we are seizing China," which "has
committed no offence against us," "by the throat," and even
projected the Chinese's government's "dispatching an ambassador extraordinary to his majesty the emperor to plead for
an evacuation of Manchuria without heavy terms for China,"
5) finally expressed the altogether heretical, anti-Bezobrazo-
vist idea that "the means of the state treasury ought not to
be invested"203 in economic enterprises in Manchuria. The
decisions of the conferences as a result proved such that
Bezobrazov acknowledged their "having no practical significance" and telegraphed the tsar his "individual opinion."204

Naturally no one even mentioned at Port Arthur (any more
than in Peterburg) the immediate and complete evacuation of
Manchuria, but here too the specter of foreign "opposition"
never ceased to hover throughout the whole sixteen sessions.

The question of introducing new troops into Manchuria never
came up at all. Under intensive preparation for war were,
apparently, understood the withdrawal of an army division
(two rifle regiments, two batteries and one sapper battalion)
from Manchuria not to the Amur province but to Kwantung,
further work on the fortress at Port Arthur in the sum of
2-1/2 million rubles and extension of the occupation for three
years, together with the stationing of troops "along the Chinese Eastern Railway line." Discarded from the list of
guarantees, to avoid irritating foreigners, were the demands
as to consuls, the non-opening of new points to trade, and
preference to Russian subjects in the obtaining of industrial
conessions (i.e., exactly the things concerning the admis-
sability of which Witte in Peterburg had "in general" just
"shared" reflections). 205 It is plain that under such conditions it was quite impossible for Bezobrazov and Alekseyev
at Port Arthur to arrive at the establishment of a "plan for
the expedient statement" of Russia's "politico-economic
tasks" in the Far East as had at first been proposed. And
the decisions made on military and political questions assumed a merely preliminary character ("until the war minister's return to Peterburg") and proved open to criticism.
    On the first news of happenings in Port Arthur both Witte
and Lamsdorf hastened to present Nicholas with their reflections in written form. Lamsdorf merely confined himself
to collating the Port Arthur list of guarantees with the latest
instructions that had been given Lessar (April 24) following
the spring refusal of the Chinese to discuss the demands,
still as formulated by Planson, and indicated in his memorandum the advantages of this old list over the new: it looked
as though Lamsdorf thought necessary to repeat Lessar's
unsuccessful excursion, without philosophizing. 206 Witte,
who prepared his report before having exact knowledge of
the Port Arthur list, presented a critique of all settlements
of the Manchurian question in his opinion possible, n.b.: 1)
formal annexation of Manchuria, which he rejected, 2) termless occupation and maintenance of the Russian administration,
even "against the will of the Chinese government," without
resort to any formal acts--which he likewise rejected, and
3) evacuation of Manchuria, which he for his part proposed.
But the direct intent of this proposal was far from "fulfillment" of the engagements made by Russia in the treaty of
March 26. First, it was proposed that Russian troops "be

withdrawn" from Manchuria and concentrated not only in the Amur and Kwantung provinces but also "in the territory of the Chinese Eastern Railway." Second, it was "as a preliminary" proposed that "certain obligations on the part of the Chinese government be stipulated," namely (we quote verbatim): "that a set of military restrictions be prescribed for it, as well as restricted terms for the admission of representatives of foreign powers, serious influence on the customs system of Manchuria be demanded for Russia, and as far as possible the preferential right of Russian subjects to railway and other industrial enterprises in this country be stipulated."

Witte was absolutely correct, of course, that such a settlement of the question would be "most in conformity with the policy that the Russian government has maintained in respect to Manchuria up to the present time," and the readers of this book will undoubtedly have no trouble identifying in this list of "obligations" the basic points of the Manchurian program that Witte had made the object of his Chinese policy ever since the Boxer uprising. But it is simply impossible to believe that Witte seriously thought that such a settlement of the question "could" even now "scarcely lead to difficulties with the Chinese government, which would, in all probability, be agreeable to assuming the above-mentioned obligations without any particular dispute," and that "at the same time it could not cause serious complications with the other foreign powers either,"--the fact was that such reflections were intended by him to give color to the idea of the possibility even now "of full protection of our interests in Manchuria,"207 as Nicholas had desired. That we are here dealing not simply with a rhetorical flourish and that Witte did truly consider it possible to carry on the old "imperial" policy in the Manchurian question is seen from the concrete practical steps that the triumvirate proposed to Nicholas in the shape of a formal statement, after having convened in full conclave on August 1 to confer.

The ministers determined: 1) that Manchuria should not be annexed, 2) that, recognizing it as no "longer possible with respect to Manchuria to adhere literally to the treaty of March 26," troops "to the required number" "be stationed" "in the Chinese Eastern Railway zone" and "the occupation" of Hunchun "be continued," 3) that before such "fulfillment" of the March treaty, China's observance of the five "exist-

ing conditions" "be demanded," since "with considerable
forces in the zone and in Kwantung province we can categorically and irrevocably declare to China what we consider
necessary for the protection of our rights and interests,"
and 4) that "it be declared" to China that "in exchange" Russia will on these terms "undertake" "the immediate removal
of garrisons" from Mukden province, "withdrawal in the
course of four months" of troops from a part of Kirin province,
and "in a year's time"208 from Heilungkian province. If,
in the words of the minutes of the conference of August 1,
the "essence of the question" (for Russia) lay "not in what
we demand of China" but in "being able" to "take suitable
measures for the attainment of our ends," even "should the
Chinese attempt in any way to oppose us," for China the gist
of the matter was evidently not whether, under pressure
from Alekseyev the Chinese were presented with something
slightly different from the five demands that the ministers
had devised, but the fact of their now being able to answer
Russia in the negative even more boldly than in the spring--
"at the instigation" of Japan, where now, by autumn, it was
already plain that the "country's two chief sources of pros-
perity, silk and rice, were alike secure for the current
year...in amounts long unprecedented,"209 and where it
was "well" understood "that each day's, well nigh each
hour's, delay was increasing the chances in favor of Russia."21
The Chinese accordingly repeated their spring answer even
though, of the demands projected by the ministers on August 1,
the one most challenging to the treaty rights of the powers was
not there."211 But in any case, even before the presentation
of the R ssian demands and before China's refusal, the fate
of the "triple ministerial alliance" had been sealed, and the
resolutions of the August 1 conference were, actually, the
triumvirate's swan-song.

Bezobrazov, who had returned to Peterburg at the same
time as Kuropatkin, in the middle of July, naturally could
not help guessing that the defeat that he had just suffered at
Port Arthur in his capacity as state-secretary was directly
connected with what had simultaneously happened in Peterburg
to Nicholas. Here--the "definitive" "decision to allow the
Japanese full possession of Korea," as Abaza had relayed
to Bezobrazov back on June 11; out there--the amicable rejection of what had become with Beaobrazov the maniacal
idea "of a st ategic screen on the Yalu," and the like amicable

demand that the timber enterprise be reduced to the level of
a commercial undertaking. Behind all this, Bezobrazov, who
had, presumably, just "come to an understanding" with the
ministers in Peterburg, could easily sense, as ever, the
scheming of the pertinacious "ringleader of the ministerial
triple alliance." The new course appeared totally insecure
and the whole thing threatened to "foul itself," or at least
remain "in the cow-pen," unless the reforms projected in
May were carried to completion and the still active influence
of the "departments"212 on Nicholas neutralized. Bezobrazov now treated the "departments" just like an "enemy camp,"
and hastened to uncover to Nicholas the subtle device whereby the triumvirate had sought to undermine the "new direction" and had created an "unhealthy business atmosphere"
that misled even the chief hope of the new course, Admiral
Alekseyev, who, incidentally, had up to the last minute
"never believed that he would be Vicegerent."213 And sure
enough, now (on July 30, o.s.) signing the edict establishing
a vicegerency in the Far East with "[its] administration"
"exempt" "from the control of the ministries" and "diplomatic
relations" "with the neighboring states" concentrated "under
the direction" of the vicegerent, Nicholas simultaneously gave
Bezobrazov, at last, the long awaited "indication" that Witte
"was to be regarded as a very transitory functionary."214
During these July days, at the height of an unprecedented
strike wave embracing the whole south, it was an easy matter for the "three mines simultaneously" "laid" for Witte's
undoing (his "arrogation of too much authority to himself,"
his pursuance of a "mistaken" policy in the Far East, and
finally the fact that he was "handsome") to "explode" in a
single detonation.

The only way Witte could have averted this would have
been to definitely decide to "fall in line,"--"join forces" and
"really pull in harness" with Bezobrazov. But even Witte
had his limit of "official equilibration": this time it was not
a matter of embracing the heresy, acknowledging the "screen"
and "showing proper respect for the Yalu enterprise," i.e.,
not refusing recurrent allocations from the treasury, but a
matter of himself participating in the demolition of his own
"special realm in Manchuria." Having, with the establishment of the vicegerency, placed matters of Far Eastern diplomatic relations and defense in the "responsible" hands of
Alekseyev, Bezobrazov now prepared to apply himself to a

detailed elaboration of his "articulated scheme" "of sound
business adjustments" for the "unification" of "state commercial-industrial enterprises" and for "just the right attraction" "of Russian private enterprise with foreign participation,"--a scheme which was to inaugurate a new era of
large profits in the Far East to replace the "present business
regime of the finance minister" under which "no private enterprise was seriously able to operate."[215]

As we shall presently see, even here no difference existed
in principle between the old economic course and the new.
But for Witte this was the last possible minute to leave the
sinking ship: on July 30/August 12, Japan had proposed that
Russia recognize and support the "principle of equal advantages for the trade and industry of all nations" in Manchuria,
throughout the negotiations insisted on Russia's recognition
of the treaty rights of the powers in Manchuria in full, and,
as has justly been noted, broke off despite the fact that
Nicholas at the last moment accepted the basic redaction of
Japan's Manchurian demand.[216] As we know, Witte even
proposed that Nicholas accept the Japanese terms in their
first July redaction, excepting only the point as to uniting
the Korean railways with the Chinese Eastern Railway and
the Shanhaikwan-Newchang line.[217] In thereby renouncing
his policy of monopolies and privileges for Russian capital
in Manchuria, Witte virtually gave consent to its "inundation"
by foreigners, and on this occasion openly took his stand outside the new course. Had Witte not now made this choice,
no alternative would have been left him but actually to find
common ground with the Bezobrazov "gang" and assume along
with it, i.e., along with Nicholas's whole government, as
occurred with Kuropatkin and Lamsdorf, the whole formal
responsbility for the war.

VI

Parting with Witte, as Nicholas finally did on August 16,
had evidently been no simple matter for him. In a moment
of frankness, just after ending this long-drawn-out affair,
Nicholas (August 19) confessed to Kuropatkin "that he suffered
agonies choosing the needful out of all that he was told,"
"that it was a heavy tax on his mind," and with unexpected
picturesqueness elucidated "that he believed this same effort
of mind in a horse would be enough to make it bolt.[218] Psycho-

logically Nicholas had reached a certain point: he was tor-
mented by a sort of "distrust in principle of ministers" as
such. When, in those same August days, Kuropatkin, after
tendering his resignation following the vicegerency edict,
expressed the hope that the tsar's "confidence" in him "would
only increase" when he "should cease to be a minister,"
Nicholas actually said: "really, you know, strange as it
may seem, this is perhaps psychologically correct."[219] In
this respect, Witte suffered most: he had in point of fact
"arrogated too much authority to himself," and, as was said
at the time, "depersonalized" "the autocracy itself."

At parting, Nicholas made no secret of his idea
of a redistribution of authority; he then and there spoke
of "dismembering the ministry of finance."[220] But Witte
was not the only one--at the time, Nicholas also remarked
to Kuropatkin: "Would it not be well to divide the war ministry" "into two parts?"[221] There is no doubt that in establishing the Far-Eastern vicegerency and subordinating it to
the Special Committee of the Far East under the tsar's
chairmanship Nicholas was, in a roundabout way, and as yet
on a strictly localized and limited scale, still gratifying this
same desire of his--to restore personality "to the autocracy
itself." It might appear that the enemy from within had now
been finally crushed, and that the "agreement" among the
ministers in opposition to the new course had "ceased to
exist." But this had still not cleared the autocracy's horizon
in the least and had done little to ease the position of the
zealots for the new course.[222]In any case, the "horse" was
no quieter as a result, and the ship of Russian diplomacy
still remained stranded, unable to budge, constantly wedging
itself tighter in the sand.

For the new course, nothing now remained but to "break
off" (September 20) the negotiations with China as to guarantees, and try to defend "Russia's whole influence in Manchuria" by diplomatic means, in the negotiations with Japan
(Russia's answer to the Japanese proposals of July 30, o.s.,
was handed to Komura on September 22, o.s.).[223] This
meant that Russia, disregarding the last date of the March
treaty, would continue the occupation of Manchuria even after
September 26, 1903, and, inasmuch as Russia's September
answer had proposed that Japan "recognize" Manchuria as
"in all respects outside her [Japan's] sphere of interests,"
the local command at Port Arthur was inevitably at once

confronted by the question of what military measures would
be necessary in the event of Japan's dispatching armed forces
to northern Korea.[224] "Bezobrazov's timber enterprise,"
which, following his June transgressions and appointment as
viceregent, Alekseyev had finally recognized as "deserving
of the high patronage to which it owed its present development"[225] was now the first thing to come under fire. It is
not difficult to imagine Alekseyev's discouragement when in
reply to the question that he now posed point-blank respecting
opposition of a Japanese landing at points, precisely indicated,
on the Korean littoral in the vicinity of the mouth of the Yalu,
he received a hasty reply from Nicholas (drawn up not by
Abaza or Bezobrazov but by Lamsdorf) categorically enjoin-
ing him to "take measures so that war should not occur."[226]
But what sort of measures was left vague to the very end,
just as "what we want in Manchuria" if not its open annexation
was becoming less and less clear as time went on.[227] But
when (on December 8) Japan categorically confirmed her
desire "to have the agreement cover all provinces of the Far
East where the interests of the two empires met" (i.e.,
Manchuria in addition to Korea,) and Nicholas at the conference
of December 15 accordingly agreed to "include" in the agreement "an article about Manchuria also," Grand Duke Aleksey
Aleksandrovich, always brief and to the point in his remarks,
being desirous of sustaining this concession in order to "obtain an agreement," declared straight out that "on the Manchurian question we play dog in the hay: can't use it ourselves
and wont let others."[228]

Meanwhile during these last months before the outbreak of
war the new course struggled with the problem of how actually
to turn the Manchurian matter so as to "let others," and themselves enjoy a certain founders' profit from industrial monopoly
On the ruins of its own economic experiment, the Bezobrazov
"gang" not only refused to abandon the idea of economic conquest of "districts beyond our Far Eastern frontiers," but,
having renounced "the previous business set-ups" of "previous
promoters" even undertook by means of "a conciliated economic program for Far Eastern affairs" "to remove the matter from the vicious circle of state economy, with its enormous deficit as a final result," and put it on the path of
"general economic well-being" in terms of the "individuali-
zation of labor and capital."[227] But here, too, Nicholas himself proved a stumbling block for the Bezobrazovists with his
"method of logical gradualism."

It is clear that with Witte's exit the threat of liquidation would overhang the Manchurian Mining Association. Even before his retirement, while manoeuvering around the "half-mad" state-secretary, who suddenly announced his claims to "possession of the better part" of the Fushun coal field, Witte had been compelled to agree to the transfer to Bezobrazov of this, the most promising enterprise among the Manchurian Association's concessions, and if the transfer never took place it was through Bezobrazov's fault exclusively.[228] Pleske, whom Bezobrazov now bombarded with his talk, projects and "formulations" of every variety, himself admitted from the first day that he was "after Witte, inevitably doomed to be a drab minister," and lacking courage to face the "weight of inherited responsibility" and the "too rapid pace" at which "we had moved [under Witte] in various matters," made up his mind to "stop this pace."[231] The result of this, as above mentioned, was a "stoppage of payments" from August 16 on, even to the Manchurian Mining Association and the Directorate of the Association, putting aside all thought of executing the projected 2-1/2 million work plan, still dragged on somehow for a time by drawing on Rothstein at the Russo-Chinese bank to pay the personnel, but at the beginning of January 1904 raised the question of releasing its members from the duties "laid" upon them.[232]

But it would be a mistake to suppose that the turn had now come for the enterprises transferred by Bezobrazov to the "Russian Timber Association" to prosper. Nothing of the sort: the same misfortune, lack of capital, simultaneously overtook this "reservoir of concessions" as well. Balashov, in Port Arthur, on-the-spot manager of the affairs of the "reservoir," had likewise not proposed to confine himself to the two millions provided, and demanded of Bezobrazov that six million rubles be "put" into the development of the timber concern alone. By the end of August 1903, it was perfectly clear to him that "the current year's operation would yield no return" and that to prevent "the whole operation for 1904 being spoiled" it would be necessary to at once make it "monopolistic through purchase of the whole forest" and put up a deposit of not less than 300 thousand rubles.[233] But, as we know, Balashov had on his hands not the timber operation alone, but coal in eastern Fushun, the electric concession with church, school and hospital, in Mukden, and even a steamship line on the Liao-ho. Nay more, G.G. Gintsburg, had just reappeared proposing to buy from the French the old Seoul-Gishu (at the mouth of the Yalu) railway concession.

Meanwhile there remained to Balashov's account at Port
Arthur (by September 15) five thousand rubles of ready money
in all, and, failing to get a definite answer from Peterburg
as to "how much" and at "what time" he might expect money,
Balashov had begged to have "something or other" sent "at
once"--but again without result. By October there were already rumors in local banking circles of the Association's
"suspension of activities," "curtailment of expenditures,"
dismissal of employees and selling off of inventory, that "it
was settled that Fushun was to be abandoned (foisted on us?),"
that a "purchaser for the electric concession is being sought,"
and so forth.[235] And by the first of November they were
already simply running in debt at Port Arthur, their "till
empty," and continuing to ask that at least "something" be
sent, and were in general prepared to reconcile themselves
in future to mere coverage of debts already incurred.[236]
At the close of navigation (early in November,) 700 thousand
rubles worth of wood in logs "of unwanted lengths" lay unsold
in the Association's yards, and even Vogak, walking in on
this catastrophe at Port Arthur (October 22) did not entirely
credit Balashov's assertion that a "down payment" of 300,000
rubles had in any case been made on the wood and that this
money had actually gone into the till.[237] The "eclipse" of
the lumber company was an actual fact and Balashov did not
succeed in "prolonging the suspense" without detriment to
the "prestige of the concern" as Bezobrazov begged him to
do.[238] Peterburg too began discussing the "collapse" of the
timber enterprise on the Yalu, Bezobrazov (by the end of
November) had succeeded in "declaring himself ill," and, as
usual, left for a rest in Switzerland, while Balashov remained
penniless as before, continuing to borrow, and not until
December 19 did Nicholas finally order that 200 thousand
rubles be remitted to him, which can scarcely have sufficed
to pay his debts.[239]
     This prolonged delay in a question so vital to the concern
was in nowise due to malevolence or heedlessness on the part
of Bezobrazov. He was merely powerless to be of any aid:
"in all his pecuniary demands" Balashov "quite forgot" that
Bezobrazov "had no discretionary funds at his disposal and
that any new allocation beyond the two millions provided must
be made in proper form" and moreover that "it was necessary to obtain the competent approval of the vicegerent, without whose cognizance" Nicholas did not wish to "authorize"

"anything."[240] The only thing that Bezobrazov could count
on while this condition obtained was the 200 thousand rubles
allotted him for his chancellery as state-secretary.[241] To
him it seemed that "Pleske was slow" about issuing this sum--
"notwithstanding a clear enough order" (from the tsar, to
whom Bezobrazov reported on money matters, and who assured him that he "had given the order").[242] Yet it was
hardly like the timid Pleske to undertake such patent infringement of a "clear order," particularly in the Bezobrazovist
sphere; and it seems more reasonable to suppose that Nicholas himself was here the cause of the delay.[243] But he may
have been disturbed by "advices as to significant abuses in-
juring the very reputation of the firm," particularly since
the advices were brought to Peterburg by no other than his
own Vonliarliarsky.[244]

There was even a moment when, under the influence of
these reports, Bezobrazov thought that "in view of the weak
business organization of the timber concern and the unreli-
ability of agents," it would be "necessary to suspend operation for a time," occupy themselves with the exemplary
punishment of offenders "in order to get rid of thievery," and
give "the concern a new organization."[245] From the purely
commercial angle, Bezobrazov could plainly see that Balashov
was unable to cope with the matter, "did not know how to
analyze out the reasons" why "goods cost more to produce
than they could be sold for," that "those chiefly responsible
for this commercial discrepancy were unquestionably" the
"specialists" (one Zhivatovsky and one Skidelsky). But to
strike the attitude of a Shchedrin hero, threaten such "specialists" with "answerability before the law" (which would be
only too easy, since both were Jews) to take it "upon himself to bring about the execution of the authors of the abuses,
something unheard of in the Far East," guided only by "personal conviction" and without resort to the procurator, "putting a wholesome fear into swindlers" and "not stopping"
until he had "ground to powder anyone at all who has swindled
me [i.e., Bezobrazov] as executor of the plans of the sovereign," [as Bezobrazov liked to fancy himself]--would all
look ridiculous and could not help matters.[246]

Vogak, sent to the seat of trouble by Bezobrazov himself
at the beginning of October, after the news "of fraud in the
timber concern" gave this advice: to set aside "execution
and grinding into powder," abandon "rummaging in ancient

history" and separate the commercial side of the matter
from the political by "ceasing to direct" it from Peterburg,
and by entrusting it to "some absolutely independent, responsible and competent person."247 The rest would look out
for itself (as Bezobrazov, as his brief access of alarm,
easily reassured himself)--as soon as they put into effect
the "full, fully completed plan of action," so calculated that
"they should not remain in constant and growing financial
deficit [in the Far East] and in an inextricable position respecting economic propagations."248

By the end of October this "plan of action" was "ready"
and was communicated by Bezobrazov through Vogak to
Alekseyev as a sort of revelation. This plan "issued from
plain common sense." But by now, Bezobrazov--from over-
exertion, no doubt--had reached an absolutely clinical state
mentally and raved on at such a rate that even his closest
collaborators and sympathizers, who knew him like their
five fingers, flatly refused to "unravel" the "contradictory
cogitations" of his verbose telegrams in cipher and besought
him to "cease" sending them: his "idiosyncratic style and
habit of employing unusual words to express the simplest
ideas" simply "nonplussed" not only Balashov and Alekseyev
but even Vogak, who knew this Bezobrazov "style" as "no-
one" else.249 No wonder that when Bezobrazov now telegraphed his plan to Port Arthur he asked Vogak to "be pen-
sive" and if there was anything he did not understand "from
the spot" to "re-interrogate betimes."250

This time the plan was, however, so simple that there
was even no need to re-interrogate. It was proposed that
the "time limit of the occupation of Manchuria and the associated military forms of administering this region" be,
without annexation, extended "until the Russian government
should receive assurance of the full security of its lawful
interests." "For the reconciliation [in Manchuria] of Russian interests and foreign" "on economic grounds" "a special
Russian company should be organized which was not itself
intended to operate but would command all the necessary
means for creating active filials in which foreign labor and
capital would find wide activity and protection." "The concession rights of this company," "to consist of carefully selected
persons, bearing personal responsibility to the sovereign,"
"will be obtained from the acquisition of Chinese Eastern
Railway company shares and from transfer to it of the rights

of the Mining and Timber Associations," and the Russo-Chinese bank "becomes industrial and emission bank" of the company. The Russian government must "recognize the exclusive right of the Chinese Eastern Railway to the possession of concessions in Manchuria" and "to obtain [from China] a monopoly over concessions" (or "deprive the Chinese of freedom to let concessions"). But, granting this last to be possible--Bezobrazov now passed to miracle with the same ease that Witte had also shown up to the last minute. He simply asserted (just as Witte had done in the report of June 27, 1903) that "there is good ground for supposing that foreigners will readily reconcile themselves to Russian monopoly of concessions in Manchuria," and the "Chinese government will be compelled to submit to our irrevocable decision."[251]

This plan was, in Bezobrazov's mind, associated (such indication exists) with the "confirmation in respect also to the Far East of the chief bases of our new empire-wide financial-economic program as already pre-indicated [by the tsar] to the director of the ministry of finance, namely: to strive toward the curtailment of state economy."[252] In any event it seemed to Bezobrazov that "Pleske was beginning to comprehend the helplessness of his department in the matter of creating real items of revenue by way of state economy," and what Bezobrazov now needed for complete success was to express himself "sufficiently clearly" in this same sense (favoring the "necessity of radical measures") to Alekseyev as well. Evidently Nicholas still stubbornly held to the principle of deciding nothing "without cognizance of" the vicegerent.[253]

The most ticklish point of Vogak's Port Arthur mission was, thus, to manage, without letting Alekseyev "notice" "the intention of teaching him anything," "to compel him to put" to Vogak "just those questions that were needful to permit [Vogak] to tell him that which it was necessary to convey or explain to him." But when Vogak had, with difficulty, succeeded in doing this, it appeared that Alekseyev "though recognizing the undoubted importance" of economic questions, now "declined to discuss them, pleading his incompetence," now pointed out the "prematureness" of any decisions on these questions "before a final decision had been reached on the Manchurian question as a whole."[254] In general, Alekseyev's "temper" "impressed" Vogak as "very unyielding, disin-

clined to compromises," and "beyond doubt" he would "firmly
insist on the necessity of retaining all Manchuria, including
Yingkow." But in the political sphere as well Alekseyev
found "decisive measures inopportune" for himself "until our
position in Manchuria had been definitively ascertained."[255]
No matter how Vogak assured him that "he could count on
the sincerest cooperation "of Plehve, Bezobrazov and Abaza,
Alekseyev still kept repeating that "he was very much dis-
heartened," that his "power was waning." It was quite obvious
that Alekseyev could not comprehend just what Nicholas actually
wanted, and all the Beaobrazovists' circumlocutions demonstrated to him that they were not on altogether firm ground
either. On one occasion Alekseyev admitted point blank to
Vogak that the settlement of the Manchurian question was
"complicated" for him by "the instruction he had received
[from Nicholas] as to the advisability of avoiding the provocation of China's lasting enmity toward us."[256] But again
the instruction he had received back in May respecting the
"defense of Russian interests in Manchuria" had put him on
his guard against opening "too easy access to Manchuria to
foreigners."[257] In Bezobrazov's plan he seemed to see just
such a danger; though on the other hand the at least verbal
tendency of this plan toward curtailing "treasury expenditures
on enterprises" in the Far East fully coincided with the
opinion announced by Alekseyev back at the June conferences
and still maintained by him now as to the "undesirability" of
future expenditures of this sort.[258]
No matter how Vogak now endeavored to "inspire" "confidence" in him that the "bases" of the plan had been "personally
projected by the sovereign himself," Alekseyev simply refused to believe this and insisted that "though you may start
no enterprises, and, more particularly, give no state money
to enterprises, you will still have to let the Sinoruss [i.e.,
the Russo-Chinese bank] do business as before." And he insisted so firmly that after two or three volleys of suggestions
all "hope of seeing him an adherent of the new economic program" was relinquished, and in future Vogak had no alternative
but to shift to the "position of silent observer" and "merely
answer questions."[259] For some time the matter of Nicholas's
adoption of the "new economic program" thus remained in
abeyance. Witte's removal alone had proved insufficient to
permit the Bezobrazovists on the new Special Committee of
the Far East to at once convert their "politico-economic"

"idea" into a government program. What actually stood in
the way of it first and foremost was, as Alekseyev had indicated, the question of "some more stable form of occupation"
in Manchuria.

But, needless to say, any pressure in this direction exerted
by the Bezobrazovists on Alekseyev directly could have no
success either: it would be necessary to obtain "a categorical
order to him from Peterburg," i.e., from Nicholas himself.[260]
The only thing Alekseyev considered himself obliged to do
was assume responsibility to Peterburg for the re-occupation
of Mukden by Russian troops, effected against Alekseyev's
order by the military commissar (Kvetsinsky).[261] But that
he should "order on his own authority" that the Timber Association be given an "exclusive concession" to the Manchurian
bank of the Yalu, something that Balashov and Bezobrazov
thought absolutely necessary for the success of their whole
"timber enterprise," was a demand impossible to make of
Alekseyev seriously as long as the "Manchurian question" remained unsolved. The project for such a solution presented
to Nicholas by Balashov from Port Arthur on November 12,
when Balashov could no longer doubt that Bezobrazov was
pwerless to save the timber enterprise from liquidation, was
calculated on the basis of putting the business on a firm
financial foundation just in Manchuria. As ranking head of
the administration of the Bezobrazov enterprises and personally doomed to go down along with them in the immediate
future unless special measures were taken, Balashov demanded decisive and immediate action: 1) open annexation
of Manchuria and Mongolia, 2) abolishment of the whole local
Chinese administration and its replacement by a Russian one,
subject to the vicegerent, 3) introduction of the "elective
principle" for "replacing lower officials" and mutual responsibility and answerableness of the Chinese population "for
all robbery and brigandage," 4) introduction of a two-ruble
poll tax (amounting to about 40 million rubles in all) to cover
all expenditures for administration, 5) assignment of the
timber monopoly on the bank of the Yalu to the Association
"by order of the vicegerent," and 6) assignment to it, by
order of the vicegerent, of the salt lease in Manchuria with
an annual revenue amounting to three million rubles.[262]

But, for a starter, even with this crafty project for financing the Association by expropriation of revenues of the
Chinese government, Balashov still had to request an im-

mediate subsidy from the Russian treasury of one million
rubles to set up the actual administration of the lease, and
this at once made the whole project suspect of being a
counterfeit as had proved to be the case with the loud touting
of fabulous returns from the Yalu timber operation started
in the spring of 1903, which had now swallowed up without a
trace the two treasury millions then issued to Bezobrazov.[263]
Moreover, the political "audacity" of the Balashov project,
which reached Nicholas in mid-December, was now altogether
outdated: Japan's categorical demand respecting the "Manchurian article" had outstripped Balashov, and Nicholas's
compromise (December 15) with Japan on this point left him
no alternative but to place the tempting project for annexing
Manchuria on file.[264]

This does not mean that the Bezobrazovists did not know
how to hit it off with their "master": it only means that the
war had overtaken Nicholas on his paths of "logical gradualism."

Notwithstanding the fact that Alekseyev had refused to support the "new economic program" and even Bezobrazov had
at the end of November "declared himself ill" and hastily gone
abroad, leaving Balashov without a kopeck, and even neglect-
ing to inform him of his departure, the question of the economic program was, by Nicholas himself, again set for discussion
in January 1904, on the very eve of the war.[265] But the conference organized under the chairmanship of Count A.P. Ig-
natyev (a member of Bezobrazov's Association) "to draw up
a program of questions subject to discussion and solution relating to Russia's financial, industrial and economic enterprises in trans-border localities of the Far East," was from
the outset designated as "preliminary," and presumably the
"solution" of these questions was to be effected in the Special
Committee of the Far East, when the working out of the whole
"statute" of the vicegerency had been completed.[266] At the
first six sessions, January 13 through February 10, the conference bickered helplessly over the points of the Bezobrazov
plan, this time expounded by Vonliarliarsky, and, having no
other "requisite materials" at its disposal, confined itself
to a restatement of these points in question form, having decided simply to request "further instructions from his maj-

esty."267 When (on February 27) Nicholas made Kokovtsov
the new minister of finance, a party to the conference, and
exhaustive factual data and explanations of the questions
previously put by it were presented to the conference; the
"new economic program" failed to pass this test: to the
Bezobraovists' surprise, the "ministry" contrived to "repudiate previous business set-ups" and, having exposed the
sham novelty of the program presented, to confront this with
its own, this time better adapted to new conditions.

The new economists, needless to say, took as point of
departure the idea of the necessity of "limiting" the policy
whereby, "while foreign states seek colonies for the material
profit of the mother country, we expend on them money
levied from the home population," and of "renouncing the
system of creating industrial enterprises on treasury money."
The "East-Asiatic Industrial Company"--"private company
de jure" and "government organ de facto"--was, accordingly,
"to stimulate private initiative and attract working capital."
On a basis of strict monopoly ("not a single concession may
be granted by the Chinese or Korean government to anyone
but the Company") it was to "unite the activity of all semi-
official and quasi-official companies already functioning in
the Far East, and halt competition among our own nationals,"
and "then transfer [the enterprises] to private hands,"--to
Russians, "or, in the event of their disinclinations," to
foreigners, on the condition that "part of the profits revert"
"to the Russian treasury." Since it was now proposed that
the Company be made "completely subordinate to the control
of the vicegerent," and the Committee of the Far East be left
to appoint a "Council of Company share-holders," and the
shares be distributed between the government (3/4) and "private persons sanctioned by his majesty" (1/4,) it was natural
that Vonliarliarsky himself, among a number of other questions "which will require" "detailed working out with the assistance of specialists," should have posed this one: "will
the East-Asiatic Company be an organ of the government and
a necessary adjunct to the Committee of the Far East, or a
pseudo-private company?"268

In either case, however, it was plain what the "newness"
of the whole undertaking boiled down to: from the existing
scheme of state economy in Manchuria, now ostensibly being
relegated to the archives, the minister of finance had been
eliminated and his place been taken by the vicegerent, who

would be assisted in performing his unifying function by members appointed to the Council of the Company (having "all the
rights of state servants"), in part, perhaps, interested partners in the business (as had under Witte been the custom
even respecting employees of his "pseudo-private" enter-
prices).[269]

Of this "most consummate galimatias," as Shvanebakh
characterized all that happened at six sessions of the conference, nothing remained by the time Kokovtsov had presented the "data" that the conference had lacked (at the session of May 10). The two enterprises most alluring to the
Bezobraovists dropped out at the first go, namely the Russo-
Chinese bank and the Chinese Eastern Railway Company.
The bank proved impossible to touch (even to put so much as
one representative of the East-Asiatic Company on the Board,
as Vonliarliarsky at first agreed) not only because "about
50 per cent of its shares were in the hands. of foreign investors" and "foreign deposits amounted to 28 million rubles,"
but also because the war loan just concluded had been made
"through the agency of the directors of the Paris branch of
the Russo-Chinese bank."[270] The Chinese Eastern Railway
likewise, in view of its political significance, "must," it
appeared, "remain [actually] under state administration,"
while its formal status could not be altered without the consent of the Chinese government. But Kokovtsov next
definitely repudiated both the very thought of the possibility
of abolishing the deficit for the Far East, since the occasion
for expenditures here was "not local needs" but the requirements of the "whole Russian state," and reliance on the possibility, after the unsuccessful Russo-Chinese bank experiment, of getting monopolistic rights for the projected company from China. Then all that would be left of the whole
Bezobrazovist undertaking would be the "compulsory mediation" of the Company, binding not on the foreign, but only
on Russian private capital. But the main thing was: while
right here in Moscow, with no special fuss or difficulty, it
is possible to get 24 per cent on discount or in the dry-goods
trade" "we are not going to find any of our industrialists
volunteering to seek their fortunes in the Far East;" "therefore the organization of such a commercial-industrial company is hardly to be expected" without treasury participation.
Moreover, "we cannot flatter ourselves with the hope that we
shall be able to confine ourselves to allowing such a company

one and one-half million to two million rubles," since "it
will need enormous sums for mining enterprises alone."271
    As over against such an "exclusively promotional" com-
pany, Kokovtsov proposed, "for the encouragement both of
individual Russians and of companies, working companies
however": 1) that we "build our financial policy in the Far
East" on the principle of "lightening customs, tariffs, taxes,
credits, and so forth," 2) "eliminate certain formalities of
company organization," and 3) renounce intolerance toward
foreigners and Jews,"--a policy which the existence of a
"monopolistic company" would only undermine. As a result,
to the profound indignation of Abaza, left in complete solitude
upon this occasion to press the bald demand for treasury
"participation without fail" in a monopolistic private company, the conference at the following session (May 24) "unanimously declared in favor of a general curtailment of state
economy in future in all enterprises of an industrial character, such as: the Manchurian Mining Association, the concessions in hunt-master Balashov's care, and certain side-lines
of the Chinese Eastern Railway Company" (i.e., the maritime
steamship line, the amalgamation of which with the railway
had so charmed Witte by its likeness to the Morgan trust).
Needless to say, the conference (except for Abaza) came out
just as "decisively" against the organization of the East-
Asiatic Company, "finding that such a turn of events would
be tantamount to the continuation of masked economy on state
means," and declared that the "attraction of foreign capital
[for the purpose of "attracting private enterprise"] should be
made part of the task of Russia's financial policy in the
Far East." But "brazen-faced" Abaza, taking up the gauntlet
for the last time, again insisted "on the uniting of all separate
companies under the aegis of a central company with treasury
participation," since only thus would "foreign enterprises and
capital" "be kept from obtaining dominant importance in the
region."
    Thus the "new economic program" was confronted by
another still newer. Both were calculated, of course, for
after the war. But Kokotsov further declared openly that as
yet "it was obviously only possible to proceed" from the
"hypothesis" of post-war preservation of the pre-war status
quo. Whereas Abaza was just then "preparing" the "expulsion of Chinese officials from Manchuria, to provoke China's
official breach of neutrality," with a view to facilitating the

annexation of Manchuria from China after the victory over Japan.[272] This "preparation" hung fire, but was not lost: as we shall see, Nicholas did not release this idea until September, after Liaoyan. This points to the supposition that Nicholas did not now, in May, set aside the idea of his "new economic program" either, without which the still future (all in good time) political act of expelling the Manchurian authorities would have had little worth.[273]

Chapter VII

RUSSIA'S INTERNATIONAL-FINANCIAL RELATIONS
DURING THE WAR PERIOD (1904-1906)

I

The Japanese war cost the treasury 6,553.8 million rubles.
Of this amount, more than half (3,943.6 million rubles) went
to pay interest on loans concluded by Russia in foreign and
domestic markets to take care of her fighting expenses. The
capital amount borrowed for this purpose during 1904-1909
totalled 2,176.1 million rubles. Thus the war expenses met
either out of "cash on hand" or budget revenue came to the
relatively negligible sum of 434.1 million rubles.[1] Take the
early weeks of the war (January-February 1904): the Russian
government cannot have commanded at the outset more than
157 million rubles in the form of "cash on hand," and the
emissive right in the reserve stood at 200 million.[2] The
problem of the conduct of the war thus acquired from the
first a doubly international character, inasmuch as its actual
financing was directly dependent on "aid" from foreign markets and must go through the regular diplomatic mill. Lacking any alliance of a nature to formally guarantee her the
direct military support, or actually provide her with the financial backing, of any other power, Russia got into the war
at a moment when she was plainly still unprepared, and ended
it in the 19th month, after financing from without had ceased.[3]
No wonder "there was a smell of loans in the air" within a
day or so of the opening of hostilities.[4] Nor is it possible to
study the effect of the war on Russian diplomatic procedure
at that time and in connection with it or Russia's international
relations as they crystallized during 1904-1906 in an environment of war and revolution except by examining them through
the prism of their financial envelopes.

By the beginning of the war about four billion rubles of
Russian state securities were reputedly held by foreign investors: of these, more than three billions were in French
hands.[5] This meant that no sacrifice could be too great for

maintaining the exchange rate of Russian securities in the
Paris market: upon it the future fate of Russian credit and
the possibility of its maximal utilization for purposes of
prosecuting the war more than half depended. In this sense
it would have been unreasonable to rely wholly on the political alliance: in the French market, Russian securities did
not lie long in bank portfolios, but were distributed to the
mass of solid investors, small as well as large, and should
a panic ever get started it would be a "real avalanche" that
nothing could check, least of all a political alliance.[6] State
loans abroad were a double burden on the Russian financial
system: they squeezed from the state economy up to 180
million rubles of its annual clear profit and subjected the
whole financial mechanism of the country to the nightmare
danger of the whole system blowing up--by a remote jolt from
a foreign land; to directly avert such a jolt out there was
impossible, it being contingent on the total international
situation, and the less accessible to influence that situation
became, the more imminent would be the threat of the jolt.[7]
One immediately available, albeit feeble, expedient in the
direction of restraint remained to the Russian government:
to beguile the French investor through the influence of the
daily press. To the fact that the latter was, in turn, susceptible only to money arguments and was utterly beyond reach
of the law, the Russian government must resign itself, and,
while periodically resorting to inflationary buying of Russian
government paper on the Peterburg bourse, systematically
provide the notorious "Bureau Lenoir" in Paris with regular
deposits for "indulging" the editorships of the Paris papers.[8]
The "lamentable manifestation of venality in the French press"
[as Kokovtsov gloomily expressed it] cost the Russian government, under the head of "disbursements for publicity" (frais
de publicité) a matter of two million francs during the course
of the war.[9]
    Russian credit was, however, threatened not alone in the
Paris market: danger lurked in the Berlin market as well.
By a goodly tradition with historical complications and at that
time not yet superannuated, "hostile speculation" might be
directed not only toward a drop in Russian securities in Paris
but toward a lowering of the exchange rate of the ruble in
Berlin. Therefore the purchase of rubles on the Berlin bourse
in sufficient quantities to hold the exchange rate at par became
a disbursement as essential for the protection of Russian

crdit as buying up government paper or bribing the press: for
the six months of the pre-war crisis alone (August 16, 1903-
February 10, 1904) this operation reached four million rubles.[10]
  In March 1904, when Kokovtsov, having just taken over the
ministry of finance, presented to the Finance Committee his
reflections "on the current financial situation and the measures
necessary in view of hostilities," these related not only to the
above-noted manipulations of the Berlin exchange rate for the
credit ruble, but also, after November, to the second-line insurance of the exchange rate through term purchase of currency and carry-over, tying up about 330 millions of the State
bank's total gold reserve of 905 million rubles, and likewise
to the sudden slump in government paper from 95.25 on
January 23 (the eve of the rupture) to 90.5 on January 28 (the
morrow of the Japanese fleet's attack on the Russian squadron at Port Arthur). Naturally, both with Kokovtsov and
afterwards in Finance Committee where his proposals were
studied, the question of currency and credit took first place.[11]
  At the moment there was a grave question as to whether
it would be possible to conduct the war without risk of mis-
appropriation and reduction of the gold reserve and still con-
serve the exchange of banknotes for gold, i.e., whether it
would be possible to obviate a stoppage of exchange. Kokovtsov's answer was: not only possible, but imperative. No
such extreme measure was indicated by conditions at the
given economic moment--conditions which in general did not
warrant apprehension--whereas the stoppage of exchange
would produce "the most serious and regrettable effects on
the welfare of the state." Though deeming this measure "as
yet" by no means justified, Kokovtsov still saw as his chief
task the obviation of its necessity in future. Moreover he
strongly emphasized the fact that his reflections as a whole
were only applicable if the clash remained confined to Russia
and Japan alone.
  Witte, supporting Kokovtsov's proposition in its entirety,
proceeded to develop the question in Committee in an ominously
prophetic manner to the logical limit--a world war. With a
localized war, even should it drag on until the cost "reached
a billion rubles" (hitherto the figure current in government
circles had been somewhere around 700-800 million rubles
for a war of a year and a half, the sum indicated by Kuropatkin),[12] "it still ought to be perfectly possible to maintain"
our monetary circulation. But "even in view of a vast

Europe-wide war, costing sums insusceptible of calculation,"
"it would behoove us to weigh carefully the probable effects
of ceasing to back our currency," though, as Witte emphasized,
"in such a war, no state would decline to back its currency."
The necessity for Russia "to back her currency" derived, in
Witte's opinion, all else apart, from the "peculiarities of our
state debt," contracted, for the most part, on a gold standard,
and, "due to lack of capital in our fatherland," allocated almost entirely abroad. Witte called attention to the fact that
"even if Russia locked her gold up in the bank vaults" she
would still have to pay it out--"in the long run, in larger
amounts, perhaps, and with incalculably greater repercussions on the welfare of the country than as if she had backed
her exchange," since the gold debt would not cease to exert
pressure on the financial system, and, in connection with the
necessity of covering the difference relative to our putative
balance, would compel the purchase of currency in steadily
dropping credit rubles, while the agio on gold would itself
cause an increasing return of our loans from abroad, "due
to confidence in them being shaken."

Ergo, exchange must not be stopped out of fear of loss of
gold reserve; on the contrary, the gold standard must at all
costs be maintained for the sake of conserving the gold reserve. Such was the conclusion drawn from the basic "pe-
culiarity" of the Russian financial system, inextricably
bound up with the French financial market, and in those days
having no independent existence apart from it. Entering the
war with his military preparations still far from complete,
yet still clinging to the idea of its victorious outcome as a
means for saving the autocracy from a revolutionary end,
and at the same time confirming the one and, for him, indisputable proposition of the specialists as to maintenance
of exchange, Nicholas, in the last analysis, placed himself,
through the French bourse, in complete dependence on the
will of the French government and involved Russia in the
basic European imperialistic conflict, already in full swing.
Calamitous military defeats and thrusts at the autocracy from
within the country were destined to change the correlation of
forces in the Franco-Russian alliance essentially, and forced
Nicholas after the war to come to an agreement both with
England and with Japan on the whole gamut of moot questions.
The possibility now exists of tracing quite accurately the path
by which Russia, none too complacently, or unresistingly,

reached her place in the ranks of the entente powers in the
event of a Europe-wide war.

II

The Sino-Japanese War of 1894-95 had already outlined
Japan's territorial program on the Asiatic mainland--seizure
of South Manchuria and severance of Korea from China to
become part of Japan's sphere of influence--as actually achieved
by Japan's triumph of 1905. The Japanese victory of 1895,
which at the time threatened to undermine substantially the
Russian government's political plans on the Pacific littoral in
connection with the building of the Siberian road, had brought
into existence in the Far East a coalition of three powers,
namely: Russia, forging ahead with the construction of the
Siberian trunk-line and, incidentally, laying claim to these
very areas; France, which had definitively freed Russia's
hands for the execution of this grandiose project by concluding
political and military agreements with her (1891-1892); and
Germany, which had just (in 1894) made her peace with Russia
in the conclusion of a trade treaty and was seeking Russia's
support for her own penetration into Chinese territory while
there was yet time. This triple coalition, after performing
its function of forcing Japan to withdraw from Manchuria and
Korea, not only received no official formulation but never
once reappeared upon the scene. That same Sino-Japanese
war which revealed the indisputable preparedness of the
Japanese army for war, and its numerical adequacy for opposing the Russians, also revealed to England her natural
ally on land against Russia, whose diplomacy in turn did
everything likely to further the actual consummation of a formal alliance. The bacchanalia of Chinese territorial seizures
by the great powers that developed immediately afterwards,
in 1897-98, and threatened the partition of all China into
closed spheres of influence, drew America, as well, into
the arena of imperialistic struggle, with an enunciation of
the principles of Chinese integrity and the "open door."
Inasmuch as Witte's policy at the time largely ran counter
to these principles, carrying Russia not only toward direct
annexation of all Manchuria, but even--and this was the more
serious matter for American capital--toward its complete
closure to foreign industrial enterprise and toward restraint
of foreign trade, the United States at once sided with the

Anglo-Japanese combination in all overtures regarding the
Manchurian question, and on the eve of the war made common
cause with Japan by signing on the same day she did a trade
treaty with China that precluded any future possibility of
Russia's assuming a monopolistic attitude toward Manchuria
(October 8, 1903) or making any sort of attempt on Chinese
sovereignty.13 As soon as the war started, Roosevelt
hastened to warn Germany and France that if they even made
a move to abet Russia, as in 1895, America would rally to
the defense of Japan.14 No doubt Roosevelt's real desire
respecting the war now started was, as he himself said, that
it should "drag on" "until both powers were utterly exhausted
(aufreiben)" and "that when peace was concluded their territorial antagonisms should still be unremoved," though before the war Roosevelt's diplomacy had on this account
stressed the idea that "the sympathies of the United States
were entirely with Japan" and that Russia's assurances concerning the "open door" in Manchuria could not be taken
seriously.15

But much as Russian diplomacy may have wished it, nothing
could any longer revive the triple grouping of 1895 in the Far
East. France was now quite hopeless in this respect. Then
she had found herself in a position of growing antagonism
against England, and the Franco-Russian alliance, fortified
by the military convention of 1892, had liberated her politically to take her chance in Africa in that it cramped England
in the Far East by in some measure fostering Russia's expansion there economically. The profoundly substantial enterprises that gave breadth to Russia's move into the Far East,
though pedantically cast in the mould of monopolistic capitalism, were the product of conditions during the early years
of the Franco-Russian alliance. And the colossal export of
capital to the territory extending from the Urals to the
Pacific was typified by the fact that private French capital
had advanced boldly into Eastern Siberia and China side by
side with Russian treasury capital either under the guarantee
of Russia's machinery of state or in alliance with international
banking capital that had previously operated in Russian ter-
ritory--in neither case seeking to assume leadership, and at
first subjecting itself to the general political direction of the
autocratic government.

Without the Siberian and Chinese Eastern Railways, where
French and American capital insinuated itself into the direct

financing, though the Russian government authorized neither, confident, apparently, that the new military-political alliance would facilitate the government's itself accommodating the French money market to the financing of these grandiose strategic construction projects in the regular course of free and unconditional administration of the empire's state budget;[16] without the Chinese loan, floated entirely on the French market by a group of Paris banks under guarantee of the Russian government, which would otherwise, i.e., solely on its own resources, have been unable to do the Manchu dynasty this political service; without the Russo-Chinese bank, which became, thanks to the breadth of its charter and the Russian government's majority on its Board, a sufficiently elastic implement of penetration and prehension for the government in its great political game on the arena of world imperialism, but, thanks to the union of French, German, and Chinese elements in its working capital, would in some measure insure the policy of its own Board against the blind subordination of commercial interests to government policy, especially the interests of French share-holders, not only as represented on the Board but as tying this Russian bank in with the whole Parisian banking mechanism:--without all this, the boldly aggressive policy prosecuted by the autocracy in the Far East for the purpose of getting the necessary strategic, political and economic vantage points for the impending international struggle in China over railways, spheres of influence, monopolies, administrative branches, industrial concessions, settlements, markets for goods and raw materials, would have been unthinkable. As long as Russia was dealing with a France having no other commitments with respect either to Germany or to England, and as long as outward political successes masked the fact that the tasks implied in the program the Russian government had undertaken in the Far East were out of all proportion to the ready cash that the autocracy had at its disposal or could bring under its "aegis"--so long would the Franco-Russian alliance make itself felt in the Far East in the readiness of French diplomacy to go hand in hand with Russian. But the Franco-Russian declaration of March 3/16, 1902 accordingly proved to be the final manifestation of the alliance in Far Eastern affairs, since France now envisaged the possibility of a very inclusive and promising agreement with England.

In March, 1903, the new French ambassador in Peterburg

(Bompar) had already "started" "throwing stones into our
garden" by openly (in the Moniteur Officiel de Commerce)
"minimizing the importance of the Siberian railway; " at the
same time Delcasse too had let drop such remarks as that
out of "an adroit flirtation with England" he "would perhaps
get more than out of our friends," while Witte and Rafalovich,
in deference to Delcasse's "Anglophilism," even thought best
to withhold support from Deloncle, a member of the Chamber
who had conceived the scheme of "introducing a motion in the
Chamber requesting that the attention of the French government be directed to the necessity of deriving commercial and
industrial profit from Russia's trans-Siberian railway," and
who had it in mind to issue "for distribution to all deputies
and senators" a special brochure on "what Russia has done
in the Far East."[17] In the spring of 1903, Anglo-French
negotiations were already "in full swing" and if information
at the disposal of German diplomacy is to be trusted, Parisian
Haute Finance, in search of a partner for future financing of
the Russian government, had at that time already started to
prepare the soil for an Anglo-Russian rapprochement.[18] By
the autumn of 1903, when suspicion was already rife in Paris
that the autocracy "would be compelled to create a diversion
abroad in order to distract attention" from the trying situation
at home, Rafalovich was, for example, unable to conceal
from his Peterburg chief the "alarm" that increasingly possessed the Parisian "commercial and industrial world" in
connection with "affairs in the Far East," and which had by
October already expressed itself "in fluctuations of Russian
stock quotations." The "adroitly launched rumor" that Anglo-
French negotiations "were getting off to a good start" Rafalovich was himself inclined to regard as a "trial balloon" from
the other side of the Channel for the purpose of "lulling French
public opinion at a moment when things might possibly go
wrong in the Far East" and of "forestalling any manifestations
against England's allies, the Japanese."

But however much it might seem to him that among "sen-
sible people" the "feeling prevailed that in the last analysis
we should succeed in avoiding an armed clash," the ruling
conviction in these business circles friendly to Russia actually was: "that our mastery of the Far East would swallow
up vast sums" for the defense of our new possessions and
"would therefore constitute a source of potential budgetary
disturbances." The "general trend of thought" appeared to

him altogether "unfavorable to us," and French diplomacy, "actually guided by Cambon in London and Barrer in Rome," not at all Russophile.[19] Even if no particular significance is to be attributed to the fact that in the military sphere as well Russia was by this time also causing the French staff some uneasiness, as Berlin heard from an Austrian source, Peterburg could in any event scarcely cling longer to the illusion of any support of Russia's pretensions in the Far East by France.[20]

During the autumn of 1903 Lamsdorf was in Paris but did not bring back to Peterburg anything positive in this sense except, perhaps, some hope of French mediation with a view to the peaceful settlement of the Russo-Japanese conflict.[21] Indirect feelers through Paris, however, came to nothing either in London or in Berlin, and on January 26, 1904 when Lamsdorf proposed that Nicholas openly resort to mediation, Nicholas was right that then it was already too late.[22] The inauspicious opening of the war for Russia could only have given France the final impetus, had such still been necessary, to conclude that exhaustive agreement with England on all colonial matters (April 8, 1904) which at the given stage of Russo-English relations might easily render questionable the future existence of the Franco-Russian alliance. Throughout the war, France maintained the strictest neutrality, which Russia never attempted to mollify in the slightest degree in her own favor, while Russian diplomacy felt that the alliance itself might be put to the test if it so much as inquired what position Russia's ally would take in the event of England's intervention in the war.[23] Thus, even though the Franco-Russian alliance had formally assumed a quasi-validity in the sphere of Far-Eastern affairs following the Russo-French declaration of 1902, it had become paralyzed by the moment when Japan's attack might have automatically created casus foederis.

Under such circumstances, Germany appeared at first glance to be exceptionally well placed just before the Russo-Japanese war to play for the break-up of the Franco-Russian alliance and the substitution of a Russo-German alliance. The Bjorko treaty, signed on July 11/24, 1905 by Wilhelm and Nicholas, represented top score for this play, and if put in force would have produced an international situation radically different from that which actually maintained during the decade from the Anglo-French agreement of 1904 to the be-

ginning of the World War. With the name of Bjorko, which
gained wide notoriety at the height of the last war, is now
linked a sudden diplomatic scandal, with difficulty hushed up
by the Russian ministers not unaided by some one of the grand
dukes, a scandal in which Wilhelm played the part of the
crook getting the victim to sign away his rights, and Nicholas
either that of a simpleton unaware of what he was doing or of
a crafty betrayer of his "allies," and in either case afterwards
forced to confess that he had signed without due consideration
of all the circumstances. Product of the personal policy of
the last two representatives of absolutism "by the grace of
God," the Bjorko treaty was not only an adventitious expression of their personal will but an objective reflection of the
complicated situation from which it represented an attempt
to break away--an attempt doomed to failure for both parties
equally.

Ever since the spring of 1895 when Wilhelm definitely
supported Russia in her action against Japanese seizures in
China, not only diplomatically but by readiness for a joint
appeal to arms, Germany's role in Russia's policy in the
Far East had never ceased to be that of rear-end locomotive.
Witte (in his Memoirs) took great pains to describe this "fatal" role of Germany, starting two years later with the seizure
of Kiaochow, which, he held, incited Nicholas II to pass to
the aggressive and "giddy" policy of seizures in the East. At
present, however, there hardly remains room for doubt that
the "fatal" knot cut by the war of 1904-1905 was tightened by
Witte's hands and Wilhelm's while Nicholas vacillated during
the spring of 1895. None but Witte then demanded the exclusion of Japan from Manchuria, even at the price of war, until
the Siberian through-route had been completed, and only
Germany's unconditional decision roused France from her
state of indecision (one eye on England) and moved her to become a party to the ultimatum that forced Japan to alter the
terms of the Chinese peace treaty already signed at Shimonoseky. Inasmuch as no grounds existed for supposing that the
Japanese government would, for no good reason, simply renounce, in Liaotung, the naval keys to South Manchuria, and
calmly await the completion of the Siberian railway, with a
strategic and political significance hard to overestimate (especially in view of its having been laid through Manchuria in
full consciousness of inevitable Russian offshoots in any
direction, to Peking perhaps, or to the Yellow Sea), the date

of the inevitable military settlement of the Manchurian question might be established as directly dependent on the date of
completion of construction. That Japan must endeavor to get
into Manchuria before this date had been conceded back in
1895.[24] In this sense, perhaps, Wilhelm (and Witte with him)
did actually assume a "fatal role" in Russia's Far-Eastern
policy practically nine years before the fatal denouement--no
more so, however, than the French, who, though not so sure
at the first moment when intervention was undertaken, nonetheless gave the autocracy most substantial support shortly
afterwards in the development of the success attained.

Naturally this friendly act on the part of German diplomacy
at a moment so decisive for the fate of Witte's imperialistic
plan at once made Germany an exacting associate when it
came to sharing such political advantages as might be extrac-
ted from the situation created in Peking by their joint efforts,
and to some extent put Russian diplomacy under an obligation.
It was not only a matter of the engagements that Wilhelm got
from Nicholas at Peterhof--inexact, to be sure, in their for-
mulation--but, for Witte, the assurance also that for the
future realization of his plan he need not be exclusively dependent on the French. Such was, in part, the meaning of Witte's
refusal to repeat the Russo-French loan to China at the beginning of 1896, on grounds of giving "friendly" Germany a
chance this time.[25] Such was the meaning of the fusion, in
1895, in the Russo-Chinese bank, of a fresh affluent of
French capital, channelled through several Paris banks, with
Disconto-Gesellschaft capital, through the St. Petersburg International Commercial Bank, now launched by Witte upon the
Far-Eastern scene as constitutor of Russia's new bank.[26]
Such too was the fusion of capital assembled in Paris by
business agents of the St. Petersburg Discount and Loan Bank
(likewise founded with the aid of the Disconto-Gesellschaft),
with capital from the Discount and St. Petersburg International
banks in the Russian Gold-Mining Company, founded in May
1895 in the expectation, linked with near completion of the
Siberian road, of operating throughout the expanse from the
Urals to, and including, the Maritime province: in 1901, as
we have seen, it reached out for the Manchurian gold-fields
as well.[27] Such, finally, was the Syndicate for the investigation of the mineral resources of China, founded in June
1897 on the initiative of the Russo-Chinese bank and the Russian Gold-Mining Company, with the considerable aid of the

St. Petersburg International bank, which, in turn, founded
in 1900 the Mining Company of the Tushetukhan and Tsetsenkhan aimaks in Mongolia, with practically half participation
by a group of Belgian capitalists.[28]

If his entire trans-Ural plan is viewed as a single whole,
Witte (with the indispensable aid of his factotum Rothstein,
who sat on the boards of all the above-enumerated "founda-
tions") may be said to have succeeded in mobilizing under the
Russian autocracy's "aegis," immediately after the 1895 intervention, a considerable amount of capital, by European
Russian standards, of extremely varied national origin, giving its monopolistic tendencies a promising organizational
unity, and interesting it in the successes of the autocracy's
foreign policy in the Far East. Expecting, as an ally, to get
a railway to the very capital of the Chinese empire, first
consolidating the alliance of the two greatest continental
powers by support of the Manchu dynasty and the old political
order in China, and proposing, on the basis of this alliance,
to get to "all the riches" of China by "new methods" for the
"peaceful conquest of culturally backward countries," Witte
must now have felt himself in full trim for capitalistic battle,
and well aware of the dangerous character of the duel he had
entered on with the incalculably mightier capital of England,
made the most of his opportunity (in Peterburg, in the summer
of 1897) to picture to Wilhelm an aging Europe, enfeebled by
land armaments, as doomed to destruction in the struggle
with "trans-oceanic" countries, and to develop his plan for
salvation through a continental alliance against England.[29]

The fact that Wilhelm now remained deaf to this idea of
a triple alliance, immediately afterwards brought pressure
to bear on Nicholas, muddled Russian diplomacy's cards by
invading Shantung, and remained just as deaf to Witte's naive
appeal that he renounce this seizure; that, finally, when the
last chance for an agreement with England was lost, and England had veered to the policy of encircling Germany (and
driving Russia from Manchuria), Wilhelm launched the formula of the "two admirals," keeping the Atlantic Ocean for
himself, and luring Nicholas with the Pacific (as Witte had
himself once lured Alexander III with the prospect of "the
domination of the Russian navy in Pacific waters"), and
prosecuted the policy of diverting Russia's armies to the
east, away from the western border--all this taken together
proved incapable of distracting Witte's diplomacy from a

sober evaluation of all the drawbacks connected with an exclusive French alliance, or making him relinquish his concept of the necessity of something to counterbalance the attitude of our French friends, which would inevitably grow
even more exacting.

Upon occasion, as noted in the proper context, Witte was
not averse to boasting, even before his associates, of the
French and autonomous character of the Russo-Chinese bank,
and of the Russian government's being obliged to regulate
even basic lines of policy by its frangible banking instrument.
But the participation of French share-holders in the administration of the bank, as stipulated at the outset, in point of
fact proved embarassing to Witte himself, giving him not
only the commercial interests of foreign stockholders to
reckon with but even political intervention in the affairs of
the bank by the French government. As we know, even at
the bank's founding the French founders did not at once agree
to the inverse proportion of their participation in the capital
of the bank (5/8) and the number of places allotted them on
its Board (3/8): interested French circles out in China had
hoped to "play the leading part" in the new bank's affairs.
Within two years of the time when Rothstein had succeeded
in persuading the French in Paris, relations between the
Russian and the French element in Shanghai had become so
strained that Witte was about ready to split the bank along
national lines, which would, of course, have entailed competition unprofitable for both.[30] Moreover, the Parisian
directors apparently preferred to implicate Hanotaux in the
matter by renewing their plea, so that (in August 1897)
Netslin approached Witte merely as a go-between transmitting the "desire of the minister of foreign affairs": 1) for
the addition of "Franco-" to the name of the bank, 2) for
reinforcement of the "French element in the administration"
of the bank, and 3) for the subsequent opening of a branch
bank "in the south of China."[31] All these "desires" encountered definite objections on the part of Russian directors
in China and were unhesitatingly rejected by Witte.[32] The
French again yielded, but there was no guarantee that such
episodes would not be repeated--and the very next year Witte
resorted to increasing the government's share in the capitali-
zation of the bank and got an article into the charter of the
bank concerning confirmation of the Board's personnel by
the Russian minister of finance.[33]

Sure enough, in October 1899, at the first signs of economic difficulties in Russia, the question of putting a French
member on the Board of the bank in Peterburg was revived
by Theophile Delcasse, this time in a form that betrayed the
initiative of the French government in the matter, while the
candidate indicated by Delcasse left no doubt that the point
now was to establish the French government's immediate
control over procedures of the Board: the man proposed by
Delcasse for the post was M. Verstrat, French commercial
agent in Peterburg, and known at the time as none too well
disposed toward Russia. But even with such a guarantee,
Delcasse was not only disinclined to renew the talk of extending the bank's activity to the south of China, but even raised
the question of delimiting the spheres of influence of the
Indo- and Russo-Chinese banks, with the latter operating "to
the north of Shanghai."[34] And, having just compromised
with his enemies the English in the direction of limiting the
railway-building of the Russian bank, Witte did not feel he
could now refuse to "do something to please Count Delcasse,"
and so agreed to limit the area of its commercial-credit
operations as well. This was just as much a compromise on
his part and in making it Witte did not hide his "doubts" from
Delcasse, which boiled down to the fear that, "when banks of
other European states, notably England, are competing with
French and Russian banks, the Russo-Chinese bank's renunciation of operations in certain sections might be less to the
advantage of the Indo-Chinese bank than to that of the English
institutions of credit."

Upon this occasion, Witte also yielded in the matter of the
fourth French member and agreed to its being Verstraat.
Obstinacy on this point would have been the more awkward
inasmuch as, in 1898, when he bought up the second issue
of stock for the Russian treasury, Witte had also put through
an enlargement of the Board from nine members to eleven
and seated two officials from his own ministry. But Witte
did not neglect also to bring it home to his pertinacious French
colleague that "it would have been more civil to raise this
question through the Paris directors of the bank," and
Verstraat was inducted into his new office (in December 1899)
only after Peterburg had received a respectful letter of thanks
addressed to the minister of finance and signed by Netslin and
Hottinguer, who had been "touched" by this attention on the
part of the Russian minister.[35] But Witte's separative policy

in China, shunning out of hand any such "hard and fast alliance"
as that proposed by Delcasse in the summer of 1900, while
threatening to bog Russia down in Manchuria financially and
diplomatically, also put the French government on its guard
respecting Russia's competence in the west, thus affecting
the destiny of the Russo-Chinese bank: 1) through its future
"nationalization" by assumption into the Russian government's
portfolio in 1902 of the whole third issue of shares, and 2)
by excluding industrial promoterism in Manchuria from the
bank's purview at the very moment when the general diplomatic formulae bearing on the Chinese government's recognition of the industrial monopoly of the bank were passing
over into the actual engagement of bank capital in the fren-
zied chartering of companies and the buying up of concessions
in Manchuria from individual Russians and even from companies prepared to sell their concession rights in the open
market and let Manchuria be "overrun" by foreigners--a
prospect as appalling to the Russian government as it was
inconsequential, to say the least, from the viewpoint of the
bank's French stock-holders.[36] Netslin and Hottinguer were
at the same time concerned in the floating of Russian state
loans on the French market and must from the first have
shared the above-mentioned fears of Parisian Haute Finance
respecting the threats to the balancing of the Russian budget
that Russia's future consolidation in the Far East would inevitably entail.

Apropos of the dictatorial terms of the French loan of
1901, it is well to observe that when Nicholas went to Danzig
in the autumn of 1901 in response to Berlin's cordial summons
of that spring, he did so not only as a matter of personal inclination but also, it turns out, in pursuance of suggestions
from Witte and Lamsdorf that he interest the German government in their Manchurian policy by confiding to Berlin the
text of the projected separate treaty with China.[37] Furthermore, at the beginning of 1902, Witte not only arranged a
loan "for the realization of the Chinese indemnity" in Berlin,
when he might just as well have done it in Paris, but refused
for the "time being" to consider any French proposals of this
nature.[38]

Whereas, in the spring of 1903, when it was already plain
to be seen that the Russian loan floated by Mendelssohn was
blithely passing into French hands, Rouvier most uncivilly
left unanswered Witte's "personal letter" requesting "a

quotation on the Russian consolidated 4 per cent loan, already
quoted in Berlin, London, and New York." And when Rafalovich reproached Bompar with this he also took occasion to
"allude to the serious threat overhanging those railroads that
we should never have started had our Paris friends not insisted."39 Acid interchange had by that time become possible
within the Franco-Russian alliance, as we can now see, not
so much because Nicholas, driven by his ministers and his
dynastic instinct, had started up the slippery path of rapprochement between the admirals of the two oceans as because Witte had at the same time undertaken to seek an anti-
dote to the political demands of French friends by switching
his credit operations to Berlin. Witte may have expected
that such an internationalization of the autocracy's finances
would facilitate its manoeuvering to "confirm the peace of
Europe." But when at the same time he hypnotized himself
with the hope of "securing" support for his Manchurian plans
from France and Germany simultaneously, he was, of course,
heading straight for the diplomatic fiasco that led to the
triumph of the Bezobrazovists.40

In the spring of 1903, when the latter began their transition
to "staff" status and undertook to carry Witte's monopolistic
Manchurian program to completion, they posed point-blank
the question of the necessity of Russia's choosing between a
German and an English orientation, setting France aside as
totally inadaptable to Russia's Far-Eastern plans. And this
question was, of course, decided in favor of Germany, on account of "Wilhelm's constant desire to get together with Russia."41 But to get German diplomacy to assume any formal
obligations took more than wishing. Berlin was not in the
least disposed to bind itself by anything beyond promises (to
Tokyo and Peterburg alike) that it would remain neutral in
the event of war, and preferred to bide her time when Russia
herself asked aid, sure that time was working in Germany's
favor.42 German diplomacy set aside all thought of intervention in the Russo-Japanese conflict for the purpose of
averting war; kept a sharp look-out lest in a moment of
weakness Russian diplomacy be stampeded into the path of
an understanding with Japan and England, or she herself betray her impatience to "fall on Russia's neck;" forced Nicholas at Wiesbaden to be the first to broach political subjects,
and not even reiterating to him there the usual assurances
about "covering his rear," with satisfaction gleaning the in-

formation that France was not even thinking of interpreting her alliance relations with Russia more broadly, and that Lansdowne was spurring Japan to action by assurances that England and France would endeavor to localize the war. German diplomacy was guided by the certitude that "regardless of which side won, Russia or Japan," the approaching war "would advance the political power of Germany," provided the Germans "sat tight."[43]

Actually, in the spring of 1903, what with the power in Russia in process of transition to open partisans of the German orientation and opposed to any compromise policy in the Far East; the establishment of a complete understanding between Russia and Austria on Near-Eastern affairs that enabled Russia to withdraw two whole army corps from the Austrian border even before the opening of hostilities;[44] the breaking off of negotiations with China and the re-taking of Mukden, Russia really created the universal impression of a power which, secure to the rear, along its western border, and with its Eastern facade roughly repainted in battle hues, had resolved not to shun war or seek a peaceful exit. After awaiting the opening of hostilities, it only remained for Germany to adopt a policy of super-friendly neutrality, virtually making her Russia's only ally, and then strike at the Franco-Russian alliance diplomatically, by reminders about the "Crimean" combination, seizing upon and exaggerating the slightest outward symptoms of its renewal.

But the above-noted revamping of the Russian machinery of government remained far from complete by the beginning of the war and was halted midway when only the machinery of administration in the Far East had been tackled--thus just sufficing to avert the hasty diplomatic retreat suggested to Nicholas from the depths of the old governmental nucleus (Kuropatkin's memorandum on the return of all southern Manchuria and Liaotung to China). Not only that nucleus, but Nicholas himself, still felt the full weight of the economic chains that consolidated the Franco-Russian alliance, and they would still have to attempt to make use of this alliance during the war for financial purposes. Plainly, with Manchuria continuing to hang heavy, Russian diplomacy's ability to remain equilibrated between France and Germany became increasingly problematical: in a moment of weakness even Witte could not restrain himself from scheming against one of the strategic railroads dictated by the interests of the

French alliance, while to Bezobrazov it was completely beyond comprehension how time and money could be wasted in
the autumn of 1903, at the height of Japanese war preparations,
on great manoeuvres along the western border, when, in the
event of the Manchurian dispute culminating in war, this front
would have to be left to look out for itself.[45] When the war
began, Lamsdorf's formula: to "let nothing sour our relations
with Berlin, or loosen our grip on Paris either," since "only
by preserving equilibrium shall we derive the utmost advantage from either side," actually, due to the timing of the war,
proved equivalent to acknowledging the inevitability of a Russo-
German alliance as well, for it became increasingly evident
as time went on that the question would not be how they might
derive "utmost" "advantages" but what demands they would
be compelled to meet.[46]

The prospect of a split into two inter-defensive and mutually
exclusive alliances, a triple alliance being out of the question,
paradoxical though it may appear, was, nonetheless, conceivable in view of the absolutism's typical element of double
diplomacy. The Russo-German alliance accordingly became
a problem for Nicholas's personal policy.

III

The losses sustained by the Russian fleet at Port Arthur
on the first day of the war left no doubt that the war now
started would be no mere matter of weeks, and by the very
beginning of February 1904 it was already rumored in Paris
that "in the immediate future" Russia would be obliged to
conclude a loan. In February, when this rumor arose, it
was at once "categorically denied" by the Russian government, but by March, as we know, the latter had resolved to
maintain the exchange, and conduct the war, however long it
might last, on foreign credit.[47] One is tempted to think that
loan negotiations were first started "at the beginning of the
current year [1904]" not in Paris but in Berlin.[48] At least,
Nelidov, Russian ambassador to Paris, had from the first
come out so definitely for postponing a loan on the French
market that Kokovtsov somewhat pettishly took it for a refusal to support the loan in future negotiations with the
French.[49] But negotiations with the Germans led to the ver-
dict that operations in Berlin must also be postponed--until
the results of the Russo-German trade treaty conferences

had been ascertained.[50] The situation thus created was such as to force Kokovtsov to summon the French bankers to Peter-burg unbeknown to his associates and then act as though they had come of their own accord.[51] But Nelidov was not the only one to advise delaying the appeal to the Paris market: Rafalo-vich, the finance ministry's agent in Paris, also warned: 1) that "the later" the loan, "the better for our national pres-tige," and 2) that 150-200 million francs (50-70 million rubles) would be all we could expect--a sum which Kokvtsov was justified in regarding as a mere "pourboire" when 800 to 1,000 million francs were actually needed to guarantee prose-cution of the war only until the end of the current year of 1904.[52]

Kokovtsov was quite right that any further postponement of the loan was out of the question: the summer season, un-favorable for any major operations, was approaching, our own resources could only last until August, and, chief of all, it was impossible to bank on "hostilities taking a turn in our favor": this, Kokovtsov regarded in April as "beyond our powers to foresee."[53] And meanwhile, now, in April 1904, when French negotiations were only just approaching a favor-able conclusion, even the Russophile Parisian press at last mentioned the possible fall of Port Arthur, the mood of France changed markedly, and even Arthur Rafalovich him-self saw nothing else for it but to "pray God for more favor-able news from the theatre of war within the next few weeks."[54] Under such conditions, to postpone the loan was the greater risk and we were obliged to accept it on frankly disadvantage-ous terms (6.5 per cent actual) and at the same time bind ourselves by a promise to "give France preference" in the matter of Russian government orders abroad--which would plainly be to the detriment of the treasury.[55]

The future only confirmed that further postponement had indeed been impossible. By June it was "apparent" from what the director of the French credit chancellery said "that he wished to indicate to us some other source [for meeting war costs] in future, for example, Berlin."[56] Though it may have been lacking in courtesy, this hint found fertile soil in Peterburg: at the time, Witte and Bülow were just opening negotiations in Berlin toward the conclusion of a Russo-Ger-man trade treaty. These led not only to its signing (July 15) but also to an exchange of notes enabling Russia to conclude a loan on the German market up to April 1, 1905.[57]

Inasmuch as the April loan of 1904 in Paris had guaranteed
Russia's war costs in full up to the beginning of 1905, she was
now disengaged for a matter of many months from insurmountable dependence (in the conduct of the war) on the French
government--capable of refusing to permit quotations of a
future loan on the Paris bourse, i.e., of killing such a loan,
even though it had the consent of the French banking houses.
At a period when the axis of the war still passed through Port
Arthur, the orientation toward Germany was prompted by the
war situation itself as well as by this freedom to choose her
source of financial support. While the April "Anglo-French
agreement [1904] was having the one chief result of keeping
France from aiding Russia" by sending her fleet to Port
Arthur...until the Baltic fleet should arrive," as Wilhelm
suggested to Nicholas in his letter of June 5, 1904; while
Paris, in August, was already quoting the expected fall of
Port Arthur as the inevitable occasion for a panic in Russian
stocks, for the mitigation of which our Paris representatives
demanded ever new allocations for the French press; while
the mere news of Russia's organizing a second land army,
sign of further prolongation of the war, was causing a drop
in Russian stocks on the Paris bourse, and voices were being
raised in the press in favor of the Japanese loan in France
projected by Russia's bitterest enemy, the American banker
Schiff,[58] Berlin was not only rejoicing Nicholas's imagination
by the prospect of the Baltic fleet "chasing the Japanese fleet
to its ports" and "restoring your [Nicholas's] domination by
sea"[59] but was actually aiding the progress of Rozhdestvensky's
squadron by providing it with coal and by doggedly sustaining
the optimism of the court at Tsarskoe Selo, which, even after
Liaoyang still continued to live in dreams of a future Japanese
indemnity and of the annexation of Manchuria away from China
and in devising means to provoke the Chinese government to
a breach of neutrality to this end.[60]
    The moment of choice between France and Germany
arrived, however, not at the beginning of 1905, but in October
1904--in connection with an attack launched upon Nicholas by
Wilhelm for fear of a "premature" end to the Russo-Japanese
war on a basis of "cordial consent." At the very beginning
of October, Berlin received news of the arrival in Paris of
Kurino, former Japanese minister to Peterburg, "empowered
to seek the mediation of France and England in Japan's behalf
for the purpose of concluding peace," and Wilhelm immediately

relayed this information to Nicholas to demonstrate that "Japan's forces in men and money would soon be exhausted," and in full confidence that his correspondent "would never be a party to any such intrigue." Wilhelm's communication had the desired effect: it raised for Nicholas the specter of an international "peace conference," where the "Crimean combination" was invoked to aid a weakening Japan and to force Russia to stop playing before she was out of trumps--the initiative coming "from across the channel."[61] And the signal of the "true signaller," as Wilhelm called himself, was rewarded not only by heartfelt "thanks for your true friendship, in which I feel supreme confidence," and by Nicholas's assurance that the war would go on until the expulsion of the last Japanese from Manchuria, but with an actual shift in the direction of formal and responsible rapprochement with Germany.[62]

As luck would have it, this shift assumed a distinctly abrupt character. In point of fact, two days before Wilhelm's message, a commissioned representative of the Credit Lyonnais had arrived in Peterburg with the proposal that "instead of postponing our new credit operation on the Paris market until the beginning of next year, we take the matter under advisement at once." Kokovtsov was given fair warning that "in the very near future the glut in the Paris money market might easily be succeeded by a stringency" in view of foreign loans projected by other countries, and was led to believe that "as matters stood, he might as well make the most of the present moment," "inasmuch as a new loan was inevitable." The representative of the Credit Lyonnais left a few days later with Kokovtsov's consent in principle "to look into the proposals of the French financial group," the arrangement being that Kokovtsov might expect "a proper proposal in the course of the next few weeks."[63] But by the time Kokovtsov had finished with the French, Ernst von-Mendelssohn-Bartoldi had arrived in Peterburg from Berlin in person--"to continue the negotiations begun in the spring." Mendelssohn made the earlier conclusion of the loan in Germany as compared with Paris an indispensable condition, but offered more advantageous terms than the Credit Lyonnais. Since the requirement as to the timing of the operation clearly indicated that the German loan would actually be allocated in Paris, with the Germans prepared to accept a more modest commission, preference for the German offer over the French would

assume in French eyes a preeminently political character.
And it was precisely the political significance implied in "the
German government's readiness to cooperate in the proposed
operation" that moved Nicholas, who made the final decision,
to give this readiness "special consideration" and accept
Mendelssohn's proposal. And Kokovtsov had to plead the
will of the tsar when he made his lengthy apologies to our
Paris ambassador for the turn the incipient French negotiations had taken. [64]

True, it shortly became known that the Credit Lyonnais
had stolen a march on the other banking groups and made
this sortie at its own risk, without consent of the French
government--so that the whole incident assumed a less acute
aspect than it might have. But the meaning of what had happened was plain, and from Paris (from Rafalovich) came the
warning "not to wound French self-esteem...by a demonstration of too great friendship with Germany," thereby accelera-
ting their rapprochement with England. [65] Rafalovich never
suspected what a monstrous demonstration of "friendship"
had been put in preparation along with the petty demonstration
in the financial sphere that he here had in mind.

Another stroke of luck--the tempest raised by the Hull
incident--was also utilized by Wilhelm at this juncture to
further a Russo-German alliance. The telegram Wilhelm
sent at 4:28 a.m. on October 14/27 found Nicholas in a state
of the "greatest indignation at England's conduct" "in promul-
gating unacceptable terms in a note like a bolt from the blue."
In this telegram, Wilhelm proposed the organization of a
"mighty combination of the three strongest continental powers"
(i.e., Russia, Germany and France) against England, which
now threatened to forbid the Russian squadron's being supplied
with coal by Germany and consequently to halt its further
progress toward the Far East, and declared that "not for one
moment" would he give in to England's "unjust threat." Nicholas at once responded by proposing that "the project for such
a treaty be drafted," agreeing that "France would have to join
her ally" (Russia) "as soon as it was adopted" by Russia and
Germany (tel. Oct. 16/29); and on October 17/30, Wilhelm
sent the finished project that he and Bulow had drawn up, with
a letter saying that it had been kept a secret even from the
German ministry of foreign affairs. [66]

Recently published documents reveal that the alliance
treaty question had by no means remained a topic for the

secret diplomacy of the two monarchs.[67] At just this time--
two days, to be exact, before the tsar--Baron Osten-Saken,
Russian ambassador to Berlin, had been drawn into a conversation on the same subject, and an analogous project communicated to him by Baron Fritz Holstein, adviser to the
German ministry of foreign affairs. In informing Lamsdorf
of this (in a "strictly private" letter of Oct. 14/27), Osten-
Saken did not conceal his impression that Germany here had
two irons in the fire, was aiming either to "disrupt our alliance with France," should the latter refuse to support Russia against England, or to herself secure the support of Rus-
and France against England. Nonetheless, Osten-Saken
recommended that instead of treating the German proposal
"as an ordinary intrigue" we should take advantage of Berlin's mood in view of the "Anglo-American coalition" against
Russia in the Far East, "created to obstruct our reaping the
fruits of our victories."

In presenting this letter of Osten-Saken's to Nicholas
(October 16/29), who had, in turn, now had time to get Wilhelm's above-mentioned telegram, Lamsdorf "fully" recognized the "necessity of a closer rapprochement with Germany"
but was opposed to asking France "any categorical questions"
respecting her position in a potential conflict between England,
on the one side, and Germany and Russia on the other--and
instantly learned, from Nicholas's notation, that the latter
was "not fully in agreement" with him: "you will see from
my answer to the German Emperor's telegram that I am at
the present time strongly in favor of such an agreement with
Germany and France; it will save Europe from England's
outrageous impudence, and be very helpful in future." This
means that the tsar's answering telegram of October 16/29,
above quoted, had been made known to Lamsdorf at the source:
he knew that in it Nicholas had also expressed the idea that
France would inevitably ("would have to") subscribe to the
treaty following its adoption by Germany and Russia. And
in future Lamsdorf became an advocate of the projected
agreement.

The treaty project forwarded from Berlin in Wilhelm's
letter of October 17/30 had been so drawn up (by von Bülow)
that Nicholas "burst out laughing as he read it" and telegraphed
Wilhelm that his "answer would follow in a few days."[68]
Lamsdorf was summoned to Tsarskoe Selo (October 20) to
draw up a counter-project and the necessity was pointed out

to him of "looking out for our own interests but sparing the
auctorial pride of the other party." Nicholas had laughed at
the German project: 1) because the treaty of defensive alliance was confined to the period of our war with Japan, 2)
because the terminology of the project throughout only allowed for two parties ("both of the high contracting parties"),
3) because not Russia, but "both" powers would have recourse
to "reminding" France of her obligations by the "Franco-
Russian treaty of alliance," and (only) "in case of need," and
4) because a special article (III) extended the efficacy of the
new alliance to the period after the Russo-Japanese war if
Germany's acts during the war (i.e., her coaling of the Russian squadron) should be serviceable in connection with the
conflict.

　　Lamsdorf drafted his treaty project accordingly. In it:
1) simply "high contracting parties" appeared (without the
"both"), 2) the "reminder" to France by "both" and "in case
of need" was replaced by "necessary steps" to be taken by
Russia alone for the purpose of "acquainting" France with
the treaty and "prompting" her to subscribe to it, and 3) to
the extension of the efficacy of the agreement was added "in
the event of difficulties arising during the peace negotiations
between Russia and Japan."69 As we see, Lamsdorf's counter-project happily combined the viewpoints of all three of
the Russians concerned in the negotiations: all the super-
ficial awkwardness with respect to France above indicated
was removed (Lamsdorf), attention was called to the danger
of an "Anglo-American coalition" when peace was in process
of conclusion with Japan (Osten-Saken), and the agreement
with Germany in any case concluded (Nicholas). In this form,
the Russian counter-project was duly sent by Nicholas to Berlin, with a "nice letter" (of October 25/November 7). 70 If
Wilhelm agreed to it, it would only have to be signed, and
steps then taken, in fulfillment of article I, toward "acquainting" France with it and "prompting" her to subscribe to it
"as an ally." What happened nine months later at Bjorko,
in July 1905, without the participation or knowledge of the
Russian minister of foreign affairs--a Russo-German treaty
of alliance parallel to the Russo-French treaty of alliance--
all but happened in October 1904 with the participation and
knowledge of Count Lamsdorf.

　　But Wilhelm suggested corrections, and the affair hit a
snag. To judge from the documents known to us, the cor-

rections themselves challenged no outright objections, but
their sense apparently moved Nicholas to wonder whether he
ought not first to show the project to the French. What Wilhelm actually proposed was that for the straightforward indication that the treaty of alliance extend to possible "difficulties" in connection with Japanese peace negotiations, a flat
general clause be substituted concerning Germany's "not
subscribing" "to any action whatsoever" "in which intentions
hostile to Germany could possibly lurk," and that all mention
of the Russo-Japanese war be eliminated, making the treaty
termless (with notice of severance a year in advance). Otherwise, as William explained, "the whole world would come to
the conclusion that instead of a defensive alliance we were
founding some sort of company for effecting annexations" (in
the Far East, of course).

It thus came about that Nicholas was offered: 1) sweet
solitude at the future peace conference or, mayhap, even
congress, and 2) an alliance worked out not in terms of the
current war's troublous moments, but with the time limit
left in principle vague and hence extensible to the general
European situation as such.[71] In the published documents
there exist as yet no sure data for asserting that it was at
the instance of Lamsdorf and not of his own accord that Nicholas now responded (November 10/23) with the request that he
be authorized to acquaint the French with the treaty project
preliminary to its signing.[72] Upon merely receiving in return
Wilhelm's telegram of November 13/26 suggesting that it
would be better "to refrain from concluding any treaty whatsoever" than to notify France beforehand, and have her notify
England, and thus invite "catastrophe"--Nicholas passed this
and Wilhelm's other telegrams on to Lamsdorf "for review."[73]
Obviously Nicholas had it in mind to utilize what Lamsdorf
promptly (November 15) tendered as his "review," i.e.
actually the text, in finished form even stylistically, of a
circumstantial argument in favor of France's preliminary
knowledge of the project "so superbly conceived by Emperor
Wilhelm," in a second attempt to convince Wilhelm. In the
event of the latter succeeding, Lamsdorf also tendered the
tsar, simultaneously with the "review," a "memorandum as
to highly confidential communications that might be made to
the French government," already couched in the first person,
as emanating from Nicholas himself.[74]

These documents reposed with the tsar for ten days and

were returned to the minister on November 25, after Nicholas (November 24/December 7) had got round to sending Wilhelm for approval the project of his communication (or "Notice") to the French--in a self-written letter which we now know only through the Berlin archive.[75] But by then it was too late: Berlin had recognized from Nicholas's first response by telegram (November 10/23) that the move had been a mistake and premature and had decided to gently quash the alliance negotiations for the time being "to keep the tsar from blocking a possible Russo-German agreement in future."[76] Instead, Berlin raised the particular question of what guarantees Russia could give Germany in the event of conflict with England and Japan over the coal question.

Wilhelm's letter in this sense went to Peterburg on November 24/December 7, the very date of Nicholas's letter enclosing the project of the "preliminary" communication, so that the two letters crossed. Wilhelm "did not wish to hurry" Nicholas "about an answer" in connection with the general "defensive treaty," but gave categorical notice that he would "at once" countermand the supplying of coal unless Nicholas gave guarantees that Russia would "honorably fight shoulder to shoulder" with Germany in the event of an attack by England.[77] Not until the required promise had been given by Russia (in a note of November 29/December 12) and the question of the general defensive treaty from the viewpoint of Anglo-German relations been presented by Bülow for the resolution of the German ambassadors in London, and the dangers connected with such a treaty been pointed out by the latter, did Wilhelm answer Nicholas's letter of November 24/December 7. Wilhelm's answer testified to his obduracy on the French point ("it is impossible to initiate France into our negotiations until we have reach a final agreement"); "rather let the parties remain independent of each other as before."[78] But Nicholas was no less obdurate.[79] Negotiations were broken off, and for six months matters remained at a standstill.

The "demonstration of too great friendship with Germany" finally broke down in December 1904, under conditions that no longer favored its forcing at all costs. During those October days when it had been put in preparation, we had again gambled on Port Arthur, on Rozhdensky's fleet gaining supremacy, on the fortress's situation by land being eased by the concentration of full command in the hands of Kuropat-

kin (with Alekseyev's removal on October 12). At that time,
while awaiting the new army that was in special process of
preparation, we were still toying with the idea of a future
victorious peace after the expulsion of the last Japanese from
Manchuria and the possibility of combating an "Anglo-American coalition" when the moment came for reaping the fruits
of victory.[80] Now, in December, the days of the abandoned
fortress were already numbered, peace receded into the vague
and distant future, compromises had to be made at home (the
December 12 order)--and in the field of international relations
we had been forced to "regulate our aspirations," as Lamsdorf expressed it, by the "stern admonitions" of military and
financial actuality.

Back in October, evidently inspired by simultaneous indications from Wilhelm, Nicholas and Osten-Saken that the problem of concluding a victorious peace under circumstances of
an Anglo-American coalition was next on the schedule, Lamsdorf had made the statement (in his report of October 19) that
it "would be an irreparable mistake if we should now concentrate all our attention and all our energies on winning" a complete victory "and lose sight of the fact that...another essential and no less difficult problem was in store for Russia,
namely that of holding on to all the gains that had cost such
terrible sacrifices," and that it was therefore "not enough to
attend to the concentration of large land and naval forces in the
theatre of hostilities to make up for losses sustained: they
must look ahead and canvas every means toward raising Russia's combat efficiency as a whole by the time the war ended."[81]
This declaration of Lamsdorf's had led to the calculation of
the actual military and financial resources at the country's
disposal by the end of the first year of war (in Kokovtsov's
report of November 19) that left no doubt of the chimerical
character of a maximal peace program.

Any increase whatsoever in Russia's combat efficiency
by the moment of negotiations was out of the question considering that: 1) during all of 1905 not more than 500 million
rubles could be borrowed in the only markets accessible to
Russia, those of France, Germany and Holland, 2) this amount
would just barely suffice for eight months of war (at 60 millions per month), 3) in the regular budget for 1905 a deficit
of 40 millions was foreseen, to be covered out of the amount
above indicated, and 4) an increase in the existing tax-rate,
which Kokovtsov considered exorbitant as it was, and ruinous

for the country, would scarcely cover the interest on the loans. Thus any thought of "large expenditures on military preparations in the eventuality of an armed clash with other powers besides Japan" automatically dropped out.[82] "This open statement"--as Lamsdorf expressed it in his final letter of December 25 to Kokovtsov--"must, so to say, serve as the yardstick for our future pretensions and a stern warning against the dangerous enthusiasms always possible at the moment when with God's help Russia shall have victoriously crushed her enemy."[83] But at the same time it also became the "yardstick" for diplomatic projects such as that which was all but put into effect during those November days when the finance minister's sobering report was in preparation, in that it implied the necessity of conserving all of our three financial markets even to continue the war for eight months.[84]

The German market (order of December 15, 1904) had just set about realizing the 231 million ruble loan, to be paid into the Russian treasury by driblets in the course of the year 1905. It was the Paris market's turn, with a quota of not less than 270 million rubles by the above computation. The Franco-Russian alliance was to be put to a second test-- this time not by Russia.

IV

The 9th of January and subsequent revolutionary events of 1905 abruptly reversed Russia's war prospects and injured her position internationally: a Russia simultaneously at war and in revolution obviously lost standing as a great power and competent member of the world concert. The most serious thing at the moment was the irreparable blow to Russian credit in France, where, by the middle of February, distrust already threatened to assume a general character.[85] Verneuille, syndic of the Paris stock-brokers, called on the Russian ambassador to apprise him of the extreme anxiety of the president of the republic and the premier in connection with "the possible repercussion of Russian events upon France." Until these events it had still been possible to combat the impressions created by the assaults of Russia's socialistic and hostile press upon Russian credit. But "now it was an entirely different matter." The war up to now had been nothing but an unbroken series of fiascos. Advices as to the home situation were "highly alarming" and "there existed no means for ex-

erting moral influence upon the press" in restraint of its circulation of alarming reports every morning. Banks and
stock-brokers were besieged with inquiries from holders of
our securities as to future prospects and as to whether they
had not better unload. "If things once got started, it would
be a veritable avalanche." "We shall have everyone down
on us from the humblest servant or laborer to the richest
nobleman: they have all invested in Russian securities. For
the French government this will mean a frantic attack on the
ministry. Rouvier and Delcasse will be unable to withstand
the blow, and the Russian alliance will disappear along with
them."[86] In reporting this, Nelidov justifiably pointed out
that the radical remedy under such circumstances was restoration of peace and order in Russia: discontinuation of the
war could here be of no assistance whatever per se.[87] And
at this point Verneuille, an "official personage," as Kokovtsov afterwards indignantly remarked, "made a demand for
which it would be hard to find a fitting epithet": that we spend
750 thousand francs on the press in the next three months,
out of an estimated three millions for the year.[88]

From the fact that, despite all this, the French bankers
now left for Peterburg to negotiate, the two-month time limit
stipulated by Mendelssohn for withholding the loan from the
French market having expired, it may be judged that all this
ado was not without some modicum of design.[89] Outside the
press, Kokovtsov could even point to direct dissatisfaction
in French industrial circles over the preference shown German as against French firms in connection with certain orders
placed in December 1904. And he was now prepared to over-
pay the French by about 1-1/2 million rubles for shrapnel,
as before, if only he might get as "good a press" as possible
by the decisive moment of fixing the amount and cost of the
loan. Therefore, immediately upon receipt of Verneuille's
demand, the ministry of finance remitted to Rafalovich's
order 235,000 francs toward the tri-mensual allotment.[90]
In any event, despite Verneuille's jeremiad, it is clear that
no direct prohibition of the Russian loan by the French government now as yet supervened.

Negotiations with arriving representatives of the Credit
Lyonnais, Hottinguer and the Paris-Netherlands bank coincided with the period of the battles of Mukden and were
"rather protracted," since the bankers "upon receipt of each
new bulletin from the theatre of war thought necessary to

telegraph their firms for instructions." Nonetheless, negotiations were carried to a conclusion, the contract was drawn
up and examined by February 27 (news of the abandonmnet of
Mukden had reached Peterburg on the 25th), on the 28th
Netslin and Hottinguer waited on the chairman of the finance
committee and reported the satisfactory completion of the
job, in the evening dined at Kokovtsov's, and on the next day,
March 1, were to appear at 11 a.m. to sign the text of the
contract. But then an unheard-of breach of decorum supervened: instead of appearing at the hour appointed, the bankers
gave notice by letter that during the intervening night they had
received orders to return to Paris without signing any contract.[91] There is no need to seek hints in the future correspondence on this question in order to assert that this directive was given at the behest of the French government. What
happened could have only one meaning: that France flatly
refused to give the Russian government money to fight a revolution and a war simultaneously, when the signs so clearly
pointed to defeat on both fronts.

Back in October 1904, before Port Arthur, while in Peterburg on Russian loan business and mingling in "banking and
commercial circles," Mendelssohn-Bartholdy got the impression that here, as with an overwhelming majority of the
population of the country, the desire for "immediate peace"
prevailed, and that only the court, the military, and "official
personages" were "holding out." Then, Kokovtsov was among
those "official personages."[92] But now, even Kokovtsov
could not fail to see that the end had come, and immediately
"after the Mukden retreat" (or, as is now plain, the tail-
turning in the matter of the French loan) he submitted a
"circumstantial memorandum" to Nicholas demonstrating the
impossibility of carrying the war on any longer.[93] This
memorandum was examined "at the beginning of March" in a
"special conference under the chairmanship of Grand Duke ,
Nicholas Nikolayevich," but its "conclusions" had no success
there, even though all were of a financial character, based
on exact computations, and apparently indisputable. Kokovtsov pointed out that thirteen months of war had already cost
a billion rubles, that to continue the war would require "expenditures just as vast," that "all sums provided for carrying
on the war" were already "completely" "exhausted," that no
domestic credit operations were possible "without complete
derangement of our whole monetary system," and, finally,

that "to obtain the necessary means through foreign loans
was either absolutely impossible or attended by difficulties
bordering on the impossible."[94]

As we can see, Kokovtsov weakened his position by leaving any hope at all of its not being absolutely impossible to
get money abroad. It obviously gave Nicholas a loop-hole to
decide to continue the war, cost what it might to obtain the
money. Kokovtsov did succeed in obtaining money at the beginning of April 1905, but this was the last wartime foreign
credit operation (and a short term one at that, in the form
of a discount on state treasury bonds) and Nicholas had of
course here been rescued by Berlin.[95] But it came to only
half the amount that was needed and that had been expected
from the French in February (not 300, but 150 million rubles):
it actually settled nothing, and only provided a respite, long
enough for a new defeat, but too brief to let Russia's disordered land forces in the Manchurian theatre get back into
full combat trim after Mukden.

The interest Mendelssohn reaped from this operation was
so high in absolute terms (7 per cent actual) that for some
time the French bankers were inconsolable, and the theme
of a Paris loan by no means disappears from subsequent correspondence. Benac, head of the Paris-Netherlands bank,
spoke with unconcealed annoyance of Mendelssohn's triumph
and intimated to Rafalovich the necessity of Kokovtsov's immediately consulting Rouvier: he had only to say the word
and "it would be no trouble at all to complete the operation."[96]
And Kokovtsov could not very well help renewing negotiations,
the more so since the French ambassador to Peterburg also
mentioned the February "fiasco" to him before leaving for
Paris. Bompar was intrusted with a special letter stating
what had occurred and Nelidov was simultaneously charged
to come to an explanation with Rouvier "for the purpose of
ascertaining the French government's viewpoint" and indicate
to him that despite "the unpleasant impression" the February
episode had produced upon the tsar, no "impediments" on the
part of the Russian government to a renewal of negotiations
"would be encountered."[97]

And six days later, on May 16, before Tsushima had as
yet been made public, Rafalovich could already write from
Paris that "the air again smells of loan" and that the bankers'
envoy had left for Russia. And what was more, even after
Tsushima, Rafalovich had no doubt of "the desire [of the

bankers] to put through a big operation with Russia in order
to profit by the present state of the market, a desire fanned
by envy of Mendelssohn's successes," and by "the ulterior
consideration that peace was inevitable"; and Benac said
straight out: "even should you be defeated on land as well,
you will still find money here." Rafalovich thought that the
"French public" (not the bankers) had only one "prejudice"
against Russia--the "internal state of the empire."[98] Meanwhile, Kokovtsov was informed that Rouvier had "expressed
the opinion that at the present time it would be inadvisable to
bring any great pressure to bear on the bankers for the purpose of obtaining success in the present matter."

Virtually, this was a tactful way of refusing the loan, and
for Kokovtsov now to ask Rafalovich to try to influence the
bankers to take the initiative, as he did (on May 28), was to
attempt to force a sealed door.[99] Actually, a letter of May 28
from Nelidov that crossed his put a damper on this whole attempt to secure financial support from France--whether for
the continuation of the war or to avoid being placed in an ultimative position in the event of peace negotiations. According
to Nelidov, Rouvier pretended he did not see how the bankers
could accuse him of having been unsympathetic to the February
operation, "plainly" declared that "no obstacles of government
origin would present themselves" to any future operation
either, even added that when the bankers came to him after
Mendelssohn's April operation to complain of Russia's "having slighted" the French market, he had answered that "it
was their own fault and that they must do what they could to
iron it out themselves." Ostensibly, that's how it was "before the battle of Tsushima." "Lately"--Rouvier gloomily
concluded his explanation--"the bankers' visits have ceased."[10]

Any further attempts by the Russian government to utilize
the alliance before the signing of peace terms with Japan also
ceased.

V

That to continue the war after Tsushima--in view of happenings at home--would be madness even from the immediate
viewpoint of the fate of the dynasty became clear even to
those in Peterburg who had still continued to entertain hopes
after Mukden, and in the matter of a few days the question of
starting peace negotiations was decided in the affirmative.

Wilhelm himself made an abrupt volte face, and now talked
of nothing but the necessity of peace in order to save Nicholas from an unnatural death--which would, in his opinion, be
attended by "disastrous" consequences for Russia, and "danger" to "the rest of the world"--and had no trouble enlisting
the intervention of Roosevelt, who had up to Tsushima still
seen in the continuation of the war a "mutual extermination"
"of two nations" that would be "salutary" for the interests of
"the rest of the powers in the Far East."[101]

To Nicholas, in the very difficult position that had been
created for him personally, Wilhelm's letter of May 21/June 3
on this delicate theme meant everything.[102] It argued exhaustively and along conventional lines not only the necessity
of stopping the war but the moral obligation, and relieved
Nicholas of an inglorious search for mediation by proposing
that Wilhelm himself act as mediator. The concluding lines
of the letter gave him clearly to understand that "the soil
for peace" was already prepared and that the tsar had only
to summon the American ambassador, and the mechanism
of negotiations would duly be set in motion. Finally, in
future as well, Wilhelm's "friendship" with Roosevelt would
remain at the service of Nicholas, as the least painful method
of influencing the course of negotiations now that France's
refusal of a loan had left Russia defenseless to break them
off should need arise.[103]

As to France, she reappeared on Russia's financial horizon after an interval--on the eve of the Russian plenipotentiaries' departure for Portsmouth, and in the "Crimean" combination with England. From our London ambassador's letter
of June 29/July 12 we know that within a month of the time
when their Russian negotiations broke down, the French
bankers were negotiating with London regarding its participation in a Russian loan "after the conclusion of peace."
Their further idea was to dispense with the cooperation of
the Jewish house of Rothschild to avoid "difficulties in connection with the Jewish question," thus promoting the Baring
Brothers banking house, which agreed to act, on two conditions: 1) provided Russia's political position should cease
to be hostile to England, and 2) provided "a state of affairs
capable of inspiring confidence" should be established within
Russia.[104] Needless to say, the latter condition did not
seem possible of fulfillment at the time: on the contrary, the
"Potemkin" incident (June 18-19) might have appeared only

a beginning, the harbinger of "a like event, sudden and dis-
tressing, that would naturally weaken Russian credit," as
that same representative of "Baring's," Lord Revelstock,
expressed it in secret code a month later in elucidating this
second condition. But even then, in mid-July, Revelstock's
opinion, when sought by Benkendorf at Peterburg's behest,
was that "conditions for this [i.e., for official negotiations]
are not yet ripe."105

As opposed to the English, French bankers entered into
no negotiations with Russian representatives this whole time,
and Kokovtsov resolutely kept from opening the subject with
them after the earlier fiasco, particularly since even the
Paris press, after showing some moderation in connection
with the above-mentioned February allotment, was again
starting to manifest a "coolness toward Russia" and a "tendency to present our position in a false light," despite the
fact that regular payments out of the 235 thousand francs
continued to be made promptly in June and July to conduce to
its "felicity."106 With both England and France the matter
evidently turned on the one point--peace.107 But for those
days, the main thing was that the seamy side of its financial
prospect was now for the first time turned toward the Russian government: to escape the consequences of its "financial
indiscretions" even after the conclusion of peace would only
be possible at the price of changing its "political attitude"
toward England, which was now preparing to reap the fruits
of diplomacy at the conference opening in Portsmouth.108

Such were the circumstances under which the notorious
Bjorko treaty of July 11/24, 1905 was signed when "suddenly"
presented to Nicholas by Wilhelm ready made at their meeting on the yacht "Polar Star."109 That the signing of the
treaty was not the result of momentary weakness on the part
of Nicholas may be seen from the message Kokovtsov sent
Witte at Portsmouth in this connection a week later. According to his impression, Nicholas was "extremely happy about
the meeting, evidently trusted his neighbor's sincerity"
(July 19.) And five days later still (July 23): "his majesty
continues in an excellent frame of mind, is evidently much
more cheerful since his meeting with the German emperor."110
Moreovoer, until August 30 (old style) Nicholas kept the signing of the treaty a dead secret even from his minister of foreign
affairs and "confessed" "the whole thing" to him (as Lamsdorf
expressed it) on that date only because concealment was no

longer possible: the treaty was to go into effect "immediately upon the conclusion of peace with Japan," that treaty had
been signed at Portsmouth on August 23, o.s., and now only
remained to be ratified. In revealing his secret to Lamsdorf,
Nicholas explained his silence as having been due to the fact
that Wilhelm had exacted his promise to tell no one of "the
act that had been signed and that was only destined to go into
effect after the conclusion of peace with Japan."[111]

Immediately the matter was thus placed in Lamsdorf's
hands, the plan made back in October 1904 was put in operation: feelers were sent out respecting the possibility of
France's subscribing to the continental agreement against
England, and when the answer was negative, a supplementary
declaration was proposed to Wilhelm invalidating the Russo-
German alliance engagement regarding France, and further
affirming that the alliance with the latter was defensive. Thus
--by all the documents as yet known to us--the Bjorko treaty
formally remained unabrogated, and theoretically retained
its defensive significance against all except France, i.e.,
against England, a fact that was duly noted in Osten-Saken's
letter of November 16, 1905 as the positive result of the
diplomatic "commotion" that had been going on for the past
2-1/2 months.[112]

There is absolutely no reason to suppose that the dress-
rehearsal for Bjorko held in October 1904 with Lamsdorf
and Osten-Saken participating was simply forgotten by Nicholas by July 1905. Specifically, the ticklish point about France's
subscribing to the treaty subsequently had, to be sure, been
rejected by Nicholas himself at the time. Its reappearance
now was a direct concession to Wilhelm. New also was the
point about the treaty becoming operative after the conclusion
of peace with Japan: in October 1904, the treaty was to have
been operative "during the peace negotiations." The thing
that suited Nicholas down to the ground both in October and
in July was the anti-English nature of the treaty as a whole.
The immediate risk of the French point was in July 1905 considerably lessened by the "flexible" character of the date for
the treaty's becoming operative: now it would have been infinitely more risky, positively hazardous, to settle the French
question before concluding peace negotiations.

In September-October 1905, when--as Nicholas had perhaps not failed to foresee--the diplomatic machine worked
without a hitch on the cancellation of the French point, the

whole international situation so differed from that of July
that it was easy enough to breathe an indulgent sigh of pity
over the "poor monarch's" "inadvertent" "indiscretion."[113]
As for the situation in July the question to be asked is: what
did the signing of that "unfortunate" treaty give Nicholas in
the immediate present, in the middle third of July? Completely forsaken internationally, and politically driven to the
wall at home, what Nicholas got at Bjorko, illusory though
it may have been, was psychological support.[114] And con-
versely: what would his refusal to sign the treaty have meant
at that moment, a voluntary refusal of his only friendly offer,
and made for the second time, if not a rupture? A rupture,
when there was no assurance that peace would be concluded,
i.e., that an agreement, rather than capitulation, would prove
possible. Of this, even Witte himself had no assurance: nay
more, at the moment it actually seemed to him (there at Portsmouth) that "an agreement would not be reached."[115] But
what if the agreement with Japan failed to come off?--should
we then continue the war in absolute diplomatic isolation? In
view of this possible turn to the question, Nicholas could
hardly refuse to sign the treaty, less because he preferred
this redaction to the other (incidentally Bülow and Holstein
did consider that the one Wilhelm proposed was more to Russia's advantage than the one they had prepared)[116] than because he must not spurn his nearest geographical neighbor,
when the latter had maintained a friendly attitude throughout
the war, had really helped start peace negotiations, was now
demanding a reward for all this, and was naturally the best
qualified to extend a helping hand in the event of some irrevocable personal or even dynastic catastrophe within the country. For Nicholas was face to face with revolution, had just
witnessed the first ominous flash of a naval mutiny, and
could not remain without hope of support.[117]

That Nicholas did not keep his word to the letter but told
Lamsdorf about the Bjorko treaty before the Portsmouth
treaty had been ratified (its ratification followed, on October 1/
14) still does not provide solid ground for suspecting him of
knowingly giving his signature at Bjorko but making a "mental reservation" and consciously heading for a breach of agreement on the French point. Recent documental publications
bear witness that even after the peace Nicholas did not (or
perhaps pretended not to) consider France's subscribing to
the continental agreement so very paradoxical. He "still"

asserted that "if we go at it the right way we may get there."118
And Lamsdorf had to spend practically all of September on the
diplomatic clarification of the French government's attitude
toward this question, until finally Nicholas undertook to inform
Wilhelm that a lengthy preliminary interchange with France
would be necessary.

But of course Witte too had at this same time, as he afterwards expressed it, been crying up "the wise principles enunciated as Bjorko."119 He not only acclaimed them on the way
to Peterburg, at Rominten, but, to the no slight embarassment and disapproval of the French, also touched on this question in a talk with Rouvier on the way back from America,
and likewise lauded Wilhelm to the skies to the editor of
Temps. With Witte at this time the idea of the necessity of
Russia's enlarging the narrow frame-work of the French alliance swung toward broad internationalism in the financial
sphere both for the large credit operation that was then in
order, and presumably, for the subsequent development of
Russia's state economy as well.120

VI

With the conclusion of the Portsmouth peace, prospects of
a large financial operation on the foreign market suddenly
opened out in all directions for the Russian government. French,
Americans, English, Germans appeared in turn on the scene.
Naturally none of them did any real soliciting. Rouvier first
introduced the subject with the Russian ambassador in Paris
even before Kokovtsov had sat down to write the latter his
long and circumspect letter sounding him out on this theme.
Rouvier, rather than scatter his efforts, was working toward
a large "basic" loan, which, as he pictured it, would be only
the beginning of a series of subsequent loans "to get the country's economic life running normally."121 At about the same
time, Morgan gave Witte an opportunity to discuss the future
loan with him and expressed his readiness to embark upon
preliminary negotiations with the Russian government, provided the latter would refrain from dealing with Schiff's Jewish group and would grant the American market special advantages." And Baring Brothers, after getting the English
government to agree "not to oppose" a Russian financial operation, "placed themselves completely at" Kokovtsov's "disposal"
and proposed a loan without Rothschild, "to make the present

loan and any future Russian loans independent of the Jews."[122]

There could now be no question of bartering this broad internationalism, in any case requiring a cautious approach owing to its extreme novelty, for the possibly fatal complications that would attach to any open execution of the Russo-German treaty of July 11/24. And there was, on the contrary, every reason for expediting the consolidation of this sudden financial situation before the "favorable impression" produced by the war's end had worn off, or there were new flare-ups at home, or, as Nelidov had already pointed out, the new Duma mechanism for confirming loans had become a fact.[123] And although they could not bring themselves to object openly to an internationalized loan, especially in view of America's unprecedented move, the French apparently perceived from the first the threat that such a novel turn of affairs would create for the dual alliance. On September 8, Rouvier, "under the impression of his talks with state-secretary Witte" (and this, as we now know for certain, was "very unfavorable"),[124] had already made it understood that only the French part of the loan would be released for quotation on the Paris bourse, plausibly explaining that "his reason for opposing an international loan issue at first" had been simply his knowledge that the Germans and Americans would still dump their quotas on the French market and just take their commission.[125] Moreover, the intrusion of American capital promised in the long run a gradual destruction of the financial fabric of Franco-Russian relations, if the full significance of this first attempt of Morgan's in Russia could be properly understood. So that in summoning the bankers of Paris, London, New York, Berlin and Amsterdam to Peterburg for a conference on October 2, 1905, Kokovtsov might well consider the success of the international operation not only "far from sure" but even "doubtful."[126]

A document discovered by us not long ago through happy accident testifies, however, to the fact that at the bankers' congress held in Peterburg between October 6 and 17 Kokovtsov was dealing with "delegates of the international consortium" as fully constituted, and had representatives of the Peterburg banks sitting in as well.[127] The numerous conferences with them that took place during this time ended in an exchange of declarative letters: a collective letter of October 17/30 from the consortium delegates, enclosing a memorandum summarizing the negotiations (the text of this

is not as yet known to us), and a letter of October 18/31 from
Kokovtsov to the delegates, plural, now published by us. As
appears from this letter, full agreement was reached on the
total amount of the loan--1,250,000,000 francs, but the questions of issue price and moment for execution of the operation
were left undecided. Negotiations were broken off by the
delegates, and the date for their renewal was left to be fixed
by the members of the consortium themselves, "depending
upon the internal conditions of the Russian social fabric."
Thus the international loan mechanism that had been set up
was kept together, and its further functioning merely postponed, and Kokovtsov's letter memorialized the fact that
"this had, of course, happened not through any lack of good-
will [on their, the bankers' part] or of readiness to meet
[their] general views on the subject half way [on his, Kokovtsov's part]." The Russian government had now only to await,
as also there specified, "notice" from the consortium of its
desire to resume the loan process so inopportunely halted by
the October strike.

But subsequent revolutionary events only made the possibility of this more remote, and, in the end, excluded it entirely. A disclosed (for that time) unprecedented drainage of
gold from the coffers of the State bank, together with withdrawal of deposits from savings banks, had by November
already made the money situation "extremely critical."[128]
And in December Witte's government was forced to seek salvation from bankruptcy on the foreign market, without awaiting "notice" and start the loan process virtually from the
beginning and under conditions not only infinitely more unfavorable in general but such as to modify the previous frail
international loan scheme. Kokovtsov's journey abroad for
the purpose of "thoroughly clearing up" "Russia's present
situation" "in its unvarnished form" with the right persons
there, and concluding a loan was settled upon in the very
heat of the Moscow armed uprising, on the one hand, and of
an obstinately mounting stock-market panic on the other. On
the day of Kokovtsov's departure (December 17, 1905) the
emission right of the State bank was already exhausted and
its gold deficit increased from day to day (a deficit of 47 million rubles on December 23, a deficit of 80 million rubles on
January 1, 1906).[129] As may be seen, neither the nature nor
the tempo of domestic events would permit even the thought
of any cumbersome coalitional finance combination of the

October consortium type. But even regardless of that, the
past two months had injected into international relations elements hostile to the internationality of the original loan project.

To begin with, American participation, which had served
as a sort of connecting link between the two European groups,
had become problematical since Kokovtsov's courteous and
carefully worded reply in the negative to Morgan's letter of
inquiry concerning the possibility of giving the "American
industrial market" certain orders.[130] And as it afterwards
turned out, Morgan did cool to the Russian loan the moment
"the lure of industrial orders fell away."[131] The German
prospect became equally unpromising from the middle of
November when Nicholas's above-noted supplementary declaration cancelled out the French section of the Bjorko treaty.[132]
Finally, Franco-German relations had become strained to
the breaking point in these last two months: in France, military preparations were in progress along the border, "many
banks were arranging the removal of their archives and securities from branches and agencies located on the German
border," credits began to be tight, the discount rate at the
bank of France shot up "with astounding rapidity" as private
banks cut down their active operations, and the discount rate
at the Imperial bank in Berlin rose to the "unprecedented
height" of six per cent.[133]

It is not surprising that the October consortium was now
not once even mentioned. There may also have been some
connection between this and the fact that Witte's personal
letters of introduction--requesting a hearing for Kokovtsov
and cooperation in "aiding my country"--were, except for
Rouvier and Bülow, sent only to the London and Paris Rothschilds, who had not only been non-participants in the previous
consortium but its chief competitors.[134] Especially emble-
matic was the resort to Rothschild London: it meant not only
capitulation to an enemy who proposed to "manage Russian
matters," as Benkendorf had just made known, on definite
political terms, but betrayal of Barings, who had risked a
hazardous clash with Rothschilds to join the Russian consortium, as Witte well knew.[135] But apparently Rothschild
London made no response whatever to the summons, and
London was ignored: Kokovtsov made straight for Paris,
without stopping at Berlin, and concentrated every effort on
concluding a "separate" loan, a French one.

Kokovtsov's December trip to France thus became the "moment" from which Russia's straight financial course to a triple agreement may be traced: after a long period of fluctuation in Russian policy as the Anglo-German conflict mounted, all the weights were assembled and tossed on the scales, which in future showed an unmistakable dip to the agreement side. The promise given Wilhelm by Nicholas in November 1905 that in the Morocco affair he would cooperate toward a "general agreement" now took the concrete form of instructions to the Russian delegates at the Algeciras conference "in accord with the interests of France," and over and above this the French government was given the assurance that "in general, his majesty, in view of their relations of friendship and alliance, was prepared to support the French government."136 Rouvier,in turn, now exerted pressure on the bankers, Rothschild in particular, toward a loan on the spot, "in the interests of France."137 However, the "cowardice" and "extreme financial ignorance" of the bankers-- Kokovtsov fairly splashed on the colors in his angry sketch of them afterwards--prevented Rouvier's efforts being crowned with the success he thought they deserved.138 And it was only under the direct threat of discontinuance of the exchange Witte had set up on December 25 that the bankers finally accede to the asked minimum of 100 million rubles-- in the form of short-term annual notes to avoid a direct appeal to the public.

Their roles had been reversed since the spring of 1905: then the bankers were willing to make a loan, and the French government boldly risked weakening the political alliance; now the bankers, for narrowly financial reasons, obstinately refused to risk financial loss, and the government for political reasons, gambled on tsarism in its struggle with revolution. Naturally the bankers would not now make any formal engagement to conclude the "present" loan in two months, as the Russian government urged, and the question of a future loan remained open.139 But such a loan, if it should come off, must now, in the Paris bankers' opinion, assume only a "partly international character": while attaching importance to the English market's participation in the loan, they this time took a frankly negative attitude toward the German and American trumps already, and consequently the auspices for an international loan, as reported by Kokotsov from Paris at the beginning of February 1906, did not appear very favorable.

The now published correspondence of January-April 1906
on the question of concluding the "large" loan bears no evidence, on the part either of Russia or of France, of anxiety
lest the loan drag or fall through upon new flare-ups of the
revolutionary movement in Russia.[141] On the contrary, it
was now evident that the "government would be capable of taking all necessary measures for the final eradication of the
revolutionary movement," as Lamsdorf wrote Osten-Saken
on February 10, 1906--provided the requisite amount of currency were placed at its immediate disposal with the utmost
speed and, moreover, before the convocation of the Duma.[142]
The one impediment and object of anxious impatience to the
Russian government during these months was the negotiations
of the powers at Algeciras over the future fate of Morocco,
for the French would not even hear of embarking on the large
Russian financial operation until the Algeciras conference
had reached a favorable outcome.[143] The Russian government was only given the opportunity to work out in private
the bases of the operation, which were, however, to be kept
a secret up to the moment of official authorization for the
opening of bank negotiations by the French ministry of finance.
For this private working out of the loan project, Witte, who
had assumed complete responsibility in the matter, chose
Netslin, representative of the Paris-Netherlands bank, who
not only worked the whole thing out afresh, just with him, no
other bankers participating, in the seclusion of Tsarskoe Selo,
but in the future process of dealings with the other bankers,
of all nationalities, acted as Russia's agent to the end.[144]
This was quite natural, inasmuch as the French group assumed
half the total amount of the loan, the other half being destined
for division in small lots among the seven remaining national
groups.

Actually, of course, the loan proved only "partly" international, due to refusals from the Americans, Germans,
Italians and Swiss.[145]   Out of 2,250,000,000 francs, France
took 1 milliard 200 millions, England 330, Russian banks
500, Holland 55.   The entente character of the operation
was successfully screened in some degree by the modest
participation of Austrian banks (165 million francs)--at the
price of "certain special privileges."[146] But this detail did
not in any way alter the political aspect of the matter. The
position maintained by Russia at the Algeciras conference
was distinctly in the spirit of the French alliance, and on all

questions Russia and England acted as one.[147] Germany's
very refusal to participate in the loan, which apparently also
influenced others to refuse, followed immediately upon the
conclusion of the Algeciras negotiations (March 23, o.s.)
and only gave final emphasis to what had happened.[148] On
March 22, o.s., the day before Mendelssohn was enjoined
from participating in the loan, the French ambassador in
Peterburg had delivered to the Russian minister of foreign
affairs the program for a conference of the allied staffs to
the end of revising and renovating the Franco-Russian military convention along lines more advantageous to France
than five years previously, and the list of questions proposed
by the French general staff to the Russian chief of staff for
discussion at this conference.[149] And another coincidence
in dates can scarcely have been accidental: despite the loan
contract being ready by April 3, old style, the French "absolutely" insisted on postponing the publication of the order
concerning it until April 9, o.s., while the protocol of the
staff conference just mentioned, altering the original text of
the military convention in France's favor, was signed (likewise in Paris) on the eve of that date, April 8.[150] And, to
round out these chronological correspondences: on April 20,
eleven days after the publication of the loan order, a highly
secret despatch from Nelidov in Paris brought word of what
the French minister of foreign affairs had told him as to
Sir Edward Grey's having offered (in connection with a revival
of the Bagdad railway question) "to enter into an agreement
with the Russian government respecting the construction of
a railway from Russia through Persia to the Tigris valley
and the Persian gulf"--an offer which Bourgeois at once
commended as a "point of departure for an agreement between
Russia and England respecting their mutual position and
interests in Persia, now the most troublesome point for any
effort at Anglo-Russian rapprochement."[151]

And by May 25, 1906 the Anglo-Russian rapprochement
project, proposed, as indicated, through the French government, was already entering the stage of direct negotiations
between the two interested parties: on this date, the English
ambassador called on Izvolsky and stated "that he had been
commissioned to enter into negotiations with the imperial
government for the purpose of arriving at a formal agreement on a series of questions having equal interest for England and for Russia," and "should the idea meet with [Russia's]

approval, he would suggest the adoption of the same system that had at the time led to the conclusion of the Anglo-French agreement." This "system," of course, consisted in examining "all interesting questions" "one by one" "but without arriving at a final decision on them separately," and thereafter, "when the possibility of complete unanimity had been ascertained," concluding a "general agreement on all questions in the aggregate."152 Reference to the French example left no doubt that full "accord," such as had been established in Anglo-French relations two years before, was intended.

Thus the "diversion abroad" in the form of a "small victorious war" produced not victories but a threatened "precipitation" of the autocracy into disastrous "financial indiscretions," and forced Nicholas to seek a "big loan" by way of "broad" political agreements.

Russia began the war with such a meagre supply of odds and ends of ready cash that the Russian government was at once confronted by the question of possible suspension of exchange. Having settled on the maintenance of exchange at all costs, it was forced to conduct the war by means of foreign credit, and this made its prosecution, continuation and chance of success completely dependent on the international money market. The French market abandoned Russia in the spring of 1904, in connection with the Anglo-French political agreement in April of that year. A shift to the German market, where soundings had been taken at the beginning of the war, proved possible only on the basis of certain concessions, which Russia accordingly made in the July addendum to the trade treaty of 1894. The attempt of one of the French banks to get in ahead of the Berlin market in October 1904 was frustrated by Nicholas to Germany's advantage and in favor of a German loan (made public in December 1904). Wilhelm's further attempt in October to draw Russia into an alliance with Germany very nearly succeeded with Nicholas, due to an exacerbation of Anglo-Russian relations over the North Sea episode and the generally passive attitude of France in the war. It failed, however, in the end, in view of its manifest riskiness with respect to the Franco-Russian alliance, since plain calculation demonstrated that the German market would by itself be incapable of providing for the future con-

duct of the war, complicated to the extreme by the fall of
Port Arthur (December 1904). Internationally speaking, this
calculation forced Russia to cling not only to the dual alliance
but to all available markets outside the English and American
markets, then plainly still hostile.

The "outbreak" of revolution in January 1905 gave the war
its coup de grace in that month. A continuation of hostilities
proved possible at this time wholly and only by looking to
Germany, since the French government enjoined the French
banks from making a loan for war purposes. After Mukden,
in view of France's refusal of a loan, Kokovtsov stated to
Peterburg point blank the question of stopping the war. But
the decision was to first exhaust all German financial possibilities as well (the April loan of 1905.) The Tsushima
defeat precluded all possibility of continuing the war, and
Nicholas's consent to enter upon peace negotiations at once
opened to the Russian government the prospect not simply
of a French but of a joint Franco-English loan. But both
groups of bankers (i.e., both governments) insisted upon
more than the mere opening of peace negotiations, explicable
on Russia's part by the pressure of revolutionary anxieties,
and up to the last minute virtually binding her to nothing if
the internal danger blew over: the loan was made conditional
upon the actual conclusion of peace. The Russian government
thus found itself in the grip of a genuinely ultimative situation:
it was obliged to make peace, and doomed to accept whatever
terms might be dictated. Personally, Nicholas also succumbed to the pressure Wilhelm brought to bear at Bjorko, not
daring to reject the second offer of a German alliance in the
face of the "Crimean combination" that had shown no consideration for the fate of the dynasty at that trying moment.

After the conclusion of peace, Witte's task consisted in
getting Russia not only out of the German alliance, which had
now lost even the meagre significance it had once had, but
away from the unilateral Anglo-French financial combination,
which was drawing Russia into the imperialistic conflict that
had ripened in the west. However, when the eight-member
banking group had no more than barely got in working order,
it was scared off by the October strike, and subsequent events
within the country brought the Russian government catastro-
phically close to bankruptcy. Thus the dream of keeping
Russia out of the gathering imperialistic conflict that Witte
and Nicholas had cheriched in different forms was shattered

during Kokovtsov's December negotiations in Paris and
trampled underfoot at Algeciras in January-February 1906.
Through neglect to make sure of America even at the cost
of considerable, but in the case of a trial venture commercially necessary, concessions, and the resulting impossibility of refusing to support France at Algeciras, Russia was
swept into the entente channel, where the Russian government found both a loan and "friends" ready this time to back
the Russian "crown" against the Russian "parliament." But
as a preliminary the Russian government must sign a document altering the terms of the Franco-Russian military convention in favor of France, and during the realization of the
loan, enormous in absolute terms, but a pittance relatively
speaking, must seek political agreement with England as
well.

The conglomerate of conditions in the Far East resulting
for Russia from the war not only did nothing to counteract
the position into which Russia had got herself in the west but
even led to agreements with Japan that sealed Russia's mem-
bership in the circle of the entente.

Chapter VIII

"LARGESCALE ENTERPRISES" IN MANCHURIA
AFTER THE WAR

I

Though preceded by a renewal of the military convention
with France, and immediately accompanied by the proposal
that Russia enter into the broad agreement with England
which actually let her into the game of imperialistic interests
being played by the dual "cordial agreement" in the Near and
Middle East, the "big" "liquidation" loan was still only intended for the emergency liquidation of budgetary gaps made by
revolution and war. It yielded "ultimately" the round sum
of 677 million rubles. But meanwhile the 1906 rent roll alone
showed a deficit of 481.1 million rubles; 180 million rubles
of expenditures from 1905 were still not covered; and the
150 million ruble short-term German loan of 1905 must be
repaid. Thus the total deficit at the moment when the "big"
loan contract was signed came to 811 million rubles, and the
two ends again threatened to remain un-met. By September
1906 a way out of the situation nonetheless opened up, thanks
to the facts that a revenue surplus of a billion rubles already
existed and that it proved possible to borrow 34 million rubles
from the savings banks, which just covered the total amount
of the deficit. But then the ministry of finance was promptly
deluged by new demands reaching 155 million rubles (including eight million rubles, at two millions a month, for the
maintenance of military divisions levied to suppress internal
disorders). Kokovtsov's desperate secret letter of September 6, 1906 to Stolypin, describing an impossible state of
affairs where it had become necessary to seek credits from
sources that did not exist in nature, somehow got into Temps
and naturally started a commotion in the European press at
large by revealing the figures just quoted.1
That the "big" loan would in point of fact be a mere pittance,
and that its actual payment in rigid installments over a period
of more than a year "would keep the state in terrible pecuniary

straits" was not foreseen by Witte alone. Kokovtsov also
heard "from the lips of financiers" in Paris, in April 1906,
"persistently repeated assertions" that "even before the year
was up" he "would be forced to seek money abroad all over
again."[2]   And Rouvier, on the morrow of Portsmouth, when
discussing the imminent loan with the Russian ambassador,
made direct reference to the fact that "for several years after the war" Russia would "still" have to "resort to credit
many a time, spreading the loans over several years."[3]
This now made the proviso appear all the more rhetorical
with which R. Poincare, the new minister of finance, at the
last minute surrounded the French government's consent to
the loan: the loan, it seemed, was "unthinkable" unless Kokovtsov gave written pledge for the Russian government that
it "would not resort to France for credit until a minimum of
two years had expired." This was further followed by an
attempt to bind the Russian Government to an elastic interpretation of this pledge in the sense that "should Russia during these two years be obliged to resort to foreign credit"
then "even if the Russian government had no intention of turning to the French market" it would still be bound to "inform
the French government of the fact."[4]   To be sure, the attempt
was made to pretend that this proviso was simply "a political
manoeuvre, to be explained by the vicious attacks made on
the French government for authorizing the loan."[5]   But in
reality it imposed on the tsarist government a type of financial
interdict hitherto unknown in the practice of the Franco-Russian alliance.

At best, the liquidation loan only allowed for the maintenance of a balanced budget and a stable currency during
1906, created only the outward, most urgent, but of themselves still inadequate, conditions for "restoration of the
normal course of economic life," which alone could restore
the country's credit in the course of the given probationary
period. What with the extreme tension of the money market
at the time, the subsequent bad harvests of 1905 and 1906,
and the still far from bright foreign-political prospects, the
liquidation loan had by no means solved the problem of the
restoration of the industrial life of a country racked by war
and revolution. The task of attracting some broad new stream
of foreign capital specifically to industrial rehabilitation, in
the face of symptoms that threatened a protracted depression,
thus confronted the Russian ministry of finance full size from
the moment the loan was concluded.

Meanwhile, in France, according to Netslin, who now became the Russian minister's constant correspondent, "competent circles had already begun to realize" that France's
status of "world banker" demanded a series of "reforms" both
in her credit institutions and in the bourse itself. The Paris-
Netherlands bank, "for the first time since the moment of its
founding, forty years before," set about increasing its basic
capital, and next in line stood a project for creating in Paris
"a large private bank with a capital of 50 million francs" to
work the North-American United States "in the province of
trade as well as in that of industry" (Kunn, Loeb and Company in New York, "our London friends" and others.)[5] Inasmuch as the Franco-American bank was headed by Netslin
himself, who at once declared that this did not mean his exit
from Russian affairs, it was to Netslin that Kokovtsov im-
parted, in his answering letter of congratulations, a "certain
regret" that "this enterprise was destined to operate exclusively in an alien [to him, Kokovtsov] land,"--"at a moment when
my own land, more than any other, is in need of free capital
and presents a vast field for productive activity, given proper
organization and the direction of able and energetic men."
Kokovtsov further emphasized that his regret related "not so
much to questions of the finances and credit of the country as
to the interests of industry, which at the present time merited
the exclusive attention" of Paris, of this "veritable reservoir
of world wealth." "Let us hope"--Kokovtsov concluded this
virtual proposal--"that the trans-Atlantic republic will still
not crowd out the empire of the tsars and we be forced to
avail ourselves of capital unrelated to you."[7]
How exactly this appeal from Russia coincided with the
mood of Parisian Haute Finance may be judged by the speed--
in somewhat less than two weeks--with which Kokovtsov found
on his table a businesslike response to it. Verneuille, himself head of the Paris stock-brokers, after having icily refused
any support a month back in reply to Kokovtsov's routine complaints about the behavior of the French press, now presented
a project for organizing in Paris a "powerful financial group"
for the "investigation of Russian commercial and industrial
enterprises capable of wide development with the aid of French
capital." The "present moment, morrow of the Japanese war"
impressed him as "propitious to embarking on these enterprises under favorable conditions" "which would admit of
large rewards to interested capital." Participation of the

"largest Russian banks" in the proposed "combination" was
a further "absolutely necessary" condition, as the "material
and moral" guarantee of success. But to undertake an organization which contemplated profiting by the country's disaster
through the participation of Russian banks and seizing the most
viable enterprises on a monopolistic basis, was, obviously,
not worthwhile until full guarantee of the Russian government's
support had been obtained from the minister of finance.[8]
Needless to say, Peterburg did not keep Paris waiting a single
day but sent a prompt, unconditionally affirmative answer,
"promising" the "widest support," and by the very beginning
of January 1907, representatives of the Russian banks that
were to participate in the proposed consortium were already
in Paris. It was now, visibly, no longer a question of transferring the deposits of the mass of French investors, through
a bankers' subscription of the loan, to the Russian government's unrestricted disposal, but of a systematic sinking of
French finance capital, through the machinery of Peterburg's
home banks, directly in the Russian national economy. The
Russian finance minister had now summoned French capital
to the "organization" of "productive activity" "under the direction of able and energetic men." At the moment, Kokovtsov apparently hesitated to propose less to the French; but
what more could he have proposed?

The readiness this move showed on the part of Kokovtsov
to enter upon a course that opened up to French capital the
future possibility of seizing Russian large industry and assuming direction, stemmed primarily from the pressing need of
the Russian government at the given moment. It was in an
immediate state of alarming uncertainty about the morrow's
budget and under the imperative necessity of elevating and
maintaining its credit on the international exchange and of
obtaining solid success in this direction as soon as possible
--in any event by the liquidation date for the 300-million
French war loan of 1904, i.e., by the spring of 1909. Inasmuch as the Russian government was under the necessity of
revising its foreign policy program to meet new conditions
and reconcile it to the country's cash on hand, there was now
no question of anything beyond "husbanding its powers for
the settlement of major questions in Europe" and not "wasting
its resources on the Far East."[9] By the day of that military
conference of January 3, 1907, where Izvolsky expressed
himself as definitely opposed to reinforcement of armies in

the Amur district, and advanced the above program, tantamount to renunciation of the active policy in the Far East,
the question of the liquidation of those Manchurian enterprises
that had dictated Russia's aggressiveness in the preceding
period was already well launched.

II

It was imperative that foreign capital should appear on the
scene in the sphere of Russian interests in the Far East after
the lost war, if only because it could formally be placed beyond reach of the influence of those international-legal acts
whereby Japan was desirous of consolidating her victory.
This was, for example, the idea in back of a project for drawing the American, Clarkson, into a concession "for the exploitation of all fishing, mining, timbering and trapping trades on
Sakhalin," early in April, after the Mukden defeat, when a
Japanese landing on the island was seriously expected.[10]
This project the Russian military agent in Korea (Colonel
Nechvolodov) had already presented by the middle of March
1905, he and the American having agreed upon the following
terms: 1) that the American "provide all capital necessary
for exploitation," 2) that the concession be issued in the name
of Clarkson and Nechvolodov, and all revenues be divided between them equally, 3) that if Sakhalin remains to Russia,
the concession be recoverable on condition that Clarkson be
accorded "preferential right over others in competition for
the customary leases and concessions on Sakhalin," and have
equal rights with Russian subjects in his enterprises in the
Maritime province, 4) that, should Sakhalin pass to Japan,
the Russian government have the right to capitalize the half
of the revenues due it: (with the concession timed at 50 years,
its value "on the American exchange" was reckoned at 100
million rubles.) Here the whole calculation rested on "due
support of the American government, if Japan shall dispute
the right" of the American concessionary. As Lamsdorf reported the project, Nicholas reacted to it "very sympatheti-
cally." But doubts subsequently arose respecting the validity
of this artful scheme and there was even fear of a scandal
should the American "betray the confidence" of the Russian
government, and the project fall through.[11] Simultaneously
with the idea "of securing revenues" from Sakhalin industries,
i.e., also in March, a similar plan for a deal with Belgian

capitalists respecting the Manchurian Mining Association's
concessions, the most valuable portion of which now proved
to lie in the Japanese army zone, originated in Peterburg.
But in view of the extreme vagueness of the situation, times
were not yet right for this deal either.[12]

On the other hand, no sooner had the peace delegation been
finally constituted for negotiations with Japan than the Bezobrazovists became agitated about the Russian Lumbering Association. By this moment all of them except Abaza and
Matyunin, who had actually been fictitious share-holders,
were out of the Association by notarial order, receipts anticipated by the treasury of the Association (419, 187 rubles)
Abaza himself declared to "be very dubious," while such
debts as Peterburg succeeded in rounding up, and which must
be paid to avoid scandal, amounted to 265,952 rubles, "an
underestimate" by Abaza's admission, and the Association
had the air of a thoroughly bankrupt enterprise.[13] Abaza
attempted to transfer it bodily to the charge of the finance
minister, but Kokovtsov, "to guard his good name," resolutely declined the "liquidation" of the Association's "business," insisting that Nicholas entrust it to Abaza and Balashov.[14]

In the matter, however, of "transfer" to the finance ministry of "all rights and concessions hitherto appertaining to
the Association," on the "assumption that means would be
found to coordinate the exploitation of these concessions with
the rest of the enterprises in Manchuria falling under its
jurisdiction," Nicholas remained firm, and all documents on
rights and concessions were delivered to the ministry.[15]
Abaza further urged the formal transfer of "rights" before
the signing of the peace treaty, oddly enough justifying his
insistence on the ground that only private property could be
relied on "to withstand Japanese pretensions" and at the same
time emphasizing that the "Association's rights had the character of private ownership."[16] It thus appeared possible to
transfer the rights to anyone at all, with the sole exception of
the ministry of finance, and at this point the thought of the
Manchurian Mining Association automatically intruded itself.
But by that time this "private enterprise" was in no better
state than its former competitor. Of its three most valuable
concessions, two (Fushun and Chapigou) "had passed into
enemy hands," and "in the region of the Kwanshan gold fields"
the "attacks of Khunkhuz" had so "increased in frequency"

that any effort at defense had become futile--and, on August 4,
1905, Kokovtsov followed in Abaza's footsteps and brought
up with Nicholas the question of "temporary suspension of
operation" of the Manchurian Mining Association, with an
allocation of 175,000 rubles for the "liquidation of all accounts," exactly half as much as the Lumbering Association.[17]
This did not mean, of course, that Kokovtsov simply wrote
off his state Association. But, in the form in which it had
hitherto existed, to combat Japanese diplomacy in its defense
with a plain denial of its state nature would have been altogether hopeless.[18] And this alone saved Kokovtsov from
having to hurry about taking the Bezobrazov enterprises under
his wing.

At the first, back in June 1905, there was momentary
thought of making "declaration of the Manchurian Mining Association's rights in the name of the Russo-Chinese bank"
during the impending discussions with the Japanese. But to
"interest France" in the Manchurian Mining Association enterprises was soon recognized as still the more reliable
method. It was accordingly proposed that Netslin "become
a member of the Association, to replace the deceased Rothstein (d. early in 1905), and Lamsdorf was to enter into negotiations with the French government as to backing Russian
diplomacy and the possibility of really "attracting French
capital to the utilization of Association concessions in the
event of a successful defense of their private character."[19]
But it turned out that Netslin himself, "apart from the fictitious entry" in his name of shares "accounted as having
belonged to Rothstein," intended to acquire "as full owner"
Association shares in the amount of 100,000 rubles and "attract to this undertaking, quite privately, two or three trustworthy Haute Banque personages" on the same provisional
bases as had earlier been proposed respecting Sakhalin.[20]
It is further known that Netslin's terms were accepted by
Peterburg and that the transaction was destined to be put in
official form when he came to Russia for the "international
loan" negotiations in October 1905. As may be surmised,
this deal was never consummated, for the same reason that
dictated the international consortium's refusal to conclude
a loan with a government locked in its capital by the October
strike. And the matter ended (November 18, 1905) in the
appointment ot the Association's board of P.A. Bok, a member of the Board of the Russo-Chinese bank respecting whom

it might be asserted that formally he was an American subject.[21]

When the October cabinet was organized, with I.P. Shipov
replacing Kokovtsov, Abaza attempted to renew his reminders
and presented a detailed inventory of the property of the Lumbering Association (1,567,178 rubles' worth), requesting that
it be protected from Japanese seizure, "as juridically private
property but actually the property of the treasury, since in
the whole matter there had actually been no participation by
private persons."[22] But Shipov's attempt to appeal this matter to the Russo-Chinese bank met with a rebuff: not only did
the bank (in the person of A.I. Vyshnegradsky) flatly refuse
to have any hand in the fate of Bezobrazov's concessions, but
Vyshnegradsky himself, now on the board of the Manchurian
Mining Association, pleaded, on the Association's behalf, that
intervention in the Bezobrazovist concerns would only "compromise" the question of the Manchurian Mining Association's
rights.[23] But in February 1906, when Shipov nonetheless
started a correspondence about the protection of the Lumbering Association's property and even about the restitution of
its rights, as though it still continued to exist (and formally
it had by no act been liquidated to a finish), suddenly Nicholas
himself quite unexpectedly intervened in the matter. On
March 14, 1906 the minister of finance received a memorandum on a small sheet of notepaper: "give hunt-master Ivan
Petrovich Balashov the documents held in the Ministry of
Finance (number 60) respecting the Lumbering Association's
concessions."

In 1905 these documents were presented by Rear-Admiral
Abaza to "state-secretary Kokovtsov.N." And on March 15
documents, and enterprises as well, "constituting treasury
property" left the hands of the minister of finance. The
secret removal of the documents and theft of the rights were
not explained until six months later when Balashov, in requesting Izvolsky not to make "any attempts to defend the rights
of the Russian Lumbering Association to the Fushun mines"
conveyed the information that "our whole lumbering concern
has with his majesty's consent been transferred by us to the
Americans."[24] Actually, on July 6, 1906 Abaza and Matyunin
had concluded at the St. Peterburg notary Zabelsky's a
notarial contract with the American citizen William Smith for
the sale of their rights in the Fushun mines for two million
rubles, with the provision that "if by July 1, 1908 he shall

not have paid the Association the sum agreed upon for the
mines, all his rights in these mines shall revert to the Association...."But this sly move did not succeed: Fushun was
firmly occupied by the Japanese, and Smith's "account with
the Association remained unsettled" "not only on July 1, 1908,
but"--on Balashov's testimony--"throughout the period of
grace granted him and now expired [1914]."25

The fate of the Manchurian Mining Association enterprises
was, in the last analysis, no better, though all the forces at
the government's command were mobilized to rescue this
nurseling of the "emperor's policy." Efforts to "denational-
ize" the Association were redoubled. Had it not been for
Netslin's withdrawal, the Association would have looked entirely foreign by July 1906, since, apart from the "American" Bok, entered as holder of the Putilov shares, Rothstein's place was now taken by a "Bavarian," one of the directors of the International bank, O.O. Weber.26 And negotiations were at the same time continuing (through Vyshnegradsky and Wouters) with the Belgian group of Mongolor
stock-holders not only as to screening Russian concessions
behind yet another national mask, but also regarding the
actual investment of capital for their exploitation in a large
way. Of all the Association concessions, the most tempting
to the Belgians was, needless to say, the Fushun mines,
which promised sure revenue at once; but in this connection
a formal difficulty of a capital nature might also be foreseen:
before their seizure by the Japanese they had actually been
exploited by the administration of the Chinese Eastern Rail-
way--by which token they were in point of fact subsequently
brought under article VI of the Portsmouth treaty.27

There was however a moment, previous to the publication
of the treaty, when the Belgians were all but persuaded to
purchase "the whole Manchurian Association without delay
for one million rubles" and assume "the entire risk arising
from the possibility that the Japanese might be unwilling to
give Fushun back." Vyshnegradsky, conducting these negotiations in Paris on the eve of the Portsmouth treaty, had
used high pressure methods, the essential point of the transaction being that if the Belgians assumed the risk they paid
the Russian government not in hard cash but in privileged
shares of Mongolor. This applied, however, "only in the
event that [the deal] was put through immediately, before
clarification of the Fushun question"; in the contrary event,

the Belgians were threatened with exaction of the whole million in cash.[28] But with the ratification of the peace treaty on October 1, and the estrangement of the whole business world from the Russian government while uncertainty remained as to the shape in which the latter would emerge from the revolution and the financial crisis, the transaction was incapable of revival on the terms originally projected.

In July 1906, a week after Balashov's provisional sale of his part of Fushun to Smith the American, there could no longer be any question of anything but a provisional sale to the Belgians of the Manchurian Association concessions either. It was now plainly to be seen that "Russia's current financial position would in the near future scarcely permit the spending of state means on mine development in Manchuria," and the Russian government was compelled to accept Mongolor's proviso regarding its right to return "all ceded rights" if Japan and China did not recognize Mongolor's rights to the Fushun mines within two years.[29] Meanwhile the Chinese government now flatly refused to recognize any validity in concessions obtained by the Russians during the occupation of Manchuria after 1900, and the only Manchurian Mining Association concession absolutely free of any claims on Japan's part (the Kwanshan) had to be returned to the Chinese.[30] All the rest of the Association concessions proved to lie south of the proposed line of demarcation between Russian and Japanese spheres of influence, negotiations concerning which led in July 1907 to the signing of the open and secret Russo-Japanese treaties.[31] As a result, by May 1907 the ministry of finance considered the realization of the Mongolor deal hopeless, and in future there is nothing to note beyond certain attempts to obtain from the Chinese government, through diplomatic channels, the satisfaction of Russia's "claim" (amounting to 642 thousand rubles) for restitution by China of the Association's expenditures on concessions returned by the Association to China.[32] The report on the state of the Association's accounts drawn up in 1915 shows, however, that this claim remained unsatisfied, the Association itself unliquidated, and a "loan" at one time made by the State bank on Association shares uncancelled.[33] Here, of course, no claim was ever entered with the Japanese regarding Fushun such as Balashov had undertaken in behalf of the Lumbering Association.

III

The question of the liquidation of the Chinese Eastern Railway, left to Russia by the Portsmouth treaty in the truncated form of the main line and the stump of the South-Manchurian branch from Harbin to Kwanchengtse, was immeasurably complicated by the single fact of being linked with a grandiose financial deal which would demand the mobilization of foreign capital to the amount of not less than a half billion of rubles.[34] Conversations with Peking as to "pre-term redemption" of the Chinese Eastern Railway had, to be sure, been started back in 1905 both by English and by Americans, who even offered the Chinese government money for this purpose.[35] But at the time only rumors of this had reached Peterburg, and, so far as we know, no proposal in this sense was then made to the Russian government. This is quite comprehensible: the South-Manchurian line was of prime interest to foreign capitalists (and to their respective governments from the political viewpoint), and agreement must be reached with Japan before Russia was approached. Negotiations with Japan were, in fact, begun "back in 1906 shortly after the peace of Portsmouth" by the American railway king Harriman, director of the American "Union Pacific" and "Southern Pacific," owners of 154 million dollars worth of railway stock; but negotiations at that time came to nothing and Russia remained out of the picture.[36]

Even regarded as a purely commerical operation, for the Russian government to put the Chinese railway up for sale on the international market of its own accord would have been consciously to invite complete disaster or a bad bargain. But the question of liquidating this railway was at the time a political question as well for the Russian government, if for no other reason than that the trunk line of the Chinese Eastern Railway was the only "thread"--however easy now "to break"--that united the empire with its Pacific possessions. Liquidation of the Chinese Eastern Railway was therefore not to be thought of until the Amur link of the Siberian road should be built. Even before the war, Kuropatkin had suggested to Nicholas that "it is essential that we extend the road from Sretensk to Khabarovsk," and the rent roll for 1905 had included an assignment of 700,000 rubles for preliminary surveys for the Amur line. True, in the autumn of 1905, upon curtailment of the budget, this assignment was cancelled, but in

the spring of 1906 the question of the immediate execution of
surveys was urged as next in turn, and, due to total lack of
means, there was some thought of attracting foreign concessionaries, Americans preferably, to the work of construction. However, since an attempt to organize a "private company" for the purpose was unsuccessful, the building of the
road, figured to require five years and a capital of 130 million rubles, was postponed until some indefinite future date.[37]
And Russian diplomacy in the Far East was obliged to take
into account all the consequences that ensued from the mere
fact of preserving to Russia the dominant strategic line in
Northern Manchuria and the railway settlement that had been
growing and spreading under Russian military protection.[38]

To begin with, Peterburg consistently tried to act as if
nothing particular had happened and effected only those changes
in the state of the Chinese Eastern Railway that were exactly
stipulated as between Russia and Japan in the Portsmouth
treaty, i.e., reduction of scale and prohibition of use for
strategic purposes. In relation to China it would presumably
be possible to return to the "peaceful" principles of 1896 and
base the future policy of the Chinese Eastern Railway on the
fundamental contract and all subsequent supplementary agreements which this "private" railway company had succeeded
in concluding with the Chinese government. The "Special
conference for the examination of questions touching upon the
function of the Chinese Eastern Railway Company," organized
in Peterburg in 1906, accordingly set to work elaborating
legislative acts, not "for general consumption," but destined
to regularize the position of the Russian settlement--to the
distinct detriment of the sovereignty of China.[39] But the
first attempt along this line--to introduce a statute of civil
administration in the railway zone--evoked protests from the
Chinese government, and met with no encouragement from
foreign powers, since it conflicted with the interests of
foreigners, who naturally desired to preserve their extraterritoriality in the region of the Russian road on the same
terms as in the rest of China. No sooner was the Russian
government's above described tendency revealed than Russo-
Chinese relations centering in the Chinese-Eastern Railway
fell into a state of chronic and increasingly bitter conflict,
daily inhibiting the commercial development of the road and
driving Russian diplomacy to desperate measures that only
complicated its position still further.[40] Moreover, the

weaker Russia's military situation in general, and in the Far
East in particular, and the more signs there were of the growth
of a national movement in China and the reorganization of its
armed forces, particularly in the Manchurian area, the more
reasonable became Russian diplomacy's besetting "fear" "that
to defend the company's right to administer the Chinese Eastern Railway zone might be impossible without risk of war."[41]

But even had it not been for that, the absurdity of persever-
ing in this direction became more apparent every day. "Through
interminable quarrels, small incursions into the sphere of
rights appertaining to us, all manner of reprisals and other
manifestations of active and systematic malevolence, the Chinese have undoubtedly contributed in no slight measure"--as
the Russian mission in Peking remarked--"to the fact that
the development of our trade and industry in North Manchuria
has been arrested, that the freight turnover of the Chinese
Eastern Railway does not improve, that the influx of Russian
pioneers into the region has diminished," that (as Kokovtsov
complained) "an impossible situation is created, upsetting all
the Chinese Eastern Railway Company's calculations and de-
priving it of the ability to derive profits from its enterprise"
--nay more: Khorvat, superintendent of the road asserted
that "the behavior of the Chinese in North Manchuria had produced results tantamount to enormous losses, even though
eluding exact calculation."[42] The Chinese Eastern Railway
as conceived and executed under Witte was too much of a load
for Russia after the Japanese war in every respect. Russia's
"whole behavior" even after the war was "by no means such"
as to give the Chinese cause to believe "that we had now renounced our former designs touching the seizure of North
Manchuria," and Russian diplomats in Peking were balked
at every turn "by the Chinese idée fixe": "the Chinese Eastern Railway is an encroachment on the sovereignty of China."[43]
To continue such a policy solely at his own risk and on his
own responsibility, "regardless of other countries," as
Nicholas would rather have liked to do[44] proved all the more
impossible in that the position occupied by Japan on the
Asiatic mainland after the war virtually robbed Russia of any
opportunity to pursue an independent and active policy.

True, the secret political agreement with Japan of July 17/
30, 1907, viewed in conjunction with the Anglo-Japanese
treaty of alliance of July 30/August 12, 1905 and the Franco-
Japanese agreement of June 10, 1907 would appear to have

neatly reconciled the mutual interests and rights of Russia
and Japan in Manchuria, Korea and Mongolia and to have established Japan's absolute disinterest in North Manchuria
above a line drawn from Hunchun to Birten and along the
Sungari to the mouth of the Nonni. But all reports from Russian diplomatic representatives in Korea, Tokyo and Peking
unanimously testified to the fact that Japan was with the
greatest celerity and system making preparations for a new
war, turning South Manchuria and Korea into her bases and
hinterlands, with railway lines, ammunition dumps, arsenals,
camps and so on adapted to attack in a northerly direction.[45]
By the spring of 1909 a situation had been created which would
admit of Japan's appearing in the Amur province with eleven
divisions within two weeks of the opening of hostilities against
Russia, after first taking a few days to liquidate Vladivostok,
which was absolutely unfitted for defense by land, let alone
by sea.[46] And Russian diplomats well knew that the favorable
attitude toward Russia assumed by Japan in the Russo-Chinese
complications might, in the situation described, be no more
than a component part of a political program designed to in-
veigle Russia into an armed clash with China that would give
Japan an easy pretext for banishing Russia from the seacoast
altogether.[47] Russian representatives continued to note "the
most highly amicable, courteous and cordial attitudes on the
part of the Japanese," who "as before spared no efforts to
conciliate the Russians," but, putting these over against the
"hurried outfitting against Russia" were "constrained" to
recognize that "these amiable attitudes were beginning to have
an air of transiency."[48]

Under such conditions it is no wonder that the thought of
losing no time about getting out of Manchuria "with honor"
while this could still be done without material losses should
have with ever increasing insistence sought admittance to the
political program of the Russian government. In June 1908
a bill passed the Duma for setting about the construction of
the Amur railway by treasury means, negotiations with French
and London bankers were in full swing relative to a new Franco-
English loan which should not only cover the whole amount of
the short-term notes of 1904 but leave something over (136
million rubles "actual") for the Russian government's free
disposal, and the idea of a recession in the Chinese Eastern
Railway question thus gained some degree of reality. If we
are not mistaken, the first timid step in this direction was

proposed by Kokovtsov--in the form of a suggested reduction
in the number of the guard along the road such as would give
the Chinese to understand that Russia had no aggressive designs in North Manchuria.[49] This proposal next received
full support from Peking (in the cited memorandum from
Arsenev), supplemented by the counsel that China be at
once advised "of our decision to liquidate, within a fixed
time, the enterprise appertaining to us in North Manchuria."[50]
Simultaneously the ministry of foreign affairs in Peterburg
put forward, for preliminary discussion, a proposal to conclude "a triple agreement with America and China" "on all
questions, not only as to Manchuria but as to the state of
Pacific affairs in general"--on the basis of "the Chinese Eastern Railway administration's total non-intervention in the
government of railway zone cities and populated points, which
were to be governed according to the pattern for foreign
settlements."[51] And on January 17/30, 1909 Korostovets in
Peking was "astonished" by an offer from Lian Dunien, minister of foreign affairs, transmitted to him through the Englishman R. Bredon, inspector of maritime customs, to redeem
the Chinese Eastern Railway.[52] Then, finally, on January 19,
Korostovets was handed Ching's note constituting China's
official offer in this sense, and expressing confidence that
the Russian government would give an affirmative answer and
that "all questions touching the road would thus be settled
and the friendship of the two states consolidated."[53]

This offer by the Chinese government was undoubtedly
backed by American capitalists. But indications exist that
the latter were drawn in by the Russian government itself.
In the summer of 1908, Peterburg was visited by the finance
ministry's Washington agent Vilenkin, connected, through his
American wife, with American banking circles. Two questions were discussed with him at Kokovtsov's, possibly on his
own initiative: as to drawing the Jewish banking house of Kuhn,
Loeb and Company into Russian financial operations and as to
compromising with Japan the question of the simultaneous
sale of the South-Manchurian and Chinese Eastern Railways
to an "international syndicate." Izvolsky was also let in on
the matter, and in future Vilenkin acted with the "approval"
of both ministers. Upon arriving in New York, Vilenkin "had
two interviews with Jacob Schiff, head of the banking house
of Kuhn, Loeb and Company," and, "having convinced himself
that Schiff's acquaintance with the Jewish question in Russia

was one-sided," urged Schiff to come to Peterburg himself
and "get an all-round understanding of the state of the question that interested him": Schiff even agreed in writing that,
if Kokovtsov invited him, he would come to Peterburg "for
joint discussion" of the question of opening the American
market to the placing of Russian loans--"provided the Russian
government would agree to discuss the question of removing
the restrictions upon Russian Jews to the end of giving them
equal rights with the rest of the population."[54]

Apparently the matter of Schiff's trip went no further and
there was no invitation from Kokovtsov. But not long afterwards, at the end of November 1908, Schiff was attracted to
the financial interests of the Russian government, neither by
the "lure" of plain "industrial orders" as might well have
happened with Morgan in 1905 had this "lure" not then been
denied him, nor by equal rights for the Jews, without which
it had looked as though Schiff would not even hear of financial
aid to the tsarist government, but by the lure of the release
of a railway enterprise colossal in dimensions and capital
investment and the wide commercial, financial and political
prospects associated with it. Vilenkin proposed to Schiff that
he "assume the initiative in realizing a project" for redemption of the Manchurian railroads through an issue of guaranteed
bonds, i.e., as Schiff expressed it, a project for the "internationalization of both Manchurian roads." Both Vilenkin and
Schiff considered as "prime and principal condition for the
success of this project" "Japan's consent to participate in it
and acquiesce to the sale of the South-Manchurian road," and
it was on this condition, i.e., that "Russia and Japan act
jointly," that Schiff agreed to assume the initiative in organizing a "syndicate at least nominally in American hands"--"provided conditions were right." In December 1908, when these
negotiations were in progress, calculations respecting Japan
were based on Baron Goto, minister of roads, with whom conversations had been initiated back in July from Vilenkin's side,
and on Tatakami, director of the bank of Japan, who had
promised Schiff his cooperation.[56] Collaterally with the tri-
lateral negotiations thus already begun, only the American
side could (or was supposed to) have dealings with the Chinese
government; and the latter had hurried to extend the Russian
government its official proposal of pre-term redemption of
the Chinese Eastern Railway (January 19, 1909) with these
negotiations still incomplete.

But now, just when Russia's undertaking might have appeared to be approaching a happy conclusion, things assumed
an altogether different aspect--with Japan's flat refusal to
"do anything about the Manchurian road." In the interval,
Japan had succeeded in realizing a South-Manchurian loan of
two million pounds sterling on the London market, which enabled her to "take her time," and such "political events" had
managed to occur in China as the death of the empress dowager
Tzu Hsi (November 15) and the fall of Yuan Shi-k'ai (January 2)
happenings that impelled the Tokyo government to "await
patiently the further development of events."[57] True, both
Schiff and his companion-at-arms Harriman were, as before,
prepared to "enter into negotiations [with Russia] as to acquiring the Chinese Eastern Railway for China" independently
of how the matter of the South-Manchurian line ended. But
Peterburg, following Japan's lead, apparently decided to take
its time too and "play a strictly waiting game in order to avoid
having the initiative in the transaction emanate from the Russian government or any agent thereof," and it was proposed
that Vilenkin "suspend all negotiations with American capitalists and leave matters to take their natural course, in the
expectation that foreign capitalists or the Chinese government
would of themselves make us reasonable offers."[58] And in
the meantime China was given the "favorable answer" that
Russia "did not in principle reject her proposal, assuming
the possibility of its effectuation after the Amur railway had
been built."[59]

Meanwhile, Japan not only had no thought of renouncing
her share of the South-Manchurian line but in the summer of
1909 manifested such activity in South Manchuria (the ultimatum of July 30 to China and the agreement of August 22 as
to the Antung-Mukden and Khorien-Kirin Railways, the Kando
area, and confirmation of the Fushun and Yantai mines to the
Japanese) as to evoke an outburst of indignation in interested
American circles and give rise to thoughts of the "impossibility
of concerting with Russia in view of Japan's threats against
the independence of China, in defiance of the agreements."[60]
At the beginning of November 1909 when American diplomacy
attempted to convince Peterburg "of the necessity of Russia's
approaching Manchurian matters arm in arm with the United
States" and Rockhill proposed to Izvolsky a "combination" designed to set a "final and so to say international limit to further seizures on the part of Japan," this turned out to be still

the same plan for "commercial neutralization of the Manchurian railway network" that Vilenkin had proposed exactly
a year before.

But even had the neutralization of Manchuria been "formally"
put through on a military footing as Rockhill suggested to
Izvolsky, this would still not have settled the problem of the
inviolability of Russia's Pacific possessions from attempts
by Japan: on the contrary, there "might" "even be reason to
fear" that if Japan "lost her preferential position in South
Manchuria through pressure from without she would seek to
recoup herself at our expense" in the Maritime province - -
which Izvolsky duly pointed out to the American ambassador.61
And when, that same day, "immediately after Rockhill,"
Motono presented himself to Izvolsky bearing the proposal
that existing relations between Japan and Russia be converted
into a "formal alliance" before which "not only China but all
the other powers would have to bow," and which would consequently enable Russia "so backed by Japan, to be bold in
defence of the rights appertaining to the Chinese Eastern
Railway Company on the strength of the 1896 contract," and
when Russian diplomacy was thus faced by the "necessity" of
"at once making final choice of the course our Far-Eastern
policy was to take," to Nicholas "personally" it was already
"quite clear what course Russia must now choose: namely
that of entering into a hard and fast agreement with Japan."
- -Seen in perspective, this course actually led, as Izvolsky
observed, to "joint Russo-Japanese guardianship over Manchuria and even over all China, as opposed to the tendencies
of America and the western-European powers."62 And for
the immediate future such an agreement was of prime importance as guaranteeing Russia's rear in the event of a general
European war.

The other course, indicated by Rockhill, not only led to
the "neutralization of Manchuria under the guardianship of
America and the western-European powers" but might finally
give the tsar's government access to the American money
market. A cautious attempt by Kokovtsov to feel out the
ground in this direction with Schiff himself was made in the
summer of 1908 collaterally with negotiations over the regular
entente loan for payment of war debts and construction of the

Amur railway, and testified to some intention of broadening
the autocracy's financial base in order to obviate the necessity of exclusive dependence on Anglo-French banking capital
in financial operations and matters of policy. At the time
when Vilenkin in New York was conducting the negotiations
entrusted to him, the exacting attitude of the French government "at times" led Kokovtsov to think "that France's consciousness of her own wealth and conviction that her gold was
indispensable to Russia were breeding [in French governmental circles] the strange view that Russia must not do what
was most to her advantage at home without first inquiring
whether this measure or that of a purely domestic nature met
with the approval of whatever group was at the given moment
the most influential factor in the political life of France"--
and Kokovtsov "for all his calm and composure" was constrained
to remind Paris officially that "alliance and friendship are
not synonyms for yoke and slavery."[63] By deciding in favor
of the "hard and fast agreement" with Japan just when this
devil's "comedy" of concluding a loan of 525 million rubles
nominal* had been happily brought to a close, and a good harvest and symptoms of the long awaited industrial rise were
already present, Nicholas's government had for a second time
let slip the opportunity to knit business relationships with the
financial aristocracy of the U.S.A.[64] Tsarskoe Selo succumbed to the temptation to accept the alliance obstinately
thrust upon it by Japan and return to an active policy in the
Far East--even if only within the bounds set for Russia by
the consortium of her imperialistic "friends."

*Of nominal current value--Ed.

NOTES

FOREWARD

1. The introduction is a revision of the survey "Basic Moments of Russian Policy in the Far East," printed in Sibirskii Ogni, (Siberian Fires), 1926, No. 4; the first and second chapters are a development of sections I-V of an article on the "Li Hung-chang fund" in the review Bor'ba klassov (Class War), Leningrad, 1924, No. 1-2, pp. 77-110.

2. This would have been particularly desirable in connection with the Introduction and Chapter I, especially the second section.

3. Later on, in footnotes to the text, when reference is made without mention of the source, simply to No. so and so ("doc. No....,") it will indicate that the paper belongs to the archives of the Third Department of the General Chancellery of the Minister of Finance. When a collection is mentioned with location undesignated, the Leningrad Central Historical Archive is to be understood. Location of a source in Moscow is always specified.

INTRODUCTION

1. From the report of November 6, 1892 made to his Majesty by the head of the ministry of finance. See below, Chap. 1, pp. 55-60.

2. See "Statisticheskie svedeniia o torgovle Rossii s Kitaem" (Statistical Data on Russia's Trade with China), in Trudi statisticheskogo otdeleniia departmenta tamozhennykh sborov (Transactions of the Statistical Division of the Customs Department), St. Petersburg, 1909, pp. 21 and 8.

3. Ibid., pp. 11 and 15, particularly the figures on imports into China by five-year periods from 1851 to 1890 (in thousands of rubles): 9,272; 8,366; 5,585; 4,635; 3,984; 2,487; 2,126; 2,186.

4. After seizing the Maritime province, Russia sold Alaska to America (1867) for 1,432 million rubles and ceded Japan the Kurile Islands, regarded by the latter as primordially Japanese, in exchange for the southern half of Sakhalin (1875).

5. Cf. H.B. Morse, The International Relations of the Chinese Empire, London, 1918, Vol. III, pp. 6-19. Comparative figures for trade turnover with Korea from 1886-1894 are: China, from 455,337 dollars to 3,226,573, Japan from 2,508,830 dollars to 5,697,633. During these same years the Russian turnover grew from 14,243 dollars to 218,572. (See Opisanie Korei [Description of Korea], pubs. Chancellery Min. Fin., part III, Appendices, St. Petersburg. 1900, pp. 176-179.)

6. Cf. E.D. Grimm, "Kitaiskii vopros v 1895-1914 gg." (The Chinese Question, 1895-1914), Novyi Vostok (New East), No. 6, p. 50.

7. Hostilities opened July 20, 1894. Temporary traffic on the Siberian railway opened in August, 1894, but only as far as Omsk.

8. Cf. the peace treaty of Shimonoseki between Japan and China, articles 1 and 2 (in Sbornik dogovorov i diplomaticheskikh dokumentov po delam D. Vostoka. 1895-1905 (Collection of Treaties and Diplomatic

Documents on Affairs of the Far East, 1895-1905), pub. MID (Min.
For. Afr.) St. Petersburg, 1906). Formosa and the Pescadores, demanded by Japan, lie opposite Fukien province itself. In 1898, China
was forced to give Japan her pledge not to alienate Fukien, in 1915 not
to permit foreigners to construct docks, coaling stations, or naval bases
there and not to employ foreign capital for this purpose (see Izv. MID,
1915, book IV, p. 70.) Relative to Liaotung, Japan demanded permanent
cession (not leasehold), not only of the Liaotung peninsula within the
limits to which it was afterwards leased to Russia, but of all territory
from the mouth of the Yalu to Fenghuangcheng-Haicheng-Yinkow, these
three points included. The possession, in particular of Yinkow--then
chief port of Manchuria--would have secured to Japan economic control
over all Manchuria.

9. Reference is to the trade treaty between Russia and Japan, of
May 27/June 8, 1895, articles XVII and XVIII of which abrogate the exterritoriality of Russian subjects in Japan.

10. See below, chap. 2, pp. 99-100.

11. Reorganized in 1900 as the "stock company for the mining industry
of the Tushetukhan and Tsetsenkian aimaks in Mongolia" ("Mongolor").

12. America's annexation of the Hawaiian Islands (1897) and her taking
of Cuba, Porto Rico and the Philippines from Spain (1898) the Anglo-
French clash over Fashoda (Central Africa, 1898-1899), the Anglo-Boer
war (South Africa, 1899-1902), the seizure: by Germany of Kiaochow and
Shantung (1897-1898), by Russia of Liaotung (1898), by France of Kwang-
chow (Kwangtung, 1898), by England of Weihaiwei and the Kowloon peninsula, finally the treaty of Japan and China regarding the non-alienation
of Fukien (1898).

13. Shantung was taken by Japan in 1914, returned to China at the
decree of the Washington conference of 1921-1922.

14. Telegram of the Russian ambassador from Paris 14/26 I '98,
LTsIA, Chanc. M.F., No. 51/2.

15. The Spanish war cost America 776 million rubles.

16. For the two years immediately preceding (1897-1898) Europe paid
America a trade balance of 1,897.3 million rubles.

17. See E.D. Grimm, "Doktrina 'Otkrytykh dverei' i amerikanskaia
.politika v Kitai (ot 1899 do 1921-22 g.g.)" (Doctrine of the "Open Door"
and the American Policy in China from 1899 to 1921-22) in Mezhdunarodnaia
Zhizn, (International Life) 1924, No. 4-5, pp. 114-115.

18. Cf. the letter of the American Secretary of State, Hay, under date
of May 22, 1903, quoted by E.D. Grimm. Mezhdunarodnaia Zhizn, (International Life), 1924, No. 4-5, p. 118 and Tyler Dennett, Roosevelt and
the Russo-Japanese War, New York, 1925, p. 2.

19. Expression used by Lansdowne in a conversation with the Russian
ambassador, see Lansdowne's telegram of August 12, 1903 in the English
Blue Book (China No. 2), No. 142.

20. See T. Dennett, Op. cit., p. 137.

21. A like evaluation of the position of America before the Russo-
Japanese war also appears in T. Dennett's op. cit., pp. 118, 115.

22. The "opening" of Harbin and other points in Manchuria to foreigners
was stipulated in article I of the supplementary agreement to the Sino-
Japanese treaty of 9/22 December 1905 (Sborn. dogovorov i diplomaticheskikh
kikh dokumentov po delam Dal'nevo Vostoka, (Collection of Treaties and

Diplomatic Documents on Affairs of the Far East) pubs. MID SPb. 1906, p. 756.) An agreement between Russia and England as to the compliance of English subjects with Russian laws and ordinances in the Chinese Eastern railway zone, worked out on the 17/30 of April, 1914, followed on the 26th November/3rd December 1914 (see Izv. MID, (Izvestiia Min. For. A.) 1915, book II, pp. 1-10;) an analogous agreement with France was concluded the 30th January/12 February 1914 (ibid., 1914, book III, pp. 39-40).

23. See, for example, the two letters of Kokovtsov to Stolypin, September 6 and November 14, 1906, published by us in the collection Russkie financy i evropeiskaia birzha v 1904-1906. (Russian Finances and the European Bourse in 1904-1906) Tsentrarkhiv, 1925, No. 222 and No. 227.

24. See the report of the minister of finance to the State Council, March 6, 1908.

25. See the resolution of Nicholas II upon Pokotilov's telegram of April 29/May 12, 1906: "In China we ought not to identify our interests with the interests of the states of Western Europe; we must endeavor to continue our pre-1898 policy, i.e., act pacifically and apart from other countries" (Moscow Archive of the revolution and of foreign policy, reports to his majesty by the minister of foreign affairs for the year 1906).

26. See T. Dennett, op. cit., pp. 161, 178, 179.

27. Ibid., p. 157. This idea was expressed by Conger, American minister plenipotentiary in Peking.

28. Ibid., pp. 112-114. -- On American proposals to purchase the South-Manchurian branch, see Payson J. Treat's Japan and the United States, 1853-1921, 1921, pp. 190-191.

29. See McMurray, Treaties and Agreements, Vol. I, p. 769.

30. The secret agreement of June 21/July 4, 1910 was published in A.M. Zaionchovsky's Podgotovka Rossii k mirovoi voine v mezhdurnarodnom otnoshenii, (Russia's Preparation for the World War in Its International Aspect), Moscow, 1926, p. 370--the open agreement of the same date in E.D. Grimm's Sbornik dogovorov i drugikh dokumentov po istorii mezhdunarodnykh otnoshenii na Dal'nem Vostoke (1842-1925) (Collection of Treaties and Other Documents on the History of International Relations in the Far East), Moscow, 1927, p. 176.

31. See the above-quoted study by E.D. Grimm in Mezhdunarodnaia Zhihzn (International Life) for 1924, No. 4-5, p. 125.

32. See doc. No. 178 for Von Heuer's dispatch of August 19/September 1, 1908: "Between Russia and Japan under present circumstances there can be no war, there can only be a pitiless slaughter of Russians."

33. For the text of the project of the secret agreement of 1912 see Siebert's Diplomatische Aktenstücke zur Geschichte der Ententepolitik der Vorkriegsjahre, Berlin, 1925, pp. 288-289. For the Russo-Mongolian agreement of October 21/November 3, 1912, see Izvestiia Min. For. Afs., 1913, I, p. 46 f. and II p. 6 f.--Russia's agreement with China as to recognition of the autonomy of outer Mongolia followed on October 23/November 5, 1913 (Izv. Min. For. Afs., 1914, I, p. 15 f.) The triple agreement of Russia, China, and Mongolia on the same subject was signed May 15, 1915 (see Ibid., 1915, p. 6 f.) The diplomatic correspondence on Mongolian affairs for August 23, 1912-September 2, 1913 was published as an appendix to Book II Izv. for Afs. for 1914. For Russia's agreement of September 17, 1914 with the Urga government as to railways in Mongolia, see Ibid. 1915, I, p. 1 ff.

34. The "21 demands" were published in Izv. Min. for Afs. 1915, Book III, p. 95 f.; the Sino-Japanese agreement of May 26, 1915, ibid., 1915, Book IV, p. 57 ff.
35. See E.D. Grimm, op. cit., pp. 126-127.
36. For the secret agreement of 6/20-7/3, 1916, see pubs. N.K.I.D. Sborn. sekr. dok. iz arkhiva b. MID (Collection of Secret Documents from the Archives of the former Min. For. Afs.) No. 1, p. 5 fol.

CHAPTER I
1. See Zapiski gen. Kuropatkina o russko-iaponskoi voine. Itogi voiny (Notes of Gen. Kuropatkin on the Russo-Japanese War: War Totals), Berlin, I. Ladyschnikoff, 1909, pp. 173 and 174. Kwantung-Liaotung.
2. See D.I. Subotich, Amurskaia doroga i nasha politika na Dal'nem Vostoke (The Amur Road and our Policy in the Far East), St. Petersburg, 1908, pp. 19-32.
3. See Dnevnik Kuropatkina (Kuropatkin's Journal), entry of December 3, 1903, Kr. Arkhiv (Red Archives) Book II, p. 91.
4. See ibid., entry of December 11, p. 93.
5. See ibid., p. 91.
6. See the memorandum drawn up in the ministry of foreign affairs: "Vozrazheniia na broshyuru Manchzhurskii vopros (Objections to the Brochure the Manchurian Question), Dos. No. 105. The memorandum in the original was sent Witte by Lamsdorf when he returned the brochure itself. On the memorandum is Nicholas's notation: "Prekrasnyi otvet" (splendid answer), dated July 19, 1902.
7. See Dnevnik Kuropatkina, entry of December 3, 1903. (Kr. Arkhiv, vol. II, p. 91.)
8. See S. Iu. Witte, Vynuzhdennye razasneniia po povodu otcheta gen.-ad. Kuropatkina o voine s Iaponiei (Necessary Explanations in Connection with the Accounting of Ad.-Gen. Kuropatkin on the War with Japan), Moscow, 1911, p. 48.
9. See ibid. The text of this brochure by Witte was ready in 1909, but its publication was not authorized until 1911.
10. See G.D. Dement'ev Vo chto oboshlas' nashemu Gosudarstvennomu kaznacheistvu voina s Iaponiei. Statisticheskoe issledovanie, sostavlennoe po otchetam Gosudarstvennovo Kontrolia i po svedeniiam Ministerstva Finansov (What the War with Japan Cost Our State Treasury: a Statistical Investigation Based on the Accounts of the State Control and the Audits of the Ministry of Finance), Petrograd, 1917, p. 34.
11. See Dnevnik Polovtsova (Polovtsov's Journal), entry of March 30 (Kr. Arkhiv, vol. 3, p. 87.)
12. See ibid., entry of August 19, p. 103.
13. See Dnevnik Kuropatkina, entries of February 19 and March 22, 1903, pp. 33 and 39.
14. See item No. 129: "O dokhodakh i raskhodakh kazny na Dal'nem Vostoke"(On receipts and disbursements of the treasury in the Far East).
15. See Dnevnik Kuropatkina, January 1903, pp. 22, 24.
16. See the report to his majesty of March 14, in our study: "Likhunchangskii fond" (the Li Hung-chang Fund), (Bor'ba klassov, No. 1-2, pp. 117-124).
17. See ibid.
18. See Witte's Vospominaniia (Memoirs), Vol. I, pp. 98-100.

19. See B. B. Glinskii, Prolog russko-Iaponskoi voiny (Prologue to
the Russo-Japanese War), St. Petersburg, 1916, p. 56. On the origin
of this publication see B. A. Romanov, "Vitte nakanune russko-iaponskoi
voiny"(Witte on the Eve of the Russo-Japanese War), in the collection
Rossiia i Zapad (Russia and the West), Petrograd, 1923, p. 162.
20. Vospominaniia, I, pp. 108-115. Part of the documents on this
affair are published in Kras. Arkhiv, Book 2, pp. 287-293.
21. Vosp., I, p. 115. -- Emphases are ours.
22. Ibid., p. 43. -- Emphases are ours.
23. Before 1905, while withdrawals from the "fund" were, on the
whole, made for expenditures connected with affairs in the Far East,
correspondence relative to the withdrawals also has a political character.
After 1905, the (quite considerable) remainder of the fund proved a complete political orphan, due to Russia's extreme weakness in the Far East,
and was spent for the most varied "needs:" correspondence about it is
laconic, assumes almost the character of accountant's entries. During
the years 1908-1910, Nicholas II, each time at his own autograph request,
was, by sealed packet conveyed to the palace by a special official, "presented," in nine installments, with a total of 1,030,000 rubles. By January 1, 1914, the fund had been reduced to 373,714 rubles 59 kopeks.
Amount spent in 16 years--4,492,151 rubles, 50 kopeks. See Obshch.
Kants. Min. Fin., sekr. delo No. 51 (General Chancellery of the Ministry
of Finance, secret dossier No. 51), in four parts: "Ob obrazovanii osobovo fonda i vydachakh iz nevo raznym litsam" (On the organization of
the special fund and withdrawals from it by various persons). The detailed "statement" as to withdrawals, drawn up on February 6, 1914, was
published by us in the article: "Lihunchangskii fond," see the periodical
Bor'ba klassov, No. 1-2, pp. 124-126.
24. See Vospominaniia, Vol. III, p. 354.
25. See the printed Spravka (reference sheet) on the Chinese railways
compiled by Pokotilov in 1895 for the minister of finance.
26. On the history of the question of the building of the Siberian railway see Sibirskaia zhel. dor. v yeyo proshlom i nastoyashchem (The
Siberian Railway Past and Present), ed. A. Kulomzin, St. Petersburg,
1903, pp. 1-128.
27. Witte proposed to resort at first to a sort of financial trick--the
diversion of 92 million rubles of banknotes subject to retirement to the
expenses of construction--and calculated on covering this sum later by
borrowings from budgetary funds. See B. B. Glinskii's Prolog pp. 15 ff.
28. Vospominaniia, Vol. III, pp. 354 ff.
29. See B. B. Glinskii, Prolog, pp. 10 ff. From this point on, we
shall use the copy of the report of November 6, 1892 exisitng in the dossier of the General Chancellery of the Ministry of Finance, 1892, div. II,
"Ob Osobom Soveshchanii po voprosu o sooruzhenii velikovo Sibirskovo
puti" (On the Special Conference on the Question of the Construction of
the Great Siberian Road). Emphases in quotations from this report will
from now on always be ours.
30. See our critique of Vol. III of Witte's Vospominaniia in Bor'ba
klassov, No. 1-2, p. 342.
31. Textually: "With all the rest, the Canadian railway has in a very
short time caused a notable development of agriculture in the erstwhile
wastes of central Canada, thanks to the methods adopted by the administration of the road for the settlement of this tract, to which end anyone so

desiring was allotted a farm of 160 acres. Back in 1880 (before the
building of the Canadian railway) the said extensive province had produced grain in quantities scarcely sufficient for its own few inhabitants,
while in 1891--five years after the opening of the road--the harvest, in
this same province, of wheat alone yielded a surplus of 30 million bushels
for export. Along the main line and its branches, of which there are now
already 1,200 miles, large cities have sprung up, such as: Brandon,
Portage, Regina, Calgary, as well as many minor settlements. During
the brief period of its existence the Canadian railway has, at large expense, brought to life and fecundated the vast wilderness that it traverses.
But then again this enterprise now already shows a clear profit of more
than 8 million dollars, though the province which it crossed had a population only half as great as Siberia's at the present time."
    32. See Vospominaniia, I, p. 39.
    33. Badmaev's memorandum, along with certain other documents
hereafter quoted, was published by V.P. Semennikov in the book: Za
kulisami tsarisma. Arkhiv Tibetskovo vracha Badmaeva (Behind the
Scenes of Tsarism: Archive of the Tibetan physician Badmaev), Leningrad, 1925, pp. 49-75. Emphases in quotations are ours.
    34. Witte's report--ibid., p. 81--was presented to the tsar along with
the memorandum before February 24, date noted on the tsar's resolution
on the report.
    35. Witte's report to the tsar, ibid., p. 81.
    36. Badmaev's memoranda to Witte of June 19 and August 28, 1893,
ibid., pp. 83-85.
    37. Badmaev's letter to Alexander III of July 22, 1893, ibid., p. 85.
    38. Ibid., p. 85, Badmaev's memorandum of August 28, 1893.
    39. Ibid., pp. 87 and 106.
    40. Toward the estimated total for operations of the first stage Witte
had at his disposal the 92.7 million rubles in banknotes that constituted
the debt of the State Bank to the State Treasury. On the financial details
of Witte's plan see Sibirskaia zheleznaia doroga v proshlom i nastoyashchem,
pp. 118-122.
    41. See Morse, The International Relations of the Chinese Empire,
Vol. III, p. 19.
    42. Ibid., pp. 19-25.
    43. Lamsdorf so formulated Russia's "primordial" tasks in the Far
East in the memorandum presented by him in reply to Vogak's accusatory
memorandum, apropos of the treaty of March 26, 1902, read at the conference of May 7, 1903, see Dos. No. 120.
    44. See Morse, op. cit., p. 29.
    45. For the minutes of the conferences of August 9, 1894, January 20
and March 30, 1895, see copies in dos. No. 20. On the fourth conference,
April 4, 1895, see Witte's Vospominaniia, I, p. 37. -- Emphases in
quotations are, from now on, ours.
    46. See Morse, op. cit., p. 41. The plenipotentiaries arrived in Kobe
on January 30, new style. Their credentials were not recognized as
satisfactory, and the war continued.
    47. See the minutes for January 20 in dos. No. 20. Besides the per-
sons mentioned in the text, the minutes were signed by O. Kremer, chief
of the central naval staff.

48. Take for example the exchange of ideas between the Russian ambassador to London and Lord Kimberley, reported in the ambassador's confidential letter of February 22 (March 6). Kimberley could say "nothing positive" about England's attitude toward Japan's possible territorial demands, and discussion was confined to an examination in "general outline" of those separate interests of the powers concerning the protection of which it would be well to reach agreement.

49. Morse, op. cit., p. 44.

50. See the copy of Lobanov's report of March 25 with the tsar's notations--in dos. No. 20.

51. The copy of Lobanov's memorandum of March 25 as well as the copies of the report and the minutes of March 30 are identical in outward form and were made in the ministry of foreign affairs.

52. Vannovsky declared that at the "given moment" we could not mobilize over 12-15 thousand men, but also that the Japanese armies were "at the present time harmless so far as we are concerned," since without adequate transport and cavalry they "cannot advance a single step." In 6 months the count of Russian troops could be brought to 50 thousand. Chikhachev asserted that, "without risking any large naval battles," our squadron might disrupt Japanese communications.

53. The decision of the conference was formulated in 2 points: 1) "to counsel Japan" "in a friendly manner" "to renounce the occupation of Southern Manchuria," stating that, in the event of refusal, we reserve our freedom of action, and 2) to notify the powers to this effect, including China.

54. Copy of the written account of Lobanov's conversation with Count Montebello, together with the tsar's rsolution in dos. No. 20.

55. Copy of Lobanov's memorandum of April 3, accompanying the minutes of the conference of March 30, ibid.

56. See Lobanov's memorandum of April 3.

57. Witte, Vospominaniia, I, p. 37. The minute book of the conference of March 30 bears the notation of April 4: "s'" (with).

58. For Wilhelm's telegrams of April 5/17 and 6/18, see Perepiska Vil'gelma II c Nikolaem II (Correspondence of Wilhelm II with Nicholas II), Moscow, 1923, p. 6.

59. See Sbornik dogovorov i diplomaticheskikh dokumentov po delam Dal'nevo Vostoka. 1895-1905, St. Petersburg, 1906, pp. 1 ff., 63 ff., 89 ff. and McMurray, Treaties and Agreements with and concerning China, Vol. I, p. 52.

60. Witte's notation, on Kuropatkin's report "On the Tasks of the Russian Army in the 20th Century," regarding Kuropatkin's statement that "for the next few years" Russia must "avoid clashes in China with European nations, and to that end limit her sphere to northern China and renounce railway enterprises south of the great wall and particularly in the Yangtse valley."-- The copy of the report with Witte's original notations is preserved in the Kuropatkin collection, in the Tsentrarkhiv. It should also be noted that in the copy of the report preserved in the Witte archives there (No. 269), all Witte's notations are reproduced in the copyist's hand and each notation is signed by Witte himself, but that the one here quoted was left unsigned and was crossed out in the same ink that Witte had used in his signatures.

61. See Perepiska Vil'gel'ma II c Nikolaem II, pp. 7, 8, 9, 15.
62. Ibid., p. 10.

CHAPTER II

1. See Sibirskaia zh. d. v eě proshlom i nastoiashchem, pp. 93-95.

2. See the Finance Minister's motion of November 13, 1892, brought in by Witte at the Special conference for discussing the question of the construction of the Siberian ry., in the above-quoted dossier of Dept. II of the Gen. Chanc. Min. Fin. on this conference.

3. For details see Sibirskaiia zh. d. v eě proshlom i nastoiashchem pp. 233-235 and B.B. Glinskii's Prolog etc., pp. 30-33. A special report on "technical difficulties discovered on the second section of the Trans-Baikal ry. and on the Amur line" is appended to the M.F.'s motion of November 11, 1896, to the Committee of the Siberian rr., No. 4250, "on the question of confirming the charter of the Chinese-Eastern Rr. Company."

4. See the memorandum of the director of the Asiatic department, presented to the minister of foreign affairs in November, 1895--in dossier No. 3 V. Ibid. for the original "Makeev report."

5. At any rate, as late as October 7, 1895, Lobanov, having received word of the Peking government's uneasiness in connection with exploratory operations by Russian engineers in Manchuria, asked Witte to see about discontinuing them; but Witte knew nothing of these operations and suspected that it might be Badmaev's lads at work (his notation on Lobanov's letter was: "Badmaev?") See Ibid.,

6. See Khilkov's report to his majesty of 28 VI, 1896--Ibid.

7. Count Cassini's despatch of April 10, 1896 from Peking--Ibid.

8. See Ibid. for Makeev's telegram of May 25, 1895 to Witte from Vladivostok. "In compliance with the desire" of Witte, Makeev had seen the Tientsin merchant Startsev who had brought this news from Shanghai.

9. For the loan contracts see McMurray, Treaties and Agreements with and concerning China, Vol. I, pp. 11-18--these totalled around 45 million rubles.

10. Article IV of the Shimonoseki treaty: see Sb. dog. i dip. dok. po delam Dal'nevo Vostoka, p. 4.

11. See the copy of Charykov's telegram of April 14/26, 1895 in dossier No. 17 "on the conclusion of foreign loans by China."

12. See Witte's telegram to Mendelssohn of April 15 and Mendelssohn's answering telegram of April 16, 1895 in the same dossier.

13. See Rafalovich's telegram of May 5, 1895 to Witte from Paris.--Ibid.

14. Witte's telegram of May 5, 1895 to Rafalovich--Ibid.

15. Times, June 9/21: telegram from St. Petersburg of June 5/17.

16. This method of procedure on the part of the Chinese is noted by Charykov in the above-quoted report of April 14.

17. See Charykov's despatch of April 20,o.s., from Berlin--in Dos. No. 17.

18. See Die Grosse Politik der Europaischen Kabinette, 1871-1914, IX B., Radolin-Hohenlohe, August 9, 1895--p. 312.

19. Ibid., p. 313.

20. Hoskier's letter of May 18/30 in Dossier No. 17.

21. Rothstein's telegram of May 29, o.s., to Witte from Paris--ibid.

22. This document is a copy of a telegram from Netslin to Rothstein, with the certificatory signature of Rothstein. The copy is stitched into Dossier No. 17 between decodings of two Rothstein telegrams of May 30, o.s., from Paris.

23. The 4 per cent Chinese loan was assumed by a syndicate made up of the following banks: Hottinguer and Co., the Paris-Netherlands, the Credit-Lyonnais, the Central Association for assisting the development of trade and industry in France, the National Discount Office in Paris, the Central Industrial and Mercantile Credit Association, and the Peterburg International and Discount and Loan, the Russian for Foreign Trade and the Volzhsko-Kamskii banks. -- The Declaration regarding the loan is published in Sborn. dogov. i diplom. dokumentov po delam Dal'nevo Vostoka, 1895-1905, St. Petersburg, 1906, pp. 56-60.

24. See Witte's letter of January 17, 1899, to Count M.M. Muravev, in Dos. No. 24 V.

25. See Witte's report to his majesty of July 14, 1895, on the Gen. chanc. Min. Fin.

26. See Witte's letter of January 17, 1899 to Count M.N. Muravev in Dossier No. 24 V.

27. Establishment of the bank was assumed by: Hottinguer and Co., the Paris-Netherlands bank, the Credit-Lyonnais, the National Discount Office and the Peterburg International bank. The fixed capital of the bank was 6 million rubles, of which 3/8 were allocated to Russia and 5/8 to France. But on the central administrative board of the bank 3 members were representatives of the French share-holders, 5 members and the chairman representatives of the Russian. French members of the Board were: Josef Hottinguer, Netslin and Chabrier; Russian: Rothstein, Notgaft, director chanc. min. fin. P.M. Romanov, and for the Far East two local Russian merchants (Startsev and Vladimirov). The Shanghai division of the National Discount office was transferred to the Russo-Chinese bank as of January 1, 1896, the Frenchman Vouillemon stayed on as its director, and a second director was added, the Russian subject Vert. The min. fin. agent D.D. Pokotilov became head of the Tientsin division. See the min. fin.'s report to his majesty of September 30, 1895 on the gen. chanc. min. fin. Negotiations with the French in Paris were conducted by Rothstein; the idea of 3 French members on the Board of the bank met with opposition from the French (see Pokotilov's report of September 19/October 1, 1895 from London in Dos. No. 1, part I.) From a conversation with Dubail, French consul in Shanghai, Pokotilov carried away the impression that the "French were counting on playing the leading role in the bank" (see Pokotilov's report of November 9/21, 1895 from Shanghai in Dos. No. 1, part I.) The hopes of the French were apparently unjustified: 2 years after the founding of the bank, French members of the Board expressed their dissatisfaction with Vert's work in the Shanghai Division on the ground that he persecuted the "French elements in the bank" and hampered its efficiency. Meanwhile from the Russian viewpoint, the Shanghai Division was indebted for its successes to this very Vert. Polkotilov; in this connection, deemed it imperative to "categorically tell the French to leave us in peace and, if dissatisfied

with the functioning of the Russo-Chinese bank, to found one of their own"
(see Pokotilov's telegram of October 20, 1897 in Dossier No. 40, part I).

28. See Witte's report of November 27, with Nicholas's notation
("s'"), in the Dossier "on the setting-up of the special fund, etc," No. 51,
part I., sheets 1 and 2.

29. See Die Grosse Politik der Europaischen Kabinette, IX B.,
Marschall-Hatzfeldt, 4 Mai 1895, No. 2260, p. 284.

30. See Sborn. dog. i dipl. dok. po delam Dal'nevo Vostoka, exchange
of notes, October 6-7/18-19, 1895, between the Russian minister to
Tokyo and the Japanese minister of foreign affairs, p. 64.

31. See ibid., sup. convention of June 8/20, 1895, pp. 14-27. For
commentary see O. Franke, Die Grossmachte in Ostasien von 1894 bis
1914, Braunschweig, 1923, pp. 109-110.

32. As an example, a very early one, of the function of the banking
alliance in Chinese affairs, take Ristelguber's telegram informing
Rothstein, for Netslin, of the concession to the Five-Lille company for
a railway from Tonkin to Lungchow and Nanningfu, since "this may
interest you." See dossier No. 25, part I.

33. See Die Grosse Politik der Europaischen Kabinette, XIV B, Radolin-
Hohenlohe No. 3654 and Schenk von Schweinsberg to the min. for. affairs
in Berlin No. 3655, pp. 18-20.

34. See Count Cassini's despatch of December 16, 1895, No. 74 in
dossier No. 3 V, sheet 29.

35. See Ibid. -- Nicholas II's notation on the original was: "verno"
(true).

36. See McMurray, Treaties and Agreements with and concerning
China, Vol. I, pp. 55-59, contract of March 26, 1896.

37. See the correspondence on the 1896 loan in dossier No. 17, part I,
especially: Witte's telegram of 18 II 1896 to Rafalovich, and the pencilled
draft, in Witte's hand, of leading points. in answer, apparently, to the
French proposal.

38. See ibid., Witte's report to his majesty of February 22, 1896, in
which he begs to present an oral report conjointly with the minister of
foreign affairs.

39. Kapnist's memorandum was sent by him to Witte in a copy dated
"November 1895" and contains a reference to the memorandum and the
concession project. See dossier No. 3 V.

40. We are here using the "summary"of Dukhovsky's note as given
in the reply to it: "Observations of the minister of finance on the note of
the Amur-province governor-general upon the question of the direction
to be taken by the Siberian trunk-line between Trans-Baikal and Vladivostok"--see dossier No. 3 V.

41. Japan "was projecting" railways along the northern shore of the
Korean gulf and on Liaotung, Germany in the person of engineer Kinder
"is now already" construction-director of the Peking-Tientsin line (this
was a mistake: Kinder was an Englishman), France had obtained the right
to build a railway inside Yunnan and was petitioning for a railway in
Kwangsi, London was discussing a project for a Burma-Chinese railway
from Rangoon to Yunnan and the English were trying to get a share in the
building of the Shanghai-Soochow railway.

42. See Cassini's letter of January 30, 1896, to Prince Lobanov, in
dossier No. 3 V.

43. Pokotilov notified Romanov of this from Peking, in a telegram of January 20, 1896. See ibid.

44. See Witte's above-quoted report of February 22, 1896, in dossier No. 17, part I.

45. See Pokotilov's report of April 17/29, 1896 to the minister of finance and his telegram of April 13--in dos. No. 3 V.

46. See the copy of the English text of Bush's concession in dos. No. 3 V. Ibid. for Pokotilov's report of April 17/29 and Cassini's despatch of April 10/22, 1896.

47. See Cassini's despatch of April 10/22, 1896.

48. Memorandum approved by the tsar November 27, 1895, but unpublished. We quote it from an excerpt cited in the publication: Kitaiskaia Vostochnaia zheleznaia doroga. Istoricheskii ocherk (The Chinese Eastern Railway: Historical Sketch) compiled by the chancellery of the Board of the Chinese Eastern Railway Company, Vol, I (1896-1905), St. Petersburg, 1914, pp. 4-5. For what follows see the copy of Cassini's report to Lobanov of April 19 (May 1,) 1896 in dos. No. 3 V.

49. In the documents, excellently preserved in the ministry of finance, relating to secret disbursements for furthering the matter of the Manchurian railway, there exists no trace of any distributions through Cassini or Pokotilov at this time. The assertion that negotiations in Peking "were conducted without the necessary speed and energy" and that the "Chinese government...could not make up its mind to refuse Russia, nor yet to give its consent" (see Prolog etc., p. 33,) is inaccurate. Cassini first raised the question of the railroad in the Tsungli Yamen on April 6 (see Pokotilov's report of April 12/24 of that year in dos. No. 3 V), Cassini's second visit and the refusal of the Chinese followed on April 18 (see Cassini's report of April 19, ibid.)

50. See Pokotilov's reports of February 1/13 and 12/24 from Shanghai, in dos. No. 26.

51. Pokotilov (in his report of November 23/December 5, 1895, dos. No. 1, part 1) noted the "readiness and alacrity with which the Tsungli Yamen gave its consent" to both of these Russian demands. -- The distinction between "intention" and "solicitation" was drawn in a report by a Chinese official published in the paper Sin-ven-bao in which this official gave his reasons for refusing to assume the status of ambassador extraordinary. We quote from Pokotilov's report of February 12, 1896--in dos. No. 26.

52. See Pokotilov's telegram of April 13/25, 1896--in dos. No. 3 V.

53. See Pokotilov's report of March 4 and 11, 1896, in dos. No. 26.

54. The mission's departure from Shanghai was set for March 16 in order to ensure its arrival at Odessa via Port-Said in the middle of April. See Lobanov's letter of March 8, 1896 to Witte--in dos. No. 18 II div. Gen. chanc. min. fin.

55. Pokotilov had given warning that in Peking "foreigners were vying with one another in attempts to seduce the Chinese ministers by bribes" (Pokotilov's report of April 17/29, 1896--in dos. No. 3 V.)

56. See Pokotilov's report of February 1/13, 1896 from Shanghai--in dos. No. 26.

57. See Pokotilov's report of March 11/23 and the special letter of recommendation to Witte from Cassini relative to Grot of February 20, 1896, in dos. No. 26.

58. See Pokotilov's above report of March 11/23.

59. Witte, Vospominaniia, I, p. 39.

60. Ibid, p. 38.

61. See Ukhtomsky's letter of October 26, 1897 to Witte, containing "diary excerpts" relating to the spring of 1896 and in general to the negotiations with Li Hung-chang. The letter deliberately brings out Witte's personal part in the affair, in which he, Ukhtomsky, could scarcely have succeeded without Witte's help--such is the tone of the letter. The "diary excerpts" sometimes become confused with the epistolary form (use direct address: "You") and create the impression of a document written at Witte's request--a method to which Witte also resorted repeatedly later on to substantiate in "documentary" form the various details essential to him of some matter in which he had participated. -- Ukhtomsky's letter is written in another hand and only signed by Ukhtomsky. In dos. No. 18 div. II Gen. Chanc. min. fin. there is a copy of the letter as well as the original.

62. A version, whereby Li Hung-chang went via Odessa rather than via Europe thanks to Witte and despite the indifference of the ministry of foreign affairs, was launched by Witte: see Vospominaniia, I, p. 40 and Prolog etc., p. 35. -- Actually the decision to go first to Russia and afterwards to Europe and America was made independently of the ministry of finance, by agreement with the ministry of foreign affairs, while Li Hung-chang was still in Peking. Only when he boarded ship in Shanghai in the middle of March did Li Hung-chang say that the Black Sea was too rough. But such talk was cut short by Cassini's remark that it would be inconvenient to change the itinerary now. See Pokotilov's reports of February 29, March 4 and 11, 1896 in dos. No. 26, and Lobanov's letter of March 8, in dos. No. 18 Div. II Gen. Chanc. min. fin.

63. See Ukhtomsky's above-quoted letter of October 26, 1897.

64. See Rothstein's letter to Witte of April 22 (May 4), 1896, giving an account of his talk with Grot, in dos. No. 3 V.

65. In speaking of Chinese shareholders, Rothstein expressed himself to the effect that "in such a syndicate there would be room for all" (see ibid).

66. Vospominaniia, I, p. 42.

67. Vospominaniia, I, p. 44.

68. The Moscow treaty of May 22, 1896, being of a secret character was published by us in the review Bor'ba klassov, No. 1-2, Leningrad, 1924, pp. 101 ff. (in English translation almost in its entirety in McMurray, Vol. I, p. 81). It was drawn up in the Chinese and French languages, with the French text regarded as the one to be followed. In dos. No. 20 there exists a copy of the French original, taken by I.P. Shipov at the instance of Witte. We quote this French text in full.

Copie

Sa Majesté l'Empereur de Russie et Sa Majesté l'Empereur de Chine, désirant consolider la paix heureusement rétablie dans l'Extreme Orient et préserver le continent Asiatique d'une nouvelle invasion étrangère, ont décidé de conclure entre Eux une alliance défensive, et ont nommé à cet effet pour Leurs Plénipotentiaires:

Sa Majesté l'Empereur de Russie, le Prince Alexis Lobanow Rostovsky, Son Ministre des Affaires Etrangères, Secrétaire d'Etat,

Sénateur et Conseiller Privé Actuel et le Sieur Serge de Witte, Son
Ministre des Finances, Secrétaire d'Etat et Conseiller Privé, et
     Sa Majesté l'Empereur de Chine, le Comte Li-Hung-Chang, Son
Grand-Secrétair d'Etat, Ambassadeur Extraordinaire et Plénipoten-
tiare près Sa Majesté l'Empereur de Russie,
     Lesquels, après avoir échangé leurs pleins pouvoirs; trouvés en
bonne et due forme, sont convenus des Articles suivants:

Article I.

Toute agression dirigée par le Japon soit contre le territoire Russe
de l'Asie Orientale, soit contre le territoire de la Chine ou celui de
la Corée sera considéré comme devant entrainer l'application im-
médiate du présent traité.

Dans ce cas, les deux Hautes Parties contractantes s'engagent à
se soutenir réciproquement par toutes les forces de terre et de mer
dont Elles pourraient disposer en ce moment et à s'entr'aider autant
que possible pour le ravitaillement de leurs forces respectives.

Article II.

Aussitôt que les deux Hautes Parties contractantes seraient en-
gagées dans une action commune, aucun traité de paix avec la partie
adverse ne pourra être conclu par l'une d'Elles sans l'assentiment
de l'autre.

Article III.

Pendant les opérations militaires, tous les ports de la Chine seront,
en cas de nécessité, ouverts aux bâtiments de guerre Russes, lesquels
y trouveront de la part des autorités Chinoises toute l'assistance dont
ils pourraient avoir besoin.

Article IV.

Afin de faciliter aux troupes Russes de terre l'accès des points
menacés et assurer les moyens de leur subsistance, le Gouvernement
Chinois consent à la construction d'une ligne de chemin de fer à travers
les provinces Chinoises de l'Amour et de Guirin dans le direction de
Vladivostok. La jonction de ce chemin de fer avec le chemin de fer
Russe ne saurait servir de prétexte à aucun empiétement sur le territoire Chinois ni à aucune atteinte aux droits de Souveraineté de Sa
Majesté l'Empereur de Chine. La construction et l'exploitation de ce
chemin de fer seront accordés à la Banque Russo-Chinoise et les
clauses du contrat qui sera conclu à set effet seront dûment débattus
entre le Ministre de Chine à St. Pétersbourg et la Banque Russo-
Chinoise.

Article V.

Il est entendu qu'en temps de guerre prévu par l'article I, la Russie
aura le libre usage du chemin de fer mentionné dans l'article IV pour
le transport et l'approvisionnement de ses troupes. En temps de paix,
la Russie aura le même droit pour le transit de ses troupes et de ses
approvisionnements avec des arrêts qui ne pourront être justifiés par
aucun motif autre que les besoins du service de transport.

Article VI.

Le présent traité entrera en vigueur à partir du jour où le contrat
stipulé à l'article IV aura été confirmé par Sa Majesté l'Empereur de
Chine. Il aura dès lors force et valeur pendant une durée de quinze
années. Six mois avant l'expiration de ce terme, les deux Hautes

Parties contractantes se concerteront sur la prolongation de ce traité.

Fait à Moscou, le 22 Mai 1896.

Signé

Lobanow   Witte

M.P.   M.P.

Space for seal and signature
of Li Hung-chang.

True to the original

Director of the General Chancellery of the Ministry of
Finance I. Shipov.

The present copy, by order of the lord minister of finance, was
made in autograph by the Director of the General Chancellery of the
Minister of Finance, State Counsellor Shipov, November 13, 1897,
in S. Peterburg.

I, Shipov

PROTOCOLE

faisant partie intégrante du traité.

Les Plénipotentiares des deux Hautes Parties contractantes ayant
arrêté les articles du traité conclu ce jour entre la Russie et la Chine,
en ont signé et scellé de leurs sceaux deux exemplaires en langues
Chinoise et Française.

De ces deux textes, dûment confrontés et trouvés concordant, le
texte francais fera foi pour l'interprétation du présent traité.

Fait à Moscou, le 22 Mai 1896.

Signé:

Lobanov   Witte

M.P.   M.P.

Space for seal and signature
of Li Hung-chang

True to the original

Director of the General Chancellery of the Minister of
Finance I. Shipov.

Both documents were entirely copied by hand by P.I. Shipov.

69. See Witte's report to his majesty of May 18, 1896 concerning Li
Hung-Chang's receipt of the proper authorizations and the setting of the
22nd as date for the ceremonial signing of the treaty--in dos. No. 18
Div. II Gen. chanc. min. fin..

70. See Vospominaniia, I, p. 43.

71. See P.M. Romanov's statement to this effect as given in the
secret minute-book of the Special meeting of the Board of the Chinese
Eastern Railway Co. on January 22, 1897, in dos. No. 7, part I. --
See ibid., Witte's letter of August 20, 1897 to Muravev.

72. See ibid.

73. See Witte's report to his majesty of March 3, 1900, in dos. No.
51, part I, sheets 30-31.

74. The original of this protocol is preserved in dos. No. 51, part I.
It is written on plain paper in Rothstein's hand, in the French language,
with graphic corrections in Witte's hand, and had no stamp. The French
language was no doubt for Li Hung-chang. The notation in Witte's hand:

"agreed" was also for him. We quote the text of the protocol:
PROTOCOLE
[in Witte's hand:] "Agreed."
Pour faciliter les negotiations de la fondation du chemin de fer de l'Est en Chine, ainsi que l'exécution de cette affaire, l'administration de la Banque Russo-Chinoise decide ce qui suit:

1) sera assignée une somme jusqu'à concurrence de Roubles Credit 3,000,000 (troid millions) pour dépenses discrétionaires à effectuer dans l'intérêt de l'affaire.

2) la somme assignée ne peut pas être versée qu'aux termes et aux conditions suivantes. On disposera: 1) d'un tiers soit R. Cr. 1,000,000 (million) après la signature et la légalisation complète de la concession et après que la trace de la ligne sera complètement arrêtée et confirmée par les administrations Chinois y ayant droit: 3) de R. 1,000,000 (million) quand la construction de la ligne sera complètement finie.

3) que les sommes en question seront mis à la libre disposition du Prince H.H. Oukhtomsky et M.A. Rothstein qui tout en observant les conditions de l'Article 2, en disposeront contre simple quittance de leur part, sans aucune responsabilité pour eux.

4) que les montants (sommes) prélevées sont à débiter à la nouvelle Compagnie de Chemin de fer de l'Est de la Chine comme frais de construction.

Moskou 23 Mai 1896
(signatures:) Prince Oukhtomsky   P. Romanoff   Rothstein

75. The project of the contract had been transmitted to Peking by telegraph back on May 26, but the Chinese government entrusted the conduct of negotiations with the bank to the Chinese minister in Berlin, Shu Ching-chen. Discussion of the project moved slowly, though no stone was left unturned to facilitate the progress of negotiations: Shu Ching-chen had been given an interest in the matter by assigning him the post of chairman of the Board of the Chinese Eastern Railway Company and Grot had remained in Russia as a link with Li Hung-chang. Threats finally proved indispensable: in July, at Grot's suggestion, the Chinese empress dowager was given to understand that if the contract was not signed, "other combinations would be resorted to and the alliance with China would remain a dead letter" (see Grot's letter of July 3/15, 1896 to Ukhtomsky--in dos. No. 3 V.)

76. See Ukhtomsky's telegram of September 2, 1896 to Witte in Yalta --in dos. No. 51, part I.

77. See Witte's telegram of September 3, 1896 to Ukhtomsky--ibid. -- The technical difficulty about transmitting the money to Grot, then in Peterburg, without special written authorization from Li. Witte thought that the Chinese themselves ought to look after the receipt of the money and suggest means of transfer.

78. See the report presented by Witte to his majesty on May 18, 1896 in connection with the agreement project--in dos. No. 18 div, II Gen. Chanc. min. fin. The report is in Witte's handwriting. Nicholas II's notation was: "It seems to me that it will be possible for you to sign the convention in such a form." The agreement as projected was in 14 articles. Of these, 13 (all but the 4th) afterwards went into the Charter of the Chinese Eastern Railway Company.

79. See Pokotilov's telegram of June 3/15, 1896 from Peking, to the effect that these items of information were being received by the French minister "from Moscow and Peterburg." (dos. No. 3 V)

80. See the Russo-Chinese bank's petition of November 4, 1896, addressed to the minister of finance and signed by Ukhtomsky and Rothstein --in dos. No. 3 V.

81. This detail is brought out in Istoricheskaia spravka o sobytiiakh na Dal'nem Vostoke s 1895 po 1903 g. (Historical Record of Events in the Far East, 1895-1903), compiled to Witte's order in the chancellery Min. Fin. Glinskii's Prolog etc. in reprinting the Record omits this detail.

82. See Rothstein's letter of December 17 to Witte--in dos. No. 7, part I. "Excellence, la souscription a eu lieu ce matin à 9 heures par une affluence considérable d'employés et a dû être clôturé quelques minutes après l'ouverture. Du public nous n'en avons pas vu l'ombre."

83. See above, p. 44 for quotations from the report on treasury receipts and disbursements in the Far East, 1897-1902.

84. We quote in full the text of the order (See dos. No. 51, part I:)

To our Minister of Finance.

On the basis of §9 of the Charter of the Chinese Eastern Railway Company as approved by the Throne, and by your agreement with said Company, it acquired from the Russian government, cred. surveys for the course of the railway in Manchuria conducted by the Ministry of Means of Communication, 4,000,000 rubles, repayment by the Company of said sum to be made at dates to be set by you.

We graciously command you to deduct from the amount of the said 4,000,000 rub., three million rubles for a special fund designed to cover disbursements connected with issuance of the concession for the Chinese Eastern Railway, one million rubles to revert to revenue of the treasury. The available sums of the said fund of three-million to be kept in a special account in the State bank or in some private bank, at your discretion, and withdrawals from this fund not to be made otherwise than with Our special authorization upon each occasion.

85. On January 31, 1897, the Finance Committee of the Board of the Chinese Eastern Railway Company resolved: "to place the first 3,000,000 rubles to be deposited on Chinese Eastern Railway Company shares in the Russo-Chinese bank, to the order of the minister of finance." The resolution of this same committee as to the yield from remaining deposits on shares to the sum of 4,500,000 rubles and the carrying of 3 million rubles of this on a special account to the order of the minister of finance was taken on March 15, 1897--see ibid.

86. See Rothstein's telegram of August 16 from Berlin, and Witte's of August 18, 1896 to Berlin, in dos. No. 3 V.

87. See Witte's telegram to Berlin on August 23, 1896--in dos. No. 3 V.

88. See the min. fin.'s speech of November 11, 1896 to the Siberian Railway Committee "on the question of confirming the Charter of the Chinese Eastern Railway Company," p. 7.

89. The basic error of this calculation is contingent on the fact that the bonded capital of the company is taken, for all 36 years, with the construction cost of the road figured at 115 million rubles. Meanwhile only to 1901, the bonded capital amounted to 272,895,200 rubles. In

fact, by the 10th year of operation, the indebtedness of the company to
the Russian government came to 733,297,212 rubles, 24 kopecks--see
"report on the Company's debt to the government to December 31, 1914,"
in dos. No. 1 supplement, lit. III.

90. See article 12 of the contract.

91. The right of the Chinese government to deposit this sum in the
Russo-Chinese bank was established both by the contract for the building
of the road and by a special agreement with the bank. For a reference
to this special agreement, see the above-mentioned "speech" of November 11, 1896, by the min. fin., p. 9.. The text of this agreement, ac-
curacy not guaranteed, is printed in McMurray, Vol. I, p. 78.

92. The only Chinese--president of the Board of the Company--was
strictly limited in his functions, which were: 1) looking after the fulfillment of the Company's obligations to the Chinese government, 2) representation of the Company in its dealings with central and local Chinese
authorities (art. 1 of the contract.)

93. Arts. 11 and 16 of the charter of the Company.

94. Both article 4 of the Russian government's agreement of May 18,
1896 with the bank and the agreement between the Russo-Chinese bank
and the State bank as to the loan on the shares were kept secret.

95. See the above-quoted speech of November 11, 1896 by the Min.
fin., pp. 6-10.

96. In the "explanatory note to the project of the charter" (pp. 4-7)
the necessity is pointed out of special treatment of the question of judicial
organization in the territory of the road. Later, the question was settled
by the introduction, by agreement with local authorities, of mixed Russo-
Chinese tribunals (Kiao-she-chui.)

97. See "explanatory note, etc.," p. 7.

98. See the commentary on art. 3 in the "explanatory note to the
project of the Charter of the Chinese Eastern Railway Company," pp. 2-3.

CHAPTER III

1. Witte, Vospominaniia, I, p. 116.

2. Compare Witte's speech at the conference of March 30, 1895, and
his strictures upon Dukhovsky's memorandum (see above, pp. 72-74 and
99-100.) -- Cf. also O. Franke, Die Grossmächte in Ostasien von 1894
bis 1914, pp. 105-145 ("Die Sphären-Politik 1895-1900") and M. Bau, The
Foreign Relations of China, pp. 37-62 ("The International Struggle for
Concessions, 1895-1911").

3. In July, 1905, Nicholas II charged Richter and Cherevansky, members of the state council, "to acquaint themselves with the data existing
in various departments as to the government's activity in the Far East
precedent to the war with Japan, starting from the moment when the idea
of our occupation of Port Arthur originated" and "on the basis of these
materials ascertain the causes that led to our military clash with Japan,"
See our article "Kontsessiia na Yalu" (The Yalu Concession), in the
collection, Russkoe proshloe (Russia's Past), No. 1, pp. 88-89.

4. See Die Grosse Politik der Europaischen Kabinette, Vol. 14, first
half, No. 3663, p. 31.

5. See, in dos. No. 40, part I, Pokotilov's telegram of March 19,
1897, from Peking, to the effect that "during his sojourn in England Li
Hung-chang made the most sweeping promises to representatives of the
English industrial world, inviting them to come to China."

6. The French text of the treaty of May 22, 1896 was quoted in the
Daily Telegraph of 15/11 1910 without the introductory and concluding
sections, without date, and without the "protocol." See McMurray,
Treaties and Agreements, Vol. I, p. 81.
    7. "Cassini's convention" is reprinted in McMurray's Treaties and
Agreements, Vol. I, pp. 79-81.
    8. A notice concerning this plan appeared in the North China Herald
of April 7/19, 1895.
    9. For further details see O. Franke, Die Grossmächte in Ostasien,
pp. 114-115.
    10. Ibid., p. 115: "mann kann ohne Ubertreibung von einem völligen
Zusammenbruch der japanischen Politik in Korea sprechen."
    11. For the Seoul memorandum see Sb. Dog. i diplom. dokum, po
delam Dal'nevo Vostoka. 1895-1905 gg., St. Petersburg, 1906, pp. 146
ff.
    12. See Lamsdorf's memorandum "Apropos of [Vogak's] memorandum
on the significance of the treaty of March 26, 1902 in the development
of the Manchurian question"--presented to Nicholas after May 7, 1903--
in dos. No. 120.
    13. See preceding note.
    14. The Moscow protocol of May 28/June 9, 1898 is published in Sborn.
dogovorov i diplomaticheskikh dokumentov po delam Dal'nevo Vostoka.
1895-1905, St. Petersburg, 1906, pp. 159 ff. -- The secret articles of
the protocol were published in full by B.E. Nolde: see his Vneshniaia
politika. Istoricheskie ocherki (Foreign policy: Historical essays),
Petrograd, 1915, pp. 246-247, note; cf. text of these in dos. No. 20.
    15. See, in dos. No. 20, the text of the "points in reply to the Korean
ambassador," with Lobanov's covering letter to Witte of June 1896,
stating that they were "approved by his majesty."
    16. For the government's statement, see Sborn. dog. i dip. dokum.
po delam Dal'nevo Vostoka, pp. 161 ff.
    17. See Vosp.,I, pp. 59-60.
    18. See Vosp., I, p. 117.
    19. See Vosp., I, pp. 59-60; negotiations in connection with "the
direct breach of the Lobanov agreement" were conducted on the Japanese
side by Count Hayashi--see "Zapiski Hayashi" (Hayashi Memoranda),
in Izv. MID, 1913, book V, p. 336. To the connection between the unfortunate turn of events for Japan in Korea and the broadening of her
military program the Russian ministry of foreign affairs itself testified,
in Obzor snoshenii po koreiskim delam s 1895 g. (Survey of communications on Korean affairs from 1895), St. Petersburg, 1906, p. 5.
    20. See Vosp., I, pp. 117-118.
    21. See Pokotilov's telegram of March 27, 1896 from Shanghai, in
dos. No. 29/1-b. In reporting that the Americans had obtained the concession for a Seoul-Chemulpo railway, Pokotilov pointed out that "the
success of promoters of other nationalities is desirable from the Russian standpoint," in view of the predominant economic influence of the
Japanese.
    22. See Weber's telegram of June 1896 from Seoul, in dos. No. 5,
part I: 1) as to the Fives-Lille Company's secret offer to the Korean
government of a loan of 5 million and 2) as to the invitation to Seoul of
an employe of an English bank in Shanghai--in view of the project founding of a private bank in Seoul.

23. See ibid., Lobanov's letter of June 22, 1896 to Witte.

24. A telegram ordering him to proceed to Seoul "without delay" as representative of the min. fin. was delivered to Pokotilov in Peking on June 25, 1896--see dos. No. 5, part I. -- Meanwhile, in July, as has been shown, Peking was still erecting obstacles in the matter of working out the contract for the Manchurian trunk-line. Cf. the above-quoted letter of July 3/5, 1896, from V. Grot to Ukhtomsky(in dos. No. 3 V) as to the necessity of threatening the Peking government with a break to compel it to agree to accept the terms of the railway contract.

25. Rumors of negotiations between the Korean government and an English bank in Shanghai had been current in Peking back in June--see telegrams of June 22 from Cassini and Pokotilov in dos. No. 5, part I-- Pokotilov arrived in Seoul on August 2 and stayed there until early November. We here have in view his telegrams of August 9, 13, 26 and 27 (see ibid).

26. See ibid.: Witte's telegram of September 3 to Romanov from Yalta, with regard to suspending the whole matter until November, Pokotilov's telegrams of September 16 and October 30, Lamsdorf's letter of September 24 to the min. fin., Witte's letter of November 2, 1896 to the min. for. afs..

27. See "Zametka o zheleznykh dorogakh Korei g-na Möllendorfa" (Mr. Mollendorf's note on Korean railways) in dos. No. 29/Ia. Mollendorf, as adviser to the Korean government, pursued a Russophile policy in the 80's and at that time presented a report on the necessity of postponing the construction of railways.

28. See Pokotilov's telegrams from Seoul of August 26, 1896, on the concession solicitations of the French engineer Grille, and of October 3 on the necessity of the revocation of the order of July 3, issued "thanks to American influence and the weakness and complaisance of our chargé d'affaires." Pokotilov on this occasion reproached the chargé d'affaires with support "goodness knows why" of the American influence in Korea. These telegrams are in dos. No. 29/Ia.

29. See ibid., letter of mgr. MFA Shishkin to MF, of Sept. 16, 1896.

30. See ibid., Witte's letter of October 10 to Shishkin and Shishkin's answer.

31. See ibid., "Zametka o. zh. d. Korei g-na Möllendorfa," supplied to the business manager of the Military-Instruction Committee of the General Staff by Vogak, military agent in China, in a letter of December 18/30, 1896. Mollendorf proposed that Russia should assume the guarantee "of at least one half of the interest," and pointed out that 1) "the Americans were least dangerous from a political standpoint" and 2) that Russia "would be afforded unimpeded transport of troops to the shores of the Japan Sea."

32. See, in dos. No. 11 a, Alekseev's telegram of January 8, 1898 to Witte concerning the constituted decree of the Korea government relative to the unlimited extension of the prohibitory order.

33. See, in dos. No. 29/Ib: Pokotilov's telegram of June 23, 1897 from Peking, Witte's letter of July 1 to Muravev, Pokotilov's telegram of July 23 proposing the purchase of all the American company's shares (Witte's notation: "decision difficult,") Witte's letter of July 29 to Muravev, Pokotilov's telegram of July 30 as to the necessity of a definite answer (Witte: "reply that I am apprehensive of stepping in, for fear of losses.")

34. See, in dos. No. 5, part I, Pokotilov's report of November 4, 1896 from Seoul.

35. See Witte's notation on Muravev's letter of January 30, 1897, in dos. No. 5/I.

36. See ibid., Witte's letter of February 12, 1897 to Muravev.

37. See Muravev's letter of March 8, same year--ibid.

38. See ibid., Pokotilov's telegram of March 8 from Peking; according to his advices,"since the king's removal from our embassy our position has deteriorated."

39. See Pokotilov's letter of April 9/21, 1897 to Rothstein, in dos. No. 7, part I, to the effect that "the state of things has noticeably altered in Korea," that "the Korean government has altered its opinion on the Russian loan," and that 1 million had been allocated to the payment of the Japanese debt. -- On the forthcoming payment of a second million see his telegram of May 22, 1897 to the min. fin. in dos. No. 5/I.

40. See the report of February 6, 1898 from Alekseev, Russian financial agent in Korea, in dos. No. 11/a.

41. See, in dos. No. 11-a: Witte's report to his majesty of May 9, 1897 on the appointment of K.A. Alekseev as commercial agent to Korea, Witte's letter of May 19 to Muravev and Muravev's letter of June 3, 1897 to Witte.

42. See, in dos. No. 5/I: Pokotilov's telegrams of February 2 and 17, 1897, from Peking, as to the necessity of promising Korea a loan to enable her to begin negotiations with Japan on the subject of pre-term payment, and Muravev's letter of March 8 of the. same year.

43. No reply of Witte's to Muravev's letter of March 8 exists in the min. fin. files.

44. Resolution inscribed on Pokotilov's telegram of February 17.

45. See, in dos. No. 13, the rough draft, in Romanov's hand, of the bases of the charter of the bank, and his reports to the minister of finance of March 27 and March 8, 1897.

46. See Witte's notation to this effect on the report of March 8--ibid.

47. In the report of May 9, Witte explained his choice simply on the ground that a person familiar with "the office of customs" was needed in Korea.

48. The instructions to the commercial agent, preserved in the form of a leave of absence in dossier No. 11-a, are date June 10.

49. See, in dossier No. 11-a, Weber's telegram of June 5, 1897 from Seoul, addressed to the min. for. afs. Weber surmised that Alekseev ought to start by setting in order the palace administration's finances.

50. See the historical sketch published by the chancellery of the Board of the Chinese Eastern Railway Company: Kitaiskaia Vostochnaia zhel. dor. (The Chinese Eastern Railway), Vol. I (1896-1905), St. Petersburg, 1914, pp. 49-50.

51. See, in dos. No. 51, part I, Witte's telegram of September 3, 1896, to Ukhtomsky from Yalta.

52. Certain observations on Ukhtomsky's journey were made by us in the study of the "Li Hung-chang Fund" in the periodical Bor'ba klassov, 1924, No. 1-2, p. 109.

53. See, in dos. No. 7, part I, the "Minutes of the Special session of the Board of the Chinese Eastern Railway Company," on the date indicated. Vice-president Kerbedz presided, present were members of the

board P.M. Romanov, Prince Ukhtomsky, E.K. Tsigler and Ia. G. Alekseev, chief engineer A.I. Yugovich and his assistant S.V. Ignatsius.

54. See above, p. 157, P.M. Romanov's report of March 8.

55. See, in dos. No. 7, part I, Witte's letter of January 29, 1897, to Muravev.

56. See above, Muravev's letter of March 8, 1897 to Witte.

57. This is how Romanov, in his report of March 8, justified the participation of the Chinese Eastern Railway in the Russo-Korean bank. He suggested for the purpose a corresponding increase in the amount of the first bonded loan of the Chinese Eastern Railway as then proposed.

58. Such, for example, as the question of what currency would be mandatory for payments in Manchuria, discussed in the conference of January 22, and as to a second Peking member of the board.

59. See, in dos. No. 7, part I, the "List of Questions for Clarification with Peking through Prince Ukhtomsky and engineer Tsigler," bearing Witte's notation of March 14 as to "confirmation by his majesty"; it is preserved in collated copy.

60. This occurred during the days immediately following the entry of German ships into Kiaochow: having heard of the alleged desire of the Chinese government to set about building a railway in southern Manchuria, Rothstein telegraphed Pokotilov on November 5/17, 1897, to the effect that if there was talk of extending the railway from Shanhaikwan to Mukden, he begged him to attempt to secure construction for the Russo-Chinese bank. See dos. No. 13.

61. See, in dos. No. 51, part I, Ukhtomsky's telegram of May 3/15, 1897, from Shanghai.

62. See, in dos. No. 7, part I, Pokotilov's telegram of May 27, 1897 from Peking.

63. Ibid., Ukhtomsky's telegram of June 4, 1897.

64. Ibid., Romanov's telegram of June 6 inquiring why there was still no answer from the Chinese as to the branch to a Korean port, and ordering that "this question be raised."

65. Ibid., Pokotilov's report of June 8 of the current year. On the question of the southerly route the Chinese expressed readiness to enjoin the chiang-chûns of both provinces to cooperate with builders in the construction of the line by the southerly route.

66. See same Pokotilov report of June 8, 1897.

67. See ibid., Muravev's letter of August 18, 1897 to Witte.

68. See, in dos. No. 7, part I, Muravev's letter to Witte of August 18, 1897, No. 253 and in dos. No. 10, part I, the August 10 report of the chargé d'affaires in Peking.

69. See Pokotilov's above-cited report of June 8, in dos. No. 7, part I.

70. See, in dos. No. 10, part I, Witte's letter of August 11 to Muravev and the August 10 report of the chargé d'affaires in Peking.

71. See, in dos. No. 7, part I, Muravev's letter of August 18 to Witte.

72. See same letter. -- Emphases are ours.

73. See, in dos. No. 7, part I, Witte's letter of August 20, 1897.

74. See, in dos. No. 10, part I, Muravev's letter of August 23, 1897.

75. See, in dos. No. 10, part I, the reports of Pokotilov of August 11 and of the chargé d'affaires of August 10, 1897: the Chinese asked for a loan of 200 thousand lan.

76. See ibid., Witte's letter of August 22 to Muravev.

77. See ibid., Witte's letter of October 11, 1897 to Lamsdorf.

78. See, in dos. No. 40, Vol. I, Pokotilov's telegrams of September 6 and March 19, 1897. Morgan himself came to Shanghai for negotiations in the winter of 1896-1897.

79. See ibid., Pokotilov's report of December 3/15, 1897: while shadowing Shackley's journey through Southern Manchuria, Pokotilov decided to resort to threat, and advised "a friend of Shackley's to amicably warn him that any intention on the part of the English to undertake anything serious in Manchuria might cause various disagreeable complications which would hardly have a salutary effect on the development of any industrial enterprise."

80. See, in dos. No. 11-a, Alekseev's telegram of September 18, 1897 from Seoul, concerning the formation "of a new cabinet" headed by a personage "devoted to Russia," and mentioning that the "temporary coolness has unquestionably ended."

81. See ibid., Alekseev's telegram of October 16 and his private letter to Romanov of October 22, 1897.

82. See ibid., Alekseev's telegram of October 14, when the order for Brown's removal was given, and the text of the contract signed October 24, 1897.

83. See the finance minister's speech of November 11, 1897 to the Finance Committee on the establishment of the Russo-Korean bank--in dos. No. 13.

84. See, in dos. No. 11-a, Pokotilov's telegram of Oct. 13, 1897 from Peking as to the protest of the English minister in Seoul and Hart's telegram to Brown: "stand firm, can confide in intervention by other powers." Ibid., Witte's letters of Oct. 24 and Nov. 20, same year, to Muravev.

85. See ibid., Romanov's telegram of Oct. 17 to Alekseev, and in dos. No. 13 a series of documents from which it appears that on Oct. 16 Witte approved the charter of the bank (with directors Ukhtomsky, Romanov, Notgaft, Vert, Pokotilov, Alekseev and Rothstein) on Oct. 20 the founders (Rothstein, Notgaft, the Belgian Cox, Ukhtomsky and Kerbedz) applied for confirmation of the charter, on Oct. 31 the tsar ordered immediate presentation of the charter to the Finance Committee; on Nov. 11 it was introduced there; on Nov. 30 the Finance Committee decreed that the charter be presented to the tsar for confirmation, accorded on Dec. 5, and on Dec. 11 petition was entered for opening a branch of the bank in Seoul.

86. See, in dos. No. 11-a, Alekseev's report of Jan. 18, 1898.

87. Ibid., Muravev's letters to Witte of Nov. 26 and 29, 1897, and his telegram of Dec. 11 of that year to Shpeier in Seoul.

88. In compensation for the successes France had attained by the agreement of June 20, 1895 in the south of China, England obtained from China, by the agreement of Feb. 4, 1897, the rectification of the Burma-Chinese boundary and the right to build a railway from Burma to Yunnan. Then France, in her turn, secured in the declaration of March 15, 1897 China's pledge not to alienate to any other power the island of Hainan (in the gulf of Tonkin).

89. Die Gross Politik der Europäischen Kabinette, 1871-1914, Berlin, 1924, Vol. 14, 1st half: No. 3654, 3655, 3659, 3663, 3664, 3666, 3668, 3672.

90. See Ibid., No. 3677, Radolin-Hohenlohe, from St. Petersburg, July 8, n.s., 1897.

91. See Ibid., No. 3679, Bulow's telegram of Aug. 11, n.s., 1897 from St. Petersburg to the min. for. afs. in Berlin giving a resume of the Peterhof negotiations.

92. See Ibid., No. 3679.

93. See Ibid., No. 3682, Radolin-Hohenlohe, of Sept. 21, n.s., 1897 from St. Petersburg.

94. See Ibid., No. 3684, Heyking of Sept. 19/Oct. 1, 1897 from Peking to the min. for. afs. in Berlin.

95. See Ibid., No. 3685, Tschirsky-Hohenlohe, of October 2/14, 1897, from St. Petersburg.

96. The murder of the missionaries in Shantung took place on Oct. 23/ Nov. 4, 1897. The order to Admiral Diedrichs to proceed to Kiaochow was prepared by Wilhelm on Oct. 25/Nov. 6, the day this news was received in Berlin. See Ibid., No. 3686, 3687, 3689; Perepiska Vil'gel'ma II c Nikolaem II (Correspondence of Wilhelm II and Nicholas II), pub. Tsentrarkhiv, Moscow, 1923, p. 21.

97. See Die Grosse Politik, Vol. 14, 1st half, No. 3693, Muravev's telegrams of Nov. 8 and 9, n.s., 1897 to the Russian ambassador in Berlin.

98. Ibid., No. 3693, Tschirsky's telegram of Nov. 9, n.s., 1897 from St. Petersburg.

99. Ibid., p. 74, Wilhelm's notations on Tschirsky's telegram of Nov. 9.

100. Ibid., No. 3694, 3695, 3697, 3699 (Muravev's telegram of Nov. 1/ 13, 1897 for transmittal to the min. for. afs. in Berlin).

101. Ibid., No. 3700.

102. Ibid., No. 3706, Muravev's telegram of Nov. 4/16, 1897; B.A. Romanov's "Witte i kontsessiia na Yalu" (Witte and the Yalu concession), Sborn. statei, posv. S.F. Platonov (Collection of Articles Dedicated to S.F. Platonov), Petrograd, 1922, p. 434). Cf. Pokotilov's report of Nov. 11/23, in dos. No. 9.

103. Of the "straining" of Russo-German relations Hohenlohe spoke on November 4/16: Die Grosse Politik, ibid., No. 3702, telegram to Hatzfeldt in London; see also No. 3708, Hatzfeldt's telegram to Berlin of November 5/17, 1897.

104. See our study: "Witte i kontsessiia na Yalu," p. 434. -- Back on Nov. 10/22 Heyking had informed Berlin that Russian and French representatives in Peking were advising the Tsungli Yamen to spin out the negotiations with Germany, in order to force her in the long run to evacuate Kiaochow: see Die Grosse Politik, ibid., No. 3716.

105. See Die Grosse Politik, ibid., No. 3707, Hohenlohe's report to Wilhelm of Nov. 6/18, 1897 and No. 3711, the note of the German min. for. afs. transmitted to Osten-Saken on Nov. 10/22.

106. See the copy of the Muravev memorandum in dos. No. 33.

107. See, in dos. No. 33 Witte's notation on the Muravev memorandum of November 11.

108. See Die Grosse Politik, Vol. 14, 1st half, p. 104, note, Radolin's letter of November 14/16 to von Bülow.

109. See Witte's "self-penned memorandum" of November 15, 1897 in dos. No. 9, sheets 13 ff.

110. See Vosp. I, p. 109.

111. See Prolog etc., p. 49.

112. See, in dos. No. 33, Pokotilov's telegram of Nov. 4, 1897 saying that he was endeavoring "to profit by this moment to compose the misunderstandings between the Chinese Eastern Railway and the governor-general of Kirin."

113. See ibid., Pokotilov's report of November 5, 1897.

114. See ibid., Pokotilov's telegram of November 16, 1897.

115. See in dossier No. 20 Pokotilov's telegram of Nov. 23/Dec. 5, 1897.

116. See Die Grosse Politik, Vol. 14, 1st half, No. 3735, Heyking's telegram of Dec. 16, 1897 from Peking to the min. for. afs. in Berlin.

117. See in dossier No. 33 Pokotilov's telegram of Nov. 28, 1897.

118. See in dossier No. 15, part I, Pokotilov's telegram of Dec. 2/14, 1897.

119. See, in dossier No. 15, part II, the "report on the question of the conclusion of a foreign loan by the Chinese government."

120. See, in dossier No. 15, part I, Ukhtomsky's telegram of June 1/13: "The loan in combination with other excellent conditions would give us quite exclusive predominance," and Witte's answering telegram: "to consummate loan at present time...very difficult matter.... But for discussion of this matter necessary to know what will be real guarantee--for a guarantee based on revenues collected by the Chinese themselves without any sort of control is a faction.... If the question is of our guarantee ...this can scarcely be made without the most substantial and entirely material benefits for Russia."

121. See Witte's telegram of December 4, 1897 to Pokotilov, in dossier No. 20. Besides the items quoted in the text, Witte demanded of China: 1) that she "confirm unconditionally the authorization for the southerly route of the Chinese Eastern Railway," 2) "permanently eliminate without exception all difficulties made by local authorities as to alienation of land, obtaining of materials for construction." 3) "release gratis all government lands needed for construction of the road, as well as government materials" and 4) remove obstacles to the navigation of a Chinese Eastern Railway flotilla on the Sungari and all affluents.

122. The covenant of organization of the "Syndicat pour l'exploitation des richesses minières en Chine" was signed by the founders on June 14, 1897. The capital of the Syndicate was set at 500 thousand rubles. On the committee of the Syndicate were: Petrokokino, Rothstein, Nerpin, Filipev, Pokotilov and Grot. Revenues were to be allocated as follows: 50 per cent to share-holders, proportionately with the number of shares, 22-1/2 per cent to the Russian Gold-mining Company, 5 per cent to members of the Committee. The Syndicate was organized at the proposal of Grot, who had in his own name taken out a concession for gold-mining in Mongolia. In 1900, the Syndicate was reorganized as the Joint-stock "Mining Company of the Tushetukhan and the Tsetsenkian aimaks in Mongolia" (see dossier No. 23, part I).

123. See, in dos. No. 20, Witte's telegram of December 11, same year, to Pokotilov.

124. News of the entry of Russian ships into Port Arthur was received in Peterburg on December 2. Nicholas notified Witte in advance as to his decision to occupy Port Arthur: see Vosp., I, p. 110.

125. See, in dossier No. 116, Muravev's December 7 telegram of thanks to Pavlov in Peking "for the perfectly friendly reception given our ships at Port Arthur" and in dossier No. 33 Pokotilov's telegram of December 10, 1897.

126. See Pokotilov's telegram of December 7, 1897, in dossier No. 15, part I, and his report of December 8, same year, on the meeting with Li Hung-chang, in dossier No. 20.

127. See, in dossier No. 33, Pokotilov's telegrams of December 10 and 11, 1897. At Witte's request (ibid., telegram of Dec. 8) Pokotilov made "careful inquiries" into Li Hung-chang's "real" attitude toward the occupation of Port Arthur, and was convinced that he "fully trusted" in Russia's having no intention of seizure.

128. See, in dossier No. 33, Pokotilov's telegrams of December 7/19 and December 10/22, 1897.

129. See ibid. Pokotilov's telegrams: of December 18/30, concerning the English loan proposal, the "abrupt change" of attitude toward Russia at the Tsungli Yamen, and the request by the Chinese that we give a written certificate; of December 17, about the concentration of the English and Japanese squadrons; of Dec. 21, as to the demand for a written certificate; of Dec. 25, on the change of attitude toward the English in Port Arthur.

130. See, in dossier No. 33, Pokotilov's telegram of December 21, 1897. Pokotilov called attention then and there to the fact that if Russia should give a written pledge without receiving the same from China relative to the December 4 demands and without stating that she "would infallibly obtain" their fulfillment, the Chinese would interpret it as "cowardly fear of Japan."

131. See in dossier No. 116 Muravev's telegram of December 23, 1897 to Pavlov.

132. See, in dossier No. 33, Pokotilov's telegram of December 27 and in dossier No. 20 his telegram of the same date giving Li Hung-chang's answer verbatim.

133. See, in dossier No. 20, the "project of a telegram to Pavlov drawn up by the lord minister of finance," and in dossier No. 15, part I, Muravev's letter of December 30, 1897 to Witte saying that he was "today" sending this project on "without change."

134. See, in dossier No. 15, part I, Pokotilov's telegrams of December 28 and 29, 1897.

135. On the opening of Talienwan see, in Pokotilov's telegram of December 28 (dossier No. 15, part I), the rumor of the opening of cities on the Hungkiang in Kwangsi and the Siangkiang in Hunan; on the pledge to make concessions to no country except England in the Yangtse valley, see his telegram of December 29 (ibid;) on January 6, 1898 the French notified the Tsungli Yamen that if the English were given "privileges in the administration of finances and mines," France would make demands relative to the southern provinces of China (Pokotilov's telegram of January 7, in dossier No. 15, part I;) it was Pokotilov who sent word about English ships at Port Arthur (see, for example, in dossier No. 33, the telegrams of December 25 and January 4, 1898).

136. On January 3, Muravev, in alluding to this possibility, had proposed that in this case Pavlov demand pledges from the Chinese "not to place at the exclusive use of any country any revenues of the Chinese treasury whatsoever" (telegram in dossier No. 15, part I).

137. See, in dos. No. 51, part II, Muravev's telegram of January 8, and in dos. No. 116 his second telegram of the same date.

138. See, in dos. No. 51, part II, Muravev's telegram of January 9, 1898 to Pavlov in Peking (published in Kr. Arkhiv, Vol. II, section 287, in the form of the "project" of the telegram; this "project" differs only slightly from the text actually sent to Pavlov and forwarded in copy to the min. fin.) and Witte's telegram of January 10, 1898 to Pokotilov (autographic draft).

139. On January 11 Pavlov and Pokotilov summoned Li Hung-chang to the embassy and offered him 500 thousand lan to arrange the loan. Li "promised full cooperation" and "gave us to understand that provided we should find it possible to arrange the loan at the exchange rate of 100 upon issuance [as the English proposed to do], he could practically guarantee success" (see Pavlov's and Pokotilov's telegrams of January 12--in Kr. Arkhiv, Vol. II, pp. 288 and 289). On January 12 a like profession was also made to Pavlov in the Tsungli Yamen. But following a conference between the Tsungli Yamen and the English minister on that same day "the ministers charged Li Hung-chang to request our chargé to renounce the continuance of negotiations as to the loan." However Li "declined to perform this mission." On the 13th, the Russians again summoned Li and promised to raise the "fee" to over a million rubles provided he arranged the dispatch of Sui Chin-chen, president of the Board of the Chinese Eastern Railway, to Peterburg for negotiations (see Pokotilov's telegram of January 13--in dos. No. 51, part II).

140. See, in dos. No. 116, Staal's telegram of Jan. 12/24, 1898.

141. See, in dos. No. 20, Pokotilov's telegram of January 14, 1898.

142. See ibid. Pokotilov's 1st and 2nd telegrams of January 14, 1898. Cf. also the following telegram of Baron Morenheim, Russian ambassador to Paris, of January 14: "Hanotaux attaches enormous importance to the question of the Anglo-Chinese loan, the success of which it would be very important to counteract by exerting pressure in Peking. He thinks that no system of compensations would be capable of counterbalancing the advantages that England would gain. He would be pleased if the imperial cabinet thought it possible to vote in favor of a project for making the loan international, with the participation of all the interested powers, not excepting, in case of need, Japan. He earnestly requested me to submit this opinion to the consideration of Your Excellency" (dos. No. 51, part II).

143. Witte's telegram of January 21, 1898 to Pokotilov in dos. No. 20.

144. Staal's telegram was sent to Witte by Muravev in copy, for comment. Witte answered Muravev in a letter of January 15.

145. See Die Grosse Politik, Vol. 14, 1st half, No. 3751 and 3753, Hatzfeldt's reports of January 10/22 and 14/26, 1898 from London. -- Hatzfeldt had the impression that London understood perfectly that Russia's chief concern was not Port Arthur and the Siberian railway at all but "to get hold of a very considerable part of the Chinese empire and cut it off altogether from world trade." Cf. ibid., p. 147, the quotation from the January 17 speech of Hicks-Beech, chancellor of the exchequer: "the government is firmly resolved at any price, and, if necessary, by force to keep the Chinese market open to itself." On the other hand Salisbury declared to Hatzfeldt that he found Russia's conduct with respect to Port Arthur "thus far" essentially "correct," and impressed this view on the Japanese ambassador as well.

146. Li Hung-chang had informed Witte back on December 27 that China would need money in March 1898.

147. See Witte's above-quoted telegram of January 21, 1898 to Pokotilov, in dos. No. 20.

148. See, in dos. No. 20, Pokotilov's telegram of January 21, 1898.

149. See the copy of the document so titled, bearing the tsar's notation of consent, in dos. No. 116.

150. See, in dos. No. 20, Lamsdorf's letter of February 4, 1898 to Witte. -- His letter of February 9 carries an enclosure--the text of the English loan terms with Russian corrections (enclosures to the letter of February 4 have not been preserved in the dossier). On 4 out of the 5 English terms the following comments were made by Russia: 1) on the right of British subjects to use their own steamship communication on the internal waters of China--that this must be made to refer to central and southern China, 2) on the right to lay English railways from Burma to the Yangtse valley--that it was necessary to point out that this would infringe on the interests of France, 3) on the opening of the ports of Nanning, Siangtan and Talienwan--that Talienwan should be omitted, since we cannot discuss it until final agreement with China, 4) on the zone exempt from the levy of likin in the region of the open ports--that the same privileges ought to be given us in the region of the Manchurian railway. Only the 5th term, as to non-alienation of the Yangtse valley, evoked no comment.

151. See, in dos. No. 20, Muravev's telegram of Feb. 8, 1898 to Pavlov. The loan terms presented to the Russian min. for. afs. by the English ambassador were already "considerably easier than those originally telegraphed us by Pavlov and Pokotilov" (Lamsdorf's above-quoted letter of 4/II). For the "declaration" of Feb. 11, n.s., as to non-alienation of the Yangtse region and the "declaration" of Feb. 13, n.s., 1898 as to an Englishman as chief inspector of maritime customs see McMurray Treaties and Agreements, Vol. I, pp. 103-104.

152. Muravev's telegram of February 8.

153. See, ibid., the Feb. 11 telegram to Pavlov and the project of a telegram to him prepared at the same time for dispatch at the necessary moment in dos. No. 51, part II. See also Lamsdorf's memorandum of Feb. 14, 1898 to his majesty in dos. No. 116, and Lamsdorf's letter of Feb. 12 to Witte in dos. No. 51, part II.

154. The agreement of the Hongkong-Shanghai and German-Asiatic banks with the Chinese government as to a 4-1/2 per cent loan of 16 million pounds sterling was signed on February 17/March 1, 1898. See McMurray, op. cit., p. 107.

155. For further details as to the course of negotiations about the leasing of Liaotung see Prolog etc., pp. 53 ff., the "Correspondence about the Bribing of Chinese Dignitaries" in Krasnyi Arkhiv, Vol. II, pp. 287 ff., our studies: the "Li Hung-chang Fund" (Bor'ba klassov, No. 1-2, Petrograd, 1924, pp. 111 ff.,) and "Witte and the Yalu Concession" (Sbornik statei, posv. S.F. Platonovu, Petrograd, 1922, pp. 434 ff.) Of the fruitless appeal of the Chinese to the Japanese and English ministers to give China a certificate that their governments would not occupy the Liaotung ports, for presentation to Russia, Pokotilov sent word in a telegram of March 3/15, 1898 (see dos. No. 20).

156. For the convention of March 15/27, 1898 and the government communiqué of March 17 of that year see Sbor. dog. i dok. po delam Dal'nevo Vostoka, pp. 331 ff.

157. See in dos. No. 18 Witte's letter of 13/III and Muravev's of 14/III, 1898.

158. The telegram of December 4, 1897 to Pokotilov, Witte drafted entirely by hand. -- French diplomacy during the critical weeks of 1897 --1897 appears in contact with Russia not only, as above noted, on the Shantung question and the question of the English loan, but in the final phase of the whole episode of the "seizure" of the Liaotung ports. Immediately after Russia's demand for them, in its definitive February redaction, the French government came forward (February 27) with the demand for a grant to France of stations for the storage of coal in South China, permission to start building railroads in Yunnan, and the appointment of a Frenchman as postal director in China; then, no sooner had Russia (March 1) set the Chinese government a limit of two weeks for meeting her demands (by March 15) than France (March 2) demanded an answer from China on her demands within 8 days; and, finally, on March 13 the French minister in Peking informed Pokotilov that "he had been instructed to give us the most vigorous support" (see Pokotilov's telegrams of February 27/March 11 and March 2/14, 1898 in dossier No. 33 and of March 13/25 in dossier No. 18). -- As to Germany, the acquisition of Port Arthur was from the very first regarded by Muravev as the necessary condition for a possible agreement with Germany "for the sake of mutual operations against our common enemy in China the English," "with a demarcation of spheres of influence in the Yellow Sea, whereby the whole north of it with the gulfs of Pechili, Liaotung and Korea would be completely at our disposal, and the southern part with the Shantung coastal strip would enter into Germany's sphere of political influence" (see Muravev's memorandum of December 2, 1897 to his majesty, in copy, in dossier No. 9. Muravev found the agreement proposed by Germany "not incompatible with our own political views" and considered it "feasible only on condition of our immediate seizure" of ports). Inasmuch as the idea of such an agreement had come to Muravev, through an "absolutely confidential source," from Berlin, in notifying the German government on December 2, 1897 of the order given on that day to the Russian squadron to enter Port Arthur, Muravev was already acting in the conviction that "Russia and Germany must and can go hand in hand in the Far East," and the answer came back from Germany that the "solidarity" of interests will "of necessity lead the two empires to regard these interests as their common concern in the face of common danger" and that "dangers which might arise from the continuing opposition of the Chinese government will at once be obviated" if Russia supports with the Chinese government Germany's demands respecting Shantung. And Russia did support the German demands (see Die Grosse Politik, Vol 14, 1st half, No. 3733, 3734, 3742: Muravev's telegram of December 5/17 to Osten-Saken, Radolin's telegram of December 17/29 to the German ministry of foreign affairs from St. Petersburg).

159. The Japanese minister sent the Russian ministry of foreign affairs a memorandum as to the terms on which Japan would like to conclude an agreement with Russia regarding Korean affairs, on Feb. 4, 1898, the very day when England conveyed to Russia for discussion the

terms of the Anglo-Chinese loan. -- Japan proposed the following terms: 1) Japan and Russia to bind themselves to guard the independence of Korea; 2) officer-instructors for the Korean troops to be appointed by the Russian government; 3) the financial adviser to be appointed by the Japanese government; 4) touching trade and industrial interests, Japan and Russia to avoid misunderstandings must in future enter into preliminary agreements previous to taking any new measure (see memorandum in dos. No. 26).

160. See above, pp. 196 and 197.

161. See, in dos. No. 11-a, Romanov's telegram of January 12, 1898 to Alekseev in Seoul.

162. See, in dos. No. 20, Witte's letter of February 6, 1898, to Lamsdorf: "the appointment of the Russian chief financial adviser having once taken place, his withdrawal would be detrimental to Russia's prestige in the Far East."

163. See Sborn. dog. i dip. dok. po delam D. Vostoka, 1895-1905, pp. 346 ff.

164. See ibid., p. 335, art. VIII.

165. See McMurray, Treaties and Agreements, I, p. 127.

166. See details in Prolog etc., pp. 66-70.

CHAPTER IV

1. "For such period as Port Arthur shall remain in the possession of Russia" (see the agreement concluded between England and China on June 19/July 1, 1898, in Sb. dog. i dip. dok. po delam Dal'nevo Vostoka, 1895-1905, St. Petersburg, 1906, p. 352.) Muravev mentioned the plan proposed by Germany for a partition of spheres of influence on the Yellow Sea in the report to his majesty of December 2, 1897 (see above, p. 206, footnote). As Osten-Saken, Russian ambassador to Berlin, afterwards reminded him, he had succeeded in obtaining from Bülow such a letter and from Wilhelm such "personal promises" as "ought to have served as a sort of prelude to a treaty," but Muravev "had not cared to take up this idea" and "had contested the necessity of an official agreement between the two governments" (the promises had been formulated in Bülow's letter of December 17, 1897; see Osten-Saken's letter of December 8/21, 1900 to Lamsdorf in Krasnyi Arkhiv, Vol. 14, p. 43.)

2. For the supplementary protocol of April 25/May 7, 1898, see McMurray Treaties and Agreements, Vol I, p. 127.

3. See above, pp. 175 and 176. The loan was issued in two installments: 200 thousand in August and 400 thousand in December 1897-- after the consent of the French members of the Board of the bank (see Romanov's memorandum of Nov. 28, 1897 to Witte in dossier No. 10, part I). Of the fact that such loans would lead only to "temporary elimination" of the English from participation in construction Witte warned Muravev in a letter of Aug. 22, 1897. (See ibid.)

4. See Pavlov's telegram of Feb. 14, 1898 from Peking in dos. No. 10, part I.

5. See Lamsdorf's letter of Feb. 12, 1898 to Witte with copies appended of Bush's letters of January 8/20 and 9/21, 1898 to the Russian chargé d'affaires in Washington--in dos. No. 10, part I.

6. See, ibid., Witte's letter of February 15, 1898 to Lamsdorf as to the "absolute" undesirability of "permitting the English, the Americans or any other foreign company to build railways in southern Manchuria," and Lamsdorf's telegram of February 16, same year, to Pavlov in Peking in this sense.

7. See the English China Association's appeal to Salisbury of April 14/26, 1898, in connection with the British cabinet's policy in Chinese affairs, as published by the English government in its Blue book (China No. 1, 1899, p. 23); for a translation of this document see E.D. Grimm's Sborn. dogorov i drugikh dokumentov po mezhdunarodnykh otnoshenii na Dal'nem Vostoke (1842-1925), Moscow, 1927, pp. 123 ff.

8. For details see Prolog etc., pp. 80 ff. Russia's protests against an English loan led to her being given by the Chinese government a pledge not to conclude a loan on security of the road associated with financial control or participation of foreigners in the administration and operation of the road (July 19, 1898 exchange of notes with the Russian chargé d'affaires in Peking).

9. See undated letter of Nicholas to Wilhelm in Perepiska Vil'gel'ma i Nikolaia II, pub. Tsentrarkhiv, p. 26, and Prolog etc., pp. 83 ff.

10. See the "translation of the project for an agreement between Russia and England presented by the ambassador of Great Britain," sent to the ministry of finance with Lamsdorf's letter of Sept. 9, 1898, in dos. No. 24-V.

11. See copy of the translation of "the project for agreement verbally presented by Sir Charles Scott," sent to the min. fin. with Lamsdorf's letter of Sept. 17, 1898, ibid., sheet 45.

12. See Romanov's telegram of Sept. 5, 1898 to Pokotilov, ibid.

13. See ibid., Romanov's telegram of Sept. 5 to Pokotilov and the memorandum presented by Romanov on August 27 to Muraviev "on the participation of the Russo-Chinese bank in economic enterprises in China."

14. See the memorandum transmitted to Lamsdorf on Sept. 11, 1898 by Romanov, and Romanov's letter to him of Sept. 18, in dos. No. 24-V. The tenor of the memorandum of Sept. 11 is given in Prolog etc., p. 85 under the guise of "cogitations" of the "minister of finance."

15. See above, p. 91, footnote.

16. Witte's telegram of Sept. 16, 1898 to Romanov from Berlin in dos. No. 24-V.

17. See Lamsdorf's letter of September 14 to Romanov in forwarding ("in view of Your having graciously undertaken the task of drawing up a counter-project") the English ambassador's supplementary explanation. The latter "considered it essential to have immediate agreement": 1) on railway tariffs and differential treatment, and 2) as to the exact demarcation of spheres. The ambassador defined the Yangtse area as "the provinces bordering on the Yangtse, and likewise Hunan and Szechuen"--and awaited "advices from the Russian government respecting the definition of Manchuria to be inserted in the agreement." Both documents are in dos. No. 24-V.

18. See ibid., Romanov's letter of Sept. 18, 1898 to Lamsdorf.

19. See ibid., Romanov's telegram of Sept. 19, 1898 to Pokotilov. -- In reply to the question of what compensations he would consider it necessary to demand from China, Pokotilov, by agreement with the chargé, proposed the following: 1) to demand a concession in Newchwang, 2) to

obtain the exclusive right over all foreigners to exploitation of ores, organization of industrial enterprises and acquisition of real estate for a
distance of 50 to 100 versts on either side of the Chinese Eastern Railway, 3) obtain for Russians the preferential right over foreigners to
build railways, exploit ores and organize industrial enterprises throughout the area beyond the Great Wall. See ibid., Pokotilov's telegram of
September 23, 1898.

20. See, in dos. No. 8, Muravev's telegram of Feb. 19, 1898 to
Shpeyer in Seoul.

21. See Muravev's report to his majesty, submitted on January 25,
1900--in Krasnyi Arkhiv, Vol. 18, p. 16. Muravev held that "only after
firmly consolidating ourselves in Port Arthur and linking it by railway
branch with Russia would we be able to get our own way in Far Eastern
affairs and, if required, maintain it by force."

22. The undated draft is preserved of a report to his majesty by the
minister of finance, possibly so left in project, where side by side with
acknowledgement of the "desirability" of an agreement with England had
been gathered the arguments against the demarcation of spheres of influence from the viewpoint of "Russia's financial and economic interests"
(see portfolio No. 16/s). -- The project was drawn up after Witte's return from abroad (there are references to conversations with French
and German political functionaries) and before the opening of the October
negotiations. This report is not preserved among the authentic fair
copies of reports to his majesty by the minister of finance as found in
the General Chancellery. There likewise exists in the original file neither
fair copy nor copy of the negotiations with England (No. 24).

23. See above, p. 80.

24. This excerpt from Sir C. Scott's letter of Oct. 21/Nov. 2, 1898 to
Salisbury was published in the English Blue Book, against Romanov's
better judgment ("would think better not publish"). See, in dos. No. 24-
V, the copies of excerpts earmarked for publication sent by Scott to the
min. for. afs. for consideration.

25. See, for example, ibid., Scott's telegram of Dec. 23, n.s., and
his letter of Dec. 25, n.s., 1898.

26. See the text of the "English communication of Nov. 18/30, 1898,"
conveyed to the min. fin. with Muravev's letter of Nov. 23, in dos.
No. 24-V. -- Emphases in text are ours.

27. For Witte's project see dos. No. 24-V. See, ibid., Witte's letter
of November 25, 1898 to Muravev.

28. For the supplementary article project, see ibid.

29. See, ibid., Witte's letter of November 25, 1898 to Muravev. Witte
"did not deny its profound significance in the sense of guarding Manchuria
from English claims," but found its rejection the more imperative since
"it spoke not only of railroads but in general of all manner of financial
and economic enterprises and even of commerce."

30. See Scott's telegram of Dec. 23, n.s., and his letter of Dec. 24,
n.s., 1898, in dos. No. 24-V. -- Ibid.: "Muravev did not, however,
make me any more direct allusion to this disagreement and evidently desired me to consider as strictly confidential everything that he said about
the existing difference of opinion between him and Count Witte."

31. See Kuropatkin's private letter of Dec. 27, 1898 to Witte, in his
own handwriting, in dos. No. 24-V. -- Emphases are ours.

32. See, in dos. No. 20, the copy of a private letter of Oct. 25/Nov. 6, 1898 from the ambassador in London to Lamsdorf. -- Staal warned that "if complications arise between us and the English in the Far East, they will be more serious than before," and that "France and England would come to an agreement on the Sudan affair and then the St. James cabinet would rear its head in other places;" and Staal urged the speeding up of our agreement.

33. See Muravev's letter of January 14, 1899 to Witte in dos. No. 24-V.

34. See ibid., Witte's letter of January 17, 1899 to Muravev. --cf. pp. 90-91 above.

35. See, in dos. No. 24-V, Witte's pencilled note on a copy of the English proposals of September 9 opposite the line about Manchuria as the Russian sphere: "And Mongolia?"

36. The text of the note of January 26 is not preserved in the files of the min. fin. It may easily be reconstructed by a comparison of the English ambassador's answering note of February 22/March 6, 1899 and Muravev's letter of February 25, same year, to Witte, in dos. No. 24-V.

37. See Witte's letter of January 25, 1899 to Muravev, in dos. No. 24-V. Witte called Muravev's attention to the fact that this was counter to both of the English proposal projects. Cf. also C. Scott's letter of Jan. 25, n.s., 1899 to Salisbury, in dos. No. 24-a.

38. See, ibid., the English ambassador's note of Feb. 22/March 6, 1899 and Muravev's letter of Feb. 25, same year, to Witte.

39. See Muravev's letter of Feb. 25, 1899 above quoted.

40. See Witte's pencilled notations on Muravev's letter of Feb. 25 and Witte's letter to Muravev of Feb. 26, 1899 in dos. No. 24-V.

41. For the Russo-English agreement (exchange of notes) see Sborn. dog. i dip. dok. po delam Dal'nevo Vostoka, 1895-1905, St. Petersburg, 1906, pp. 358 ff.

42. See Witte's letter of Feb. 26, 1899 to Muravev. -- Muravev replied that "unfortunately we are completely incapacitated for taking any such steps in this direction, since this question was settled between England and China" (Muravev's letter of Feb. 28, 1899, ibid.)

43. See, in dos. No. 24-V, Muravev's letter of March 16, 1899 to Witte.

44. See Witte's letters of March 28 and 30, 1899 to Muravev in dos. No. 10.

45. See, in dos. No. 24-a, Witte's telegram of April 17, 1899 to Pozdneev in Peking.

46. See, in dos. No. 10, Muravev's letter of May 2, 1899 to Witte.

47. See Prolog etc., p. 87.

48. See ibid., pp. 88 ff.

49. See, Izvestiia MID, 1914, book IV, appendix, pp. 62 ff., the Chinese ministers communication of May 20, 1899 to the Russian ambassador in Peking and the Russian minister's answering note of June 5, 1899, which contained the warning that, though not insisting on immediate construction of the line, "nonetheless Russia could in nowise renounce her demand for the concession to this line, which was a necessary compensation for the Chinese government's indisputable and direct violation of positive obligations assumed by it in the communication of July 19 of the past year." In consenting to such a postponement, Witte in a letter of

May 6, 1899 to Muravev, confessed that previous to the completion of the Chinese Eastern Railway trunk-line--proposed for 1902--the line to Peking would not be built, and suggested that "by firmly and consistently pursuing this aim and choosing convenient moments, he gradually obtain the principal agreement of the Chinese government" and "settle the terms of its construction" (see dos. No. 10).

50. See Pozdneev's telegram of April 23, 1899 from Peking in dos. No. 24, part II.

51. See Witte's report to his majesty of July 3, 1898 "on acquiring for the State treasury shares of the Russo-Chinese bank," copy in dos. No. 20, sheets 213 and 214.

52. See Pozdneev's telegram of May 1, 1899 in dos. No. 24, part II.

53. See, in envelope No. 14 of the accumulation of the Peking divisions of the Board of the Russo-Chinese bank and the Chinese Eastern Railway Company under the title: "Correspondence respecting the cession of the Tientsin-Shanhaikwan-Newchang line to the Chinese Eastern Railway Company," the following documents: a) Pokotilov's memorandum to Witte on the July 1, 1899 negotiations with Koch, b) blue pencil memo in Witte's hand to Pokotilov, requesting him to draw up with Rothstein a "project of the basic items of negotiations with the English bank respecting the Peking road," v) rough draft (in French) of Pokotilov's letter of July 3/15, 1899 to Rothstein, giving a summary of the project worked out between Tsigler and Koch, and g) the "list of questions" (with Witte's notations) presented by Pokotilov on June 21 of the same year.

54. See, in dos. No. 10, Pozdneev's telegram of May 9/21, 1899 concerning his explanation with Sui Chin-chen, president of the Board of the Chinese Eastern Railway, on the question of the Russian demand.

55. See, in envelope No. 14 of the accumulation of the Peking division of the Board of the Russo-Chinese bank and Chinese Eastern Railway Company, Pokotilov's memorandum to Witte of July 6, 1899, giving a resume of Rothstein's telegrams from Ishl.

CHAPTER V

1. See Kitaiskaiia Vostochnaia zh. d., historical sketch compiled by the Chancellery of the Board of the Chinese Eastern Railway Company, Vol. I, pp. 72, 73, 75, 58, 163, 299, 59-63, 131-134, 297, 43-45, 67. Of the Company's 13 ships, 5, with a carrying power of 5,819 tons, were bought outright in 1899, and 8, with a carrying power of 9,850 tons, were ordered at the same time. -- For the Russo-Chinese agreement respecting the Bureau of foreign and railway affairs see, in supplement to Izv. MID for 1916, books III and IV: "Agreement between Russia and China on railway, postal-telegraph and customs questions," pp. 21 ff and 26 ff. (May 19/31, 1899 respecting Kirin province and November 20/December 2, 1899 respecting Heilungkiang province.) -- To the beginning of 1901 the total outlay on Liaotung was figured at more than 20 million rubles (see, in dos. No. 75, part 4, Witte's letter of July 23, 1901 to Lamsdorf).

2. See the report on this question in dos. No. 120. On a world scale, according to this calculation, England had spent during the years indicated 1,917,500,000 rubles, France--345,331,000 rubles, Germany (in Shantung) 13,880,000 rubles, Belgium--37,500,000 rubles. War expenditures of Spain and the United States equalled 720 million rubles plus

776 million rubles, or 1,496 million rubles in all. For 1897-1898 Europe had, besides, paid the U.S.A. 18,973 million rubles in trade balance.

3. For the exchange of notes on this question with France, Germany, Italy, Russia and England, see McMurray Treaties and Agreements, Vol. I, pp. 221-235.

4. See above-quoted report on colonial expenditures, in dos. No. 120. Cf. above, pp. 84, 102-103 and 211. -- The participation of the U.S.A. in trade with China had by this time (1899-1900) reached the figure of 848 million rubles (imports into China 261 million rubles, exports--587 million rubles), with the trade turnover of England 755 million rubles, of France 87 million rubles, of Japan 596 million rubles and of Russia 51 million rubles. Counting in the trade with Hongkong the correlation is somewhat different: England 1,134 million rubles, Japan 1,078 million rubles, U.S.A. 1,053 million rubles (see M. P. Fedorov, Soperni-chestvo torgovykh interesov na Vostoke [Commercial Rivalry in the East]), St. Petersburg, 1903, p. 84.

5. See Witte's letter of December 14, 1899 to Muravev, in dos. No. 20. -- Cf. in dos. No. 50: Witte's letter of October 18, 1899 to Lamsdorf; Muravev's of November 16 to Witte, enclosing Cassini's telegram of November 14 concerning the desirability of an agreement with America on the basis of granting Russia in her sphere "the privilege of exclusive building and exploitation of railways and other industrial enterprises," but with equality of railway tariffs for all; Witte's of November 18 to Muravev (disagreeing as to tariff equality); and Muravev's of December 18 to Witte as to its being impossible after the affirmative answers of the other powers "to go counter to a politico-economic prin-ciple generally accepted by the powers, and, by undermining the existing friendly relations between Russia and the U.S.A., create occasion for the organization of a coalition of powers in the Far East very dangerous for our interests."

6. See McMurray, op. cit., I, p. 234.

7. See Witte's letter of December 14.

8. Reference is here made to Muravev's memorandum to his majesty and the ministers' answers to it (especially Witte's) of January-February 1900, published in Kr. Arkhiv, Vol. 18, pp. 4 ff.

9. See Pokotilov's questionnaire of June 21, 1899, in envelope No. 14 of the accumulation of the Peking Division of the Chinese Eastern Railway Company and the Russo-Chinese bank. Only respecting Manchuria did Witte consider that they "ought" to continue to "maintain in the Chinese the conviction" that railway construction, and exploitation of the mineral resources of Manchuria, "might not be otherwise promoted than by the means and with the aid of Chinese and Russian capitalists and engineers." But on the question of German promotional attempts on the hither side of the Wall, Witte confined himself to the mere advice "not to encourage" them. And on the question of our attitude toward English concessionary demands between the Wall and the Yangtse, Witte gave no "precise" an-swer, but left this question "open."

10. The advices through the prism of which the Russian government was at this time obliged to scan its chances in China are assembled in the Prolog etc., pp. 70 ff. and 90 ff.

11. For an allusion to the special "benevolence" toward Russia of Li Hung-chang and the express alike that cannot be taken otherwise than as indicating that Tzu Hsi had also been implicated in the notorious million, see above, p. 163, Kerbedz's declaration at the conference of January 22, 1897.

12. See, in dos. No. 51, part I, Witte's report to his majesty of March 3, 1900. Cf. our "Likhunchangskii fond" (Bor'ba klassov, No. 1-2, p. 113.)

13. See Morse, The International Relations of the Chinese Empire, III, pp. 279, 196, 201, 203; Krasnyi Arkhiv, Vol. 14, documents on the Boxer uprising, pp. 12 and 14, Girs's telegrams of May 25/June 7 and May 27 (June 9,) 1900 from Peking; Die Grosse Politik etc., Vol. 16, No. 4515; according to a message of May 22/June 4 from Kettler, German minister to Peking, the French and American admirals were anchored at Taku awaiting the arrival of the English, Russian, and Japanese admirals; the German admiral reached Taku on May 26/June 8.

14. In Seymour's detail were assembled 915 Englishmen, 540 Germans, 312 Russians, 158 French, 112 Americans, 54 Japanese, 40 Italians and 25 Austrians (Morse, op. cit., p. 202). See also Muravev's report to his majesty of May 25, 1900 on the dispatch of a shore detail of 4,000 in Kr. Arkhiv, Vol. 14, p. 13.

15. See Muravev's report to his majesty of June 4/17, 1900, Kr. Arkhiv, Vol. 14, pp. 14 and 15.

16. See, ibid., Lamsdorf's report to his majesty of June 30/July 13, 1900 and his telegram of June 15/28 to Admiral Alekseev, pp. 18 and 16. Muravev died suddenly on June 8, 1900.

17. See Nicholas's notation on the project of August 24 for a letter to the Russian ambassador in Paris, in Kr. Arkhiv, Vol. 14, p. 31; Witte, Vosp., I, p. 146; the 60,000 Chinese laborers were mentioned by Muravev in a report of June 4, 1900, Kr. Arkhiv, Vol 14, p. 15; on the taking of Taku and the declaration of war, see Morse, op. cit., pp. 207,220, Prolog etc., pp. 103-105.

18. See Kitaiskaia Vostochnaia zhel. dor. Istoricheskii ocherk, comp. Board of the Chinese Eastern Railway Co., Vol. I, p. 77.

19. See in dos. No. 69: Li Hung-chang's telegram of June 13/26, Witte's telegram of June 14/27, Ukhtomsky's telegram (text in cipher) of 14/27. No decoding of Ukhtomsky's telegram exists in the dossier. Ukhtomsky was accustomed to deliver to the chanc. min. fin., for sending texts in his own hand ready ciphered. The date proposed by Ukhtomsky for his journey is known to us from Li Hung-chang's answering telegram of June 16/29 to Witte, in which, among other things, he "besought" Ukhtomsky to hasten his arrival.

20. See Witte's telegram to Yugovich, in dos. No. 51, part III. Witte was in such a hurry that the telegram was dispatched on June 15, but only referred to and approved by the tsar on the 16th.

21. See Witte's report of June 18, 1900 in dos. No. 69. In his answering telegram Li Hung-chang said that he had appealed to the Mukden governor to protect the road.

22. See Prolog etc., pp. 110-111.

23. See Prolog etc., p. 115, and, in the letters of Witte to Sipiagin published by us (Kr. Arkhiv, Vol. 18,) the letter of July 7, 1900: the bombarding of Blagoveshchensk by the Chinese did not disturb Witte in

the least, on the contrary he took evident satisfaction in the fact that this gave the Russians "occasion to demolish Aigun as an example." Witte did not doubt that the Chinese campaign "would cost much money and many lives" but thought "better lose money than prestige." Cf. the entry for September 8, 1901 in Polovtsov's diary (Kr. Arkhiv, Vol. 3, p. 104) to the effect that Kuropatkin had shown the author a record of the words spoken to him by Witte at the beginning of the Chinese war concerning the necessity of sending as many troops as possible to China: "what a misfortune, their having to go by sea." And Kuropatkin, as can now be seen, was justified in complaining at that time of its having been on him that "recriminations were heaped, for sending not 50 thousand, but 150 thousand, thus giving the war exaggerated dimensions." As we see, it was Witte himself who thought of 150 thousand men.

24. See Nicholas's notation on the project of September 10, 1900 for a telegram to Alekseev (Kr. Arkhiv, Vol. 14, p. 34,) and Prolog etc., pp. 114-117.

25. See Lamsdorf's report to his majesty of June 30, 1900, in Kr. Arkhiv, Vol. 14, pp. 18-19.

26. See Die Grosse Politik, Vol. 16, No. 4537, 4548, 4552, and Osten-Saken's telegram of June 17/30 from Berlin, in Kr. Arkhiv, Vol. 14, p. 17.

27. Die Grosse Politik, Vol. 16, No. 4553.

28. Ibid., No. 4548. Kuropatkin said, among other things, that there were now already in Manchuria (i.e., that is before the order of June 26 for the introduction of Russian troops into Manchuria) "6000 men." It is possible that the troops here understood are those military divisions which "the minister of finance had asked the minister of war to propose Admiral Alekseev's sending to Yinkow to guard railway property" even earlier than June 16 (cf. Prolog etc., p. 112.)

29. Ibid., p. 35, Lauenstein's telegram of July 4, n.s., from St. Petersburg and the remarks of sub-state-secretary Richthofen apropos of Kuropatkin's communication.

30. These were also brought out by Richthofen (see preceding note).

31. See ibid, pp. 27 and 28, note.

32. Ibid., Lamsdorf's telegram of June 22/July 4, 1900, pp. 40-41.

33. Ibid., p. 42, Wilhelm's series of wrathful notations on Bülow's telegram conveying Lamsdorf's text to Wilhelm.

34. Ibid., No. 4558, Wilhelm's telegram of July 8, n.s., to Bülow and No. 4573, Bülow's telegram of July 18, n.s., apropos of Radolin's telegram of July 14, n.s.

35. See Lamsdorf's report to his majesty of June 30, 1900 (Kr. Arkhiv, Vol. 14, p. 19) and Witte's letter of July 14, 1900 to Sipiagin (ibid., Vol. 18, p. 34.)

36. See, in dos. No. 69, Li Hung-chang's telegram of July 13/26, 1900 and Witte's autograph report to his majesty of July 15.

37. See, ibid., Nicholas's notation on Witte's report of the 15th as to an appointment for a personal report "tomorrow, Sunday, at 2 o'clock," and Shipov's memorandum of July 18 as to advancing Ukhtomsky 20,000 rubles for travelling expenses out of the 12-million reserve fund, with Witte's resolution of consent.

38. See Delcasse's telegram of July 19/August 1 to Montebello, the project of the Russian answer, same date, and Lamsdorf's report to his majesty of July 20--in Kr. Arkhiv, Vol. 14, pp. 19-22.

39. See, ibid., Wilhelm's telegram of July 24/August 6, 1900, to
Nicholas (p. 22,) and Nicholas's answer, in Die Grosse Politik, Vol. 16,
No. 4602.
40. See Witte's letter of July 25, 1900 to Sipiagin (Kr. Arkhiv, Vol.
18, pp. 35-36.)
41. See, ibid., Witte's letter of August 6, p. 38; and the letter of
August 10, p. 39 ("nor should we wait for Waldersee and his pogrom").
France did not answer Berlin assenting to Waldersee's appointment until
August 1/14, 1900: see Die Grosse Politik, Vol. 16, p. 91. Cf. the tele-
gram of July 29/August 11 from the Russian ambassador in Paris, in Kr.
Arkhiv, Vol. 14, pp. 24-25.
42. The general conviction was that before September an advance on
Peking was impossible on account of the rains and lack of forces (see
Wilhelm's telegram of July 24/August 6 in Kr. Arkhiv, Vol. 14, p. 22;
Witte's letter of August 10 to Sipiagin, ibid., Vol. 18, p. 39; Morse,
op. cit., p. 265). The taking of Peking came as a complete surprise to
Lamsdorf and Witte, and they accused Kuropatkin of having, behind their
backs, given ("Of himself or under orders?") Linevich instructions to
march on Peking (see Witte's letter of August 10). Cf., however, Morse,
op. cit., pp. 267-268: the initiative of the English command at the end
of July was supported by the American commander, General Sheffy, to
whom suitable instructions were issued from Washington at the request
of the American minister in Peking, Conger, the Americans and English
then managing to overcome the passivity of the Japanese and Russians.
Cf. also Die Grosse Politik, Vol. 16, p. 92, note.
43. See Witte's letter of August 10, to Sipiagin, Prolog etc., pp. 118
ff., and the Russian government's circular note of August 12, 1900 in
Kr. Arkhiv, Vol. 14, pp. 28-29.
44. See Prolog etc., p. 110 and Morse, op. cit., pp. 315, 317. The
French participated in the punitive expeditions, but as a rule entered into
an agreement with Li Hung-chang on such occasions.
45. Morse, op. cit., pp. 306-307. Cf. the telegram of August 15/28
from the Russian ambassador in Paris (Kr. Arkhiv, Vol. 14, p. 29),
Die Grosse Politik, Vol. 16, No. 4627, 4628, 4638, 4639.
46. See Die Grosse Politik, Vol. 16, No. 4613 (text of Lamsdorf's
telegram of August 3/16), and No. 4625, note (Wilhelm's notations on
Radolin's telegram of August 30, n.s.) Cf. Morse, op. cit. p. 306. Li
Hung-chang was appointed authorized agent for negotiations on July 27/
August 8 (ibid., p. 272).
47. See Morse, op. cit., pp. 330-340. Cf. documents on the Boxer
uprising in Kr. Arkhiv, Vol. 14, No. 25, 27, 28, 29, 32, 39, 40, 42,
43, 44, 47, 49, and Die Grosse Politik, Vol. 16, No. 4614 (Wilhelm: "if
Li Hung-chang falls into our hands at Taku or in Chihli, we shall take him
as a hostage"), 4615, 4618, 4622, 4623. At the very first news of Boxers
on the Yangtse, June 6/19, Wilhelm had expressed himself as in favor of
a "large military undertaking of a general character" for the purpose of
"razing Peking to the ground," and "would be pleased" to contribute a
general of his for the chief command, see ibid., No. 4527.
48. See Morse, op. cit., p. 342. For the final protocol of August
25/September 7, see Sb. dog. i dip. dok. po delam Dal'nevo Vostoka,
pp. 459 ff.

49. Morse, op. cit., p. 343. Cf., in dos. No. 120, Lamsdorf's memorandum, composed apropos of Vogak's memorandum, read at the conference of May 7, 1903, on the significance of the treaty of March 26, 1902 in the development of the Manchurian question. Of the total compensation of 450 million lan, Russia was allotted 28.97136 per cent, i.e., 130,371,120 lan or (at the ruble exchange rate of 1.142) 184,084,021.44 rubles (see, in dos. No. 93, part 7, sheet 30, the report drawn up in July 1905 on Russia's war compensation). Witte estimated all losses and expenditures resulting form the hostilities of 1900 at 170 million (see, in dos. No. 12, his letter of May 28, 1901 to Lamsdorf). Of this sum, 70 million represented damage to the Chinese Eastern Railway, and 100 direct war expenditures.

50. On the attempt of England and America at financial control, see Girs's telegram of October 9/22, 1900 from Peking, in Kr. Arkhiv, Vol. 14, p. 39, and Pokotilov's telegram of Oct. 21/Nov. 3, 1900, in dos. No. 75, part 1.-- For Witte's report to his majesty of Oct. 11, 1900 "on the question of the forthcoming peace negotiations with China," see dos. No. 75, part I. As examples of such "privileges" Witte pointed out "extension of the railway concession time-limit, purchase of Kwantung province, etc." For further details of negotiations on the financial question, see Prolog etc., pp. 122-123 and 128-131.

51. See Pokotilov's telegram of September 16/29 to Witte from Shanghai, in dos. No. 75, part I, and Morse, op. cit., pp. 251 and 305. Li Hung-chang left for Peking on October 3, n.s. He had been appointed viceroy of Chihli by an order of July 9, n.s.

52. See Ukhtomsky's telegram of September 18/October 1, 1900 to Witte from Shanghai, in dos. No. 75, part I.

53. The decision to conduct parallel negotiations on the general question, touching all the powers, and on the particular, touching "future regulation of Russia's relations toward China,"--was confirmed by Nicholas on September 13, see Lamsdorf's telegram to Girs at Peking in Kr. Arkhiv, Vol. 14, p. 35.

54. See Pokotilov's telegram of September 20/October 3, 1900 to Witte from Shanghai, in dos. No. 75, part I.

55. See Ukhtomsky's telegram of September 23/October 6, 1900 to Witte from Shanghai, in dos. No. 51, part I.

56. See Witte's telegram of September 25, 1900 to Ukhtomsky in dos. No. 51, part I. Opposite Witte's words: "Li had absolutely no right to pretend to me that I did not keep my promises, inasmuch as the events that have transpired have broken all Li Hung-chang's own promises and inflicted stupendous losses upon us"--is Nicholas's notation: "konechno" (exactly).

57. See Ukhtomsky's telegram of September 29 to Witte, ibid. -- Ukhtomsky had "answered that he honestly could not mention any such sums and considered 200 thousand the maximum to which Russia would as yet agree," but that if Li Hung-chang "should frame the negotiations to our mind" he could "count on their [father and son] being given something more substantial besides."

58. See, ibid., Witte's telegram of September 29, 1900 to Ukhtomsky, and Ukhtomsky's telegram of October 16, 1900: "Li Ching-fang in extreme disillusionment after polite refusal to talk money with him, and constant greetings from Li Hung-chang have suddenly ceased."

59. Pokotilov's first telegram from Peking was sent on October 21 (see dos. No. 75, part I). Ukhtomsky had counted on leaving Port Arthur and being in Tientsin on October 17, his first telegram from Peking is dated November 6, o.s. (See Romanov's telegram of October 17 to Witte at Yalta and Ukhtomsky's telegram of November 6 from Peking in dos. No. 69). Kuropatkin's telegram of September 24 to Admiral Alekseev, Alekseev's of September 29 to Kuropatkin, engineer Girshman's of October 3 from Port Arthur and Witte's letter of October 4 to Kuropatkin are in dos. No. 67, part I.

60. See, in dos. No. 67, part I, Lamsdorf's letter of November 18, 1900 to Witte. -- McMurray, Vol. I, p. 329, gives the text of this agreement in an absolutely fantastic redaction. We quote in full the text as given in the copy conveyed from the min. for. afs. to the chancellery of the min. fin. on January 3, 1901 (see dos. No. 67, part I):

PRELIMINARY AGREEMENT.

His majesty the emperor, desiring to preserve the long-standing friendship with Chin, has recognized the possibility of restoring in the province of Mukden, now occupied by imperial troops, the former administration headed by the chiang-chün, in which connection it has pleased his majesty to authorize the commander of Kwantung province, Vice-Admiral Alekseev, to enter into negotiations with chiang-chün Tseng toward the conclusion of an agreement.

Now in consequence of the arrival at Port Arthur of the daotai Choumyan, the functionary Chuyan of the rank of canton head, and Chanwenhai of the rank of district head, with authority from the chiang-chün for the conduct of negotiations, Vice-Admiral Alekseev has on his side authorized a functionary of his from the diplomatic office, Korostovets, to conclude with the said officials, sign for the central authority, and seal, the following preliminary agreement in nine points which shall thereafter be presented for the confirmation, by seal and signature, of Vice-Admiral Alekseev on the one side and the chiang-chün on the other.

1) With the entrance of the chiang-chün upon the execution of his former duties in the administration of the province, he shall become responsible for the maintenance in the province of order and tranquility, for the unimpeded progress of operations connected with the construction of the Chinese Eastern Railway and for its preservation.

2) To safeguard the railway under construction and guarantee order in the country, Russian troops will be stationed at Mukden and certain other points in the province; these the chiang-chün's administration must respect and must assist where necessary in the matter of quartering, purchase of provender, and so forth.

3) The Chinese troops remaining in Mukden province must, as having participated in the revolt and the demolition of the railway, be disarmed and disbanded by the chiang-chün, but will not be held answerable for their previous acts if they execute this order without resistance. Arsenals, guns, arms, all manner of military depots and stores not yet taken by Russian troops shall pass under the control of the Russian military authorities.

4) At points where Russian garrisons do not exist, all fortifications of various denominations (forts, batteries, etc.) shall be subject to levelling at the order of the Chinese authorities in the presence of a

representative of the Russian military authority, and ammunition depots which the Russian military authorities do not propose to use shall
in like manner be demolished.

5) At the city of Yinkow and other places where Russian civil government has temporarily been introduced, its replacement by Chinese
shall be effected in the measure of actual restoration of order in the
country, at the discretion of the imperial Russian government.

6) For the direct maintenance of order in the cities of the province,
the chiang-chün is given the right to organize a foot and mounted police
guard without guns, directly subject to him; on the same principles a
rural police shall be organized in villages and settlements. The number of the guard and its arming shall be fixed by special agreement.

7) The chiang-chün shall be provided with a Russian commissar
for convenience of communication with the central authority of Kwantung province. This commissar must be informed as to all more important matters and as to the chiang-chün's decrees.

8) In the event of the inadequacy of the police organized by the
chiang-chün to preserve the security of the maritime or overland border of the country or to guarantee order within, the chiang-chün has
the right to appeal through the aforementioned commissar to the commander of the Russian imperial troops.

9) For the interpretation of the eight points above set forth the
guiding text shall be the Russian.

The preliminary terms above set forth shall go into effect on the
day of Chiang-chün Tseng Chi's return to Mukden and may be supplemented or altered only by mutual consent of the central authority of
Kwantung province and the chiang-chün of Mukden, or if both governments recognize this to be necessary.

Concluded at Port Arthur on October 27, 1900. Signed by the functionary of the diplomatic office Korostovets and the Chinese plenipotentiaries.

61. See the minute book of the conference of October 31 in dos. No.
67, part I.

62. See, in dos. No. 67, part I, the original of the project bearing
Kuropatkin's signature of October 30, 1900. -- The "principles of Rus-
sian governmental control" in their final redaction are summarized in
Prolog etc., p. 139.

63. Compare the manuscript corrections and additions inscribed in
the chancellery min. fin. on Kuropatkin's original with the redaction
adopted; both documents are in dos. 67, part I. -- Two supplementary
articles of Witte's not mentioned above (15 and 18 by final count) only
further defined Kuropatkin's redaction: (article 15) as to the relations of
army heads outside the three provincial cities with authorities "up to and
including the fudutun" and within the three cities with the chiang-chüns
directly, in the absence of the military commissar, and (article 18) as
to identifying chiang-chüns and fu-tu-t'ungs with governors and district
heads. The article on turning local residents over to the military tri-
bunal embraced Witte's addition: "in cases where it shall be deemed
necessary."

64. See the above-mentioned manuscript corrections on Kuropatkin's
original, in dos. No. 67, part I. Ibid., Witte's letter of October 25, 1900
to Kuropatkin apropos of a telegram from Grodekov, governor-general

of the Amur province, proposing that, on the basis of measures afterwards proposed by Kuropatkin, on October 31, Manchuria be made subject to the governor-general of the Amur province. Witte expressed
himself as in favor of subordinating Manchuria to the central authority
of Kwantung province, Alekseev, and agreed to "exceptional measures"
only "until final agreement with the Chinese government": "the occupation
may be prolonged for many years and to maintain the exceptional measures all this time would be inexpedient." Kuropatkin (letter of October 29
to Witte) disagreed with Witte on both points. As we see, the disagreement respecting the subordination of Manchuria was compromised (by
the division of control over Manchuria between the two--Alekseev of
Kwantung and Grodekov of Pri-Amur,) and that respecting "exceptional
measures" decided against Kuropatkin.

65. See assertion on page 139 of the Prolog etc. There exists in dos.
No. 67, part I, a justified memorandum drawn up in the chancellery
min. fin. concerning alterations desired in Kuropatkin's project. All the
details there indicated were afterwards introduced as additions and corrections and adopted in the final text. Only one last wish of the memorandum went begging--that into the title of the document be introduced
the word "temporary" (principles). This alteration in the title could
hardly have changed the fact of the matter, when the temporary character of the "principles" was obvious both from the 2nd article and from
the last.

66. See, ibid., the minutes of the conference of October 31, and
article 3 of Kuropatkin's project as above quoted in the text.

67. See Pokotilov's telegram of October 21/November 3, 1900 from
Peking, in dos. No. 75, part I.

68. See Pokotilov's telegram of October 21/November 3, 1900, in
dos. No. 75, part I: the Chinese minister in Peterburg had informed
Li Hung-chang of Witte's professed "readiness to evacuate Manchuria in
the near future"; and Witte's telegram of October 25 to Pokotilov, ibid.

69. See Witte's telegram of October 20/November 2, 1900, to Ukhtomsky, in dos. No. 69, in reply to his question as to just what he was to
demand of Li Hung-chang at their meeting.

70. See Ukhtomsky's telegram of October 21/November 3, 1900 from
Tientsin in dos. No. 69: "from this our mutual interests can only gain,"
and Witte's answering telegram of October 23 that "it might breed a
whole lot of misunderstandings" and was "unthinkable." Nicholas's
notation on Ukhtomsky's telegram was: "Ukhtomsky all over."

71. See, ibid., Ukhtomsky's telegram of October 23/November 5, 1900
from Tientsin, Witte's telegram of October 30 to Ukhtomsky, and Ukhtomsky's telegram of November 6/19 from Peking.

72. See Ukhtomsky's telegram of November 6/19, 1900 from Peking
in dos. No. 69. Li Hung-chang undertook to meet Ukhtomsky ceremoni-
ously outside the city gate, but the latter entered in "through another
gate." But even so, Ukhtomsky's arrival in Peking started "idle talk
among the foreigners."

73. See Pokotilov's telegram of November 7/20, 1900 from Peking,
in dos. No. 75, part I.

74. See Witte's telegram of November 9/22, 1900 to Ukhtomsky, in
dos. No. 75, part I. That a treaty was being proposed in the name of
the Chinese Eastern Railway was here first declared by Witte.

75. See, ibid., Witte's telegram of November 10/23, 1900 to Ukhtom-sky. Both telegrams are in Witte's own handwriting.

76. See Ukhtomsky's telegram of Nov. 13/26, 1900, in dos. No. 75, part I.

77. See Witte's telegram of Nov. 15/28, 1900 to Ukhtomsky and Witte's telegram of Nov. 20 to Romanov from Yalta, in dos. No. 75, part I, and Ukhtomsky's telegram of Nov. 21/Dec. 4, 1900 in dos. No. 69.

78. See Ukhtomsky's telegram of November 28, 1900, telling of the understanding with Girs and requesting "permission to leave for home" "if I can be of absolutely no use to you," in dos. No. 69, and Girs's telegram of November 28 to the minister of foreign affairs, in dos. No. 75, part I. Until this latter telegram, we found no communications to Peter-burg on Li Hung-chang's concession proposal either from Girs or from Pokotilov.

79. See Kuropatkin's letter of December 3, 1900 to Lamsdorf, in Kr. Arkhiv, Vol. 14, p. 41, and Witte's of December 5, 1900, read by Nicholas at Yalta on December 12 and undisputed by so much as a single mark, in dos. No. 75, part I. The project of the program of the separate agreement with China, forwarded in copy to the min. fin. with Lamsdorf's letter of December 21, was confirmed by the tsar at Yalta on December 13, and consequently was sent there not later than the 9th (dos. No. 75, part I).

80. Even Kuropatkin, see his above-mentioned letter of December 3.

81. Even Witte: see his above-mentioned letter of December 5. Of Nicholas's confirmation of the "principles, etc." on December 4 Witte informed Kuropatkin in a letter of Dec. 4 (see dos. No. 67, part I).

82. Cf. Kuropatkin's above-quoted letter of Dec. 3 and Witte's of Dec. 5.

83. See Witte's telegram of Dec. 4, 1900 to Yugovich, in dos. No. 75, part I.

84. See the collective telegram of Kerbedz, Yugovich, Ignatsius and Gen. Gerngross from Vladivostok, of Dec. 17, 1900, in dos. No. 67, part I. In their opinion, until the signing of a general peace treaty with the powers, the return of the court to Peking, the withdrawal from China of foreign troops, and confirmation of all three chiang-chüns in Manchuria by the emperor and until the lapse of three or four months of probation thereafter, there could be no question of withdrawing the regular troops from Manchuria. Until then, they set the total figure for regular troops in Mukden, Kirin, Tsitsihar, Ninguta, Kwangchengtse, Tiehling, Liaoyang and along the Sungari at "not less" than 12 battalions of 6 batteries.

85. See Witte's letter of December 5, 1900 to Lamsdorf in dos. No. 75, part I.

86. See his letter of December 5.

87. See quoted project of program in dos. No. 75, part I. On the instructor question in Manchuria, Chihli province and Chinese Turkestan, see the "promemoria" transmitted to Bülow by Osten-Saken on January 1, n.s., 1898, published in Die Grosse Politik, Vol. 14, 1st half, pp. 134-135. The "promemoria" even quoted an agreement not to permit foreign instructors in this region said to have been made by the Chinese govern-ment "in terms of a formal engagement" (dans les termes d'un engage-ment formel).

88. See telegram No. 2 of December 9, 1900 from Lamsdorf to Girs, in Kr. Arkhiv, Vol. 14, p. 46.

89. See, ibid., telegram No. 1 of December 9 from Lamsdorf to Girs (p. 45).

90. See in dos. No. 75, part I, the quoted "project for program, etc." and Nicholas's notation on it. The "project" stipulated that the concession question would be further discussed, "to the end that...only such concession demands be made as we actually propose to prosecute in the immediate future." -- As to even acquiring Liaotung permanently cf. above, p. 262, note, Witte's report of October 11, 1900.

91. See, ibid., Lamsdorf's letter of December 21, 1900 to Witte, and his letter of January 4, 1901, Witte's letter to Lamsdorf of the same date. Witte had categorically declared in favor of conducting the negotiations at Peterburg in a letter to Lamsdorf back on December 5, 1900. -- Yan Yu was the Chinese minister at Peterburg.

92. See, in dossier No. 75, part I: "list of privileges, etc." and "explanatory memorandum" to it, drawn up by I.P. Shipov and P.M. Romanov and peppered with pencilled notations and corrections by Witte, and the two projects, fair copies of which were sent to the min. for. afs. in Witte's letters of January 9 and 11, 1901. On Lamsdorf's letter of January 9 telling of the Chinese minister's receipt of powers and requesting that he "give resolution" to the program of December 13, is Witte's notation: "must work faster, we are keeping everyone waiting." -- A few things on the "list," Witte decided not to include in the projects, namely: 1) closing of the river Liao to steamers competing with the Chinese Eastern Railway ("hardly feasible"), 2) pushing forward the pre-term redemption of the Chinese Eastern Railway from 36 years to 54 and transfer gratis to China of the Chinese Eastern Railway from 80 years to 120 ("this is a topic for subsequent agreements"), 3) grant to the Chinese Eastern Railway of 1 sq. verst in Chihli province near Kaiping for the mining of coal ("hardly feasible for us to poke in there"). On the other hand, Witte had "ordered" included in the list "extension to all Manchuria of the right of free trade," but it was explained to him that "no state" bordering on China possessed such a right (see ibid., sheet 188, investigation into this).

1. The project for the "separate agreement of the governments" is divided into "articles"; the project for the agreement with the Chinese Eastern Railway Company into §§. In future we shall strictly observe this designation.

93. Formally this was, of course, expressed thus (§ 2): "in view of the difficulty for the Chinese government of payment in a single install-ment" the Company "agrees to postpone payment, etc." But the project gave China no alternative.

94. In the event of redemption of the railway, the whole amount of the debt still owing, together with accrued interest, must be paid the Company in full, and China would not enter into possession of the road "until all payments due on this debt had been paid to the Russian State bank" (§ 2).

95. See above, pp. 126 and 127.

96. See Witte's report to his majesty of March 14, 1903, published by us in a study of the "Li Hung-chang Fund" (Bor'ba klassov, No. 1-2, pp. 117 ff).

97. See Witte's letter of January 9, 1901 to Lamsdorf, in dos. No. 75, part I.

98. In the summer of 1899, when Pokotilov asked, in view of the possible introduction of the dollar throughout China, "whether we ought not by all means to strive for the introduction at least in Manchuria of the lan instead of the dollar," Witte demurred "that it would be difficult to decide this question now" (see "List of questions" in envelope No. 14 of the accumulation of the Peking Division of the Management of the Chinese Eastern Railway).

99. On the right of foreigners to trade in "open ports" and the most favored nation principle see, for example, E.D. Grimm's Sb. dog. i dr. dok. po ist. mezhdun. otn. na D. Vostoke, Moscow, 1927, pp. 7-16.

100. A demand, contradicting article 1 in the crudest and most elementary manner, for the introduction of Russian civil government in the city of Chinchowting was squeezed in at the very end of the text, in article 15, in the form of China's mute "consent" to the "abrogation" of article 4 of the supplementary protocol of April 25/May 7, 1898. Articles 11, 12, and 16 of the separate agreement, unmentioned above, included China's engagements: to enter into an agreement with the Russo-Chinese bank concerning compensation for its losses, to make good the losses of private persons and make payments on the 1895 loan in monthly instead of semi-annual installments. The project for the separate agreement contained 16 articles in all.

101. See above, p. 245 and p. 219, note 1.

102. As Witte explained in a letter of January 16, 1901 to Lamsdorf (see, in dossier No. 75, part I), he recognized the concession for the Peking line as "one of the most important objects of the agreement"--"not with a view to utilizing this concession, but in order that, having secured it, we might obtain transfer to our hands of the Shanhaikwan-Yinkow-Hsinminting railway." For the treaty of March 26, 1902, see Sborn. dog. i diplom. dok po delam Dal'nevo Vostoka. 1895-1905, St. Petersburg, 1906, pp. 538 ff.

103. See Witte's letters of July 14, August 6 and 10, 1900 to Sipiagin (Kr. Arkhiv, Vol. 18).

104. See, ibid., Witte's letter No. 10, undated (c. September 18, 1900). "The elimination of Manchuria as a province of China," to which, in Witte's opinion, Kuropatkin's "impossible" demands "strictly speaking" boiled down, was "perilous" precisely because the Japanese would in such a case "demand Korea for themselves" (letter of August 6).

105. See Obzor snoshenii s Iaponiei po koreiskim delam s 1895 g., (Survey of relations with Japan on Korean affairs from 1895) pub. MID, St. Petersburg, 1906, p. 15.

106. See, ibid., the memorandum of the Japanese minister to Peterburg of January 9/21, 1901, appendix No. 9, p. 66.

107. See Osten-Saken's letter of December 8/21, 1900 to Lamsdorf from Berlin (Kr. Arkhiv, Vol. 14, p. 43). Cf. O. Franke, Die Grossmächte in Ost-Asien, pp. 149-150. For documentary material on the agreement of October 3/16, 1900 see Die Grosse Politik, Vol. 16, pp. 197 ff.

108. Cf. Witte's letter of Dec. 5, 1900 to Lamsdorf, in dos. No. 75, part I.

109. See Die Grosse Politik etc., Vol. 16, p. 312, note.

110. See The English Blue Book (China No. 2, 1904), No. 8, 9, 10, 12, 13 (Russian edition in Materialy po Dal'nemu Vostoku (Materials on the Far East), pub. chancellery of the Special Committee of the Far East, St. Petersburg, 1904, pp. 7-12.

111. See Lamsdorf's letters of Jan. 16 and 22, 1901 to Witte, in dos. No. 75, part I.

112. All departures of the final redaction from Witte's text are underlined; everything taken over in to the final text from Witte's project is set in ordinary type. -- For the projects delivered to the min. fin. on Jan. 16, 22, and 25, and likewise for the final redaction as established at the conference of Jan. 26 and delivered to the min. fin. on the 28th as well as the copy here quoted, see dos. No. 75, part I.

113. In Witte's project, the sentence began instead: "Independently of the guard...".

114. Witte's project had continued: "Commensurately with the pacification of the country and the completion of construction on the Chinese Eastern Railway, the Russian government will gradually reduce the number of troops stationed in Manchuria. This reduction has already started. If order remains undisturbed, the number of these troops will be reduced in the following sequence:...[see p. 288 above].

115. This obligation was also laid on the Russian troops in article 9 of the "principles of Russian governmental control."

116. In Witte's project: "and the Chinese Eastern Railway."

117. Lamsdorf's project of January 16 had: "...until Russian military forces shall have been recalled from said province." The redaction in the final project was established at Witte's desire (see his letter of January 16 to Lamsdorf in dos. No. 75, part I).

118. In Witte's project the same thing was differently formulated: "On the chiang-chüns of Manchuria, the fudutuns and other local officials, is laid the responsibility of preserving order and tranquillity in the country generally and in particular of preventing attacks on the Chinese Eastern Railway, its enterprises and its employees. The Chinese government pledges that upon declaration of the Russian minister to China of non-compliance with this condition of his tenure by any one of these officials up to and including the chiang-chüns, it will immediately replace this official."

119. Witte's project only had: "In view of practical inconveniences that hamper the application of art. 4 of the St. Petersburg supplementary protocol of April 25/May 7, 1898, the Chinese government agrees to the abrogation of this article."

120. Other omitted items from Witte's project were those concerning the "preparedness" of the Russian government "to charge the whole sum due it or a part thereof to the Chinese government's account with the Chinese Eastern Railway Company" and those concerning the Company's addition "of the compensation it paid the Russian government to the amount of its own damages."

121. Still another item omitted in its entirety was art. 10 of Witte's project, enumerating the concessions to be given the Chinese Eastern Railway Company.

122. Another point from Witte's project omitted was: "A special agreement between the interested parties may be instituted concerning the substitution for this concession of the right to finish and exploit the

Shanhaikwan-Yinkow-Hsinminting railway, with liquidation of the Chinese government's existing liabilities on these lines."

123. See, for example, Witte's letter of February 22, 1901 to Lamsdorf, in dos. No. 75, part 2. Witte recognized the "great importance" of prohibiting foreign instruction.

124. In the project that Lamsdorf sent Witte on January 16 for consideration there was no article about a line to Peking. For Witte's urgent entreaties, see his letter of January 16 to Lamsdorf (dos. No. 75, part I).

125. Even Li Hung-chang objected to art. 11: see Girs's telegram of February 12, 1901 in dos. No. 75, part 2.

126. See Witte's report to his majesty of February 10, ·1901 in connection with presentation of the project of a telegram to Pokotilov: "I authorize you to notify Li Hung-chang that immediately upon conclusion of the understanding with us you will transmit to him or to whomever he wishes, in token of our gratitude, 500 thousand rubles. In addition, convey to him that, with his majesty's consent, I shall be in Arthur and probably in Peking in September, and, if our affairs go well, shall transmit to him or to whomever he wishes another like sum" (dos. No. 51, part 3).

127. See, for example, in dos. No. 75, part 2, Girs's telegrams of February 8 and 12 and Pokotilov's of February 12, 1901, and in dos. No. 51, part 3, Pokotilov's telegram of February 14.

128. See Izvolsky's telegram of February 18, 1901 from Tokyo, and Cassini's of the same date from Washington, in dos. No. 75, part 2.

129. See telegrams of February 12 from Pokotilov and Girs, Witte's letters of February 17 and 22 to Lamsdorf, in dos. No. 75, part 2, and Pokotilov's telegram of February 14, 1901, in dos. No. 51, part 3. Witte agreed to renounce Mongolia but not the districts "rich in gold," of Kashgar, Yarkand, Khotan and Keriya (letter of February 17).

130. In the text offered on February 28 the following corrections had been made in compliance with China's wishes: 1) any mention whatsoever of Mongolia and the other districts had been absolutely excluded, 2) instead of pledging not to maintain armies in Manchuria, China was to pledge that she would "enter into an agreement" with Russia as to "the number and places of cantonment of Chinese troops in Manchuria," 3) art. 6, concerning foreign instructors, was deleted, 4) prohibition of import of arms into Manchuria was given a "temporary" character, pending the "unanimous" settlement of the general question of import of arms into China in conjunction with the other powers, 5) from the article concerning a line "to the Great Wall," the phrase "in the direction of Peking was deleted, 6) provision was made for concluding the agreement as to compensation of the Chinese Eastern Railway Company "on the basis of general principles to be worked out on the compensations question by representatives in Peking and confirmed by all the powers (see the project of February 28, 1901, in dos. No. 75, part 2). -- See also Witte's telegram of February 28, 1901 to Pokotilov, in dos. No. 51, part 3, and Pokotilov's telegram of March 11 from Peking (received March 12) in dos. No. 75, part 2.

131. See Scott's telegram of March 26, n.s., 1901 to Lansdowne from St. Petersburg, telling of the Japanese minister's meeting of March 12/25 with Lamsdorf--in the English Blue Book (China, No. 2, 1904), quoted Russian edition, p. 28.

132. See Witte's telegram of March 15 to Pokotilov and Lamsdorf's ⟨ letter of March 15, 1901 to Witte, conveying the opinion of Nicholas, in dos. No. 75, part 3.

133. See Li Hung-chang's telegram of March 22, 1901 to Ukhtomsky, in dos. No. 75, part 3.

134. See the copy of Cassini's "extremely confidential letter" of March 15, 1901 to Lamsdorf, ibid. -- Emphases are ours.

135. A lengthy government message giving a survey of the Russian government's policy in Chinese aggairs, starting from 1900, was published in the March 24, 1901 No. of the Pravit. Vestnik.

136. See E. Satow's telegrams of March 6 and 19, n.s., 1901 to Lansdowne from Peking in the Blue Book (China No. 2, 1904) No. 25 and 30.

137. See, ibid., C. Scott's report of January 25/February 6 to Lansdowne, and Lansdowne's telegram of March 4, n.s., 1901, to C. Scott, No. 11 and 20, C. Scott's telegrams of March 26, n.s., and April 12, n.s., 1901 to Lansdowne, No. 34 and 39.

138. See Izvolsky's telegram of February 18 from Tokyo and Pokotilov's telegram of March 11, 1901 from Peking in dos. No. 75, part 2.

139. See Lamsdorf's letter of May 23, 1901 to the ministers of war, navy, and finance, "approved" by Nicholas, published in our collection: Russkie finansy i evropeiskaia birzha v 1904-1906 gg. (Russian finances and the European bourse, 1904-1906), Moscow, Tsentrarkhiv, 1926, dok. No. 39, appendix. -- Emphases are ours.

140. See Die Grosse Politik, Vol. 16, No. 4008, 4812 and 4813.

141. See ibid., No. 4817, Eckardstein's report of February 3/16, 1901.

142. See ibid., p. 325.

143. See ibid., No. 4826 and 4821, Hatzfeldt's telegrams of February 20/March 5 and February 15/28, 1901.

144. See ibid., No. 4820, Eckardstein's telegram of February 15/28, 1901.

145. And, consequently, to emphasize the uselessness of an agreement with Russia. -- See, ibid., No. 4821, Holstein's telegram of February 16/ March 1, 1901 to Hatzfeldt, p. 329.

146. See ibid., No. 4829, Hatzfeldt's telegram of Feb. 23/March 8.

147. See O. Franke, Die Grossmachte in Ost-Asien, p. 172.

148. See ibid., pp. 173, 174, 178, 179.

149. See Die Grosse Politik, Vol. 17, No. 5038, Eckardstein's telegram of April 4/17, 1901.

150. See ibid., No. 5037, his telegram of April 3/16, 1901.

151. See O. Franke, Die Grossmächte in Ost-Asien, p. 183.

152. See ibid., pp. 184-192. For a brilliant analysis of the general volte-face of British policy against Germany at just this time see E.V. Tarle: Evropa v epokhy imperializma (Europe in the Epoch of Imperialism), Moscow, 1927, pp. 65-66 and 117 ff.

153. See Witte's letters of May 24 and May 28, 1901 to Lamsdorf in dos. No. 68, part 4, and No. 12. -- Cf. above, pp. 70-74.

154. See Witte's letter of June 11, 1901 to Lamsdorf, his report of June 15 to his majesty as to organization of the special conference, and the minutes of the conference of June 28 --in dos. No. 81. The Peking line proposal was not in the letter of June 11; it first appeared in the minutes of the conference. All correspondence on the conference was

conducted in the chancery of the minister of finance. -- On Li Hung-
chang's objections see Pokotilov's telegrams of February 14 and 25, 1901,
in dos. No. 51, part I.

155. See Alekseev's telegram of June 17, 1901, which figured in the
conference correspondence, as to "reconnaissance operations" and "increased activity" of the English along the "coast from Taku to Chinwang-
tao" for the purpose of fixing points suitable "for the landing"of Japanese
--"in the Tientsin-Shanhaikwan-Chinwangtao region" for occupation of a
"broad sector" there, and likewise as to the reinforcement of the English
garrison at Shanhaikwan and "persistent demands" of the English for
transfer to them of an extra fort there.

156. See Lamsdorf's letter of July 19, 1901 to Witte, in dos. No. 75,
part 4. Lamsdorf proposed that they decide "finally and irrevocably"
whether it was "advisable for Russia to retain either all of Manchuria as
occupied by our troopsor one of its provinces?" Lamsdorf's letter did
not touch on the question of setting a time limit for the evacuation.

157. See Kuropatkin's letter of July 30, 1901 to Lamsdorf, ibid. For
an exposition of Kuropatkin's letter see Prolog etc., pp. 175 ff.

158. Witte's answer to Lamsdorf's letter is reviewed in Prolog etc.,
p. 174. -- For Hayashi's communication ("strictly confidential") concerning Witte's proposal, see Die Grosse Politik, Vol. 17, No. 5041;
in Eckardstein's telegram of July 26, n.s., 1901, Hayashi stated that
Sutemi had conversed with Witte "quite recently."

159. See Die Grosse Politik, Vol. 17, No. 5040, Eckardstein's telegram of July 6/19, 1901.

160. See translation of "Hayashi's Notes" in Izv. MID, 1913, book V,
p. 324. Cf. O. Franke, Die Grossmächte in Ost-Asien, p. 192. These
proposals were made, Hayashi was told, at the wish of Edward VII.

161. See "Zapiski Gayasi" (Hayashi's Notes), pp. 324-325 and O.
Franke, op. cit., pp. 193-194.

162. See Pozdneev's telegram of July 20, 1901 to Witte in dos. No. 51,
part I, and Girs's telegram of July 28, 1901, in dos. No. 75, part 4.

163. The instructions given Li Hung-chang for the negotiations with
Girs were so formulated: see Girs's telegram of August 18, 1901 from
Peking in dos. No. 75, part 4.

164. See Pozdneev's telegram of July 20, 1901 from Peking, in dos.
No. 51, part 3.

165. See Girs's tel. of July 28, 1901 from Peking, in dos. No. 75,
part 4.

166. See Lamsdorf's report of August 4, 1901, to his majesty, in
dos. No. 75, part 4.

167. See Girs's quoted telegram of July 28, 1901, in dos. No. 75,
part 4, and E. Satow's reports of August 14 and 21, n.s., 1901, to
Lansdowne in the English Blue Book (China No. 2, 1904), No. 40 and
42. With the report of August 21 Satow enclosed a comparative text that
he had made of all three redactions of the Russian project (the February,
the March, and the August), showing the August one to be a verbatim
combination of the first two.

168. See, in dos. No. 75, part 4: Lamsdorf's telegram of August 14,
1901 to Girs, and the "project for an agreement with China respecting
Manchuria" sent to the minl fin. on August 6 (Witte's comment: "answer
that I have no remarks").

169. See above, pp. 288 and 315.

170. See, in dos. No. 75, part 4: Kuropatkin's letter of August 12, 1901 to Lamsdorf, Lamsdorf's telegram of August 22 to Girs, and the "new redaction" of the agreement project forwarded to the min. fin. with Lamsdorf's letter of August 8, 1901. The "new redaction" omitted point V of art. 4 concerning the grant to the Chinese Eastern Railway Company of the concession for a branch "to the Great Wall at the boundary of Manchuria and Chih-li province," evidently introduced into the first redaction from the minutes of the conference of June 28, 1901 on trans-fer of the railways to China (see above, p. 314).

171. See Girs's tel. of Aug. 18, 1901, in dos. No. 75, part 4.

172. See ibid., Pozdneev's tel. of Aug. 19/Sept. 1 to Witte.

173. See Lessar's telegram of Sept. 23, 1901, ibid. Besides the three editorial changes, Li Hung-chang asked that in art. 3 the clause about the two governments concluding a "special agreement fixing the number and places of cantonment of Chinese troops in Manchuria" be altered to read that the two governments "see to ordering the Russian military authorities and the chiang-chüns to arrange respecting the fixing" of same. Cf. Witte's tel. of Sept. 26 to Lamsdorf as to the acceptability of this correction.

174. See, ibid., Witte's letter of Sept. 28 to Lamsdorf enclosing Yugovich's telegram from Harbin, and Lamsdorf's letter of Sept. 30, 1901 to Witte. From the very beginning of the occupation of Manchuria advices had never ceased to come in from Russian agents of the Chinese Eastern Railway as to the impotence of Russian troops to cope with the swiftly moving "khunkhuz" detachments.

175. See Lamsdorf's quoted letter of Sept. 30, 1901, in dos. No. 75, part 4.

176. See Lamsdorf's tel. of Sept. 30, 1901 to Witte, ibid. -- Komura was Japanese minister of foreign affairs.

177. See ibid, Lessar's tel. of Oct. 2, 1901 from Peking.

178. See Lamsdorf's telegram of Oct. 31, 1901 to Lessar. Lamsdorf offered the following "arguments" in favor of delaying negotiations: "since the moment when dates were set for evacuation, approximately 3 months have already passed and the time of year is approaching when it will with each week be more difficult to start withdrawing troops from remote dis-tricts of Manchuria," and Lessar "as a preliminary to signing the agree-ment, would need to request thorough instructions for setting new evacu-ation dates for such army divisions as would have to leave certain regions of Manchuria during the present year of 1901."

179. See, in dos. No. 51, part 3, the telegram of July 27, 1901 to Pozdneev that Witte submitted to Nicholas, and Pozdneev's tel. of July 29/August 11, 1901.

180. See, ibid., Pozdneev's tel. of July 27/August 9, 1901. Cf. above, p. 321.

181. See, in dos. No. 51, part 3: Witte's tel. of July 27, 1901 (on giving Li Hung-chang "suitable remuneration") and his tel. of August 3, 1901 ("he might be paid three hundred thousand rubles, but only after the agreement is finally confirmed"), and, in dos. No. 75, part 4: Lams-dorf's tel. of August 14, 1901 to Girs, and his tel. of August 22 to Girs ("the official communication given you bearing the signatures of Li Hung-chang and Ching we consider sufficient").

182. See, in dos. No. 75, part 4, Lamsdorf's tel. of August 18, 1901 to Girs, Witte's tel. of August 16 to Pozdneev, Lamsdorf's tel. of August 22 to Girs, and Witte's letter of August 23 to Lamsdorf, mentioning that the banking agreement "must be concluded earlier than, or simultaneously with, the agreement as to the evacuation of troops, but on no account after the latter."

183. See, ibid., Pozdneev's tel. of Aug. 21, 1901. The talk proceeded "in a very friendly tone," though Pozdneev did not speak of compensation until the next day (with Li Hung-chang's younger son Li Ching-mai, who "immediately went to report this to his father and expressed almost absolute certainty that the agreement could be signed"): see Pozdneev's tel. of Aug. 22, in dos. No. 51, part 3.

184. See, in dos. No. 75, part 4, Witte's tel. of Aug. 23 to Pozdneev.

185. See, ibid., Pozdneev's tel. of Sept. 24, 1901. -- Li demanded that Pozdneev show formal authorization to negotiate, and this was telegraphed to Peking by Ukhtomsky, as chairman of the Board of the bank, on October 1 (see Ukhtomsky's telegram, ibid.) "in the likely supposition that this agreement will be concluded" and inasmuch as it was "obvious that in said agreement the Russo-Chinese bank was a figurehead," Witte thought it "imperative that, when the agreement was signed, the Board immediately give the ministry of finance a pledge that it would make no decisions relating to the present agreement without approval of the ministry of finance...and that the Board be obliged to execute without dispute all orders of the minister of finance as to this agreement provided they involved no disbursements by the bank," and that "at the first general meeting" thereafter "this pledge [of the Board's] be confirmed by the general meeting of share-holders." Witte charged Shipov to project such a pledge (see, ibid., Witte's letter of Sept. 26 to Shipov and the "treaty" project in 7 points drawn up by Shipov). -- We quote the text of the project:

"Between the Russian minister of finance, on the one hand, and the Russo-Chinese bank, on the other, a treaty has been concluded to the following effect:

Exclusively on the strength of the Russian government's support and protection, the Russo-Chinese bank concluded with the Chinese government on October...of this year an agreement concerning the bank's prior right to obtain industrial concessions in Manchuria. In view of this, the Russo-Chinese bank assumes the folowing obligations to the Russian government.

1. The Russo-Chinese bank engages to report at once to the minister of finance any concession offered it by the Chinese government.

2. The Russo-Chinese bank engages to present to the minister of finance for preliminary approval the project of any concession which it may propose to accept from the Chinese government on the basis of the above mentioned agreement with said government. The bank will likewise present for the preliminary approval of the minister of finance the projects of any treaties that the bank contemplates concluding with the Chinese government in connection with said agreement. The bank shall have the right to accept from the Chinese government only those concessions and conclude with this government only those treaties respecting which the consent of the minister of finance shall be forthcoming.

N o t e . On the basis of a charter confirmed by his majesty, the Russo-Chinese bank has the right to acquire in China concessions for the construction of railways and the laying of telegraph lines. In view of this, should the question arise of granting the Russo-Chinese bank, on the basis of the aforementioned agreement with the Chinese government, any other industrial concession in Manchuria--the bank as a preliminary to acceptance of such a concession shall be obliged to petition the Russian government in the regular order for a suitable addendum to its charter.

3. The Russo-Chinese bank engages, if this shall not be attended by expense to the bank, to accept, upon request of the minister of finance, any concession offered by the Chinese government, or petition said government for grant to the bank of any concession that the minister of finance shall indicate to the bank.

4. The exploitation of concessions received by the Russo-Chinese bank on the basis of the aforementioned agreement with the Chinese government, the bank engages to convey to stock companies organized in conformity with Russian laws or to private persons in good standing, at the discretion of the minister of finance. The charter of such companies shall be worked out by the Russo-Chinese bank in accordance with the instructions of the minister of finance; in the conveyance of concessions to private persons the bank shall impose on the latter such conditions respecting the organization of the enterprise as shall be indicated by the minister of finance.

5. Any concession that the Russo-Chinese bank refuses, may, on the strength of the above-mentioned agreement with the Chinese government, be transferred by the latter to such persons and institutions as will in the exploitation of these concessions avail themselves exclusively of the services of the Russo-Chinese bank as banker.

6. The Russo-Chinese bank engages, in general, to act on all questions in any way connected with the aforementioned agreement between the bank and the Chinese government in accordance with the instructions of the minister of finance.

7. The present treaty is exempt from payment of any taxes or levies to the treasury."

186. See Pozdneev's tel. of Sept. 26, giving complete text of the agreement, and of Sept. 27, 1901, in dos. No. 75, part 4.

187. See, in dos. No. 75, part 4, Pozdneev's tel. of Oct. 2, 1901.

188. See, ibid., secretary min. fin.'s tel. of Oct. 9 to Shipov and Pozdneev's tel. of Oct. 12, 1901.

189. See Pozdneev's tel. of Sept. 17, Oct. 12 and 13, and secretary min. fin.'s tel. of Oct. 10, 1901 to Shipov, in dos. No. 75, part 4, and Witte's tel. of Oct. 14 to Pozdneev in dos. No. 51, part 3.

190. See in dos. No. 75, part 4, Pozdneev's tel. of Oct. 17, 1901.

191. See, in dos. No. 51, part 3, Witte's tel. of Oct. 25 to Pozdneev and Pozdneev's of Oct. 26, 1901 to Witte. For the present, Pozdneev had given orders "to our agents to cement friendly relations with all newly constitutued officials enjoying the favor of Wang Wen-shao and Yuan Shih-kai, and had allowed 500 lan for entertainment and gifts" (about 700 rubles). Witte licensed this expenditure by telegram of Oct. 27 (see ibid.).

192. See Lamsdorf's above-quoted letter of September 30, 1901 to Witte, in dos. No. 75, part 4.

193. See "Zapiski Gayasi," In Izv. MID, 1913, book V, p. 325.
194. See the tel. of Sept. 2, 1901 from Yokohama of the min. fin.'s
agent in Japan, Alekseev, who had obtained this information from the
French consul. Not until the latter half of October did the min. fin. receive the detailed report, and with it copies of the Frenchman's corresponding report to his own government in Paris (see dos. No. 12).
195. See Witte, Vosp., I, pp. 183 ff., Morskoi, Razocharovaniia v
chestnom maklerstve. T. Ruzvelt i Portsmutskie soveshchaniia (Dis-
illusionments of Honest Brokerage: T. Roosevelt and the Portsmouth
Conferences), Moscow, 1911, p. 12, and Prolog etc., p. 189.
196. See Lamsdorf's letter of Oct. 29, 1901 to Witte, in dos. No. 12:
"Today I gave Butiron a memorandum for the guidance of Delcasse in the
matter of his negotiations with Marquis Ito. I also remarked to him
parenthetically that it was of course impossible for France to promote
the Japanese loan without knowing how secure peace was in the Far East,
and that the preservation of peace and tranquility was directly dependent
upon good relations between Russia and Japan. We desire the establishment of such relations, ask nothing better, but cannot renounce our
rights and certain conditions, which I then indicated in general outline.
So I hope that Ito will be prepared for the talks ahead of him in St. Petersburg, and that France before concluding the loan will prudently await the
results of Ito's sojourn in Russia."
197. This confession Li Hung-chang made to Pozdneev at precisely
the moment when, having exhausted all devices for delaying the bank
agreement, he changed his "plan of action" and, still without telegraphing
the court as to the agreement with the bank, began erecting obstacles to
the general agreement (see Pozdneev's telegrams of Oct. 12, 13, and 17,
1901, in dos. No. 75, part 4).
198. See Lamsdorf's tel. of Oct. 31, 1901 to Lessar, in dos. No. 75,
part 5.
199. Ito arrived in Paris on November 1, o.s.
200. Ching first summoned Pozdneev on November 28. Ito had left
Peterburg on Nov. 21. See Pozdneev's tel. of Nov. 28, 1901, in dos.
No. 75, part 5.
201. See the report of Dec. 4, n.s., 1901 of Alwensleben, German
ambassador to St. Petersburg, published in Die Grosse Politik, Vol. 17,
pp. 144-145, and Alekseev's report of March 25, 1902 from Yokohama
on his meeting with Ito's secretary Suzuki, who, speaking for his patron,
so characterized Ito's conversations with the two ministers, in dos.
No. 97.
202. See Lamsdorf's letter of Nov. 27, 1901 to Witte, in dos. No. 12,
giving an account of the two conversations that Lamsdorf had had with
Ito. -- Cf. "Ustnyi obmen mnenii mezhdu rossiiskim ministrom in-
ostrannykh del i markizom Ito" (Oral exchange of opinions between the
Russian minister of foreign affairs and Marquis Ito), published in izd.
MID. Obzor snoshenii s Iaponiei po koreiskim delam s 1895 g. (Survey
of Relations with Japan on Korean Affairs from 1895), St. Petersburg,
pp. 68 ff., and excerpt from said letter of Nov. 27 to Witte. Cf. also
Witte, Vosp. I, p. 183.
203. See Lamsdorf's letter of Nov. 27, 1901 to Witte in dos. No. 12.

204. See Witte's letter of Nov. 28, 1901 to Witte in dos. No. 12.(This is printed in Glinskii's Prolog etc., pp. 243 ff., as of November 1902). Witte proposed no changes in the Japanese text of articles 2 and 3 except deletion of the words "against each other." -- The text common to both projects is given in regular type; Russian corrections are in italics; spaced sections in square brackets are words of the Japanese text omitted from the Russian. For the Japanese and Russian projects see Obzor snoshenii s Iaponiei po koreiskim delam s 1895 g., St. Petersburg., 1906, pp. 67 and 71.

205. The Russian project left Japan a choice of two formulations: one mutual, the other unilateral.

206. It is very possible that the whole 5th article was inserted at Witte's direction: see Hayashi's "Zapiski" in Izv. MID, 1913, book V, p. 330.

207. See Alekseev's report of March 25, 1902 from Yokohama, in dos. No. 97.

208. Cf. also the interview with Ito published in the Japanese newspaper Hochi Shimbun for June 22, 1902. To Ito's statement that "should Korea be recognized as falling within Japan's exclusive sphere of interests, then peace in the orient would without doubt no longer be in danger," Witte replied: "Quite true,provided Russia is allowed to occupy a point on the south-Korean littoral, in which case she is prepared to immediately renounce all pretensions to Korea." But if by this point Masampo was implied, then "Japan,"--remarked Ito--"could not agree to such a compromise , for Masampo is the Gibralter of the Korean gulf; to lose it would mean losing all Korea" (see dos. No. 12). In 1899, when at the instance of the navy department, which had from the start pointed out the unsatisfactoriness of Port Arthur, a section of coastal strip was secured in Masampo, the ministry of finance had declared that "it would appear advisable" to obtain strips of land not only in Masampo but also in Sonchinpo and Pengyang, but "especially in Masampo." See, in dos. No. 55, Witte's letter of April 22, 1899 to Muravev. For the treaty concerning Masampo see Sb. dog. i dip. dok. po delam Dal'nevo Vostoka, St. Petersburg, 1906, pp. 388 ff.

209. See Die Grosse Politik, Vol. 17, No. 5042, Alwensleben's report of Dec. 4, n.s., 1901 from St. Petersburg. The words "bis 1904" were written in the margin by Wilhelm.

210. See above, p. 330.

211. See Ito's letter of Dec. 10/23, 1901 to Lamsdorf in izd. MID. Obzor snoshenii s Iaponiei po koreiskim delam, pp. 74-75.

212. See O. Franke, "Die Grossmächte in Ost-Asien," p. 198. In his "Zapiski" Hayashi puts the assertion into Ito's mouth that since the talks with Lamsdorf and Witte he "could feel confident of the conclusion of an agreement with Russia," and had so telegraphed Tokyo. It hardly seems probable that Ito would not have indicated in the telegram, however briefly, the terms on which Peterburg was prepared to compromise with Japan in Korea. The more so since at a conference previous to Ito's departure for Europe Tokyo had considered "recognizing" "Russia's freedom of action in Manchuria" "only in an extremity" (see Izv. MID, 1913, book V, pp. 330 and 327).

213. Even before Ito's return to Tokyo, Alekseev had reported, on January 7, 1902, from Yokohama that "the government here has been officially notified that Russia's intentions respecting Manchuria remain 'inflexible.'"

214. The project of the Anglo-Japanese treaty was delivered to Ito in Peterburg by courier on November 20/December 3, 1901 for consideration (see Izv. MID, 1913, book V, p. 329). Both Russian ministers were thrown off the track by their own agents, who now sent word of the impossibility of Japan's making a loan in Paris, now explained Japan's refusal at the beginning of January to intervene jointly with England in Russo-Chinese negotiations as due to her hope of an agreement with Russia, now again sent word about the continuance of Japanese loan negotiations in Paris (see, in dos. No. 12, the telegram of December 26, 1901 from the ambassador in Paris, Lamsdorf's letter to Witte and Witte's to Lamsdorf of January 7 and 10, 1902).

215. See Pozdneev's tel. of Nov. 28, 1901 and Lessar's tel. of Nov. 30, same year, in dos. No. 75, part 5.

216. See Pozdneev's telegrams of November 28 and December 5, and Witte's of December 1, 1901, ibid.

217. See Pozdneev's telegram of December 7 concerning the first preliminary call on the minister by the whole group of Chinese plenipotentiaries (Ching, Wan Wenshao, Liang Fang and Takshin) and Lamsdorf's letter of December 15 to Witte enclosing the text of the emendations proposed by the Chinese, in dos. No. 75, part 5.

218. See Witte's letter of December 17, 1901 to Lamsdorf, ibid. -- Witte found, 1) that the reduction of the evacuation cycles "would be attended with certain inconveniences in view of the fact that we shall not have succeeded in completing the equipment of the Chinese Eastern Railway by that time and the numbers of the border guard of the trans-Amur district will not as yet have been brought to the proposed figure" (25,000 men), 2) that "limitation of the number of Chinese troops as far as possible" "had been made one of the main conditions of our evacuation of Manchuria, and there would appear to be no grounds for backing down from this condition at the present time," 3) that unless guns are forbidden, "artillery divisions" will be formed from the police guard, 4) that it was not a question of the Chinese government "permitting" a "foreign power" "to occupy" the railroads, but simply of China being responsible for the appearance there of "foreign troops," 5) that disbursements must be repaid "as a preliminary to" transfer of the railways and without any discussion. -- The amount to be repaid was calculated at about 1,120,000 rubles--a "hard condition for penniless China" (see Lessar's tel. of Nov. 3, 1901, in dos. No. 75, part 5.)

219. See, in dos. No. 75, part 5, Pokotilov's tel. of Dec. 26 and 30, and Lessar's tel. of Dec. 31, 1901; cf. Alekseev's report of Dec. 29 from Yokohama, in dos. No. 97.

220. See Alekseev's report of Jan. 7, 1902 from Yokohama, and Lamsdorf's letter of Jan. 5, 1902 to Witte in dos. No. 75, part 5, and his letter of Jan. 7, 1902 in dos. No. 12. From Yokohama, Alekseev warned that "intrigue" was afoot around Izvolsky and that he had mistakenly supposed that Japan had "flatly refused" when she had merely temporarily "declined to give an answer as yet and would preserve [Alekseev here stumbled completely] a waiting attitude until Ito's return

from Europe." Confident of the latter, Alekseev did not telegraph, but sent his report by post, figuring that it would reach Peterburg in a month, and Ito was "not expected before the end of February." Alekseev also cautioned that the Americans had replied in the affirmative to the English proposal and "would always go hand in hand with England as desiring a negative settlement of Russia's special treaty respecting Manchuria."

221. Cf. Witte's telegram of January 5 to Pokotilov, Pokotilov's of January 11, Witte's tel. of January 15, and the collated text of the agreement project, dated in the chanc. min. fin. January 15, 1902. In the excerpt from the project reproduced, words are underlined that Witte insisted upon and that Ching would not agree to; spaced words in round brackets are those that Ching insisted on including and to which Witte would not agree.

222. See Lamsdorf's tel. of Jan. 18, 1902 to Lamsdorf, in dos. No. 75, part 5.

223. See Pokotilov's telegram of Jan. 20, 1902, and Witte's tel. of Jan. 22 to Pokotilov, ibid.

224. See the United States ambassador's note of Jan. 21/Feb. 3, 1902 in dos. No. 75, part 5. The note was transmitted to Lamsdorf on Jan. 23 (see, ibid, his report of the 23rd to his majesty).

225. See project for note of reply to the United States ambassador, forwarded to the chanc. min. fin. with Lamsdorf's letter of Jan. 24, Witte's letter of the same date to Lamsdorf ("I fully share the considerations set forth in the project"), and especially Lamsdorf's tel. of Jan. 27, 1902 to Cassini, asserting among other things that the ministry "was not precisely informed of all the details of the bank's agreement with the Chinese government" (in dos. No. 75, part 5). The American note did not admit of any other interpretation of its clear and forthright sense. The second paragraph said: "I am authorized to say to you that the government of the U.S.A. cannot view without alarm any agreement whereby China would grant a commercial company exclusive privilege to exploit mines in its own territory as well as to build railways or enjoy other industrial rights."

226. See, ibid., Pokotilov's tel. of Jan. 24 and Lessar's of Jan. 25, 1902. Even the American minister in Peking told Lessar "apropos of the Russo-Chinese bank's Manchurian agreement": "had Russia not insisted on this, no one would have opposed the political convention" (see, ibid., Lessar's tel. of Jan. 21). Hay in an explanation with Cassini likewise "fully recognized the expediency of concluding the convention respecting the gradual evacuation of Manchuria," only objecting to the "complete exclusion of foreign industry" (see, ibid., Cassini's tel. of Jan. 26, 1902).

227. See, ibid., Pokotilov's tel. of Jan. 29, received in Peterburg on the 30th. Ching had referred to "categorical protests on the part of America and Japan."

228. See Die Grosse Politik, Vol. 17, No. 5047, Alwensleben's tel. of Jan. 31/Feb. 13, 1902 from St. Petersburg.

229. Of the Anglo-Japanese treaty, Izvolsky in Tokyo had, up to the moment of its publication, "absolutely no suspicion" and was "in great chagrin" about it (Alekseev's tel. of Jan. 31/Feb. 13, in dos. No. 12;) Lamsdorf was also "completely taken by surprise" (vollständig uberrascht: Die Grosse Politik, Vol. 17, No. 5047) by the minister's communication.

230. See, in dos. No. 75, part 5: Lessar's tel. of Feb. 12, Alekseev's tel. of Feb. 16 to the minister of war from Port Arthur, Witte's letter of Feb. 20, 1902 to Lamsdorf, Lamsdorf's letter of Feb. 22, 1902 to Kuropatkin, and Lamsdorf's letter of Feb. 25 to Witte; in this last, Lamsdorf proposed agreeing to China's new addendum concerning evacuation and transfer of civil government, of Newchwang before September 26, 1902, in exchange for which China agreed to extend the time limit of evacuation from 12 to 18 months; Adm. Alekseev's tel. of Feb. 16 from Port Arthur, telling of the appearance in Manchuria of "many Japanese subjects," "travelling about freely by rail" for the purpose of "espionage," of the "strange reserve" of Japanese merchants in Port Arthur about contracting for supplies and of unfavorable alteration in the conduct of the chinag-chün of Mukden, was made known to Lamsdorf precisely on Feb. 25.

231. See Witte's telegram of March 11 to Pokotilov, and Pokotilov's to Witte of March 16, in dos. No. 51, part 3.

232. See, ibid., Pokotilov's telegrams of March 18 and March 29, 1902. In all, 40,656 rubles, in Russian money, were paid over. After this payment from the four-million ("Li Hung-chang") fund, there remained in the finance minister's account in the Russo-Chinese bank 2,342,228 rubles, 24 kopecks (see, ibid., folio 63, chanc. min. fin. statement).

233. See Morse, The International Relations of the Chinese Emprie, Vol. III, pp. 228-9.

234. See, in dos. No. 12, Witte's letter of Nov. 28, 1901, to Lamsdorf.

235. See p. 308, above.

236. See Die Grosse Politik, Vol. 17, No. 5047 and 5048 (Bülow's notation on Wilhelm's impressions of the report of the ambassador in Peterburg as to the French minister's having repeated to him Lamsdorf's words on first learning of the Anglo-Japanese treaty).

237. See, ibid., No. 5049, Alwensleben's tel. of Feb. 3/19, 1902 from St. Petersburg.

CHAPTER VI

1. See Die Grosse Politik, Vol. 17, No. 5186, Metternich's tel. of Jan. 17/30, 1902 from London. -- On the secret non-agression and neutrality pact of 1902 between Italy and France, see A.M. Zaionchkovskii, Podgotovka Rossii k mirovoi voine v mezhdunarodnom otnoshenii (Russia's preparation for the World War in its International Aspect), Moscow, 1926, p. 116.

2. See Izvolsky's dispatch of May 5, 1902 from Tokyo, in dos. No. 12.

3. See above, p. 294, note 2, and p. 209, note 1, also Die Grosse Politik, Vol. 17, No. 5049, Alwensleben's tel. of Feb. 3/19, 1902--the Danzig meeting occurred Aug. 29/Sept. 11--Aug. 31/Sept. 13, 1901 (on it, see Ibid., Vol. 18, part I, No. 5385-5396.)

4. See Die Grosse Politik, Vol. 18, part 1, No. 5384, 5385 (April 7/20 and 8/21, 1901 exchange of telegrams between Wilhelm and Nicholas), No. 5386 (Bülow's memorandum of May 29/June 11, 1901 on the terms of the meeting as transmitted by Nicholas to Wilhelm through the naval agent Pauli;) Vol. 18, part 2, No. 5893, 5894, Alwensleben's telegrams of May 24/June 6, 1901 concerning Pendezec's February negotiations in

Peterburg (cf. A. M. Zaionchkovskii's Podgotovka k mirovoi voine v mezhdunarodnom otnoshenii, Moscow, 1926, p. 91.)

5. See Die Grosse Politik, Vol. 18, part 1, No. 5402, p. 41, Bülow's notation on Alwensleben's letter of Feb. 14/27, 1902 concerning Osten-Saken's words: "You assured us at Danzig, that in the Far East we should proceed together." Cf. the letter of Sept. 3, 1901 from Obo-lensky, assistant minister of foreign affairs to Witte, stating that "Lams-dorf requested him to inform" Witte "that he remained completely satis-fied by the Danzig negotiations and furthermore had not had to communi-cate the text of our proposed agreement with China as to the evacuation of Manchuria" (dos. No. 74, part 4).

6. See Die Grosse Politik, Vol. 18, part 1, No. 5395, Bülow's memo-randum on the Danzig meeting of Sept. 1/14, 1901, and No. 5399, his memorandum of Oct. 22/Nov. 4, 1901 on Prince Heinrich's advices con-cerning his talks with Nicholas at Spala.

7. See Ibid., Vol. 17, No. 5052, Alwensleben's tel. of Feb. 13/26, 1902 on his "big" talk with Nicholas of Jan. 14/27 of that year.

8. See Ibid., No. 5048 and No. 5050 (Bülow's instructions of Feb. 9/22, 1902 to Alwensleben.)

9. See Ibid.: No. 5050, No. 5051 (Bülow's memorandum of Feb. 12/25, 1902 on the talk with Osten-Saken), No. 5057 (Alwensleben's tel. of March 4, n.s.), No. 5052 (ditto of Feb. 13/26,) No. 5186 (Metternich's tel. of Jan. 17/30, 1902 from London); Vol. 18, part 1, No. 5399, 5408 (Richthofen's memorandum to Bülow, of March 21/April 3, 1902 on Wil-helm's talk with Paul), No. 5404 (Alwensleben's letter of March 2/15, 1902 to Bülow), No. 5409 (Bülow's tel. of March 23/April 5, 1902 to Wil-helm).

10. See, ibid., No. 5057 and 5408 (as Wilhelm expressed himself: "Das Liebeswerben Russlands ist sehr warm und sehr auffällig. Sie müssen doch grosse Angst vor irgend etwas haben.")

11. See ibid., No. 5416, Bülow's communication of July 26/Aug. 8, 1902 to Metternich in London.

12. See Wilhelm's letters of April 13/26, 1895 and Sept. 2/15, 1902 to Nicholas, in Perepiska V. i N., pp. 7-8 and 41.

13. See Witte's letter of July 12, 1901 to Sipiagin (Kr. Arkhiv, Vol. XVIII, pp. 45-46: "...Bezobrazov is no less than twice a week closeted for hours with the sovereign.... His majesty is in a state of perplexity, with ideas of some sort in process of fermentation.")-- See above, pp. 40-42, on the Berlin brochure dated May 1902. Of the Japanese seizure of Korea as casus belli for Russia, Nicholas had spoken to Hein-rich of Prussia at Spala in the autumn of 1901 (see Die Grosse Politik, Vol. 18, part 1, p. 35).

14. See Wilhelm's tel. of Oct. 18/31, 1902 to Nicholas, in which he "proposed" the following formulation of the answer to Edward or his ministers if they should inquire about the Reval meeting (Perepiska Vil' gel'ma i Nikolaia, p. 43): "His Majesty the Emperor of all Russia, as head of the dual alliance, and I, as head of the triple, both have in view the one great aim of securing peace for our nations and our friends. We are therefore laboring for the maintenance of peace, with an eye to the interests common to continental nations desiring to consolidate and develop their trade and their economic position." It is not known that Nicholas "approved" the "proposed answer" (see his telegram of Oct. 19/

Nov. 1, 1902, published in Die Grosse Politik, Vol. 18, part 1, No.
5418). Thereafter, Wilhelm several times circulated this formula, see
Perepiska Vil'gel'ma i Nikolaia, p. 44.
    15. For the declaration of March 3/16, 1902 see Sb. dog. i dip. dok.
po delam Dal'nevo Vostoka, p. 533. -- To incline France to this move,
Lamsdorf, in the note of Feb. 7, 1902, promised that "in the event of
any misunderstandings with England in southern China, France could
always count on the support of Russia" (see S. Tomsinskii, "K voprosu
o sotsial'noi prirode russkogo samoderzhaviia" (On the question of the
social nature of the Russian autocracy), in Vestnik Kom. Akademii (Com.
Academy Herald), Vol. 15, p. 273). -- Compare Die Grosse Politik,
Vol. 17, No. 5065, Eckardstein's tel. of March 8/21, 1902 from London:
the English cabinet had considered the "possibility of France intervening
on Russia's side and, in consequence, the opening of casus foederis for
England" "excluded," and now the declaration of March 3/16 "had shattered
this illusion and given scope for a certain feeling of insecurity" (Unsicher-
heit.) -- The French ambassador in Berlin was likewise "alarmed" by this
joint move with Russia against England and Japan (see ibid., No. 5064,
Marquis de Noailles' conversation of March 7/20, 1902 with Bülow).
    16. For the exchange of remarks between Lamsdorf and Scott see the
Blue Book (China, No. 2, 1904), No. 52 and 53. Scott remarked that
the notorious proviso would in the event, for example, of "disorders in
China" release Russia from her obligations, and asked: "How true are
the items that have appeared in the Russian press concerning new disorders in Manchuria?" Lamsdorf replied that he "had always included
this clause in his explanations" and that he ascribed no significance to
newspaper reports--for example, on his part, "saw no necessity for requesting Lessar to make any official inquiry" as to the truth of items about
disorders in South China (the English sphere). In general, Lamsdorf observed, he "found himself in grave doubt respecting the final result of
those arrangements for the attainment of which the powers had made so
many sacrifices," and feared "a renewal of the difficulties through which
we recently passed." -- On the secret conferences in Tokyo and the
adoption of Yamamoto's third naval program, see: in dos. No. 12,
Alekseev's telegram of May 12/25, 1902 from Yokohama ("powerful increase of army of Eastern Siberia and constant reinforcement of squadron
in the Pacific since the Manchurian agreement understood by Japan as a
demonstration.... Reliable information as to repeated conferences recently of all ministers, with participation of heads of war and navy
staffs;") in dos. No. 79, part I, Izvolsky's telegram of May 30, 1902
from Tokyo, denying the "serious significance" of reports communicated
by Alekseev, and, ibid., Alekseev's report of Oct. 13/26, 1902 that
"as a result of the conferences of Japanese ministers...Adm. Yamamoto's
project for execution of the third program for strengthening the Japanese
fleet is now approved by the cabinet council." See also Pokotilov's tel.
of Feb. 27/March 12, 1902 in dos. No. 79, part I: "in Shanghai and Port
Arthur most alarming rumors of Russia's supposedly inevitable war with
Japan stubbornly persist," and Stein's tel. of April 17, 1902 from Seoul
in dos. No. 12: "...in the strip bordering on Manchuria are many assorted Japanese. In the large towns Japanese officers and non-coms are
instructing Korean soldiers. Japanese officers are everywhere conducting careful reconnaissance.... Among the population there is an ob-

stinate rumor of war between Russia and Japan in May.... The Japanese
are everywhere buying up rice, exporting it to Chemulpo and Genzan."

17. See Kitaiskaiia Vostochnaia zhel. doroga. Istoricheskii ocherk
(The Chinese Eastern Railway: Historical Outline), compiled by the
chanc. of the Board of the Chinese Eastern Railway Co., Vol. I, p. 236;
see also Witte's report to his majesty on his trip to the Far East in the
autumn of 1902: "Complete interruption of passenger service (at Baikal)
continued for 18 days in the winter of 1900-1901, for 29 days in the spring
of 1901, for 4 days in the winter of 1901-1902, for 8 days in the spring,
and freight transfer was suspended even longer."

18. See above, p. 42.

19. See above, p. 342. -- By the opening of hostilities no plan had
been settled on for the transport of troops over the Chinese Eastern Railway, the Khingan tunnel (opened May 14, 1904) was not ready, a steady
water-supply existed at 44 points out of 92, the railway shops were not
finished. The Trans-Baikal road gave passage to four pairs of trains in
24 hours, whereas the Siberian and Chinese Eastern Railways could ac-
commodate seven pairs (see Kitaiskaia Vostochnaia zhel. dor. Istoricheskii
ocherk, comp. chanc. Board Chinese Eastern Railway Co., Vol. I,
pp. 236 ff.)

20. See Witte's letter of Feb. 4, 1902 to Lamsdorf, in dos. No. 98.

21. See above, p. 326, note.

22. See Witte's letter of Jan. 30 to Lamsdorf, Lamsdorf's of Feb. 2
to Witte, and Witte's of Feb. 4, 1902 to Lamsdorf, in dos. No. 98.

23. See Witte's telegram of Feb. 4, 1902 to Pokotilov, in dos. No. 51,
part 3, and Shipov's of Feb. 5, same year, to Pokotilov, in dos. No. 98.

24. See Pokotilov's tel. of Feb. 9/22 and Feb. 15/28, 1902 from
Peking ("the Japanese are trying to get concessions to the coal mines
around Mukden. From Kirin comes word that Americans have already
secured a concession to work the silver ores around Kirin,") in dos.
No. 98.

25. See, ibid., Witte's tel. of Feb. 13, 1902 to Yugovich at Harbin.

26. See, ibid., Yugovich's tel. of Feb. 24, 1902 from Harbin. -- In
the matter of coal, Yugovitch reported that back in June 1901 he had obtained from the chiang-chün a concession to the prior right of prospecting
for and mining coal in Kirin province, and that negotiations to the same
effect had just been successfully concluded with the chiang-chün of Tsitsihar on Feb. 4, 1902. -- Yugovich preferred to obtain a like general concession respecting Mukden province. The negotiations now started by him
in this sense were, so far as is known, without result.

27. It was presented to Nicholas for confirmation on March 8, 1902
(see Witte's report to his majesty of March 8, in dos. No. 51, part 3).
Expenditures aimed at "disposing the local Chinese authorities in our
favor" Witte proposed to charge against the "Li Hung-chang fund," expenditures on acquiring parcels of land for the road, against the funds of
the Chinese Eastern Railway.

28. E.I. Alekseev collection, dos. No. 29, Lyuba's report of
Feb. 24, 1901 to Alekseev from Kirin.

29. See, in dos. No. 5, the copy of Lyuba's "preliminary agreement."
Russian subjects must address all applications respecting discovery and
operation of mines to the official of the ministry of foreign affairs. The
right to prospect was issued for one year. Permission to operate must

be put into effect within a year of its receipt. Every mine must be headed by a Chinese official. The discount of the Chinese treasury was 15 per cent of the gross earnings. This agreement was "confirmed by the Chinese emperor in July 1901."

30. See, ibid., Lyuba's report of Sept. 7, 1901 to the min. for. afs. The right to prospect was granted: 1) to coll. ass. Astashev for the upper stretch of the Sungari in the Hunchun and Ninguta districts, 2) to the Russian Gold-mining Company in the Tunhwashan district (headwaters of the Mudan-kiang), 3) to the nobleman Troitsky in the southern part of the Sansin district (lower course of the Mudan-kiang and the river Taoken), 4) to Gen. Shaniavsky in the northern part of the Sansin district, 5) to the Upper-Amur Gold-mining Company in the Binchow and Azhekho districts (all direct tributaries of the Sungari from Sansin to Bodune).

31. See, ibid., the copy of Krotkov's agreement of Sept. 19, 1901. The whole region from Lake Talai-nor to the river Sungari was divided among five concessionaries: the Upper-Amur Gold-mining Co., Astashev, the Gold-mining Company of Counts Apraxin, Popov, and Emelianov, the United Stock Company, and the Russian Gold-mining Company.

32. See, in the collection of the Peking Div. Mgmt. Chinese Eastern Ry. and Russo-Chinese bank, "file on concessions in Manchuria (special file IV)," Drezemeier's letter of Feb. 15/28, 1902 to Pokotilov from Shanghai. -- The military commissar in Mukden had demanded "communication of your [Pokotilov's] secret code, quoting the ruling that forbids private persons to exchange coded telegrams," see, ibid., Nezabytovsky's tel. of March 21, 1902 to Pokotilov from Mukden.

33. See, ibid., Drezemeier's tel. of March 11, 1902 to Pokotilov, and, in dos. No. 98, Pokotilov's report of July 9/22, 1902 on the activity of agents of the bank in securing concessions.

34. See, in dos. No. 98, Pokotilov's report of May 6/19, 1902 and his letter of June 16/29, 1902.

35. See Pokotilov's letter of May 6/19, 1902 to Witte from Peking, in dos. No. 98.

36. See ibid., Pokotilov's letter of June 16/29, 1902 to Witte.

37. See, in dos. No. 98, Pokotilov's report of July 9/22, 1902. -- Hunt was to get 1/8 of the shares of the Anglo-Russian company.

38. See ibid.

39. See, ibid., Pokotilov's account and the special report on Pokotilov's dispatches and telegrams compiled in the chanc. min. fin. in August 1902.

40. See Pokotilov's report of July 9/22, 1902.

41. See Ukazatel' deistvuiushchikh v Imperii aktsionernykh predpriiatii (Index of Active Joint-Stock Enterprises in the Empire), ed. V.A. Dmitryev-Mamonov. St. Petersburg, 1903, p. 37. On the government's securing the whole issue, see, in dos. No. 134, the "report" compiled by P.M. Romanov in March 1904. Thus 36,200 shares out of 80,000, i.e., c. 41 per cent, were in the hands of the government.

42. The report to his majesty on the founding of the M.M. Ass'n (No. 2297 in the chanc. min. fin.) was confirmed by Nicholas on July 5, 1902. The treaty of association was signed by the share-holders on June 26, same year (see Mongolor collection, dos. No. 12, original treaty of organization of the Assn.). The shares were divided: to Putilov 3334, to the other two 3333 apiece.

43. See rep. to his majesty of July 5, 1902, No. 2297.

44. See Assn's treaty of June 27 with the Russo-Chinese bank and the protocol of the constitutent meeting of shareholders of June 27, 1902, in the Mongolor file, No. 12.

45. So Witte presented the matter to Nicholas in his report of July 5.

46. See, passim, dos. No. 106, in the nine parts of which all Assn. correspondence is concentrated. Direction was entirely in Rothstein's hands.

47. See above, p. 157.

48. As was projected, for example, in turning the Anglo-Russian company into a stock company in which the M.M.A. proposed to participate "jointly with the Russo-Chinese bank."

49. See, in dos. No. 106, pt. 1-b, the Assn's July 1903 report.

50. See Witte's report to his majesty of July 5, 1902, No. 2297, and in dos. No. 106, pt. 1-b, the Assn's January 1904 report.

51. See, for example, Rothstein's correspondence with Pokotilov apropos of participation in the Chinese company, founded at the Mukden chinag-chün's initiative, "Gi shensin" (Mukden Mining Company) in dos. No. 106, pt. 6.

52. See estimates in the annual report of the Association to July 1903, in dos. No. 106, pt. 1-b. The management asked for an additional assignment of two million rubles.

53. The autumn expeditions of 1902 covered about 3500 versts and examined 14 beds in Kirin and Mukden provinces, see ibid.

54. This engagement was provided in Astashev's agreement of August 27, 1901 with the chiang-chün of Kirin (see Mongolor accumulation, dos. No. 12). The M.M.A. paid Astashev's heirs 25,000 rubles for the transfer of rights.

55. See, in dos. No. 106, pt. 9, the letter of April 1, 1903 from the chairman of the Board of the Rus. Gold-m'g Co. to the M.M.A. -- Terms of the transfer: yhe Rus. Gold-m'g Co. to be repaid 60,198 rub. 44 kop. of its expenditures and allowed 25 per cent of the annual net profit (without participating in the management, however), the Russo-Chinese bank to receive 200 rubles of each pood of gold mined, engineer K.E. Pfaffius 175 rubles, and 2 per cent of the profits to go to the chiang-chün of Tsitsihar (see, in dos. No. 157, the schedule of the M.M.A.'s concession rights).

56. See ibid.; terms of transfer: former owners to receive 25 per cent of the net profit from each pood of gold dust: A.E. Den to receive 375 rubles, A.I. Kazarin, 375 r., engineer K.E. Pfaffius, 200 r., A.E. Pfaffius 150 r., and A.B. Nagel, 150 r.

57. However, the M.M. Assn's right to these shares was only made official by the bank's letter of August 7, 1906 (see ibid). By January 1904 the Assn. figured that it held a total of 1190 shares out of 2000 (see in dos. No. 106, pt. 1-b, the report of Jan. 4, 1904).

58. See, in dos. No. 157, schedule of the M.M. Assn's concession rights. Declaration of the desirability of the Russo-Chinese bank's participation in the Mukden company had been made by the chiang-chün himself (see, in dos. No. 106, pt. 6, Pokotilov's tel. of Sept. 2/15 and 3/16, 1902 to Putilov). However, the affair ran into difficulties in Peking, and Pokotilov had to pay 32 thousand lan to see it through (to Wang Wen-shao, minister of finance, Ching's eldest son and others), see, ibid., Pokotilov's tel. of April 14, 1903.

59. In event of the organization of a stock company for the exploitation
of this Company's concessions, the Russo-Chinese bank "engaged to transfer half its shares to the M.M. Assn.," on condition of reimbursing the
bank "for half its expenditures" (see, in dos. No. 157, the minute-book
of the special committee of the ministry of finance, confirmed August 8,
1906, on transfer of the M.M. Assn's rights to Mongolor).

60. See, in dos. No. 106, pt. 1-b, report to July 1903.

61. See, in dos. No. 106, pt. 1-b, the July report of the Management
of the Assn.

62. See, ibid., the January 1904 report, and, in dos. No. 12 of the
Mongolor accumulation, the list of the stockholders presenting shares at
the organization meeting of August 14, 1903: K.V. Berg--5 shares, P.A.
Bok--40, L.F. Grauman--40, A.A. Davidov--40, K.M. Yoganson--5,
S.I. Littauer--40, Pokotilov--40, Putilov--40, A. Iu. Rozenfeld--5,
A.E. Soloveichik--5, G.I. Yagodin--5, and (over and above the 5,200
shares for the concession) the M.M. Assn.--535.

63. As the Management of the Assn. complained of in the report of
Jan. 4, 1904, on August 16, 1903 precisely, the State bank stopped advancing sums on the security of shares, having previously advanced
400,000 rubles in all. -- By the time this report was drawn up, the problem of first importance was the operational reorganization of the Fushan
coal bed, where the Hwasinli company was using "primitive Chinese
methods." To raise production to 25 million poods per annum would require 1,025 thousand rubles of capital; construction of a communicating
road would come to 1,533 thousand rubles.

64. See, in dos. No. 98, the copy of Matiunin's memorandum of
Jan. 30, 1902.

65. See the copy of Lamsdorf's report to his majesty of Jan. 31, 1902,
and the projected telegram to Lessar confirmed by Nicholas (sent on
Feb. 1)--"to enter immediately" upon negotiations with the chiang-chün
of Mukden as to issuing the concession to Matiunin for the term of 25
years, with a discount to the Chinese government of 20 per cent of the
net profit.

66. See above, pp. 368-369.

67. See above, p. 178.

68. See M.N. Pokrovskii, "Iaponskaia voina" (The Japanese War) in
the collection 1905. Istoriia revolutsionnogo dvizheniia in otdel'nykh
ocherkakh (1905: A History of the Revolutionary Movement in Separate
Eassays), Moscow, 1926, Vol. I, pp. 571, ff., and B.A. Romanov,
"Nikolai II i kontsessia na r. Yalu" (Nicholas II and the Yalu Concession)
(Russkoe proshloe [Russia's Past], Petrograd, 1923, No. 1, pp. 97 ff.)
Matiunin who had served as consul in northern Korea, came to Peterburg,
seeking a new appointment, not later than September 1897 and stayed
there until the beginning of February 1898, when he left for Seoul to act
as charge d'affaires having instructions from Nicholas (in oral form, at
the time of his presentation on December 1) and from Muravev, in the
sense of the then accepted Witte program for Korea. Matiunin spoke of
the Briner concession to Vonliarliarskii (his fellow-lyceist) at their first
meeting on Jan. 1, 1898. On Vonliarliarskii's own admission, he took
his project for a stock company to exploit the natural resources of Korea
higher up only "after two or three interviews" with Muravev, when "it
had become plain" to him "that Witte would not permit the emergence in

the Far East of a competitor to the Russo-Chinese bank" (see Vonliarliarskii's Materialy dlia vyiasneniia prichin voiny s Iaponiei (Materials for Ascertaining the Causes of the War with Japan), p. 6, and appended copy of Matiunin's letter of Oct. 25, 1905 to A.M. Abaza). -- V.M. Vonliarliarskii, retired colonel of the guards, former orderly to Grand Duke Nicholas Nikolayevich in the war of 1877-78, large Novgorod landholder, "had conducted large lumbering operations," "headed two cotton mills in Siberia," was president of the Novgorod Society of agriculture and agricultural industry and member of the Society for the Advancement of Russian Industry and trade, owned "gold-fields in the Urals" (see cited letter of Matiunin to Abaza, likewise Witte's letter of July 12, 1901 to Sipiagin, in Kr. Arkh., Vol. 18, p. 45, and Vonliarliarskii's Materialy, pp. 13 and 14).

69. See, in dos. No. 213, the copy of Briner's power of attorney of May 5, 1899 to D.A. Neratov to annul his first treaty with off. min. of the court Neporozhnev (as to cession of rights to the concession of May 11, 1898) and to "cede all" Briner's "rights" by it "without exception" to Neporozhnev, for 65 thousand rubles, (by the treaty of May 11, 1898 Briner ceded his rights for 80 thousand rubles worth of company shares, see Vonliarliarski's cited Materialy). Ibid, in dos. No. 213: copy of the June 26, 1899 act of sale of the concession by Neporozhnev to Matiunin and Albert for 30 thousand rubles, and copy of the "pledge" of Matiunin and Albert given Fredericks on July 9, 1899, certifying that "all sums which had been paid for the transfer to us of rights by said concession were entered by Mr. V.B. Fredericks in accord with special instructions and that all rights in this concession appertained to us only nominally."

70. See, in dos. No. 278, the "absolutely secret memorandum" of April 30, 1898 "transmitted through Grand Duke Alexander Mikhailovich to his majesty the emperor after the money had, by report of Mr. Fredericks, been allocated to the sending of an expedition to northern Korea," and, ibid., the "memorandum" of Feb. 26, 1898 "given his majesty the emperor." These two memoranda, like all the other documents in dos. No. 278, are in copy. -- See above, p. 286.

71. See, ibid., the memorandum of Feb. 26, 1898.

72. See Vonliarliarskii's Materialy, p. 12: "his right hand man [Vorontsov's, in the svyshchennaia druzhina] was A.M. Bezobrazov."

73. See, ibid: "with respect to...the powers" "an intelligent assignment of property rights must be consistently prosecuted and affiliation of the most friendly of the claimants to participation in such material advantages as shall fall to the share of the East-Asiatic company."

74. See ibid. This memorandum does not mention Rothstein by name.

75. "We are the staff" is Vonliarliarskii's expression (see his letter to Grand Duke Alexander Mikhailovich, written after the expedition's return in the spring of 1899, in dos. No. 278).

76. See, in dos. No. 16/s, the copy of the "project" of March 28, 1900.

77. See in dos. No. 278, Vonliarliarskii's letter of Dec. 25, 1899 to Grand Duke Alexander Mikhailovich.

78. See, ibid., the unsigned memorandum given Nicholas by Fredericks on June 2, 1900. In 1898 all orders and allocations for the Korean concession and expedition had gone through Fredericks and he well knew

that the latter, "though equipped for thorough clarification of the matter," "had given but scant information and no exact analyses."

79. So Vorontsov expressed it in a letter of June 4, 1900 to Nicholas (see, in dos. No. 278).

80. See, in dos. No. 278, the unsigned memorandum given Nicholas by Fredericks on June 2, 1900. Both the fact that it was not signed by Fredericks and the fact that it so categorically referred the matter to the ministry of finance incline one to suppose that there had been a preliminary agreement with Witte, and that the memorandum had gone unsigned because it was drawn up in another department. On the other hand, the details noted in the text, as well as the whole structure and style, make it plausible to suppose that the memorandum was drawn up in the ministry of finance. In any event, had it been proposed that Witte dispute Bezobrazov's project, he would have had trouble adding anything to what was said in the memorandum quoted.

81. See, in dos. No. 278, Vorontsov's letter of June 4, 1900 to Nicholas ("Fredericks has nothing to fear. Capital should be returned from first profits"). Vorontsov proposed to see Nicholas, and "take leave of him" before departing on the 5th, "in the presence of Grand Duchess Maria Georgevna;" it may be that Vorontsov also proposed, in passing, so to speak, to obtain, and did obtain, Nicholas's "instructions" in the matter of the charter; Nicholas's resolution (as to turning the charter over "to the committee of ministers for examination" and Abaza's buying of shares), was written on a plain sheet of foolscap with a black pencil, and after obtaining this sheet from Vorontsov on June 6 Bezobrazov in his own hand wrote at the very bottom of the sheet that it was "his majesty's resolution, received June 5, 1900 and relating to the projected charter of the East-Asiatic Industrial Association" (see dos. No. 16/c).

82. See dos. No. 16/s: this "order" of Nicholas's is written on the same sheet of foolscap in Witte's hand and dated "Peterhof, June 1900." Both the charter and the above-described project of March 28 are enclosed, in the dossier, in this sheet.

83. See Vonliarliarskii's Materialy, p. 35: after March 9, 1899, he "received an order to prepare...an estimate on railway surveys from Kirin to Pektusan and along the Yalu to Gishu." Cf. also, from Bezobrazov's memorandum of March 2, 1898: "to come out at the Korean gulf and then join this point by rail with Vladivostok," "bending the railway line to Kirin and Mukden will compel passage through a settled part of China, which will be harder to snip off."

84. See, in dos. No. 278, Bezobrazov's letter of July 15, 1900 to Grand Duke Alexander Mikhailovich. -- Emphases are ours.

85. See, in dos. No. 278, the "memorandum" Bezobrazov prepared for Nicholas on July 23, 1900, and Vorontsov's letter to Bezobrazov in connection with the memorandum, giving corrections (undated).

86. See above, p. 293.

87. This was not indiscriminately aimed merely against foreign capital: "the company must be wholly Russian, and not merely under the flag of the fatherland, the participation of foreign interests [as before] is quite permissible, but without any foreign domination."

88. See Vonliarliarskii's Materialy, pp. 32. ff., Bezobrazov's memorandum of July 26, 1900, entitled "project for a statement of principles of the question."

89. See Bezobrazov's letter of July 15, 1900 to Grand Duke Alexander Mikhailovich,in dos. No. 278: "Quite a time will go by, before things clear a little and decision finishes brewing."

90. See above, pp. 289-305.

91. See, in dos. No. 278, Bezobrazov's letter of June 17, 1901 to Nicholas. Bezobrazov "came to an agreement" with Witte "on certain questions," and Witte even confessed "to certain blanks in his own program," but "around" Witte, Bezobrazov "endeavored to state questions in their most terse form in order to avoid untoward hazards." Upon this occasion the 200 shares were to be turned over not to the Cabinet, but to the treasury in return for the transfer of the Soochan forest to the Company. Witte's "trick" apparently consisted in his striking from the list of founders at the last moment persons in government service (Yusupov, Hendrikov, Abaza, Vonliarliarskii, and Serebriakov) and replacing them by Albert and a certain F.M. Kruz, not so employed, which, in Bezobrazov's opinion, made the "matter still-born" "through fault of the accoucheur" (see, ibid., Bezobrazov's letter to Alexander Mikhailovich). Cf. also Prolog etc., pp. 251-252, and B.A. Romanov, "Nikolai II i kontsessia na Yalu," in Russkoe proshloe, Petrograd, 1923, p. 102.

92. See Witte's letter of July 12, 1901 to Sipiagin, in Kr. Arkhiv, Vol. 18, p. 44; Witte, Vosp., Vol. I, p. 149; B.A. Romanov, "Vitte nakanune russko-iaponskoi voiny" (Witte on the Eve of the Russo-Japanese War), in the col. Rossiia i Zapad (Russia and the West), Petrograd, 1923, p. 166; "Dnevnik Kuropatkina"(Kuropatkin's Diary) in Kr. Arkhiv, Vol. 2, p. 58.

93. See, in the State bank collection, ser. No. 124, dos. No. 155, Nicholas's resolution on the finance committee minutes of Dec. 25, 1901: "To be discussed, the question: Would it be impossible, in the opinion of the chairman and the majority, to aid the State bank by eliminating Poliakov. Moscow would be rid of the Hebrew nest, the domestic (local) economic crisis might be relieved."

94. See Witte's letter of July 12, 1901 to Sipyagin.

95. See B.A. Romanov, "Nikolai II i kontsessia na Yalu," p. 102, and Witte's letter of July 12, 1901 to Sipiagin. (Kr. Arkhiv, Vol. 18, p. 45).

96. See above, p. 307.

97. See above, pp. 314 ff.

98. Vorontsov had refused to be a founder from the moment of the shift to transfer of shares to the treasury rather than to the cabinet. The rest struck after their non-confirmation. In the latter half of 1901 there were some signs that a break-up had begun within the "staff." For example, Grand Duke Alexander Mikhailovich one fine day informed Bezobrazov through Vonliarliarskii that he "did not consider" A.M.'s "participation" in the Company "possible" and "had forgotten former business arrangements." From Bezobrazov's letter to A. Mikhailovich in this connection it may be gathered that in an effort to restrain the fleeing bodyguard of shareholders, Bezobrazov had spread a report as to A. Mikhailovich's "future participation in the affair" of which someone had "mistakenly informed" him (see Bezobrazov's letter to A. Mikhailovich in dos. No. 278).

99. See, in dos. No. 278, Bezobrazov's report to his majesty of Jan. 20, 1902.

100. See, in dos. No. 278, Bezobrazov's report to his majesty of Jan. 20, 1902.

101. See, ibid., his report of Jan. 31, 1902 to his majesty.

102. See, ibid., Bezobrazov's "memorandum," presented to Nicholas with letter of Jan. 31, 1902.

103. See above, pp. 377 ff.

104. See, in dos. No. 213, copies of Gintsburg's pledges of May 2, 1902 to Matiunin (concerning mineral resources in Hamheung province) and of Dec. 20, 1902 (ditto in Pinyang province:) "purposing to obtain a concession" and "proposing to form a company."

105. See the lithographed collection (untitled, with Witte's notations copied in the margins), analogous to Vonliarliarskii's and Abaza's collections and, by certain indications, from Matiunin's pen, dated December 1905. There is no reason to suspect this evidence, inasmuch as two other figures, as well as their sources, are given correctly in the collection: in 1898, 250 thousand rubles from the Cabinet and in 2,200,000 rubles from the treasury.

106. See, in dos. No. 98, Pokotilov's telegrams of March 21/April 3, Oct. 29 and Nov. 20, 1902: the Mukden chiang-chün would not take it upon himself to issue the concession and recommended that Lvov, Matiunin's representative, approach Peking; in October, Lvov still hoped "to secure the cooperation of the Russo-Chinese bank" but "the order" "to our agents" "not to intervene in this matter" had been "confirmed," and the chiang-chün, with whom the bank was at that time starting a serious flirtation on the subject of the Mukden Mining Co., was given to understand that the bank was not a party to it; up to October 29 the bank knew of the transfer of 75 thousand rubles to the Matiunin agent; the Chinaman whom Lvov sent to Peking in November still had no success with solicitations.

107. See the agreement project proposed by Japan on July 22/Aug. 4, 1902, in Obzor snoshenii s Iaponiei po koreiskim delam s 1895, pub. min. for. afs., 1906, p. 78. That it was there designated as a projected agreement on the "Korean question" is a contribution to the "Korean theory" of the origin of the Russo-Japanese war. The agreement concerned the "Manchurian question" equally. On the "Korean theory" see: M.N. Pokrovsky's "Iaponskaia Voina"(Japanese War) (1905. Ist. rev. dvizh. v otd. ocherkakh, I, Moscow, 1926, pp. 595 ff.;) cf. our article "Nikolai II i kontsessia na Yalu" (Russkoe proshloe, No. 1, 1923, pp. 107 ff.)

108. See Witte, Vosp., I, p. 186; his Bozniknovenie rus.-iap. voiny, Vol. II, p. 533, the copy of Nicholas's letter of 19/I, 1903 to Witte (in the Witte accumulation in the Tsentrarkhiv;) Prolog etc., p. 260, "conspectus of the report" of Bezobrazov on his trip to the Far East; Kuropatkin's "Dnevnik," Kr. Arkhiv, Vol. 2, pp. 59 ff.

109. See cit. copy of Nicholas's letter of Jan. 19, 1903. For an excerpt from it see M. Pokrovsky's "Iaponskaia voina," p. 578. In the copy, the letter has the wrong date: 1902. As we know, in January, 1902, Bezobrazov was "liquidating" affairs "to get out of them" (see above, p. 398)-- Nicholas's order was transmitted to him through the palace superintendent Gesse. In October 1902 Witte inquired of Pokotilov as to the position of "Matiunin's undertaking," and he replied with information as to the transfer to the Russo-Chinese bank in Mukden of 75 thousand rubles (see in dos. No. 98, Pokotilov's tel. of Oct. 29, 1902; the tele-

gram does not state to whom the transfer was made). That these 75 thousand rubles have no relation to the two-million credit is seen from the "report on sums paid by the Russo-Chinese bank to State Secretary Bezobrazov against the credit of two million rubles allowed him by his maj.," in dos. No. 213: from February to November 1903, the whole two mill. rubles were paid out in their entirety.

110. See Prolog etc., pp. 260 ff., "conspectus of the report" of Bezobrazov on his trip to the Far East. This enumerates the following "undertakings," transmitted by Bezobrazov to I.P. Balashov, as "practically completed in the manner projected [by Bezobrazov]": 1) The timber concern on the Yalu, "has so far cost 320 thousand rubles, and will cost 180 thousand rubles more," 2) the Fushun coal mines (eastern part of the bed), area 250 square versts, 3) "Fushun-Telin district for Russian settlements," c. 500 square versts "of excellent plough-land," 4) steamship line between the mouth of the Yalu and Port Arthur, 5) steamship line on the Liao-ho, 6) concession to electric lighting and channels of approach in Mukden and Kirin provinces, and 7) mineral waters of Tanheze.

111. To this attempt of Witte's to adapt himself to the triumphant "Bezobrazovshchina" in January-February 1903 we have devoted a special study, to which we refer the reader (see "Vitte nakanune russko-iaponskoi voiny," in the symposium Rossiia i Zapad, Petrograd, 1923, pp. 140-167). When Vonliarliarskii, after Bezobrazov's departure for the East, approached Witte, pleading the tsar's "command," Witte "expressed his readiness" to inform Vonliarliarskii of "the measures he had taken to get as large a number of concessions in Manchuria as possible" and offered to transfer them to Vonliarliarskii "for equipment with the aid of foreign capital" (see in dos. No. 278, Vonliarliarskii's report to his majesty of February 12, 1903).

112. The "mangy triumvirate" was "Nozdria"(Nostril), "Teterka" (Grouse) and "Golovastik" (Tadpole), as the Bezobrazovists among themselves called Witte, Kuropatkin and Lamsdorf (see the letters of Bezobrazov and Abaza for 1904 as published by us, Kr. Arkhiv, Vol. 17, pp. 70 ff.).

113. See, in dos. No. 120, Abaza's memorandum, read at the conference of March 26, 1903, and the minutes of the conference. Cf. "Dnevnik Kuropatkina," p. 38, and Prolog etc., pp. 277 ff.

114. For resolutions of the conference of March 26 in full, see Prolog etc., pp. 281-282. Thus, the projected amalgamation of all Manchurian concessions was dropped, even though Plehve supported it at the meeting, and the M.M. Assn. continued its independent existence. Cf. B.A. Romanov: "Vitte nakanune russko-iaponskoi voiny," in the symposium Rossiia i Zapad, pp. 162 ff.

115. See minutes of the conference of March 26 in dos. No. 120 and Kuropatkin's "Dnevnik," Kr. Arkhiv, Vol. 2, p. 40. Under "got his own way" Kuropatkin apparently only understood that by point 2 of the resolutions of the conference of March 26 the obtaining of the concession to the Manchurian forests on the Yalu river was entrusted to him, Witte.

116. See Kuropatkin's "Dnevnik," Kr. Arkhiv, Vol. 2, p. 38.

117. See B.A. Romanov, "Vitte nakanune russko-iaponskoi voiny," in the symposium Rossiia i Zapad, Petrograd, 1923, p. 145.

118. See Kuropatkin's "Dnevnik," Kr. Arkhiv, Vol. 2, pp. 41 and 42.

119. Back in March 1903 he had feared that "as a result" of "Bezobrazovist" management in Manchuria it might be "handed over to foreigners" (see Kuropatkin's "Dnevnik," Kr. Arkhiv, Vol. 2, p. 39).

120. See, in dos. No. 120, Nicholas's tel. of May 2, 1903 to Alekseev.

121. See, ibid., Nicholas's tel. of May 2, 1903 to Kuropatkin.

122. In the telegrams of May 2 Bezobrazov was already called state-secretary. Judging from the minutes of the conference of May 7, 1903, (see in dos. No. 120), the said telegrams of May 2 were read there and a memorandum by Gen. Vogak (a Bezobrazovist): "Znachenie dogovora 26 marta 1902 v razvitii voprosa o Manchzhurii" (Significence of the treaty of March 26, 1902 in the development of the Manchurian question). This indictment ended with the deduction that "with the signing" of this treaty, "after enormous sacrifices," "Russia is now worse off in the Manchurian question than before 1902," since with the "open door," foreigners "will soon nip any buds of Russian trade and industry that have appeared in Manchuria," "the railway and the Russo-Chinese bank will serve foreign interests, and their activity will be restricted by the competition of the Shanhaikwan railway, already in the hands of the English, and of branches of foreign banks that will probably be opened in Yinkow and Dalny."

123. Cf. Kuropatkin, "Prolog manchzhurskoi tragedii" (Prologue to the Manchurian tragedy), in the Tsentrarkhiv symposium: Russko-iaponskaia voina, Leningrad, 1925, p. 24.

124. See, in dos. No. 120, the minutes of the special conference of May 7, 1903, and Prolog etc., p. 285, where the resolutions of the conference are stated; they relate only to the question of the company.

125. See Kuropatkin's "Dnevnik," Kr. Arkhiv, Vol. 2, p. 44.

126. See Vorontsov's letter of May 9, 1903 to Witte, in dos. No. 120. It is quoted practically in its entirety in our article: "Vitte i kontsessia na Yalu," in Sb. statei, posvyashchennykh S.F. Platonovu, Petrograd, 1922, p. 439.

127. See above, p. 345.

128. See Vorontsov's letter, just cited.

129. "Sufficient" meant defensability of Port Arthur for six months, and the ability to set up an army of 100,000 in the Far East "without resort to our European forces" (see, in dos. No. 120, Witte's answer of May 9, 1903 to Vorontsov); Witte simply did not choose to mention the fleet: he himself knew that "Japan's fleet is stronger than ours," as Vorontsov had written and as had been demonstrated to him by the official report of the ministry of the navy of November 1902 (Russian fleet in the Pacific ocean: tonnage, 114,436, personnel, 8,532, French, t., 45, 499 and p., 3,862, Japanese, t., 211,702 and p., 15,891, English, t., 125,- 588 and p. 8,850; see, in dos. No. 79, pt. I, report of Nov. 20, 1902, signed by Lieutenant A. Petrov).

130. See, in dos. No. 120, Witte's cited letter of May 9, 1903.

131. See, in dos. No. 112, Witte's report to his majesty on his trip to the Far East in 1902, pp. 55-56. In the Prolog etc., this report is quoted almost entire (see pp. 189-242), but the reference omitted.

132. See, in dos. No. 107, pt. I, the report of the comm. of the trans-Amur district Div. Border Guard Corps, March 18, 1903.

133. See above, p. 370, and Witte's cited report on his trip to the Far East, pp. 50-54. Up to May 1903, 143,700 desyatinas had been bought up "for settlement," 100,000 of these at railway stations (Witte's report to his majesty of Aug. 1, 1903, in dos. No. 11). "Regulations concerning the settlement of Russian

134. See Witte's report to his majesty on his trip to the Far East, pp. 49-50.

135. See ibid., p. 33.

136. See ibid., p. 32.

137. See above, p. 279.

138. See Kuropatkin's "Dnevnik," Kr. Arkhiv, Vol. 2, p. 22, and, in dos. No. 107, pt. 1, the minutes of the special conference of Jan. 25, 1903.

139. See, in dos. No. 107, pt. I, Kuropatkin's letter of July 13, 1902 to Lamsdorf, and Lamsdorf's of July 23, 1902 to Kuropatkin. Lamsdorf did not see how, on the strength of such considerations, the Russian government could, four months after the signing of the agreement and a few weeks after his majesty's ratification, make declaration to the Chinese government of the unsatisfactoriness, and so forth."

140. See Kuropatkin's proposal at the conference of Jan. 25, 1903 to maintain occupation to the north of this line, in dos. No. 107, pt. I.

141. For Lamsdorf's formulation: see ibid., minutes of the conference of January 25.

142. See the Anglo-Chinese trade treaty of August 23/Sept. 5, 1902, art. 8, sec. X and XI (Sb. dog. i dip. dok. po delam D. Vostoka, St. Petersburg, 1906, pp. 609-610).

143. Witte complained of this in the cited report of 1902 (p. 22).

144. For copies of the minutes of the conferences of Jan. 11 and 25 see dos. No. 107, pt. I. For a detailed review of them see, in Prolog etc., pp. 245-247 and 269-275. Rozen's memorandum of Sept. 12 and Pavlov's of Sept. 25, 1902 are in dos. No. 26; Lessar's memorandum of Jan. 4, 1903 is in dos. No. 107, pt. I.

145. Rozen's memorandum of Sept. 12, 1902, all covered with Witte's notations, is in dos. No. 26. It was written apropos of the Japanese proposal of July 22, 1902, but embraces the whole question of Russia's policy in the Far East in connection with the general international situation and harshly criticizes the whole previous policy of "peaceful" conquest of Manchuria and "its conversion into a forbidden province"--"an endeavor" "all the more strange" "in that the natural resources of Russia herself are still so largely being exploited by foreigners for lack of capital at home."

146. See, in dos. No. 107, pt. I, the minutes of the conference of Jan. 11. In the Prolog etc., this detail is, needless to say, omitted.

147. See, in dos. No. 107, pt. I, the minutes of the conference of Jan. 25. -- A week before the ministers' conference of Jan. 25, Witte "sat for a long time one evening" with Kuropatkin for the purpose of clearing up and "ending" their "mutual irritation about things," promising Kuropatkin to "put himself on a footing of equality" and "increase the budgetary limit" (for the war department). Witte succeeded in this attempt at an above-board explanation: the collocutors "parted friends" (see Kuropatkin's "Dnevnik," Kr. Arkhiv, Vol. 2, pp. 25-26).

148. See Kuropatkin's "Dnevnik," <u>Kr. Arkhiv</u>, Vol. 2, pp. 21-22, and the minutes of the conference of January 11.

149. See minutes of the conference of January 25.

150. See ibid.

151. See, for example, in dos. No. 26, Witte's memorandum of Dec. 28, 1902 apropos of the above-mentioned memoranda of Rozen and Pavlov.

152. By January 28, 1903, Kuropatkin had received Nicholas's order: 1) to start the evacuation of Mukden province at the middle of February and complete it in one month, and 2) to withdraw troops from the southern part of Kirin province in the expectation of their arriving in the Amur district "during the summer of 1903" (see, in dos. No. 107, pt. I, Kuropatkin's letter of Feb. 7, 1903).

153. Such was the "resolution" of the January 11 conference of foreign ministers. Japan had on July 22, 1902 <u>for a second time</u> proposed annulling all previous agreements (see above, p. 336).

154. See, in dos. No. 107, pt. I, Planson's two telegrams of March 13 and Lamsdorf's tel. of April 2, 1903 to Planson. -- The project of the "preliminary instructions" to Planson, examined at the January 25 conference, consisted of only 3 demands: 1) non-modification of the internal ordering of Mongolia, 2) non-transfer to any power whatsoever of evacuated "localities" "under any guise whatsoever (cession, lease, concession, and so forth)" and 3) isolation, in the event of foreigners being invited to manage any branches of the Chinese administration, "of the affairs of northern China" "as an absolutely special department" and entrustment of their management to Russians. -- In Planson's project of March 13, the first point was dropped but five new ones appeared: 1) non-alienation of areas in evacuated localities, 2) non-opening to foreign trade of new points in Manchuria and non-admission to them of consuls without preliminary communications with Russia, 3) non-invitation of foreigners to the administration of Manchuria, 4) reservation to Russia of the Port Arthur-Mukden-Yinkow telegraph line, 5) reservation to the Russo-Chinese bank in Yinkow of obligations of the local bank even after the evacuation of the city, 6) reservation to Russians of all rights acquired during the occupation even after the withdrawal of troops, and 7) appointment of Russians to the posts of physician and commissar of customs in Yinkow. -- For final text of the note, see <u>Prolog etc.</u>, p. 274.

156. See, in dos. No. 107, pt. I, the project of Lamsdorf's tel. to Adm. Alekseev, delivered to the chanc. min. fin. on March 24, 1903, in connection with Alekseev's proposal to include among the guarantees: 1) autonomy of Chinchowting and 2) confirmation by the Peking government of the Manchurian timber concession of the Yalu (Lamsdorf answered that "abrogation of the autonomy of Chinchowting [see above, pp. 281 and 298] might actually take place without any dealings with the Chinese government," and respecting the second point discreetly inquired whether it would not complicate "an already difficult matter.") Ibid., Witte's letter of March 19, 1903 to Lamsdorf as to having no objections to the Planson project.

157. See, ibid., Planson's tel. of March 19, 1903. Planson had not replied to Ching's official request that Russian representatives be appointed for the transfer of the area under evacuation. When he responded to a second inquiry by notice of the projected presentation of conditions, Liang Fang exclaimed: "What further conditions can there be, when all conditions were provided for in last year's agreement."

158. See, ibid., Planson's tel. of March 12 and Pokotilov's of March 24, 1903. Cf. also B.A. Romanov, "Vitte nakanune russko-iaponskoi voiny," in the symposium Rossiia i Zapad, Petrograd, 1923, p. 161.

159. See, in dos. 107, pt. I, the note of the Chinese ambassador to St. Petersburg of April 9, 1903.

160. See, in dos. No. 107, pt. I, Cassini's three dispatches of April 23, 1903 from Washington, especially dispatch No. 44. Cf. also the Blue Book (China No. 2, 1904), No. 74 ff.

161. See, in dos. No. 107, pt. I, Cassini's dispatch No. 44 of April 23, 1903. Cassini had received this information (as to what was then being said in the Japanese embassy in Washington) from a "confidential source."

162. See the Blue Book (China No. 2, 1904), No. 91, 92, 97, and Cassini's quoted dispatch No. 44.

163. See, in dos. No. 107, pt. I, Cassini's cited dispatch of April 23, 1903.

164. See the Blue Book (China No. 2, 1904), No. 110, 114, 117, 120, 119, 121, 140, 141, 145. -- The demand concerning ports and consuls was already absent from the demands projected at the Port Arthur conferences with Alexseev at the end of June 1903. -- See Prolog etc., pp. 306-307.

165. See the Blue Book (China No. 2, 1904), No. 79-82.

166. See, ibid., No. 87 and 88. -- When, at the beginning of June 1903, Ching expressed the assurance that the Manchurian question would "shortly" be settled between China and Russia "without any loss of their sovereign rights," the English minister in Peking found this "strange" (see ibid., No. 143).

167. See Prolog etc., p. 276. This time Russia (in the instructions of April 24 to Lessar) had withdrawn the points as to consuls and ports and the deposit of customs levies at Yinkow in the Russo-Chinese bank.

168. See Witte's 1902 report to his majesty, in Prolog etc., pp. 214, 216.

169. See the Blue Book (China No. 2, 1904), No. 118, MacDonald's report from Tokyo as to the Japanese press on the Manchurian question, and, in dos. No. 107, pt. I, Alekseev's letter of May 11, 1903 to Witte, dated "St. Petersburg." "Our Japanese secret agent" had informed Alekseev of Baron Komura's intentions "by code," as follows: "Baron M. has specially requested me to notify you at once of the following plan of Baron Komura's that has been approved by the supreme authority," namely 1) "first of all to learn the will of the British government and the degree of its preparedness to aid Japan in the event of a breach of peaceful relations with Russia," 2) "as soon as the will of Britain shall have been ascertained, to make a proposal to the governments of Russia and China in the following form: a) that the railway guard inside Manchuria be limited numerically, b) the more important points in Manchuria be opened to all foreigners equally, c) free residence of her subjects in Manchuria be guaranteed to Japan, with provisions for their personal and property rights in this country;" 3) "in the event of an unsatisfactory answer from Russia or non-fulfillment of the pledge given by her respecting withdrawal of troops, to resolve on an extreme remedy--regard Manchuria as restored to its previous state, dispatch Japanese engineers thither, and in the event of an attempt on their lives or freedom of action,

equip a parallel military detachment, using for this purpose the division
now in North China."

170. Sic. in the account in Kuropatkin's "Dnevnik" (Kr. Arkhiv, p. 43)
of the conference of the triumvirate (plus Lessar) that took place on
April 13, 1903 "on the question of the evacuation of Manchuria": troops
remained in Harbin, Tsitsihar, Fuliardi, Ninguta, Hailar, Hunchun,
along the Sungari and along the Tsitsihar-Blagoveshchensk highway. Cf.
in dos. No. 107, pt. I, Witte's letter of April 11, 1903 to Lamsdorf:
Witte agreed, in "deviation" from the March 26 treaty, to the "establishment of military posts along the Chinese Eastern Railway and the Amur
and Sungari rivers"--"in the event of the Chinese government's refusal
to produce the supplementary guarantees demanded by us."

171. We quote in translation an excerpt from the parliamentary report
of July 11, 1903 in dos No. 107, pt. I. -- Very likely there was a connection between this declaration in the House of Lords and Benkendorf's
attempt to discuss with Lansdowne "the possibility of a more complete
understanding" between England and Russia "on Chinese affairs" (see,
in the Blue Book, China No. 2, 1904, under No. 139, Lansdowne's letter
of July 16/29, 1903 to Ch. Scott:) but Benkendorf understood certain concessions on Russia's part respecting the Yangtse, while Lansdowne "indicated" to him Manchuria and Newchwang.

172. See Materialy po D. Vostoku (Materials on the Far East), pub.
Spec. Com. of the Far East, St. Petersburg, 1905, pp. 170, 173 and
177. Respecting Manchuria, the Japanese proposed on July 30/Aug. 12
to include in the agreement: 1) recognition of the independence and territorial inviolability of the Chinese and Korean empires and support of
the principle of equal advantages for trade and industry to all nations in
these countries, 2) Russia's engagement "not to hinder the possible continuation of the Korean railway into South Manchuria to a junction with
the Chinese Eastern Railway and the Shanhaikwan-Newchwang line,"--on
the other hand 3) Japan's recognition of "Russia's special interests in
railway enterprises in Manchuria" and 4) her recognition of Russia's right
to send troops to Manchuria for the protection of these interests or the
suppression of uprisings and disorders. -- On the same day, July 30/
August 12, in London, Lansdowne emphasized the fact to Benkendorf that
an Anglo-Russian agreement on Chinese affairs was possible only on
condition of the "Manchurian question" being included in it (Blue Book,
China, No. 2, 1904, No. 142.)

173. See Kuropatkin's "Dnevnik," Kr. Arkhiv, Vol. 2, p. 43.

174. See the symposium Russko-Iaponskaia voina, pub. Tsentrarkhiv,
Leningrad, 1925, Bezobrazov's letter of May 29, 1903 to Nicholas, p.
143; Kuropatkin's "Dnevnik," p. 86.

175. See B.A. Romanov, "Bezobrazovskii kruzhok letom 1904 g."(the
Bezobrazov clique in the summer of 1904), Kr. Arkhiv, Vol. 17, p. 79,
Bezobrazov's letter of July 8, 1904; "Dnevnik Kuropatkina," p. 60.

176. See, ibid., p. 94.

177. See Count S. Iu. Witte, Vynuzhdennye raz'iasneniia po povodu
otchëta gen-ad. Kuropatkina o voine s Iaponiei (Interpretations Given on
the Occasion of the Report of Lord High Admiral Kuropatkin concerning
War with Japan), Moscow, 1911, pp. 87, 89, 90-92. The extracts from
documents relating to the conference of May 7, 1903 here published by
Witte were by us collated with the copies in dos. No. 120 and prove to be
absolutely accurate.

178. See, in dos. No. 120, the memorandum presented by Lamsdorf after the conference of May 7, in reply to the memorandum by Vogak that had been read there.

179. See Prolog etc., p. 308, and Kuropatkin's "Dnevnik," p. 105, the entry for Jan. 15, 1904.

180. See, in dos. No. 120, the minutes of the conference of May 7, 1903.

181. See, in dos. No. 107, pt. I, the telegrams from Protasev (commissar for finance of a part of Kwantung province) of May 24 and June 9 and from Pokotilov of June 7, 1903.

182. See, in dos. No. 107, pt. I, Protasev's tel. of May 24, 1903 from Dalny.

183. See, ibid., Protasev's tel of June 9, 1903.

184. See Bezobrazov's letters to Nicholas of June 2, May 8, May 11, and the two of May 29, 1903 (in the symposium, Russko-Iaponskaia voina, bub. Tsentrarkhiv, Leningrad, 1925, pp. 143-144, 136, 137, 141-143.)

185. See Bezobrazov's cited letter of June 2, 1903 to Nicholas.

186. See Witte, Vynuzhdennye raz'iasneniia etc., Moscow, 1911, p. 92.

187. See Bezobrazov's letter of May 23, 1903 to Nicholas, in sym. Russko-Iaponskaia voina, p. 139. Cf. Kuropatkin's "Dnevnik," Kr. Arkhiv, Vol. 2, p. 47: "the greatest secrets are being aired in the street," and Sakharov's letter to Kuropatkin, ibid., p. 62.

188. See Bezobrazov's letter of June 2 to Nicholas, in symposium, Russko-Iaponskaia voina.

189. For the treaty of association for founding the "Russian Lumbering Association in the Far East" see Prolog etc., p. 290. There was no further levy of stock capital: the government's two millions were as yet far from exhausted.

190. See, in dos. No. 120, the copy of the minutes of May 7 with resolution, and Bezobrazov's cited letter of June 2, 1903 to Nicholas.

191. See Kr. Arkhiv, Vol. 2, pp. 47 and 62.

192. Cf. Abaza's letter of June 21, 1904 in Kr. Arkhiv, Vol. 17, p. 78.

193. See Sakharov's letter of June 12, 1903 to Kuropatkin, Kr. Arkhiv, Vol. 2, p. 61.

194. See Lamsdorf's letter of June 11, 1903 to Witte, in dos. No. 11, and Lessar's first telegram of June 3, 1903 to Lamsdorf, in dos. No. 107, pt. I.

195. See Lessar's cited first tel. of June 3, 1903.

196. See Lessar's second tel. (sequel) of June 3, 1903, ibid., and Witte's letter of June 23, 1903 to Lamsdorf in connection with Lessar's two telegrams, where Witte thus resumed Lessar's proposal, expressed with some confusion and prolixity in the telegram, and perhaps even defective textually. Witte's understanding of Lessar is important to our further exposition.

197. See, in dos. No. 107, pt. I, Rozen's tel. of June 13, 1903 to Lamsdorf.

198. See Witte's notations on the copy of Rozen's tel. and on Lamsdorf's letter to Witte of June 11, 1903, enclosing Lessar's telegrams of June 3, in dos. No. 107, pt. I.

199. See Abaza's letter of June 14, 1903 to Nicholas, the symposium Russko-Iaponskaia voina, pp. 144 ff.

200. Two weeks after Abaza had adjusted Nicholas's Korean decision with Grand Duke Aleksey Aleksandrovich, on June 28, Nicholas interested himself in learning: "Why Rozen does not continue...negotiations respecting Russia's giving Japan freedom of action in Korea?" (See M. N. Pokrovsky, Iaponskaia voina, p. 599.)

201. See Abaza's letter of June 14, 1903 to Nicholas, symposium, Russko-Iaponskaia voina, pp. 144 ff.

202. See Abaza's two letters of June 16, 1903 to Nicholas in the symposium Russko-Iaponskaia voina, pp. 146 ff.

203. See Prolog etc., pp. 293 ff., where the course of the Port Arthur conferences is recounted in detail. Cf., in dos. No. 120, the minutes of conference on the Manchurian question No. 1, June 18, 1902, and, in dos. No. 107, pt. II, Pokotilov's tel. of June 25, 1903.

204. See Bezobrazov's letter of August 2, 1903 to Nicholas in the symposium Russko-Iaponskaia voina, p. 157.

205. See complete list of the guarantees adopted at Port Arthur: Prolog etc., pp. 306-307. -- Point 10 of the demands, as to preference in obtaining industrial concessions, was to be presented, they decided, only if Lessar deemed it convenient.

206. See, in dos. No. 120, the "memorandum on the guarantees worked out at the Port Arthur conference," presented to Nicholas on July 6, 1903 by Lamsdorf. On it is Nicholas's resolution: "This must all be discussed after the war minister's arrival. The objections and corrections of the ministry of foreign affairs deserve serious attention." -- Cf. Blue Book (China No. 2, 1904), No. 138.

207. See, in dos. No. 107, pt. II, the release of Witte's report to his majesty, dated June 27, 1903.

208. See, in dos. No. 107, pt. II, the minutes of the conference of Aug. 1, 1903. The five terms were: 1) non-cession to foreigners of restored territories, 2) Russian military posts on the Sungari and the Amur, 3) ditto on the Tsitsihar-Blagoveshchensk highway, 4) exclusion of North China from foreign management, and 5) protection of the commercial interests of the Chinese Eastern Railway.

209. See the report of August 28, 1903 from Raspopov, financial agent in Japan, in dos. No. 79, pt. II. -- Moreover the revenue from silk proved to be 1100-1150 yen per picul instead of the average 900-950 yen.

210. See, ibid., copy of the report of Aug. 20, 1903, from Capt. Rusin, naval agent in Japan. From April to June 1903 check-up and practice mobilizations were carried out in Japan "in practically all army divisions," and likewise in the navy (his report of June 5/18, 1903). For the whole summer of 1903 Japan's armed forces were kept "in tense fighting trim" and during Rusin's whole stay in Japan "he had never observed, nor had there been, such a serious all-round preparation for immediate war" (report of Aug. 8/21, 1903).

211. See Prolog etc., p. 346; Blue Book (China, No. 2, 1904), No. 147, 148, 149, 150, 151, 156; Kuropatkin's "Dnevnik," pp. 52 and 54; Alekseev's tel. of Aug. 23/Sept. 5, 1903 from Port Arthur, in dos. No. 107, pt. II. Nicholas wished to know Alekseev's opinion regarding the August 1 resolutions of the ministers. Alekseev protested against changing the guarantees adopted at Port Arthur. As a result, the presentation of the demands to China was delayed until Aug. 24/Sept. 6. There were five of these. The first three of the August 1 demands had been

preserved, the 2nd and 3rd been made into one. The fourth, on the exclusion of North China from the purview'of foreigners, had been omitted. Two essentially insignificant ones had been added: on the guarding of the branches of the Russo-Chinese bank by Chinese troops and on the inclusion of a Russian physician in the make-up of the sanitary commission at Yinkow. With the foreign powers the whole thing went like clockwork: the Russian demands were immediately communicated by the Chinese to the English and Japanese, who, finding them contrary to the open door principle, advised the Chinese to give a negative answer.

212. See Abaza's tel. of June 11, 1903 to Bezobrazov in Port Arthur in the Crimson Book (published by the chanc. Spec. Committee of the Far East," "on manuscript authority," under the title: "Dokumenty po peregovoram s Iaponiei 1903-1904 gg., khraniashchiesia v kantseliarii Osobovo Komiteta Dal'nevo Vostoka" (Documents on Negotiations with Japan 1903-1904, Preserved in the Chancellery of the Special Committee of the Far East), doc. No. 1; Sym. Russko-Iaponskaia voina, Bezobrazov's letters of Aug. 2 and 4, 1903 to Nicholas, pp. 156 ff.

213. See Bezobrazov's letters of July-August 1903 to Nicholas in symp. Russko-Iaponskaia voina, doc. No. 14-17. Bezobrazov accused the ministers of "adapting the truth to suit their own purposes," of actually bringing things to the point where, in the event of war "we should have to abandon South Manchuria, take up a position to the north, in the Siberian forests," and, in proposing to concede Korea to the Japanese, of actually permitting Japan to make of Korea "a secure base for operations against Russia on the continent" to "dislodge us in time from Manchuria."

214. See, ibid., doc. No. 16, Bezobrazov's letter of Aug. 2, 1903.

215. See Kuropatkin's "Dnevnik," Kr. Arkhiv, Vol. 2, p. 60; on August 2, Bezobrazov had the impression that Witte might not know "how to fall in line" (symp. Russko-Iaoponskaia voina, doc. No. 16), but it was "perfectly clear" to him "that he will never really pull in harness with me" (ibid., doc. No. 17;) even on August 12 it was supposed in "diplomatic circles" "that Witte had joined Bezobrazov" (Kuropatkin's "Dnevnik," p. 54); "immediately after Witte's release, Bezobrazov was with him and reproached him, Witte, with having refused to go along with him and having therefore fallen (ibid., p. 81); "to show proper respect for the Yalu enterprise" is Bezobrazov's formula (ibid., p. 44); Plehve explained to Kuropatkin how it happened that "influence got into bad hands," those of the Bezobrazovists: "the whole trouble was that preparations were being made to erect a special realm in Manchuria (Witte's realm, naturally)" (ibid., p. 83"; on Bezobrazov's "articulated plan" see doc. No. 17 and 14/III in the symp. Russko-Iaponskaia voina."

216. See M.N. Pokrovsky's Iaponskaia voina, p. 604.

217. See Prolog etc., p. 343; Kuropatkin's "Dnevnik," p. 98: even after his dismissal, Witte still hoped "for a peaceful settlement of the Japanese business," convinced that "we shall not be turning tail but giving ground."

218. See Kuropatkin's "Dnevnik," Kr. Arkhiv, Vol. 2, pp. 58-59.

219. See, ibid., p. 49, entry for August 4.

220. See, ibid., pp. 60, 55.

221. See, ibid., p. 57.

222. See Kuropatkin's "Dnevnik," Kr. Arkhiv, Vol. 2, p. 60.

223. See Crimson Book, No. 6, 7, and 8, Alekseev's telegrams of
Sept. 12, 15 and 20, 1903 to Nicholas; the Japanese White Book, doc.
No. 17, Komura's tel. of Sept. 22/Oct. 5, 1903 to Kurino. -- The "sudden" breaking-off of negotiations with the Chinese, to which Nicholas
gave his sanction on September 20, was "a very clever move on the part
of the vicegerent, who was obviously afraid that the Chinese might at the
last minute express consent to our demands, inasmuch as these were excessively to their advantage, since they may be said to have reduced our
privileges over foreigners to practically nil." (See Balashov's memorandum of Nov. 12, 1903 to Nicholas, in "file of the ministry of the interior,"
No. 119/3, "on the Far East;" this was forwarded to the chanc. Spec.
Com. Far East on July 29, 1904 in a bundle"of V.K. Plehve's papers" in
relation to P.N. Durnovo). -- Balashov ascribed to Alekseev the fear
that such counsel would be given China by the foreigners--her "allies."
The advice given was of course quite the opposite.

224. See same documents. Alekseev, in a tel. of Sept. 20, proposed
that in the event of Japan's landing "even one brigade" on the shore of the
Korean gulf the Japanese government be notified that further landing
"would entail our taking military measures as well." These measures
were: "in the event of a landing at Chemulpo, Chinampo or the mouth of
the Yalu, first--to oppose by main force at sea the landing of further
echelons, second--immediate mobilization of the troops in Kwantung
province and those stationed in Manchuria."

225. See, in dos. No. 107, pt. 2, Alekseev's tel. of Aug. 23/Sept. 5,
1903, protesting against the resolutions of the ministers' conference of
August 1.

226. See Kuropatkin's "Dnevnik," pp. 78 and 80, and the Crimson
Book, doc. No. 9, Alekseev's tel. of Sept. 25, o.s., 1903 to Nicholas.
--Alekseev objected, to Nicholas, that "complete agreement with China"
was "impossible, that the result of negotiations conducted in the spring
of this year, and recently, had confirmed" that "restoration of a trusting
attitude toward us on the part of the Chinese...must be recognized as
absolutely unattainable, even should we renounce everything that we had
by grievous sacrifices secured in Manchuria."

227. As to this, Lamsdorf questioned Nicholas on December 15, 1903
(Kuropatkin's "Dnevnik," p. 95); palace superintendent Gesse put this
same question to Abaza, "but could get nothing out of Abaza's lengthy
answer" (ibid., p. 93); even Plehve, with whom the Bezobrazovists were
in closest contact, confessed to Kuropatkin that he did not "know where
we are headed for" (ibid., p. 83); needless to say, Benkendorf was even
less able to do more than "decline to answer" a similar question from
Lansdowne (ibid., p. 102).

228. See the Japanese White Book, doc. No. 35, Komura's tel. of
Dec. 21, o.s., to Kurino; Kuropatkin's "Dnevnik," pp. 94 and 95.

229. See Bezobrazov's letter of Oct. 14, 1903 to Nicholas in the symposium, Russko-Iaponskaia voina, pp. 160 ff.

230. See, in dos. No. 106, pt. I-b, the report of the Directorate of
the M.M. Assn. to the head of the min. fin., of Jan. 2, 1904. According
to data of Engineer Kalistratov's expedition, "the supply of coal in the
Fushun field to the depth of 60 sazhens may be fixed at 675 million poods,"
i.e., would yield 25 million poods per annum for 25 years.

231. See Kuropatkin's "Dnevnik," p. 61.

232. See cited report of the M.M. Assn's Directorate of Jan. 2, 1904.
233. See Balashov's tel. of Sept. 6, 1903 to Bezobrazov, in dos.
No. 119/3 of the chancellery of the Spec. Com. of the Far East. -- In
this dossier, assembled in the ministry of the interior under Plehve, are
copies, to be cited by us hereafter, of two invaluable correspondences:
1) that of Balashov and Bezobrazov from August 25 through November 10,
1903, and 2) that of Vogak and Bezobrazov for Oct. 18-Nov. 3, 1903.
There is no evidence that decoded telegrams came into Plehve's hands.
But letters exchanged by Abaza and Bezobrazov in the summer of 1904
are known to have been censored, and extracts prepared in the police
dept. for report to Plehve. These excerpts are published by us in Kr.
Arkhiv, Vol. 17. It is curious that the collection preserved in the files
of the dept. breaks off at the letter of July 17, 1904 in which Abaza
mourns the death of this "ally" of his. Ironically enough, our correspondents "feared the mails" since "everything is read" and the "enemy"
(i.e., Witte) is informed of everything "done to oppose him" (see for
example Abaza's letters of May 26 and June 10, 1904), and sought "means"
to send letters under Plehve's guarantee of secrecy.
234. See Balashov's tel. of Sept. 3, 1903 to Bezobrazov, ibid.
235. See ibid., Balashov's tel. of Sept. 16 and 17 to Bezobrazov, and,
in dos. No. 120, Dmitrev-Mamonov's tel. of Oct. 2 and letter of Oct. 26
from Mukden to Pokotilov in Peking.
236. See Balashov's tel. of Nov. 6, 1903 to Bezobrazov in dos.
No. 119/3 of the chanc. Spec. Com. of the Far East.
237. See, ibid., Balashov's tel. of Nov. 10, 1903 and Vogak's letter
of Oct. 18 to Bezobrazov from the cap. city of Manchuria.
238. See, ibid., Bezobrazov's tel. of Aug. 26 to Balashov, and in dos.
No. 120 Dimitrev-Mamonov's letter of Oct. 26 to Pokotilov.
239. See Kuropatkin's "Dnevnik," p. 86, entries of Nov. 26 and 27,
and, in dos. No. 44/47 of the chanc. Spec. Com. of the Far East, Balashov's tel. of Dec. 14, 1903 to Bezobrazov threatening to "stop everything;" on the tel. is Abaza's notation of Nicholas's "order" to the minister of finance to remit 200 thousand rubles. Ibid., the letters of Dec. 22
of Romanov, head of the min. fin., as to execution.
240. See Bezobrazov's telegrams of Sept. 18 and 9, 1903 to Balashov
in dos. No. 119/3 of the chanc. Spec. Com. of the Far East.
241. See tel. of Sept. 18, Oct. 2, 22 and 30.
242. See tel. of Oct. 22 and 30, ibid. "Official formalities are slow-
ing down the remittance"--and Bezobrazov only awaited the return of
Nicholas, who was passing just these days in Germany.
243. In line with the tsar's pretended order to Pleske was his "order"
to Bezobrazov to undertake nothing "without a report." See Bezobrazov's
tel. of Nov. 7 to Balashov, ibid.
244. See Bezobrazov's tel. of Sept. 21 to Balashov, ibid. Bezobrazov
also asked Balashov to communicate "the information as to this year's
timber operations necessary for a report to his majesty."
245. See, ibid., Bezobrazov's tel. of Oct. 11, 1903 to Balashov.
246. See, ibid., Bezobrazov's tel. of Oct. 25, 1903 to Vogak.
247. See ibid., Vogak's tel. of Oct. 27, 1903 to Bezobrazov.
248. See ibid., Bezobrazov's tel. of Oct. 29, 1903 to Vogak. Cf. his
tel. of Oct. 22.

249. See ibid., Bezobrazov's telegram of Oct. 29 to Vogak, and Vogak's of Oct. 27 to Bezobrazov; cf. Vogak's letters to him of Oct. 24, in which Vogak complained that he had spent "the whole day" deciphering Bezobrazov's telegram, and of Oct. 18, where Vogak expresses his hope that this letter will find Bezobrazov "already abroad: " "you certainly ought to take a rest, to go on this way is impossible."

250. See Bezobrazov's cited tel. of Oct. 29.

251. See Bezobrazov's tel. of Oct. 30, 1903 to Vogak, ibid., and "extract from the memorandum of State-Secretary Bezobrazov of Nov. 11, 1903, " in dos. No. 134. -- Cf. above, p. 440.

252. See mem. cit. of Bezobrazov of Nov. 11.

253. See Bezobrazov's tel. of Oct. 22 to Vogak in dos. No. 119/3 chanc. Spec. Com. of the Far East.

254. See, ibid., Vogak's letter of Oct. 24 to Bezobrazov, and his tel. of Oct. 28.

255. See Vogak's letters to Bezobrazov of Oct. 22 and 23 and tel. of Oct. 27, 1903, ibid.

256. See Vogak's letter of Oct. 22 and tel. of Oct. 28, ibid.

257. See same telegram. Cf., above, pp. 409 and 430.

258. See same telegram.

259. See, ibid., Vogak's telegrams of Oct. 31, Nov. 1 and 3, and Bezobrazov's of Nov. 1 and 3, 1903.

260. See, ibid., Balashov's tel. of Oct. 19, 1903 to Bezobrazov.

261. See, in dos. No. 120, Dmitrev-Mamonov's letter of Oct. 26, 1903 to Pokotilov, giving details of the occupation of Mukden "from very good sources: " "the vicegerent was in a fury, but 'to save the honor of the Russian uniform (his very expression) reported to Peterburg that it had all been done at his order." Vogak, who happened to be in Port Arthur just at the time of this episode, had, with a view to "reassuring" Alekseev, asked Bezobrazov what impression the taking of Mukden had produced in Peterburg. But Bezobrazov in reply burst forth in one of his usual verbose telegrams on his own approving attitude toward the event, but never said a word as to the attitude of Nicholas (see, in dos. No. 119/3 chanc. Spec. Com. of the Far East, Vogak's telegram of Oct. 24 and Bezobrazov's of Oct. 24, and Vogak's letter of Oct. 24 reproaching him in this latter connection).

262. See, ibid., copy of Balashov's memorandum of Nov. 12, 1903. This had been written at Port Arthur and if sent at once could not have reached Peterburg until a month later, in mid-December.

263. Cf., in dos. No. 107, pt. 2, Protasev's tel. of July 15, 1903 from Port Arthur to the effect that the central government not only did not have revenue from Kirin and Heilungkiang provinces but even made a supplementary annual payment to each of approximately 300 thousand lan.

264. Kurino transmitted to Lamsdorf verbally the note requesting that "all provinces of the Far East where the interests of the two empires meet be covered by the proposed agreement" (i.e., Manchuria) on Dec. 10/23. Kurino also threatened "that in the present situation serious difficulties and even complications might arise should we fail to come to an agreement" (see the Japanese White Book, No. 35 and 36).

265. See Kuropatkin's "Dnevnik," Kr. Arkhiv, Vol. 2, p. 86; Balashov's tel. of Dec. 14 1903, demanding a "categorical answer" as to whether

the "200 thousand rubles promised in November" would be sent, had been addressed to Bezobrazov, but, in his absence, was reported to Nicholas by Abaza (see dos. No. 44/47 for 1903, chanc. Spec. Com. of the Far East.)

266. Analogous files "on the preliminary conference etc." exist in the collection of the chanc. min. fin. and in that of the chanc. Spec. Com. of the Far East. We have used the former, No. 134. The reform of Far Eastern administration dragged. Before the war only two "edicts" had been promulgated--that inaugurating the post of vicegerent, July 30, and that establishing the Spec. Com. of the Far East, Sept. 30. The working out of the vicegerency "Statute" had been assigned to a special committee under Plehve's chairmanship and proved a long-drawn-out affair. Appointments to the Committee were constituted only in part: Bezobrazov was made a member, Abaza business manager, and Matunin assistant business manager. The only vice-chairman appointed, the tsar being chairman, was Plehve. No further members were appointed, and, so far as can be judged from the correspondence of the Committee chancellery as preserved, not a single meeting of the Committee was ever held.

267. See, in dos. No. 134, Vonliarliarskii's memorandum of Jan. 17, 1904, the "explanatory memorandum to the program of questions etc.," and the "program of questions, etc." Members of the conference were: mem. state coun. Cherevansky, ass. min. agriculture Shvanebakh, and Abaza. "Guests" Vonliarliarskii and Matiunin assisted at early sessions.

268. See, in dos. No. 134, Vonliarliarskii's memorandum of Jan. 17, 1904.

269. See A.M. Abaza's letter of May 30, 1904. (Kr. Arkhiv, Vol. 17, p. 74). Kokovtsov told Abaza that he "well understood the advantage of the company for certain persons seeking additional income."

270. See, in dos. No. 134, Shvanebakh's letter of March 16, 1904 to Kokovtsov, forwarded with the documents of the first sessions, and minute book No. 2 of the session of May 10, at which Kokovtsov first appeared. -- Total deposits in the Russo-Chinese bank by the report for 1902, were figured at 31,890,000 rubles.

271. Kokovtsov was referring to the fact that in Manchuria "every enterprise that arose ended by seeking treasury aid."

272. See A.M. Abaza's letter of June 1, 1904 (Kr. Arkhiv, Vol. 17, p. 75).

273. When the downfall of the East-Asiatic Company enterprise even in the Ignatev conference was ascertained, Abaza still did not lose heart but anticipated that Ignateev "would be removed" and "be told to turn the thing over to Plehve," under whom, in turn, Abaza "felt sure that everything would go as it should." Only when Plehve was assassinated did complete confusion seize upon Abaza, so that he did not "even" know "to whom to turn all this over." (See, ibid., Abaza's letters of June 1 and July 17, 1904, and our introduction to the letters, p. 72).

CHAPTER VII

1. See G.D. Dementev, Vochto oboshlas' nashemu gosudarstvennomu kaznacheistvu voina s Iaponiei (What the War with Japan Cost Our State Treasury), Petrograd, 1917, pp. 32-33. -- Collated "lists" for 1903-1904 and for 1905 "of expenditures on preparatory measures and hostilities

in connection with the war with Japan" and the "list of sums allocated in
1906-1907 to the fund designated by the 1906 schedule for expenses in
connection with the Russo-Japanese war and event consequent upon it"
(preserved in the archives of the department of the state treasury)
give the following figures on expenditures: for 1903--10,650,000 rubles
(3,000,000 by the min. of war, and 7,650,000 by the navy dept.), in 1904,
up to the war, nine million rubles (five mill. on Dec. 31, 1903 and two
mill. rub. on Jan. 23, 1904, by the war dept. and two mill. on Jan. 23,
1904 by the navy dept.), in 1904 after the opening of hostilities--657,191,
-005 rub., in 1905--985,348,750 rub., in 1906--415,586,788 rub., or
2,077,776,543 rub. in all.

2. See Document No. 40 in a collection of documents published by
us: Russkie finansy i evropeiskaia birzha v 1904-1906 gg. (Russian
finances and the European bourse, 1904-1906), pub. Tsentrarkhiv, Moscow, 1925. Future references to this work will emply the abbreviation:
"Rus. Fin.," No. so and so.

3. Moreover, the war started when the Russian government had no
actual minister of finance: Pleske, appointed on Aug. 16, 1903 (after
Witte's dismissal), fell ill and left the ranks on Nov. 22, and the manage-
ment of the ministry of finance was temporarily left to ass. min. P.M.
Romanov--a situation which dragged on until Feb. 5, 1904, when
Kokovtsov was appointed.

4. See Rus. Fin., No. 1 and 2.

5. See ibid., No. 3 (pp. 33-34) and 43-44 (pp. 127-128).

6. See ibid., No. 44.

7. See ibid., No. 3, p. 34.

8. Even in Russia the use of administrative measures against foreign
correspondents was altogether ineffectual: see Rus. Fin., p. 238.

9. See ibid., No. 63, p. 172.

10. See ibid., No. 3, p. 10.

11. See ibid., No. 3 and 4. Cf. Kuropatkin's "Dnevnik," Kr. Arkhiv,
Vol. 2, pp. 99 and 105.

12. See, in dos. No. 120, Kuropatkin's deposition in the minutes of the
conference of March 26, 1903.

13. In connection with the ratification of this trade treaty, Hay "suddenly"
came out with a statement in which "the American government serenely but
unequivocally rallied to the defense of China's sovereignty in Manchuria"
(see Die Grosse Politik, Vol. 19, pt. 1, No. 5941, Holstein's memorandum of Jan. 15, n.s. 1904, p. 32).

14. See T. Dennett, Roosevelt and the Russo-Japanese War, New York,
1925, p. 2, Roosevelt's letter of July 24, 1905 to Spring-Rice: "as soon
as this war broke out, I notified Germany and France in the most polite
and discreet fashion that in event of a combination against Japan to try to
do what Russia, Germany and France did to her in 1894 (sic), I should
promptly side with Japan and proceed to whatever length was necessary
on her behalf." -- Respecting America, even Nicholas himself apparently
entertained no illusions, confessing that "America alarmed him too"
(see Kuropatkin's "Dnevnik," Kr. Arkhiv, Vol. 2, p. 93, entry for Dec.
8, 1903).

15. See Die Grosse Politik, Vol. 19, pt. 1, No. 5992, see Speck von
Sternburg's tel. of March 8/21, 1904 from Washington, and No. 5978,
his tel. of Jan. 24/Feb. 6, 1904.

16. On the French proposal of 1891, see dos. No. 24, 1892, 2nd div. chanc. min. fin. ; on the American proposal of 1896, dos. No. 12, div. 3, chanc. min. fin, M. Rutkovsky's report of April 17/29, 1896 to P.M. Romanov on the proposal of Vanderbilt's intimate, Creighton Webb, that they "let the contract for building part of the Siberian railroad to the American Syndicate." The French proposal issued from the society for the study of the trans-Siberian railway, organized in Paris in 1890 by three senators (P. Deves, G. Lesueur, P. Decauville) and three contracting-engineers (A. Courreux, L. Coiseaux, E. Letelier). The society undertook to complete the line in six to eight years (from 1892) at a cost of 300 million rubles. The financial side of the proposition boiled down to the Russian government's settling with the Society in bonds of the 3 per cent loan of 1891 at an exchange rate somewhat lower each time than the mean for the preceding three months (provided, however, this mean was not higher than the rate for the last month) to be established in accordance with quotations from Paris, Amsterdam and Berlin, and in addition pay the Society a certain percentage commission, counting not the actual but the nominal value of the bonds. Lesueur approached the Russian government twice: on Feb. 25/March 9, 1891 and on Jan. 29/ Feb. 10, 1892. Finally, on Feb. 16/28, 1892 he and Decauville were received by Alexander III and got no for an answer (Alexander III's notation on their report of this date is: "I told them again the same thing that you [Vyshnegradsky] had told them, not to count on this, since it was settled that the treasury would itself build the Siberian road.") -- Whether negotiations with Cr. Webb took place is uncertain.

17. See Rafalovich's letters of March 15 and 23, 1903 to the minister of finance, in dos. No. 2, 1902. of the Secretarial section chanc. min. fin. (Witte's notation on the letter of March 15 as to preparation of the brochure is: "say not to meddle.")

18. See Die Grosse Politik, Vol. 17, No. 5369, Eckardstein's memorandum of May 10, n.s., 1903, and No. 5374, Radolin's tel. of May 5/18, same year from Paris. -- Eckardstein underscored that he "definitely" knew Haute Finance was working Delcasse round not only to an Anglo-French but also to an Anglo-Russian rapprochement; Radolin based his statement on a direct communication of the Rothschild agent Betzhold. Betzhold had asserted that Rothschild London, under the influence of a letter from Rothschild Paris was, along with Chamberlain, working on Balfour to make the Manchurian question appear no obstacle to an Anglo-Russian rapprochement and that Edward VII was "not unsympathetic" to Russia. True, Betzhold did not anticipate the possibility of an English loan to Russia for a year or more, but "thought it his duty" to inform Radolin of these "future possibilities" so that the Germans "could lay counter-mines."

19. See A.G. Rafalovich's letters of Aug. 9 and Oct. 10, 1903 to the minister of finance, in dos. No. 3, 1903, Secretarial section chanc. min. fin., and of Oct. 14, same year, ibid., dos. No. 2.

20. See Die Grosse Politik, Vol. 18, pt. 2, No. 5919, the communication of Nov. 7, n.s., 1903 from Romberg, chargé d'affaires in St. Petersburg, to the effect that Gen. Pendezek had expressed great irritation "at Russia's slackness in constructing the strategic railways in the direction of the western border that had been promised France upon the occasion of the last French loan," and "that "France had made representations to St. Petersburg respecting the matter."

21. See ibid., Vol. 18, pt. 2, No. 5917, Radolin's tel. of Oct. 16/
29, 1903. -- Lamsdorf was in Paris Oct. 29/31, n.s.

22. See ibid., No. 5944, 5936, 5931, 5959, 5948 and especially 5941
and 5917. -- Kuropatkin's "Dnevnik," Kr. Arkhiv, Vol. 2, p. 109.

23. See A.M. Zaionchkovskii, "Franko-russkie otnosheniia do voiny
1914 g." (Franco-Russian Relations Before the War of 1914), (in the
symposium Kto dolzhnik? [Who is Responsible?], Moscow, 1926, p. 51),
Lamsdorf's tel. of Oct. 20, 1904 to Nelidov in Paris.

24. Ito who was, presumably, the last to give his consent to the break
with Russia, had, back at the very beginning of March 1903, provided
"much food for alarming rumors" by his speech at a Party meeting in
Kofu, where he said, in passing: "...World affairs show abrupt changes˗
with each decade. The Great Siberian railway, uniting the Far East with
the Far West is already almost completed and the distance that separated
them may now be traversed in a matter of two weeks. It should not be
forgotten that such a shortening of distances demands our most serious
attention from the viewpoint of national security. Recent improvement
in means of communication is producing a complete revolution in the
relative position of peoples. To give an example--ten years ago, no
western power could ever have dreamed of sending an army of one hundred
thousand to the Far East. But conditions have so changed since then that
it has now become possible to transfer in a matter of two or three months
an army of several hundred thousand men. Of course, all nations desire
peace. Nonetheless, not one of them will venture to forget that the storm
may burst any minute. This is what robs me of peace day and night and
this is why I never let slip an occasion to remind my fellow-countrymen
of the necessity of unity and accord." (See, in dos. No. 79, the report
of March 8/21, 1903 from Raspopov, financial agent in Japan.)

25. See above, p. 96.

26. See above, p. 91, and E. Granovskii, "Monopolisticheskii kapi-
talizm v Rossii" (Monopolistic Capitalism in Russia), Istorik Marksist
(The Marxist Historian), No. 4, p. 40.

27. The Company was founded (the official founders being Th.I.,
Petrokokino, large stock-broker and shareholder in the Discount bank,
and K.A. Vargunin vice-director of the same bank) with a capital of
5,000,000 rubles, divided into 50 thousand shares. At the organizational
meeting on May 26, 1895, 16,561 shares were presented by "foreign
share-holders," not counting the 2253 shares that Th. I. Petrokokino
entered to his own name on the list of "foreign share-holders," evidently
intending to place them in foreign hands later on. The foreign share-
holders were headed by the Paris-Netherlands bank with 3539 shares and
the International bank in Paris with 2500 shares. The Discount and Loan
bank presented 4113 shares, the St. Petersburg International only 1,875.
At subsequent meeting in 1895-98 the International bank's parcel increased (4,000, 8,000, 9,300), the Discount bank's diminished (1,200,
500, 150, 600). See below, appendix II.

28. See below, appendix II.

29. See Witte, Vosp. I, pp. 99-100.

30. See above, p. 91, note.

31. See, in dos. No. 64, the tel. of Aug. 13, 1897 from the director
of the chanc. min. fin. to Pokotilov.

32. See, ibid., Pokotilov's telegrams of Sept. 4 and Sept. 12, 1897.
Pokotilov and Vert both thought it "inadvisable" "to scatter the forces"
of the bank and enter into competition with the Indo-Chinese (French)
bank in the south of China (Witte's notation is: "if to the bank's disadvantage, must not be done.") At those lines of the telegram where Pokotilov expressed himself as in favor of breaking with the French if they
didn't like the policy of the Russian directors, Witte endorsed: "Should
stick to this." See, ibid., the tel. of Nov. 4, 1897 from the dir. chanc.
min. fin. to Pokotilov, saying that Witte "fully shared" Pokotilov's
opinion "as to the necessity of a categorical answer to the French in connection with their relations to the bank."

33. See above, p. 236.

34. See, in dos. No. 64, Rafalovich's two letters of Oct. 15/27, 1899
to Witte. Rafalovich did not mention the Paris members of the bank's
Board as having anything to do with this transaction. The proposals to
be transmitted to Peterburg were made to Rafalovich by Delcasse himself. After this conversation, Rafalovich was further informed that the
proposal of a fourth seat for the French had at one time been made by
Rothstein. When interrogated in connection with Rafalovich's advices,
Rothstein clarified only the question of delimitation, to the effect that at
one time there was talk of a boundary at the Yangtse with branches of
both banks operating in Shanghai and that "as the French government saw
it" the Russo-Chinese bank would in such an event have "played the same
part in the north, as the Indo-Chinese in the south, of China" (see, ibid.,
Rothstein's letter of Oct. 27, o.s., 1899, to Shipov).

35. See, ibid., Witte's letter of Oct. 26, 1899 to Rafalovich, and
Hottinguer's and Netslin's letter of Dec. 9/21, and Verstraat's of Dec. 23.

36. See above, pp. 257-258, 376. -- For example, the gold concessions in Manchuria taken up in 1901 by the Rus. Gold-mining Co. and
A.A. Troitsky were acquired by the Man. Mining Assn. in 1903 just because they had been offered to "foreigners" (see, in dos. No. 106, the
report of the Board of the M.M.A. for Jan. 2, 1904).

37. See Polovtsov's "Dnevnik," Kr. Arkhiv, Vol. 3, p. 103.

38. See Die Grosse Politik, Vol. 18, pt. 1, No. 5406, Bülow's tel.
of March 5/18, 1902, and in dos. No. 3, 1903, Secretarial div. chanc.
min. fin. Rafalovich's letter of Aug. 12, 1902 to Witte to the effect that
"Rouvier was very hospitably inclined to a Russian operation if allowed
to choose the moment." Witte's notation on the passage is: "I am unprepared for the time being to conduct any operations in Paris." --
Bülow went at Mendelssohn hammer and tongs to get him to refuse the
loan unless Witte gave his "written promise" not to raise the Russian
tariff in response to the impending rise in the German import duty on
wheat. But in view of the possibility of Witte's going over to the French
market, Bülow's idea went begging (Die Grosse Politik, Vol. 18, pt. 1,
No. 5404, 5405, 5407.)

39. See Rafalovich's letter of Dec. 1, n.s., 1902 to Witte, in dos.
No. 3, 1903, Secretarial div. chanc. min. fin., and his letter of May 10,
1903, ibid., dos. No. 2, 1903.

40. See Polovtsev's "Dnevnik," Kr. Arkhiv, Vol. 3, p. 103.

41. See, in dos. No. 120, Vorontsov's letter of May 9, 1903 to Witte:
"Once we have entered the arena of world politics, we shall need an agreement either with England or with Germany." Vorontsov preferred "the
latter power, as more dangerous to us, but also more in need of us."

42. See Die Grosse Politik, Vol. 19, pt. I, No. 5920, 5923, 5927, 5943, 5950, 5951, and Vol. 18, pt. I., No. 5421.

43. See ibid., Vol. 18, pt. 2, No. 5917, Radolin's tel. of Oct. 16/29, 1903 from Paris, telling of his talk with Germain, director of the Credit Lyonnais, who plainly indicated that the peaceful issue of the Russo-Japanese conflict depended entirely on Germany, that it was hers to "dictate" (Wilhelm's notations are: "I never even dreamed of this," and: "the French are afraid of losing their money in a Far-Eastern scuffle and want us to restrain the Russians, I would never think of it") ibid., Vol. 19, pt. I, No. 5924, Mühlberg's memorandum of a talk with Osten-Saken on July 2/15, 1903 about the state of affairs in Manchuria (Osten-Saken manifested great "diffidence" and expressed the hope that Russia would find "support" in Germany; Bülow's notation is: "We must not permit Russia to so far give way to fear as under any circumstances to come to an agreement with Japan"); No. 5943, Bülow's memorandum of Jan. 3/16, 1904, in which Bülow, discussing what counter-demands Germany might make if Russia asked for support, declared in favor of great caution in the formulation of demands, so that "the Russian government would not get the idea of an understanding with Japan, England and America or future compromises;" ibid., Vol. 18, pt. I., No. 5421, Holstein's tel. of April 3/16, 1903 to Bülow, giving a detailed demonstration of the necessity of a "'waiting policy"; ibid., No. 5422, Bülow's memorandum of Nov. 7, n.s., on the Wiesbaden meeting that took place on Nov. 4 and 5, 1903: Wilhelm "avoided" being the first to mention "foreign policy," and on the 2nd day of the meeting Nicholas saw that he would be "forced" to "open the subject" himself; moreoever Bülow underscored that Wilhelm made no "promise" respecting coverage of the rear; ibid., Vol. 19, pt. I, No. 5931, Metternich's tel. of Jan. 8, n.s., from London: Lansdowne had "categorically announced" to the Japanese ambassador "that England would in future exert no pressure on Japan in the sense of maintaining peace and would herself conscientiously fulfill her treaty obligations," and "that France would remain neutral;" No. 5936, Bülow's tel. of Jan. 12, n.s., to the effect that Rouvier had assured Luzzati that casus foederis would arise for France only in the event of England's attacking Russia in European waters; cf. also No. 5945.

44. See Die Grosse Politik, Vol. 19, pt. 1, no. 5939.

45. See Kuropatkin's "Dnevnik," Kr. Arkhiv, Vol. 2, pp. 44, 47, 62. On the great manoeuvres in the Warsaw military district at the end of August 1903, see ibid., pp. 69 ff.

46. See Lamsdorf's letter of Oct. 28, 1904 to Osten-Saken, Kr. Arkhiv, Vol. 5, p. 15.

47. See Rafalovich's tel. of 10/23 to Kokovtsov and Putilov's of Feb. 12/25, 1904 to Rafalovich (Rus. Fin., No. 1 and 2).

48. See Kokovtsov's letter of Oct. 20, 1904 to Nelidov (ibid., No. 34).

49. See Nelidov's letter of March 25/April 7, 1904 to Kokovtsov (ibid., No. 5).

50. See Kokovtsov's cited letter of Oct. 20, 1904.

51. See Kokovtsov's letter of April 11, 1904 to Lamsdorf (ibid., No. 14, p. 93).

52. See Rafalovich's letter of March 31/April 13 to Kokovtsov and Putilov's of April 5/18, 1904 to Rafalovich (ibid., No. 6 and 9).

53. See Kokovtsov's letter of April 11, 1904 (ibid. No. 14, pp. 92 and 94).

54. See Rafalovich's letter of April 24/May 7, 1904 to Kokovtsov (ibid., No. 18).

55. The loan issue order was constituted on April 29, and by April 30, Bompar, the French ambassador, was already reminding Kokovtsov to utilize the services of French industry: see exchange of letters between Bompar and Kokovtsov of April 30/May 13, May 1/14 and May 3/16, 1904 (ibid., No. 20-22). On overcharges on French orders as compared with German prices see Kokovtsov's letter of Feb. 26, 1905 to Nelidov (ibid., No. 46, pp. 163-164).

56. See Rafalovich's letter of June 19/July 2, 1904 to Kokovtsov (ibid., No. 23).

57. The Russo-German trade treaty of Jan. 29/Feb. 10, 1894 expired on Dec. 18/31, 1903. A new customs tariff and a new customs law had been passed by the Reichstag on Dec. 25, 1902. As applied to Russia's export to Germany of wheat, spelt, rye, oats and brewing barley, the new tariff would exceed the old by a minimum of 78 million marks and a maximum of 110. The Russian government responded on Jan. 13, 1903 by publishing a new tariff of its own which taxed goods, principally from Germany, coming overland across the border, 20 per cent higher than those coming by sea. Dates when the new tariffs would be put into effect were not announced by either party. On January 8, 1903, Germany proposed entering into negotiations on the basis of the new German and the old Russian tariff. By note of Jan. 20, 1903 the Russian government agreed to negotiate, but on the basis of the new Russian tariff hastily published on January 13. Negotiations were opened, but by Dec. 30, 1903 had come to a standstill with Russia proposing terms whereby German exports to Russia would be taxed 26 million marks per annum more than under the status quo, and with Germany proposing terms whereby Russian exports to Germany would be taxed 33-1/2 million marks more. Things had reached a deadlock when, at the instance of Wilhelm, (see Perepiska V. i N., p. 58). Nicholas entrusted the question to a special conference under the chairmanship of Witte for revision. The conference of May 1, 1904 "reached the conclusion that the effectuation of a trade treaty with Germany might be possible on the basis of the minimal German tariff imposts, " and in July Witte went to Germany for direct negotiations with Bülow. By the finance ministry's calculations, the addendum to the trade treaty accepted by both sides on July 15, 1904 taxed the Russian export of agricultural products 11,603 thousand rubles more than before and the German export of manufactured products 13,482 thousand rubles more (see the min. fin.'s presentation of Jan. 22, 1905, No. 547).

58. See Wilhelm's letter of June 6, 1904 to Nicholas (Perepiska V. i N., pub. Tsentrarkhiv, Moscow, 1923, p. 62;) Nelidov's letters of Aug. 10/23 and Sept. 16/29 and Kokovtsov's of Aug. 26, 1904 (Russk. fin., No. 27-29).

59. See Wilhelm's letter of Aug. 19, n.s., 1904 to Nicholas (Perepiska V. i N., p. 65).

60. See A.M. Abaza's letter of Sept. 9, 1904 to Adm. Alekseev (archives of the Chancellery of the Special Committee on Far Eastern Affairs, dos. No. 114/95/s). Through Abaza, Nicholas asked Alekseev what his ideas were on the Manchurian question, "viewed" "in the following light": "Taking into consideration, first, the impossibility of actually getting an adequate war indemnity from ruined Japan, and, second, the

relative worthlessness of Korea economically, Russia's only palpable indemnity for the present war might appear to be the annexation of Manchuria. A prolongation of Chinese neutrality will not only lead to the conservation of the existing vague and, to us, damaging situation in Manchuria, but might even worsen it by obliging us to profess feelings of gratitude to China for her ostensible cooperation through the preservation of neutrality during the war. Consequently a breach of neutrality by China would be to our advantage and is hence to be desired. Granting that, in the present phase of the war, an outright break with China may be considered premature, it is nonetheless impossible not to admit that it will not do to let slip a suitable moment for the first serious step in this direction, the more so since upon our further accumulation of troops and after our first successes, a breach of neutrality by China will become less likely. Bearing this in mind, it might appear possible to utilize the perpetual disturbances and hostilities of the Khunkhuz for announcing to the Peking government that, to guarantee peace in the country, we demand the removal from Manchuria for the period of the war all chiang-chŭns and fudutuns incapable of preserving order and safeguarding the civilian population and the railway. After taking over the higher administration of Manchuria, we might leave the lower native administration as it is, though of course completely subordinating it to ourselves." --Alekseev replied (see, ibid., his letter of Oct. 7, 1904 to Abaza from Harbin) that "until we have crushed our chief enemy it will be absolutely necessary for us to deter China from breach of neutrality and avoid any provocative acts that might embolden the celestial emperor's government to come out openly for Japan." Alekseev's reply was composed by Planson, diplomatic officer to the vicegerent of the Far East (see Planson's diary, preserved in the LYsIA, entry for Oct. 10, 1904; for ability to use the transcript of the diary, I am indebted to P.A. Sadikov, who prepared it for the press and was so kind as to lend me his own copy of the transcript). In September, even before he learned of the Abaza-Nicholas project, Alekseev, located in Harbin, had indulged in pessimistic reflections as to the war and its probable results (according to Planson's diary): "We are rocking like an old coach on unsteady wheels. I have been in the business for 40 years and say with assurance that we can't put up a fight. We must end the war somehow, for I see no possibility of its satisfactory conclusion; the worse the more of it" (Sept. 8); "as to the future fate of Manchuria, the vicegerent stated that it was now very hard to say whether we should be able to annex Manchuria even if we conquered Japan" (Sept. 13); Planson tried to persuade Alekseev that "we must without fail take all Manchuria and endeavor to derive revenue from it," but "the admiral said that we were incapable of this, hadn't the men or the knack, we were simply good for nothing" (Sept. 19).

61. See Wilhelm's tel. of Oct. 6/19, 1904, to Nicholas, Perepiska V. i N., pp. 68-69. In this case the news, emanating from the Japanese representative in Stockholm, proved false: to an inquiry from Bülow, the German minister in Tokyo, Count Arko, replied that Kurino was in Tokyo and that nothing was known of his taking a trip to Europe (see Die Grosse Politik, Vol. 19, pt. 2, Arko's tel. of Oct. 12/25, 1904, No. 6166). Hayashi's attempt to start peace talks with Witte, "confidentially through intermediaries," apparently dates from this same time. Witte himself saw the only obstacle to the conclusion of peace in Nicholas, who still

"believed" that "the war might end victoriously for Russia" (see ibid.,
No. 6167, Mendelssohn's message of Nov. 2, n.s., to Bülow, giving
Witte's exact words, p. 387).

Roosevelt received word at the same time
that England and France intended to propose that, in accord with Japan's
wish, America act conjointly with them in the interests of a mediated
peace (ibid., No. 6271, Sternburg's tel. of Nov. 11, n.s., 1904 from
Washington). Bülow was prepared to be a party to the mediation only if
Russia so desired. But when the Germans attempted to get his opinion
on the matter, Lamsdorf replied that "the tide of war was beginning to
turn against Japan" and that from Russia's viewpoint it was an unfortunate
moment for intervention (ibid., No. 6168 and 6169, Bülow's and Romberg's tel. of Oct. 30/Nov. 12, 1904).

62. See Nicholas's tel. of Oct. 10/23 in E.V. Tarle, Zapad i Rossiia
(The West and Russia), Petrograd, 1918, p. 204.

63. See Kokovtsov's letter of Oct. 8, o.s., 1904 to Nelidov in Paris
(Russk. fin., no. 33).

64. See Kokovtsov's letter of Oct. 20, o.s., to Nelidov (ibid, No. 34).
After returning from Peterburg, Mendelssohn had informed Bülow "in the
strictest secrecy" that the following year Russia would need one billion
marks and that half of this amount would be borrowed in Germany and
half in France (see Bülow's memorandum of Oct. 20/Nov. 2, 1904,
Die Grosse Politik, Vol. 19, pt. 2, P. 388).

65. See Nelidov's letter of Oct. 25/Nov. 7 to Kokovtsov and Rafalovich's
of Nov. 8/21, 1904 (Russk. fin., No. 35 and 36).

66. See Perepiska V. i N., pp. 70-72.

67. Secret, that is, from their ministers of foreign affairs. -- See
"Russko-germanskii dogovor 1905 g. zakliuchennyi v B'orke" (The Russo-
German Treaty of 1905 Concluded at Bjorko) (documents published in
Kr. Arkhiv, 1924, Vol. 5, pp. 6-49) and chap. CXXXV, in Vol. 19, pt. 1
of Die Grosse Politik, pp. 300-350.

68. See Nicholas's memorandum of Oct. 20 to Lamsdorf in Kr. Arkhiv,
Vol. 5, p. 12 and Bülow's memorandum of Oct. 17/30 to Wilhelm, enclosing projects of the letter in reply to Nicholas and the treaty text, published
in Die Grosse Politik, Vol. 19, pt. 1, No. 6120.

69. See Kr. Arkhiv, Vol. 5, p. 12.

70. This letter of Nicholas's lacks Russian publication. For its text,
see Die Grosse Politik, Vol. 19, pt. 1, No. 6124. -- A reference to it
exists in Wilhelm's letter of Nov. 4/17 (Kr. Arkhiv, Vol. 5, p. 17).

71. See Wilhelm's letter of Nov. 4/17 and the German counter-project,
in Kr. Arkhiv, Vol. 5, pp. 17-21. All three put a great deal of work on
the text of the letter: Bülow and Holstein as authors, and Wilhelm as
English translator (7 hours), see Die Grosse Politik, Vol. 19, pt. 1,
p. 313, Wilhelm's notation and editorial note.

72. See Nicholas's tel. of Nov. 10/23, 1904 to Wilhelm, in E.V. Tarle,
Zapad i Rossiia, p. 207 (in Perepiska V. i N. , pub. Tsentrarkhiv, this
tel. is undated, see p. 83).

73. See Wilhelm's tel. of Nov. 13/26, ibid., p. 83; Lamsdorf's "review" (report) is in Kr. Arkhiv, Vol. 5, pp. 22-23.

74. See ibid., p. 23.

75. See Nicholas's letter of Nov. 24/Dec. 7, 1904 and the "Notice"
(which exactly corresponds with the text published in Kr. Arkhiv, Vol. 5,
p. 23) in Die Grosse Politik, Vol. 19, pt. 1, No. 6131, pp. 322-324.

Unless Wilhelm agreed to the preliminary notification of France in the proposed form, Nicholas proposed to delete all mention of France from the treaty.

76. See the letter relating to this of Nov. 10/23 from Wilhelm to Bülow apropos of the telegram received from Nicholas,and Bülow's memorandum of Nov. 11/24 to Wilhelm giving the draft of the answer actually sent St. Petersburg on the 13/26th--in Die Grosse Politik ibid., pp. 316-319.

77. See Die Grosse Politik, Vol. 19, pt. 1, No. 6129, Bülow's letter of Nov. 23/Dec. 6, 1904 to Alwensleben. Wilhelm's letter of Nov. 24/Dec. 7 is published in Perepiska V. i N., p. 85.

78. See Die Grosse Politik, ibid., No. 6137, Lamsdorf's note of Nov. 29/Dec. 12; No. 6139, the list of questions that Bulow put to the German ambassador in London, Count Metternich, on Dec. 16, n.s.; and No. 6140, Metternich's memorandum of Dec. 18, n.s. -- For Wilhelm's letter of Dec. 21, n.s., 1904 to Nicholas, see Perepiska V. i N., p. 87.

79. Nicholas's answering letter of Dec. 12/25, 1904 is published in Die Grosse Politik, ibid., No. 6145. In it, Nicholas did nothing beyond making a "declaration on the coal question" in the sense of an "explicit guarantee on our part such as to permit Russia and Germany to continue undisturbed the line of action that they had adopted some months back." About the general treaty Nicholas never uttered a word. Wilhelm took this as "a plain refusal to even consider an agreement without the pre-liminary information of France," but Bülow consoled him by saying that the Russians did not "as yet" realize the true value of the opportunity to enter into an alliance with Germany (see ibid., pp. 346-347).

80. Back in June 1904 Nicholas had "reassured" Abaza that "by No-vember new divisions will have been formed all over Russia to replace those that have left for the East, and we shall have the same number of troops here as we had before the war;" see B.A. Romanov, "Bezobraz-ovskii kruzhok letom 1904 g." (The Bezobrazovist Clique in the Summer of 1904), in Kr. Arkhiv, Vol. 17, p. 76.

81. See Lamsdorf's letter of Oct. 28, 1904 to Kokovtsov, carrying a reference to the report of his maj. of Oct. 19 (Russk. Fin., No. 39). From the fact that Lamsdorf also mentioned the episode of the spring of 1901 above described (pp. 306-307 and 312-313), when he had likewise raised the question of calculating Russia's material resources in con-nection with Russian diplomacy's taking decisive steps on the Manchurian questions, one wonders whether now too he may not have had it in mind to use that same inter-ministerial discussion pattern to pour cold water on the heated imaginings of any who still thought that Russia's hands were not tied in this war or the final results absolutely contingent on the com-plicated game of international relations on a world scale.

82. See ibid., No. 40, Kokovtsov's rep. to his majesty of Nov. 19, 1904.

83. See ibid., No. 41.

84. Nicholas's proposal that preliminary notice of the defensive treaty be given the French did "not surprise" Wilhelm, since Nicholas had no one else to lean on in the matter of loans (see Die Grosse Politik, Vol. 19, pt. I, No. 6126, Wilhelm's letter of Nov. 10/23, 1904 to Bülow).

85. Curiously enough, the Paris market started to react to "events in Peterburg" on January 5 (agitation had opened in the Peterburg factories on January 3): on January 9 at 4:07 p.m., Them. I. Petrokokino telegraphed Kokovtsov from Paris that "for four days now all the people who subscribed provisionally to the new Russian loan have been cancelling their subscriptions" and that "the heads of all credit institutions are gravely distressed about it" (see Petrokokino's tel. of Jan. 9/22, 1905, in dos. No. 1, 1904, Secretarial section chanc. min. fin.).

86. See Nelidov's letter of Feb. 17/March 2, 1905 to Lamsdorf (Russk. Fin., No. 44)..

87. Cf. Witte's desperate letter of Jan. 19, 1905 to Kuropatkin, in Kr. Arkhiv, Vol. 19, pp. 73 ff.

88. See Kokovtsov's letter of March 4, 1905 (Russk. Fin., No. 49).

89. Ibid., No. 44, p. 131.

90. Kokovtsov's letter of Feb. 26, 1905 (ibid., No. 46).

91. See Kokovtsov's letter of May 10/23, 1905 to Nelidov (ibid., No. 53).

92. See Die Grosse Politik, Vol. 19, pt. 2, No. 6167, Bülow's memorandum on Mendelssohn's communications of Nov. 2, n.s., 1904, following his trip to Peterburg.

93. See Krasnyi Arkhiv, Vol. 6, p. 14, mention in Kokovtsov's letter of June 20, 1905 to Lamsdorf of the fact that he, Kokovtsov, had presented this memorandum.

94. We have not as yet succeeded in finding the text of Kokovtsov's memorandum among the documents of the finance ministry archives, A rough draft has however been preserved of Kokovtsov's letter of March 13, 1905 to Gen. F.F. Palitsyn, Grand Duke Nicholas Nikolaevich's chief of staff, enclosing "the conclusion to my reflections, with which you [Palitsyn] are conversant, on the question of resources for conduct of the war," and so has the used postal wrapper on which Kokovtsov made a pencil draft of these "conclusions" in nine points, with the date: "13/III," and carrying the notation of off. sp. dep. Dorliak: "executed that same day." The text of "the conclusions" will be published by us in full in Kr. Arkhiv in the article "Konets russko-iaponskoi voiny" (End of the Russo-Japanese War).

95. The initial impression of the Mukden defeat almost impelled Wilhelm to make a false move: he considered the "annihilation" of the Russian army likely in the near future and was prepared to make all sorts of advances to the Japanese (promise not to oppose their occupation of Port Arthur, and even congratulate the Mikado on his victory). Bülow succeeded, however, in averting this, and the idea gained ascendancy in Berlin that "if the tsar kept on" and refused to make peace at once as Witte and all the liberals seemed to wish, then "the situation would improve for the tsar and deteriorate for the Japanese." Bülow was fortified in his conviction that "time was in Russia's favor" by the fact that it was the "friends of Japan" and the "enemies of tsarism" who were insisting on peace. The immediate conclusion of peace, he feared, might lead to the assassination of Nicholas and the regency of Mikhail, with Witte's active participation, and this might easily end in the conversion of the tsarist monarchy into a republic, attended by "grave perils" for Germany. Wilhelm was readily persuaded of this and decided not to take any responsibility or intervene with any offer of mediation, as Roosevelt was now apparently

of a mind to get Germany to do (see Die Grosse Politik, Vol. 19, pt. 2, No. 6187, 6189, 6191, 6295 and 6296, correspondence of Feb. 26/March 11-March 17/30, 1905). -- Concerning the impression of the Mukden catastrophe on the Manchurian army itself, see Linevich's diary (in the symposium, Russko-Iaponskaia voina, p. 90, entry for Feb. 28): "Everywhere it was said that peace would come by February 28."

96. See Rafalovich's letter of May 2, 1905 (Rus. Fin., No. 52).

97. See Kokovtsov's letter of May 10/29, 1905: Bompar, "who is leaving shortly" (Rus. fin., No. 53).

98. Rafalovich's letter of May 25/June 2, 1905 (ibid., No. 55).

99. Putilov's letter of May 28/June 10, 1905 to Rafalovich (ibid., No. 56).

100. See Nelidov's letter of May 28, 1905, ibid., No. 57.

101. Back at the beginning of May Bülow had seriously figured in "the possibility of a Russian victory by sea" that would establish the Russo-Japanese "balance" in the Far East desired by America (see Die Grosse Politik, Vol. 19, pt. 2, No. 6306, Bülow's tel. of May 17/4, 1905 to the German ambassador in Washington). At that time, having learned of Delcasse's mediatory attempts, Roosevelt sounded out the Japanese and Russian ambassadors, and both gave him to understand that "their governments had firmly resolved to continue the war": Russia in expectation of a naval victory, Japan of a decisive attack on Harbin and Vladivostok (which gave Roosevelt occasion to speak of the utility of their mutual extermination, see ibid., No. 6310, Speck von Sternburg's tel. from Washington on his talk of May 11/24 with Roosevelt). Roosevelt gave telegraphic instructions to von Langerke-Meier in Peterburg to approach the tsar with an offer of mediation on May 23/June 5, after receiving the telegram of May 22/June 4 from the American ambassador in Berlin saying that Wilhelm had entrusted him to tell Roosevelt "that he [Wilhelm] recognized Russia's situation to be so serious that when Peterburg learned the truth about the latest defeat the tsar's life would be in danger," and that he, Wilhelm, had suggested the president's mediation to the tsar (see Tyler Dennett, Roosevelt and the Russo-Japanese War, New York, 1925, pp. 217-219, Tower's tel. of May 22/June 4 and his letter of May 27/June 9, 1905 to Roosevelt; for the text of Roosevelt's telegram of May 23/June 5 to Langerke-Meier, which Meier was to show to Nicholas, see Die Grosse Politik, Vol. 19, pt. 2, No. 6314).

102. See Perepiska V. i N., Moscow, 1923, pp. 102 ff.

103. Wilhelm's letter of May 21/June 3 was received in Peterburg on May 23, and "the next day" (i.e., May 24) Langerke Meier, having received his instructions, requested an audience and was received by Nicholas on the 25th. Thus Nicholas neither had to ask Wilhelm to "communicate with Roosevelt," as he had offered to do, nor yet "summon" the American ambassador. Lamsdorf answered Cassini's communication concerning the American offer of mediation on May 24/June 6, and his answer was that "Russia could sue neither for peace nor for mediation" and that peace negotiations were out of the question until the Japanese terms were known. The contradiction between Lamsdorf's answer and Nicholas's consent the next day (May 25/June 7) to accept Roosevelt's offer is perhaps explained by the fact that Lamsdorf was not invited to the "military conference" held at court, with Nicholas presiding, on May 24, o.s., which resolved to resort to mediation (see Die Grosse

Politik, Vol. 19, pt. 2, pp. 425 and 424; Tyler Dennett, op. cit., pp. 223 and 193); the minutes of the May 24 conference, with stenographic transcript of what was said, will be published in Kr. Arkhiv; only the military attended, including Grand Dukes Vladimir and Aleksey; Vladimir spoke the most decidely in favor of an attempt to take steps toward the conclusion of peace and Nicholas supported him).

104. See Benkendorf's letter of June 29/July 12, 1905 to Lamsdorf from London (Russk. fin., No. 58).

105. See Benkendorf's letter of July 18/31, 1905 to Lamsdorf, ibid., No. 60.

106. See Lamsdorf's letter of July 15 to Kokovtsov, and Kokovtsov's of July 20, 1905 to Lamsdorf, ibid., No. 62 and 63.

107. See Kr. Arkhiv, Vol. 19, p. 80, Witte's letter of June 23, 1905 to Kuropatkin: "foreign credit is already absolutely closed to us," and Die Grosse Politik, Vol. 19, pt. 2, pp. 427 and 472-473: Radolin's tel. of July 12/25, 1905 to Bülow from Paris ("Rothschild and other representatives of Haute Finance, it is rumored, will conduct negotiations with Witte, but on every hand I am assured that large sums will be forthcoming only in the event that peace is achieved") and Bülow's tel. of July 14/27 to Wilhelm (Rouvier told Radolin that "financially speaking, if the war continues Russia has not the slightest hope of finding money in France").

108. See Kokovtsov's tel. of July 19, 1905 to Witte in Paris, requesting that on his way back he "urge upon Paris the necessity of a loan, as the sole means of preventing our being pushed to financial indiscretions" (Kr. Arkhiv, Vol. 6, documents published by us on the Portsmouth negotiations, p. 23). But even Witte was then disinclined to approach "the English channel" (see Die Grosse Politik, Vol. 19, pt. 2, No. 6198, Radolin's tel. of July 12/25, 1905, p. 427).

109. With the purpose, as Bülow forumulated it, of leading Nicholas so far as to make it impossible for Witte and Lamsdorf to form a triple Anglo-Franco-Russian accord immediately after the conclusion of peace (see Die Grosse Politik, Vol. 19, pt. 2, No. 6212, Bülow's tel. of July 7/20, 1905 to Holstein).

110. See Kokovtsov's telegrams of July 19 and 23, 1905 to Witte, Kr. Arkhiv, Vol. 6, pp. 22 and 24. It is not impossible that the loan offer made Russia at this time...by the Darmstadt (family) bank also contributed to the tsar's "excellent frame of mind." But the proposed sum (47 million rubles) was, in Kokovtsov's opinion, "quite inadequate to meet the requirements" of Russia, while the short-dating (nine months) "might only damage our credit," so that Kokovtsov's reaction to this proposal was "completely negative." The question of admitting the Darmstadt bank to participation in Russian credit operations already had its history. During the war certain "communications" on this question had passed between Nicholas and the grand duke of which Kokovtsov knew nothing at all. At the beginning of January 1905 Nicholas expressed to Kokovtsov his "desire that something be done for this bank," and Kokovtsov had to open a credit there to the account of the State bank "and enroll it among the correspondents of the latter." Now, after Bjorko, the Darmstadt bank aspired to having the Russian ministry of finance "influence" Mendelssohn in the sense of getting the latter to include this bank in his group in connection with future Russian loans. But Kokovtsov protested this point as well, since it appeared that the Darmstadt bank had "taken

an active part in the subscribing" of the last Japanese loan. On this,
see Kokovtsov's letter of July 25, 1905 to Lamsdorf in reply to Lamsdorf's letters of July 20 and 23 in connection with these two demarches
of the Darmstadt bank, in dos. No. 1, 1904, Secretarial section, chanc.
min. fin.

111. See Lamsdorf's letter of Sept. 26/Oct. 9, 1905 to Nelidov in Kr.
Arkhiv, Vol. 5, p. 36.

112. See ibid., p. 47: "On the other hand we are now completely
freed of the possibility of an agreement between Germany and England
to the detriment of our interests." -- Cf. ibid., p. 36. -- "Actually
(thatsächlich)--as even Wilhelm grasped--this was not only a return to
the status quo, but the establishment of a "triple military coalition."
For him the only question that remained was "whether this was entirely
clear" to Nicholas. Formally, the German min. for. afs. continued to
regard the Bjorko treaty as "juridically existent" even, for example, in
July 1907. (See Die Grosse Politik, Vol. 19, pt. 2, No. 6255, Wilhelm's
letter of Nov. 13/26, 1905 to Bülow, and p. 528, note, the memorandum
presented to Wilhelm in July 1907 before the meeting at Svinemund.)

113. Nelidov's and Lamsdorf's expressions: see Kr. Arkhiv, Vol. 5,
pp. 30, 35 and 43.

114. Prince Holstein, who by no means looked at Wilhelm's venture
through rose-colored glasses, considered it in the highest degree advisable that at their meeting, Wilhelm wait for Nicholas himself to mention
the alliance. He considered that Russia was now much more dependent
on France financially than six months before, and for Russia saw only
one argument in favor of a German orientation (rather than an English,
as, in his opinion, France would propose, as well as Witte, Lamsdorf,
and the two tsaritsas), namely, that Germany was proposing the alliance
"here and now, before the conclusion of peace," thereby "improving
Russia's position relative to Japan at the peace table, whereas England
could only join Russia after the peace, and would consequently exert no
influence on the Japanese peace terms" (see Die Grosse Politik, Vol. 19,
pt. 2, No. 6207, Holstein's tel. of July 9/22, 1905 to Bülow).

115. See Witte's tel. of August 1/14, 1905 to Lamsdorf (Kr. Arkhiv,
Vol. 6, p. 31).

116. Bülow even thought of resigning unless Wilhelm consented to drop
from article I of the treaty the clause that bound the allies to aid each
other "in Europe." This clause, in the opinion of Bülow and Holstein,
reduced the value of the Russian alliance in an Anglo-German clash,
where they had pictured Russia's aid as taking the form of a campaign
against India and a threat to England's Asiatic possessions as a whole.
At the end of July, o.s., there was a plan for having Wilhelm propose to
Nicholas that the debatable article be altered. It was dropped for fear
Russia (Lamsdorf) might take the opportunity to make a revision of the
treaty that would reduce it to nil. (See Die Grosse Politik, Vol. 19,
pp. 450-451.)

117. This was just what the Germans had gambled on: see Holstein's
tel. of July 13/26, 1905 to Bülow ("until the contrary is proved, I hold
that isolation in between" France and England "is more terrifying to the
tsar for reasons of domestic than of foreign policy," Die Grosse Politik,
Vol. 19, pt. 2, No. 6223, p. 470) and Bülow's tel. of July 9/22, 1905 to
Wilhelm, ibid., No. 6208, p. 445 ("if at the forthcoming meeting your

majesty takes the warm and cordial tone with the tsar that informed your whole demeanor during the war, it will please him very much at so diffi- cult a moment. Your leitmotiv always was: We desire only that the Rus- sian dynasty shall emerge unscathed and Russian might unimpaired from this crisis.")

118. See Kr. Arkhiv, Vol. 5, p. 36.

119. See Witte's tel. of March 22/April 4, 1906 to Mendelssohn (Russk. fin., No. 173.) Cf. Nelidov's letter of Sept. 22/Oct. 5, 1905 to Lams- dorf: "Witte in his talk with me here seemed disposed toward an alliance with Germany, for, said he, "everyone is changing alliances and we shall be left alone" (Kr. Arkhiv, Vol. 5, p. 32). And in June 1905 on his way to Portsmouth Witte in a talk with Radolin in Paris returned to the "old" idea of a triple continental agreement against the "trans-oceanic" (über- seeischen) countries, and Radolin carried away the impression that Witte "had not yet approached the English channel." (See Die Grosse Politik, Vol. 19, pt. 2, No. 6198, Radolin's letter of July 12/25, 1905 to Bülow, p. 427.)

120. See Nelidov's letter of Oct. 2/15, 1905 to Lamsdorf, Kr. Arkhiv, Vol. 5, p. 39. -- On his way back from Portsmouth Witte told Radolin that he had "at the last moment" turned down the large loan proposed for Russia by England and France jointly, with Germany excluded (see Die Grosse Politik, Vol. 19, pt. 2, No. 6241, Radolin's letter of Sept. 10/23, 1905 to Bülow, likewise No. 6243, Bülow's tel. of Sept. 12/25, 1905 to Wilhelm). Witte also told Wilhelm at Rominten that he had turned down the Anglo-French loan offered Russia, since he "wanted an international loan with America and Germany participating" (see ibid., No. 6359, p. 663, Wilhelm's notation on Bernstrof's report of Sept. 12/25, 1905 from London).

121. See Nelidov's letter, telling about Rouvier's proposal "the other day," dated Aug. 31/Sept. 13, and Kokovtsov's letter of the same date to Nelidov (Russk. fin. No. 75 and 74).

122. Witte's talk with Morgan took place on Aug. 27/Sept. 9, see Kr. Arkhiv, Vol. 6, pp. 46-47. For Rutkovsky's tel. to Kokovtsov of Sept. 1/ 14 about Barings, see Russk. fin. , No. 76. On Aug. 29/Sept. 11, the Times had printed a correspondence item from Paris ("Rossiia posle voiny"), noting the satisfactory state of Russia's finances and indicating that "for the reorganization of her army and navy" "Russia will without any trouble find sufficient financial aid to meet her needs." -- According to advices reaching Peterburg at the beginning of October, Paris was even discussing Japanese participation in the Russian loan. The same source reported that as soon as the [Anglo-Russian] Persian Gulf agree- ment was signed and Lansdowne said the word, the English public would subscribe to this and all future Russian loans as one man," and that Lord Rothschild himself had said that if Russia would institute "an open and generous attitude toward Jews," then, "not to mention himself" (i.e., Rothschild), "all the 109,000 Jewish bankers throughout the world who were pledged to obstruct Russian financial operations would at once gladly join the other financial interests in Russian transactions." (See the two letters of the American, Judge Ch. Mayer, entrusted to Kokovtsov when he was making his scouting tour of the European capitals in connection with the Russian loan, October 8/21, 1905, in dos. No. 4, 1903 (sic.), Secretarial section chanc. min. fin., folio 29 ff.).

123. See Nelidov's letter of Aug. 31/Sept. 13 to Kokovtsov (Russk. fin., No. 75).

124. See Nelidov's letter of Oct. 2/15, 1905 to Lamsdorf, in Kr. Arkhiv, Vol. 5, p. 39.

125. See Nelidov's letter of Sept. 9/22, 1905 to Kokovtsov (Russk. fin., No. 82). To Mayer as well the Paris situation in October seemed "very complicated": on the one hand, the French government would have liked the loan bonds printed in different colors for France and the other participants, who would also be obliged to retain their portion for two years, and to have the Russian government give preferential rights to the French trade; on the other hand even in the financial world there existed no "group at the moment" "that could command the general confidence of the public" (see Mayer's cited letter of Oct. 8/21, 1905).

126. See Kokovtsov's tel. of Sept. 16/29, 1905 to Rutkovski in London (Russk. fin., No. 83 and p. 223, note).

127. See our publication (Russk. fin., No. 88) of Kokovtsov's letter to the delegates of the international consortium of Oct. 18/31, 1905. A rough draft of the letter was found by us among a mass of separate papers from various archives of the institutes of the ministry of finance at the time of their dismantling.

128. Witte, Vosp., II, p. 180.

129. See Witte's tel. of Jan. 2/15, 1906 to Kokovtsov in Berlin (Russk. fin., No. 129:) Cf. the letter of S. Timashev, manager of the State Bank (unaddressed and undated, but apparently written very soon after Dec. 23): "Balance to December 23 compounded. Situation very bad. Reduction of gold to 59.6 million rubles, increase of bank notes by 20 million rubles, total deterioration of the emission right, 80 million rubles. Emission law broken in the sum of 46.8 million rubles. Even if gold is obtained in Paris, the balance to December 23 will still remain illegal. I anticipate new bank-note issues, data coming in from Siberia and Trans-Baikal point to their being wholly destitute of currency--they have neither metal nor bank-notes. Accountings made there wear down our ready money still further. We cannot get along without an extension of the emission right. This will be necessary even if we get gold from Paris. In any event the balance to Dec. 23 is unpublishable, but to withhold publication for more than a few days is unthinkable; the impression created will be one of desperation. S. Timashev." (See State Bank archives ser. No. 124, dos. No. 162.)

130. See Kokovtsov's letter of Oct. 18/31, 1905 to Morgan (published by us, in translation, from the pencilled English draft, in Russk. fin., No. 89).

131. See, ibid., Netslin's tel. of March 22/April 4, 1906 to Witte, No. 171.

132. The text of the declaration was approved for forwarding to Berlin on Nov. 10/23, 1905 (see Kr. Arkhiv, Vol. 5, pp. 44 ff.). For the letter from Nicholas of Nov. 10/23, 1905 that accompanied the declaration, see Die Grosse Politik, Vol. 19, pt. 2, No. 6254.

133. See Kokovtsov's report of Janaury 15, 1906 on his trip abroad (Russk. fin., No. 131).

134. See ibid., No. 94 a-g.

135. See also Benkendorf's letter of Dec. 2/15, 1905 to Lamsdorf.

136. See Nicholas's tel. of Nov. 19/Dec. 2, 1905 to Wilhelm (Perepis-ka V. i N., Moscow, 1923, p. 127, where the date is not indicated; in E.V. Tarle, Zapad i Rossiia, Petrograd, 1918, p. 217--with date) and Witte's tel. of Dec. 22/Jan. 4, 1905/6 to Kokovtsov in Paris (Russk. fin., No. 107).

137. See ibid., No. 116, Kokovtsov's tel. of Dec. 26/Jan. 8, 1905/6 from Paris.

138. See ibid., No. 116, Kokovtsov's tel. of Dec. 24/Jan. 6, from Paris.

139. See ibid., No. 117, Kokovtsov's tel. of Dec. 26/Jan. 8 to Shipov.

140. See ibid., No. 131, Kokovtsov's report, p. 263.

141. See Russk. fin., No. 132-216.

142. Lamsdorf's cited tel. is quoted in Witte, Vosp., II, p. 186.

143. See Rafalovich's tel. of Jan. 26/Feb. 8, 1906 to Witte (Rus. fin., No. 132). All Witte's attempts to get the loan before the end of the conference were balked (see. ibid., No. 134, 141, 148, 153); Witte proposed "executing the operation" at the end of February, and Poincare's permission "to begin negotiations with bankers" followed on March 18/31, 1906 (see ibid., No. 159).

144. This situation was established after Witte's Tsarskoe Selo negotiations with Netslin at the beginning of February 1906. Before Netslin came, Witte had not yet given up the idea of immediate feelers--with the Rothschilds, for example (see Russk. fin., No. 134 and 137).

145. See Kokovtsov's tel. of March 30/April 12, 1906, Russk. fin. No. 189 (with the refusal of Germany, "America and Italy and the insignificance of Holland's participation the international character of the loan is practically lost.")

146. See, ibid., Witte's tel. of March 30/April 12, 1906 to Kokovtsov in Paris, No. 187 ("It will be very annoying particularly from the political angle if Austria refuses") and Kokovtsov's tel. of March 31/April 13 ("after incredible efforts" "succeeded in securing participation of Austria" "at the last minute" "by certain special privileges" "relating to term of usufruct" of their portions, "deal otherwise threatened to fall through.")

147. See Witte, Vosp., II, p. 185.

148. See Mendelssohn's tel. of March 23/April 5 to Witte (ibid., No. 174).

149. See A.M. Zaionchkovskii, "Franco-russkie otnosheniia do voiny 1914" in symp. Kto dolzhnik?, Moscow, 1926, p. 29, and his Podgotovka Rossii k mirovoi voine v mezhdunarodnom otnoshenii, Leningrad, 1926, pp. 117-124.

150. "Publication of the order must absolutely be" on April 9, "not earlier, not later," "on this the bankers insist" (see Russk. fin., No. 196,201 and 204, Kokovtsov's telegrams of April 3 and 4, o.s.). -- A.M. Zaionchkovsky, op. cit., p. 30.

151. See dos. No. 4, pt. I, 1910, chanc. min. trade and industry.

152. See ibid., Lamsdorf's report to his majesty of May 27, 1906. -- Arthur Nicholson was with Izvolsky "on Thursday": the nearest Thursday to the report fell that year on May 25.

CHAPTER VIII

1. See Russk. fin., No. 222.

2. See Russk. fin., No. 197. Payments by foreign participants in the

loan were placed at the disposal of the Russian government in eight installments, from May 2/15, 1906 to May 24/June 6, 1907 (see ibid., p. 379); "actually" this only obstructed any payments abroad, "formally" it did not take away the "right of extension of emission" on the scale of the total amount of the loan (see ibid., No. 198). On the Paris "pessimists" see Kokovtsov's letter of July 2/15, 1907 to Verneuille, in file of the Secretarial division K.M.F. on the conclusion of the 1909 loan.

3. See Russk. fin., No. 75.

4. See ibid., No. 197 and 198. This engagement was couched in the form of a letter of April 16, n.s., 1906, from Kokovtsov to Poincare. The elastic interpretation was already present in Poincare's reply of April 19, but at that time Netslin, in transmitting the letter, gave "verbal assurances" that the idea here was "to admit the possibility of turning to French credit even during the two-year term." But in Bompar's "verbal note" of June 16/29, 1906 Russia's elastic engagement already figured without any such commentary and had the "precise sense" of a limitation of Russia's independence in the choice of a foreign market for the entire two-year terms (see Kokovtsov's letter of June 16/29, in which he resolutely declines such an interpretation of his engagement and declares that the Russian government "reserves complete freedom in the event of its seeking credit from a country other than France,"--in dos. No. 4, 1903, Secretarial section K.M.F.)

5. See Kokovtsov's tel. of April 3/16, 1906 from Paris (Russk. fin., No. 198).

6. See Russk. fin., No. 225, Netslin's letter of Nov. 7/20, 1906 to Kokovtsov.

7. See Kokovtsov's letter of Nov. 14/27, 1906 to Netslin, Russk. fin., No. 228.

8. See Verneuille's letter of Nov. 30/Dec. 13, 1906 to Kokovtsov, and Kokovtsov's of Dec. 8/21 to Verneuille, Russk. fin., No. 230 and 231. S. Ronin (Inostrannyi kapital i russkie banki [Foreign Capital and Russian Banks], Moscow, 1926, pp. 54 and 55) erroneously dates these letters 1907. They were published by us from copies remaining in the general chanc. min. fin. when the originals were sent to the Special chanc. for the credit section. They were sent there in a letter of Jan. 6, 1907 from off. spec. dep. Dorliak, No. 13, the rough draft of which is preserved in the General chanc. Dorliak's letter enumerates, indicating contents and dates, the two letters (dated 1906) and Dorizon's telegram (of Jan. 18, n.s., 1907) to Kokovtsov, "received today," requesting that the Northern bank, "which had been approved by the Russian delegates," be included in the consortium. We verified the date of Dorliak's letter by the outgoing register of the gen. chanc. for 1907: it is actually on record there under Jan. 6, No. 13. This dating of our letters establishes their immediate connection with Kokovtsov's cit. letter of Nov. 14, o.s., to Netslin, which Netslin "showed" to "some of a very small group of eminent persons," its data on the Russian budget for 1907 producing "a most highly favorable impression" upon the readers. Undoubtedly Verneuille was among these "eminent" persons (see Russk. fin. No. 229).

9. See A.A. Polivanov, Memuary (Memoirs), Moscow, 1924, p. 16.

10. See, in the files of the Civil Accounting dept. of the State Control for 1897, under "Secret papers of the dept.," the tel. of Chief-Lt. Andreev (loc. com. armies pri-Amur district) to E.I. Alekseev from Nikolsk-on-Ussury, March 20, 1905.

11. See in dos. No. 121 of the chanc. Sp. Com. of the Far East the copy of Alekseev's report to his major of (?) March 1905 setting forth the project and the ministers' reactions to it. Kokovtsov in particular only tolerated adoption of the project on condition that the concession treaty be given a "pre-war" dating--"to lend the transaction greater force on the formal side." The minister of justice pointed out the possibility of a betrayal of confidence on Clarkson's part "in the event of his receiving some more advantageous offer from Japan, and of acts on his part that might be injurious to the prestige of the Russian government." Nicholas's resolution was: "better refuse."

12. See, in dos. No. 106, the tel. of March 25, 1905 from the Belgian Wouters to A.I. Vyshnegradsky saying that in general he considered the Association's enterprises attractive, but as requiring further preliminary study.

13. If Vonliarliarskii is to be credited (Materialy dlia vyiasneniia prichin voiny c Iaponiei,·pp. 198 ff.), a meeting of the members of the Lumbering Association was held "at P.P. Gesse's apartment" upon A.P. Ignatev's initiative, and Gesse, Gendrikov, Vonliarliarskii, Yusupov and Serebriakov signed a protocol suspending the efficacy of the treaty of May 31, 1903, and to the treaty was appended an indorsement certifying their exit from the Assn. acknowledging the efficacy of the treaty as suspended without any mutual claims on the part of associates, and reserving to Abaza and Matiunin "the right of use of the firm name of the Russian Lumbering Association in the Far East and the right of organizing an Association."

14. See B.A. Romanov, Vitte i kontsessiia na Yalu, in the symposium of articles dedicated to S.F. Platonov, Petrograd, 1923, pp. 453-457; also dos. No. 213: Abaza's letter of July 2, 1905 to Kokovtsov, Kokovtsov's report to his majesty of July 7, Abaza's letter of July 15 to the same, Kokovtsov's report to his majesty of August 4.

15. See Kokovtsov's report to his majesty of Aug. 4, 1905 and Abaza's letters of July 18 and Aug. 18 same year (first), ibid.

16. See, ibid. , Abaza's two letters of Aug. 18, 1905.

17. See Kokovtsov's rep. to his majesty of Aug. 4, 1905 "on suspension of operations of the M.M.Assn., for liquidation of the business." Abaza was given 350,000 rubles for its "liquidation."

18. See, in dos. No. 106 I-b, Polkotilov's letter of July 29, 1905 to Lamsdorf.

19. See, ibid., the exchange of letters between Vyshnegradsky, July 22/Aug. 4, and Netslin of July 28/Aug. 10, 1905, and Kokovtsov's letter to Lamsdorf of Aug. 1, 1905.

20. See, ibid., the report of the Board of the M.M. Assn. for Aug. 10, 1905 (with Kokovtsov's notation: "agreed"). Netslin proposed: 1) to date the transaction "as previous in time to the Mukden defeat," when Fushun was not yet in Japanese hands, 2) to make an "informal" engagement to the effect that the Russian government had the right to recover the French shares "at double the nominal price." But Russia proposed over and above this: 1) to accord Netslin "for services rendered" 5 per cent of the total profit, and in the event of the conversion of the Assn. into a stock company--5 per cent of the fixed capital free of charge, 2) to figure 5 per cent on his paid shares before apportionment of the profit among other shares.

21. See, ibid., Shipov's rep. to his majesty of Nov. 18, 1905.

22. See, in dos. No. 213, Abaza's two letters of Nov. 28, 1905 to Shipov and Balashov's letter of Nov. 18, same year, to Abaza enclosing the property inventory.

23. See ibid., A.I. Vyshnegradsky's letter of Dec. 30, 1905 to E.D. Lvov.

24. See B.A. Romanov, Vitte i kontsessiia na Yalu, pp. 455-456.

25. See the files of the chancellery of the ministry of the imp. court No. 103, under schedule No. 194/2682, "correspondence on Korea," Stolypin's letter of Nov. 22, 1907 to N.D. Obolensky and I.P. Balashov's letter of June 16, 1914 to S.D. Sazonov "to make my demands known to the Japanese government"--for return of the mines and indemnification of losses from 1904. Cf, on the other hand, Vonliarliarsky's assertion (Materialy dlia vyiasneniia prichin voiny s Iaponiei, p. 201): "I know from Bezobrazov's words that all concessions acquired by him both in Korea and in Manchuria he had an opportunity to sell at a profit after the conclusion of peace with Japan and recoup all the expenditures he had made." But if there were even a particle of truth in this, the question would still remain: where did the sums received go? In any event not into the resources of the treasury (see B. A. Romanov, "Vitte i kontsessiia na Yalu" in Sb. Statei, posv. S.F. Platonovu, Petrograd, 1923, pp. 456-457).

26. See Kokovtsov's rep. to his majesty of July 14, 1906.

27. By this article, all mines appertaining to the Chinese Eastern Railway or exploited in its interest in the region of the portion of the South-Manchurian branch to be ceded to Japan, passed to Japan.

28. See, in dos. No. 157, A.I. Vyshnegradsky's personal letter of Aug. 23/Sept. 5, 1905 to A.I. Putilov from Paris.

29. See Kokovtsov's rep. to his majesty of July 14, 1906 and, in dos. No. 4 of the Mongolor accumulation, the treaties signed by Mongolor and the M.M. Assn. on Aug. 9 and 17 of that year.

30. See, in dos. No. 51, pt. IV, the memorandum of the director chanc. min. fin. of May 23, 1907.

31. See E.D. Grimm, Sb. Dog. i dr. dok. po istorii mezhdunarod. otnosh. na D. Vostoke, Moscow, 1927, pp. 168 ff., treaties of July 17/30, 1907.

32. See, in dos. No. 106, pt. I-v, Kokovtsov's letter of Sept. 27, 1909 to Sazonov. The indicated total included "uncovered disbursements" on the Kwanshan (114,000 rubles) and Sansin (101,000 rubles) concessions, but no Fushun expenditures.

33. See, ibid., the report, signed by Grauman as representative of the M.M. Assn. The running account of the Assn. in the Russo-Asiatic bank in Petrograd showed 41,509 rubles on Jan. 1, 1915 and that of the Hwasinli Co. in the same bank, 185,234 r. 50 kopeks (in the report for 1906 under the same heading appear: 38,670 r. and 161,016 r.; see report, in dos. No. 157).

34. On Jan. 1, 1909 the indebtedness of the Chinese Eastern Railway Company to the Russian government amounted to 550,577,386 r. (including: bonded debt, 275,414,025 r., loans, 1903-1909, 81, 988, 010 r., operational subsidy 1903-1904 and 1907-1908, 54,112,495 r. and 1904-1906, 66,115, 829 r.).

35. See, in dos. No. 214, Davydov's tel. of June 23, 1905 from Peking to the minister of finance, telling of a "principal preliminary exchange of opinions" between the Englishman Walter Hillier and the Chinese government concerning a "loan for the redemption of the Chinese
Eastern Railway"; in dos. No. 105, pt. II, Pokotilov's despatch of
Oct. 18, 1905 to the minister for. afs., concerning a proposal that had
been made to the gov.-gen. of Nanking "by American capitalists" "to
lend China the sum needed to redeem the Manchurian railways."

36. See, in dos. No. 214, G. Vilenkin's letter of Feb. 9/22, 1909 to
Kokovtsov. At that time "joint control and management of the South-
Manchurian Railway by Japan and an American syndicate" was in question.
This project was approved by Ito and Katsura, but the deal fell through
on account of Komura's opposition (see ibid., Schiff's letter of Dec. 4,
1908 to Vilenkin).

37. See Kuropatkin's "Dnevnik," Kr. Arkhiv, Vol. 2, p. 50: August 5,
1903. Nicholas "agreed" with Kuropatkin "that it is essential that we
extend the road from Sretensk to Khabarovsk."--Cf. in dos. No. 4, 1903,
Secretarial section K.M.F., the letters of Oct. 8/21, 1905 and March 16/
29, 1906 from Ch. Mayer, the American, to Dorliak and Dorliak's of
May 18/30 and Sept. 1/14, 1906 to Ch. Mayer. The latter expressed a
desire not only to "undertake the building of the Amur road as soon as
possible" and finish it in 5 years but also "to devote himself" to a Russian "development program" "for the next five years," wherefore in
the spring of 1906 he was interested in the "prospects for successful
study of serious enterprises in St.P." whither he was planning to journey
in June 1906. Borliak, on his side, kept Mayer informed in detail both
on the question of the Amur road and in general on the "serious enterprises" awaiting foreign capital (for example, the Kerchensky works,
the Nevsky factory), and up to date on rumors capable of stimulating
the American's jealousy ("It is said in town that an Anglo-Franco-Belgian
syndicate has been organized in Berlin for buying up all metallurgical
enterprises in Poland," letter of Sept. 1/14, 1906). In the spring of 1906
the Russian government, according to Dorliak, conducted negotiations
with M.W. Jackson as to linking the Baltic and the Black Seas and as to
the Amur railway. But Jackson stipulated the expropriation of too "large
an area of land on both sides of the railway," and his proposition was
rejected. In the autumn of 1906 Mayer was informed of four foreign
proposals to organize a "private company" to build the Amur road, two
of them associated with American capital ("Messrs. Harrison, Gould
and Co." and "Loicq de Lobel's American Syndicate.")

38. At the close of the war, in 1906, the local management of the
Chinese Eastern Railway had resumed the buying up of lands in the region of the road and in one year succeeded in buying up 140 thousand
desyatinas (see Kokovtsov's rep. to his maj. on his trip to the Far East
in the autumn of 1909).

39. See the accumulation of the Council of Ministers, minute-books
of the "Special Conference" of July 25, 1906 (on the organization and
composition of the railway divisions on the Chinese Eastern Railway
line, specifically with reference to their numerical reduction to the norm
of the Portsmouth treaty, 15 men to the kilometer); of Oct. 17, 1906 (on
the organization of postal communication along the Chinese Eastern Railway); of Oct. 17 and 24, 1906 (on the organization of civil administration

in the Chinese Eastern Railway territory, and more particularly on general administration in populated points along the road "on the model of Russian and foreign settlements in the Far East"); of March 20, 1907 (on the commercial and tariff policy of the Chinese Eastern Railway: "in no event to aid the manufacturing industry of Manchuria" and to take every measure for the encouragement of Russian import into Manchuria); of March 20, 1907 (on the organization of police supervision along the Chinese Eastern Railway line, "acting in the name of the Company" but "officially" "under" "the direction" of the ministry of the interior), etc.

40. See the minute-book of the Special Conference of July 28, 1909: When representatives of the U.S.A., England and Germany "expressed doubts as to the equity of investing a private company with powers of a public character," Russian diplomacy "made an attempt to explain [to explain [to Peking] the possibility of replacing the concession of 1896, issued to the Chinese Eastern Railway Company, by a government concession as had been proposed at the very commencement of construction." As was to have been expected, "this proposal, however, encountered decisive objections on China's part, and at the same time the actions of the Chinese authorities started to assume an increasingly hostile character expressed in a series of clashes with the administration of the Chinese Eastern Railway."

41. Moreover the min. for. afs. "in its correspondence on this subject with the ministry of finance repeatedly pointed to the Chinese Eastern Railway as the basic source" "of misunderstandings" with China and "the other foreign powers." See minute-book of the Sp. Con. of July 28, 1909. -- By the beginning of 1909 the Chinese army in process of reorganization ("up-to-date troops") had been brought up to 175,000 men, in ten divisions and sixteen brigades. The proposal was to bring it to 400,000 by 1913-1914 (see f.-Goier's report of May 28, 1909 to the minister of finance on his trip to Japan in April 1909, in dos. chanc. Council of Ministers No. 106).

42. See the memorandum of B. Arsenev, first secretary of the mission in Peking "on the status and political rights of the Chinese Eastern Railway," dated Dec. 22, 1908 (we utilized the copy in the Planson accumulation).

43. See same memorandum.

44. Cf., above, p. 29, note.

45. See, in dos. No. 106 chanc. Council of Ministers, the correspondence of Russian representatives in Seoul, Tokyo and Peking, 1907-1909, there collected, passim.

46. See minute-book of the Sp. Conf. of April 14, 1909, Unterberger's statement. In 1909, Japan already had at her disposal "an army of almost a million" (see in dos. No. 106 chanc. Council of Ministers, the report of the military agent in Japan of Oct. 9, 1909).

47. See cit. memorandum of B. Arsenev of Dec. 22, 1908.

48. See, for example, Somov's despatch of Aug. 29, 1909 from Seoul, in dos. No. 106, chanc. Council of Ministers.

49. See Kokovtsov's letter of Oct. 30, 1908 to Stolypin, No. 708. It was not discussed in Sp. Con. until April 14, 1909 and Kokovtsov's proposal was then waived--"until completion of the Amur railway."

50. See Arsenev's cit. memorandum of Dec. 22, 1908. Nicholas's notation on it was: "It would be well to undertake the settlement of this important question immediately. The memorandum is excellently written.

51. See the min. for. afs. memorandum (unsigned) of Dec. 14, 1908 (copy in the Planson accumulation).

52. See, in dos. No. 214, Korostovets's tel. of Jan. 17/30, 1909.

53. See ibid., Korostovets's tel. of Jan. 21, 1909.

54. See ibid., Vilenkin's letters of Sept. 15/28 from New York and of Nov. 21/Dec. 4, 1908 from London to Kokovtsov, and the copy of Schiff's letter of Oct. 8, n.s., 1908 to Vilenkin.

55. See ibid., Vilenkin's letters of Nov. 21/Dec. 4 and Dec. 1/14, 1908 to Kokovtsov, Schiff's letter of Dec. 4, same year, to Vilenkin and his telegram of Dec. 8. Vilenkin emphasized that "this would be a first step on the part of the banking house of Kuhn, Loeb and Co. toward participation in Russian financial operations" and that it "would untie the hands of the Jewish firms that had hitherto considered themselves morally bound" and "we shall thus obtain the cooperation of these firms without any provisos touching the Jewish question in Russia."

57. See ibid., Vilenkin's letter of Feb. 9/22, 1909 to Kokovtsov from Tokyo.

58. See ibid., Kokovtsov's letter of March 9, 1909 to Vilenkin.

59. See minute-book of the Sp. Con. of July 28, 1909.

60. See Somov's tel. of Aug. 29/Sept. 11, 1909 from Seoul bearing Nicholas's notations: "At last" (archive of revolution and foreign policy in Moscow, cart, rep. to his majesty of 1909).

61. See ibid., Izvolsky's rep. to his majesty of Nov. 8, 1909.

62. See same report of Nov. 8, and Nicholas's notation on it.

63. See in dos. No. 1, 1908 Secretarial section K.M.F., Kokovtsov's letter of Aug. 31-Sept. 13, 1908 to Rafalovich. Kokovtsov here had in mind the representation made by the head of the French government to Izvolsky in connection with the rumor that Russia had placed an order for warships in Germany.

64. See ibid., Kokovtsov's letter of Aug. 22-Sept. 4, 1908 to Revelstock saying that it "had required great efforts" on his part to make the French government concede that "the circumstances in which Russian credit found itself now were very different from those maintaining in April 1906" and telling how the "comedy" of the Paris negotiations was progressing.

SUPPLEMENT I

The Russian Gold-prospecting Company[1]

Opened operations on May 26, 1895. Founders: Th. I. Petrokokino and K.A. Vargunin. Stock capital 5 mil. rub., divided into 50 thous. shares. Of these 6,750 shares were turned over to Mr. G.E. Gintsburg in exchange for 225 shares of the Lena Gold-prospecting Assn. (out of a total of 900). The board of the company comprised: Th. Petrokokino, K. Vargunin, A.F. Maslovsky and A.I. Nerpin. The Council: G.E. Ginstsberg, D.I. Petrokokino, A. Iu. Rothstein, L. Villar, A.A. Pomerantsev, N.N. Bogdanov, K.D. Benardaki, R. Charlié and T.R. Lombardo.

At the general meeting on May 26, 1895 shares were presented by: 1) the court office of Grand Duke Nicholas Nikolayevich (250); 2) Alchevsky A.K. (500); 3) Baimakov F.F., employee Dis. and Loan bank (16); 4) Benardaki N.D. (312); 5) Benardaki K.D. (156); 6) Bogdanov N.N., mem. coun. Rus. bank for For. Trade (312); 7) Bogdanov N.A. (62); 8) Buge F. (62); 9) Vavelberg G. (750); 10) Valtsov D.P., bus. mgr. to Gr. Duke Nich. Nik. (50); 11) Vargunin K.A., vice-pres. Board Disc. and Loan bank (1,250); 12) Weber, O.O., trustee Internat. Com. bank (62); 13) Gerberts B.V., dir. Don.-Yur. company (125); 14) Gintsburg G.O. (125); 15) Gintsburg D.G. (500); 16) Glokov L.K., trustee Disc. and Loan bank (20); 17) Goldenberg, M.D. (50); 18) Goldshtand I.L., mem. Board Internat. Com. bank (250); 19) Golubev V.F. (375); 20) Grube R.I., stock-broker (62); 21) Guber K.K. mem. Board Kaz. ry. (18); 22) Desmon R.I., trustee Disc. and Loan bank (16); 23) Zhuravlev M.N., vice-pres. Board Disc. and Loan bank (375); 24) Kartavtsev E.E., mem. Counc. Rus. bank for For. Trade (125); 25) Kestlin I.I., asst. dir. Rus. bank for For. Trade (62); 26) Kostylev N.A., mem. Board V.-Kam. bank (250); 27) Kokh A.F., mem. Board Intern. Com. bank (250); 28) Lombardo T.R., Board S.-Eastern ry. Co. (125); 29) Lepenau G. (62); 30) Makarov N.V., trustee Disc. and Loan bank (19); 31) Mak-

491

simov I.M. (125); 32) Manasevich T.A. (37); 33) Maslovsky
A.F., pres. Board St. P.-Tula bank (200); 34) Maslov A.N.
(15); 35) Meyer E.M. and Co. (625); 36) Moor M.A., trustee
Disc. and Loan bank (15); 37) Murany A.I., dir. St. P. Priv.
Com. bank (312); 38) Mukhin A.F., dir. V.-Kam. bank (750);
39) Nerpin A.I., asst. mgr. Upper-Amur and Amgun Co.
(300); 40) Netslin E., dir. Paris-Netherlands bank (250);
41) Novitsky Z.O. (21); 42) Notgaft F.K., dir. Internat. Com.
bank (250); 43) Palashkovsky S.E., engineer (1,250); 44)
Petrokokino Th. I. (1,134); 45) Petrokokino D.I., dir. Disc.
and Loan bank (438); 46) Petrokokino A.I., commissioner
(312); 47) Petrokokino F.I., stock-broker (250); 48) Petrokokino brothers (250); 49) Podmener K.G. (187); 50) Pole-
zhaev N. M., mem. Board Disc. and Loan bank (1,250);
51) Pomerantsev A.A., pres. Council Rus. Merc.-Indus.
bank (125); 52) Popov V.V. (62); 53) Pfeifer F.A., trustee
Internat. Com. bank (62); 54) Ramseier Iu. I., trustee Disc.
and Loan bank (24); 55) Rafalovich A-dr F. (62); 56) Rafalovich Art. F., mem. Board Russian bank for For. Trade
(125); 57) Romanov V.A. (62); 58) Rothstein A. Iu., dir.
Internat. Com. bank (1,125); 59) Sementovsky-Kurilo K.M.
(62); 60) Skalkovsky P.A. (62); 61) Smit Bertold, Rus.
Marine Ins. Co. (62); 62) St. P. Internat. Com. bank (1875);
63) St. P. Discount and Loan bank (4,113); 64) Uteman F.V.,
mem. Board Disc. and Loan bank (312); 65) Utin Ia. I.,
vice-pres. Board Disc. and Loan bank (125); 66) Frenkel
A.O., dir. Rus. bank for For. Trade (375); 67) Khessin P.
Ia., rent-broker (62); 68) Charlié René, mem. Board Disc.
and Loan bank (62); 69) Shereshevsky G. and Co. (125); 70)
Sheftel M.I. (125); 71) Schmidt K.F., mem. Board Amur
steam navigation and trading Co. (62); 72) Schneider M.V.
(20); 73) Ebenau R.I., trustee Disc. and Loan bank (17);
74) Evmorfopulo G.I., stock-broker (200); 75) Erk N.P.,
deputy Disc. and Loan bank (62); 76) Yunker I.V. and Co.
(500); 77) Viazmitinov N.P. (70); 77a) Petrokokino Th.I.
(6,750)--[total in the hands of Russian shareholders
31,250]; foreign shareholders[2]: 78) Paris and Netherlands
bank [Erk] (3,639) 79) Heine and Co. [Ramseier] (625); 80)
Hottinguer and Co. [Ramseier] (312); 81) K. Hogel and Co.
[Schneider] (312); 82) Widow Kinen and Co. [Schneider] (312);
83) International bank in Paris [Lombardo] (2,500); 84) Yefrusi

and Porzhes [Desmon] (1,0u0); 85) A.I. Steri and Co. [Des-
mon] (875); 86) Demachi and F. Selier [Markov] (400); 87)
G. Bamberger [Makarov] (500); 88) Count Germini [Novitsky]
(337); 89) Eug. Huen [Novitsky] (400); 90) Netslin E.
[Glokov] (362); 91) Isidor Sall [Baimakov] (82); 92) Artur Rafalovich
[Baimakov] (250); 93) Jozef Tors [Glokov] (200); 94) L. Villar
[Moor] (325); 95) James Hirsh [Moor] (125); 96) Hugo Teisier
[Skalkovsky] (125); 97) Hugo Finali [Skalkovsky] (125); 98)
V. Mac Sweeney and Co. [Ebenau] (500); 99) N.I. and S. Bar-
dak [Ebenau] (500); 100) A. Tardier [Smit] (250); 101) K.
Bloch [Smit] (125); 102) E. Teri [Huber] (62); 103) Raf. George
Levi [Huber] (75); 104) Ern. Dutilel [Buge] (300); 105) Raf.
Bauer [Buge] (334); 106) Chopen de Janvri [Romanov] (82);
107) Ed. Chevrau [Romanov] (164); 108) Louis de Steiger
[Viazmitinov] (77); 109) Eug. Lates [Vyazmitinov] (18); 110)
Willi Kan [A. Petrokokino] (25); 111) K.H. Dumen [A. Petro-
kokino] (75); 112) Henr. van Vik [Palashkovsky] (25); 113) Josse
Allard [Charliér] (25); 114) Count Ferd. Ultremon [Lombardo]
(25); 115) Count Ivan Ultremon [Nerpin] (25); 116) Herm.
Stern [Nerpin] (60); 117) Nik. Hurtado [Schmidt] (25); 118)
K. Belzer [Schmidt] (30); 119) Aug. Leon [Charliér] (38);
120) Louis Bauer [Grube] (25); 121) Kassel and Co. [Grube]
(30); 122) H. Rulofs [Bogdanov] (13); 123) Fr. Filipson [Bog-
danov] (30); 124) Sigm. Bernstein [Goldenberg] (13); 125) R.
Reitins [Utin] (25); 126) F. Pollak [Utin] (125); 127) Jack
Gintsburg [Weber] (100); 128) M. Berton (75); 129) I. Lusson
and Co. (75); 130) P. Krinos (190); 131) Ad. Chamansky
[Erk] (150); 132) Th. I. Petrokokino (2,253). -- Total, 50,000.

For two years after first increasing the basic capital to
7-1/2 million rubles the Company scattered its efforts widely.
By June 1897 6/7 of the capital was invested in 1) shares of
the Lena Gold Assn., 1,500,000 r.; 2) mines in Trans-Baikal
450,000 r.; 3) Mari mines 25,000 r.; 4) South-Ural mines
350,000 r.; 5) shares of Pri-Amur Gold Assn. 150,000 r.
6) shares Amgun Gold. Co. 3,700,000 r.--total, 6,025,000 r.
A profit (67,362 r. 27 k.) was for the first time shown in
the report for 1898, but as early as 1899 the special commission assigned to investigate the state of affairs in the company
had recognized this as unsatisfactory. At the meeting of May
27, 1900 the St. P. International bank's representatives Vavelberg and Yunker moved a supplemenetary issue of preferred
shares in the sum of 2-1/2 mi. r. However, by the end of

1900, the Company's shares were quoted at 20 r., and a new issue appeared impossible. In March 1901, when a meeting of stock-holders determined to reduce the fixed capital to 2 mil. r. by substituting 20 thousand new shares at 100 r. for the 50 thousand old shares at 150 r., and after that put through the supplementary issue at 2-1/2 million rubles, the Company's losses had already reached 223,750 r. The Company's largest enterprise, the Amgun Co.'s mines, became so involved that in 1902 the only way out was recognized as being to deposit the shares of the Amgun Co. belonging to the Company in the State Bank.

From 1898, the Board was re-elected annually: December 1, 1898--bar. N. E. Wrangel, Rothstein, K. Vargunin, Lombardo; November 3, 1899--A.A. Davidov, N.D. Nikiforov, I. Efron; December 8, 1900--Wrangel, Rothstein, Lombardo; December 1, 1901--Davidov, Efron, Kolberg, Shaikevich; February 4, 1903--Wrangel, S.I. Littauer, Rothstein.

We cite a collated list of shareholders and the number of shares presented by them at the annual meetings of June 27, 1896, June 5, 1897, December 1, 1898, November 3, 1899, December 8, 1900, December 1, 1901 and February 4, 1903 (shares presented at the Paris and Netherlands bank are marked by an asterisk).

Share-owners:	1896	1897	1898	1899	1900	1901	1903
1) Alvang A. E., mgr. Anchor Const. Co.	--	--	10	--	--	--	--
2) Amiragov G., merch.	25	--	--	--	--	--	--
3) Antipov V.N., mgr. Nik. ry.	--	--	--	--	25	25	25
4) Arkhangelsky V.V., St.P. Circ. Trans. S.	--	--	--	--	--	25	--
5) Assafrei A.F. eng. trans. s.	--	--	10	--	--	--	--

Share-owners:	1896	1897	1898	1899	1900	1901	1903
6) Bagnitsky D.R.	--	--	--	--	--	--	12
7) Bari V.V., St. P. merch..	.--	--	100	100	25	25	25
8) Bastian F., stockbroker..	--	25	--	--	--	--	--
9) Bashilov A.P., St. P. property holder, St. P. Exch. Cred....	--	--	60	--	--	--	--
10) Bedriag A.V.	--	--	25	50	--	--	--
11) Beliustin N.I. dir. dept. customs duties...	--	--	12	--	--	--	--
12) Benardaki K.D.	131	131	131	35	35	--	--
13) Count Berg G.G., gen.-m.....	--	1000	--	--	--	--	--
14) Berenzon I.D.	--	--	--	25	25	35	25
15) Biler......	--	50*	--	--	--	--	--
16) Bistrom F.R., St. P. property holder.....	--	--	75	75	--	25	--
17) Bogdanov N.N., mem. Coun. Rus. bank for Ex. Tr......	35	35	35	35	35	--	35
18) Von Breveri N.O.	100	100	--	--	--	--	--
19) Brodsky Lazar	--	--	--	2025	2025	2025	2025
20) Bumagin M. Ia.	--	--	--	1	1	1	1
21) Vavelberg G.,							

Share-owners:	1896	1897	1898	1899	1900	1901	1903
22) Vargunin K.A., mem. Board Disc. and Loan bank	675	70	675	70	70	--	--
23) Vargunin A.I. and Co..	--	605	--	--	--	--	--
24) Warsaw Com. bank.	640	--	--	--	--	--	--
25) Weber O.O., trustee St. P. Int. bank	--	--	--	--	200	200	200
26) Von Vendrikh A.A., mil. eng.	25	--	200	--	--	--	--
27) Villar L.	35 50*	35 50*	35 50*	35	35	--	--
28) Vinterfeld V.Ia.	--	--	--	--	--	50	--
29) Witte N.A., dir. adm. Azov steam navig.	--	--	30	--	--	--	--
30) Vorobev A.M.	--	--	--	--	25	25	25
31) Voronin N.A., St. P. merch.. . .	--	--	175	--	--	150	--
32) Bar. Wrangel N.E., min. eng.	--	--	50	70	70	70	70

Share-owners:	1896	1897	1898	1899	1900	1901	1903
33) Vulfson B. (L.?), mem. St. P. Loan-office	--	15	80	--	--	--	--
34) Vystavkin V. K., book-keeper State Control	--	--	--	28	24	24	24
35) Ganel and Co. . .	86*	-	--	--	--	--	--
36) Heine and Co. . .	200*	--	--	--	--	--	--
37) Gintsburg, G.E.	1535	1635	--	--	--	--	--
38) Goldstand I., mem. Bd. Int. bank	200	--	--	--	100	100	100
39) Goldstand L. . .	--	--	--	--	252	172	172
40) Gelstrem A. . .	40	--	--	--	--	--	--
41) Gordon S.	--	115	115	--	--	--	--
42) Grankin N. . . .	--	1	5	--	--	--	--
43) Grentser S.A., merch. 1st guild	--	25	--	--	--	--	--
44) Grüning B. . . .	--	--	75	--	--	--	--
45) Huen E.	100*	100*	100*	--	--	--	--
46) Gurileva F.A., wife of merch. 1st guild	30	100	--	--	--	--	--

Share-owners:	1896	1897	1898	1899	1900	1901	1903
47) Gutman A. E.	--	--	--	--	--	150	--
48) Davidov A.A., trustee St. P. Int. bank	--	--	50	170	170	170	345
49) Demachi and Seler	100*	100*	100*	--	--	--	--
50) Dobrotvorsky A. Ia.	--	--	--	--	15	--	--
51) Diumen Ch	25*	25*	25*	--	--	--	--
52) Eroshenko A.I., exch. shop owner	--	--	15	--	25	10	25
53) Ershov D.M., St. P. property-holder	--	32	--	--	--	--	--
54) Efron I.A., dir. pub. house	--	--	--	50	70	70	70
55) Zhuber A.V., French eng.	--	35	35	35	35	--	--
56) Zhokhov P.K., ret. cap.	--	'20	--	--	--	--	--
57) Zhuber	150*	--	150*	--	--	--	--
58) Zelenoi I.A., palace mgr. to Gr. Duke Const. Const.	--	25	1	1	1	1	1
59) Zering A.I.	--	--	--	--	12	50	12

Share-owners:	1896	1897	1898	1899	1900	1901	1903
60) Zobov I.V., St. P. merch..	--	--	--	--	80	10	80
61) Isaev I.G. . . . . . --		--	25	--	--	--	
62) Kadetov I.M., St. P. pawn- broker . . . . . --	--	--	1	5	--	--	
63) Karalli N.I., stockbroker. . . --	--	50	--	--	--	--	
64) Kartavtsev E. E., mem. Counc. Rus. bk. for For. Tr. . . . . --	--	150	--	--	--	--	
65) Kashinsky I. . . . 5	--	--	--	--	--	--	
66) Kvitte F.M., merch. . . . . . . --	25	--	--	--	--	--	
67) Keyzerling A.G., dir. Aldr. quarry Co. . . . . --	--	75	--	--	--	--	
68) Kobylkin S.A., St. P. merch. . 200	--	--	--	--	--	--	
69) Kobychev A.A., mem. Coop. com. and indus. Co. 12	12	12	--	12	12	12	
70) Kozlov S.S., civ. eng. . . . . --	12	--	--	--	--	--	
71) Kolesov K. . . . --	25	--	--	--	--	--	

Share-owners:	1896	1897	1898	1899	1900	1901	1903
72) Kolberg G.A., min. eng. . . .	--	--	--	70	70	70	70
73) Konasov N.A. . .	25	--	--	--	--	--	--
74) Konasov I.N. . . .	--	10	--	15	15	15	15
75) Korepanov V.A.	--	--	15	--	--	--	--
76) Korobkov A.I., M. Nelken banking house	25	--	50	--	--	100	100
77) Kokh A.F., mem. Board St. P. Int. bank	255	255	1000	500	170	431	661
78) Krotte R.	--	--	20	--	--	--	--
79) Kukhta K.P., sp. off. Min. Fin.	--	100	--	--	--	--	--
80) Littauer S.I., min. eng. . . .	--	--	--	70	70	70	70
81) Lombardo T. R., mgr. O. S.-E. ry.	35	35	110	70	70	70	70
82) Makriukov S.M.	--	--	15	20	20	20	20
83) Maksimov P. A., St. P. householder . . .	60	--	--	--	--	--	--
84) Mandel E.S., bailiff Com. court.	--	25	--	--	--	--	--

Share-owners:	1896	1897	1898	1899	1900	1901	1903
85) Matusovsky B. .	--	--	50	--	--	--	--
86) Matusovsky N. .	--	--	25	--	--	--	--
87) Meyer and Co., banking house .	740	--	--	--	--	--	--
88) Meniaev K.s., St. P. property holder, Duma leader	--	12	25	12	50	--	50
89) Nelken M., owner of a St. P. banking house	--	1200	--	--	--	--	--
90) Nerpin A.I., asst. mgr. Upper-Amur and Amg. Gold Co.	280	70	130	70	70	--	--
91) Nikiforov N.D., Gent.-of-the-bed-chamb. . .	--	--	3	70	70	70	70
92) Nikolay Iu. F., trustee St. P. Int. bank	--	--	--	--	--	100	100
93) Nosov I.N., St. P. house-holder	--	20	--	--	--	--	--
94) Notgaft T.	50	--	--	--	--	--	--
95) Osipov A. . . .	--	20	--	--	--	--	--

Share-owners:	1896	1897	1898	1899	1900	1901	1903
96) Pazukhin P. . .	--	--	5	--	--	--	--
97) Palashkovsky S.E., eng.	--	--	5	--	--	--	--
98) Palibin M.I. .	--	100		--	--	--	--
99) Paris and Netherlands bank	686*	419*	929*	--	--	--	--
100) Penshon Mrs.	15	--	--	--	--	--	--
101) Petrokokino Th. I.	1270	1110 60*	1370 33*	1440 33*	--	1070	1070
102) Petrokokino D.I., mem. Board Disc. and Loan bk. .	535	285	320	35	35	--	--
103) Petrokokino F. I., stockbroker	100	--	--	--	--	--	--
104) Pechenkin and Co., banking office	--	15	25	--	25	--	--
105) Podgorny K.P.	--	--	100	--	--	--	--
106) Polezhaev N. M., Disc. and Loan bk. . . .	685	685	--	--	--	--	--
107) Polezhaev N. N., Rus. bk. for For. tr. . .	25	25	90	--	--	--	--
108) Poluektov A., exch. shop . . .	--	--	30	15	--	--	12

Share-owners:	1896	1897	1898	1899	1900	1901	1903
109) Pomerantsev A.A., pres. Counc. Rus. Com.-Ind. bk. .	35	35	35	35	35	--	--
110) Popov D.A., St. P. merch. .	--	250	250	--	--	--	--
111) Prelin A.S. . .	--	--	--	--	--	25	--
112) Prokhorov M.F.	5	22	--	--	--	--	--
113) Pfeifer F.A., trustee St. P. Int. bank	--	37	--	--	200	200	200
114) Ratkov-Rozh- nov V.A., St. P. mining chief	--	200	1350	1350	1000	915	915
115) Ratkov-Rozh- nov Ia. V., dir. Airship Co.	--	--	815	500	--	1000	1000
116) Rafalovich A. F., mem. Board Rus. bk. for For. Tr.	--	--	25	--	--	--	--
117) Rezvitsov A.D.	--	--	--	--	24	24	24
118) Reztsov A.D. . .	--	--	--	28	--	--	--
119) Rodzevich A. A., owner St. P. techn. off.	--	--	--	20	--	--	--

Share-owners:	1896	1897	1898	1899	1900	1901	1903
120) Romashov N. M., cap. 2nd rank	--	--	40	--	--	--	--
121) Rothstein A. Iu., mem. Bd. St. P. Int. Bk.	516	336	3035	1070	1441	1070	1233
122) Russian Commercial-Industrial bk.	140	--	--	--	--	--	--
123) Smirnov I.I.	--	300	--	--	--	--	--
124) Smirnov N.I.	120	--	--	--	--	--	--
125) Sokolov A.A.	--	--	--	15	--	--	--
126) Soloveichik M.A., asst. dir. Sib. T. bank	--	25	--	--	--	--	--
127) Songailo L. K., min. eng.	--	--	--	70	70	70	70
128) Spittser G.K., mem. Bd. St. P. Int. bk.	--	--	500	100	210	--	701
129) St. P. International Commercial bank	3500	8000[3]	5000	4000	4585	4800	4800
130) St. P. Discount and Loan bank	500	150	600	300	--	--	--
131) Stern and Co.	175*	175*	100*	--	--	--	--

Share-owners:	1896	1897	1898	1899	1900	1901	1903
132) Sushchov N.I., mem. Counc. Rus. bk. for For. Tr.	100	--	--	--	--	--	--
133) Teise	25*	25*	25*	--	--	--	--
134) Terk G.T., dir. Bd. Bogatov sugar refinery, dep. Disc. and Loan bk.	150	--	--	--	--	--	--
135) Trube A., St. P. merch.	25	--	--	--	--	--	--
136) Uteman F.B., mem. Board Disc. and Loan bk.	300	--	--	--	--	--	--
137) Utin Ia. I., vice-pres. Bd. Disc. and Loan bk.	315	235	270	35	35	--	--
138) Fedorov A.S.	--	--	25	--	--	--	--
139) Fedorov I.F.	--	--	15	--	--	--	--
140) Fileva E.E.	--	12	--	--	--	--	--
141) Furman B. E. architect	--	25	25	--	--	--	--
142) Shabishev S.S., mem. liq. com. Glebov works	--	--	1	1	1	1	1

Share-owners:	1896	1897	1898	1899	1900	1901	1903
143) Shaikevich E. G., mem. Bd. St.P. Int. bk.	--	--	50	200	200	1062	381
144) Charlié R., mem. Bd. Disc. and Loan bk. . . .	380	170	240	70	70	--	--
145) Chevran	25*	25*	25*	--	--	--	--
146) Sheftel M.I., advocate	--	--	12	--	--	--	--
147) Shlumberger O.A.	--	--	50	--	--	--	--
148) Shliakov P.A., dir. St. P. Int. bk., ass. dir. Rus.-Chi. bk.	--	--	--	--	25	25	25
149) Chopen de Janvri	20*	20*	20*	--	--	--	--
150) Shpanov V.S., advocate	--	--	25	25	--	--	12
151) Shtibel, E. Ia.	--	35	--	--	--	--	--
152) Shtifter M.V., trustee Nelken banking house . .	--	--	25	--	--	--	--
153) Ellers V.G. . .	--	--	20	--	--	--	--
154) Erk N.P., deputy Disc. and Loan bk. . . .	30	30	50	--	--	35	--

Share-owners:	1896	1897	1898	1899	1900	1901	1903
155) Essen	25	--	--	--	--	--	--
156) Iunkers B.F., inv. bank for Yunker and Co.	--	--	--	--	100	50	100
157) Iunker I.V. and Co.	100	100	90	100	100	100	100
Total	15201	22174	23800	17731	13972	14828	15454

The Syndicate of 1897 and Mongolor[1]

"The syndicate for investigating mineral wealth in China" (Syndicat pour l'exploration des richesses minières en Chine), was founded, by agreement of June 14, 1897 among the participants, with a capital of 500,000 r., divided into 100 shares, with provision that profits should be divided: 50 per cent to members of the Syndicate, 22-1/2 per cent to the Russo-Chinese bank, 22-1/2 per cent to the Russian Gold-mining Company, and 5 per cent to members of the Committee, consisting of Th. I. Petrokokino, A. Iu. Rothstein, A.I. Nerpin, N.I. Filipyev, D.D. Pokotilov and V. Iu. Grot.

Syndicate participants signing the agreement were 1) Th. I. Petrokokino (10 shares); 2) St. P. International bank (10 shares); 3) I. Goldshtand (3 shares); 4) A. Rothstein (4); 5) A. Kokh (4); 6) S. Palashkovsky (1); 7) G. Vavelberg (3); 8) D.I. Petrokokino (2); 9) Ia. Utin (1); 10) R. Charlié (1); 11) A.A. Pomerantsev (2); 12) A.I. Nerpin (2); 13) N.N. Bogdanov (2); 14) I.V. Yunker and Co. (2); 15) I. Kestlin (2); 16) N. Kostylev (1); 17) N. Filipyev (3); 18) S. Kerbedz (1); 19) Iu. Rothstein (1); 20) A. Kan (2); 21) D. Shereshevsky (1); 22) Evmorfopulo (2); 23) F. Pfeifer (1/2); 24) K. Notgaft (1); 25) O. Weber (1/2); 26) Zigler von Schafhausen (1); 27) K.A. Vargunin (1); 28) E. Ukhtomsky (1); 29) V. Iu. Grot (1).

Syndicate participants who informed the Russo-Chinese bank by letter of their consent to participate were: 30) F.I. Petrokokino; 31) Mendelssohn, Berlin; 32) Ern. Mey, Paris; 33) the bros. Dzhamgarov, Moscow; 34) E. Netslin; 35) L. Brodsky, Kiev; 36) Société Générale pour l'Industrie en Russie, Paris; 37) Mosc. Branch St. P. International bank.

On January 26, 1900, the Syndicate's committee decided to organize a stock company for the exploitation of gold-mining concessions obtained by Grot from the Chinese government within the boundaries of the Tushetukhan and

Tsetsenkhan aimaks in Mongolia (along the river Orkhon
and its affluents), with a capital of 3 mil. r., divided into
12 thous. shares at 250 r. each (charter conf. April 4, 1900).
Of these, 1 mil. r. were assumed by the "Belgian group."
The Board of the company consisted of: Ukhtomsky, A. Brown
de Tiège, Grot, Rothstein and A.A. Davidov. Grot was appointed Director-Manager and Company Representative in
Mongolia.

According to certain indications there was from the outset no thought of limiting the activity of the company merely
to exploitation of the gold fields of the enormous area left to
Grot in May 1899 for 25 years by "order" of the chiang-chün
of Ulyasutai.[2] By the spring of 1900 the Russo-Chinese bank
had moved into Ugra and Ulyasutai with its agencies on the
heels of the Company, and Grot, to whom their organization
was entrusted, posed the question point blank of "subsequently" founding a Mongolian bank there "in connection with the
gold-mining company."[3] Nay more: immediately upon receipt of his concession, in July 1899, Grot had seen Witte
in Peterburg and obtained from him "principal consent" to
"his [Grot's] obtaining the concession for a line to Kalgan,"
i.e., in that same direction of Peking, to which, as above
narrated (pp. 237 ff.), Witte was at just that moment seeking a means of approach through redemption of the loan on
the Shanhaikwan railway from the English; and when in the
spring of 1900, before the appearance of the Boxers, Grot
was slow about making efforts in this matter, Girs undertook to remind him of the "advisability" of "efforts toward
this end."[4] After a talk with Rothstein in January 1901 and
a meeting with Witte, who on this occasion as well "wished
him complete success," Grot finally, in the spring of 1901,
when the Bosers were done with, sent two Swedish engineers
"to survey the distance from Peking to Kalgan," and at the
same time men to open an agency of the Russo-Chinese bank
in Kalgan--fully convinced "that he was acting with the complete approval of our government."[5] It is no wonder that
not only Grot himself but even such an ever alert agent of
Witte as, for example, Pokotilov, who knew how matters
stood, should have been totally unprepared for the explosion
produced in Peterburg by the report of the Russian consul
in Ungra on the proposed journey of the engineers--in the
summer of 1901. At Witte's categorical request, Grot was

immediately discharged from the service of the Russo-Chinese bank, with him was buried all thought of a Peking-Kalgan railway, and it was all made to look as though Peterburg had never even dreamed of such a thing. July 1899 was, indeed, entirely different from the summer of 1901, "economic conditions" were now quite "bad," the Manchurian noose was being drawn ever tighter, no end was in sight to expenditures on the Chinese Eastern railway, and, in the meantime, more than a thousand versts of new track would now clearly have to be laid, likewise at the treasury's expense. The Belgian million in the Mining company had by the autumn of 1901 entirely run out, and the danger of failure immediately impended over the Company's gold-mining enterprise itself.[6]

By all the existing data, Grot, though having "no evil intention" and "acting to the best of his understanding," conducted the business in an extremely imprudent and incompetent manner" and in less than two years "laid out, practically to no purpose, and chiefly on the purchase of various machines in America, all the capital that had been placed at his disposal," and then, powerless as before to set up the "proper exploitation" of the mines prospected, existed for some time on credit partly at the Russo-Chinese bank, partly with local Chinese. When, finally, in the autumn of 1903, the Board of the Company decided to break with Grot and dispatch an expert engineer to the scene, and Grot himself, "without a penny to his name," went to America "as a common laborer" in the California mines, the Company's debt to the Chinese amounted to around 120,000 r. and to the bank around 500,000 r., while the balance-sheet loss for October 1, 1904 came to 666,889 r. In November 1904 a "representative of the Belgian stockholders" came to Peterburg and "having investigated the state of the concern, proposed to suggest that his principals invest another 500-600 thous. r. in it in an attempt to put the whole enterprise on its feet." But by the end of December Peterburg had received information that the Belgian's plans had fallen through, "the chief obstacle being the extremely unfavorable political conjunction"--and the Board of the Russo-Chinese bank raised the question of "liquidating the whole affair."[7] However, "from the political point of view" Kokovtsov regarded it as "inopportune just now to enter upon the liquidation of the only large-scale Russian industrial enterprise in Mongolia, a country which would, with the arrival of the Dalai Lama at Ugra acquire particularly serious significance for us, " and the Company was given a loan of 50,000 r., to "enable it to continue operations on a modest scale for the ensuing year, in the expectation that within this time the political situation in the Far East would clear up, and along with it the attitude of the Belgian stockholders toward the continuation of the Company's activity be definitely settled."[8] As soon as the war was over, the "attitude of the Belgian shareholders" was successfully "settled" in the affirmative, as we know, by the lure of transferring to Mongolor the whole assortment of coal and gold concessions that the Russian government in Manchuria had at its disposal (see above pp. 552 ff).

We cite a collated list of shareholders and the number of shares presented by them at the meetings of April 14, 1901, June 21, 1902, December 30, 1903, September 24, 1905 and August 8, 1906. The list for 1900 is compiled on the basis of quittances of the International bank on the receipt of quittances of the Russo-Chinese bank as to payments on shares (dos. No. 24, Mong.).

Share-owners:	1900	1901	1902	1903	1905	1906
1) Aron I. 28		--	--	--	--	--
2) de Bats, French eng. . . . 12		--	--	--	--	--
3) Berg K.V., trustee Russo-Chinese bank . . --		--	--	--	30	--
4) Berendt E.R. . . --		--	60	60	60	--
5) Bertels A. . . . . --		--	--	--	--	150
6) Bikhner E.A., St. P. property holder . . . . --		--	1	1	1	--
7) Bleiler K.s., trustee Russo-Chinese bank . . --		--	100	50	50	100

Share-owners:	1900	1901	1902	1903	1905	1906
8) Bogdanov N. . . .28	--	--	--	--	--
9) Bok P.A., trustee Russo-Chi. bank. . . . . --	30	30	30	30	85
10) Brodsky Lazar . .14	--	--	--	--	--
11) Brodsky Lev . . .14	--	--	--	--	--
12) de Brown de Tiège A. . . . 1520	5320	5320	--	840	750
13) de Brown de Tiège K. . . . . --	--	--	--	500	700
14) Bunge Edouard --	--	--	--	500	700
15) Busse V. Iu. . --	--	40	--	--	--
16) Vavelberg G., owner banking house 84	--	--	--	--	--
17) Vapereau Ch. . --	8	--	--	--	--
18) Vargunin K.A., vice-pres. Bd. Disc. and Loan bk. 14	--	--	--	--	--
19) Weber O.O., asst. dir. Russo-Chinese bk. . . 7	7	7	7	--	--
20) Wert A., dir. Shanghai Branch Russo-Chinese bk. 28	--	--	--	--	--

Share-owners:	1900	1901	1902	1903	1905	1906
21) Villar L.	14	--	--	--	--	--
22) de Wouters d'Oplinter Em. .	--	--	--	--	500	700
23) Vyshnegradsky A.I., vice-dir. Sp. C. for Cr. Div.	--	--	--	--	59	30
24) Gede F.	--	--	1	1	1	--
25) Geftler M.F. .	--	--	40	--	--	--
26) Goldshtand I. . .	42	--	--	--	--	--
27) Gordon I.S. . .	--	36	--	--	--	--
28) Gotson D. . . .	--	--	40	--	--	--
29) Greynert I.I. . .	--	--	60	--	--	--
30) Grot V. Iu., off. Chi. service	1232 400*	1232	1232	1114	--	--
31) Gurev A. (N. ? mem. Disc. Cred. Min. Fin. . . .	--	--	1	1	1	--
32) Davidova T. E.	--	--	5	5	5	--
33) Davidov A.A., trustee St. P. Int. bank	2	36	30	30	30	85

---

* Chinese persons

Share-owners:	1900	1901	1902	1903	1905	1906
34) Deviler L. . . . --	--	60	--	--	--	
35) Deitrick J. . . . 24	56	--	--	--	--	
36) Dehoepre A. . . --	--	--	--	--	150	
37) bros. Jamgarov, banking house . . 14	--	--	--	--	--	
38) Evstifeev N.P. . . . . --	1	--	--	--	--	
39) Efron I.A., dir. publishing house 34	94	34	--	--	--	
40) Fern. de Jardin . . . . . --	--	--	--	500	700	
41) Kan Albert . . . 56	--	--	--	--	--	
42) Kappler Genrukh (Urga) . . . --	--	--	--	--	12	
43) Kerbedz S.I., asst. pres. Bd. Chi.-E. ry., pres. Coun. St. P. Int.bk. . . 28	--	--	--	--	--	
44) Kestlin I.I., mem. Bd. Rus. bk. for For. Tr. 28	--	--	--	--	--	
45) Cordes I. . . . --	--	--	--	50	80	
46) Korobkov A.I., trustee St. P. Int. bank . . . . --	--	200	100	--	--	

Share-owners: 1900 1901 1902 1903 1905 1906

47) Kostylev N.A.,
     mem. Bd. Vol-
     zhsko-Kamsky
     bank 14   --   --   --   --   --

48) Kokh A.F.,
     mem. Bd. St.
     P. Int. bk. . . . 98   70   70   70   --   --

49) Kripin V.L. . . --   --   75   30   50   --

50) Levenson V.A. --   --   --   --   100   60

51) Levy G. . . . . --   --   1   1   1   --

52) Littauer S.I.,
     eng. . . . . . . --   30   40   40   40   40

53) Liakhovsky
     V.A. . . . . -- --   20   20   20   60

54) Maheo, Zh. . . --   --   --   30   30   100

55) Manteufel V. . . --   --   --   35   35   100

56) Meier N.I.,
     trustee St. P.
     Int. bank . . . . --   --   75   50   50   --

57) Meier E.M.
     and Co.,
     banking house . . 84   --   --   --   --   84

58) Mendelsohn
     and Co., Ber-
     lin 56   --   --   --   --   --

59) Mols Alexis . . . --   --   --   --   500   --

60) Mushkin I. Ia., . --   --   --   --   20   --

Share-owners:	1900	1901	1902	1903	1905	1906
61) Mey Ernst	28	--	--	--	--	--
62) Nerpin A.I., asst. dir. Upper-Amur Gold Co.	60	--	--	--	--	--
63) Netslin E., dir. Paris-Netherlands bank	224	--	224	224	224	224
64) Nolken N. bar . .	6	14	--	--	--	--
65) Palashkovsky S.E., eng. . . .	14	--	--	--	--	--
66) Pauli G.L., secretary to dir. St. P. Int. bank . . .	--	--	20	20	--	--
67) Petrokokino Th. I.	88	--	--	--	--	--
68) Petrokokino D.I., mem. Bd. Disc. and Loan bank	28	--	--	--	--	--
69) Pimenov V. . .	--	--	--	45	--	--
70) Pokotilov D.D., mem. Board Russo-Chinese bank in Peking .	20	--	20	20	20	--
71) Popov P., gen. consul in Peking	--	8	--	--	--	--

Share-owners:	1900	1901	1902	1903	1905	1906
72) Pfeifer F.A. asst. dir. Russo-Chinese bk. mem. directorate St. P. Int. bk.	7	7	7	7	7	--
73) Rozenfeldt A. Iu., trustee Russo-Chinese bk.	--	--	--	50	--	--
74) Russian Gold-mining Company	630	570	630	630	630	630
75) Rothstein A. Iu., mem. Board Russo-Chi. and St. P. Int. bks.	200	200	30	30	--	--
76) Russo-Chinese bank	630	1734 1174*	630	630	630	570
77) Serezhnikov D.I., trustee St. P. Int. bank	--	--	59	59	--	--
78) de Serce, Count	--	14	--	--	--	--
79) Soloveichik A. E., trustee Russo-Chin. bank	--	--	200	100	100	100

---

* Shanghai branch of bank.

Share-owners:	1900	1901	1902	1903	1905	1906
80) Société A.E., trustee Russo- Chin. bank . . .	112	--	--	--	--	--
81) Spitser G.K., mem. Board St. P. Int. bk.. .	28	28	--	--	--	--
82) St. P. Inter- national bank . .	504	532	810	810	810	810
83) Startsev A.D., St. P. property holder	--	28	--	--	--	--
84) Stevens H. . . .	--	--	--	--	--	150
85) Stefansky L.K.	--	--	20	20	20	75
86) Stirikh A.A. (Stirig)	--	--	--	30	--	100
87) Syrkin M.S. . . .	--	--	--	--	45	100
88) Tors J.	14	--	--	--	--	--
89) Trakhtenberg I.G., bus. mgr. Mongolor	--	--	--	--	--	70
90) Utin Ia, I., vice-pres. Board Disc. and Loan bk. . .	14	--	--	--	--	--
91) Ukhtomsky E. E., pres. Board Russo- Chinese bk. . . .	48	48	48	128	128	128

Share-owners:	1900	1901	1902	1903	1905	1906
92) Ushinskaia M. .	14	--	--	--	--	--
93) Filipev N.I., mem. Board St.P. Int. bk. . .	62	--	--	--	--	--
94) Friling Willy .	--	--	--	--	460	150
95) Khrulev S.S., pres. Board St.P. Int. bk. .	--	--	40	40	40	40
96) Shaikevich E. G., mem. Board St.P. Inter. bk. . . .	--	--	200	200	200	--
97) Schenck Albert	--	--	--	--	500	150
98) Shleziger G.F. dep. bookkeeper Board Vladik. ry.	--	--	1	1	1	--
99) Shliakov P.A., mem. direc- torate St.P. Int. bank	28	28	28	--	--	--
100) Shmidt K. Mrs.	14	--	--	--	--	--
101) Shchutsky S.M.	--	1	--	--	--	--
102) Evmorfopulo G.I., stock- broker	28	--	--	28	5	--
103) Engelman I.G.	--	--	40	40	40	--
104) Erk N.P. . . .	--	--	--	--	30	--

Share-owners:	1900	1901	1902	1903	1905	1906
105) Ettinger M.N. .	--	--	--	--	30	--
106) Iunker I.V. and Co., banking house .	28	--	--	--	--	28
107 Iakobs F.S., trustee St. P. Int. bank . . .	--	--	100	50	50	--
Total . . .	7878	10132	10649	4837	7973	7799

NOTES TO SUPPLEMENTS

Supplement I
    1. Data for this report were taken by us from the accumulation of
the Rus. Gold-pros. Co., dos. No. 339-353.
    2. Persons who signed the roster for the owners are indicated in
square brackets.
    3. At the meeting extraordinary of June 30, 1898, the St. P. Inter-
national Bank presented a parcel of 9,300 shares.

Supplement II
    1. Data for this report were taken by us from dos. No. 23, div. 3
K.M.F., and from dos. No. 24, 19, 11, 15, 6, 4 and 8 of Mongolor.
    2. See translation of the "order" in dos. No. 23, pt. I.
    3. See, ibid., Grot's tel. of Aug. 18/31, 1900 to Rothstein.
    4. See Pokotilov's personal letter of Jan. 16, 1902 to Shipov, ibid.
    5. See, ibid., the report of May 4, 1901 from Shishmarev, consul
to Ugra, and Pokotilov's cited letter.
    6. The abrupt turn taken by the Grot affair is, however, to be ex-
plained not only by the nature of the matter and the absurdity of the new
railway project, but also by circumstances of an altogether personal
character. When Lamsdorf questioned Witte about Grot's engineering
expedition, Witte replied that he was "unaware even of any project for
the construction" of a Kalgan line. Lamsdorf then gave Witte an excerpt
from Shishmarev's report, the sense of which in no wise tallied with
Witte's assertion but tended to the conclusion that the Company "as constituted"--and participants were thereupon enumerated--"was in closest
touch with the functioning" of the ministry of finance and that the "minister of finance was chief participant in and guiding spirit of both the Company and the bank, albeit secretly" (see, in dos. No. 23, pt. I, Lamsdorf's letter of August 8 and Witte's of August 5, 1901). Such a story,
which at first glance could only have originated with Grot, roused Witte's
indignation. Cf. his notations, on the excerpt from Shishmarev, as to
Grot: "son of a b.," and on Lamsdorf's letter "answer the min. for.
afs. asking that it take measures to have the Chinese government prohibit the surveys. Request that Shishmarev be informed that no one in
the min. fin. was a party to this affair and that this was a lie spread by
interested persons. The min. fin. was absolutely unaware of Grot's
activity and in no way connected with it. I have simultaneously ordered
that Grot bear no part in the Russo-Chinese bank, finding the given
plurality of office inconvenient. I demand that this be immediately put
into effect. When Rodstein returns, I ask that he be informed of my
extreme dissatisfaction with Grot's arbitrary actions and that I am tired
of constantly having unpleasantness over the actions of Count
Rodstein, that if this is again repeated I shall be forced to take measures. To the dir. of the chancellery for punctual execution."

7. See, in dos. No. 23, pt. II, Liuba's report of July 23, 1904 from Ugra, and Dolbezhev's of March 26, 1904 from Ugra, Pokotilov's memorandum of Sept. 2, 1904 and the letter of Dec. 29, 1904 from the Board of the Russo-Chinese bank to the minister of finance. Cf. also the reports of the Mining Co. of the Tushetukhan and Tsetsenkhan Aimaks in Mongolia for 1901 and 1902-1904.

8. See, in dos. No. 23, pt. II, the min. fin.'s report to his majesty of Jan. 7, 1905.

CONCORDANCE

The concordance below will make it possible for the reader to refer from the present text to corresponding pages in the Russian original; and also to refer from any mention in the Russian indexes, which follow, to relevant pages in the text of this translation.

In the tabulation, the Russian original is represented by the letter R; the translation by T.

R.	T.	R.	T.	R.	T.	R.	T.
3	1	37	27	71	53	105	78-79
4	1-2	38	27-28	72	53-54	106	79
5	2-3	39	28-29	73	54-55	107	79-80
6	3-4	40	29-30	74	55-56	108	80-81
7	4	41	30-31	75	56	109	81
8	4-5	42	31	76	57	110	81-82
9	5-6	43	31-32	77	57-58	111	82
10	6	44	32-33	78	58-59	112	82
11	6-7	45	33-34	79	59-60	113	82-83
12	7-8	46	34	80	60-61	114	83
13	8-9	47	34-35	81	61	115	84
14	9	48	35-36	82	62	116	84-85
15	9-10	49	36-37	83	62-63	117	85
16	10-11	50	37	84	63-64	118	85-86
17	11-12	51	37-38	85	64	119	86-87
18	12	52	38-39	86	64-65	120	87
19	12-13	53	39-40	87	65-66	121	87-88
20	13-14	54	40-41	88	66-67	122	88-89
21	14-15	55	41	89	67	123	89
22	15-16	56	41-42	90	67-68	124	89-90
23	16-17	57	42-43	91	68	125	90-91
24	17	58	43	92	68-69	126	91
25	17-18	59	43-44	93	69-70	127	91-92
26	18-19	60	44-45	94	70-71	128	92-93
27	19-20	61	45-46	95	71	129	94
28	20	62	46	96	71-72	130	94-95
29	20-21	63	46-47	97	72-73	131	95-96
30	21-22	64	47-48	98	73-74	132	96-97
31	22	65	48-49	99	74	133	97
32	23	66	49	100	74-75	134	97-98
33	23-24	67	49-50	101	75-76	135	98-99
34	24-25	68	50-51	102	76-77	136	99-100
35	25	69	51-52	103	77	137	100
36	25-26	70	52-53	104	77-78	138	100-101

R:	T.	R.	T.	R.	T.	R.	T.
139	101-102	188	137-138	237	170	286	202
140	102-103	189	138	238	170-171	287	202-203
141	103-104	190	138-139	239	171-172	288	203-204
142	104	191	139-140	240	173	289	204-205
143	104-105	192	140-141	241	173-174	290	205
144	105-106	193	141	242	174	291	205-206
145	106-107	194	141-142	243	175	292	206-207
146	107	195	142	244	175	293	207
147	107-108	196	142-143	245	175-176	294	208
148	108-109	197	143-144	246	176-177	295	208-209
149	109	198	144	247	177-178	296	209-210
150	109-110	199	144-145	248	178	297	210
151	110-111	200	145	249	178-179	298	211
152	111	201	145-146	250	179-180	299	211-212
153	111-112	202	146-147	251	180	300	212-213
154	112-113	203	147	252	180-181	301	213-214
155	113	204	147-148	253	181	302	214
156	113-114	205	148	254	181-182	303	215
157	114-115	206	148	255	182-183	304	215-216
158	115-116	207	148-149	256	183-184	305	216
159	116	208	149-150	257	184	306	216-217
160	116-117	209	151	258	184-185	307	217-218
161	117-118	210	151-152	259	185-186	308	218-219
162	118-119	211	152	260	186	309	219
163	119	212	152-153	261	186-187	310	219-220
164	119-120	213	153-154	262	187	311	220-221
165	120-121	214	154	263	187-188	312	221-222
166	121-122	215	154-155	264	188-189	313	222
167	122	216	155-156	265	189	314	222-223
168	122-123	217	156	266	189-190	315	223-224
169	123-124	218	156-157	267	190-191	316	224
170	124-125	219	157-158	268	191	317	224-225
171	125	220	158	269	191	318	225-226
172	125-126	221	158-159	270	191-192	319	226-227
173	126-127	222	159-160	271	192-193	320	227
174	127-128	223	160	272	193	321	227-228
175	128	224	160-161	273	193-194	322	228-229
176	128-129	225	161-162	274	194	323	229
177	129-130	226	162-163	275	195	324	229-230
178	130	227	163	276	195-196	325	230
179	130-131	228	163-164	277	196-197	326	230
180	131-132	229	164-165	278	197	327	230-231
181	132-133	230	165	279	197-198	328	231
182	133	231	165-166	280	198-199	329	231-232
183	133-134	232	166-167	281	199	330	232-233
184	134-135	233	167-168	282	199-200	331	233
185	135	234	168	283	200-201	332	233-234
186	135-136	235	168-169	284	201	333	234-235
187	136-137	236	169-170	285	201-202	334	235

R.	T.	R.	T.	R.	T.	R.	T.
335	235-236	384	267-268	433	299-300	482	333-334
336	236-237	385	268	434	300-301	483	334
337	237	386	268-269	435	300-301	484	334-335
338	237-238	387	269-270	436	301-302	485	335-336
339	238-239	388	270	437	302-303	486	336
340	239	389	270-271	438	303-304	487	336-337
341	239-240	390	271-272	439	304-305	488	337-338
342	240	391	272	440	305	489	338
343	240-241	392	272-273	441	305-306	490	338-339
344	241-242	393	273-274	442	306	491	339
345	242	394	274	443	306-307	492	339-340
346	242-243	395	274-275	444	307-308	493	340-341
347	243	396	275-276	445	308	494	341
348	243-244	397	276	446	308-309	495	341
349	244-245	398	277	447	309-310	496	341-342
350	245-246	399	277-278	448	310	497	342
351	246	400	278-279	449	310-311	498	342-343
352	246-247	401	279	450	311	499	343
353	247	402	279-280	451	311-312	500	343-344
354	248	403	280-281	452	312-313	501	344-345
355	248-249	404	281	453	313	502	345
356	249-250	405	281	454	313-314	503	346
357	250	406	281-282	455	314-315	504	346-347
358	250-251	407	282-283	456	315-316	505	347-348
359	251-252	408	283-284	457	316	506	348
360	252	409	284-285	458	316-317	507	348-349
361	252-253	410	285	459	317-318	508	349
362	253	411	285-286	460	318	509	349-350
363	254	412	286	461	318-319	510	350-357
364	254	413	287	462	319-320	511	351
365	254-255	414	287-288	463	320	512	352
366	255-256	415	288-289	464	320-321	513	352-353
367	256-257	416	289	465	321-322	514	353
368	257	417	289-290	466	323	515	353-354
369	257-258	418	290-291	467	323-324	516	354-355
370	258-259	419	291	468	324	517	355
371	259	420	291-292	469	324-325	518	355-356
372	259-260	421	292	470	325-326	519	356
373	260	422	292-293	471	326-327	520	356-357
374	260-261	423	293-294	472	327-328	521	357
375	261-262	424	294	473	328	522	357-358
376	262-263	425	294-295	474	328-329	523	358
377	263	426	295	475	329	524	358-359
378	263-264	427	296	476	329-330	525	359
379	264-265	428	296-297	477	330-331	526	359-360
380	265	429	297	478	331	527	360
381	265-266	430	297-298	479	331-332	528	360-361
382	266	431	298-299	480	332-333	529	361-362
383	266-267	432	299	481	333	530	362

R.	T.	R.	T.
531	362-363	558	380-381
532	363-364	559	381
533	364	560	381-382
534	364-365	561	382
535	365	562	382-383
536	366	563	383-384
537	366-367	564	384
538	367-368	565	384-385
539	368	566	385-386
540	369	567	386-387
541	369-370	568	387
542	370	591	491
543	370-371	592	492-493
544	371-372	593	493-495
545	372	594	495-498
546	372-373	595	498-501
547	373-374	596	501-503
548	374	597	503-506
549	374-375	598	506-507
550	375-376	599	508-509
551	376	600	509-510
552	376-377	601	510-511
553	377-378	602	511-513
554	378	603	513-515
555	378-379	604	515-518
556	379-380	605	518-520
557	380		

*Words appearing often which are omitted: Russia, China, Far East,
Manchuria (as a whole; Southern and Northern Manchuria are included).